BEYOND RECOGNITION

BEYOND RECOGNITION

A Story of Triumph Against All Odds

PART ONE

Written By: Sandra L. Lawson

XULON ELITE

Xulon Press Elite
555 Winderley Pl, Suite 225
Maitland, FL 32751
407.339.4217
www.xulonpress.com

© 2024 by Sandra L. Lawson

All rights reserved solely by the author. The author guarantees all contents are original and do not infringe upon the legal rights of any other person or work. No part of this book may be reproduced in any form without the permission of the author.

Due to the changing nature of the Internet, if there are any web addresses, links, or URLs included in this manuscript, these may have been altered and may no longer be accessible. The views and opinions shared in this book belong solely to the author and do not necessarily reflect those of the publisher. The publisher therefore disclaims responsibility for the views or opinions expressed within the work.

Paperback ISBN-13: 979-8-86850-631-4
Ebook ISBN-13: 979-8-86850-632-1

Table of Contents

Section 1

Salt Water	3
The Cove	4
Dirty Hands	7
Different Stuff	9
No Hitting	11
Same	14
Up Next	17
The Highway	20
Tell the Truth	23
Get Back Up	26
Double Standard	31
Nancy and the Secret	34
The Movies	38
Praying Mantis, Scarecrow, and Grandma	41
Hypocrite	44
No Crying	46
BCGs	49
Peas	51
Quiet	54
Heroes	56
Dolls	59
Shredded	63
Tomahawk	65
Toys	67
Retribution	69
Jump	72
Bite Down	75
Jay	83

Now	87
Montana	89
Ponytails	92
The Fox	94
Promise Me	96
You're Not Going	101

Section 2

The Aquatic Abyss	107
Sea Bag	110
GATE	112
Don't Become the Bully	115
That's My Brother	118
God is Watching You	121
Run for Your Life	124
Can I?	126
Don't Be a Burden	129
You Can't Go in There	133
You're Still Gonna Get It	135
Gray Mouse	139
Scarlet Letters	142
The Surprise	145
Set It on the Table	150
Leaves	152
Got Tacos?	156
Tiger Cruise	158
Forbidden	159
Backwards	161
The Cartoon	165
Looming	167
Mediums	169
Most Outstanding Student	171
Goodbye	173

Section 3

Texas Happened	179
Pale and Darkness	183

Living Hell 185
VHS 187
Stained 188
Dive-bombed 192
Die-hard 194
Logs 196
Phone Calls 198
Letters 200
Toothbrush 203
Post Holes 207
If You're There 210

Section 4

Golden Plates 217
Questions 223
Battlefield 226
The Holy Ghost 229
Obedience 232
Reinvent Yourself 234
Short-alls 236
Lunch 240
My Testimony 243
A Bone to Pick 246

Section 5

Magic 251
Mara 255
Flowers 258
Why? 261
Broken 263
Paul 268
Bible Study 271
The Name of Jesus 275
UPC 277
Jesus' Name Baptism 282
Still Unsure 285
Beg 287

You're Doing It 289
Sister Nebiyah 292
Test Me 294
Alice 295
Caden 298
The Conductor 302
Salad 304
Fishing 305
Deer Season 307
Bruises 311
Doom 315
Alice Was Right 318
Loophole 320
The Backslider Prayer List 322
Spunky 329
Checkmate 331
Two Storms 336

Section 6

Fire 343
First Bedroom to the Left 348
Just a Game 351
A Second Generation 358
Goody-Goody 363
Defend Yourself 366
Red 369
Opportunity 371
Encourage 373
Female 376

Section 7

Good Eye 381
Fish 384
Cool It 386
Nicki 388
Varsity 390
Ruby 392

Not Stupid	395
Mammon	397
Sadie	399
I Said It	401
You'll Learn	404
Mrs. Weather	406
Scouts	409
Lessons	412
Mack	416
Sweet Sixteen	421
Running Your Mouth	424
Oliver	426
Dance	428

Section 8

Deleted	433
Ditch the Girl	435
Launched	438
What's Your Emergency?	441
Odd	446
Goals	449
Indifference	451
Peacock	453
Armageddon	456
Amin	460
Coach Gather	465
Words	472
Thad	473
Degrading	475
Dear Nancy	477
Welcome	478
Help Us	481
Mascot	484
Don't Look Back	490
Closing Thoughts and Prayer	494

Introduction

I'm an overcomer of childhood narcissistic abuse… *among other things*. To practice discretion, I have altered or completely omitted many individuals' names.

Although I'm non-denominational now, Jesus the Messiah has led me on a journey through several religious congregations. While in their company, I met various individuals that changed the course of my life, for better or for worse. To this day, I avoid sectarianism, but appreciate the valuable lessons I learned in my pursuit of Truth.

Much of what you're about to read is brutally raw and may be triggering for some. We're all in need of healing and forgiveness. Do your best not to cleave to the same judgement that took me so long to unload. If we recall when we've wronged others, humility will find us. The *real* villains are Satan and his demons, but we're *all* responsible for what we think, say, and do… or don't do.

Vignettes construct the layers of my testimony and represent chronological memories that I've refused to whitewash by portraying only victories and concealing my disgusting sin. My story is perilously messy and Jesus has proven to be exactly who Yahweh sent Him to be, *my Savior*. Over time, the Holy Spirit has been tirelessly cleansing and restoring my thought-life of the residue left behind from years of trauma and gaslighting. Consistent prayer, worship, Scripture reading, and deliverance have led to a life of intense healing and restoration.

If you dare to explore the Truth pertaining to each situation, I encourage you to read the referenced Scriptures at the back of this book to determine *for yourself* if what had occurred ever lined up with Messiah's teachings or missed the mark completely. Before diving into the story, I strongly suggest that you pray and ask for protection from Satan and his demons, who will attempt to distract you as you read my testimony. The accuser doesn't want to see you delivered from whatever situation, trauma, or form of C-PTSD you might be facing.

If you remember nothing else, understand that through the blood of Jesus and by sharing our testimony with others, we defeat Satan… and with the Messiah leading you, anything is possible, even the radical freedom and restoration of a wretched, ignorant, misled, abused, neglected, deceived, depraved, violent, foul-mouthed, unforgiving and blundering sinner… like *me*.

Dedication

For 'Jay'.

I will no longer be silent.

Acknowledgements

All esteem belongs to Jesus the Messiah, I assure you. Putting my testimony in writing was His idea entirely. He even burned the cover image into my mind and gave me the title in a moment, all while I worshipped Him on a friend's porch. One miracle after another made this task possible, and some of those miracles have names and birthdays.

To the loving friends and relatives that supported me spiritually, emotionally, financially, and sometimes physically through this arduous process, *thank you*. Your obedience to our Messiah has eased my load, softened my heart, and helped me attain a lifelong dream of being a published author. You've done more than you'll ever know on this side of mortality. May you receive every reward for your kindnesses, in Jesus' name.

SECTION 1

Salt Water

I was born a sailor's daughter.

Aircraft carriers, battleships, cruisers and nuclear submarines made a crawling passage through the Pacific coastal waters that enveloped my view. The monumental size of the mechanical beasts docking and departing left me awestruck. Being old enough to understand *much* of what was occurring around me with no way to stop it, I waved goodbye to the only stability I had ever known and watched him walk up the ramp to enter his *other* home. [1]

My father left his household for another six-month deployment with the United States navy, casting a shadow over the turbulent, onyx-tinted waters of my life. As the steel monstrosity crept toward the horizon, reality pierced my side and squeezed my delicate throat with a despair of the densest variety. I *knew* what my father's ever-shrinking aircraft carrier signified. [2]

Thanks to educational children's programming, I could read and write by the age of five. However, despite my precociousness, I still lacked the capacity to articulate the dread that crippled me. Tears filled my eyes as I wailed, *"Daddy!"* I struggled against a rebelling diaphragm, forced another deep breath, and repeated, *"Daddy!"* The sobs dragged on and led to exhaustion for all parties in the immediate vicinity.

"It's time to go," my mother announced as she pulled me away from the familiar smells of oil, metal and sea.

Once loaded into the car, the woman pulled up to a familiar drive-through window. A small burger, some crispy fries, and a plastic toy were never enough to cause the *amnesia* needed to forget what I had just lost. After finishing my meal, the man's face and uniform came to mind and compelled me to continue where I had left off.

For days, the memory of his most recent departure intrusively shoved my body into heaving sobs that dropped me to my knees. In another desperate attempt to silence me, my mother lifted my tiny frame to buckle me into a mounted child-seat on her bicycle, pedaling me around the neighborhood. I fell asleep to the sensation of the wind on my face as the sun-kissed trees cast wispy shadows across my closed eyelids. That all-but-worshipped sailor was the first thought of the morning and the last image in my mind as I lay my anxieties down to sleep.

The Cove

With my father being stationed in California, the ocean's vastness had become a coveted distraction from the darkness that commonly surrounded me. To escape the confines of navy housing, my mother packed my brother and me up for a day at the beach. [1]

Barnacle covered rocks lined a reinforced-concrete seawall that protected my favorite cove from deceptive rip tides and turbulent waters. When the timing was right, a geyser-like splash would catapult itself in an exhilarating spray. Safely on the other side, a calmer ocean offered a roaring metronome of lapping waves, leaving behind damp sand and shells. I chased the greedy seagulls that filled their bellies with beak-watering bread and stale popcorn. Life under water was precious and fascinating to me, so much so that even a local restaurant's aquarium could render me mesmerized. [2]

Waiting for the opportunity, I broke away from my distracted mother and rushed toward the forbidden tide pools that bordered the seawall. It took a brave and sure-footed individual to navigate their treachery, especially shoeless. Using my toes, I felt around for mucus-like algae before committing my weight to a step. One slip could cast an unfortunate explorer upon the unforgivingly jagged barnacles, sharp mussels, and shredding coral below, making the challenge irresistible. Upon reaching my favorite spot, happiness and wonder glittered within me as I discovered tiny crabs and squirting sea anemones. [3]

The swelling waters beside me were deceptively beautiful, appearing to be much shallower than they truly were. I envied each wetsuit-clad snorkeler as their flippers propelled them through an environment that I had yet to explore.

A breeze carried something unusual with it to my mother's powerful nose. Alarmed, the woman lifted her booming voice above the crashing waves and shouted, *"Kids, let's go! It smells like dead fish out here!"*

Acknowledging her call, my brother obediently ran to her side.

Not being bothered by oceanic fragrances and rarely visiting the beach, I lingered in defiance, thinking, "Come and get me, lady. You'll never get past the algae." [4]

With patience exhausted, the flustered woman roared, *"Sandra, get over here! Now!"*

I found the foul demeanor of our materfamilias' repulsive and often sought refuge in solitude, but it was fear of her wrath that dragged me toward her seething presence. Leaving my marine friends behind, I carefully maneuvered amongst the rocks to find traction and safer spots to step. Having hopped down to the sand, my happiness faded as I dug in my feet with each foreboding step towards the woman who bore me. Like any addiction, time spent on the coast seemed to increase my longing, as opposed to satisfying it. [5]

"Where are we going *now*?" I whined.

"Somewhere that doesn't stink!" the termagant huffed, grimacing. "Listen to me, little girl. When I call you, you come. *Do you understand me?* Grab your towel. I'm not carrying all of your **** too." We ventured along a sidewalk that strayed from the ocean's edge to a parking lot. "*Wow. The smell is getting even worse! What is that? I thought I could just walk away from it. Yuck! Let's just go home. I think it's coming from over there.*" The woman pointed back towards the blue waters.

"That way?!" I chirped, already running. "Let's find out what it is!"

"*Sandra! Get back here! I'm not chasing you! If you don't come back, I'm leaving you here!*" she howled, which sounded more like a reward than a threat. "*Someone could take you and do God-knows-what!*" [6]

"Okay! Sounds good!" I quipped, longing for a good kidnapping. Upon reaching the edge of the man-made cliff, I pointed to an area down below and announced, "*Look! The rocks are moving!*" [7]

"*Whatever, Sandra!*" my brother scoffed from beside our mother. "*We're not falling for that! Rocks don't move, dummy!*" [8]

"*I'm not kidding, Sandra! We're leaving you here!*" the woman repeated abrasively.

Ignoring her words, I pondered aloud, "He's right. They *can't* be moving rocks." Focusing harder, I gasped and became fascinated with the jostling and laborious maneuvers below. "*Guys! You're missing it! C'mon! Look!*" At that, the woman and her son begrudgingly approached, gazing over the side and down. "See?! They're sea lions! What are they doing here?! This is amazing! I've never seen them in the wild before!"

"We walked all the way over here for that?!" she scoffed. "Okay. We saw them. Now, let's go. The smell is nauseating."

"I don't understand. We've been here a bunch of times and have never seen them in this area before. How is this not interesting to you?" I wondered aloud. "Don't you care?"

"No, I don't care. It's nothing new. I've *seen* sea lions before and they smell. We're leaving," she barked, tightly grabbing my arm with a yank.

"*Let go!*" I demanded, breaking free to walk towards the vehicle out of arm's reach.

"Someone could grab you!" the woman warned.

"Like *you* just did?" I snipped. "At least it would be a *stranger* doing it." Before I climbed into the vehicle, the woman opened the passenger door to create a visual barrier and lowered herself to pinch my arm. Wincing, I cried out, "Ow! Why are you always hurting me?!" [9]

"*Shut up, you little monster,*" the woman forcefully whispered. "*Listen to me. When I tell you to do something, you'd better do it.*" [10]

I furrowed my brow at her and thought, "I'm not the monster."

With gnashed teeth, she bent down and growled, "*You demon from hell.* I don't care *what* you're looking at! *I'm* an adult and *you're* just an ignorant child. If you don't obey me, I won't bring you to the beach anymore. I'll just go while you're both at school." [11]

Fighting tears, I climbed into the back seat and buckled up.

"*What's wrong with you?*" my brother hissed from beside me. "*Just do what she says or you're gonna screw things up for me, too.*"

"Don't think you're gonna get away with what you did today," the woman added from the driver's seat. "When we get home, you're getting a spanking. *Here I am*, trying to do something nice for you, and all you want to do is ruin it. *You're a spoiled little brat.* This was a really good day until *you* started acting up. *You ruin everything.* I wanted a little girl my entire life. When I was fifteen, I said, '*I'm going to have a little girl and I'm going to name her Sandra.*' Then *you* came along and all I got was an unappreciative little *monster*. I hope you have a bunch of brats *just like you*. After you were born, my life was *over*..." [12]

I stopped listening and pondered, "If I'm anything like her, I'll *never* have children."

Dirty Hands

While visiting a local park, I saw a sandbox that hosted a little boy playing alone and enthusiastically greeted, "Hi! I'm Sandra!" He cheerfully divulged his name just before we dug our fingers into the sand.

"*Sandra!*" my mother abruptly shouted, gripping my attention and causing me to sit erect. *"Get over here, now!"*

I peered over at my sandy friend and murmured, "Excuse me," before scurrying back to her.

The materfamilias forcefully whispered, *"You can't play anymore. We're leaving."*

"Aw! Really?! Why?!" I whined. "We just got here!"

"Don't argue!" she sharply rebuked. "Now, let's go!" [1]

"Okay. Hold on," I mentioned, just before trotting back to the sandbox. "It was a pleasure to meet you, sir, but I have to go now. Bye!" Wishing to be polite, I shook his hand and returned to the red-faced woman.

My mother snatched me by my wrist and pulled my tiny body toward the vehicle, gruffly whispering, *"You'd better wash your hands."*

"Why?" I inquired with a scrunched nose, trying to keep up to prevent being dragged. "Is it because the sand is dirty?"

"You just shook that black boy's hand!" she divulged. "You don't know where he's been or if his hands are clean!" [2]

My mind whirled with confusion. As she drove us home, I silently pondered, "How can I possibly see if someone's hands are clean? Sandboxes are boxes of sand. Sand is on the beach. Doesn't that make the entire beach dirty? Is she talking about germs? My book says that germs are micro-organisms, but I would need a microscope to see them. I *like* shaking people's hands. Will I have to stop?"

Back from deployment, my father arrived home from the local base and stepped through the front door. Instead of tackling his legs to sit on his foot, I furrowed my brow and lingered at the mouth of the hall.

"What's on your mind, squirt?" the man inquired.

Cocking my head to the side, I queried, "Daddy, how can you tell if someone's hands are clean?"

"Why do you ask?" he wondered aloud. [3]

"Well… at the park, Mom said that I needed to wash my hands because I touched a black boy and couldn't see if he was clean," I rattled. "I'm confused because sand was on my hands, too, and I couldn't see anything. Was she talking about germs? If she was, why does it matter that he's black? I don't understand. We were only at the park for *five minutes* when Mom made me leave!" [4]

The man sighed and shook his head in disapproval, instructing, "Sandra, treat people the way *you* want to be treated. I have met people from *all over the world*, of every race and nationality. Disliking someone because of their skin color is as ignorant as *favoring* someone because of it. If you stay away from an individual, let it be because of their lack of character, bad behavior, or poor choices. Don't judge someone by their nationality." [5]

"I get it!" I chirped. "You're saying that I don't have to stop shaking people's hands. *Right?*"

He grinned and said, "That's right. You don't have to stop shaking people's hands." Feeling the burden lift from my chest, I smiled and gave my father a warm hug. [6]

"Daddy makes sense, but Mom doesn't," I internally concluded as I stepped into my room. "Technically, unless they're washed, *everyone's* hands are dirty." [7]

Different Stuff

A distinct sound traveled through the air, signifying that my day was coming to a close. While filling the tub with warm water and some bubbles, my mother shouted from the hallway, *"Bath-time! Get in here!"* [1]

My brother and I scurried over. By the time my mother finished turning me around and removing my clothing, my sibling was already sitting in the tub. I carefully joined him and started playing with the foam. Since my sibling could bathe himself, the materfamilias focused on me and roughly scratched my scalp with her nails as I winced and moaned. Tilting my head back with force, she grabbed a cup of bathwater and rinsed off the shampoo. The woman soaped an abrasive washcloth and raked it over my skin. As she violently scrubbed, my bottom and the area between my legs became raw. [2]

"Ow! That hurts!" I complained, peering down to check the tender region that was stinging the most. The suds weren't as thick and fluffy as in previous baths, which allowed my peering through the water's surface. My focus went from my body to my brother's and then back to me. Confused, I queried, "Mom, why is *his* stuff different from *my* stuff?" [3]

My sibling confidently replied, "That's because I'm a *boy* and you're a *girl*." [4]

Wide-eyed, the woman removed her son from the tub and announced, "You're clean. Here's your towel. Go to your room and put on your pajamas." As he trotted away, the woman glared down at me with disgust. "Why were you looking at your brother's private parts?! That's dirty! I thought I was doing a *good thing* by bathing you two together to save water, but I guess not! Looking at your brother's private parts is a sin! God is going to get you for that, you little *demon!*" [5]

My mother abandoned me in the water and firmly shut the door behind her. Confused and ashamed, I surmised that asking the woman a simple question was a dangerous business. [6]

Since the water was still warm with a remnant of suds, I cheerfully squeaked to myself, "Wait a second! Don't feel bad, Sandra! You have the *whole tub* to play in! Now you can swim!" Enjoying the sounds of swirling water and the sensation of splashing, I felt calm and safe again to enjoy the bath until my fingertips wrinkled and the liquid became uncomfortably tepid. Beginning to shiver, I carefully dried off with the remaining towel and shouted, *"Mom! I'm done! What do I do now?!"* In response to my cries, she raised the volume of the living room television. Not knowing if I was to wait for her to bring my pajamas or do as my brother had done and carefully wear the towel into my room, I hesitated. Unwilling to guess incorrectly and upset the woman even further, I shivered under the damp towel and waited. Wondering if I was *still* making a mistake, I called out, *"Help me! I'm done and I don't know what to do now!"* I waited further, but no answer came. [7]

Discomfort eventually outweighed my apprehension and inspired action. Determined to avoid sleeping naked on the bathroom floor or forgetting a wet towel in my room for my mother to discover later, I attempted to hang the damp item on the door rack beside its counterpart. The targeted hook was uncomfortably high and difficult to reach. I silently climbed onto the slick counter and stretched myself toward the curved hardware with the towel in hand, feeling quite accomplished when it actually stayed. Safely back on the ground, I opened the door and peeped around its frame to discover an empty hallway. At once, I sprinted to my room naked and shut the door behind me. Still shivering, I pulled out pajamas from my dresser and frantically covered my body. Listening intently through the closed door, I heard the woman get up from the sofa and stomp down the hall to drain the tub. Unwilling to encounter her wrath, I switched off my ceiling light and jumped into bed. That was the last time my brother and I bathed together, which was nice. [8]

No Hitting

*H*orror washed over me as my mother led me to class on my first day of kindergarten. The elementary school seemed massive and labyrinth-like in layout. Without considering the consequences, I instinctively cleaved to the woman's hand and confessed, "I'm afraid of getting lost! What if I don't remember where I'm going?!" [1]

My mother yanked my arm and growled under her breath, *"Stop it. You're embarrassing me. Come on."* [2]

To distract myself, I observed the pebbled texture of some exterior walls and several murals on others. One path hosted the depiction of a wooden ruler that leaned against a short stack of novels. Another displayed a red apple that hosted a spectacle-clad worm with a small open book before it.

"Ha! I get it! A *book*worm!" I chirped. "I can remember *that*! If I get lost, I'll look for the bookworm." My mother dropped me off and silently departed, leaving me to step forward into the unknown by myself. [3]

A sweet woman with a crinkled smile was already waiting for me and greeted, "Hello! I'm your kindergarten teacher! It's so nice to meet you! Come on over here and have a seat. You're a bit early, but that's okay." Soon after, other students arrived and appeared as nervous as I had felt. "Come in! We're sitting over here! Join us on the rug!" The kind stranger counted us as we huddled together on a colorful mat covered in math problems and geometric shapes. "Let's learn everyone's names." We formed a circle and introduced ourselves. "Okay! This is a new school for each of you, so let's go for a walk to look around! Stand in a line by the door and I'll help you find your spots." We followed her around the campus like amused little ducklings. Each step behind our smiling leader eased my mind as we retraced some of my steps beside the mural covered walls and gained familiarity with our new surroundings. [4]

We visited the school counselor who shared a captivating story while puppeteering a turquoise dragon that caused us to giggle. Afterward, the woman's intelligence and vocabulary dazzled me as she asked us thought-provoking questions. When speaking, it was the first time I felt as though my opinions *mattered* to an adult.

Beyond Recognition

"What makes you afraid?" the counselor queried to our class. "Think about your answer before you speak and raise your hand when you're ready. I'll call on you."

After volunteering and being selected, a student cautiously responded, "Do you mean being afraid of things like *spiders*? I don't like spiders."

"Exactly, if that's what you're afraid of," she clarified. "With this question, there are no right or wrong answers. Just tell the truth. Who else wants to share?" Monsters, ghosts, snakes, scary movies, and the dark were among the confessions.

One boy stood and abruptly exclaimed, *"Pizza!"*

As our class erupted into laughter, the woman lowered her voice to hush the students and warned, "Don't laugh, boy and girls. If he's afraid of pizza, we should be respectful and let him express it without judgement." [5]

"Ha-ha!" a classmate playfully taunted. "You're afraid of pizza!"

The boy hid his face and whimpered, *"I am not."*

Hushing the children once more, the counselor directed her attention to the self-proclaimed pepperluciophobic and warmly asked, "Young man, are you *truly* afraid of pizza?"

He wiped his tears and sniffled to confess, "No, ma'am. I was just joking." [6]

"Are we going to take class discussions seriously from now on?" she gently queried, causing the boy to nod humbly. The counselor offered a gentle smile, which calmed the child and inspired a grin in return. "Very good." [7]

Day after day, our kindergarten teacher taught vital lessons while radiating all the kindness one could hope for. I learned new things each day, such as how to add, subtract, and count money. The instructor had a gift of making learning fun and I loved her for it. [8]

I experienced recess with a lingering sense of urgency to find an activity early, since my time outside seemed far too brief. Discovering the jewel of the playground, I rushed to its inviting seats. The swing set provided coveted sensations of a breeze and the thrilling pull of centrifugal force. I practiced my pendulum technique in order to achieve maximum height, craving the elevated perspective that followed each forward and backward thrust. Launching myself upward, I dared to push the limits of gravity and my nerves. When my timing was interrupted and I lost inertia, the swing would suddenly drop and jerk the chains. The weightlessness and plunge became a relished experience that I sometimes committed intentionally at the end of my turn.

Wielding a coach-whistle, a teacher's aide was always present to monitor our swing sessions. An abrupt *"Next!"* always followed her loud tweet, which signaled that our turn was over. Once we dug our feet into the gravel to stop ourselves, most of us would immediately get back in line. If I was *very* fortunate and the line was shorter than usual, I had enough time for a *second* turn before recess ended. [9]

Growing tired of the waiting, I left behind my favorite activity and selected the monkey bars to join some unfamiliar children on their perch. Before my hand could touch the welded metal, a tall boy blocked my path and aggressively snipped, "You can't get on the monkey bars with *us*." [10]

With pigtails dangling and a hand on one hip, I slapped the child, and sternly rebuked, "How dare you?! You have no right to stop me! There's room and I'm climbing!" His lip quivered, redirecting the flowing tears as he ran to the most intimidating teacher's aide on duty. I thought, "*Oh no.* Thanks to the *tattletale*, my recess is about to be cut short." [11]

I quickly jumped onto the cube-like monstrosity and climbed to the top. The fast-paced jingle of dangling keys was all the warning I needed as I closed my eyes and sighed at her approach. "Come down from there," the woman ordered. I obeyed her and stood face-to-face with my judge as she bent down low. "Now, I saw what happened and heard every word that was said. I don't think you should be in trouble. He was wrong for trying to stop you from playing. *However*, if I see you hit someone again, you *will* be in trouble. *No hitting.* Come to me next time, before resorting to violence. Now, go play."

I walked away, stunned. Although I expected *punishment*, I experienced understanding, forgiveness, and grace. [12]

Same

*A*fter bedtime, relentless curiosity over my belly button prevented me from falling asleep. Hours prior, I had an encounter with a child hanging upside-down on the monkey bars, and their exposed belly button piqued my curiosity. Its appearance was entirely different from my own and the image burned in my mind.

I silently wondered, "Why do I have a belly button? Is it some sort of plug? Would I have a big hole in my tummy if the plug ever fell out?" The concept made my eyes widen further and mind spin with dread. I wanted answers. [1]

Afraid to disturb my mother about *anything*, I resorted to asking my trivia-laden sibling for mental relief. Above all else, I desired to know if *he*, too, had a belly button, and if it was like mine. My task was a high-risk operation, involving the breaking of a cardinal household rule. We weren't to get out of bed after seven o'clock unless we were sick or needed to use the restroom. Well, I was sick of being ignorant about belly buttons. [2]

I crawled out from under the covers and walked towards my bedroom doorway, attempting to gain night vision spontaneously by opening my eyes wider than usual, which didn't work. However, turning on any additional lights would only alert the fire-breathing materfamilias in the living room and cause me to fail my mission completely. [3]

Quietly opening my door, I noticed how the dull glow from the television down the hall shifted all the shadows at once, over and over. I maintained focus on the opposing door frame to keep my bearings, tip-toed over to my brother's room, and gently whispered, *"Hey. Are you awake?"*

"What do you want, Sandra?" he whispered back with irritation.

Ignoring his tone, I softly inquired, *"Do you have a belly button?"* [4]

"Yes. Everyone does. Why?" he quietly huffed.

"Well... does yours look like mine?" I continued, still paused at his door.

The question must have piqued his interest. With wonder, he replied under his breath, *"Hmm... I don't know."*

He slipped out of bed and stepped onto the floor. We tried comparing belly buttons by facing one another, but couldn't see much of anything since my body was blocking the little light we had. We simultaneously rotated ninety degrees clockwise, but could only capture a weak side-light that created more shadows.

Recalling how I became exposed to the other child's belly button in the first place, I softly suggested, *"Let's try a different angle."*

I crawled onto my brother's comforter, flipped belly-up with my feet pointing away from the door, and carefully scooted my body towards the doorway's glow. Using my legs as a counterbalance, I bent backwards over the mattress' edge and allowed my head to dangle upside down, exposing my belly button to the dim light. My sibling understood the approach and did the same thing parallel to me.

After a quick examination, we discovered our belly buttons *matched*. I completed my mission and finally experienced a sense of relief. However, noticing my dangling brother's voluminous hair made me giggle. My standing strands must have been just as comical to him, since neither one of us could muffle our laughter. [5]

Sounds of joy traveled down the hallway far more effectively than the television light, for our mother had heard us and rapidly approached to investigate. Too distracted to hear her stomping nearer, we laughed until the materfamilias flipped the lights on and startled both of us.

The woman gnashed her teeth at our exposed stomachs, glared at me and shouted, "*Ah-ha!* I caught you! What are you doing in your brother's bed with your shirt up?! That's demonic!"

"No! That's not true!" I corrected, wide-eyed in disbelief. "We were trying to see if our belly buttons were the same and…" [6]

"I don't believe you!" she brutally interjected. "You're going to *hell* for whatever you were doing in the dark!" The woman snatched my arm and violently yanked my body off of my brother's bed. After violently spanking me, the woman tossed me onto my bedroom floor and coldly warned, "I better not catch you in your brother's room at night or you'll get it again! God is going to get you for that, *you little demon.*" [7]

At that, she shut the door and stomped into the living room to watch her favorite glowing companion. Stinging and confused, I drowned in shame, feeling sub-human. [8]

I wondered to myself between deep, trembling breaths, "How in the world could belly buttons be evil if everyone has one? That doesn't make any sense. How am I going to hell for not being in bed? Does God hate me? What just happened?" I crawled under my covers, thought about how peaceful it would be to never wake again, and cried myself to sleep. [9]

The following morning, just before our mother was to walk both of us to school, she prepared our sack lunches. While the woman was busy, I approached my sibling and quietly asked, *"I'm sorry if I got you in trouble last night, but do you know why Mom was so mad? Am I going to hell? I don't understand what happened."*

Refusing to discuss the recent belly button incident and seeming fearfully traumatized, my brother turned in a shunning manner and hurried away, avoiding eye contact and proximity during the entire walk to school. [10]

Up Next

Once my mother trekked the half-mile to school on foot and brought us home, the woman immediately made her way over to the sofa to continue her weekday routine. Using the remote control to turn on the television set, she found her favorite talk-show as my bother hustled to his bedroom to enjoy an evening of children's programming.

Suddenly remembering a confusing experience on the playground that day, a question weighed on my mind and caused me to deviate from compulsively following my sibling into the other room. Forgetting myself, I tapped the lounging woman on her shoulder and whispered, *"Mom? Something happened today and…"*

"Shh! It's four o'clock!" the scowling woman hissed. "If you wanted to say something, you should have said it while we were walking! You had your chance! Now, go away!" As my mother refocused on the screen, her demeanor immediately flipped from enraged to completely vacant, displaying an unflatteringly blank gaze and droopy countenance. [1]

Her sudden transition caused me to note internally, "Well, *that's* disturbing."

Sensing my lingering study of her odd behavior, she spouted, "What are you staring at, *you little monster?!* Go find something to do! Leave me alone! Am I asking for something impossible?! Am I asking for the moon?!"

Retreating into the backyard and up my favorite tree, I cried and murmured, "I should have known better. Why did I try to ask her a question? She hates me." [2]

Weary of isolation, I returned to the occupied living room and sat down on a separate couch to find out what had taken my place in her heart.

A talk show headline read, *"Is YOUR Man Cheating? UP NEXT!"*

"You've got to be kidding me," I thought to myself. "No wonder my parents are always fighting."

It was clear to see the connection between the warped scenarios of daytime television and my mother's twisted version of reality. Individuals volunteered to have their stained private lives broadcasted as entertainment and feed the gluttonous insecurities of the woman raising me.

The televised wife claimed, "Well, my husband keeps working late and doesn't bother calling. I tried talking to him about it and asked him to be home more, but he won't listen. I didn't know what else to do, so I called the show for help. Things can't go on like this."

Watching the guest sob, the host replied, "We're here to help. Guess what? After your call to us, we had your husband followed. Do you want to know what we found out?" The audience cheered with approval. While showing footage from a hidden camera, the host revealed multiple occasions where the spouse had been meeting up with another woman while claiming to be at the office. "We have your husband here with us today in a soundproof booth. He thinks he's here to see the results of a makeover. Are you ready to confront your husband?" The host led the unsuspecting man to sit down beside his wife and showed him the footage. He confessed to committing adultery and apologized to his sobbing wife. It wasn't enough. The merciless studio audience openly booed and ridiculed him, including several women with a microphone shoved in their face. [3]

At the end of the show, they interviewed the private investigator, who claimed to have ways for anyone to detect a philandering spouse. My mother gobbled down each generic clue as an indisputable and irrevocable detection of guilt. [4]

During the ending credits, the woman peered over at me to utter, "A woman *knows* when her husband is cheating on her. If he's not getting it from me, he's getting it from somebody. I'm going to hire a private detective to follow your father."

"You really *should* hire a detective," I advised, having recalled the theme-song to a police-show we watched regularly. "All suspects are innocent until proven guilty in the court of law. It would be worth the money to discover the *truth*. Then you'd know if you're wrong about Daddy and can finally relax." [5]

"*Shut up!*" she barked. "I shouldn't have said anything to you! You don't know anything! Besides, private detectives are expensive! *Innocent*. Ha! If he's found innocent, how do I know that the detective isn't lying just to protect your father?! Men stick together." [6]

I rolled my eyes and shook my head at the woman's frustrating logic and inquired, "It sounds like you actually *want* him to cheat on you. What's more important? Do you want *the truth* or to be right?" [7]

"Just wait until *you* get married and *your* husband cheats on *you!*" she viciously retorted. "*Then*, you'll know what it's like." [8]

"No, thanks." I said matter-of-factly. "If arguing is all there is to marriage, I don't need it." [9]

"*Ha!* You're six! You shouldn't even be *thinking* about marriage!" she ridiculed. "Marriage is for adults!" [10]

"*Exactly*," I added, leaning forward with sass. "So, stop talking about it." [11]

"You don't tell me what to do! I'm the mother and you're the child! You don't pay the bills, so you don't have a say in *anything*!" the woman announced bitterly. "Get the hell out of here, you little demon, before I give you a spanking!" [12]

I casually retreated to my bedroom and mumbled under my breath, "*You* don't pay the bills either. My daddy does. So, that means *you* shouldn't have a say. Nice logic, idiot." [13]

The Highway

While I traveled in the passenger seat, my mother drove the two of us deeper into the city and parked near a strip mall. I unbuckled my seatbelt to let myself out when the woman grabbed my arm and whispered, *"What are you doing? Close the door. We're not going in."*

Confused, I plainly asked, "Why are we here if we're not going inside?"

*"Shh! That woman that just walked into the building is ******* your father,"* she cautiously whispered. *"I'm waiting for her to come back out."* [1]

Shocked, I scanned the area and queried, "Really? What woman? How do you know? Do you have any evidence? What happened? Did you hear them talking about it or witness them together?"

"Be quiet," she continued under her breath. *"I just know… and don't question me. I shouldn't have brought you. I don't have to explain myself to you. You're just an ignorant child."*

"Why are you whispering? If she's inside the building and we're inside the car, she can't hear us," I reasoned, shaking my head in frustration.

My mother shot me an aggressive look and quietly ordered, *"Shut up."* Having lost track of how long we were sitting, I gasped when the stalker growled, *"There she is. That little ****."*

The target entered her vehicle and pulled away from the parking lot. Hastening to catch her, my mother tailed the car and followed it onto the highway. The stranger may have assumed that her gas tank was open or that we needed help, because the driver pulled off of the road and came to a full stop with her window rolled down. Fearing for the stranger's life, I tried to come up with a way to warn the victim before my mother unleashed her wrath.

"*Mom?* What are you going to do? What's happening?" I prodded, clinging to the hope that the stranger would wise up and drive away. As our vehicle pulled up closer to the unsuspecting young woman, my mother hunched down and shut off the engine with gnashed teeth and narrowed eyes of hatred. "This is a bad idea, Mom! You're acting weird! I want to go home!" [2]

"Shut up," the termagant snapped quietly. *"Stay in the car. Keep the doors locked until I come back."* The materfamilias charged toward the suspected mistress and alarmed the woman with her threatening demeanor. The victim better secured herself by rolling up the window and locking her doors.

"Finally," I murmured, clinging to my seatbelt as the scene unfolded.

Keeping her back to traffic, my mother shouted toward the driver side window, *"I know who you are, you ******* *****! Stop ******* my husband! If I ever catch the two of you together, I'll kick your ***! Do you hear me?!"* [3]

At that, the woman peeled out and sped away, leaving her accuser to be peppered with roadside gravel. The materfamilias stomped back towards our car and climbed inside to drive us home. Minutes of silence passed when my curiosity won out and caused me to inquire, "I couldn't hear what she was saying. What happened?"

"She was *lying* and said that she didn't know what I was talking about or who my husband was," the jealous wife confidently replied.

I slapped my palms to my thighs and conveyed, "I believe her! If she has never seen you before and doesn't know your name, how could she possibly know who your husband is?"

"I'm not telling her my name so she can do something to me!" she reasoned.

Ashamed, I hung my head and concluded, "This didn't solve *anything*."

"Yes, it did! If she's sleeping with a married man, she'll stop," the woman boasted.

My mouth dropped open in disgust, scolding, "*If?!* You chased a woman down the highway and threatened her over something you weren't even *sure* about?! That's awful! Do you know how *crazy* that is?!" [4]

"Shut up… and don't call me crazy!" the woman warned. "I followed your father and saw them talking, so I followed her afterward."

"What?! Where did you see them talking?" I interrogated. "Was he working?"

My mother's face turned crimson as she roared, *"Stop asking me questions or I'll spank you! Whose side are you on, you little brat?! God is going to get you for that, you little demon! Do you want some **** to take your father away from us?! I'm not raising two brats all by myself so she can spend all his money! No way!"* [5]

I looked out the window and ignored the rest of her rambling monologue. [6]

After being home for a few hours, a familiar jingling caused me to gasp in delight. Popping up from watching a cartoon, I sprinted over as the sound of metal raking upon metal tickled my ears. It was my father's key sliding into the lock. Claiming my prize, I tackled my father's leg and sat on his foot before he could remove his shoes.

He laughed and grunted, "Sandra, you're getting too big for this." [7]

"I love you, Daddy," I assured, trying to strengthen the man's spirits before they shattered completely. [8]

A far less appealing sound alluded to a brewing storm that tensed my tiny shoulders. To intimidate her next victim, the termagant's bare heels thumped from their bedroom at the end of the hall and drew nearer until she stepped into view. [9]

The woman raged, *"You're eight minutes late!"* Releasing my father's shin, I slipped into the nearby kitchen and actively listened out of sight, lingering feet away from the altercation. "I see what's going on here! You think I'm stupid, don't you?! *I know what's happening!* Who were you ******* this time?! God's gonna get you for what you're doing, you mother ******!" [10]

An eruption of vulgarity blasted forth from her lips, spewing whatever steaming, molten-filth had been building up inside of her troubled mind throughout the day. [11]

Ignoring his wife's ravings, my father removed his shoes and found a ballgame to watch on the television. Although the woman progressively grew louder and increasingly vulgar, the man's eyebrows didn't so much as twitch. However, in order for the hours of badgering to end, he capitulated to his wife's long-awaited expectations and delivered a heated rebuttal. It was then that unhinged woman drew closer to him, balling up her fists as she had so many times before. [12]

I couldn't passively observe, so I abandoned my hiding spot, stood beside my father, and demanded, "Leave my daddy alone!" [13]

The termagant peered down and shouted, *"Get out of here, you demon from hell! Go watch TV or I'll spank you!"* [14]

Her husband turned to me and angrily shouted, *"Go to your room, Sandra!"*

Shocked and wounded, I retreated down the hall and found my brother watching a cartoon. I joined him on the floor as he turned up the volume to drown out the fighting.

Tell the Truth

When my brother played with his movie-themed dinosaur set, I wanted to join in. If my sibling liked a specific television show, I wanted to like it and watch it with him. While he played with a neighborhood boy in the backyard, I wanted to be included. As a result, nearly every day, I irritated my older sibling until he snapped and hit me. When it happened again, I cried and ran into the living room to report my brother's actions to my father.

"Well, Sandra… were you pestering him?" the man coldly questioned. "I had four sisters and was the only boy. I know how girls can be. I received spankings for things that didn't even happen… for the lies that they told. You were probably messing with him until he finally hit you. I'm going to teach you to leave your brother alone. *You're getting the spanking.*" [1]

Off came the tooled-leather belt from my father's hip. The disciplinarian rapidly delivered three stinging swats, which had been his standard amount for most infractions. Although I *had* been bothering the boy, I was the only one who received punishment when reporting his violence. [2]

One afternoon, I disrespected the materfamilias in public and received a vicious spanking after returning to the house. Her *discipline* didn't stop until she grew tired or broke a blood vessel in her hand. "Stay in your room! You can't watch TV or play with your brother! I'm telling your father when he gets home! Then you're *really* gonna get it!" [3]

Stinging and tender, I spent hours in solitary confinement until my father arrived through the front door from work. The materfamilias greeted him with her demands. At once, my bedroom door swung open and revealed a very irritated man, scolding, "You disobeyed your mother in public?! You're getting a spanking."

As he removed his leather belt, I pleaded, "I don't understand! Mom already spanked me for that!"

"Well, she didn't tell *me* that," he sternly replied. "Turn around or this will hurt more than it needs to." Obeying, I received three controlled swats on an already red and throbbing area.

Later, I confronted my mother and rebuked, "Why didn't you tell Dad that you already hit me?! You're a hateful woman and a liar! I don't know how you sleep at night." [4]

"Ha! You think *that* was bad? That was a *piece of cake* compared to what happened to *me* growing up! When *I* was bad, my mother would beat the **** out of me and I deserved it! My father came home drunk every weekend and then beat up my mom. It was a *nightmare*! When he would come after *us*, my mother would get in the way to protect us. I *love* my mother. You're going to miss me when I'm dead and gone. *You'll see.*" She might have been wrong about that. Imagining her funeral only inspired small jigs and cheerful songs. [5]

I clumsily spilled my drink on the table at dinner. My eyes filled with dread as the termagant stood and rounded its corner. A violent spanking begun as the materfamilias shouted, "How many times have I told you to watch what you're doing?! All you ever do is make more work for me! I'm just a slave in this house! All I ever do is cook and clean!"

"I'll clean it!" I cried out in a sob, being gripped in place by my thin arm while her hand cracked at my bottom half.

"Shut up! What good will that do! All you'll ever do is make things worse!" she snarled, tossing my appendage away from her. "Stop crying and get out of my sight!"

While out and about at a discount store, I noticed a popular slime for sale that I had seen in a commercial. Assuming the woman would refuse to buy it for me, I took a chance and asked. To my surprise, the materfamilias purchased it.

For days, I played with it constantly until it slipped out of my hands and onto the floor, picking up dirt and hair. Figuring it just needed a good wash, I brought it into the bathroom and ran water over it, but the undesired particles were not coming out. Giving up and accepting the gritty slime as it was, I attempted to dry it off with a bath towel. The slime clung to the towel and caused me to panic.

Dreading what my mother would do to me if she found out, I shoved the towel behind the washing machine and thought, "No one will know." [6]

My father stepped into my room with evidence in hand, querying, "Is this towel stained with *your* slime?" [7]

Fearful and trembling, I sheepishly claimed, "I don't know." [8]

The man shook his head in disappointment and sighed. Squatting down, he explained, "Usually, when I ask you a question, *I already know the answer.* This stain *is* from your slime. You probably got it dirty, tried to wash it, attempted to dry it, and got it stuck to the towel. It was obviously an accident." My mouth dropped open, amazed at his powers of deduction. As my father struggled to remain stone-faced, he continued, "What *wasn't* an accident was you hiding the stained towel behind the washing machine. If you break something or make a mess, just come tell me. You probably won't get a spanking. However, if you *lie* about it, you'll get *two* spankings. One for the mess and one for lying. I will eventually find out what happened, so it's best to just tell the truth from the start." [9]

"*Wait a second*," I interjected, mind blown. "You're telling me that if I *admit* to making a mistake and tell you about it right away, you might just *fix it* and moved on?" [10]

He smirked, confirming, "Yes, depending on what it is."

"Wow," I replied. "That's *amazing*. I understand. With mom, I get spanked for just spilling milk. I get spanked no matter what happens, but with you, I can avoid them. I'm sorry for messing up the towel, Daddy." [11]

My father stood up and calmly announced, "Thank you for coming clean. However, you still need to be disciplined. It's time for two spankings since you lied."

"Is that two *sets* of three swats?" I inquired. After he nodded, I continued, "So… *three* swats… times *two* sets… equals *six swats total*."

"Very good," he encouraged. "Now, come on. Let's go to your room and get this over with."

Get Back Up

~~~~~

The weather was beautiful and inviting, which inspired the materfamilias to open the windows for a cascading breeze to flow through the entire house. My brother and I pleaded to our matriarch, "Can we go outside and ride our bikes?"

"Fine, but don't go too far. If I have to get out of my chair to look for you, you're getting a spanking and we're going back inside. You could get kidnapped," she warned. "If someone touches you, I'll kick their ***!"

While exiting through the back door, I mumbled, "I guess *you're* the only one that's allowed to hurt me."

With an icy drink in her hand, the materfamilias retrieved her favorite lawn chair from the garage and sat comfortably to keep an eagle eye on her offspring. As I followed behind my sibling, the woman shouted, *"Stay out of the street and watch for cars! Stay close to your brother! Someone could take you!"* [1]

I rolled my eyes and whispered, "Someone, please, *take me*."

Growing bored with pedaling up and down the same sidewalk, my sibling and I took turns piloting a red metal wagon. We hauled it up to the top of the hill and steered the contraption down the sloped sidewalk by its handle, intentionally crashing it onto the plush neighboring lawns. When that grew tiresome, I laced on some roller skates from a local garage sale while my brother navigated his red scooter. In time, we mounted our bicycles all over again.

My father observed us and announced, "Sandra, you're too old to be riding your bike with training wheels. You're going to learn how to ride like a big-girl." [2]

"Is she ready?! You better not hurt her!" his wife warned from her seat. "What if she falls down and cracks her head open?!" [3]

"If you can't handle watching, then go inside!" he shouted, receiving a nasty glare from his wife as she abandoned her post and huffed away. [4]

Taking the bicycle from my hands, he opened the meticulously organized garage to retrieve the appropriate tools. My bicycle's double-amputation caused me to tremble like a novice acrobat watching the removal of their safety net. "If I fall down and crack my head open, will I *die*?" I nervously inquired. [5]

"You're *not* going to die," the man confidently assured, tightening a bolt. "*Training* wheels were designed to *train* you how to ride a bicycle. They were never intended to be permanent. You may not realize it, but you don't use your training wheels when you pick up speed. The dependency is all in your head." [6]

I made a quizzical face, wondering aloud, "In my head?" [7]

"*Yes.* For example, you don't use crutches to walk around because you can walk without them. Training wheels are like crutches. You don't need them to ride your bicycle anymore," he clarified, adjusting the height of my seat. "Okay, Sandra. Everything looks good. Climb on and give it a shot." [8]

Wearing a helmet and matching joint pads, my eyes filled with tears as I earnestly expressed, "Don't let go of me, Daddy! I'm scared!" [9]

"I'm right here," he reassured. "I'm not going anywhere." [10]

"What if I fall down?" I murmured. [11]

"Then, you will get right back up and try again," the man coached, walking beside me while holding onto my seat and handlebars. I pedaled through the terror. "Keep steering. I think you have the hang of it now." [12]

"Uh…no, I don't," I corrected. The idea of making a mistake in front of my father horrified me. I hoped to ride effortlessly on the first try. However, his hovering body position required me to tilt my head sideways to avoid his arms and chest, making the entire exercise awkwardly offset.

Ignoring my discomfort, the man firmly insisted, "Yes, *you do.*"

"No, I *really* don't," I rebutted. Undeterred, my father hunched over beside me and ran. My heart pounded harder with every stride. Panic set in as I cried out, *"I can't do this! Why are you doing this to me?!"* [13]

"*Steer, Sandra!*" the man shouted. "*Steer!*"

He released me, causing me to wail, *"What are you doing, Dad?! No!"*

No longer hearing his footsteps or breathy huff, I twisted my entire body with the handlebars to peer backwards. The front tire cut a hard left, carrying my body's momentum over and down to the sidewalk, painfully scraping my knee against the unforgiving cement and jarring my body. I sobbed, discovering my kneepads resting loosely at my ankles. Being far too thin, the safety gear couldn't stay in position during a wreck. [14]

"*Stop crying*," my father ordered. "Let's go, again."

Grabbing my shoulders, he pulled me to my feet and allowed me to reposition my knee pad over my bleeding skin as I rebutted, "Dad… I just fell! Shouldn't we stop?" [15]

Irritated, he sternly warned, "If you don't get back on that bike right now, you *never* will. Pick it up and roll it to the top of the sidewalk. You fell because you turned your body and lost focus of where you were going. Learn from your mistakes and don't get distracted. When I let go, *you have to steer*. Focus on pedaling. Forward momentum keeps you upright. You can do this. Let's go." African drums seemed to beat under my sternum as the man began again. After he released me, I continued pedaling and felt astonished by my success. Suddenly, my father shouted, *"Okay! Now, turn around and come back!"* [16]

Panic swarmed me as I futilely tried to drag my feet, remembering that he had raised my seat. Gasping, I thought, "Oh, yeah! I need to pedal backwards to stop!" My feet failed to reconnect with the speedily revolving pedals. Desperate, I turned the handlebars and surrendered myself to physics as it brutally slammed me onto the asphalt street. [17]

From our distant driveway, my father ordered, *"Get up, Sandra! Grab your bike! Let's try again!"* [18]

"No!" I defiantly sobbed as I stood myself back up. *"I don't want to! This is supposed to be fun, and it isn't!"* [19]

"Then put away your bike and go inside!" the man loudly replied. *"Quit! I'm done teaching you! You're on your own!"*

Humiliated, bruised and bleeding, I rolled the bike up that hill with drooping shoulders and my chin to my chest. My father's words stung. I refused to be a quitter. Wiping away hot tears and the drips from my nose, I lifted my gaze with a squint and resolved, "I'm going to do this. I'll show *everybody*. Pedal, but not too fast… and practice stopping. Since I have to come back, I shouldn't go very far away." Unwilling to be just another crash-test dummy like the ones I watched on television, I cautiously mounted the contraption and pedaled in a jerking manner to engage my brakes. As I picked up confidence and speed, I squeaked, *"I'm doing it!"* [20]

I ventured farther than ever before and passed some unfamiliar houses as the slope increased significantly. At once, the momentum to became too great for my twiggy-legs to counter. Blurred pedals snagged my dangling shoelaces, jammed the crank arm, pinned my ankles onto the speeding metal frame, and stopped the bike. Centrifugal force showed no mercy as my body launched forward and violently met the pavement.

Panic clawed from within my chest as I wondered if anyone would notice that I was missing. Afraid that I would starve to death on the sidewalk or bleed out from my scrapes in forgotten solitude, I screamed for help. [21]

The father of a neighboring family gently opened his front door to approach me with overwhelming gentleness and asked, *"Do you need some help, sweetie?"* [22]

His masculine appearance and deep voice soothed me. My sobs diminished as I replied, "Yes. I'm stuck and I can't move." [23]

"Well, let me help you," he offered with a smile, squatting down to investigate while the rest of his household huddled before me in sympathy. "First, let's get these shoes off of your feet. That will make things easier." [24]

Grinning, I remarked, "That's so smart! I don't know why I didn't think of that. Thank you for helping me. You're really nice." [25]

"Everyone falls down," he warmly informed. "We all need help now and again." [26]

With my socked feet liberated, the gracious man unraveled my laces while his wife helped me up and the eldest daughter patted my clothes clean. [27]

"Would you like some water?" another daughter offered, handing me a miniature bottle. [28]

"Wow!" I exclaimed, unaccustomed to that level of generosity. "Thank you so much!"

"*Sandra! Where are you?!*" the materfamilias aggressively called from just out of view, panicked and in a rage. [29]

I lifted my voice and replied, *"I'm okay! I'm over here!"* As the woman stormed nearer with a spiteful trod, the man finished up and gently set my shoes neatly on the sidewalk. The termagant snatched up my bicycle with one hand and violently grabbed my wrist with the other, yanking my body away from our benevolent neighbors. Resisting her, I exclaimed, "Wait, Mom! I need to get my shoes!"

"*They tried to steal your shoes?!*" she yelled. [30]

Horrified, the family gasped in unison as the eldest girls covered their mouths. Shocked that the thought could enter her mind, I frantically explained, "No, Mom! My shoelaces got stuck and I crashed my bike! They heard me crying and came outside just to help me! This nice man took off my shoes and got me untangled while his family cleaned me up! They even brought me bottled water!" I pogo-jumped and queried, "Can we be friends with them?" [31]

"No!" she snapped, staring down at me. "You have your shoes. Now, *let's go*." [32]

Wrenched away, I looked back over my shoulder at my rescuers and shouted, *"Thank you!"* Each one waved goodbye with a pity-drenched smile and slowly made their way up the driveway and into their home. Turning to my mother, I boldly chided, "You were terrible to those nice people! You accused them of stealing my shoes, but they didn't! They *helped* me!" [33]

Other neighbors stepped out of their home to witness my body being forcefully pulled along the sidewalk. The termagant took notice and growled, "*You don't know that and be quiet. Do you want to wake the whole neighborhood?*"

At full volume, I sternly rebuked, "In case you weren't aware, it's the afternoon! The neighborhood is already awake… and yes, I know exactly what happened because *I was there!* That nice family helped me… and I know *exactly* why you don't like them! You don't like them because… because… because they're *black!*" [34]

Exposed before a navy-housing community, humiliation clung to her like a rotten egg to the face as she averted her eyes from the multiracial glares. Once inside, she locked the door and tossed my tiny body to the vinyl floor, roaring, *"Get inside, you demon from hell! God is going to get you for embarrassing me!"* [35]

"I'm not the one that's embarrassing," I thought with an elevated brow.

The following morning, I became determined to ride my bike without a traumatic scene. As I exited, the materfamilias continued to stare at the television and coldly remarked, "If you fall, don't expect me to help you." [36]

"I *never* expect help from you," I bitterly confessed, shutting the door behind me. [37]

Rethinking my father's initial strategy, I chose a completely different starting position and pedaled somewhere flatter, practicing how to break and smoothly turn. Realizing that maintaining control was far more pleasant than losing it and attempting to regain it, I finally stopped crashing. [38]

Double Standard

~~~~~

Someone was lightly rapping at the door while my brother and I were watching cartoons down the hall. Irritated at the interruption of her regularly scheduled program, the materfamilias arose from the sofa and investigated through the peephole. The woman's stomp prompted me to tiptoe over to see who had visited. [1]

Before touching the doorknob, the termagant harshly whispered, *"I don't want any brats inside my house. They'll just steal something."* Waiting to see if the person would grow impatient and leave, the woman silently monitored through the peephole. They knocked once more with even greater confidence. As if movie cameras were rolling, the materfamilias opened the door with a contrived smile and sweetly greeted, "Hi!" [2]

A dark-skinned little girl nervously fidgeted to request, "Hello. Do you have a *daughter* that I can play with?" [3]

"I'm sorry. She isn't home," the woman dryly stated.

"Oh, okay. Thank you," replied the child, who quickly departed. [4]

Astonished and wounded, I queried sharply, "Why did you *lie* and say that I wasn't home? I was right behind you and wanted to play! I'm not *grounded*, I don't have homework, and it's a sunny day! Why did you do that?!" [5]

"I have my reasons! Stop questioning me! I'm the mother and you're the child! You go where I say you go and you do what I say you do!" the termagant berated. [6]

"Well, I get *spanked* for lying. You talk about sin and God all the time, but isn't *lying* a sin? Isn't God going to get *you* for that?" I openly mocked, causing her to snarl at me. [7]

Shortly afterward, there was another knock at our door, prompting the liar to stand up begrudgingly and grumble, "Can't I have any peace around here?" She turned the knob and cheerfully greeted, "Hi!" [8]

The fair-skinned boy next door queried, "Can your kids come outside to play?"

With feigned kindness, she replied, "You can play in the *backyard*, but don't go into the front yard. If I catch you guys playing in the front yard, *they'll* be in trouble and *you'll* have to go home. Okay?"

"Okay!" he agreed with enthusiasm, waiting for my sibling and me to meet him at the backyard gate. "You guys have the best climbing tree in the neighborhood!"

I couldn't understand why the woman permitted visitors that came for my brother, but not for me. The double standard became clearer the day he quoted lines from a movie I hadn't seen and referenced video games he had played when we didn't own a single console.

"How are you playing video games?" I interrogated.

"I play them at my friend's house," he replied casually, reclining on the floor while watching a military cartoon.

Slack jawed, I raised my hands and commented, "Wait a second! You get to go to a *friend's house!* Mom never lets me do that! I'm not even allowed to use the phone or invite friends over! That's messed up! How do you even get there?! Mom never leaves!"

He divulged, "They just come and pick me up."

"Are you allowed to use the phone, too?! *What's going on here?!* That's not fair! I'm trapped here all the time and you get to do whatever you want! How often does this happen?!" I angrily questioned. [9]

After that, the boy became silent and ignored me.

On another day, a fair-skinned girl knocked and inquired, "Can Sandra come over to *my* house to play? We have a trampoline!"

"*No*," the woman harshly declined. "You both will play in *our* backyard or she doesn't play *at all*."

"Okay!" the child exclaimed. "Let me go tell my mom! I'll be right back!"

In the child's absence, the materfamilias lectured, "I'm not letting you go over to someone else's house so you can get *molested!* Even *my father* molested me... and I think my brother did, too. I couldn't go play at a cousin's or friend's house without someone trying to do something *dirty*. One time, I walked with a friend to her house and her dad answered the door in his underwear with all the lights off. It was really dark in there. I don't remember what happened after that. I think I blocked it out or something. I'm pretty sure I was molested that day, too."

"Listen. I hear what you're saying, but I've never played on a trampoline before. Why don't you just come *with* me?" I suggested. "No one will molest me if you're right there. You could even bring your own lawn chair and a drink! Who knows? What if her mom is a *nice person* and you make a new friend to talk to?" [10]

"What do I need friends for... so they can know all my business and stab me in the back?! I don't think so!" the woman reasoned. "Besides, I'm not rearranging my day just for you to jump on a trampoline. You can't always get what you want." [11]

"Well, *my brother* apparently can!" I protested, boldly indignant. "I have to stay home, but *my brother* can leave to play video games and watch movies with his friends at *their* houses! That's not fair! Why is it okay for him and not for me?!"

"Because he's a boy and you're a girl!" she revealed, matter-of-factly.

"Does that make him *molest-proof*?!" I rebutted.

The woman's eyes narrowed with malice as she replied, "Boys *can* get molested, but he's *big* and can defend himself! You can't! *Look at you.* You're skin and bones! They could just throw you and that's it!" [12]

Angry tears filled my eyes and streamed down burning cheeks as I concluded, "No matter how big I am, I'll *always* be a girl! I can't change that! So, because I'm not *a boy*, you'll never let me go over to a friend's house?!"

She flippantly tossed her hands into the air and quipped, "I guess not!" Pleased with herself, the materfamilias donned a megalomaniacal grin and returned to her television.

Nancy and the Secret

Another day, another knock. The materfamilias inspected through the peephole and quickly opened the door to a tanned little girl. Determined to play, I strategically stood in her view and waved.

Glancing over, the child spotted me and offered a perfect smile, greeting, "Hello! My name is Nancy. Can your daughter come outside and play?"

"What a pretty little girl! Look, Sandra! Do you see how *polite* and *respectful* she is? You should be more like *her*," the woman cruelly goaded, noticing my defiant eyebrow. Without pause, the materfamilias returned her attention to the preferred child and gently charmed, "You're more than welcome to play *here* in the backyard. Since the weather is so nice, I'll go get Sandra's table and play dishes out from her room so you both can have a little tea party." [1]

Shocked, I ran toward the backyard and half expected to see airborne pigs doing barrel rolls in the sky. It was then that the situation became clear. Nancy, who was being treated as an honored guest, just so happened to be the same race as *my mother*. [2]

True to her word, the termagant gently placed the plastic table under the shade of our neighborhood-famous tree. The materfamilias even prepared the rarely served, yet highly coveted, sweet-red-drink and completely forbidden animal crackers. Prior to that moment, my mother had only purchased the cookies for herself to consume. When I requested to eat them, it resulted in aggression and threats of a spanking. The woman returned once more with a selection of colorful freezer popsicles, leaving me slack jaw. For me, touching the refrigerator or freezer was against house rules, since I might 'leave fingerprints'. I was completely unaware that we possessed treats like that and certainly hadn't eaten them. [3]

Although the woman's behavior toward my playmate was out of character and *very* suspect, I joined in the act and pretended that she was a loving mother. I was thankful for the fortunate turn of events. Nancy's arrival had immediately benefited me. The materfamilias showed unusual hospitality and had never hosted a tea party before, especially for me. My mother must have run out of edible surprises to display and finally left us alone.

Conversation with my new friend covered a broad range of topics. We were the same age, enjoyed climbing trees, played with dolls, and possessed the most vivid of imaginations. United through navy-housing, we shared a deep understanding of missing our fathers during their long deployments. [4]

"Let's toast," I chimed, refilling our teacups. We pinched the tiny plastic handles and lifted our red liquid high. "To being best friends, forever! *Cheers!*"

"*Cheers!*" she chirped, gently tapping her cup to mine before downing the remaining drops. Observing one another's ruby red lips, teeth, and tongues, we laughed. "It's getting hot out here, Sandra. Can we go play in your room? I want to see the dolls you were talking about earlier."

Suspecting that the materfamilias was always listening through the back screen-door, I leaned forward and whispered, "*You don't want to go into my house. My mom is mean.*" [5]

"Really?" Nancy quietly replied. "*She seems so friendly.*" [6]

Exercising further discretion, I continued all the more softly, "*Yeah… to you. My parents fight every night. They hate each other. Sometimes, I worry about my mom trying to kill my dad, but then I remember that if he dies, my mom would have to work. Since my mom doesn't like doing anything but watch TV, maybe she won't kill him.*"[7]

Nancy stood up with a heavy expression on her face and gently ordered, "Sandra, come here. You need a hug." [8]

Her offer of comfort moved me, so much so that I cried in her arms and whispered further, "My mom *hates* me, but I hate her *more*." [9]

"I'm so sorry, Sandra," Nancy soothed, refraining from releasing me until I let go to dry my eyes and clean my nose.

Suddenly, I perked up and suggested, "You know what? I don't want to be *me* anymore. Let's be *spies* and fight crime!"

Her eyes enlarged as she jubilantly reciprocated, "Yeah! Good idea! I want to be a ninja!"

We scurried up the textured bark of the crooked and knobby tree to conduct a brief meeting. "Okay," I began. "You're a highly skilled ninja and I'm a government spy. Our job is to make the city safer by bringing criminals to justice."

"Okay. I like it," she confessed with a grin. "What's our first mission?"

"Well, let's pretend that it's nighttime and we're sneaking up on a robbery in progress," I conveyed, acting as though I could really see the events unfolding.

Responding in kind, Nancy gasped and said, "Look! They're stealing jewels!"

"This job is for Ninja Nancy!" I exclaimed. "What are you going to do?!"

"I'll use my ninja stars to knock out the lights and then judo-chop the bad guys!" she declared, keeping her fingers together as she sliced through the air. "Hi-yah! Hi-yah! Oh, no! I need help, Sandra the Spy! There's way too many of them!"

"I'm coming!" I announced, pretending to grab a holstered sidearm. "Stop right there! Drop the merchandise or you'll be sorry! Guy in the hat, put down that pipe and back away from my friend. *Nice and easy, dirtbag.* I'd hate to stain that diamond necklace in your hand. All of you, put your backs against the wall and keep your hands where I can see them. I've already called for backup. They're on their way..."

Daylight weaned, signifying that it was time to part ways for the evening. I walked Nancy to the gate, hugged her, and solemnly informed, "I hate that you have to go home. I miss you already. Hopefully, I'll see you again tomorrow."

Putting her hand on my shoulder, she encouraged, "Everything is going to be okay, Sandra. See you then."

Once Nancy had exited the gate, my mother's voice raked across my soul, forcefully whispering, *"Sandra, get in here."* Having delayed her wrath until a sound barrier was present, she shut the doors behind me and cornered my body in the mudroom. "Why did Nancy tell you that *everything was going to be okay*? What are you telling your friends about me?!" I shrank back in silence as she loomed over me. "Don't go around telling everybody what happens here! What goes on in this house isn't anyone else's business! It's a *sin* to talk bad about your parents! *God is going to get you for that!* You're just an *unappreciative little brat.* Look at what I did for you today! I let you have your little friends over and set up tea parties for you! Well, no more!" Terrified at her threats, I sobbed. "How dare you talk bad about me! If you want to have friends over, don't go blabbing about what goes on in this house or I'll stop you from seeing anyone! Keep running your mouth and someone will call the cops! They'll take you away, put you in a foster home, and you'll be pushed around from house to house!" [10]

"*Wait a second,*" I confidently interjected. "Are you telling me that someone can *legally* take me away from you? *That can happen?!* Is there a *hotline*? Do you have the number?"

"You think you can find a better home out there?! *Ha!* Go ahead and try! Call them!" the woman prodded. "You don't even know what you're talking about! *No one wants you.* You think I'm such a terrible mother and that your foster parents will be sweet and nice? They'll molest you and do God-knows-what! You're not safe out there! You have it way better than I did! I drove my mother crazy, and when she spanked me, I deserved it! My mother used to beat the hell out of me... and I *love* my mother! You're so spoiled. You have dolls and a bicycle! I didn't have *anything* when I was little! We grew up poor in the projects! My father would come home drunk every weekend and my sister had to call the cops on him when he started beating my mother when she tried to protect us! My childhood was a living hell! No one was there to help me! My brother was running the streets and my sister was working all the time! I had to steal her clothes to wear something nice! I buy you pretty clothes! You're the little girl I always wanted! I had your name picked out when I was sixteen!" Her words meant nothing to me, and it showed. "Go to your room, *you demon from hell*, before I spank you!" [11]

The following morning, I intently watched a public service announcement on television about missing and exploited children. After scribbling down their number, I opened my dictionary and looked up the word *exploited*. Within seconds, I crumpled up the number and threw it away, mumbling, "Those poor kids. I'm not missing or used. Those kids need that hotline for *real* dangers with strangers and bad men. Maybe something's wrong with me. Maybe I *am* spoiled and *deserve* to be hated. After all, my mother *did* let me have a tea-party."

The Movies

"Put your backpacks in the trunk and get in the car," the materfamilias ordered after our typical walk home from school.

Suspicious that the woman was about to stalk another innocent person or worse, I inquired, "Why are you being so sneaky? Where are we going? Are we going to do something bad?" [1]

Before entering the vehicle, my brother remarked, "Shut up, Sandra. Does it even matter? Just get in the car and stop asking questions. She's going to get what she wants anyway, so don't make her mad." [2]

The materfamilias pulled up to a drive-through window to purchase fast food. An aroma of juicy burgers and crispy fries filled the vehicle as my mouth watered, ready to consume the contents of the oily paper bag. [3]

Before we could get our hands on some freshly fried potato strings, the woman interjected, "Don't eat it yet. Just wait." My stomach growled at the grocery store where our mother insisted, "Pick out your favorite candy from where it says *three for a dollar.*" After exiting, she handed us two quarters each and ordered, "Take this change and pick out a drink from that soda machine." Cold cans slammed down into the black dispensing slot, one after another. "Okay, bring those to the car." Finally, we pulled up to a classic-style cinema where my mother parked and grabbed her oversized purse. [4]

"What?!" I exclaimed. "You're taking us to the movies?! Wow! Yay! Why didn't you just say so?"

"I wanted to surprise you. Now, *you better behave*," she threatened. "If I have to get after you while we're in there, I'm going to spank you and we'll *never do this again.* Do you understand me?! Hand me your cans of soda, the bag of food, and the candy. *See?* Look what a *good* mother I am! You can't say I never did anything for you. Now, pay attention to what I'm telling you. We have to wait until the movie starts before eating, so don't even ask or complain that you're hungry. I'll hand you your food and drinks when the time is right. *Don't embarrass me. Let's go.*" [5]

Once inside, I read aloud a posted sign that stated, "Outside food and drinks are… *pro-hi-bi-ted.* Mom, what does *prohibited* mean?"

The Movies

My sibling rolled his eyes and sighed as our mother pursed her lips and forcefully whispered, *"Stop talking and don't touch anything."* We approached the ticket counter where the woman queried, "Wednesdays are your dollar-matinees, right?"

"Yeah," the concession attendant confirmed. "On Wednesdays, we play our previously released films for a dollar."

"Perfect. One adult and two children, please," the materfamilias requested.

"Oh, wow! That's cheap! Good job, Mom!" I congratulated. The woman nervously laughed with the attendant and yanked me away from the counter as I whispered, *"What did I do?"*

Once settled, the materfamilias gave further instruction and whispered, *"When the movie starts and it gets dark, I'll hand you your burgers and drinks. Wait until there is a noisy part of the movie before opening your soda can."*

"I don't understand why we need to be so sneaky," I quietly commented.

My brother huffed at me and shook his head as the woman snapped under her breath, *"Just do as I say or we won't come back."* [6]

As the sconces dimmed, automatic curtains pulled away from one another to reveal a large white screen. Various advertisements illuminated the once blank surface to sell name brand jeans, snacks, and refreshing beverages, which caused my stomach to growl furiously. The opening credits finally burst forth and led straight into an action movie, causing me to cheer. It was time to eat. I munched on a lukewarm burger and limp fries while sipping from a room temperature soda can. Eating discount candy bars before a steroid-injected action-hero became a beloved distraction from an existence riddled with *authentic* hostility. [7]

When vacating the movie theater, the sunlight was blinding. The materfamilias slid on her sunglasses and prodded, "Now, what do you say to me for buying you food, candy, drinks, and a trip to movies?" [8]

"Thank you!" my sibling and I shouted. [9]

Once in the car, I asked, "Mom, why did you get mad when I told you 'Good job' today? I thought you *liked* clearance racks and sales?"

She shook her head and huffed, "That was embarrassing! Everybody doesn't need to know about me saving money! Going to the movies is *expensive*, especially with two brats! If something is cheap, you don't have to tell me. I already know. That's why I'm buying it. Don't do that again." [10]

Once home, I looked up the word prohibited and gasped. Realizing that we had *smuggled* outside food and drinks into the cinema, I scurried into the living room and informed, "Mom! The word *prohibited* means you're not allowed to do something!

Outside food and drinks were *prohibited* at the movie theater. We broke the law! That's why we had to be so sneaky, because you knew!" [11]

The woman scoffed from the sofa, "Oh, no… *I've sinned*. Shut your mouth, little girl! We didn't break the law… just a rule… so don't judge me! Are *you* going to pay for the expensive snacks they sell at the movie theater?! Do *you* have money?! *No*. So, if you want to do this *every Wednesday*, keep your mouth shut or I'll leave you *both* at home!" [12]

My brother chimed in from his room down the hall and shouted, *"You better not screw this up for me, Sandra! Why do you have to question everything?! I want to go to the movies, so shut up!"* [13]

Praying Mantis, Scarecrow, and Grandma

~~~~~~

While lounging on a branch in the backyard, my shoulders nearly pinched my ears when the materfamilias abrasively shouted, *"Dinner is ready! Come and eat!"* [1]

Hungry and having no eye for portions, I scooped a large helping onto my plate and sat down. By the time I had consumed half of my meal, I was no longer hungry.

"I won't let you waste food," my father reminded me, getting up from the table with his empty dish. "Sit there and eat until it's all gone. Eventually, you'll learn to serve yourself smaller portions." Full of dinner and anxiety, I lost another hour at the table. While I sat uncomfortably alone, the man passed by and goaded, "Sandra, staring at your plate won't make the food disappear. Keep taking bites. Eventually, it will be gone." [2]

A separate dinner experience comprised a hotdog and bun served with peas and macaroni. The meal was bland and difficult to finish, which extended my time at the table. Shifting in my chair and sore from sitting, I grew bold. Verifying that the coast was clear, I finished the undesired peas and rolled my hotdog directly under the dish cabinet before putting away my plate. [3]

Later that evening, I relaxed on the floor in front of my sibling's small television to watch a science program. Observing various insects and their hunting methods, I smirked and imagined myself on a jungle adventure to net such a specimen.

Unexpectedly, the materfamilias poked her head into the room and announced, "Look, Sandra, it's *you!* Your face is so gaunt! You look like that praying mantis! Yucky! Ha-ha-ha!" [4]

Our eyes met as I coldly replied, "Wow. Your cruelty amazes me. Did you *really* step into the room just to say that? You're a *terrible* human being and a worthless example of a mother. Go away and leave me alone before you cause any more damage." [5]

Enraged, she rushed toward me and growled, "Do you think you can just say whatever you want to me?! You're just a child! Don't *ever* tell me what to do!" Grabbing my arm, my mother lifted my body from the floor to rapidly swat me as I dangled. Suddenly dropping me like a sack of dirt, the termagant held her own fingers and calmly informed, "I think I broke a blood vessel on your bones." Nursing her injury, the woman awkwardly left without emotion. [6]

Days later, I pulled my long hair into a bun and passed the materfamilias in order to play outside. The woman taunted, "*Ha!* Why do you put your hair up like that? It doesn't look good. You're so thin! You look like a little old *grandma!*" [7]

"Stop calling me that," I enunciated through my teeth. "I *hate* it when you call me that. You're not even clever with your insults. Read a book and learn some new words."

In the manner of a cartoonish kindergartener, the grown woman jeered, *"Grandma! Grandma! Ha-ha-ha!"* [8]

Waiting for her to grow tired of her own voice, I rebutted, "I'm not the one who's *old.*"

The materfamilias furrowed her brow at me and then instantly switched into some dramatic form of hubris, turning up her nose and snapping, "Shut up! I look *good!* Your father is younger than me and looks older! He's lucky to have me! I'm beautiful!"

"He's aging faster because he's married to *you,*" I brutally revealed while exiting the house.

The following day, I left my hair down before we left for the store. The materfamilias peered down her nose at me with cruel disdain and ordered, "Do something with that flat hair! You look like a scarecrow! *Hey!* That'll be your Halloween costume this year! I won't even have to spend any money! *Scarecrow!* Ha-ha-ha!" [9]

With my strands tied up or left down, I couldn't win. Her poorly applied eyeshadow, mascara, rouge, and red lipstick left me wincing, so I quipped, "I'd rather be a scarecrow than a demonic clown."

During another drive toward the naval base PX, a song played on the radio with the word *bones* in the lyrics. Turning up the volume, my mother pecked, "Sandra, *your song* is playing! Ha-ha-ha!" [10]

Aunt-T and her husband, Uncle M, visited us all the way from Texas during my winter break. The kind woman hugged me and playfully greeted, "Hello, Sand-wah! It's nice to see you, pretty girl!"

"Go serve yourself some turkey… *grandma.* You're skin and bones!" my mother ruthlessly badgered in front of her visiting sister. Understanding house rules, I seated myself at the children's table. "Look at how skinny Sandra is! Yuck! She looks like a praying mantis! Doesn't she?! Ha-ha-ha!"

"That's not nice. You're being mean to your daughter," Aunt-T corrected, being ignored as her sister diabolically laughed alone. [11]

Uncle-M joined the rest of the adults at the dining table. Since I ate far too slowly, my sibling finished his plate and left me to sit alone. With an unblocked view, I stared out the sliding glass door at the swaying branches of my favorite tree. Uncle-M quickly grew weary of the materfamilias' vulgarity and left the dining table to sit awkwardly beside me in a child-sized chair. "Hey, Sandra," he greeted. "You looked lonely over here. How've you been?"

"Don't you think you're a little tall for this table?" I questioned. "Sitting like that must hurt. You don't have to give up your spot at the big table for *me*. I'll be okay."

Almost in a squat position, he gently smiled with understanding eyes, rubbed my vertebrae-ridged back and confessed, "I like it better over here with you." [12]

Hypocrite

After parking the car at a store, the materfamilias led my brother and me toward the entrance and noticed a woman who clearly out-weighed our trio put together. In a catty tone, the termagant whispered down to me, *"Look at that woman over there. Does my butt look like that from behind?"* [1]

Nearly foaming at the mouth to wound her vulnerable ego, I paused and chose self-preservation while considering elements of the truth that I could safely divulge. Since my mother's pronounced posterior took on an alternate shape than that of the stranger's, I informed, "No, your butt does not look like that."

While shopping, I silently pondered, "Why does Mom say mean things about other people's weight when she struggles with the exact thing? If she's trying to lose weight and makes fun of how thin I am, why doesn't she allow me to eat the snacks that she hides? Why does she even tease me about being boney if she's trying to lose weight? There has to be a vocabulary word for that." [2]

Back at the house, I grabbed my dictionary. Ignorant of a way to look-up a word by its *definition*, I approached my father during a televised football game as he queried, "What's up, squirt?" [3]

"It can wait until a commercial, Daddy," I replied, unwilling to disturb his relaxation. I studied the screen to determine which teams were playing and who was ahead. Finally, an advertisement interrupted the game. "Daddy, is there a word that describes a person who *says* one thing and *does* the opposite?"

He looked upon my confusion with a furrowed brow, scolding, "Sandra, don't be lazy. If you don't know a word, look it up in the dictionary. That's why I bought one for you. I'm not just going to give you the answer. You need to learn how to figure things out for yourself." [4]

I respectfully stood my ground, inquiring, "Yes. I understand that, but how do I look up a word in the dictionary by its *definition*? That's my problem. I don't know the word I need to look up."

His stern face mellowed, confessing, "I see your point. I'll help you *this time*, but you'll need to start reading higher level books to learn new words or expand your vocabulary with a thesaurus."

"What's a *thesaurus*?" I wondered aloud with a scrunched nose.

"It is a book of synonyms which allows you to find words that all mean similar things to the ones you already know," he divulged. "Since you don't have a thesaurus yet, I'll answer your question. The word you're looking for is *hypocrite*. That's someone that doesn't *practice what they preach*. If a person creates or enforces certain rules that they don't follow themselves, it makes them a *hypocrite*." [5]

"A hypocrite. Okay. *Mom* is a hypocrite," I chirped. Unwilling to lose the word, I repeated it quietly, "*Hypocrite. Hypocrite. Hypocrite,*" until I made eye contact with my amused father and added, "Thank you, Daddy." Doing an about-face, I quickly scampered down the hallway and passed my mother while I repetitively whispered, "*Hypocrite. Hypocrite. Hypocrite…*" [6]

The materfamilias raged into the living room and accused, "What are you telling Sandra to call me?! I might need to lose some weight, but *you're* already graying and look like an *old man!*" [7]

Overhearing her provocation and becoming confused, I tip-toed back toward the developing scene to observe.

My father laughed, correcting, "I was teaching Sandra a new word. She was saying *hypocrite*, not *hippo*. You misheard her."

"I'm not stupid! I know what you're calling me! I'm almost ten years older than you and just look at me! I hardly age! *I'm beautiful!* People think *you're* the older one! Ha! You're *lucky* to have a wife that looks as good as I do!" Holding out her arms, the termagant displayed herself with a prideful rotation as if awaiting roaring applause. [8]

"Well, stop coloring your hair and then tell me what people think," the man casually replied, provoking his wife's infamous glare and gnashed teeth. [9]

No Crying

    Wearing tennis shoes, shorts, and a sports t-shirt, my father grabbed a football from the garage as his children scurried to the backyard. Although my older sibling was far more coordinated and physically developed, I couldn't bear the thought of him receiving more training in a sport than I did. [1]

    My brother marked the end zone with toys just before the man threw the first pass. The football spiraled directly to my brother, who made an effortless catch and an instant touchdown. Being too short to intercept, too slow to tag my sibling, and the only defender, I grew frustrated. The man wisely prohibited tackling, for I itched to knock the golden child to the ground.

    "Okay, Sandra. You can be the quarterback for this play. Just get the ball to me," my father coached.

    My taller sibling towered over me, waving his arms. Intimidated by his presence and confused by the pressure, I tearfully complained, "Daddy, he won't let me pass it! He's too big and I can't see anything!" [2]

    Grasping his daughter's intense desperation, my father attempted to even the playing field and ordered, "Take a step back, son. Give her some space." He obeyed. "Okay! Throw it, Sandra!" I panicked and remained motionless. "You have to throw the ball to me or we'll just keep standing here!" [3]

    I didn't understand many rules of American football or much of the lingo when watching a televised game. Trying to avoid my brother's reach, I blindly threw the ball as hard as I could and over both of their heads, causing it to flip into a grassy resting place.

    "I'm sorry, Daddy! I was scared!" I tearfully confessed, causing my brother to shake his head in irritation. "I don't understand what I'm doing!" [4]

    "No crying. Suck-it-up or go inside," the man sharply ordered. "If you don't understand something, ask questions, but don't start crying. I'm not putting up with it."

    Stuffing my wounded pride down into my play-shoes, I calmed myself, swallowed hard and queried, "Daddy, how do you throw the football to make it spin?" [5]

Although I clumsily chunked the oddly shaped ball, he effortlessly snatched it from the air and replied, "Do you mean a *spiral pass*?"

I nodded vigorously, clarifying, "Yeah. How do you throw a spiral pass?"

He walked over to me, bent down and coached, "Well, your hands are way too small for this football. However, if you hold it towards the rear, you'll have a bit more control. As your hand grows, you can slowly adjust your grip to be more forward. Eventually, you might be able to grip the laces. Give it a try. Let the ball roll off of your fingertips as you throw it forward. That's what makes it twist." He walked away from me, turned around and encouraged, "Go ahead, Sandra. Throw it."

The throw might as well have been a dead goose falling from the sky. "I'm sorry, Daddy!" I shouted. "****!"

"Hey! Watch your mouth! Don't talk like that," he rebuked.

I muttered, "*Mom* does it."

My father walked over, popped me on my bottom and rebuked, "You're *not* your mother. You're *my* daughter… and don't talk-back to me." With a quivering lip, I teared up again. "Stop crying. Do you want to learn this or not?"

"*Yes*," I muttered. [6]

"Okay. You tried to throw the ball *too hard*," he continued, passing the ball back to me. "Speed and power can come later. Right now, let's focus on accuracy and a smooth spiral. Roll it off your fingertips." I tried another pass, exaggerating the roll to feel the ball grip each pad of my fingers. [7]

When it went straight to him, a jig commenced as I cheered, "*I did it!*" [8]

"Very good," he encouraged, increasing the distance between us. "Throw it *again*. If you can do it three times in a row, it's a *skill* and not by chance."

He threw a spiral pass that slipped through my hands and caused me to chase it. I growled to myself, "*Come on, Sandra. Stop making mistakes. Get it right.*"

"If you're going to learn how to throw a spiral, then you'll need to learn how to catch one, too. Since your hands are so small, you'll need to get your *entire upper body* ahead of it. It might sting a little at first, but you'll have a better chance of success. Don't be afraid of getting hit," he added. "Remember, you're *trying* to stop the ball, so it *will* hit you. You'll either figure out how to do it in a way that won't hurt or simply get used to the pain. Now, throw it back to me. Roll the ball off of your fingertips like I showed you." [9]

The spiral pass went over his head as I shouted, "Sorry, Daddy!"

"That's okay! That was better!" the man ensured. "Now, for accuracy, snap your wrist and point to me with your throw." Another dead goose flipped and flopped at his feet. He picked the ball up, readying it in his hand. "Get in front of it." He spiraled the pigskin to me, watching the ball slip between my palms and thud onto my chest, scraping my forearms as I caught it without a wince. "Very good, Sandra! You'll get better with practice. Now, throw it back to me. Remember what I told you." [10]

Each weekend our father was home, he would play a different sport with my sibling and me, rotating them. Eventually, I could catch a baseball in a mitt without flinching, volley in badminton, play croquet with accuracy, make a ducky-hand to catch a Frisbee… and throw a *skilled* spiral pass. [11]

BCGs

It was a Saturday morning when I heard my father in the kitchen and whispered, *"If I want to have Daddy to myself, I need to hurry before Mom spoils everything."* [1]

I cautiously opened my bedroom door, allowing the delightfully distinct aroma of freshly brewed coffee to fill my nostrils. A warm illumination from beyond the hall invited me to press on and warily slip past the slumbering-dragon's layer, having trained my feet to roll on their outside edge to eliminate the sound of steps. [2]

Sitting alone in the living room, the man quietly watched television and sipped from his anchor mug. Sunlight poured through the sliding-glass door, enveloping my father and offering a surreal glow that seemed to ignite each dust particle that floated by. Although my heart overflowed with adoration, I remembered a severe error and practiced restraint.

A few months back, I spontaneously executed a flying-squirrel leap onto my father's lap while he held a cup of freshly brewed coffee. As a result, the scalding liquid spilled over his belly and caused the once-stoic sailor to cry out in agony. Mortified to have caused him pain, I swore to never be so careless again, no matter how overjoyed I was to see him. [3]

My father possessed a slightly different appearance that morning while wearing some hideously brown navy-issue nylon spectacles, also known as BCGs or birth-control-glasses. More interested in his company than his eyewear, I silently stepped into view and gently whispered, *"Good morning, Daddy."* [4]

Warmly amused, he made eye-contact with me, gently grinned, and whispered back, *"Good morning, squirt."* [5]

I gingerly climbed onto the sofa as the man elevated his powerful arm, like the wing of a bird, to receive me. With my tiny body snuggled up between his ribcage and bicep, I found comfort in listening to my father breathe. [6]

"This is perfect, just like the coffee commercials on TV," I thought to myself.

The materfamilias poked her head out from the hallway and baited, "Where are the *nice* glasses that you just bought?" My father remained motionless, lifelessly staring at the television screen. "Did you leave them at your *whore's* house?!" [7]

My father responded plainly, "Well, they were on the nightstand a few days ago until they mysteriously disappeared. Where did you put them?" [8]

In a huff, his wife completed a cartoonish about-face and stomped out of view, making my shoulders tense. [9]

"Oh, no!" I silently fretted. "I'm on the wrong side of him and can't protect him from here!" As the termagant stomped her way back, I felt like a coward and worried that my hesitation could cost him. [10]

Without a word, the materfamilias returned and threw an unidentified, yet remarkably delicate object in our direction that slapped the sofa's backrest and lightly landed beside my father's other hip. I had flinched, tucking my chin to gasp at the approach of the projectile. However, my father had remained astonishingly controlled and tranquil.

Unsuccessful in her efforts to alarm him, the materfamilias removed herself as quickly as she had arrived and stomped all the way back to their bedroom to slam the door. My father casually lifted the item from the neighboring sofa cushion, removed the BSGs, and slipped on his formerly missing spectacles. [11]

With a furrowed brow, I queried, "So... *Mom* had your glasses *the whole time*?" [12]

"Yup," he blankly stated, focused on the television screen.

"...and she still accused *you* of leaving them at someone else's house?" I continued. [13]

"Yup," he repeated.

Confusion scrunched my face as I remarked, "That's strange." [14]

Impressed at my observation and a little saddened by it, my father made eye-contact with me and calmly confirmed, "Yes, Sandra. It *is* strange, isn't it?" [15]

Peas

~~~~

I followed my father into the kitchen and witnessed him open the pantry doors to whip something up for lunch. [1]

"What's all of this?! I shouldn't have to search this hard for a can of tuna!" he exclaimed as he beckoned his wife to walk over to him. After a deep breath, her husband politely inquired, "Why do we have nine cans of peas? There are a lot of the same things in here. Just look at the shelf below it. We have four *huge* cans of baked beans. Why do we have a bulk-sized one-gallon tub of mustard? How much mustard could we possibly eat? They use *that* size at concession stands."

She furrowed her brow and passionately rebutted, "Mustard doesn't go bad! We'll eventually eat it! I use it to refill the little containers! You like mustard, too!" [2]

"You make a valid point," he admitted. "However, *it's a lot of mustard*. This will last us a very long time. Please don't buy any more mustard."

"Why are you complaining?!" the woman shouted. "All of it was on sale! I'm just trying to save money! If you don't like it, *go shopping yourself!*" [3]

"Yes, I understand that you're trying to save money. I didn't intend to start a fight, but you're buying peas, baked beans, and mustard as if that's *all we eat*. You're not *really* saving money if you buy a lot of things that we don't consume just because they're *cheap*. It doesn't make any sense. That's *hoarding*. This ties up money in canned goods that could be applied somewhere more useful. Please, don't do that anymore. You'll save more money by simply *not* buying it. We're going to be eating peas for a long time with just what I see here. Looking at this, I don't know how anyone can see what we have with everything mixed up like this. This pantry is a *disaster*. I'm fixing it right now." [4]

"*Whatever*," the termagant dismissively commented as she returned to the sofa and plopped down.

My father meticulously removed everything from the pantry and placed the items on the kitchen floor. Concluding that I wouldn't be an asset in such a tight space, I joined my brother to watch Saturday-morning cartoons in his room.

"Okay. Come look," my father urged his wife, prompting me to hide nearby and listen. [5]

"While making an inventory, I found even more peas and beans. So, here's what I did to help," the man casually conveyed. "I put the *repeated* items in rows directly behind what's displayed in the front and faced all the cans forward so you can see what they all are. If you keep the pantry organized like this, you can see what we have in stock and won't buy more of it accidentally. Okay? Don't buy peas for a while, even if they're on sale. We don't need them. We should eat down what we already have." [6]

The materfamilias turned crimson and roared, *"Don't tell me what to do, you piece of ****! **** you! I'm not stupid! You think you're so ******* smart! You're not better than me! I'll buy whatever the **** I want! I'm the one raising these little brats while you're gone doing God-knows-what overseas! You're only in the navy because of me!"* [7]

Blinking in amazement, her husband corrected, "That's not true *at all*. I was in the navy before I ever met you! I *wanted* a career in the navy! I'm not going to let you take credit for *that*." [8]

She leaned in and shouted, "You're still in the navy because of *me!* I could make you get out of the military and stay home, *but I don't!* What have I done?! Have I committed a sin?! Oh no! I bought too many cans of peas!" The materfamilias pressed her palms together and peered upward like a Roman Catholic painting and mocked, "I'm such a terrible person! Strike me down, Lord! I don't deserve to live!" He stared at her, dumbfounded. "At least I'm not running around on you, ******* every Tom, Dick or Harry, like these other women! I could do it, too, *but I don't!* I'm a good wife and mother… and if I see something on sale, *I'm buying it!* Kiss my ***!" [9]

"Watch your filthy mouth! The children can hear you! Lead by *example*… and I didn't call you *stupid*, but hoarding peas and intending to buy even more is pretty ridiculous," he added. "I know that I'm gone a lot, but I'm here *now*. I meant to help you, but it looks like it's not appreciated. I just thought you were forgetting what you already had and simply needed a boost, but now it sounds like you *want* to live like this. *Fine*. Eat canned peas every day. Do whatever you want." [10]

My father walked outside and caused me to think, "Oh no! If he doesn't feel appreciated, he might leave us! Not on my watch!" Swiftly abandoning my post in the hallway, I stepped past my mother's view to pursue the emotionally bruised sailor and offer a hug. [11]

"Ha! I caught you! What were you doing, *you little brat*? *Eavesdropping?!* Mind your own business and stay inside, *you little demon*," the termagant ordered. "Your father doesn't want you following him everywhere like a puppy, annoying him. If he wants to be outside, let him be outside!" [12]

Peas

I casually examined my father's organizational skills and chirped, "Wow! I love what he did! The cans are in order and easy to count. It *really is* a great way to do things. This was a lot of work. Instead of being mean, you should *thank* him."

Standing over me, the woman narrowed her eyes and barked, "What are you doing opening up cabinets?! You're not even allowed in here! Get out, you little *monster*!" [13]

Too excited to be afraid, I suggested, "Oh! Now that we know what the problem is, we can buy *green beans* instead… or spinach… or some carrots!"

"*No!*" the materfamilias spitefully snapped. "What do you mean '*we can buy*'? You're just a child and can't buy ****! So, shut up! You don't have any say in this! *Ha!* When I was little, we were poor and lived in the projects! My mother would keep milk in the refrigerator, but she never let me drink it. She was too afraid we would need milk and wouldn't have any. It was like she was saving it for a rainy day, but it always went bad! No one ever drank it! Even though she did that, I *still* loved my mother. Because of that, I don't like running out of *anything*, so I buy a lot of what I like!" [14]

I pursed my lips and timidly confessed, "I don't like peas."

The materfamilias inhaled deeply and roared, "You unappreciative little brat! You should be *grateful* you even have food to eat! Besides, *I don't care* what you like! I like peas and that's what we're eating! Your opinion doesn't matter! You don't even know what you're talking about. You're just a *daddy's girl*. You agree with *anything* your father says, no matter what it is." [15]

I couldn't have radiated more hatred in my stationary position. The foulest of grimaces lingered on my face as I imagined lasers shooting from my eyes and burning the materfamilias alive. [16]

Unnerved at my boldness, the woman leaned forward and raged, "Why are you staring at me, you little demon?! I'm sick of *looking* at you! Get out of here before I spank you!" [17]

Quiet

~~~~~~~~~~~~~~~~

While my father and I relaxed on the sofa to watch a basketball game, I realized how ignorant I was of the many rules, especially why the referee had been calling fouls. [1]

During the commercial break, I queried, "Daddy, how did the *dribbling* player foul the guy that was standing in his way? The same sort of thing happened earlier, but the foul was called on the other team. Why?"

"Just as in football, basketball has an offense and a defense. In basketball, a team frequently switches from being on offense one moment and defense the next, depending on who has possession of the ball. During the foul, the *defender* had both of his feet planted on the court and was standing still when the offensive player was coming toward the basket. The defender didn't lift his feet to catch himself when the offensive player knocked him down. That particular foul is called a *charge*," the man explained. [2]

"A *charge*? So… if the defender *had* moved his feet, would the foul have been counted against the *defender* and not the offence?" I inquired.

"Correct. That's called *blocking*. The defender has to stand firm with both feet, not react to the push, and fall down for the foul to be called on the offensive player." [3]

I nodded my head slowly and mumbled, *"Interesting."*

While the game was still in play, the materfamilias noisily stomped down the hallway, made her way to the living room, and angrily halted on the center of the rug to gawk at her husband. Despite her domination tactic, the phlegmatic man stared through her as though he had the clearest view of every lay-up, three-pointer, and passing play.

I fixed my eyes on the termagant as she interjected, "Why are you so quiet? Are you thinking about your *whore*?!" Although *my* shoulders ached from the tension, her husband remained perfectly still, as if nothing had changed. Amping up intensity and volume like a whistling teakettle, the woman roared, *"Don't ignore me… or I'll do something to you!"* [4]

Motionless as a discerning fawn, my eyes flicked over to witness my father's stoney tolerance of the materfamilias as each wave of her tempest broke against his tranquil humor. Seeming to be at a loss for words, the woman theatrically lingered before him with her hands on her hips in the manner of a hormonal juvenile, utterly maladroit in her attempts to intimidate and fluster. [5]

Observing in total silence, I wondered, "Is she plotting something right in front of us? What's she gonna *do*? *Kill* him?" [6]

With narrowed eyes, the materfamilias continued, "I bet your *whore-of-a-mother* ignored your father, too! *She's* the reason he's dead!" [7]

My father's countenance changed entirely as the man quickly rose to his feet, inspiring the beast-of-a-woman to take a step back while he passionately rebuked, "You have no *idea* what you're talking about! You'll say *anything* to get a rise out of me! You pester and pick until you start a fight! I don't understand you, woman! Do you *hate* peace?! Are these the only thoughts dancing around in your head?! Did you come out here to start something because you were *bored*?! Can a day go by without you accusing me of something or insulting me?! I'm tired of it! Shut your disgusting mouth! I'm sick of hearing your perverted words and warped ideas! Get away from me!" She lingered, dumbfounded. "*Well, what do you want?!*" [8]

As would a pouting child, she whined, "You're gone *all the time* and you never pay any attention to me!" [9]

"Are you joking?! Is this one big *game* to you?! There are better ways of getting my attention than making up lies and setting me off! It's pretty hard to be around someone that accuses me of cheating and calls my mother names!" he reasoned, articulating my thoughts perfectly. "You wanted my attention?! Well, *you have it!* If this is what you were after, *you win!* I'm paying attention to you now!" [10]

A cruel blend of hatred and fear mingled within me. The woman had repeatedly snuffed out any happiness I had enjoyed while in my father's presence. During their voluminous combat, I internally fretted, "Why is she doing this to him... *to us?* What makes him come back home... and then *stay?* Will he finally get fed up with her and abandon us all together? What if this is the last straw? It can't be. I can't stay here alone with *her*. I'd rather die." Overwhelmed and tangled in the thorny vines of dread, I sobbed amidst the chaos. [11]

With his mouth already twisted upward, my father shifted his anger down at me and shouted, "*Sandra! This has nothing to do with you! Go to your room!*"

Shooed away, stinging and powerless, I obeyed, only to further absorb their scantly muffled altercation from the other side of the sheetrock. Even with the door shut and hands over both ears, there was no escaping the toxic blasts that carried down the hall. No man-made walls could contain the residual effects of their volatile relationship. [12]

Heroes

~~~~~

*A*ny daily pressure or inconvenience turned my mother into a raging storm at sea, and I was an isolated dinghy at her mercy. Despite being detained alongside a maniacal dictator, my mind floated free and created its own means of escape to survive. Cartoons coupled with my vivid imagination were one such mode of transportation. [1]

While watching an animated series, I mentally immersed myself within the fictional epicenter of crucial missions and exotic adventures. With the press of a button, I joined an eclectic team of military personnel who resisted a malign juggernaut that relentlessly pursued global domination. As expected, the skilled ensemble uncovered the deception and thwarted a diabolical plot, which forced the overpowered regime to flee. Putting a bow on the entire experience, the thirty-minute episode neatly closed with a public service announcement that patriotically encouraged me to pay attention to my surroundings and practice wisdom. [2]

My sibling switched the channel to another program that ushered my imagination into standing with some teenagers who touched their rings together to summon an eco-friendly superhero. Deforestation and oil-spills were no match for the tenacious do-gooders. After restoring order to the environment, another public service announcement encouraged me to reduce, reuse and recycle without littering. [3]

Having waited for the toy commercials to end, my sibling and I smiled as a catchy tune filled our ears. We cheerfully sang along and pumped our fists with the music. I envisioned myself being loaded into a converted ambulance and felt the weight of my battery-powered, laser-stocked backpack as I stormed the streets with eccentric men who caused more damage to property than the translucent villains we hunted. I relished the idea of delivering people from their torment, and it was the heroes' literal *business* to capture destructive spirits and transport them into a specialized vault for safekeeping. [4]

Noting the time aloud, the boy flipped back to the previous television station. After singing every word to the theme song, I accompanied sewer-dwelling, crime-fighting, oversized reptile brothers as they opposed theft and mischief. After watching their first movie in theaters and seeing the same creatures on stage at a local concert, I became absolutely convinced of their existence and desperately wanted to introduce myself. [5]

My stomach rumbled and snapped me back into reality. It was time for lunch. Just like I had practiced after watching a kung-fu movie, I pulled my legs up and flipped my body upright, joyously scurrying to the living room until I glimpsed at the lounging materfamilias. Sobering up from the fantasy world, I remembered where I was and who I needed to deal with.

"*Mom?*" I warily interjected. [6]

"What is it?! Can't you see I'm watching TV?! What do you want?!" she hissed, preferring codependent, philandering couples over me.[7]

"Could you make me a peanut butter and jelly sandwich, please?" I sheepishly requested. "I'm hungry."

"Make it yourself!" she snapped, rolling her eyes and throwing her hand in the air. "What am I, your *slave*?!" [8]

"But… I'm *not allowed* to touch the refrigerator. How can I make a peanut butter and jelly sandwich if the *jelly* is in there?" I respectfully pointed out. "Besides, I've never been allowed to use the kitchen. I don't know where anything is. I'll have to look into the cabinets, even though you told me *never to do that*. Have the rules suddenly changed? Am I allowed to be in the kitchen now or is this a one-time thing?" [9]

"I don't care *what* you do, you little demon! Just leave me alone!" the termagant roared. Obeying, I slowly backed into the kitchen as she shouted, "…and don't make a mess! All you ever do is give me more work!" [10]

I tearfully stepped into the kitchen and sighed. Nearly everything I required was out of my reach. Stuffing down my shame, I grabbed a stepstool out of the adjacent mudroom and returned with determination to construct a delicious sandwich. Within the forbidden refrigerator was the jelly and milk. Taking advantage of my situation, I laboriously removed the coveted drink from its shelf and slid it onto the counter beside the jelly. Gently adjusting the stool each time, I systematically searched for a loaf of bread, the jar of peanut butter and a clean knife. [11]

Seeking a chalice for my beverage of choice, as well as a sandwich plate, I climbed onto the counter and traversed it. Its width didn't exceed that of the upper cabinets but by a few inches, making it a difficult feat to lean away and twist sideways to open each door and effectively search. Clutching the items, I silently retraced my steps and lowered myself to the stool, using only my balance.

Feeling empowered at my independence, I grinned and slathered a layer of peanut butter over the bread's porous face, evenly covering every square inch. The second slice received delicate treatment, finally allowing jelly to meet its counterpart. My tiny arm hoisted up the cumbersome gallon jug and painstakingly poured its contents, allowing some white deliciousness to dribble onto the counter. Recalling that each spilled drink resulted in a brutal spanking, I snagged the washcloth near the sink to wipe away the pale liquid. Paranoid about how much the freshly cleaned spot stood out against the rest of the surface, I wiped down the entire counter by sidling the stepstool as needed. Treading softly, I lifted my plate, carried it to the table, and returned promptly to retrieve the glorious cup of milk.

The drama on television resonated in the background as I shook my head, took a bite, and concluded, "I don't *need* a mother. I know where the stepstool is."

Upon finishing my satisfying meal, I fretted over the dirty cup, knife, and plate. Trepidation jolted through my shoulders like the current of a taser. Peeking out from the kitchen entry, I apprehensively queried, "Mom, what do you want me to do with the dishes?" Ignoring me, the woman intently stared at her electronic idol. At that, I left the dishes in the sink. [12]

Hours later, well after my seven o'clock bedtime, I was wide awake to notice the brilliant moonlight pouring into my room, illuminating everything it touched. I desired to peer through the window, drawn by the glow, but the materfamilias forbade me from doing so. She often warned that perverts, rapists, and pedophiles stared through little girls' windows, but her words didn't sway me. I firmly concluded that if my own mother found me hideous, I could never tempt a pedophile. [13]

Cautiously, I listened for my mother's heavy trod, parted my curtains, and sat on the sill that faced our street. Remaining stationary, I peered through the glass and patiently waited for my heroes to emerge from the sewer to whisk me away and create in me their fifth ninja warrior.

"C'mon guys," I whispered. "*You always know when someone's in trouble. Where are you? Am I not worth saving? Am I not pretty enough?*" I certainly didn't resemble any of the women in the marathon of cartoons that showcased curvy hips, penetrating eyes, and flowing hair. I possessed no Kung Fu skills or a flattering-yet-tactical wardrobe. "*They're not coming and I don't blame them. Why should they waste their time on someone like me?*" [14]

Dolls

~~~

A new commercial radiated from the television screen and ignited a gasping smile. Proportionate to the height of my dolls and inspired by one of our favorite shows, an upgraded series of action figures was being advertised.

"Whoa!" I alerted my brother, who was watching the same screen. "Look at *that*! They're so tall and have *real* hair! My guy only has *painted on* hair. *Wow.* I want one."

"Who cares about hair?! They have tactical clothing, combat boots, and a gun!" the boy corrected. [1]

Since they had intended the toys for male children, I didn't bother asking the materfamilias to buy one for me. Instead, I hoped that her beloved son would acquire it for his birthday. Before long, that very action figure was in my brother's possession. Historically, I would have been sick with jealousy. However, on that particular occasion, I celebrated his persuasiveness. The boy's maternally aimed charm had finally benefited me directly. [2]

While my brother was away at a friend's house, I snuck into his room and found the replica of a lead character in the cartoon series. Noting exactly where and how my brother had placed it among his other possessions, I lifted the soldier and examined his realistic accessories. The uniform was flattering and tailor-fit to his muscular design. [3]

To the soldier in my hands, I whispered, *"Don't be nervous about your first date. You're perfect for her. She'll love you."*

Awestruck by the chiseled jawline, masculine features and tactile hair, I gently carried the dashing male to my favorite tropical-themed doll, ready and staged in my room for a surprise introduction. Originally donning her from-the-box bathing suit, I dressed my little friend in elegant dinner attire and matching shoes from one of her plastic peers. Lowering myself to the floor and laying belly-down, I set the action figure upright on his heavy boots and admired that he could stand on his own two feet. [4]

To puppeteer the scene, I spoke for the inanimate objects and became engulfed in an epic narrative of my creation, mentally setting the stage.

Minutes prior, the soldier's red-eye flight landed on a remote tropical island, leaving the man famished and jet-lagged. In his wandering, he came upon a restaurant with a dazzling view overlooking a sandy beach with crashing waves. As they glistened and frothed in the moonlight, he resigned, "That'll work." If he had seen one waterfront venue, he'd seen them all, and already knew that establishments that catered to the wealthy rarely welcomed a man in camouflage.

While waiting for a server to acknowledge him, he examined his surroundings, only to behold a beautiful woman in a stunning dress tabling her napkin and calmly rising from her chair. A yuppy with perfectly gelled hair arrogantly shouted, "Where are you headed, huh?! How mad can you be?! I'm the only guy on this island! You'll be back!" [5]

Fueled further by his insulting presumptions, she pushed open the glass doors and traversed the back deck. With her face like flint, her heart hardened. Anger had proved to be an easier pill to swallow than the pain, and she refused to allow the man's stinging pretensions to conjure tears. [6]

Staring forward, she declared, "It's high tide," and proceeded down the weathered steps to where she felt strongest and most secure. The roaring sea drowned out the voice of her tormentor. "Maybe it's time for one last swim," she contemplated with closed eyes, focusing on the droplets of sea spray that collected on her exposed skin. [7]

"What is she doing?" the soldier remarked, observing the tossed waters she approached. Neglecting his hunger, the man abandoned the long-awaited server and barreled past the worthless egomaniac on his way out, nearly knocking him down. "Wait!" he urgently pleaded, stepping to the deck and racing down the stairs onto the cool sand below. [8]

Curious, the beauty hesitated, not recognizing the masculine voice emanating from behind her. She turned to discover a uniformed man, rugged in appearance and holding out a scarred hand to introduce himself. Although healthy, it was obvious, even under moonlight, that his body had withstood overwhelming abuse. Touching his fingers, she fondly recognized the callouses of manual labor. [9]

"Hello," she politely greeted, managing a smile.

"Hello," he nervously replied, taken aback by her radiance up close. "I saw what happened and overheard some of what that idiot said. He doesn't know his elbow from his… well… I'm sorry. I just wanted to make sure you're alright." [10]

His genuine concern felt so foreign to her. She had not experienced such a display of kindness. "Thank you for checking on me, but I'm fine," the professional surfer lied. She had just scorned her manager, and bills were due.

Being a native, she had grown accustomed to the isolation of the island. Having learned the hard way to be cautious and distant to protect herself, the woman starred at the moon and longed for the waves to take away her worries permanently. Although she had grown more reserved over the years, a dazzling evening gown cascaded down her toned and shapely figure. [11]

She discreetly peeked at the soldier as he openly stared, unashamed and resolute. Their eyes met, revealing his wisdom, kindness, stalwart power, and a longing. He sensed her unyielding strength, hope, and thirst for life. His scars were plainly seen, but the picturesque specimen before him carried deeper wounds that needed mending. Delicately clasping her fingers, the winsome soldier dauntlessly drew them to his face to kiss her hand, causing a wave of heat to rush up the woman's neck. [12]

Side movement caught the seasoned warrior's attention. Her former suitor, gallivanting in lime-green shorts and a floral shirt, was observing from inside the venue's window. Seeming more like a tourist than a resident, the toad gazed down his nose in disdain. What the man lacked in humility, he made up for in cunning. For fear of bodily harm and further embarrassment, he acquiesced to defeat, turned, and approached an unsuspecting woman seated at the bar. [13]

The camouflaged veteran returned his gaze to the leading lady and stated, "He walked away without a fight. I wouldn't have." [14]

Cocking her head to the side, she laughed, "Fight? With you? Ha! How could he possibly win?!" *Her eyebrow playfully lifted as she chuckled and continued,* "Maybe he would've risked it if you were more like him, reeking of fear… and tanning oil." [15]

The man huffed in amusement. She was smitten, and struggled to maintain composure. His silent presence had already defended her, running off the enemy while drawing her in. To distract herself, the woman redirected her focus onto the glittery horizon.

Possessing the innate ability to size-up others quickly had allowed the soldier to destroy oppressive forces and terrorist plots over the years, taking many lives and saving so many more. Although he had only known of the captivating creature for a few moments, he perceived her level-head, honesty, resilience, and steel backbone. The confident soldier placed his powerful arm around the waist of the glamorously decorated civilian to pull her in close. [16]

The stilettos slipped from her heels as the warrior effortlessly lifted his treasure into the air with a spin, sweeping her off her feet to reveal, "There's something about me you should know. I work all over the world and can't limit myself to just one location." *Devastated that he wouldn't remain with her on the island, she fought back tears, regretting that she had allowed herself to hope. Cradling her, he continued,* "However, I don't want to leave without you. You have far more to offer than being someone's trophy… and far more to receive than human weakness. Do you believe this?" [17]

Relieved, with countenance beaming, her body relaxed as she processed his words. Despite all her past disappointments and years of regret, she responded, "Until now, I didn't think more was possible." [18]

Looking down at the bundle in his arms, he proposed, "Join me. Come and be a part of something bigger than yourself. Let's offer aid to others and defeat tyranny, one battle at a time." *Her countenance shifted from that of ecstatic expectation to deeply forlorn. Sensing apprehension, the warrior cautiously lowered her bare feet to the sand. Caressing her cheek, he inquired,* "Don't you want more than the same every day?" [19]

She gently stepped back and retrieved her elegant footwear to dust them off. With a deep inhale, the woman stood up straight, summoned her bravely, and informed her pursuer, "I'm not qualified." *Her chest tightened, forcing an involuntary sob brimming with tears. Ashamed of her vulnerability, she covered her face with both hands. A moment was all it took to breach the fortified walls she had spent a lifetime building. Compelled to reach complete transparency, she confessed,* "I'm not what you think I am. I'm not rich or sophisticated. These shoes and this dress aren't even mine. I borrowed them from a friend to have dinner tonight. I'm… I'm…" *she stuttered, feeling her throat constrict. Resisting her anxiety, she conceded,* "I'm just a surfer. This island is all I've ever known. I'm not enough." [20]

The soldier laughed heartily. Embracing the sun-kissed athlete, he gently pressed his lips to her forehead and caught the sweet fragrance of her hair. With a full heart, he peered down to wipe away her tears with his thumb. His lethal hands tenderly held the woman's face to regain her lost gaze.

"Even better," he whispered. *The woman collapsed into his arms, soaking in his strength. With unwavering resolve, he kissed her cheek and sought confirmation of her change of heart.* "Was that all that was stopping you?" *Awaiting her answer, he held her close to his chest, allowing his heart to be felt without a word spoken.* [21]

The surfer closed her eyes and inhaled deeply, slowly nodding to convey, "Yes. That's all. I can't think of a single reason to stay and I'm not afraid of the unknown… not if I'm with you." [22]

Tracing his fingers down her arms, he slid his hands around hers. With a backward lean, he tugged, "Well then, come on. Let's get off of this island. Others could use our help. Whatever you need to know, I'll teach you." [23]

An abrupt knock on our front door startled me out of my daydream. Assuming that my sibling had just been dropped off, I rushed into his room and quickly returned the action figure to its original location.

Before scurrying back, I whispered to the warrior, *"See you soon."*

Shredded

~~~~~~~

Before dawn, my ears captured the jingling of keys that stirred me alert. I popped my eyes open and gasped, rarely awake in time to hug my father before he left for the base. Cheerfully whispering, *"Daddy,"* I leaped out of bed to ninja-step past my parent's bedroom and down the hall, becoming slack-jawed as my eyes scanned the skin of the sailor's face. Forehead to chin were deep scratches speckled with dried blood. My eyes watered at the thought of him in pain. "Daddy, what *happened* to you?"

He dryly replied, *"Your mother."* [1]

That was all he needed to say for anger to fill my heart. I ached for the man as I empathized over how embarrassing the domestic abuse must have been. The sailor was required to show his face and military identification to be cleared by base security. The man was about to traverse populated grounds on foot to board a bustling aircraft carrier in full uniform, salute with eye contact, and eventually give orders to subordinates. [2]

Carrying his pain on my little shoulders, I tightly hugged my father. As if I could hold the pieces of his heart together with my tiny arms, I reassured, "I love you, Daddy."

"I love you, too, squirt," he replied, pulling away as I cleaved. "Okay, Sandra. I have to go."

Unwilling to delay him further, I promptly released the man to exit my view and lock the door behind him. Indignation stirred my already turbulent hatred toward the snoring materfamilias down the hall. Her peaceful rest disgusted me as I remained motionless, processing the overwhelming wickedness behind my father's mauled countenance. [3]

Moments later, the assailant emerged and inspired my brow to elevate with pleasant surprise. I disguised my grin with a forced wince and tightened my face into submission as the termagant showcased what I instantly judged as a well-deserved black-eye. [4]

"Did *Daddy* do that to you?" I inquired and hoped that he had.

"*No*," she snapped. "I tried to punch your father last night, but he caught my fist. When I pulled my hand away, I hit myself in the eye." A fear of her swift retribution snuffed the desire to laugh. [5]

While returning to my room, I imagined my father collecting our personal items to take my sibling and me away on the ship, abandoning his abusive wife to her own devices. Noticing my brother tranquilly watching a television show, I shifted my course and entered his room instead. Before sitting down to join him, I stared at his oblivious demeanor in awe. [6]

"What are you looking at?" the boy snipped. "Quit being weird."

"How are you so calm? You always know everything before I do, but you might not know *this* since I got up early. Mom and Dad fought last night," I reported as my sibling rolled his eyes. "Seriously. It was *really bad*. You should've seen Dad's face. It's *shredded*... and he had to go to work like that this morning. And have you seen *Mom's* face? She has a *black eye*. I asked her if Dad did it, but he didn't. Get this. She *actually admitted* that she tried to hit him, but Dad caught her fist. When she pulled away, she hit *herself* instead. If Mom and Dad get divorced, one of them has to take us. I'm choosing Dad. He's *sane*."

As if I knew nothing, my brother shook his head at me and replied, "They won't divorce... and *if they do*, I'm staying with Mom. She gives me whatever I want." [7]

Tomahawk

By comparison, I believed other children lived in *real* homes. My daily environment felt more like a domestic dojo, with my father and me as the sparring dummies. Each time the materfamilias balled up her fists during an open argument, I readied myself to protect and defend her primary target. The woman often shouted in my father's face, almost touching her nose to his to provoke him. The sadist bored into her husband like a power drill to the skull. He eventually caved from the torment and shouted for it all to stop. [1]

Unable to stand aside and merely observe, I often accomplished what I could and wedged my underweight body in between them to prevent his murder. Each time they pushed me aside, I cried loudly to create a diversion and strategically drew her attention down to me. More often than not, the woman completely forgot about her argument with my father and directed her profanity at me. Her vicious words stung, but I preferred experiencing the abuse over witnessing it happen to the sailor. [2]

On one occasion, her husband had offered a witty response to one of her incoherent rants and inspired me to sit up to monitor her hands. I stood as the termagant snatched up the television's remote control and cocked her arm back. She tomahawked it toward my father's head while the ballgame distracted him. Willing to die for the man, football instincts kicked in. I dove in front of the projectile before impact and bore the brunt with my chest.

Completely ignorant of what had just occurred, my father became irritated and shouted, "Sandra, quit horsing around and diving in the living room!" [3]

Although the man didn't welcome the violence or intense vulgarity of his wife, he took no definitive action to stop it. Dissuaded by nothing, the woman raged on, saying and doing whatever she wished to manipulate her husband into joining her self-induced conflict. [4]

"Leave my daddy alone!" I shouted, tearfully standing between them once more. My father angrily picked me up to transport me to my bedroom. Unable to protect him from there, I twisted my body and protested, "No, Daddy! Let me go!"

The frustrated man released me and watched on as I positioned myself between them, convinced that the materfamilias wouldn't murder my father if there was a witness. [5]

"Sandra, this is none of your business! Go to your room! Get out of here!" he ordered.

Wounded and unable to articulate my intentions, I fled to my brother's room and wondered aloud, "What if she kills him?" [6]

"You just make things worse," the boy callously replied. "They fight. It's what they do."

Seated at a table in a restaurant setting, my father corrected his wife with a quip that caused me to chuckle. Offended, the woman sadistically smiled and thumped the back of her hand to his chest.

He leaned away from her with a wince and moaned, "Ow! Knock it off."

Thwacking my father on the arm, she altered her voice to match that of a child and remarked, *"You're mean to me."* [7]

"I don't like that. Quit hitting me," he ordered.

"Keep making fun of me and you'll get it again," she threatened through a toothy grin to throw off passersby. "I'm not hurting you. Those are just *love-taps*. Wait until we get home." [8]

"Don't hit my daddy," I warned from across the table. "You're the one who's mean." [9]

"You'd better shut up or I'll spank you," the woman hissed under her breath, narrowing her threatening eyes with a forward lean. *"Do you think you're safe because we're in public? You're gonna get it when we get home. Who allowed you to speak? Children are to be seen, not heard. Say something else and you won't be allowed to come out to eat with us. We'll just leave you both at home."* [10]

"Be quiet, Sandra," her son added. "You're getting *me* in trouble, too. I want to go out to eat." [11]

"Sandra, don't disrespect your mother," the sailor scolded. [12]

Tears swelled as I silently wondered, "Why am I all alone in this?" [13]

Toys

During his birthdays and at Christmas, my brother received the *exact* gifts he wanted. I couldn't understand how the materfamilias repeatedly knew what to buy the boy, while not knowing me at all. I wasn't privy to witness or take part in any conversation where the woman truly sought anyone else's wants or desires. [1]

Blown away by his fortune, I approached my sibling and inquired with absolute sincerity, "Your toys are amazing. What's the trick? If I ask for something in a store, Mom tells me *no*, or that *it is too expensive* and that *I'm spoiled enough*. Dude, I ask for doll clothes. How does Mom even know what to buy you?"

"Well, that's easy," he calmly replied. "I make a list each year and hand it to her."

"What?! Really?! That's it?!" I exclaimed. "How do you even know what toys are out there to buy?! We aren't allowed to ask for anything from the toy aisle when we go shopping and we don't go to any toy stores. How do you remember what to ask for? I'm so confused. Do you base your list off of toy commercials?"

"Sometimes, but I usually use the toy catalog that comes in the mail," he informed.

Donning anti-gravity eyebrows, I wondered how so much pivotal information could have evaded my awareness. In that moment, the thought occurred to me that a process may have been in place before my birth and I was simply never privy to it. [2]

"There's a catalog for *toys*?!" I squeaked. "Can I see it?!"

"Sure," he replied. "It's from last year. I don't need it anymore."

"Wow. Thanks!" I chirped. Already beginning to examine its contents, I walked into my bedroom and pondered, "Maybe I'm *not* forgotten. Maybe Mom just doesn't know what to buy me."

Grabbing a pencil, I circled the toys I desired most and compared their prices to the toys my brother had already received. The items I had selected were far lower in cost, allowing me to hope that I would receive at least one of them that following year. [3]

Despite submitting a written request for a dollhouse, board games, and an outdoor activity, I didn't receive any of those items for my birthday or Christmas. Determined to provide something special for my miniature friends, I created a variety of backdrops out of construction paper, magazine clippings, shoeboxes, and glue.

Comprehending the stark difference in favor, I waited in the hall for a commercial break, approached the occupied sofa and queried, "Mom, do you love my brother more than you love me?" [4]

The woman pressed her hand against her sternum and theatrically deflected, "How can you even ask me that?! What kind of person do you think I am?! I'm a *good* mother!" [5]

"Well, it *feels* like he's your favorite," I confessed, wiping away tears. "Why does my brother get the best toys as gifts when I don't get anything I ask for? He has movie dinosaurs, the official play set, a matching vehicle, and the action figures. I saw the prices in the catalog that he showed me. I'm good at math, Mom. *That's not cheap.* He has miniature soldiers and matching accessories, along with buckets of building blocks, including the space vehicle sets. If I get something I asked for, it's usually a used toy from a *garage sale*. That's not fair. Why is he so special? Do you *hate* me?"

"You ungrateful little *monster!*" the termagant growled. "I'll tell you why he gets better toys than you! Your brother does what he's told and isn't disrespectful! I shouldn't buy you anything at all! Why should I reward you for evil? *You're* the reason your father and I fight! *It's your fault!* You talk back and think you can say whatever you want! All you do is cause problems! If we get a divorce, *it's because of you!* I can't even talk to him without you sticking your nose into our business!" [6]

Arching my eyebrow, I challenged, "Talk to him?! You call accusing-him-of-cheating *talking?!* I'm not the problem! Your *mouth* is the problem! That man can't take a step in the door without you yelling at him or saying something mean! I'm surprised he comes home at all! *I sure wouldn't!*" With a slap on my legs, I added, "You know what? *I don't care* that you love my brother more than me. I don't want *anything* from you." [7]

The vicious woman cocked her head back and mocked, *"Ha!* Say what you want. You think I'm a bad mother, huh? Well, you'll miss me when I'm dead and gone! Maybe I should just kill myself! Then where would you be? Do you think your father will just quit the navy and stay home to raise two brats?! *No way!* You'll be stuck in foster care and get passed around to a bunch of child molesters and who knows what else!"

Staring directly into her eyes with a forward lean, I rebutted, "At least I'd be getting hurt by strangers and not by my own mother."

The materfamilias roared, *"Get out of my sight, you demon from hell!"*

I became more familiar with the step stool as days of cruel silence followed. [8]

Retribution

My brother had proclaimed his allegiance to the materfamilias, who benefited him in tangible ways. I grew increasingly jealous of his growing fortune and waited for my sibling to take a bathroom break so I could bury a few of his miniature soldiers in the backyard dirt. [1]

While he was away at a friend's house, I noticed the boy had left his favorite action figure out in the open. Boiling with malice, I snatched it up and twisted the toy's upper-half until the internal rubber band had snapped, causing the item to fall apart in my hands. Immediately, I felt my actions had gone too far. Filled with remorse, I penitently attempted to repair it with another rubber band, but lacked the proper tools and dexterity to undo what I had done. Horrified of the consequences, I placed the toy pieces upright on his desk to appear wholly intact and hid in my room. [2]

When the soldier collapsed into separate sections as my sibling touched it, he shouted, *"Sandra! What did you do?!"*

I ran into his room and cried, "I tried to fix it, but I couldn't!" [3]

"Mom!" the boy alerted. *"Sandra broke my toy!"*

I heard the sofa springs loudly relax as the materfamilias quickly arose from her vegetable-like state to storm down the hallway and yell, *"Sandra, are you breaking things?!"* Guilty of sabotage and having already confessed, dread filled me. Rushing into the room, the woman snatched up my arm and shouted, *"Who's going to pay for it?! You?! You're getting a spanking!"* She swatted my thin legs, bottom and back, over and over, as my sibling watched on. Expecting the child to relish her violence against me, he instead appeared mildly disturbed. Out of breath, the termagant released me and dropped my body to the floor. *"Leave your brother's things alone, you demon from hell! Can't I get any peace around here without you causing problems?!"* [4]

Days later, after playing in the backyard with Nancy, I returned to my bedroom and gasped in absolute horror. A bone-chilling shriek erupted from my depths as my brother burst into infernal laughter, delighted by my classic reaction to his retribution.

Set with thumbtacks and string around each of their necks, all of my dolls were hanging from my bedroom ceiling, suspended in mid-air to produce what appeared to be a gangland crime scene in effigy. The open eyes and perpetual smiles of my dangling companions tormented me, causing an immediate and severe meltdown of emotions. Having lived an entire fantasy-life through my plastic friends, I reacted as though I had stumbled onto a genuine homicide. [5]

"*Who's hurt?! What happened?!*" my father questioned as he raced over to stop just short of our rooms. Unsure of how our patriarch would respond, his son grew still and silent.

Hungry for justice, I sobbed and pleaded, "*Look! Look what he did!*" Seeing both of his children standing near my bedroom's threshold, the man stepped around the corner to behold whatever heinous act his son had apparently committed. The man hesitated to take in the scene. Abrupt laugher exacerbated my trauma. "*Daddy! My dolls! He murdered them! What sort of person does something like that?! Serial killers?!*"

"She broke my action figure!" the boy interjected. "I was getting her back!" [6]

I glared at the male child and rebutted, "I already got spanked for that! How many times do I need to be punished?! You're a horrible and twisted person! I can't stand you! How can you look at yourself in the mirror?!"

My father laughed all the more. His male offspring dropped all expectations of discipline and rolled on his back in hysterics.

"Well, Sandra, that serves you right for breaking his toy!" the cynical man concluded. "You even admitted it! I had four sisters who did terrible things to me all the time. When I did something back to them, they cried to our father. My father whipped me and sent me to bed without supper. You won't get any sympathy from me!" [7]

"*What's going on over here?! I hear screaming, crying, and laughing! Why is there so much noise?! I'm trying to watch my show!*" the materfamilias angrily huffed. The man grabbed his wife's shoulders and pointed her toward their son's masterpiece. Observing the dolls, she became unsettled with mouth agape until the woman noticed my tears and her son's laughter. Her initial expression of concern morphed into irreverence as she guffawed along-side the males and added, "See?! I told you to leave your brother's things alone! Didn't I? That's what you get!"

In the presence of our parents, the Machiavellian child convincingly offered, "Let me take them down, Sandra. *I'm taller.* It's easier for me to reach." [8]

"*Don't touch my dolls again!*" I loudly warned. "*You're dead to me! I hate you! Stay away from them!*" [9]

The golden child threw his hands in the air to display surrender, passed between our parents on his way back to his room, and turned on the television as if nothing unusual had occurred. [10]

"Sandra, quit your belly-aching," my father sternly ordered. "You're overreacting. He didn't hurt anything. Just take them down. If you don't stop crying, I'll *give* you something to cry about." [11]

When my situation lost its entertaining appeal, both parents dispersed. Unwilling to look upon my lounging sibling, I shut my door and trembled at the lofty task before me.

Retrieving their plastic bodies, one by one, was an excruciating process. Being far shorter than my older brother, I clutched a child-size chair and precariously set it in various places on my twin-sized bed. Delicate balance was required to reach each cherished companion. While standing tip-toe on the seat, I gently tugged at their pointed toes until the tacks slipped from the popcorn ceiling and dropped onto the bed. As I cradled several dolls in my left arm, one slipped out and bounced off of the back of the chair, hitting the floor with a crack.

Believing that my dolls had endured far too much that day, I whispered, *"Oh no. I'm so sorry."* Lidless eyes stared up at me as I silently contemplated, "What if I were to throw *myself* down? I could smash my head on the floor and die. *Then* they'd be sorry." I imagined my skull splitting open upon impact, spraying copious amounts of blood over my bedding and furniture. However, as my imagination snowballed, tears rolled down my cheeks. Even in my fantasy, my dead body remained undiscovered until a horrid stench emerged. "No one would miss me. Once someone found me dead, they would laugh and get the others. If I was still dying, no one would help me off the floor or take me to the hospital. My parents would *let me die* and be relieved, happy to raise their *favorite* child without distraction. My death would solve their problems. Maybe I *am* the reason that my parents fight. *Wait a second*. What if I make a mistake and just hurt myself or end up with permanent brain damage? Things would get even worse! I'd get another spanking for creating a mess and then have to clean up all the blood myself! Never mind. It's not worth it." [12]

At that, I carefully climbed down, put the chair back and offered comfort to my dolls.

Jump

"H-m-m-m-m... I need some cardboard. I'm pretty sure Dad has some broken-down boxes in the garage," my brother plainly stated, as if talking to himself.

The boy piqued my curiosity, so I asked, "What do you need cardboard for?"

"I'm going to build *wings*. I saw how to do it on TV and want to test it out from the roof," the boy conveyed, observing me. My eyes grew wide at the thought of aeronautical adventure. "You can't get too excited or loud. If Mom finds out, we'll get into trouble. She can't know anything about this, so be quiet." I silently nodded and tailed my brother to the garage, where he grabbed a large cardboard box, two trash bags, and some rope.

"How do we get on top of the roof?" I queried.

"I'll show you," he replied, leading me around to the back of the house on the opposite side of the yard. "The side tree has a branch that grows over the house. See? We just climb up and get on the roof from there."

"Wow! I never noticed that!" I exclaimed, having completely forgotten the narrow portion of our yard. To prevent getting stuck, I observed where he placed his feet and replicated his steps. "Have you done this before... climb the tree up to the roof?"

"Stop asking questions," he ordered. "Once you're on the roof, step softly or she'll hear us." Our lofty test site provided a grand view of our neighborhood. Feeling liberated and alive, I enjoyed the altitude and explored the entire surface area. As I did, the boy fiddled with the rope and instructed, "Now, this loop goes over this wing and that loop goes over that wing. See? Now you have something keeping the cardboard under your arms. Then, you just jump with your arms out and glide down. It's pretty simple."

Eager, I exclaimed, "I want to go first!" [1]

"*Shh!*" he hushed. "You're right. Good idea. You're lighter. You *should* test it first."

"Like that?" I queried, tightly gripping the rope as my sibling nodded in approval.

I stepped forward and stood at the edge of the overhang. After gazing beyond the branches of my favorite climbing tree, I peered down at the grass below. Adrenaline coursed through my veins, making me quake with anticipation and caution. Unwilling to seem cowardly, I summoned my courage and jumped, landing with an awkward roll as the cardboard flopped over me.

"You're such an idiot!" my brother laughed from above. "I can't believe you fell for that! Cardboard wings could never work on people! You weigh too much, dummy!" [2]

"Fell for what?! You're the dummy!" I shouted up at him. "That was *fun* and I'm doing it again!" I snatched up the cardboard and rope, climbed back up, and stood next to my brother. "The cardboard is bent now, so it probably won't slow my fall as much as it did last time. What are the trash bags for?"

"Parachutes," he replied confidently. "You hold on to the sides and then jump. Air should fill the bag and slow you down."

"Give me one," I demanded.

"Wow! You're so dumb!" He laughed again. "This won't work either! I'll admit, I feel kind of bad about the wings because you didn't know it was a prank, but I'm telling you now. This *won't* work." [3]

"I don't care," I remarked cavalierly. "It's not that far down. You might be too scared, but I'm not. Hand me one." [4]

My brother just shook his head in amazement and ordered, "Get it yourself. You're the dumbest person I know."

I took the black plastic, shook it open, held the two opposing sides, and jumped without hesitation. The thin plastic didn't catch air or slow my fall in the slightest. After my quick landing, I looked up and informed, "You're right. That didn't work. I want the wings again. *Those* actually helped."

"They did?" my brother wondered aloud, only to shake his head. "No, they didn't. You're dumb. I don't believe you. Anyway, we should stop. If we keep this up, we might get caught. I didn't think you'd actually jump more than *once*." He gathered all the materials and threw them to the ground before climbing down safely. "You're such an idiot. You'll do *anything*." [5]

"Whatever," I huffed. I grabbed the trash bags and followed the boy back into the garage. As we put away the supplies, I continued, "You're just mad because your plan *backfired*. I *liked* jumping from the roof. In fact, you missed out. Thanks for showing me how to get up there. The view was amazing and I like the feeling I get when I'm falling."

"You're crazy," my sibling scoffed. While shoving the cardboard back into its original storage spot, he warned, "Seriously, don't jump off the roof anymore. You'll end up getting yourself killed."

I chuckled and reminded, "It's possible, but you didn't seem too concerned about that when you suggested all of this. It's nice to know that you care *so much* about me. You're an *amazing* brother." [6]

"Shut up," he dismissed. The boy put away the rope, rolled the unopened trash bag in with the others and shoved the failed parachute into the garbage.

"Dang. No wonder you don't get caught doing anything wrong. There's no evidence. I'll have to remember that," I noted. [7]

"I'm going back inside," the knave announced. [8]

Once he was out of sight, I quickly returned to the roof to locate the best vantage point on the highest ridge. Feeling secure and at peace, I laid down on the sun-warmed shingles. The coarse material gripped my t-shirt, shorts and skin, keeping me from slipping downward as I examined the clouds passing overhead. Before long, I heard the screen door open.

"Sandra, where are you?! I can't see you!" the materfamilias shouted. [9]

"Well, that was short-lived," I thought, remaining silent and undetected. Refraining from panic, I carefully boarded the leafy tree as my leg raked over a jagged protrusion just before I answered, *"Coming!"* and raced to where the woman was impatiently standing.

"You better not have been on the roof!" she successfully guessed, analyzing my reaction for confirmation.

Unwilling to lie, but possessing no desire to reveal my new hiding place, I replied, "I was climbing the side tree and scraped my leg." [10]

Satisfied with my answer, the woman ushered me inside for dinner.

Bite Down

The climbing tree provided ample space for multiple adventurers, boasting a gently sloped trunk and core branch arrangement that somewhat resembled a relaxed wrist with palm up and fingers slightly curled. The firmly set bark and copious knots established traction and foot-holds for climbers of every skill level. However, what was most impressive was the robustness of each bough. Except for an occasional dry twig, which was removed quickly and discarded down to the knuckle-like root system below, the woody perennial plant indisputably endured the brunt of each swinging, dangling, leaping, and reclining person without compromise.

Sloping between the two lowest branches was a five-foot-long zipline my brother installed using the rope from the garage. The challenge was to find something to grasp that could support our weight, was comfortable for our hands, and cascaded us down smoothly.

Recalling various movie scenes, my sibling and I were confident that a simple household item might suffice, as opposed to expensive rigging. Hearty sticks either snapped under the pressure or slipped to the side to cause rope burn. Plastic bucket handles and flexible metal bits were unforgiving, digging into the pads of our fingers and leaving painful indentions.

"There has to be something that will work," I assured myself. Stepping into the garage, I scanned the walls that displayed the shelving my father installed and his meticulously organized possessions. A red shop rag caught my eye and was within reach. "It's worth a shot." Excited over its potential, I snatched the grimy cloth, scurried to my brother, and yelled, "Let's try *this!* Me first! I found it!"

"*Okay. Okay.* Just let me move," the boy conceded, reaching his foot to the base of a neighboring limb to observe.

I tossed the grease-stained shop rag over the weathered cotton rope and performed a firm test-yank. The makeshift substitution for a T-bar had qualified for an attempt. Intrepid and determined, I threw myself into the mercy of its fibers, pinching the rag's corners with a white knuckled grip. Down the line I went, without discomfort, to land firmly on my feet.

"*Sweet! It works!*" I shouted. "*Try it! Try it! Wow! Oh my gosh! I'm doing it again!*"

"*Nice!*" my sibling cheered as he stepped forward. After carefully examining the cloth, the boy nodded his head in approval. The greasy shop rag had maintained its integrity. Preceded with his own firm test-yank, my sibling finally took a brief turn down his own zipline. "*Yeah! Awesome!*"

Much like ants harvesting an abandoned plate of cake, my brother and I instinctively developed an unspoken system of finishing a turn, handing the rag up to the other and climbing the trunk to receive the rag back for another go. There was no bickering or the suppression of jealousy. We unified under the banners of innovation and exhilaration, and continued to zipline in blissful harmony until sunset. [1]

The materfamilias pushed open the screen door and shouted, "*What are you monsters doing?! Take that down! I better not see you doing that again! Come inside! It's time to eat!*"

"*Okay!*" her son submissively replied, sounding perpetually innocent.

The boy leaped from his perch and sprinted toward the garage to retrieve a screwdriver. Climbing to regain his position, he began a vigorous attempt to dig the tip of the Phillips head into the highest knot to loosen it, fiddling with the rope until twilight engulfed us.

"*Come inside now!*" the termagant roared.

Abandoning the treed line, the boy returned the screwdriver and shop rag to their rightful locations and ran into the house with me on his heels. While I forced myself to eat whatever had been served, I became obsessed with our newfound thrill.

During bath time, I grinned, thankful that my brother failed to dismantle the zipline. While brushing my teeth, I relived memories of laughter, climbing and cheerfully taking turns. Resting my head on my pillow, I hoped to fall asleep quickly and fast-forward myself into the morning where the rope, shop rag, and I could reunite. Rest patiently waited for my mind to still its incessant wiggles of expectation, ultimately finding me in sleep.

After daybreak, sunlight poured from the window above my headboard. Stirred awake, I gasped and whispered, "*The zipline. It's still there.*"

Hearing the materfamilias speak gently to someone in the dining area opposite the kitchen, I grew confused. During most summer mornings, the woman would traditionally be fast asleep or already seated on the sofa to watch daytime television.

I stepped softly through the living room to discover my brother seated in a hunch at the dining table as his beloved mother encouraged, "*Sound it out. You got the first part. Don't get frustrated.*"

Utterly distracted from my mission by overwhelming curiosity, I inquired, "What are you guys doing?"

"I'm helping your brother with his reading," the woman informed. "Don't interrupt." I peered over his shoulder at the page. "Get out of here! You're bothering us! Besides, you're too young to read," the materfamilias snapped. [2]

I laughed and confidently reported, "That's not true at all! You *know* I can read! I read signs all the time!" [3]

"Whatever! No, you can't! Get over here and read this, you little *liar*," the materfamilias challenged.

Snagging the opportunity to impress the woman and gain her favor, I stepped up and clearly read aloud, "The boy ran up the hill and was out of breath. It was more difficult than it seemed…"

Pleasantly surprised, the woman chirped, "Very good, Sandra!" Prodding my brother, she antagonized, "Look! Even *Sandra* can read this, and she's *younger* than you." My sibling's face grew crimson. The materfamilias glared at me and gruffly ordered, "Go away, Sandra! You're not helping! Find something to do outside!" [4]

I peered through the sliding glass door that displayed my favorite tree and the rope that was waiting. In a flash, I snagged the rag from the garage and rushed up the tree, confidently tossing it over the rope. Pulling straight down, I slung my feet away from the tree as I had countless times the day before. The zipline slipped off the branch and ripped away from the cloth in my fists, as if my brother had never tied the rope at all, causing my left arm to thud firmly onto my chest. Falling face down, my wrist became sandwiched between my sternum and a knuckled root as the inertia of my body slammed down, releasing a distinct crack.

As I hit the ground, the impact knocked the breath from my lungs and left me grounded like a freshly caught trout. Unable to inhale or speak, my mouth was nothing more than a pulsing gape. I was suffocating. Any attempt to breathe tweaked my clamped wrist on the exposed root and surged pain through every nerve in my arm. Pulse racing and on the verge of passing out, my rigid body involuntarily relaxed and allowed me to take my first deep breath. A frightful howl escaped my lips which rattled even *me*.

No one came.

The pain seemed to intensify without limit, causing my body to spasm. When I moved, my wrist tweaked. The agonizing sensation forced another blood chilling howl from my tightly distorted face. Tears landed on the root and soaked into the soil near my cheek. As I attempted to flip myself over with the other arm, I quickly discovered that increased blood flow exacerbated the agony.

Remaining face down, I screamed over and over. Using my words, I cried out, *"Help me! Someone, please help me!"* In return, I heard a forceful knock on the glass. It was the same knock heard when Nancy and I joyously played outside too loudly. With increasing intensity, I cried out once more, *"I hurt my arm! Please, help me! Help me!"* [5]

No one came. [6]

I lingered among the roots, sticks, grass, and soil as insects crawled past my face and over my right arm. Mustering willpower in the absence of human aid, I forced my right arm to flip the rest of my trembling body over. Pangs surged through my throbbing limb. I focused on breathing and whimpered to exhale. I attempted to adjust my body with instant regret. A wave of searing pain made me rigid and locked me in place. Surrendering all efforts to cry out for help, I allowed time to pass. The scenario confirmed my suspicion. The woman preferred my sibling and considered me expendable.

Our screen door eventually opened and slammed shut just before an aggressive trod drew nearer. The termagant scolded, "Can't you see I'm trying to help your brother read?! What's wrong with you?! You're such a crybaby! What did you do?! Didn't I tell you to take that rope down?! That's what you get! Stand up, right now!" [7]

I peered up in amazement to witness a soulless creature standing over her greatest inconvenience. At that moment, I recalled a television episode about insects and preferred to be consumed alive by African driver ants than be subject to her version of care. [8]

Calming my thoughts, I slowly informed, "My arm is broken and I can't get up. When I try to move, the pain stops me. I need help. If you won't help me, would you please go get my brother?"

"I don't believe you! You're a liar! Your arm isn't broken!" she accused. "Let me see it!" The woman snatched my throbbing left wrist and hoisted me off of the ground by it, causing me to howl in torment. "Shut up! You cry about everything! You're just faking it! I'm not taking you to the hospital so they can tell me that nothing's wrong with you! Let me look!" [9]

With a firm grip over my injured wrist, she forcefully pulled and twisted it upward as I cried, *"Stop! Stop! What are you doing?! Let go! Let go of me! Why are you doing this?!"*

"Shut up! Stop crying, you demon from hell, or I'm going to spank you!" the termagant growled, refusing to release my wrist from her tightening clutch. "Get inside now, before the whole neighborhood hears you!" [10]

"Good!" I tearfully snapped with gritting teeth. "Maybe one of *them* will hear what's happening to me and take me to the hospital!"

Using my injured wrist, she pushed me backwards through the opened screen door, across the entire kitchen, down the hallway, and ultimately into my bedroom where she threw my underweight body to the floor and shouted, *"Shut up or I'll spank you! You're faking it!"* The woman exited and slammed the door behind her as I wailed with all my soul. Uncontrollable sobs filled the atmosphere and resurrected the woman's wrath. She threw open the door and shouted, *"Stop crying! Your arm isn't broken!"*

The materfamilias lunged toward me, attempting to lift me once more by my injured wrist. From a fetal position, exactly where she had forced me to the ground, I shrank back and shrieked, *"Get away! Don't touch me!"* [11]

Cradling my left arm with the other, I scrambled to my feet as tears flowed and anger swelled. My mind pulsed with a graphic mental image of me tearing the woman apart using only my teeth. [12]

"You're driving me crazy!" the materfamilias screamed. "What do you want me to do?!" [13]

Furiously blown away at her reckless stupidity, I slowly enunciated each syllable with overt exaggeration and growled, "Take… me… to… the… hos-pi-tal." The materfamilias remained motionless, boasting a facial expression categorized somewhere between a raging bull and catatonic. Offering the sadist an incentive, I bribed, "If my arm *isn't* broken, you can spank me *all you want*."

The woman simply stared, hesitating further in arrant vacancy. [14]

"Mom," her son interjected. "Sandra can't fake her arm turning *blue*."

Being snapped out of her stupor, the woman pivoted, marched to her bedroom, and huffed, "Now I have to go put on make-up!" [15]

In his mother's absence, the boy stepped toward me to confess quietly, *"Yesterday, when I got the screwdriver to untie the knot, it worked. I was pretending to still be untying it, so Mom would think that I couldn't undo it… so it could be left up. I was going to tighten the knot the next time I was out there. I didn't think you'd use it without looking at the knot first. You couldn't see that the rope was barely hanging there?"* [16]

Scowling, I replied through my teeth, "Well, if I saw that, we wouldn't be *having* this conversation." I shook my head and sighed. "I don't understand why you untied it in the first place if you were just going to leave it there. You made it seem like the knot was too tight to take apart and that it wouldn't go anywhere. Why should I check something that worked so many times before and couldn't be undone with a screwdriver? Dude, that's messed up. You should have said something to me."

He shrugged and continued, "Well, I *really* thought you saw what I was doing… and the idea of leaving the rope up hit me after I had already untied it." He shook his head. "Dang. After this, we'll *for sure* have to take the rope down."

I displayed my blue arm and murmured, "You think all of this is *my* fault? *Wow.* I get blamed for everything." I glared at my brother. "*Wait a minute.* You *knew* why I was screaming and didn't say anything?" [17]

"I told Mom that she should check on you, but she kept ignoring you and making me read," he corrected.

"If you would have told her what you did with the rope, she might have believed me and not grabbed my arm or twisted it. You just didn't want to get into trouble," I surmised. "*You're unbelievable.* I don't know why you even worry about that. Mom *loves* you. *I'm* the one she hates." [18]

"I'm ready," the termagant announced. "Let's go… and that arm *better* be broken." Looking down at my brother, she ordered, "*You stay home.*" The car ride was silent and left me worried that there would be no witnesses if I were to be murdered and disposed of. [19]

In the waiting room with the termagant beside me, my arm throbbed in my lap as I inquired, "Can someone *die* of pain?" A frigid pause lingered in the air between us as I peered up at the woman, pleading with my eyes for a shred of civility.

"*No,*" she growled, drenched in disdain. [20]

My soul choked on the blackest ink of despair, as if to orate, "*I am alone. Futile in all my ways, I scream grievances to the deaf, display evidence to the blind, and await the mute to lift their voice on my behalf. Unworthy of love, I exist to be an outlet for frustration and madness. Shame cradles my head each night as I pull a sheet of bloodstained rejection up to my chin, shivering beneath it. I am a broken thing. No one will come for me. I am less than forgotten, for one must first be considered. I am not missed nor worthy of remembrance, but a detestable and cumbersome burden slung over an unwilling back, a lopsided load to make one unstable. At my core, I crave to be disregarded. Perhaps I'd find peace. Yet I remain linked to misery personified, shackled to childhood and my lingering weakness.*" [21]

"Sandra? Sandra *Lawson*?" announced a feminine stranger in scrubs.

Hearing my name spoken into the air had delivered a spark of life to my downcast being and inspired me to chirp, "That's me!" [22]

I grinned at the woman, who gently smiled back and greeted, "Hello, Sandra! Let's get you fixed up. *Follow me.*" We quickly proceeded down a long, sterile hall. "Okay, Sandra. What happened that caused you to be here today?" [23]

Feeling seen, I replied confidently, "I fell from a tree branch onto a root. My arm was under me and I heard a pop. It hurts really bad, so I'm pretty sure it's broken."

"It might be. Roots can be pretty unforgiving. This is the x-ray room where we're going to take special pictures of your arm to find out exactly why you're in so much pain. If it's broken, we'll see it," the woman explained. "In this room, you'll need to wear a lead gown, but I'll help you with it. *It's heavy.* Now, once inside, I'll need you to take your clothes off. If you would feel more comfortable, your mother can join us for that." [24]

"No, thank you," I quickly replied. [25]

Controlling an expression of suspicion, the woman professionally turned to the materfamilias and ordered, "Wait here. This should only take a few minutes." [26]

The technician closed the door behind us and separated me from my tormentor. I examined my surroundings and relaxed in the pleasant company of a woman that was knowledgeable and kind. With all the machines and monitors around me, I imagined myself as an astronaut prepping for a mission.

Curious about my floppy armor, I inquired, "Why am I wearing this heavy poncho?"

Muffling a chuckle, she chirped, "Well, we don't want to *fry your eggs!*"

"Fry my eggs?" I parroted, hiking an eyebrow.

A grin emerged as the technician valiantly suppressed her laughter. She carefully and methodically positioned and repositioned my delicate arm for the x-ray machine and continued, "Let me explain. Radiation can harm your reproductive system. We have you in a big iron gown to protect your body so you can have children in the future… *if you want them.*"

Through a foul grimace, I commented, "I don't want children. Can this machine make it so that I can't have them? If I take this gown off, is that what will happen?"

The technician pursed her lips, moved my arm for one last x-ray, and said, "Ok. Perfect. Hold your arm right there. Don't move." She paused and answered, "Well, Sandra, you might not feel the same way when you get older. Thankfully, you don't have to make those kinds of decisions right now. I'm just protecting your body so that you can choose *later.*" She shut off the machine. "We're all done here! Let's get that *poncho* off of you," she sweetly teased.

Within moments, I was in another waiting area.

A tall man in a white lab coat entered my view with a big smile and greeted, "Hello, Sandra! *Follow me.* Let's examine those photos of your arm together." He sat me on an exam table beside a glowing wall of white light. Quickly, he slid some x-ray transparencies up under a lip to hold them in place. "Yup. You see that? *That* is a broken arm." [27]

Glaring at the termagant, I abruptly confirmed, "*See?* I told you it was broken." [28]

The doctor suspiciously eyed the woman, bathing her face in shameful crimson as she attempted her sweetest smile to appear innocent. Since the original break had been an accident, I kept the rest of the story to myself. [29]

The doctor redirected his attention toward me and conveyed, "Ok, Sandra. I need to set your arm. This will hurt *a lot*." The man wrapped some gauze around a few tongue depressors and handed them to me. "Bite down on *this*." I obeyed and clamped my teeth onto the combined materials. Without hesitation, he clutched my wrist. Sharp pain shot through my arm, up my neck, and clamped my jaw down. "Keep breathing, Sandra. I know this hurts, but you're doing *great*." Right away, I trusted that man more than I had ever trusted the woman who bore me. I knew the pain that he was inflicting was to *correct* the damage and not to harm me. "Alright. That part is over. Now, I need to wrap your arm in a cast." [30]

The doctor layered the fabric drenched in a chalky paste around my left arm from thumb to armpit. "Oh, wow. That's cold," I remarked, managing a smile.

"Now, your arm is very thin, so I need to make the cast tight enough so that it stays on when it's dry. I'm going to squeeze this cast as close to your arm as possible. This will hurt." Without being told, I reinserted the tongue depressors, clenched my jaw, and nodded like a bull rider. Red faced and sweating, one tear welled up and rolled down my cheek. The doctor released my arm. He lowered his face to my level with unwavering eyes and remarked, "Sandra, *that was amazing*. Not a sound and only *one* tear. You're one tough kid." He stood up straight and ordered, "Now, let that dry. *Don't move your arm*." [31]

My cast hardened with my heart. I remained motionless and silently pondered, "Not crying can impress a doctor? Maybe he's on to something. Every time I cry at home, things get worse. Hiding my pain is definitely *safer*."

Jay

~~~~~

First grade placed me before a few familiar faces, creating a cheerful and uproarious reunion. Until our eyes met, I had not realized how much I missed their company.

"What happened to your arm?" a girl asked, examining my cast.

"I fell out of my tree, but it doesn't hurt anymore," I reassured.

"Can I sign it?! Let me find a marker!" she exclaimed as students giggled and huddled around to do the same. "My name is Nam, by the way."

"I'm next!" declared a boy, gently stabilizing my arm as he scratched out his name. "I'm Josh. Sorry about your arm."

Another stranger brazenly approached us and added, "I'm Jay. Wanna hear a joke?" Smitten by his contagious grin, I lost track of his words, but laughed anyway.

Folding-tables somewhat formed a large U-shape that faced the centered chalkboard where a frigid woman stood to scribe her name.

The teacher turned and sternly announced, "Alright, class. You're not in kindergarten anymore. You're *first-graders*. You all have assigned seats, so find your spot and *be quiet*. I won't tolerate any disruptions. If I have to tell you to stop talking, your name will be written on the board. If I have to tell you three more times, a note will appear in your progress folder and sent home with you to be signed by your parents. However, if you make it to the end of Friday without your name on the board, you'll be awarded a stick of licorice. Let's see how well this class follows directions." [1]

I sighed and whispered to my neighbor, "Getting older is hard." [2]

"What's your name, little girl?" the instructor probed.

Trembling, I replied, "Sandra." Shame and disbelief weighed my jaw down as chalk scratched my name at the top of the board.

"If you have something to say, Sandra, raise your hand. There will be no side conversations in *this* classroom," she warned. "Am I being perfectly clear?" [3]

"*Yes, ma'am*," I murmured, looking forward to the last day of school for the first time.

A student's defiant tongue poked out as the woman turned her back, causing Jay to chuckle quietly to himself. [4]

The disciplinarian lifted her chalk, whipped around, and snarled, "Do you think disrupting this class is funny? What's *your* name, sir?"

"Jay," the child despondently informed with a lingering frown… until his name appeared directly under mine and prompted us to smirk at one another. When recess finally arrived, Jay playfully goaded, "I bet I'm *faster* than you."

"You're on!" I accepted with a smile, rushing to stand toe-to-line on the blacktop. We felt like Olympians with a single-minded focus. [5]

"Ready, set… *go!*" a classmate shouted, releasing us to sprint across the blacktop.

The California sun baked the tar-like surface and radiated blistering heat, creating visible waves in the air just above it. Sweat poured down my face and arms, soaking the girlish clothing the materfamilias had just purchased for me days prior.

"It's hot. I'm gonna get some water," I announced, sprinting across the sizzling playground to wait in line for the fountain.

I sensed a tap on my shoulder and turned to discover who it was, but none of the strangers in line were looking at me. A snicker from below drew my attention downward. "Oh, my gosh!" I laughed. Jay peered upward from a crouched position. Thinking about our names on the board, I commented, "I'm pretty sure the teacher hates us." [6]

"She must be allergic to *adorable children*," the boy quipped, batting his lashes.

I huffed at his endearing display and somberly added, "I miss my kindergarten teacher. She was really nice and hugged us, but this lady scares me. If she doesn't like children, she shouldn't teach. I don't like her at all. First grade is going to *suck*."

"No, it won't. It'll be *better* than last year. Now you have *me*," Jay reminded with a nudge, making me blush. "Besides, I'm not afraid of her. In fact, I'm not afraid of anything."

The last bell rang that Friday and excited each student as we stood up with our backpacks in hand. "Sit down!" the woman demanded. Terror-struck, our class frantically returned to our seats. "The bell may have rung, but I haven't dismissed you! Do *not* do that again."

Our instructor slowly erased the board, leaving only the list of names. We sat motionless until she ordered, "Quietly stand with your things and line up at the door." The instructor handed each student a stick of licorice, skipping the listed students as we stepped past. Week after week, I spoke out of turn at least once. My name decorated the board each week, except for once. I was sick for three days and returned on a Friday. Being far too social, I became accustomed to her disapproval and invented a distaste for red licorice. [7]

Monday morning, I chirped, "Hi, Jay!" He smiled with a wince. The child arrived at school with a swollen bottom lip and bruised arms. "That looks *painful*. Are you okay? Did you crash your dirt bike this weekend?"

"Yeah… that's what happened. I crashed my bike," he confirmed with a nervous laugh. "Don't worry about it, Sandra. I'm fine."

"Jay! Sandra! Sit down!" the teacher barked. "Class is about to start!"

We were inseparable at recess and constantly competed, often tripping onto the grating black top or skidding across the grassy field together. Scraped knees and green stains were daily occurrences, ruining the pants the materfamilias had picked out for me to wear each morning.

On another Monday, Jay gingerly entered the classroom with cuts and facial bruises. Confusion distorted my once elated expression as I drew closer to him. "Jay, what happened to you?" I queried. "Did you lose a fight?"

After a brief hesitation, he rattled, "I was going *really* fast on my bike and crashed super hard. I rolled all the way down a hill."

"Okay. How did you get the black eye?" I wondered aloud.

"The black eye?" he sheepishly parroted. "Oh. That must be from when I ran into the doorknob. It's not *that bad*. It doesn't even hurt."

"Sandra! Jay! Sit down and be quiet!" the woman abruptly ordered. "The lesson is about to start! I'm growing very tired of telling both of you to sit each morning. You're testing my patience."

"*Race ya!*" the boy challenged as he bolted from the classroom when the recess bell sounded. Already a few strides ahead of me, he sprinted to the starting line and skid to a stop with his biggest grin.

The blacktop offered us hop-scotch and a set of monkey bars, where we scrambled up and made the other laugh with jokes we had learned. Jay and I would simply look at one another and burst into contagious laughing fits that often spread to anyone near us. [8]

On a Friday afternoon, sunlight flooded into our classroom through the propped-open doorway, signifying that the bell would soon ring for dismissal. That day, the class was unusually quiet and attentive to the lesson being scraped on the blackboard. Unexpectedly, a shadow dimmed the room with a disturbing chill. The teacher turned her face from the board towards the open doorway.

With salt in her voice, she menacingly warned, "Jay, you'd better *straighten up*. Your father is at the door." [9]

The child slowly drew his gaze from the notebook and shrank back, allowing his pencil to hit the desk and roll off to the carpeted floor. Sunlight shimmered from Jay's swelling tears and prompted the rest of his classmates to stare at the entrance.

Blocking the doorway was a slender man with a baleful expression on a gaunt face. His lanky elbow leaned against the metal frame, showcasing an unusually tall, gelid presence as he relished the paralyzing fear of his son. [10]

That evening, while trying to fall asleep, I pondered, "What happened today? That woman is *evil* and I hate her. Why did she have to say that to Jay's father? He wasn't talking or laughing or *anything*. Does she *enjoy* getting us into trouble? I don't understand what she was thinking. Didn't she see his face? He was so scared, he *cried*. Something's up. Cuts? Bruises? A black eye? If that man is hurting Jay, then I hate him, too." [11]

Now

My father had returned from another prolonged deployment at sea. Soon after, the man intricately planned a family road trip, intending to complete a five-thousand-mile loop of the western United States in just two weeks' time. Among our list of stops were national parks, various monuments and the homes of select relatives.

The shore-leave that the sailor had accrued didn't coordinate with my elementary school's winter, spring, or summer breaks. However, since the district catered to the military families of navy housing, he simply notified the main office that my brother and I would be absent from class on those days.

By the time we backed out of the driveway, our patriarch had already mapped and scheduled each stop to streamline the route, focusing on the timing of departure to minimize city traffic delays. His wife packed picnic food and provided her son and me with coloring books, markers, toys, word searches, and games to keep us distracted and quiet for as long as possible.

Hours later, despite the wall of pillows and folded blankets that were stacked between our two back seats, I slipped my hand between the quilts and poked my brother in the ribcage.

"Stop it, Sandra," he warned. My hand returned to me speedily as I silently giggled. I forced my stuffed turtle through the quilts and popped it out on the other side to puppeteer a mesmerizing turtle-dance. The boy laughed at the lifelike and rhythmic movements. Without warning, I poked him once more. "Ok, Sandra. Stop it," my sibling ordered, firing his second warning shot. I reached over the plush wall and slowly progressed my finger toward his face. "Mom, Sandra won't stop touching me!" [1]

His mother's arm awkwardly reached back to slap and pinch my skin. Quickly using the seatbelt for leverage, I pulled my legs up to my chest to avoid her attack radius as she thundered, "Sandra, leave your brother alone! I bought you things to play with, so *play!* Look out the window! Go to sleep! Do something, but just *be quiet!*"

My father chimed in and announced, "*Sandra*, if I have to pull over, you're getting a spanking with the belt. *Knock it off.* I'm not telling you again." [2]

I obeyed the man and fell asleep within minutes. That first day, we stopped a handful of times for the family to eat, use the restroom and stretch our legs.

Abruptly waking me, ten hours after leaving the driveway, the termagant shouted, *"You better stop this car, right now! I can't take it anymore! Find a motel! This trip is driving me crazy!"* [3]

Her irritated husband begrudgingly pulled into the nearest motel parking lot, where I inquired, "Why is Mom yelling? Are we stopping here for the night? Do I need to put my shoes on?" [4]

Ignoring me, she loudly continued, *"No! I'm not sleeping here! Look at this place! Do you expect me to stay in a dump like that?!"*

Palming his face, the man conveyed, "Alright. Fine. Just lower your voice. I'm right next to you. You're worse than the kids." [5]

"Pull over here," the termagant demanded, quickly getting out to speak to the front desk while we waited in the car. After about fifteen minutes, she walked back, reentered the vehicle, and commented, "I'm not paying those prices! Forget it! Try another one."

"Well, if you want nicer rooms, we'll have to spend more money," the man reasoned. "We're almost on the other end of this town. I planned this entire trip already and we'll be at our stopping point *in an hour*. You'd better make up your mind or I'm gonna keep driving."

"The hell you will!" she snarled, growing even louder. [6]

"Listen, the earlier we stop, the earlier we'll needed to wake up tomorrow," my father reasoned with maintained composure. "I planned out this entire vacation and we're staying *on-schedule*. If we stop here, we'll need to get up at six in the morning."

"I don't care!" the woman raged. *"We're stopping now! I'm tired of being cooped up in this car!"*

"Well, Mom," I interjected, "shouting isn't helping anything. Why don't you listen to some music, look out the window, or go to sleep? It worked for *me*. One more hour isn't so bad."

"Shut up!" the materfamilias roared. [7]

"Stay out of this, Sandra," my father gruffly added. "You're not helping." [8]

I rolled my eyes and sighed at her hypocrisy. Incapable of following her own advice, the woman pressured my father repeatedly. We stopped four more times in that town before the materfamilias settled for a standard hotel to sleep in… two hours later. The argument repeated each day we were on the road, followed by early-morning bickering. [9]

Montana

Northern California offered massive sequoias and redwood trees that transported my mind into a realm of fantasy fiction during hikes. Miniscule beside the ancient timber, I peered straight upward to the point of falling backwards, and wondered about all that may have occurred under their mighty branches.

While in Oregon, we entered a commercial boat that ferried us to the center of a lake located inside of a crater. I beheld the most limpid waters I had ever clapped eyes on and tried to touch the submerged stones that seemed frigidly within reach. "Be careful, my dear. The bottom is farther away than it seems," the tour-guide gently warned. "Snowmelt feeds this lake, which is why it's so clear. If you fall in, you'll get hypothermia and *still* won't touch the bottom. The average depth is one hundred feet, but plummets to almost two thousand." I pulled back my hand with a smile and rubbed heat into my fingertips.

South Dakota boasted mountainside faces. Years prior, clever sculptors had strategically placed dynamite to blast away stone. The precision astounded me as I cleaved to the rails surrounding the mount, although I didn't recognize any of the men showcased.

However, before we arrived at the patriotic sculpture, there was a location the sailor wanted to visit for a couple of days. My parents owned property in Montana and intended to build a house there. In that acreage of wilderness, our father scheduled for us to stop and camp. My brother and I helped the proud land owner pitch a massive four-person pipe-and-canvas tent, followed by collecting pinecones and sticks to start the evening's campfire. [1]

At dawn, the man cooked pancakes over our portable gas stove and lead a hike amongst towering pines. Instead of shedding leaves, their needles caked the ground, feeling like sponge under my feet.

"Look!" I shouted, pointing at the forest floor. "Oh, my gosh! Someone dropped chocolate candy all over the ground! What a waste! Good thing pine needles are clean! I can eat them!" [2]

"*No!*" my parents shouted simultaneously, freezing me in my tracks. [3]

"That's *poop*, not chocolate!" the woman explained. "What's wrong with you?! You're old enough to know not to eat things off the ground!" [4]

Embarrassed, I argued, "Well, poop shouldn't come out in perfect little balls. It's misleading. Doesn't it look like candy to you?" [5]

"Sandra," my father interjected. "If you don't eat things off of the ground, you won't have to determine if it's poop. *Stop and think*. Look around you. Why would someone throw candy all over the ground in the woods? It's everywhere." Obeying, I examined my surroundings and immediately understood my father's point. As far as I could see, there were piles of perfectly round brown balls. Devastated with my stupidity, I released a shame-filled sigh. "Cheer up, squirt. You're *six* and only know the city. How would you recognize deer and elk poop if you've never seen it before? It's our job to teach you. So, what did you learn from your mistake?" [6]

"I need to think before I act, pay attention to what's happening around me, and… *not eat things off of the ground*," I replied, feeling even more ridiculous after having said it. [7]

"Very good," he encouraged. "If you learn from your mistakes, then they have purpose."

A few more steps through the woods unveiled a glassy lake, reflecting the picturesque mountains and sky. "Oh, wow! Are we going fishing?!" I wondered with a gasp.

"It's too late in the day for that. We'll come back tomorrow morning," he calmly reassured me.

True to his word, after preparing a tasty breakfast, my father returned his family to the captivating body of water as we carried folding chairs, snacks, and supplies. The sailor opened a tackle box and instructed his children on how to hook worms securely and cast their line without injury. [8]

Observing the man's patience with the rod and reel as he monitored the attached bobber, I stood beside him and queried, "Doesn't the hook hurt the worms, Daddy? I feel bad for them and this is pretty gross. Will you hook my worms for me?"

"Nope. Use the lake water to rinse the worm off of your hands. If you want to fish with a rod, you need to use lures or bait. These fish like nightcrawlers, better known as earthworms," he replied. "No matter what, if you want to go fishing, you'll have to get your hands dirty. Any fish you catch will have to be gutted and descaled so we can cook them. Fishing is messy and can be a lot of work. Do you still want to fish?" [9]

"*Yes*," I assured with desire to impress, "but the worm keeps falling off when I cast. Show me how *you* do it." [10]

As if sensing my lack of preparation, several fish flopped and rolled in that moment, just yards away from the shore at my feet. They taunted me, snacking on any unfortunate insect that gently settled onto the water's surface tension. Ripples spread themselves over the mirror-like tranquility, distorting the mountain's reflection as they rolled ever outward to the opus of bird serenade. [11]

"I'm bored!" erupted the materfamilias, fidgeting in her folding chair. "This is torture! I should have brought my radio! The silence is killing me! I can't *talk*, I'm all *sweaty*, and bugs are everywhere! Why can't I say anything?! You're not my boss!" [12]

"Be *quiet*," my father huffed forcefully. "I already told you. Loud sounds scare the fish. If you can't sit still or shut your mouth, go back to the campsite. I'm tired of your complaining." [13]

That starry night, the scent of burning pine wafted through the crisp night air as I listened to the crackling pinecones of our campfire. Warm in my sleeping bag while lounging in a folding chair, I stared at the flickering flames. After all the bitter words the woman had spewed, I sweetly announced, "I'm having fun, Daddy. I *like* camping." [14]

The following morning, my father prepared bacon, eggs, and hash browns for his family. Overwhelmed by the fragrance of sizzling pine sap, smoke, and seared meat, I rested before the fire with my plate and savored the crisp edges of perfection in a setting from the most pleasant of dreams.

"I'm *so* bored!" his wife aggressively reiterated, pacing back and forth. "How are you guys not going crazy?! There's no electricity, TV, or restrooms! I feel disgusting! My hair is going flat! I look like a man! I hate this! Camping is for the birds! I'm getting out of here to find a place to shower!" [15]

The woman commandeered the family car and abandoned us at the campsite. As she pulled away, a crushing weight lifted and allowed my tiny body to relax. Throughout the day and during the hike, not a soul complained or quarreled. Our personal chef prepared another delectable meal before twilight, followed by a treat of hot chocolate and marshmallows. I stared at the flames' glow while the three of us enjoyed the dazzling ambiance of mountains crowned by the setting sun. [16]

Sounds of an engine emanated from the darkness and steadily grew louder. Within moments, the family vehicle pulled into view and parked as I mentioned, "Oh yeah. I completely forgot about her. Maybe she'll be *nice* now that she's clean." The materfamilias stepped out of the vehicle, shut the door behind her, and walked toward us with a blank expression. "Do you feel better after a shower, Mom?"

"*No!*" the woman roared like a freshly slapped bear. "I didn't even get to shower! I drove all over the place to find a motel or hotel that would give me a discount to just use their restroom! They wanted me to pay for an *entire night* just to use the room for an hour! No way! I'm not letting them cheat me! I tried a bunch of places. They all said the same thing. Then, when I tried to come back, I got lost. I've been driving around all day!" [17]

The materfamilias angrily consumed her hot chocolate and promptly went to bed. We each followed, unwilling to be the one to wake her from hibernation.

Ponytails

Summer returned. Each day, for as long as allowed, Nancy and I basked in the sun beside one another. We slipped on our joint-pads and well-seasoned rollerblades to shred the sidewalk as our synchronized ponytails swayed under colorful helmets. For a break, we retreated to the backyard to rest within the branches of my climbing tree.

Nancy suggested, "Let's try something new today. We're always spies or cops. Let's be someone else."

"I know!" I chirped. "Let's be rock stars!" I imagining us standing on a stage before thousands of screaming fans as we performed our favorite songs from the radio. "I'll sing and play guitar!"

"Yeah! I've got the drums!" my friend declared as she smacked two twigs together. "One, two, three… hit it!" We hummed music and sang every song we knew. "Sandra, when you're famous, what will you do with all your money?" [1]

I thought for a moment and replied, "I'll buy an entire beach and build two houses on a cliff that overlook the ocean. One for you and one for me… in case we each get married and need some privacy… but you can come over whenever you want. *Next*, I'll buy a helicopter so we can go anywhere at any time. *I'll be the pilot.* We'll just get in and fly away. What would you buy?" [2]

"Well, I'd buy a house for my parents to live in, since you would've already bought one for me," she laughed. "Hey! I just thought of something! Do you wanna play a game?"

Being silly, I acted like a valley girl and replied, "Uh… *yeah*."

With a grin, she chirped, "Okay! Since its multiple-choice, we need some notebook paper and pens." [3]

"On it!" I announced as I leaped from my tree branch. After sprinting to my room, I returned with all the supplies we needed. Using every color possible, the game of chance hilariously predicted a celebrity crush we would ultimately marry and the details of our lives together. "Dude!" I exclaimed after Nancy handed me the results. "I'm going to be a movie star, live in a mansion with a superhero, own a talking dolphin, and drive a pink sports car! Life sounds pretty amazing!" [4]

"No kidding! Check this out! I'm gonna be a beauty queen, live in a mansion with a pro-football player, have a robotic dog, and drive a monster truck... *and*... we'll be beach neighbors!" Nancy proclaimed with her infectious giggle. Repositioned onto a low-swooping branch, she posed the question, "Seriously though, what *do* you want in life? Like, what do you want to do when you grow up?" [5]

"That's easy. I want to move out and get as far away from my mother as possible, somewhere she could never find me. *Then,* I want to go on adventures all over the world and help people. I want to fight crime, stop injustice, and make a difference." [6]

"Me, too," Nancy agreed, patting my hand.

"Right now, I just feel *stuck* and a kid shouldn't feel that way," I protested with restrained emotion. [7]

"One day, you'll be *big*, Sandra. Then you'll do anything you want," my friend encouraged. "Cheer up. You'll see. It won't always be this way." [8]

The Fox

~~~

On the first day of school, I approached my second-grade classroom and wondered, "Are *all* teachers mean to their students after kindergarten?" [1]

I stepped through the open door and glanced around. A gentle tap on the shoulder interrupted my dread. Turning to discover who had sought my attention, I saw nothing but giggling students peering towards the carpet.

"Gotcha, again!" Jay announced as he sprung upward.

"Oh, my gosh!" I laughed. "How do I keep falling for that?! *Hey!* We're in the same class this year! That's awesome!" [2]

"Yeah!" he cheered.

"Okay, students! Please stand in a line on the yellow tape," an adult voice sweetly conveyed from the front of the room. Remembering all that had happened the year prior, we swiftly obeyed. "Welcome to the second grade! As your teacher, I am so happy to meet all of you! Now that you've all chatted for a bit and got rid of some first-day wiggles, let's get started. If you will look, you'll see the number mat centered on the floor. I'm going to assign a number to you and that will be where you sit *all year* when I need to address you as a class. That means you'll need to remember it. Alright? If you forget, don't worry. I'll help you. When I say your name, sit on the number assigned to you. Are you ready?!" [3]

Each student eagerly nodded in compliance as one boy exclaimed, "I was born ready! I want *thirteen*. It's not unlucky to me!"

A girl chirped, "I hope I get number eleven. That's my birthday!"

During recess, I mentioned to Jay, "Last year was a total nightmare. I was treated like a criminal, but I'm a good student! That's messed up! This year is *so much* better already. Isn't our new teacher wonderful?"

"Yeah. She's pretty great," Jay confessed.

"...and a total *fox*," Josh interjected, causing Jay and me to face him. As Nam stepped forward, we unanimously nodded in agreement. "Together again, like a *posse*." [4]

"I like the sound of that. We're a *posse*," Nam added with a giggle. "A posse that loves our teacher." [5]

Apart from her beauty and gracious manner of speaking, it seemed to bring our esteemed surrogate-mother great joy and satisfaction to watch each one of us grow and bloom under her supervision. Becoming a heroine against the mundane, our captivating mentor read books aloud, practiced exciting methods of exploration in science and art, and found creative ways to apply mathematics to everyday life. [6]

"Happy Monday, class! What did all of you do this weekend?!" the captivating woman queried with a smile. Chaotic chirping ensued. With a chuckle, she added, "Okay. Okay. That was *my* mistake. Let's take it from the top. *One at a time,* please. Raise your hands and I'll call on you."

The woman provided us with information about planets and their moons, the seasons, migrating animals, and how all the topics were connected. As a result, my cravings for a broader education became insatiable. [7]

While stepping out of class together to head home for the day, I whispered to Nam, "I just love our teacher. When I grow up, I want to be just like her… smart, beautiful, and *kind*." [8]

Promise Me

*J*ay and I narrowed our competitive focus during recess to four-square and foot-races, which resulted in more tripping, falling down, rolling, and skinned knees. I arrived to class in the clean and feminine clothing that my mother had picked out for me, often matching from head to toe and covered in ruffles or glitter. By the time recess was over, sweat soaked through my grass stains and stung around the bloody holes in my patterned stockings.

One afternoon, the materfamilias gasped and aggressively questioned, "Why do I even bother buying you anything new?! You destroy it! Look at your knees! What happened today at school?! Why do you look like you've been in a fight?!"

"Well, I'm really fast, but these girly shoes don't grip the ground very well," I explained. "All my dress shoes slip on the blacktop, which is why I fall down so much. It would be *less expensive* if I just wore shorts and tennis shoes. I wouldn't fall as often during the races and…"

"Sandra!" the materfamilias interrupted. "Why can't you play calmly like other little girls?! Why do you have to act like a boy?! I want you to behave like a daughter, not a son! Your brother doesn't even come home looking like that! I waited my whole life to have a precious little girl! I had your name picked out when I was just sixteen years old! I hated *my* name, so I wanted a *good* name for my daughter. I named you the name I wanted… *Sandra*… and look what you've become! You're skin-and-bones, you talk back, and you play like a boy! What a disappointment." [1]

"All of my friends go home like this, boys *and* girls," I rebutted. "We all race and get sweaty. If you're concerned about me ruining my new clothes, then just let me wear hand-me-downs from my brother's clothes. I don't care how I look. I just want to play."

"That's the stupidest thing I've ever heard!" the termagant shouted. "You think you have all the answers?! Well, you don't! That's why *you're* the child and *I'm* the mother! I'm not dressing you like a boy! *That's even worse!* People will think that I don't care about you!"

"Correction. People will *know* that you don't care about me," I interjected. "I'm a disappointment. *Remember?*" [2]

"I don't have to listen to you!" the materfamilias roared. *"Get out of my sight, you demon from hell!"* [3]

Ready for another sunny recess, I lined up for a race and expected to see Jay beside me, but he wasn't there. I scanned the blacktop and spotted him standing alone in the shade by a wall. Right then, Nam and Josh approached him. Abandoning the line, I sought to join the rest of the huddled posse.

Sprinting their way, I shouted, "Jay! Come on! You're missing recess!" Stutter-stepping, I slowed to a stop, smiled, and chirped, "Hey, guys! Why aren't you playing?"

Stone faced, Nam pointed at our friend and ordered, "Look at Jay *carefully*." Confused, I focused and gasped. Riddled with deep cuts and skin discoloration, Jay looked as though he had survived a car accident.

"Oh no," I winced, touching Jay's shoulder. "What happened?"

"*Nothing*," he sharply replied, pulling away from me. The sting of his response pooled tears in my eyes. "Nothing happened. I don't want to talk about it."

Compassionate and assertive, Nam inquired, "Jay, *something* happened. I'm serious. What's going on?" Afraid and embarrassed, he refused to speak and looked away. "We're your friends and we love you. You can tell us." [4]

"Stop making a big deal about it. It's not that bad," Jay claimed.

"It *is* that bad. It's so bad, you're not playing or running around. That's not like you *at all*. Are you too sore to play? Let me see your back," Nam gently requested. Jay relented and allowed her delicate fingers to lift his shirt. I stood near Jay's head as Josh used his body to block the view from the blacktop. "Sandra… Josh… come look at this."

Josh went slack jaw as I grit my teeth in anger. Bruises covered Jay's rib cage and lower back, bearing deep cuts that seemed to have happened the night before. Nam lowered his shirt and allowed Jay to face us.

Defensive, the mangled child argued, "It's not a big deal, guys. *Seriously*, I just fell off my bike. Stop freaking out."

"I know that you're afraid, Jay. I can see it in your face. *Don't lie*," she rebuked. "We're not stupid. This wasn't from a bike wreck. We've all wrecked our bikes before. You look like you've been mauled by a tiger. What about this black eye and busted lip, *huh*? What's the story behind that?" [5]

"I ran into a doorknob," he tearfully muttered, trying to control his swollen lip from quivering. I stared motionless and remembered the last time Jay used that excuse.

"No. I don't believe that," Nam conveyed. "No doorknob could give you that black eye. You're too tall, so *stop lying*." [6]

Jay slumped for a moment, then perked up and announced, "I know what happened! I took my bike on some new trails and wrecked it *really bad*. The cuts are from the sticks and rocks."

"Dude, I ride a *dirt bike*," Josh informed with an eyebrow raised. "I go really fast and have crashed really hard on some gnarly trails. I can tell you right now… I've *never* looked this bad."

Nam pleaded, "We love you, Jay. We're your friends and we care about you. Those cuts are deep. *Stop lying*. How did you *really* get them?" [7]

Jay continued, "Well, my bike was *destroyed*… so I had to walk it back home. It was *expensive*. My dad got *really mad* and…" He stopped himself and closed his mouth.

"Then what happened?" Nam interrogated.

"Then…" Jay mumbled, as his gaze dropped to his worn shoes, *"… he threw me through a window."* The three of us gasped. [8]

"Now, *that* I believe," Nam remarked, crimson with anger. [9]

"Your father threw you through a window?" I growled with white-knuckled fists.

"What the heck, Jay?! That's not normal! Parents aren't supposed to do that!" Josh protested, lifting his friend's chin to regain eye contact. "Your dad… *threw you through a window…* for wrecking your bike. There's no excuse for that. That's child abuse, flat out."

"Uh… uh…" the boy stuttered. "I mean… my *uncle* did it. My uncle was visiting… got mad about my bike… and *he* threw me through the window."

"Jay, that lie isn't any better. This is serious," Nam informed. "Guys, back me up. We need to tell the teacher what happened." [10]

"*No!*" Jay shouted, causing each of us to flinch as he fought back tears and attempted to calm himself. "I'm sorry. I know you guys are just trying to help, but… *please*… don't tell anyone. You'll just make it worse. Promise me *you won't tell*." He trembled and passionately repeated, "*Promise me!*" [11]

Standing beside our pleading friend, the posse unanimously decided to put Jay's wishes above our own. We agreed to not disclose Jay's testimony unless directly asked by an adult and refused to lie about the subject. [12]

Jay didn't come back to school the following day. While he was gone, Nam, Josh, and I revisited the topic of Jay's bruised body and regretted ever giving our word to be silent.

He had been absent for several weeks in a row when the three of us approached our teacher's desk and inquired, "Is Jay on vacation? He's been gone a long time."

The compassionate woman whispered, "You noticed, huh? I'm impressed with the three of you. You're very observant students. Let me address the entire class all at once. Go ahead and take your seats on the number rug." Nam, Josh, and I quickly obeyed as she stepped away from her desk and gently ordered, "*Everyone*, I need you to stop working on your art projects and sit on the number rug."

Some classmates whined, "Aw! But I'm not finished!"

"C'mon guys!" I encouraged. "Let's do what she says!"

"Yeah, we can finish it later!" Nam added to expedite their compliance.

From the number rug, our class peered up at our teacher's emotional hesitation before she informed, "Jay… *is in the hospital*. He's in a coma."

"What's a *coma*?" I wondered out loud. "I've never heard of that."

"It is a lot like when a person is asleep… but when they're in a coma, they can't seem to wake up," she answered as a tear dripped from her cheek. "Doctors are trying to help Jay wake up."

"Do you know what happened that put Jay into a coma?" I queried as anger discreetly bubbled.

"Yeah. Is he sick, like with a virus?" another classmate wondered. "Could I go to sleep tonight and not wake up?"

"My goodness. No, sweetheart. Don't be afraid. It's not that," the woman gently replied. "He's not sick. They ran those tests already and didn't find anything. They don't know why Jay fell into a coma."

"Is Jay gonna be okay?" Nam inquired. [13]

"These are all *very good questions*. I just don't know. I only know what I've been told," she confessed. Taking a deep breath, she clasped her hands together and warmly suggested, "Why don't we all pitch in and do something for Jay?! He's our friend, right?!"

"Yeah!" the class enthusiastically agreed.

"Okay! I have been doing my research about comas and read somewhere that *hearing* is one of the last things to go and one of the first things to return in many coma patients. So, guess what?! I have a tape recorder and a bunch of empty tapes! Let's record ourselves speaking to Jay and talk to him! How does that sound?!" The entire class cheered with excitement. [14]

Josh petitioned, "Would it be okay if Nam, Sandra, and I go first? We're his best friends."

"Of course," she replied. "Just let me empty this closet. It's not soundproof, but it's quieter than the classroom. Okay, everyone… Nam, Josh, and Sandra will go in first and record. When they come out, I'll send in another group of three. You can say anything you want Jay to hear… and take all the time you need."

Our posse huddled around the device and cheerfully recorded, "*Hey, Jay!* It's Nam, Sandra, and Josh! *We miss you!*" I took the lead and shared some fresh jokes. Nam and Josh jumped in and added, "We need you to wake up and get better. You need to come back to school so we all can be together again." On the count of three, we signed off and exclaimed, *"We love you, Jay!"* [15]

After stopping the recorder, the three of us opened the door to behold a line of classmates patiently waiting for their turn.

You're Not Going

A few mornings later, I entered the classroom, placed my sack lunch in my cubby, and noticed my beloved teacher struggle to maintain composure. Behind her dainty hands, she attempted to hide red eyes and a tear-soaked face.

Nam, Josh, and I approached her together and mentioned, "You look sad. What's wrong?" [1]

Our instructor grabbed a tissue and dried her flawless face as she struggled to inhale. We stepped back as the woman gently rose from her seat and ordered, "Class, I need everyone to sit on the number rug." Having learned from the last announcement, each child obeyed without complaint. Trembling before her students, she painfully divulged, *"Jay… will not be returning to class. I'm so sorry, guys… um…"* She laced her fingers behind her crimson neck and cleared her throat. "Jay did not wake up. He passed away in the hospital. *I'm so sorry…*" [2]

Gasps and sobs erupted from classmates as one boy shouted, *"No-o-o-o-o! It's not true! That can't be right! No! No-o-o!"* The expressive child struck himself in the head and pulled his hair. *"No-o-o-o!"* [3]

Frozen with my legs crossed, I remained seated on my number, vacant and numb, unable to respond. My eyes found Nam wrenched in the fetal position with her hands shielding her face.

A sob betrayed the beloved woman as she continued, "I'm so sorry, guys. *I'm so sorry.* There will be no lesson today. I don't want to put anything else on your plate. Please tell me what can I do to help you through this. *I'm so sorry.*" [4]

Burdened with Jay's dark secret and my unexpressed love for him, I became horrified at myself and silently wondered, "What's wrong with me? They're losing it and they barely knew him. Why can't I cry? Why can't I scream? I could have helped him and I didn't. I'm a horrible friend. It should have been me. Jay should be here, and I'm to blame. I knew his father was hurting him. *I knew it.* His father killed him. I should have said something. He might have had a chance. Jay is dead and I'm a coward. I'm the one that doesn't deserve to live." [5]

"I need a hug!" the same expressive boy cried out. [6]

Responding to the child's urgent plea, our teacher lowered her knees to the floor with arms opened wide, warmly confessing, *"Come here, guys. I need a hug, too."*

The class swarmed her. As skin purposefully and compassionately touched mine, a soothing effect occurred. The raw wound of reality, although involuntarily suppressed, had met the healing properties of tender human touch. The wailing boy had inadvertently introduced to me a phenomenon. Although I joined an awkward huddle and had my ear pinned to another student's back, my heart softened at the unexpected relief and warmth of benevolent contact. [7]

After walking my brother and I home, the materfamilias sat on the sofa and ordered, "Sandra, come over here." I obeyed and wondered what crime I had committed as of late. "I heard about what happened to the little boy that died. The school called all the parents and told us everything."

"He wasn't just *a little boy*. He has a name. Jay was my *friend*," I corrected through my teeth. "Did they tell you when the funeral will be? I really want to go. We've been friends since the first grade."

"They told me about the arrangements. I think a child-funeral is too sad for you, so you're not going," the woman dryly concluded.

Cleaving to the faintest hope of gaining sympathy, I calmly pleaded, "Please, let me go to Jay's funeral. My *entire class* will be there. Losing Jay is hard enough, but not going to the funeral will make it so much worse. Please, let me go. Please."

"*No*. I'm going *alone*. I've made my decision and if you ask me again, you're getting a spanking," the woman threatened. "I said *no* and that's final." [8]

Abandoning any form of self-preservation, I shouted, *"Why are you doing this to me!?"* Tears finally swelled in my eyes, hot and burning. *"You are completely evil! I hate you! You take everything away, even burying my friend! You won't listen! You never listen! Why are you even going?! You don't even know his name! You make me sick! Don't bother coming back! I don't ever want to see you again! I hate you! I hate you!"* [9]

"You'll miss me when I'm gone," she flippantly presumed. [10]

I glared at her with frigid disdain and coldly added, "No… *I won't*." [11]

"Oh, yeah?! Keep it up, Sandra! You're about to get a spanking! Go to your room, you demon from hell!" the materfamilias ordered. [12]

I fled her corrosive presence and writhed on my bed, alone with my palpable tempest of emotions, and silently contemplated, "Maybe *death* was the only way Jay could escape his father. What if death is the only way I can escape my mother?"

The termagant left me behind and attended Jay's funeral.

"That was the saddest thing I have ever seen!" she thoughtlessly blathered as she entered and locked the front door behind her.

"Stop talking to me," I ordered, standing up from the living room television. "I don't want to hear about it from *you*."

"It was awful seeing his body like that," she mindlessly divulged.

"Stop it! What's wrong with you?!" I shouted. "Talk to someone else, lady! You didn't let me go to the funeral because you said it was too sad! So, why the hell would you tell *me* about it?!"

"Seeing him in that little casket…" she proceeded, grabbing a tissue. As she vomited more undesired information, I stared at her in unwavering horror. It was as though she had pressed a mute button during my side of the dialogue. My words meant *nothing* to her.

"You're a twisted person," I bluntly informed. "Stop talking. You're evil and I couldn't hate you more." [13]

"Everyone was crying…" she odiously recalled, "and I felt so sorry for Jay's father. He cried *so loud*. I can't imagine what he's feeling." [14]

"Are you kidding me?! You would feel sorry for that monster!" I tearfully raged. *"He beat his son to death! You should know all about that! You're both the same person! The problem is…I just won't die! Jay was my best friend, and I loved him! He was missing for weeks, right after letting us see the cuts and bruises all over his body! We didn't say anything because he wouldn't let us, and now he's dead! I'll never see him again! We were together every day since the first grade and you wouldn't let me go to the funeral! Now you won't shut up about it! I hate you!"*

"I didn't know!" she declared.

"You wouldn't listen! You never listen!" I sobbed. *"I will never forgive you! You're dead to me!"*

During recess, Nam and Josh described the behavior of Jay's father as *theatrical*, under the impression that the brute had purposefully drawn everyone's attention away from Jay and to himself.

"Jay was his victim. Let the man drown in guilt," I growled through my teeth. "If my mom would've let me go, I would've shamed Jay's father in front of everyone and forced him to explain the two years of Jay's cuts, bruises, and black eyes. Maybe the police might have locked him up right then and there. Now, what are we gonna do? I'll never forgive my mother for not letting me go. *Never.*" [15]

SECTION 2

The Aquatic Abyss

During summer confinement with the materfamilias, televised documentaries about vast waters and oceanic trenches held my thoughts captive, providing temporary relief from Jay's death and my father's elongated absence. [1]

Being seven years of age and unable to drive myself to the beach, I made a few formal requests for oceanic outings. Each plead was an act of utter futility. To survive, I compensated for my lack of physical freedom with creativity and a quirky sense of humor. [2]

While isolated in my room, I pretended to be a salty, swashbuckling pirate captain that sailed tumultuous seas to uncover hidden treasures, and exclaimed, "A-hoy there, may-tees! Prepare the plank! Let us see if this mutineer floats! *Argh!*"

I daydreamed about being a captivating siren from Greek mythology. My body launched into turquoise waters from the jagged rocks near the shore and effortlessly glided toward a dashing stranger as he strolled to the end of a long pier. Intrigued by the sight of me, the audacious man dove head-first into my domain, surfacing to tread water and gawk. Fluttering my eyelashes in feigned surprise, I openly flirted, "Oh, hello. Was it lonesome way up there?" [3]

Vivid and often extreme, my imagination plunged into exaggerated and enthralling worlds that existed far beyond my natural reach. I pictured myself as an adult, capable of experiencing absolutely *anything* I desired.

Approaching the shore, the roaring sea's aroma engulfed my senses with the hot sand as my welcome mat. I was home. Unfolding a plush lounging towel, I rested face-down in the warmth of sunbaked sand, stretching out my legs and allowing my toes to dig down into cooler pockets of crushed shells, glass, and pulverized coral. Solar rays melted the throbbing burdens from my shoulders as I turned over to watch the gulls glide above each swell of the frothy tide. Drowning out my swirling thoughts, the waves beckoned to me, inviting me to submerge into their powerful embrace. [4]

Driven by a deepening desire to experience the unknown, I slid my submergible lamp over my forehead and secured a trusted weapon to my thigh, abandoning the comforts of dry land to stretch my understanding far beyond. Crisp, churning waters slowly engulfed my body with each progressing step, swirling past my feet and breaking against my shins. Crashing waves dissolved the clinging shackles of anxiety and helplessness, freeing me from the expectations of daily terranean life. Without fear of drowning or being crushed by pounds per square inch, I breathed in the brilliant waters that teamed with vibrance. The ocean's surface swelled and sparkled above me, diffusing beams of light that traced their long fingers across my skin as I twirled in liberating weightlessness. [5]

Navigating myself amid treacherous coral and their fiery inhabitants, I pursued a school of elaborate fish that crossed paths with a prone octopus, hungry and focused on the next unsuspecting snack. Unwavering in my presence, the beast whipped its tentacles around the violently resisting meal, dragging it to her layer to feed. [6]

Beyond the labyrinth of flamboyant tube worms, crustaceans, and swaying sea grass was a daunting ridge, dropping off into the expanding vastness. My heart drummed the soundtrack of my exploration as I pressed into all that waited beyond my sight. Unidentified figures approached, appearing hazy at first, but growing clearer as their distance dwindled. Hammer heads, tiger sharks, and their assorted brethren circled me, searching for carnage and obsequious respect. Smooth and purposeful, I touched the flesh of several passersby, delighting them into a trusting bond that sensed no threat from my contact. The shiver led me outside the view of the ridge and into the abyss. There was no turning back. [7]

Barreling up from the depths, a great white brushed past, avoiding a strike to turn and circle back right above me. He spared my life, though I didn't know why. Its weaving body dwarfed the entire entourage of its kin and cast a looming shadow. Scarred from battle and hungry for flesh, its gaping mouth revealed rows of jagged teeth. Unlike his brethren, this creature had lethal intentions of the sadist variety. Little did it know, the beast would have to work for its meal. Each finger slipped around my dagger's handle, preparing for whatever end. It jerked sideways at the glimmer of my blade, recalling the seasoned warriors it consumed in times past. [8]

Tried strategies and flashes of daring victories flooded my soul, reminding me that all was not lost... not yet. Anticipating his attack, I monitored the white's whip and dash at it cut through water like lighting through sky. Grossly underestimated, I locked eyes with my adversary and dodged the strike, plunging my blade through its coarse skin and powerful flesh in a line that spilled his life, billowing a dark cloud into the depths. Robbed of its prey and sensing mortality, the predator relented and sought refuge from those drawing nearer. [9]

Squeaks and clicks filled my ears, followed by a rush of bubbles that blocked my view and swaddled my body in effervescence. Pockets of air touched my feet and rolled up my legs to escape around my chin. Making their way to the surface, they finally revealed their source. A pod of dolphin formed a barrier cyclone, having tracked my movements and rushed to my aid, blocking all potential enemy advances. Arching, bobbing, and nudging against my extended hand, the pod leader encouraged me to clasp its dorsal fin for guidance and a tow. Propelled into more frigid depths, liquid rushed past my skin and invigorated my senses, heightened by the darkness engulfing me. Having completed his mission, my escort squeaked, clicked a farewell, and quickly made its way toward the surface. [10]

However, I was anything but alone, noticing a dim speck stand out against the black void. A radiating orb cascaded and swayed, steadily growing larger and larger as each second passed. All but blind, I flicked on my headlamp and remained perfectly still in the paralyzing spirit of self-preservation. Gargantuan and fierce, possessing eyes as wide as my wingspan, a haunting creature was exposed. Swiftly, it turned its slick and semi-translucent body to narrowly evade physical contact, and I beheld its full length as it passed before my lamp's beam. I gently turned my head to maintain visual and revealed a majestic yet dreadful sight to behold. Fully equipped with needle-like teeth, the lifeform seduced its prey with a pearl of luminescence, acting as both angler and bait. [11]

Stirring me into reality, the formidable trod of the materfamilias tensed my body just before she burst through my bedroom door and scolded, "Sandra! What are you doing?! Why are you laying on the floor?! I've been calling you and calling you! Are you deaf?! Get over here! Dinner is ready!"

My imaginary world faded into the crags of reality… where the *real* danger lurked. [12]

Sea Bag

Each year, my father's extended absence tormented me with a rollercoaster of extreme emotions. While he was missing for months at a time, I didn't hear his voice or receive a single piece of mail. Sobs were all I offered the man when he left and when he returned. I cleaved to the illusion of peace and safety in his presence, and refused to release my grip as his wife pried me from his uniformed body. Within weeks of his arrival, he was gone again to reset the cycle.

I missed the distinct scent of my father's aftershave and enjoyed how infuriating the sailor's calm manner was to his wife. More than anything, I longed to hear his laughter, having become rarer with each return. With the materfamilias at the helm, if I wasn't being ridiculed or spanked, neglect stepped in and made room for thoughts about Jay. I envied the boy's eternal separation from his abuser. Tears pooled and flowed down my temples most nights as I wondered how I might *will* the life from my body to avoid blatant suicide, but my stubborn heart continued to beat. I longed to be numb and hated myself for being susceptible to pain. [1]

"I wonder where Daddy is on the globe right now?" I thought to myself, drying my face with the sheet. "Does Daddy think about me as often as I think about him? When will he be back? Why doesn't he ever call or write? Does he *enjoy* being away from us? *I would.* Why come back to a wife that hates you? Why should I stay when my mom hates *me*? If I ever get the chance, I'm gonna leave with Daddy and never come back." [2]

Our sailor finally stepped down from the aircraft carrier as we watched on to receive him. I was beside myself with tearful joy. That same day, another thunderous fight kept me awake. The materfamilias refused to control herself, even for a day. Although the woman's malignant behavior had become expected, it didn't grow easier to endure. My expectation of lasting peace between my parents had shifted to hope for divorce, then died altogether. Fed up with waiting, I laid my things in order. [3]

Before dawn, I stirred to the jingling of keys and the tap of early morning steps down the hall. Remembering my urgent mission, I slipped on a frilly dress and listened through my bedroom door.

"*Shoot. I almost forgot,*" the sailor whispered to himself. He noisily set an item down by the front door and returned down the hall into the bedroom.

While he was preoccupied, I tiptoed down the hall in my dress socks, holding my matching shoes in hand. He had abandoned a large duffle bag that toted a few loose items. I stepped into my opportunity and formed the tightest ball to zip my transportation closed from the inside. Not a muscle moved or twitched as I imagined our adventures together, far away from our nemesis.

My father's purposeful steps returned. He stopped to snatch up his luggage and whispered, "*Wow. This bag is heavy.*"

After several steps and turning a few corners, the man gently set the sea bag onto the floor as I silently concluded, "We're already on the ship! It worked! I'm a genius!"

My father slowly opened the zipper with a grin to see my smiling face. He chuckled and quietly noted, "*Well, what do we have here? You don't look like laundry.*"

With great ease, he reached into the bag and carefully plucked me out. Reality's kick struck me limp. Everything that surrounded me was horrifically familiar. There were no metal walls in sight. No cheerful men in uniform passed by to return my unnecessary salute. Although my father had carried me off, it had been a ruse.

Undone, I collapsed to tearfully plea, "*Don't go, Daddy. Please don't leave me.*"

The man scooped me up and held me close. "I have to go, Sandra," he replied. "I need to earn money so you can have a place to live and food to eat."[4]

To complete his uniform, the sailor restored the hat to his head and was gone.

GATE

~~~

Completely unaware of her intentions, my teacher had nominated me for the Gifted and Talented Education program, known as GATE. Accepted and enrolled, our class learned in our very own bungalow on the opposite side of the blacktop from the rest of the school. In that setting, both third and fourth-grade students occupied the same space, and made me feel quite honored to be considered. However, finding out that Nam and Josh were also enrolled brought me the most joy. [1]

After our first recess, the third-graders raced toward our teacher, Mrs. Blossom, who was quietly waiting in the sweltering heat. Using one hand to shade her eyes, the woman held out her other and gestured for us to stop and calm ourselves while the older students stepped forward to join us.

Our instructor announced, "Alright class, as the fourth-graders already know, each day I will have you silently line up single-file outside the bungalow door. You will not be allowed inside until you all are completely still and in control of your bodies again." The third-graders chuckled when she smirked. "Remember, the air-conditioning is *inside*, and the longer it takes for all of you to be still, the longer you will stand in the heat. Fourth-graders, if you would, please lead by example." They instantly lined up and hinted for the rest of us to file in behind them. "Very good. When I invite you to enter, silently locate your table, sit down at your assigned chair, and lay your head on the tabletop until I say otherwise." The woman paused with a gentle smile. "You may come in." [2]

Ready to escape the blazing sun, I obediently stepped into the darkness and allowed my eyes to adjust. As I looked toward the front of the classroom, I smiled. It felt as though I had entered someone else's life. A cozy armchair sat beneath a solitary floor lamp to cast a spotlight in our dimly lit bungalow. I watched the others and flattened my cheek against the cool surface while the frigid air chilled my sweaty clothing. The rapid pulse within me slowed to a resting speed and, at once, I knew Mrs. Blossom was brilliant. [3]

"You may now lift your heads," the woman gently conveyed from the chair with an open book in her hand. The seated thespian cleverly altered her voice to distinguish one character from another and caused the story to come alive in my heart as I imagined every vibrant detail. She read a captivating tale about a race of giants, a child, misunderstandings, and morality. I intently listened and became invested in each of the lively and well represented characters. Finishing the first chapter, our teacher closed the book and caused the students to groan. [4]

Mrs. Blossom smiled and added, "Tomorrow, I'll read chapter *two*."

In contrast to the standard of thirty or more students in each classroom, GATE only had twenty children in the program at a time. Hand-picked students, armed with cheerful temperaments and inquisitive natures, created a dynamic environment for intellectual progress and healthy emotional development. Since it was the fourth-graders' second year to be with Mrs. Blossom, they were very comfortable speaking up about critical-thinking topics and drawing their own conclusions based on provided information. [5]

Using funding which exceeded that of the average classroom, our class embarked on special and frequent field trips. My classmates and I explored the local zoo and an animal park that contained several exhibits of roaring animatronic dinosaurs. Sometime later, I devoured interesting facts while visiting an extravagant aquarium to feast my eyes upon an array of marine life and all their behaviors. The on-site marine biologist even provided the opportunity for students to dissect squids. [6]

"Gently cut open the fleshy outer layer of your specimen and fold back the tissue to unveil the squid's ink sac. Be careful not to rupture it," the marine biologist instructed. Our class obeyed and made the first incision as Mrs. Blossom strolled around behind us to observe. I smirked as she chuckled at the various reactions from her students. Some children gagged or openly pitied the squid, while others concentrated on the assignment to complete it as precisely as possible.

I found the experience enthralling and provided audio commentary of the entire process, chirping, "Wow! There's a hard tube inside of it! What's *that* for?"

The marine biologist smiled and instructed, "Great question, young lady! The squid draws in water through the tube and releases it again for propulsion. Think of an air-filled balloon that you're pinching to keep inflated. If you release the balloon, it can fly all over the place! In the same manner, the squid draws in water to inflate itself and then pushes the water out to zoom wherever it needs to go using that hard tube."

Another third grader exclaimed, "Look, guys! I accidentally cut open this sack and black stuff came out! I grabbed the hard tube, dipped it in the black, and wrote my name on a paper towel! It's like a quill and ink from the olden days!"

Giddy to try, many students dipped the tube in the substance and painted various pictures.

"Great observation, young man! That actually brings me to my next point!" the marine biologist cheerfully continued. "When observing the ocean's food chain, you'll discover that the squid is often a meal for larger marine life. In order for it to survive long enough to reproduce, the squid has been equipped with a natural defense mechanism called *inking* that enables it to release a black substance from its own body into the water. This creates a dark, cloud-like visual barrier between the squid and any potential danger, creating a diversion to evade predators. It is really quite effective!" [7]

A fourth-grader raised his eyebrow, looked down, and quipped, "It didn't seem to work very well for *these* guys."

Don't Become the Bully

*W*illing to get our hands dirty in order to help our classmates, Nam, Josh, and I cheerfully volunteered to dig up earthworms to for an up-and-coming science lesson.

Away from Mrs. Blossom and other students, I mentioned, "I wish Jay was digging with us right now. I miss him." Nam and Josh agreed while using a garden fork and trowel to explore the ground near the steps of our bungalow. "I think about Jay all the time and it still hurts. I want *justice*. How could Jay's father just get away with *murder* like that? Thinking about it makes me angry all over again." [1]

"I'm with you," Josh replied. "Even though we saw all those cuts and bruises, and heard what Jay told us… we can't *prove* that his father murdered him. There's no evidence, especially now. It would just be our word against his. Besides, who would've listened to second-graders?" [2]

"Jay told us *not to tell*, but I shouldn't have listened to him. He was *always* afraid of his dad," I tearfully divulged. "I shouldn't have hesitated and I blame myself for *everything*. It's all my fault. I *knew* he was getting hurt since the first grade. If I had spoken up sooner, he'd still be here." [3]

"You don't know that and you shouldn't carry all that guilt," Nam counseled. "How were you supposed to know things would turn out like that?" [4]

Josh touched my shoulder and fervently added, "We *all* saw what happened, Sandra. If *you're* responsible, then so are we. If we start thinking like that, we'll go *nuts*. We did what we thought was right. We're just kids, for goodness' sake. Jay's dad is the one who's responsible for his death, *not us*." [5]

"*That's right*. Jay begged us not to tell, and we did what he asked," Nam reminded as she joined my emotion with tears of her own. "We had never been in a situation like that before and we didn't know what to do. Now, *we know*. In the future, if I notice anything like that, I'm going to tell a teacher *right away*." [6]

"Yeah," Josh and I responded simultaneously as we wiped tears away with our sleeves.

Standing up and brushing the dirt from our knees, we group-hugged as Nam endearingly declared, "Friends forever… and, Jay, if you can hear us… *we love you*." [7]

Holding several worms in a paper cup, I reentered the bungalow and spoke in my heart, "Telling a teacher is a waste of time. If I see someone getting hurt, I'm shutting it down right there. I'm won't lose another friend to hesitation." [8]

At recess, a former classmate approached me as they dried their eyes. I wondered aloud, "What's wrong, buddy? Why are you crying? Did someone hurt you?"

"*Yes,*" she sobbed, causing my fists to tighten. "A boy said that I was fat and ugly! My feelings are so hurt, it's hard to breathe!"

I hugged her with a squeeze and encouraged, "You're *beautiful* and a very nice person. Don't worry. He won't get away with it. Point him out to me."

"He's right over there," she clarified with an extended arm.

Without hesitation, I marched over to the boy, deliberately within view and earshot of Mrs. Blossom, and interrogated, "Did you go up to a little girl and tell her she was fat and ugly?" [9]

He laughed and answered, "Yup. I sure did, because she *is* fat and ugly!" [10]

Slack jaw, I reared my hand back, slapped the villain on his cheek, and rebuked, "*That* will teach you! Stop making fun of people! You made her cry!" [11]

Alarmed, Mrs. Blossom walked up quickly as the boy loudly accused, "She just walked up to me and hit me for no reason!" [12]

Mrs. Blossom bent down to speak to the young man and said, "I saw everything and heard every word. Stop being mean and stop lying. I think you've been punished enough, so you won't receive further repercussions. Go on." As he walked away to dry his crimson cheek, the woman turned to me and added, "Sandra, I understand why you hit him. You *felt* it was the right thing to do. In that, I'm proud that you acted on your principles, but violence isn't the answer." She raised herself up. "Today, you're not in trouble. However, use *words* next time. Don't become the bully." [13]

I walked away and whispered, *"Me... become the bully? That's never gonna happen."*

Several days later, a stranger approached me and nervously inquired, "Is it true that you fight bullies?"

"What happened?" I inquired sternly, with a balled fist. [14]

"Oh, ok. I'm talking to the right person. I wasn't sure. You're even smaller than me!" the puny child commented. "Do you see that tall boy playing four-square?"

As the sun beat down, I squinted and asked, "Do you mean the one wearing the shirt with one big stripe?"

"*Yeah,*" he confirmed. "That guy picks on me *every day*. Actually, he picks on a lot of people. Will you beat him up for me and tell him to leave us alone?"

Without another word, I noted the teacher's aide stationed nearby, walked directly to the four-square group, and shouted, *"Hey! You! The tall one in the striped shirt! I'm talking to you!"*

Students around him gained his attention and motioned for him to look up. The bully dwarfed my bony stature and arrogantly scoffed, "What do *you* want, pipsqueak?" [15]

With a forward lean, I aggressively interrogated, "Do you think it's *okay* to be mean and pick on people just because you're bigger?!" [16]

"*Yeah, I do.* So, what?! What are you going to do about it?!" he laughed. [17]

Surrounded by witnesses, I dispensed a slap with such fury that my hand tingled. The speechless boy trembled and fought back tears as he nursed his swelling cheek.

The aide rushed to the scene and asked me, "Why did you hit him?" [18]

"This boy is a *known* bully and picks on kids that are too afraid to defend themselves," I confidently explained. "I can't just *stand by* and let him keep doing it. It ends today." [19]

The aide made eye-contact with the boy and inquired, "Is what she's saying true? Are you a bully?" [20]

"She's lying! I don't even know who she is! I don't pick on anyone!" he shouted. [21]

"Well, that's a shame," she commented. "Don't insult my intelligence, young man. That was your opportunity to tell the truth. Just so you know, I actually *saw* and *heard* everything. You openly admitted to repeatedly picking on the other kids! I heard it from your own mouth! You've been punished enough *for today*, but I'll be watching you very carefully. If I catch you picking on *anyone*, you're going straight to the principal's office. It's *never* okay to bully people. *It stops right now.* Do you understand me?" She gazed over at me and quickly added, "You're not in trouble. I'll take it from here. Go play." [22]

That's My Brother

"Are you the bully fighter everyone's talking about?" a little boy huffed, out of breath from his sprint. "Someone pointed you out, and I need help."

Several cries for justice came from all over the schoolyard, and I delivered a few more slaps. An assortment of teacher's aides released me without repercussions, sometimes expressing mild forms of admiration.

In class, Mrs. Blossom discreetly summoned me from my table and inquired, "Sandra, have you met the school counselor before?" [1]

I smiled and exclaimed, "You mean, the awesome lady with the dragon puppet?!" My teacher chuckled and nodded. "Yes, I met her in kindergarten. She's pretty great."

Speaking softly, Mrs. Blossom replied, "I'm glad you think so. She's going to spend some time with you."

"Nice! When?!" I chirped.

"Right now. I'll walk you over there. Let's go," the pleasant woman gently informed.

Standing before the counselor, I asked, "Are you going to use the dragon puppet today?"

"No, Sandra. You're too old for that," the woman answered flatly. [2]

The adult maintained eye-contact and engaged with me in thought-provoking dialogue over my likes and dislikes. I forgave her about the puppet and felt heard, as though I were interesting and worthy of deep exploration. Her inquiries seemed random and indirect, but the counselor gained insight into my home life and the subjects that I felt strongest about, such as self-defense, loyalty, and helping others. [3]

No one brought up my weekly visits with the school counselor in any outside conversation, nor did I ever mention them to any of my classmates. I independently concluded that evaluations from the counselor must have been a common practice with the GATE program. [4]

During another recess, I enjoyed an inverted dangle from the monkey bars as one of my co-danglers exclaimed, "Look, Sandra!" A gathering on the soccer field was in progress and roared with energetic shouts. "Do you think it's a *fight*?!"

To investigate, we flipped down and sprinted towards the commotion. Unable to see over the crowd, my undersized friend and I squeezed our bony bodies toward the interior of the circle for a better view to discover the brutal nucleus of their attention. [5]

A ruthless and beastly child had mounted a boy, pinned him to the grass, and mercilessly pummeled him in the ribcage. I gasped. Although he guarded his head with his arms, I recognized my sibling receive blow after blow.

Wrath flowed out in a war cry as I shouted, *"That's my brother!"*

The behemoth rose to his feet to search for the origin of the voice. My tiny friend and I joined forces and charged the beast without hesitation. The valiant little warrior forcefully pushed the attacker off balance as my dropped shoulder winded the scoundrel to the ground. Disoriented on his hands and knees, I scrambled over and sat on the back of his neck, repeatedly smashing the assailant's face into the grass as if his head were the seat of a see-saw. Scores of children cheered as the battle raged on, appearing much more like a rodeo bull ride than a schoolyard brawl. [6]

With my pink shoes and tiny ankles in his peripheral vision, he noticed them and roared, *"What?! You're a girl?!"*

His confidence and strength returned to him with a grunt as he launched my forty-pound body backwards with unexpected force. I landed face up and hit my head on the ground as the bully stood to his feet. Too disoriented and winded to scramble, I peered up at my towering foe as he menacingly closed the gap between us.

Two teacher's aides barreled through the dense group of children to interrupt his imminent advance and struggled to tame the flailing man-child. I quickly stood and looked on as he lunged for me. Set on my destruction, he resisted the women's authority as they tightened their grip. The boy's gaze didn't break away from mine until he was escorted away by force. Within moments, the crowd dispersed. [7]

Blown away by what had just occurred, I lingered in silence as an unknown boy ran up to me. Panting, he informed, "Do you even know who you just fought?! That was the *worst bully* in the entire school! He's in the fifth grade! Didn't you see what he was doing to that other boy?! You're so small! One punch could have killed you! You were so lucky that the aides came when they did! Why did you stick your neck out for that kid?!"

"That *kid* is my big brother," I replied, wiping off some grass from my blouse. [8]

Offering a slow nod, the stranger responded, "That makes sense. I get it now. Before you said that, I thought you were just a crazy person with a death wish! Now that I know the truth, I think that was really brave of you. I'm glad you're okay. I'd avoid him though, now that he knows who you are and what you look like. How's your brother? He took a beating." [9]

"Good question. I don't know. I lost sight of him during the fight," I admitted, scanning the blacktop for my sibling's face. "Dang. I hope he's okay. He must have run for cover when his bully focused on *me*. I don't blame him. He must be pretty sore." I looked back at the boy and continued, "Hey, thanks for warning me about that guy. I'll watch out for him." [10]

"That would be *wise*… and you're welcome," he added.

After school that evening, I noticed my brother doing homework at his desk and asked, "Are you okay? That jerk was hitting you *really* hard."

Glaring at me, he angrily growled, "It wasn't the first time. I just wish you would have just stayed out of it. Now, things are even *worse*. They all laughed at me, saying that my *baby sister* had to rescue me. I get picked on and there's nothing I can do about it, so just stay away from me." [11]

"Whoa! You're mad at me for *helping* you?!" I wondered, perplexed and irritated. "Well, I don't care what you say. If I see someone hurting *you*, I'm going to hurt *them*. I can't just leave you out there all alone! If anyone should be made fun of, it should be *that* guy! He got taken down by a third-grade girl! I'm sorry if I made things worse, but I'm not sorry for knocking that jerk to the ground. He had it coming." [12]

"Yeah? Well, *you had help*," he jabbed. "That little boy pushed him *first*." [13]

"Yeah, he did," I proudly confirmed. "That kid is super cool and *way* stronger than he looks. I didn't even have to ask. All I had to say was that you were my brother." He remained silent and wrote on some notebook paper. "*Listen*. I'm really sorry that I upset you. I was just trying to help."

God is Watching You

At the elementary school, the weather was often so inviting that students had outdoor lunch breaks under calming shade trees at cement picnic tables. Each child either brought lunch from home or stood in line to purchase a hot meal. The leafy branches above my head would cast wispy shadows that swept over the coarsely porous surface and mesmerized me in the cooling breeze.

Two parallel lines of nutrition sat on top of our table top and showcased a variety of themed lunchboxes. Their giddy owners enjoyed an assortment of sandwiches or coveted left-overs, a container of sliced fruit, juice boxes, and chips. Some children even received baked goods or pieces of candy tucked inside with a small love note from their mothers. It appeared as though each boy and girl felt a cozy nuzzle from their parents with every delicious bite. [1]

While seated, I stared at my brown paper sack and didn't need to peek to know what was inside. It had been the same each day since kindergarten. With a sigh, my hands unrolled the warm bag to retrieve what once qualified as a sandwich. Maybe the woman haphazardly slapped together the ingredients that morning or prepared it the night before. I was too leery to confirm with her. Regardless, whatever she assembled for me had lost its integrity by noon.

Watery jelly had permeated through the gluey, translucent bread to render the provision soggy and flaccid. A wasted layer of desirable peanut butter was all that held its substance together. Although I had been careful to not jostle the bag, the slightest tilt allowed the sugary goop to shift and soak through the opposite side. Much like how I felt at home, my lunch had been thoughtlessly tossed into darkness, left to suffocate, and abhorred upon inspection. Its condition was far beyond human aid. [2]

Hungry, I furrowed my brow in anger. It pained me to see *that jelly*.

Weeks earlier, at the grocery store, the materfamilias placed her hand on the same jelly that transformed a sandwich into a square of purple bread paste. Choosing to be brave, I petitioned, "Could you please buy this jar of *preserves* instead? I don't like that jelly. It's too runny for the bread and I don't like the flavor."

"No!" she snapped. "Do you think money grows on trees?! That's *expensive*, you little demon!" [3]

"I'm good at math. It's not much more," I rebutted. "You say that I'm too skinny and call me names. If I enjoyed my lunch, it would help. You don't eat that much jelly, but I'm forced to eat it every day." The materfamilias snarled at me. "Fine. If I can't have the preserves, could you at least buy *wheat* bread? It feels more solid. Maybe the jelly won't soak straight through it. The white bread just ends up floppy and wet."

"How *dare* you talk back to me, you spoiled, ungrateful little brat!" the termagant gruffly announced. "I *like* this jelly and that's what you're gonna eat! Wheat bread is too expensive! If you ask me for anything again, I'm going to spank you! *I'm* the mother and *you're* the child, and you'll eat whatever I buy!" [4]

Publicly shaming me in the grocery aisle, I avoided eye-contact with on-looking shoppers and peered at the ground in defeat. Taunting me with her brazen hypocrisy, the woman placed a box of brand-name dieter's candy bars into the cart, strictly for her consumption alone. [5]

As my arms rested on the concrete table beside my peers, that vivid memory churned in my mind and contrasted drastically against what I witnessed around me. Holding back a sob, the jelly saturated the last portions of bread and suctioned itself to the plastic sandwich bag. My stomach growled loudly. I peeled back the clear wrap and took a bite. The mush between my incisors gaged me and drew unwanted attention from dining classmates. [6]

"Sandra, *stop*. You don't have to eat that," a friend graciously mentioned. "Have some yummy food that my mom made yesterday. Here. You must be hungry." The little girl slid her container over to me and handed me her wiped-off spoon. The generosity and kindness pricked my heart as I deemed myself unworthy of the gift. [7]

"Oh, no. That's alright, buddy. I don't want *you* to be hungry, too. Thank you for offering. It looks amazing," I politely replied.

As I had each lunch period prior, I chunked the pasty mess into an outdoor trashcan on my way back to the bungalow and preferred to go hungry.

Wearied by the insanity of my circumstances, I approached the materfamilias at home and entreated, "Will you please buy me a lunchbox? My sandwiches are always smashed by the time I sit down to eat them. A lunchbox might solve the problem."

"No! Lunch boxes are too expensive, you little brat! Besides, just look at you. What did your brother call you the other day? I remember! Skinny-bone Jones! Hahaha! Look in the mirror! You're a scarecrow! You're just getting more and more gaunt! You don't even eat!" the termagant raged as I screamed internally and palmed my forehead at her limitless stupidity. "You better not be throwing your sandwiches away. I'm gonna stand on the roof of your school to spy on you. If I catch you throwing away your lunch, you're getting a spanking. God's *watching* you. He can see through your sheets. He can read your mind. He knows *everything*. There's no hiding from *Him*." [8]

Walking away from her, I thought to myself, "Well, if there is no hiding from God, then that lady is in *serious* trouble. She's either Satan disguised as a woman or his favorite employee. Hopefully, when I *finally* die, God will let me walk right into heaven since time in *hell* has already been served." [9]

That following lunch period, I examined the surrounding school buildings and determined that the materfamilias did not possess the ability to scale their sheer walls. However, remembering her stalking capabilities, I used more discretion with my jelly blob disposal.

Run for Your Life

"Don't leave the front yard… and don't talk to strangers or get in their car," the materfamilias warned us again, just before my brother and I played in the front yard. "There are evil people that do bad things to children, like steal them, molest them, and kill them. I was molested by my own father and brother. Even my cousins and my friends' fathers molested me. What do you think a *stranger* will do to you?! Do you understand me?! If something happened to either one of you, I don't know what I would do! I would just kill myself! Now, go play outside and remember what I told you! If I see you playing too far away, I'm going to spank you!" [1]

I exited the house with rolled eyes and grumbled under my breath, *"She's the real threat. If something ever happened to me, nothing would change. She'd probably be relieved and go back to watching TV. If it were my brother, she'd kill herself for sure. I wonder what it would be like to be kidnapped. As mean as she is, it might actually be a vacation."* [2]

While watching local news, a reporter announced, "Two elementary students remain missing after being snatched off the sidewalk while riding their bicycles…" The television screen displayed photos of both children, their last known whereabouts, and the promise of a cash reward for any information leading to their recovery. It startled me to learn that it happened just outside of my neighborhood. [3]

Since the threat had been near our campus, the following day, a student assembly was called to receive instructions about kidnap-prevention. A police officer stepped up to the podium and fervently instructed, "*Never* get close to a stranger's vehicle, no matter what they say, threaten, or offer. The sort of people that steal children off of the street are experienced and hardened criminals that *will* hurt you, even if they seem nice at first. Once they have you, they won't pity you because you're young and weaker. They would have *chosen* you because you're young and weaker. If you don't know someone on the street or in a vehicle, then they have *no business* talking to you. *It's a red flag*. Keep your distance and get as far away from them as you can." [4]

I nodded emphatically and pondered, *"I trust this police officer over my mom. If he says that kidnappers are bad, then they're very bad. The man knows what he's talking about. In fact, I change my mind about being kidnapped. I don't want it anymore."* [5]

"If an unknown vehicle pulls up to you while you're riding your bike, *do not let go of your bicycle*," the officer continued. "Hold on tight and scream loudly for help. Don't let go of your bike to fight off your abductor. Remember, it's much harder to pull a child *and a bicycle* into a car or van than a child *alone*. Once you're in their vehicle, your chances of survival drop drastically. Most abducted children are *never* found. *Hold on to your bicycle*. It could save your life." [6]

"That makes sense," I whispered to myself.

"If someone tries to grab you, scream as loud as you can. Don't freeze up and become silent. Scream information, like, *'Help! This is not my dad!'* If you can, try to make eye contact with passing adults and yell, *'I'm being kidnapped! Help me!'* Looking right at an adult and pleading for your life will jumpstart their protective instincts and might compel them to take action," he passionately informed. "If you aren't riding a bicycle, *fight with everything you have* to get away. I know you're encouraged not to fight in school, but in *this* situation, you *must* fight back. Resist them. *Bite, scratch,* and *kick* whoever would try to take you and *don't you ever give up*. Inflict as much pain as humanly possible. Go for their eyes and make them want to release you. If you break free, run. *Run for your life*. If they grab your jacket or backpack, slide out of it. They can keep it. *No item is worth more than your life*. Even if your friend gets snagged, *leave them*. Run anyway." [7]

The students gasped in unified horror. I quietly commented, "I won't just leave a kid to die. I'm fighting for them."

"Alright, guys. Calm down and *look at me*," the officer gently ordered. "It may sound heartless, but if you stay to help, the abductors will try to take *both of you*. Your friend's chances of survival go *up* if there's a witness. Quickly find an adult to help you call the police. Describe to the police whatever you can remember… but don't stay and stare at the kidnappers just to take notes. Get away and run for help. I know that many of you are fighters and want to defend yourself and your friends, but please remember that those criminals are bigger, stronger, and will not hesitate to hurt a child. If you break free, don't stick around to hurt them back. *Run for your life.*" [8]

Can I?

After waiting for a commercial break, I gently tapped the materfamilias and pleaded, "Mom, Nancy wants to know if I can spend the night at her house. She lives just down the street. You can even see her house from the front door. I know that you really like Nancy and I've never spent the night at anyone's house before. So, *please*, can I?"

"You don't need to be *bothering* people!" the woman replied, dousing me with derision without so much as breaking her gaze from the screen. "Nobody wants you in their house! You probably just invited yourself over. No, you can't go." [1]

As the venom of her words coursed through my veins, I made my way outside and reported, "She thinks that I'm inviting *myself* over and that you're just being nice in saying yes. I can't go." [2]

"Well, that's not true at all. *I love you.* You're my best friend," Nancy reassured. "Why don't you let me talk to her?" [3]

Panic nearly choked me as I whispered, *"No, Nancy. It won't work. She won't like that..."*

While the warning fell from my mouth, Nancy knocked on the screen door to announce, "Mrs. Lawson, it's Nancy. May I please speak with you?"

As the child summoned the materfamilias from her sofa, dread covered me. I didn't know if she would allow me to see my best friend again.

"Hello, Nancy!" the materfamilias cheerfully greeted.

"Hello! It was *my* idea for Sandra to spend the night. She's my friend and I want her to come over," the girl sweetly clarified. "With your permission, may she come over to my house and spend the night tonight?" [4]

"See, Sandra?" the woman prodded. "Do you see what a polite and pretty little girl she is? Why can't you be like that?" She returned her gaze to Nancy and countered, "Have you spoken to your mother about this? I'll need a written invitation signed by her for me even to *consider* it." [5]

"Okay! I'll be right back!" Nancy chirped.

As the child sprinted away, the termagant narrowed her eyes at me and growled, *"Get inside right now, you little monster. Why did you make Nancy put me on the spot like that? You know I hate that."* [6]

"I didn't!" I rebutted with choked-back tears as she shut the door behind us. "Nancy actually *wants* me to come over and didn't want you believing that I was just inviting myself, because it's not true!"

"It doesn't matter!" the materfamilias snapped. "I don't want you going over there! Nancy has a big brother! Who knows what he could do to you when no one is watching?!"

"What? Why are you even *thinking* like that? Nancy and I would be in the same room. We'd be together the whole time," I whimpered through forced breath.

"You're not safe anywhere but *here!"* the deluded woman barked. "I was molested by my own brother and my father and *God-knows* who else! That big boy could do anything to you! *You're so skinny and weak.* You can't even defend yourself! No one will protect you like *I* can! No one!" Backing me into a wall, she closed the gap between us. "If you ever put me in this position again, Nancy will *never* be allowed back! If you want to keep your friends, don't put me on the spot, you *demon from hell!* You're making me look bad! Who knows what you've said to Nancy?! *Just look at you.* If she's nice to you, it's because she feels sorry for you!" [7]

Right then, Nancy returned out of breath and knocked to report, "Mrs. Lawson, I have a note from my mother. Here you go." She held out a slip of paper and placed it in the woman's hand. "My mom said that she would *love* to have Sandra over for the night. She even wants to make us a really nice dinner. May she please spend the night now?"

"That was fast," the termagant scoffed, examining the penmanship with her arms crossed. "How do I know that you two didn't plan this and that you aren't just *saying* that it's okay with your mother? How do I know that you didn't just write this note *yourself*? I don't know your mother's handwriting or her signature. No. Since I can't be sure, *Sandra can't go."* [8]

Relentless and clever, Nancy politely insisted, "Well, let me give you our phone number… if you'd like to confirm. You can just call my mom for yourself. She said it was okay, so you won't surprise her." [9]

"No," the woman replied. "I don't really know if whoever answers the phone is *really* your mother or just another friend. Besides, if she really *is* involved, I don't want to bother her anymore. She has enough to deal with. I don't want to burden her with *Sandra*, too. It's better if she stays home. You both can play in our backyard, but that's it. Sandra is done playing for the day and will not be spending the night *anywhere."*

"Yes, ma'am," Nancy politely murmured.

Impassive and vacant, the unscrupulous termagant calmly locked the door and returned to her couch, alarming me with an instantaneous conversion from abject paranoia to virtual comatose.

Feeling gutted, I sobbed in my bedroom and contemplated, "Nancy jumped through all those hoops for nothing! Why did she allow Nancy to even hope?! She could have just told the truth from the beginning! I don't understand that woman at all. If I'm going to be anything like that when I grow up, I don't want children. I refuse to do this to another human being. She hits me and threatens me, but won't let me leave because she thinks someone *else* will hurt me. That's nuts. What's happening in this house? *Am I crazy?* Do crazy people *know* that they're crazy? Will it always be this way? Am I being punished by God? Does He hate me, too? He probably does. If being stuck here is all there is to life, I don't want to exist." [10]

Don't Be a Burden

A smiling friend approached me as I stepped into the GATE bungalow. Crystal slipped a beautiful invitation into my hand. She was celebrating her eighth birthday with a sleepover party, which inspired a regretful sigh.

"Wow. Thank you for inviting me and I would love to be there, but my mother won't let me go to a sleepover. I've never been to one," I replied, handing the invitation back. "Last time someone asked my mom, she wanted a written invitation signed by a parent. Even with *that* in her hand, she accused my friend of lying and writing it herself. She couldn't believe that I was actually *wanted*. Plus, she thinks that my friend's older brother would molest me. *Believe me,* my mom won't let me go to a sleepover. It's hopeless." [1]

"Well, I have good news for you. *I don't have a brother*," she divulged with a smirk. "I'll talk to my mom about everything you said. The worst thing that could happen is that your mom says no. Don't worry. Just let me try." [2]

"Okay, but don't get your hopes up," I warned. "If my mom doesn't think that your mom is actually involved, it's not happening. She lies and makes up excuses, too. I don't want her to ruin your birthday." [3]

That week, Mrs. Blossom invited parents to a class event held in our bungalow, serving punch, cookies, and cupcakes. Crystal and I were conversing near a classroom-dividing bookshelf when she subtly stopped talking and encouraged me to pay attention to something unfolding behind me.

"*Watch,*" the charming girl whispered.

Crystal's mother approached the materfamilias, politely introduced herself, and kindly stated, "I would just *love it* if Sandra could attend my daughter's birthday slumber party this weekend. It will be just myself and the girls. She is my only child and my husband is still out at sea with the navy. My daughter had been so lonely without her father around, and she speaks fondly of your precious daughter each day. It would mean the world if Sandra could come and celebrate with us. May she please attend?" [4]

"Okay. I guess so," the termagant sheepishly replied.

"Did you hear that, Sandra?! You can come!" the delightful child cheered under her breath and pulled me in for a hug as tears flooded my eyes. *"We're going to have so much fun!"* [5]

The afternoon of Crystal's birthday had arrived. I carefully pack my very first overnight bag in total disbelief, amazed that something so wonderful and special could happen for me.

As the materfamilias drove me to the party, I became giddy and wiggled in the passenger seat. With Crystal's gift on my lap, I chirped, "Thank you for letting me go, Mom! I'm so excited! Oh, my gosh! I can't believe it! This is going to be amazing!"

We pulled into a driveway that led to a stunning home and immaculate yard, garnished with well-kept landscaping and pink balloons. Even a personalized banner hung before their threshold.

Before I had the chance to escape her foul presence, the materfamilias glared at me and barbed, "Don't be a burden or act like a boy, *you little monster*. If you embarrass me in any way, I'm never going to let you go anywhere again! Do you understand me?! I didn't know that these were *rich people*. Now I *know* that they invited you because they *feel sorry* for you. Remember that, *demon*. Don't get too comfortable here." [6]

Ready to make a running dive over their perfect hedges to get away, I chirped, "Okay. Are you coming inside with me, or are you just dropping me off?" Crystal waved from under the feminine banner and donned a sparkling birthday-princess dress.

"I'm too embarrassed to even show *my face* here! You go," she ordered. "Just remember what I said. They just feel sorry…" Already clutching my backpack, sleeping bag, and pillow, I shut the door before she could finish speaking and fled.

"Sandra! You're here!" Crystal effusively cheered with her arms open wide. "Come here, Sandra! *Let me help you put down your things.* I want to hug you! I'm so happy!" [7]

When we released, I put my hand on her shoulder and admitted, "This is a miracle. Your mom is a *genius*. She knew just what to say for my mom to let me come!" Since Crystal's mother was standing beside us with a tearful smile, I peered up and said with a grin, "Good job!"

The woman chuckled as she ushered us over to the other young guests playing in their backyard. I peered around to see birthday decorations that lined the dining room and table, including pink and pearl balloon arrangements with matching streamers. It was the closest to heaven I believed I would ever get. We played party games, ate a sumptuous dinner, divided her princess themed birthday cake, and watched the *real* princess open her gifts with endearing gratitude. [8]

"Alright, girls! It's bedtime! Your sleeping arrangements are set in Crystal's bedroom and waiting for you!" her mother announced as she guided us to her daughter's closed door. The princess twisted the knob to reveal *surprise* decorations hanging from her bunk bed. Strategically arranged on the floor were pillows, neatly positioned with their corresponding sleeping bags, turned down.

"Mommy! This is amazing! I *love* it!" Crystal squeaked. "Thank you!"

As we filled the room, her mother dropped to her knees and embraced her beloved child with a kiss on the forehead. Warmed at the sight, I smiled and scanned the floor for my things, frozen from panic. My sleeping bag was not among the others. Immediately, I assumed I had done something wrong.

"Oh, no!" I silently fretted. "What am I going to do?!"

Her mother whispered to her little princess and released her from their hug. Crystal discreetly motioned and softly revealed, *"Sandra, look up there."* I climbed the wooden ladder to the top bunk and discovered my sleeping bag resting amid twinkling lights. *"Do you like it? You're my guest of honor."*

I climbed down, hugged my friend, and wept. While her mother looked on and dried her eyes, I softly peeped, *"Wow. I feel like it's my birthday, too!"* [9]

She grabbed my hand and encouraged, "My mom says that sharing your blessings makes them even better… and it's *really* true! I'm really glad you're here."

I hugged my favorite princess again before crawling back up the bunk ladder to lie down. After enjoying a few minutes of the glow and muffled giggles, the kind woman unplugged the twinkle lights and left us to rest. [10]

Before I had the chance to doze off, Crystal's mother opened the door and allowed light in from the hallway.

"Sandra, are you awake?" she softly asked.

"Yes, ma'am," I whispered, curious.

The woman gently walked over to my bunk and informed under her breath, *"Your mother is here to pick you up. She said that you called her crying and wanted to come home."* [11]

A muffled sob made its way from my trembling body. I crawled down from the bunk and dragged my sleeping bag and pillow behind me.

In the hallway light, I whispered, *"My mom is lying. I had an amazing time and I want to be here. You have to believe me. This isn't my fault. My mom lies all the time. I didn't call her. If I had it my way, I'd never leave."* [12]

Tears flowed down my face and alerted Crystal. She grew concerned and put her arm over my shoulders to squeeze me as her mother continued, *"Oh, honey, I believe you. I think your mom just misses you."*

"No. She doesn't miss me," I quietly added, failing to control my tears. *"My mom hates me and makes me feel awful every day. She's not like you. My mom takes everything away.*

Even this. I'm so embarrassed by her behavior. I love you guys. You don't deserve this at all." At that, I faced the princess and sobbed, *"I didn't mean to ruin your birthday. I'm so sorry. I…"*

"Sandra, you didn't ruin *anything*," Crystal declared as she gently stroked my back. "We had fun today. We'll always have that and I'll see you at school on Monday. Nothing is ruined. Cheer up."

"*None of this* is your fault, Sandra," her mother clarified. "You're a *good* little girl and you're *always* welcome here. It's important that you to know that. *Ok?* Everything is fine. Dry your tears and I'll help you gather your things." [13]

"What's taking so long?!" the materfamilias shouted from just outside the front door, left politely ajar. *"What's going on in there?! Do I need to come in and get her?!"* I cringed at the sound of her detested voice. The ridiculous behavior and unmerited threats of the materfamilias burned me with shame. [14]

Crystal's mother stalled so I could calm down. She stepped into the entry and graciously answered, "I'm so sorry about the delay. Sandra is just gathering her things. The girls had the lights out and were falling asleep, so it's taking a little while. She's almost ready." [15]

Outside in my pajamas, I peered backward at the kind woman and silently mouthed, "I'm sorry."

"Get in the car," the materfamilias growled under her breath.

Broken and confused, tears streamed as I inquired, "Why did you lie, saying that I called you? That was the most fun I've ever had, and you ruined it. You didn't want to be embarrassed or even show your face! Then you did *that*. I don't understand any of this." [16]

"I don't care!" she roared. "*No one* can protect you the way *I can!*" [17]

In my bed, void of twinkle lights and my loving friend, my tense body wrenched under the sheet. I muted sobs with a pillow and whispered, *"Anything can be taken away from me. Nothing is safe."*

I perceived my existence to be nothing more than a living nightmare from which I could not wake. [18]

You Can't Go in There

The beautiful day must have called for a more scenic path home from school.

"Let's walk this *other* way," the materfamilias girlishly conveyed. Her pleasant mood surprised me. Normally, the bitter woman had walked us back with annoyance, as if I were responsible for my existence and her inconvenienced life as a mother.

We explored an unfamiliar street of navy housing and followed the gradually swerving sidewalk. Although it was faint, I heard something unusual in the distance. What was almost imperceptible at first had grown louder with each step, as my ears picked up on ebullient sounds that captivated me entirely.

"Does anyone else hear that?!" I wondered aloud. "*Listen!* It's music and singing!"

"Yup. I hear it," the woman patronized, deadpanning with mild irritation.

"It's a choir! The music is coming from a church! Isn't it amazing?!" I chirped with awe. It was then when I noticed their double doors propped open. *"Let's go!"* [1]

"Sandra, *stop!* Don't go in there! Come here right now!" the materfamilias shouted as I rushed toward the service. When I hesitated at her command, she trotted over to snatch my arm. "Don't run from me like that again!" [2]

"Well, I didn't think you'd mind me being in a *church*, since you call me a demon and talk about God *all the time*," I rebutted. My attention strayed from the termagant and returned to the worship. From the front lawn of the building, I marveled with a smile. I had never experienced such a level of passion and adoration for the Messiah as what emanated from that congregation. Each harmonized and melismatic breath reached for the hemisphere with each octave change. Upbeat claps and joyful shouting caused me to dance and wiggle across the sidewalk. "Mom, they're singing about *Jesus!* Listen to them! It's *beautiful*." [3]

The materfamilias clamped her hand around my forearm, spun me to face her, and forcefully whispered through her teeth, *"You can't go in there. You're not allowed."* [4]

I gasped and rebuked, "You're wrong! *I am allowed!* Look! *It's a church!* Anybody can go into a church! They're worshipping *Jesus* in there! Listen to the words! Aren't we *supposed* to worship God?! Why would you *ever* stop a child from worshipping God?! Don't you believe *anything* you say?! Come on! *Let's go!*" [5]

As I attempted to bolt, she snatched my arm again and growled, "Listen to me. That is a *black* Baptist church and you're not *black* or *Baptist*." [6]

"How do you know that it's a *black* Baptist church?" I countered. "The sign just says *Baptist Church*. I know how to read *very well* and the word *black* isn't there." [7]

The materfamilias rolled her eyes and concluded, "You can't go because *I said so*. If you try to go in there, I'm going to *spank you*." I broke free from her painful grip and led the way home, indignant and wounded. I overheard the woman remark to her son, "We're never going to walk this way again. That's what I get for being *nice* and trying something *new*." [8]

The gap between the diabolical duo and me grew wider with my quickened pace. As the music faded away, I angrily muttered, "I wish *I* was black."

You're Still Gonna Get It

Chorale wasn't a pastime that my brother and I pursued originally. The personable choral instructor was also my sibling's teacher and enjoyed him as a student. When she convinced the boy to join her after-school program, the golden child simply asked his mother for permission and she readily agreed to it.

While he was making requests, the boy mentioned his desire for a lunchbox. That was motivation enough for the termagant to purchase *two*, a science fiction one for him and a doll themed one for me. To my surprise, his Machiavellian ways managed to benefit me once more... and so did the termagant's laziness. Since the woman wasn't about to walk back and forth between home and school *three* times in one day, I was *required* to attend chorale with him. I loved to sing and almost gasped at my extended freedom, but I dared not. To protect my joy from her sadism, I feigned indifference. [1]

"Today, after chorale practice, I need you both to walk straight home from school *without me*. I have something to do today, so I won't be there to walk with you," the materfamilias announced as she reached into her purse to hand her son the extra front door key.

I wondered what the woman couldn't accomplish or experience during business hours and casually inquired, "Where will you be and when will you be back?"

"That's none of your business! I don't answer to you!" the hypocritical materfamilias suspiciously barked. [2]

Had her husband ever withheld *his* whereabouts from the materfamilias, she would have promptly checked him into the local morgue. However, unwilling to endure a severe spanking before school, I held my tongue. [3]

During chorale, we rehearsed popular songs from animated films and sang along to the pre-recorded music. Equipped with a stapled packet of lyrics in our hands, students stood in tight rows according to height on choral risers.

When I flipped a page to the second song, the stranger in front of me growled, "*Stop it.*"

"Stop what?" I asked.

He turned his head slightly to side-eye me and angrily clarified, "Stop flipping your page by my head. It bothers me."

"Well, there's not much room and I have to turn the page," I replied frankly. I found his request absurd. Crammed onto those risers with bright clothing, we looked like an oversized crayon box. Each child pinned their elbows against their ribcages just to fit everyone. When the song ended, I turned the page. [4]

The boy's skin flashed crimson as he warned through his teeth, *"I said, stop... it."*

Mimicking the boy's manner of speaking, I informed, *"I have... to turn... the page."*

I did so and read the packet with the other sardines. While the lyrics blocked my view, I perceived movement on the choral riser. A fist socked my stomach and knocked the breath out of me. Unwilling to be disruptive, I silently recovered my breathing and finished the last song without so much as a whimper. [5]

After choral practice had ended, I needed to retie my shoes. My brother was already waiting for me outside with his lunchbox in hand. Upon seeing it, I did an about face to retrieve mine.

Finally ready to leave, the instructor called out, "Sandra!" My sibling and I stopped to turn and discovered her in a squat to talk to me. The beloved woman divulged, "Sandra, I watched you get punched in the stomach today. As remarkable as it was for you to take a hit like that and not react, I would have preferred that you had said something. I have already dealt with the student and he shouldn't bother you anymore. If anything like this happens again, come tell me. *Do you understand what I'm telling you?*" [6]

I respectfully nodded and replied, "Yes, ma'am." Satisfied with my response, the kind woman stood and went about her business. As we proceeded towards the crosswalk, I queried, "Whoa! Where's Mom?!"

My brother shook his head and reminded, "Sandra, Mom told us to go straight home. *Don't you remember?* She isn't picking us up today."

I smiled and confessed, "*Oh, yeah!* I forgot. We should be allowed to walk home by ourselves, anyway." With our house in view, we followed the sidewalk before preparing to cross the street. Paused, my brother poked my side and caused me to inquire, "What?"

"*We're being followed,*" he whispered, as he focused on something to my rear. [7]

I turned around to track his gaze and gasped. Ten yards behind us were two menacing children. I quietly informed, "Whoa. *That's* the kid that punched me in the stomach today. I don't know him *or* the other guy."

Beside the tiny featherweight contender was a taller, husky young troglodyte whose incompetent expression made me sad for our nation's future. His confused demeanor inspired doubt that the boy understood why he was even there. [8]

My brother shouted, "Who are you and why are you following us?!"

With thumb to chest, the smaller boy answered, "I'm *Willie*… and *this* is Baxter. Your sister got me into trouble."

"No, I didn't!" I loudly rebutted. "You got caught red-handed! The teacher saw everything and came to me! I didn't tell!"

Displaying an overdeveloped Napoleon complex, the pugnacious child caught his own fist and menacingly threatened, *"It doesn't matter. You're still gonna get it."* [9]

Attempting to draw first blood, Willie lunged to attack me. Although I had the footing to resist, my sibling intercepted the assailant and drove him to the sidewalk. Pressed into submission by a grappling choke, Willie became immobile while my brother *squeezed*, all but crushing the boy. Mesmerized, Baxter watched-on in slack-jawed mental paralysis. Unable to predict if the toad would make a move, I hesitated. Despite my unwillingness to exacerbate the situation, I was prepared to resist. Long seconds passed and weighed upon me with palpable tension. [10]

Like a pinball machine with a freshly inserted quarter, the stooge suddenly lit up and engaged. As he stepped forward to intervene on behalf of his asphyxiated friend, I thwarted a lopsided double-teaming and rushed the goon. Wielding my pink lunchbox like custom brass knuckles, I slammed the plastic into Baxter's temple with moxie and followed it with an uppercut to his chin. Disoriented, he tipped backward with an elephantine thud and allowed my tiny frame to mount him. Using my plastic sandwich defender as a hammer, I unleashed years of repressed rage on his disconcerted face. [11]

He didn't fight back. Instead, the henchman shielded his head from the devastating blows and reminded me of my bullied sibling, curled up and afraid. Pity infiltrated my heart as I inquired, "Have you had enough? Are you done?" [12]

With a blend of horror and gratitude, Baxter respectfully voiced, "Yes… yes, I'm done."

I dismounted and allowed the bruised boy to back away sheepishly.

My brother provided the same opportunity to Willie and asked, "Are *you* done?"

"*Yes… I'm done,*" the instigator strained, seeming to have seconds of life left. "*Let me go.*"

Released from my sibling's kung-fu grip, the defeated child struggled to his feet and stood beside his wounded counterpart to face us. [13]

"Leave us *alone*," my brother assertively warned.

As the villains slowly backed away, Willie shouted, "My brother is in *two* gangs! This isn't over! They'll be coming for you! Where do you guys live?" It was a miracle. My brother and I silently pointed in the same wrong direction, down the sidewalk and away from our house. "Why did you take the long way? That's stupid. You could have just gone straight earlier." My sibling and I just stared. "Whatever. This isn't over." [14]

We held our ground with intimidating grimaces until they were completely out of sight and earshot. Once we felt it was safe, both of us sprinted across the street and hustled inside the house to lock the door behind us.

"Do you think he was bluffing about his brother?" I queried.

My sibling nodded and replied, "No one's in *two* gangs. He's lying."

Thrilled by the rapid turn of events, I grinned and exclaimed, "Dude! I can't believe that actually happened! Is this real?! I mean... you totally tackled that little jerk and choked him out in seconds! *Good job!* Where did you even learn that?! He couldn't move... and then, *wham!* I took out Baxter with my lunchbox and beat him to a pulp! I really can't believe this! We don't even have a scratch on us! *Man,* we make a great team! Wow! Not that I want to be jumped again, but that was *amazing.* Once word gets out about what happened..."

"*Sandra,*" my brother interrupted. "You *do* realize that no one can *ever* know that we got jumped today or even that we won the fight."

"We can't control that," I rebutted. "What if Willie and Baxter try to get us into trouble?"

"They won't. *Think about it.* Those idiots aren't going to admit that they tried to jump two kids after school, *especially* since they got beat up in the process. Besides, a teacher already witnessed Willie punch you. They'd sink themselves if they ever spoke up," he concluded. "If anyone finds out about this, it will be because *you* bragged. *Keep your mouth shut.* If Mom ever hears about it, she'll *never* let us walk home by ourselves ever again. We can't talk about this to friends or mention it to anyone. If the school gets involved and calls Mom, *that's it.*" [15]

"You're right. There's no telling what she'll say or do if that happens," I conceded with a sigh. "Well, we might not be able to brag about it, but I'm going to remember this day for the rest of my life." [16]

Gray Mouse

While seated at my child-sized drawing table, I colored quietly in my room. The materfamilias frightened me when she entered and sat directly on top of my page. The proximity of her hip to my face made me nervous since she rarely positioned herself that closely. [1]

"When *I* was a little girl, I never had a birthday cake or a party thrown for me. I don't want that to happen to you or your brother, so I'm going to throw you a party next week for your eighth birthday. What theme do you want?" she tenderly inquired, as if my opinions had always mattered to her.

Amazed, I cautiously suggested, "What about pink? That should be inexpensive and easy."

"Not a color… *a theme.* I'm the mother. You let *me* worry about the price," she gently corrected, behaving out of character and making me suspicious. "What *theme* do you want your birthday party to be?"

Unsure if the opportunity would ever come again, I mentioned, "Well, what about a mermaid theme?"

"Okay. For your party, you can invite *five* girls from school. If you ask for *any more friends than that*, I'm just going to cancel the whole thing," the woman threatened. "You're inviting Melissa and Stephanie, too." [2]

"What?! I have to waste two spots on *those* twits?! We don't even *like* each other!" I rebutted. "Melissa is spoiled rotten! She blamed me for the bad things *she* did and got me into trouble for it! Don't you remember?! I don't care if I ever see that little jerk again! And Stephanie is a complete ditz that can't think of anything to talk about except *shoes* and *purses*… and you say *I'm* too expensive."

"*I'm* inviting them. I *like* those little girls. They're pretty, they wear dresses, and they don't act like little boys," the termagant barbed. "That leaves you three more girls to invite." [3]

"Are you really forcing those stuck-up little snobs onto me? Why did you even tell me to choose *five* girls, if you really just meant *three*? This party isn't *really* for me anyway, is it? Throw *them* a party, if you're just going to invite your friends' prissy daughters over here. I'm not going. One is evil, and the other is stupid," I observed. "I'd much rather have three *actual* friends over than those two twerps."

"*Why am I throwing you a party at all, you unappreciative little brat?! You'll invite who I say to invite or there won't be a party!*" the materfamilias roared. [4]

I invited Nancy within the hour, who had requested for me to play. The following morning, I stepped into class and promptly invited Crystal and Nam.

An obscure friend of Melissa's mother baked and decorated my birthday cake to accommodate the oceanic theme. The woman painstakingly illustrated images on a sheet of rice paper and laid it over white frosting with a turquoise trim. It blew me away.

"Wow! Your drawings are amazing! This looks *very* professional. Good job," I told the cake artist, wide-eyed and grateful. The woman smiled without a word and lead me to believe that she didn't understand English.

On the eve of my birthday, the materfamilias sat down to make some party favor bags and shouted, "*Sandra! Make a list of who you invited to your party and give it to me! Now!*" I sprinted to the termagant and handed her the names, excited about my big day. "Who's *Nam*?"

Sensing a problem, I informed, "Nam is my friend from class. We met in the first grade and were friends with Jay. We all played together every day… *before he died*. Nam is really smart and a very nice person…"

"*She can't come,*" the materfamilias frigidly interjected.

My throat shrank. Tears streamed down my face as I passionately appealed, "*Why are you like this?! Why ask me to invite people if you're just going to take them away from me?! Nam is my friend and I want her there! She's excited about my party and told me that she already has my gift! I don't understand! Why throw me a party when you hate me?! Why would you do this to Nam?! She's a good person!*"

"You don't know everything! You're just a child!" she viciously dismissed. "You want to know why she's not invited here?! *I'll tell you why*. Her name is *Nam*, like Viet*nam*. Her parents, *who live in the United States*, named her Nam. *It is a slap in the face to America*. The Viet Kong tortured American soldiers during the Vietnam War and slid little pieces of bamboo up under their fingernails! They even wrapped bombs on their own children to blow up soldiers who wanted to help them! *And you want her in this house?!* No way. *She can't come*. If that little girl even *steps foot* into this house, you'll be in trouble, you little *monster*." [5]

I sprinted to my room, slammed the door shut, and collapsed onto my bed to smother my shouting face with a pillow. [6]

The morning of my eighth birthday, I saw Nam in class and drew near to her before Mrs. Blossom could begin the lesson. The termagant's swamp of prejudice nearly drowned my soul in the muck of her hatred. I feared that if I didn't unload the terrible burden immediately, I would interrupt the class with an eruption of emotions. Reading my burdened body language, my empathic instructor provided ample space and monitored the interaction from nearby. [7]

When Nam noticed my approach, she gasped and cheerfully exclaimed, "Happy birthday, Sandra! You're eight years old! Yay!"

"Nam? I… I… I have bad news," I whispered, bursting into tears.

"Oh, no!" Nam exclaimed with a gentle hand on my shoulder. "Sandra, are you okay? What's wrong?"

Through sobs, I blubbered, *"My mom said that you… can't come to the party because… your name is… Nam."* Having lost control over every liquid that could come from a face, she rushed to grab me a tissue. *"Thank you.* Nam… I love you and I want you at my party. *I hate my mom.* I'm *so* sorry for putting you through all of this. You don't deserve any of it. Will you forgive me?" A tear rolled down her cheek as she gently smiled with a nod before I could finish. "You're my friend and I don't believe or feel, *in any way*, the way she does." [8]

Nam took in a deep breath and tenderly replied, "*I understand*. My parents have already talked to me about this. Some people are mean because *we are different.* Sandra, there's nothing to forgive you for. *It's not your fault.* I love you, too, and I'm still your friend. Don't worry." Nam embraced me as Mrs. Blossom dried her eyes. "Guess what?! I brought your gift to school! *Let me go get it.* It's in my backpack." [9]

My friend handed me a darling toy mouse with over-sized ears and a red fabric tongue that protruded out, followed by a beautiful hand-stitched coin purse.

"Oh, my gosh! *I love them!* The mouse is so cute!" I squealed.

"They're *Vietnamese*," she prodded, smirking defiantly as I kissed the mouse's little nose.

"*Nice.* Now I love them even *more*," I quipped defiantly.

Scarlet Letters

Mrs. Blossom gave the class an assignment first thing in the morning, stating, "Today, you will write the first draft of a *short story*. It can be about any subject you desire. Think about it and take your time. When you're finished, bring it to me. *Begin*."

Although a few children groaned, I wiggled in my seat and silently wondered, "If I were the main character and nothing held me back, what would I do? This is *my* story. Anything is possible." [1]

The short story revolved around a youthful heroine who abhorred deception and injustice, often inadvertently exposing the truth among those around her. [2]

As the character ventured to a friend's house on her bicycle, the aspiring sleuth observed evidence of a home invasion and stepped through the threshold without touching a thing. To her surprise, not a soul was in sight. Before panicking, she remembered her friend mentioning a family vacation and assumed they were blissfully unaware of the incident. Out of love for her friend, and to aid local police in bringing the antagonist to justice, she investigated the crime scene and offered a detailed report of her findings to the local police. Irritated with the nosey child, the police didn't appreciate her trespassing in a crime scene, and informed her that law enforcement *and the family* were already aware of what had occurred.

Underestimated and determined, she insisted that the detective read her notes aloud. Humoring his pest to expedite their encounter, a completely overlooked clue stood out in his seasoned mind and subtly changed his expression to that of interest. Refusing to acknowledge her findings, he disregarded it and the juvenile altogether. Dauntless, the precocious girl followed the lead herself to discover the criminals at their next target in broad daylight. While collecting indisputable evidence, the protagonist caught their attention. Chased through her neighborhood, the elementary student managed a harrowing escape from those who sought to silence her forever. [3]

Moments later, the humbled detective received a series of instant film exposures from her scraped hands. They used the stack of images as indisputable photographic evidence to file charges and put warrants out for arrests. Convicted of multiple accounts of breaking and entering, and one account of attempted kidnapping, the criminals became familiar with iron bars, jumpsuits, and the eyewitness testimony of a spunky little girl. The detective's heart grew heavy with guilt for displaying the cruel indifference that nearly led to a child's abduction. Immediately after sentencing, while surrounded by reporters, the man expressed his gratitude to the clever minor who helped close the case. [4]

After a deep breath, I arose from my seat and gleefully handed in my assignment. Our highly esteemed editor whispered, *"Thank you, Sandra. I'll have you come back to get it when I'm done making my notes. Remember to stay quiet. Other writers are still working."* [5]

Understanding her meaning, I tip-toed past my classmates and quietly sat down. In the absence of occupation, my eyes searched each wall for a clock and couldn't find one. The only time-measuring device in the room was on the wrist of our vigorously critiquing instructor. As I anxiously waited, I laid my head on the chilled table before me. [6]

"Okay, Sandra. Your story is waiting for you," our editor softly announced from her desk as she patted a few sheets of notebook paper.

Observing my poorly muffled enthusiasm, Mrs. Blossom chuckled at my approach. I returned to my seat and refocused on my beloved creation, ready to read a rave review. To my shock, red ink jumped from each page and struck my ego with an unexpected left-hook. My lip quivered while I personalized the copious spelling errors, marked out sentences, and assorted notes that seemed insurmountable to correct and rewrite. [7]

My perception became cruel and haunting as I punished myself and thought, "You're a *terrible* writer. You'll *never* have what it takes to become a published author. No one will *ever* want to read your work. Look at that mess. Do you even know English?"

"Don't get discouraged," our editor softly offered from her seat, still focused on the paper in front of her. *"Let me know if you need help."*

Upon hearing her words, I silently coached, "Sandra, if you want to be a better writer, you'll need to learn from your mistakes. Stop being a baby about it. *You can do this.* Fix one error at a time. You'll never become a published author if you quit now." [8]

Except for lunch and recess, our class revised short stories all day to create a second draft.

"Okay, everyone, put your pencils down," the editor announced. "You all have been working very hard and I'm proud of you. To give you something to look forward to, I'm going to let you in on a secret. I have a surprise for you tomorrow."

"I wonder what she'll do for us *this* time," I pondered with a grin as I made playful eye contact with Nam who seemed to share my exact thoughts. [9]

"Write a third draft of your story *tonight* and make it as wonderful as you can," Mrs. Blossom encouraged. "*Tomorrow*, I will tell you what the surprise is, but I will give you a hint. The surprise has to do with your *writing*, so don't forget to bring your story back to class. See you in the morning! Class dismissed!"

While I was sitting at my desk in my bedroom, attempting to apply all that I had learned from my instructor, something abruptly distracted me from my task. My father arrived home from work and the warning signs of another heated altercation unfolded in the living room just down the hall. [10]

Separating myself from their madness, I quietly shut the door and whispered, *"I'm not dealing with this today. Writers need to concentrate."* [11]

The Surprise

~~~

*E*xcited about my drastically improved short story and the unveiling of Mrs. Blossom's hidden plans, I rushed into the bungalow and found my seat. Unaware of exactly what the day would bring, I set my pencil, eraser, and some fresh paper beside my assignment in preparation. [1]

As the rest of my classmates filled the room, a child raised his hand and was called upon to convey, "Yesterday you told us there'd be a *surprise*." He comedically pumped his eyebrows at our scholastic shepherd. "Can we know what it is now, *please*?" [2]

Displaying an inviting smirk, Mrs. Blossom challenged, "You'll have to *guess* the surprise before it's revealed. Yesterday, I told you the surprise had to do with your writing. Now that you've had time to think, let's hear some guesses!" She grinned as her students enthusiastically flung their hands skyward to inquire about pencils, erasers, and notebooks. "Those are good guesses and you're on the right track! Those things certainly have to do with writing! I'll give you another hint. *It's a person*. What's a career that deals with *writing stories*?"

Another student, Axle, raised his hand and blurted, *"A writer!"*

"Very good!" she encouraged. "Now, what kind of writer has written *published books*?"

Nam was called upon, who confidently answered, "An author!"

"Yes!" our instructor confirmed. "That's your surprise! We have a *published author* visiting us today, and *that's* why you have worked so hard on your stories!"

Awestruck, I wondered aloud, "What? A real author is coming?"

"*Yes*. A real author is *here*, right now," the magnanimous woman revealed. "If you're daring enough, you may read your story to her *yourself* and learn from her suggestions. As you know, getting critiqued is how we sharpen our skills. I invited her here to deliver pointers to help guide you, but only present your story to her if you desire to *be a better writer*." [3]

Mrs. Blossom placed a tall stool at the front of the class, introduced our special guest, and stepped away. My heart longed for the chance to know *from a professional writer* if I possessed the talent to become an author myself. Willing to absorb anything she offered, I listened intently. [4]

"*Never* fall in love with your first draft," the author began. "When you begin a story, you are simply getting the idea out of your head and onto paper. *That's it…* and it's the hardest part. Once you do that, the rest is clipping, adding, and tweaking. Know that, when you've finished your first draft, you're not really done at *The End*." Her deadpan caused a unanimous chuckle.

Axle posed, "Are you rich?"

"*Am I rich?*" she parroted, amused at the thought. "I make a living, but if being wealthy is your main goal, *pick a different profession*." [5]

"Wealthy, best-selling authors *do* exist," a girl corrected with snobbish impertinence. "I would know. My mom and dad read their books. What makes *those* authors different from the rest?"

"A *better* question to ask yourself is this: *Why am I writing?*" the speaker redirected. "The most famous writers didn't know how successful they'd become. Many authors found themselves underappreciated and weren't widely read until *after they had died*, so don't wait around for the glory. If you really want to be a writer, let go of the idea of being wealthy. That goal creates extra pressure to just write what will *sell*, as opposed to what you really want to convey. Write what is meaningful to *you* to the best of your ability, whether it's in an essay, a letter to a friend, or… *a short story*. If you write to be rich, you'll be disappointed, and so will your readers. If you write because you have ideas *burning* inside of you, just *aching* to get onto a page, then you're a writer. Put your heart into every written word and you'll be satisfied just doing what you love. If money is a result, *great*. If not… and you still need a different job to pay the bills… at least there's a small piece of you out there for someone to read." The author slapped her legs and added, "However, you can't get your work *out there* if I'm still talking! Let's hear some of your stories! Who's first?!" [6]

Several students, myself included, raised an eager hand.

"*Me! Me! Me!*" Axel emphatically urged, becoming the first selected to stand up and read. The child positioned himself to face his peers and nervously cleared his throat. "I like cars, so I wrote a story was about racing." [7]

A few moments in his story, the author interrupted the student to inquire, "*Why* did the characters do that?" The boy thought for a moment and then explained himself. "Excellent. *Write it down.*" Axel added the note to his page and proceeded. Spotting the same plot hole in my story, I inserted the missing information in the margin. Before long, she interrupted him again and questioned, "*Why* did the characters choose that location?" [8]

"I don't know," he divulged and lingered nervously in silence. With each passing second, Axel's face took on a deeper shade of burgundy.

The author gently encouraged, "This is *fiction*, so just make something up! Have some fun with it!" Still lost, the reader manifested a pitiful expression of fear and humiliation. "It's fine! You're okay! Let me ask you the same question in a different way… to help your creativity *emerge*," the author playfully offered. "If the characters go to that location, how could they potentially *benefit* from it?" Perking up, the child blurted out an idea. "Very good! Write that down, too!"

"*Okay*," the relieved child mumbled as he rapidly scribbled on his paper.

Axel resumed where he left off and immediately referred to an unknown character. The author inhaled to speak, paused, and simply closed her mouth instead. The unmentioned error had alerted several students, who faced Mrs. Blossom with their hands raised. Understanding the delicate situation, she slowly shook her head in silent protest. Tension grew palpable in the room as Axel's precarious emotions cracked further, beading sweat on his brow. [9]

"Keep going!" the author spurred with a smile. "What happens next?" The woman refrained from making any further corrections.

"…and he won the race. The End," Axel tearfully concluded, chin to chest.

"Look up at me, sweetie," the author gently ordered. "First, let me say that it's not *easy* to stand up in front of people and expose your flaws to them. You held up your story before the firing squad… and that was *brave*." Axel's shoulders and countenance lifted as he cracked a smile. "If we are to endure pain, let's learn from it. Okay?" He nodded in agreement. "*Very good*. Your readers will only know what you put down on the page. They can't read your mind or call you at home to ask you about the missing details of your story. If something's important to the plot, establishes the setting, or reveals character development, *write it down*. When someone is crying, tell your reader *why* they're crying. If your characters show fear, explain *why* they're afraid. Why might a character *not* experience fear? Have they survived *worse* situations? What were the situations? *Tell your reader*." [10]

"This woman is amazing," I thought as I polished my assignment with a few more lines.

Filling what would have been silence, the only distracting sounds in the classroom were from my vigorously raking pencil. Noticing, I paused and made eye contact with my affable teacher, who tucked her chin at me with a playful smirk of warning. I sheepishly smiled back and felt my cheeks glow rosy.

The author had delicately continued, "Write the information in a way that your readers will understand and remember. Seek to move *them* by what moves *you*. What do you want the reader to learn, feel, or understand after they read your words? If *you* can't answer that question, neither will they."

The child nodded with vulnerable eyes and muttered, *"Okay."*

"Your plot was *very* exciting," she affirmed. "If you fix the few things I mentioned, you will have quite the story!" Emboldened, Axel quickly reclaimed his seat. *"Who's next?"* My lone hand enthusiastically emerged from a sea of apprehensive faces. "Come on up! I heard you *scribbling* over there," she lovingly roasted, which forced Mrs. Blossom to bite her tightened lips into submission. [11]

I journeyed to the front of the class and glanced over at my surrogate mother, who offered an inspirational nod. When I instinctively faced my peers, it dawned on me that the *real* judge was our special guest. Boldness wore me like a cloak and pivoted my entire body to face the author *directly*. The action touched the woman's heart and piqued her curiosity as her countenance softened. [12]

"Hello. My name is Sandra Lawson, and this is *my* story," I began, using inflections and voice changes for each character. Suddenly, I realized that some events in the text didn't transition properly. "Oops," I peeped and used the nearest table to make a note. "Please excuse me. I caught a mistake. She needed to *ride her bike* to the police station. That's how she got there. She's not old enough to drive." [13]

The author chortled and patiently waited for me to continue. Within a few seconds, the woman leaned forward with encouraging charm and caused me to await instruction.

"Simplify that sentence, Sandra. That's known as a *run-on*," she critiqued. "Break it up into two separate thoughts." Embarrassed of the flaw, I scratched out that line and read the two new sentences aloud. *"Perfect.* Keep going." [14]

With slightly less enthusiasm, I finished orating, awkwardly smiled through a wince, and expected the harshest of blows.

"Nice job!" the author chimed, which flipped my expectation on its head. "I appreciate how you took the time to include *details*, such as when your main character asked for permission to leave the house. I see what you did there. Her parents stepped back and gave her the space to figure things out on her own. Your story had a strong beginning, a good body, and a great climax, but *don't be afraid of criticism*. Continue improving and building on what you know. Excellent work, Sandra! You're a good writer!" [15]

Grateful for her valuable time and knowledgeable commentary, I bowed as if before royalty and peeped, *"Thank you."*

Her words of approval all but brought me to my knees and evoked a tearful smile with radiating joy. I clutched my short story and voyaged back to my desk, slack-jawed. A professional author had validated me publicly. I couldn't believe it. [16]

"Well, I really enjoyed spending time with all of you! Thank you for having me today and remember to *keep writing*," the woman signed off before she made her way towards the bungalow exit. [17]

"*Thank you!*" the class sporadically shouted to the author. "*You're awesome! We love you!*"

The special guest blushed with a smile as she pushed open the door.

Before the woman could clear the threshold, I loudly suggested, "*Maybe you can come back and see if we've improved!*" [18]

The author's shining eyes met mine as she broadly grinned and silently exited our bungalow.

"Okay, class!" Mrs. Blossom announced. "Your next assignment is to write the final draft of your short story using the lessons you've learned today. Use the remainder of class to edit and then finish the rest at home. Whatever you hand in to me tomorrow will be for a grade, so do your very best. *Begin.*" [19]

Recalling the author's words, I resolved to turn in the best short story ever written.

Set It on the Table

~~~

As my sibling and I were being walked home that day, I continued to ponder the author's words. Her encouragement resurrected hope within me, hope for a future filled with published novels of my own. Seated at the desk in my room, I began my fourth draft with vigor and applied her sage wisdom to my short story. I longed to produce written fruit so satisfying that literary juice would run down a reader's chin with each turn of the page, in want for another messy bite. [1]

"This is an *excellent* story," I internally concluded. "I want to read it aloud again, but Mom is the only adult here and probably won't care. Maybe I shouldn't. What if she doesn't like it? No, Sandra. That shouldn't matter because *I must not be afraid of criticism*. Sheesh. You'd think, with *this* family, I'd be used to criticism by now."

Emboldened, I waited until her favorite talk show had ended, gently touched the woman's shoulder, and requested, "Mom? We wrote short stories in class. Can I read mine to you?"

She pressed mute on the remote control, shrugged, and relented, "Okay... *I guess.*"

I stepped forward and orated with all the energy and swelling emotion I felt while writing it. With an exhale of relief, I queried, "What do you think about my story? Did you like it?"

With gooey sweetness, the woman gushed, "You read that *beautifully.*"

Taken aback, I replied, "Wow. *Thank you...* but what did you think of my *story*?" The woman shrugged and said nothing as she blankly stared at the muted television. "Did you not like it? Was it too boring? I need to be critiqued." Tension arose in the silence that made me curious. "Do you even remember what was the story was *about*?" [2]

With her intelligence insulted, the materfamilias flipped from self-conscious silence to rabid aggression and shouted, *"I don't know! I gave you a compliment, didn't I?! What more do you want from me?! Do you want me to give you the moon, too?! Stop asking me questions! I'm not in school! Why are you testing me?! Get out of my face before I spank you!"* [3]

While listening to her rant, a revelation struck me like a bolt of lightning. My eyes widened as I took it all in. The nefarious woman had lorded herself over me with her size, age, physical strength, and maternal authority, but I had surpassed her intellect and achieved an early scholastic high ground. My hardened heart beat with empowerment and superiority over the squirming, sofa-bound wretch. [4]

In my stillness, she quickly lost interest and unmuted her television just before the familiar sound of jingling keys reached my ears. Fresh from the naval base, a brilliant man walked through the front door.

I beamed with joy and exclaimed, "Daddy! A *real* author came to class today and said that my story was *excellent*... and that I was a good writer! I'm really proud of it! Can I read my story to you?!"

The unamused sailor remained focused on setting down his belongings and sternly huffed, "I will read it *myself*. Leave it on the table. I'll get to it later."

Regret had thrust its blade through my tender and vulnerable gut as the dream-giving day turned into a blood-splattered nightmare at my prompting. With a face of stone, I gently set my creation on the chopping block and mentioned, "Okay. Would you please let me know when you're done? I need it for class tomorrow." [5]

After a while, the editor stopped at the door of my bedroom to hand back the assignment and harangue, "Your handwriting is *terrible*. This paper is a *sloppy mess* and you're not turning this in until you re-write it and correct all of your spelling errors. If you would slow down a bit and write things neatly *the first time*, you'll save yourself from unnecessary work in the future. Show me your intelligence and give this back to me when you're done so I can check it. I'd start on it now if I were you. This chicken scratch needs to turn into legible handwriting before you go to bed." [6]

Waiting for the man to walk away, I closed my door and tearfully contemplated, "What about the story? Does anyone in this family have any depth? Am I all alone in this? No one in this house understands me or even wants to. Everyone is either irritated or fighting. There's no in between. Is getting ignored or being attacked as good as life gets?" [7]

I calmed myself and took another glance at my work from the man's perspective. With neatly corrected errors, I aspired for perfection and hoped I would become worthy of his approval someday. [8]

Leaves

Mrs. Blossom set our report cards face-down on the tables before us. Excited to discover if I had the highest grades in class, I flipped mine over and examined its contents with a smirk.

Blood drained from my face as I frantically commented, "What?! This can't be right. How did I get a B? How did I get a B in math?!"

Mathematics had been a consistent companion, with logical and predictable outcomes. The answers I offered were right or wrong. Math didn't involve opinions, and the targets didn't move, nor were there varying degrees of correctness to consider. I savored numbers as one would a perfectly seared filet mignon, devoured to satisfaction with a blissful hum and sigh… and yet… math had betrayed me.

With my face in my hands, tears pooled in my trembling palms as I moaned, "What's *wrong* with me?! My parents are going to *kill* me! This has never happened before! I don't want to go home. *I'm dead.*" [1]

Mrs. Blossom observed as Nam soothed, "It's okay, Sandra. It happens sometimes." A pale smile surfaced, but her words brought no comfort. [2]

"Did anybody *else* make a B?" I wondered aloud as I searched the faces surrounding me. Nam and the rest of my classmates pursed their lips and nervously looked at each other, shaking their heads. They were A-students, as I had once been. Hiding my face once more, I wailed, "I'm the *dumbest* person in the class?! What's happening to me?!" Although tears had splashed on the cardstock, nothing smeared but my pride. [3]

As if choreographed in advance, my classmates circled to embrace by wrenched body. Tiny hands gently rested all over my back, shoulders, and arms. Some children patted while others scratched or stroked. For a time, a child even held my hand. Their compassion moved me to tearful gratitude, but the dread of my parents lingered. [4]

Downcast all the way home, my thoughts remained behind my teeth in horror and anticipation of pain upon their release. I despised the trepidation and volunteered my report card to the materfamilias. "Mom, I got a B in math," I confessed. "I don't know how that happened. I'm really sorry."

"What is *this*?!" the materfamilias roared as she shook the evidence in my face. "How could you make a *B*?! What have you been doing?! Why are you not paying attention in class?! This is so embarrassing! *You just wait until your father gets home. Go to your room!*" [5]

I sobbed in privacy and wondered, "I'm the one *dying* inside. Why does *this* embarrass her? How about her psychotic behavior at the sleepover or what she said about Nam before my birthday party? *That's* embarrassing." [6]

Keys jingled at the door.

"Your daughter got a B in math! Look!" the sailor's wife shouted. "I don't know what that girl has been doing, but you need to spank her!"

Her husband directed me toward the dining table and informed, "In all my years of education, including college and nuclear power school with the navy, there was only *one time* that I ever made less than an A. In high school, there was a year where my father wouldn't allow me to join the wrestling team, since he was a farmhand and wanted my help for the harvest that season. My school was small, and the teacher was also our wrestling coach, so when he asked me if I was joining the wrestling team, I told him no and the reason. As a result, even though I had nothing but A's on each test and assignment, he dropped my overall-grade to a C to pressure me into reconsidering." [7]

"What?! How's that even possible?!" I challenged. "No one saw that long string of A's and questioned how your grade mysteriously dropped to a C?!"

"Nope," he replied. "Back then, there was no one that would overrule a teacher. It was just the way things were. Nothing could be done to change my grade and my father still had me work. In the end, neither of us got what we wanted. Unless something like *that* is going on with you, which I seriously doubt, there's no excuse for bringing home anything less than an A in every subject. We know that you're smart. All we're asking for is your best. *Don't be lazy.*" [8]

Within days, Mrs. Blossom mysteriously requested a parent-teacher conference. The materfamilias paced and interrogated, *"What's this parent-teacher conference about?! What have you been saying about me?! Have you been telling people what goes on in this house?! God's going to get you for talking bad about me! I'm your mother! God says to honor your mother! It's no one's business what goes on here! Do I need to pull you out of class and homeschool you?! If I do, say goodbye to all your friends! If I find out you're talking bad about me at school, you're going to get it when we get home! You'll be sorry! Don't think you can mess with me and nothing will happen to you!"* [9]

At a loss, I remained perfectly still and silently wondered if Mrs. Blossom was going to discuss my tears over the report card or the comments made about Nam.

During the long walk from our house to the school bungalow, the termagant growled, *"If you made me look bad, I'm going to get you back. Don't think you're going to get away with this. You'll get more than a spanking. You have a lot of things that I can take away. I buy you clothes and feed you. How dare you do this to me? This is so embarrassing. What did you do? You're in so much trouble. Don't think I'm going to forget this."*

As the bungalow door opened, the sadist flipped from a Nazi Gestapo frau to the picture of motherhood and cheerfully greeted Mrs. Blossom with a charming pseudo-smile. [10]

My surrogate mother graciously seated us and informed, "Mrs. Lawson, Sandra's scores on *all* of her preprinted math worksheets were *perfect*. However, the math problems that she had copied from the board were answered *incorrectly*. I changed the way I graded her work, and the issue became abundantly clear. The math problems that Sandra had written *did not match* what was on the board. After working out the problems she had copied, I discovered her math was *correct*."

Validated and glowing, I glanced over at the termagant, who appeared glazed and unresponsive. Shaking my head, I made eye contact with Mrs. Blossom and silently mouthed, "She doesn't get it." [11]

"Sandra needs *glasses*," Mrs. Blossom quickly added. "She can't see the board." [12]

"Oh! Really?!" the materfamilias replied. "I didn't know that! I'll take care of it right away!"

Once my mother gave a coherent response, Mrs. Blossom continued and revealed how much she enjoyed my presence in her classroom. While she walked the materfamilias and me to the door, I became overwhelmed at the woman's efforts to defend me and hugged Mrs. Blossom in front of the termagant. The precious woman offered a gentle squeeze that released my grateful tears. The beloved teacher backed away. As Mrs. Blossom's eyes met mine, her maternal gaze conveyed much. Without saying a word, I knew she loved me and believed I was worth fighting for. [13]

Jealous of my open affection toward Mrs. Blossom, the termagant expedited our exit and interjected, "I'm so glad Sandra is doing good in class. Thank you for letting me know about her needing glasses. I'll take her to get a pair right now." On the walk back home, she warned, "This is going to be *expensive*. Your teacher better be right about your eyes. Now you have *no excuses*. You'd better start making straight A's again *or else*… and don't break your glasses by acting like a boy! Glasses aren't cheap!" [14]

The optometrist explained, "Sandra has *astigmatism*." The materfamilias gasped. "No need to worry, Mrs. Lawson. It just means her eyes are misshaped, and she needs glasses. Her vision will grow steadily worse as she ages before they level off, so we'll need to see her every year for a re-evaluation of her prescription."

"Oh, wow. Okay," the woman sweetly replied before turning to me in the same manner. "Okay, Sandra. Pick out the glasses you want." With her threats in mind, I located the least expensive frames on the children's display shelf and lifted them from their perch for the termagant to inspect. The materfamilias winced in disgust and questioned, "Are you sure that you don't want to try on a different pair?" [15]

Knowing that she disapproved of the boxy brown plastic spectacles, they became even more desirable. I mocked her and cheerfully corrected, "Oh, no, Mom. I don't need to try on *anything* else. They're the same frames that my brother has! I want *these* glasses… and look! They're the cheapest ones, too!" [16]

The optician raised his eyebrow at the materfamilias from behind his designer frames, which caused the woman to shrug from embarrassment.

When the glasses were ready, the clerk opened their temples and urged, "Try them on, Sandra. Tell me how they *feel*."

Retrieving the item from his large hands, I smiled and chirped, "Thank you, sir." He grinned as I peered through his handiwork and gasped. All that was around me had become *clear*. "Whoa! I can read every *wall poster* and see the pattern on the carpet… which is *very nice,* by the way." The clerk muffled his laughter. "Whoa! I can actually see the light bulbs instead of giant glares! This is amazing! Good job!" Grinning with an open mouth, I spun around and soaked in every detail of my surroundings.

The optician chuckled as he faced the termagant and teased, "*I think she likes them!* Now, if they become uncomfortable, just bring them back. I think she's too excited to tell us right now."

On the ride home in the passenger seat, I peered through the window. Tears rolled down my face as I joyously expressed, "I can see leaves on the trees! They're so pretty and the wind is moving them! Wow." [17]

The materfamilias broke down into a sob and interrupted my road sign reading. When I glanced over at her, mascara had already dripped down her right cheek. She tearfully whimpered, *"I'm so sorry, Sandra. I didn't know that you couldn't see. I feel like a bad mother."* [18]

To express anything other than total agreement felt dishonest. Then again, she didn't qualify as a mother. She was a warden, a dictator, a tyrant, a sadist, a liar, a villain, and a fool, but not a mother. The woman didn't even seem human at times. In bitter reflection of the day's accusations, threats, and brutal manipulation, I allowed a cruel silence to haunt the air all the way back to the house. She would find no comfort from *my* thoughts.

Got Tacos?

On the way to a local park, the materfamilias pulled into the drive-through lane of a fast-food venue. I wiggled in my seat and cheered. We were about to devour a copious amount of inexpensive yet delicious tacos. [1]

"How hungry are you?" the woman inquired, gauging how many sets to buy. [2]

When the familiar aroma of crunchy corn shells and spices wafted past my little nose, I salivated and requested quite a few. With the completed order in hand, we made our way over to a picturesque location to gorge ourselves under some shade trees to avoid getting crumbs in the car seats.

Unable to finish my order, I announced, "Mom, I'm *super* full. What do I do with the extra tacos?"

"I'm full, too. I couldn't eat all of mine either. Just put the rest back in the bag and set the whole thing at your feet when we get into the car. We can snack on them later if we get hungry again," she replied as she stood from the cement table to lead me back to the vehicle. Buckled in, I sat the tacos on the floor mat. [3]

As we pulled away from the park, I relished my clear vision and read each approaching sign out loud as a game. The further the sign was from the vehicle, the more points I'd award myself. [4]

The street light changed to red at a major intersection and brought traffic to a complete stop. While scanning the area for something to read, I noticed movement a few yards ahead of us. On the concrete median stood an unkept man that faced our direction who held a cardboard sign with a message clearly scribed in dark black ink.

"*Got tacos?*" I read aloud, peering down with a gasp. "Mom! *We* have tacos!" [5]

Irritated and confused, the woman angrily questioned, "What are you talking about?! I know we have tacos! I bought them! Stop shouting!"

"No! Listen! The man's sign says '*Got tacos?*' and we *have* tacos! We have to give them to him! He's hungry and *we* can feed him!" I squeaked. "Seriously, what are the odds that we would have extra tacos *and* see his sign? Hurry! How long is this red light? We need to get his attention!" [6]

In the afternoon sun, the woman rolled down her window and assertively beckoned, *"Excuse me! Sir?!"* The fellow lifted his eyes and leisurely approached our vehicle. "My daughter read your sign and wants to talk to you."

Remaining on the median and bending low to peer inside, the sign-bearer found me in the passenger seat and stared.

Feeling a sense of urgency, I quickly chirped, "Hello, sir! We just finished eating tacos and couldn't finish them all. Then, I saw your sign! I just *know* that *Jesus* wants you to have these tacos!" The man grinned. "Just so you know, these tacos are individually wrapped and we haven't touched them, so they're *sanitary*." He chuckled without breaking his gaze. "I give these tacos *to you*, and I hope you enjoy them as much as we did! They're our favorite!" I stretched toward the man and released the bag into his weathered hands. [7]

As the traffic light turned green, he softly replied, "Thank you. God bless you." I maintained eye contact and vigorously waved as we pulled away. His hand slowly waved back until he was out of sight.

The sound of sniffling from the driver's seat drew my attention as I sat back down. The termagant used an extra napkin to dry her eyes as I inquired, "What's wrong? Why are you crying?"

"I think we just met an *angel*," the materfamilias confessed as she focused on traffic.

Confused, I cocked my head to the side and queried, "That homeless man was an *angel*?"

"When I was a little girl, my mother once told me that there was a scripture in the Bible that says to be kind to strangers, because you might be entertaining angels," she divulged. "I think he was one of them." [8]

"Wow! We met an angel?!" I exclaimed. "That's *so* awesome. That man was *really* nice. If what you're saying is true, then we learned something new today. Angels like *tacos*!" [9]

Tiger Cruise

My father walked through the front door and cheerfully called out, "Come here, kids!" Eagerly, I jumped up from watching television and sprinted toward the man to hug his leg. "I have some exciting news! A Tiger Cruise is coming up in a few weeks!"

"What's a Tiger Cruise?" I queried.

My brother sighed and rebuked, "If you'd shut up and stop asking so many questions, he'd tell us."

"A Tiger Cruise is for navy families, *with the exception of spouses*, to see what it's like to live aboard the ship," the sailor informed while I exploded with excitement beside him. It was as though all of my dreams were about to come true. "It will leave from the base, sail to Hawaii, and then bring us back."

"Wait. Am I hearing you right? This is a trip to Hawaii… for sailors and their children *only*?" I eagerly questioned. [1]

"Yes," he confirmed. "No spouses are allowed."

"*Yay! Oh my gosh! I can't believe this! I'm going to Hawaii on a ship!*" I screamed with a jump-fist-pump. "This is amazing! I'm gonna start packing right now!"

His bitter wife quickly interjected, "Sandra, it's only for *boys*."

"*What?*" I barely whispered, slowly turning to seek verification from the sailor. "*Is that true?*" [2]

"C'mon, Sandra. Don't you remember? It's an *all-male ship*," he reminded with irritation. "I'm only taking your brother." [3]

The man's reckless approach to the situation struck me like a cannonball to the chest. I teetered on the edge of madness as hope tumbled down merciless crags of cruel disappointment into a tossed sea of shattered dreams. Suffocating with jealously in the presence of the golden child, I wailed aloud and fled to my room to soak my clutched pillow with hot tears. [4]

"I wish I was a boy," I groaned. "God must *hate* me. He knows everything and is all-powerful… and He created me as an ugly girl with no freedom. Why am I even alive? Girls are *worthless*. I should just do the world a favor and kill myself." [5]

Forbidden

~~~

The materfamilias bent down low and randomly asked, "Do you see that door over there?"

I stood to my feet and wondered why the woman had interrupted my peaceful cartoon-watching for such an idiotic question. The woman's angrily pointing finger led to her closed-off bedroom. I warily acknowledged, "*Yes. I see the door.*"

"*You have no business being in my bedroom or bathroom!*" she abruptly roared, inches from my nose. My anxious shoulders tightened as my chin pulled away from her horrifying face. Only once did the occupied hall bathroom force me to enter her restroom… days prior. I had not entered it before or since. "*You have your own bathroom right there! Whatever's in my bedroom or whatever happens in my bedroom is none of your business! If I ever catch you opening that door, you're getting a spanking! Do you understand me?! And you better not be stealing from me or God's going to get you! Go back to your room and stay out of my sight!*" [1]

Confusion scraped the interior walls of my skull as I attempted to decipher what had brought on a suspicion of *stealing*. My sibling received all he desired and nothing that woman possessed was worth dying for.

That night, an argument exploded from the couple's closed-off bedroom. The door and surrounding sheetrock became nothing more than a visual barrier. Every vulgar word from the termagant's mouth rang clear in my ears. I covered my head with pillows and hummed, but their words pierced every effort for peace. With no warning, an eerie silence engulfed the house. [2]

I laid awake and silently wondered, "Did she *kill* him this time? Is *that* why we're not allowed to look inside their room, so there won't be witnesses? Oh no. If Dad *is* dead, she planned it. I watch that police show every day. Spouses kill each other… and Mom was extra crazy tonight. What if Dad's murder ends up in the next episode? Am I even old enough to testify in court? I'm really smart. Maybe they'll make an exception for me. *Hold on.* What if he's bleeding to death on the floor right now? How would I know? Why am I still laying here like a coward? What if he needs me right now and I'm hesitating over a potential spanking? A spanking hasn't killed me yet. Maybe I can find him in time and save his life. I have to do something. If he's not breathing or if I see blood, I'm calling the police." [3]

I cracked open my parent's bedroom door and shook my head in frustration. True to her suspicious ways, the materfamilias had strategically located herself between the man and their bedroom door to monitor his movements. The woman's sheet-covered body prevented me from seeing my patriarch on the other side. Standing on the very tips of my toes, a second covered body barely came into view. Convinced that the materfamilias would not hesitate to choke or stab the sailor to death and fall fast asleep beside his corpse, I needed proof of life. With my toes held in excruciating ballerina point, I could see his chest move with each inhale. Satisfied, I silently restored the door to its original position and allowed myself to fall asleep. [4]

Backwards

~~~~~

In no way did I ever wish to disturb my parents at night, especially if they had just finished trading verbal blows and finally shouted themselves to sleep. In hopes of self-preservation, I would have done just about anything to avoid poking the grizzly bear that abrasively snored beside my father. After my inspections, I knew the sailor slept, although it surprised me each time to find him alive Prepared to turn over a masculine corpse to local law enforcement, I discovered him experiencing a moment of peace and dared not rob him of it. His tormented heart continued to beat as he somehow slumbered beside a ticking time-bomb of strife and violence. Even if the woman hadn't made comic book villains seem benevolent by comparison, I couldn't fathom how her husband ever dozed off or completed a REM cycle with her voluminous sow snorts and sputtered breathing erupting right next to his ear.

"Oh, no," I fretted inaudibly as trepidation wrapped its heavy fingers around my throat. The sensation grew urgent, but I wouldn't get up to pee. An abrupt flush from the hall bathroom toilet risked far too much noise, even with the termagant's snoring. Unwilling to take any chances that might stir either of the adults awake, I opted to wait in acute discomfort and relieve myself at sunrise.

The agonizingly intense pressure lasted for hours as I held my bulging lower abdomen and crossed my legs with shallow breathing, since fully inflated lungs took up too much space in my tiny body. A trickle occurred and prompted me to swing my legs around and off the bed, but my painfully taut bladder overruled my determination to hold. An involuntary flow began. Panicked, I didn't want to create an obvious puddle on the floor, so I laid back down and attempted to hide my shame under a blanket. Urine soaked through my pajamas, sheets, and the mattress beneath me. Doom pounded out an ominous theme from within my chest as I wept over my fate and laid in my filth until morning.

Sunshine poured through my window and onto the bed as I remained damp and motionless.

"What is that *smell*?" the materfamilias wondered aloud as she exited her bedchamber, sniffing her way into my room to uncover a trembling child in wet pajamas on top of soaked sheets. *"Did you pee the bed?! Why didn't you get up?! Are you a baby?! Do I need to put diapers on you?! Why are you going backwards?! You're eight years old! If you pee the bed again, I'm going to spank you! All you do is give me more work! Now I have to strip your bed, wash your sheets, somehow clean the mattress, and let it dry before putting on clean sheets! Why did you do this?!"*

"I was afraid to wake you up and make you upset by flushing the toilet at night," I tearfully revealed. "I'm sorry." [1]

"You did this on purpose?!" the materfamilias raged as she grabbed my tiny arm. *"Don't ever pee your bed again! I don't care if it wakes me up! If you need to pee, get up and pee in the bathroom! This is ridiculous! I'm sick of looking at you! Get away from me!"* [2]

Weeks later, I woke to sensations of intense nausea and a burning fever. Unable to make it to the toilet, I vomited on my bedroom floor and panicked. The materfamilias didn't permit me to open any cabinets. As a result, I was unaware of the location of necessary cleaning products and quaked at the thought of creating more work for the termagant. Tormented by the fear of a ruthless spanking, I laid back down and baked on top of my covers. [3]

Just the thought of the snoring woman's presence filled me with intense foreboding as I considered approaching her. While my stomach felt a bit more settled, I mustered the courage and physical strength to stand. Avoiding my mess, I silently made my way to my parent's threshold and froze in crippling trepidation. Consumed with a terrible dread of stirring the beast, I lingered outside their door in sweaty pajamas and caught a chill. [4]

The strength to stand diminished as I silently turned the knob, opened the door, and hesitated once more to control my nervous breathing. My frail and shivering body was the only presence standing between their bed and the pale glow from the hallway night light. Were she to awaken right then, I would have resembled a reanimated corpse from a selection of B films. Overwhelmed at the thought of frightening her into aggression, I silently closed the door and retreated into my bed to endure the symptoms, swallowing back waves of nausea as sweat pooled on my ridged chest. Feeling *immensely* worse, the fever burned a hole through my cowardice and propelled me back toward their formidable bed. I ever-so-gently touched the materfamilias' shoulder and startled her awake.

"What do you want?" she gruffly murmured.

"I'm sick with a fever… and I threw up on the floor in my bedroom," I whispered, chattering my teeth from another chill. Sweaty pajamas clung to my thin body and soaked up my uncontrollable tears. *"I don't know where anything is, or I'd clean it up myself. I'm

sorry." The woman stood and walked past me while I was still speaking. "*I didn't want to wake you, but I need medicine and don't know what to take.*" [5]

"It's fine," the groggy woman flatly replied as she retrieved disinfectant spray and a bottle of fever reducer. "You can't help that you're sick. I'm glad you didn't get into the medicine cabinet. I have to give you the right amount or you could take too much. Drink this."

"What is it?" I questioned.

"It's medicine," she replied, irritated. "What do you think I'm giving you? Poison?" I considered her words and downed the plastic cup of thick putrescence, willing to die or heal. Stepping past me in into my room, the woman flipped on my light, looked at the floor and commented, "Well, I'm glad you threw up on the floor and not in your bed. This is easy to clean." She wiped down the tiles, sanitized the area, and returned to her pillow.

Hours later, the woman abruptly snapped me from sleep and sternly ordered, "Get up and take a bath. You smell like sweat." While clean and clothed in fresh pajamas, the materfamilias barked, "Close your eyes," and sprayed disinfectant all over my flesh. A fog of chemicals engulfed me and filled my lungs as I refrained from the largest cough. "Now, get into bed and *stay there* before you get everyone sick. No one wants your germs… and don't walk around touching everything with your *filthy hands*. If I catch you out of bed, you're getting a spanking." [6]

Upon my return to school, Nam, Josh and I volunteered to help Mrs. Blossom with another class project. While we worked, I inquired, "Hey, guys. At home, when you're feeling bad, what you do to feel better?"

"That's easy!" Josh exclaimed. "If I feel sick or have a bad dream or am sad, I go to my mom and dad! They snuggle with me in their bed and tell me that everything is going to be just fine. They always know what to do." [7]

Nam warmly added, "Yeah! Me, too… and if I'm crying or upset, my parents hold me and talk to me about it."

"*Really?*" I questioned. "What's *that* like?! I swear, something must be wrong with my family. I'm afraid to wake my mom up at night, even to flush the toilet. If I'm sad, no one cares. If I ask questions, I'm accused of talking back and being an ungrateful brat. My mom is the last person I would *ever* want around me if I'm sick. She only makes me feel worse. That woman is *mean* and told me that I have no business being in their bedroom because she thinks I'm going to *steal* from her." I leaned towards them. "I've *never* stolen from her." [8]

Josh stared at me in awe and commented, "That's messed up, Sandra. *Your own mom* thinks you'll steal from her? *Wow.* You know what? Next time you feel bad, you should just come over to my house! *My* parents will hug you!"

Offering a defeated half-smile, I replied, "That sounds *amazing*, but I'm not allowed over at anyone's house either, especially one with a *boy* living there. Sorry, Josh."

"Dang," he huffed with an amazed brow. "I'm really sorry that you don't get comforted at home. I don't know how anyone's parents could be like that."

"Especially to *you*," Nam consoled with her delicate hand on my burdened shoulder. "I'm glad we're all in the same class together. We love you, Sandra. If you're ever sad, come to *me*. I'll hug you." At that, the child pulled me into an embrace with Josh holding us both. [9]

The Cartoon

Once again, my seafaring father boarded the aircraft carrier for another long journey away and left his offspring in the hands of the deplorable materfamilias. The woman had all but convinced me to raise myself, so I attempted to avoid her and stay out of trouble, but trouble hunted me. [1]

"Electricity is expensive, you little brat! If I catch you wasting electricity, you're getting a spanking! Leave the lights *off* unless you need them!" the termagant ordered as she closed all the blinds to fill the house with shadow. I refused to hypothesize what she deemed *necessary* and trained myself to navigate by the dull glow emanating from each television.

I stepped from the darkened hallway and inquired, "Mom, since you and my brother are watching different shows that I'm not interested in, may I please watch the unoccupied TV in your bedroom?" [2]

"Fine. *I don't care...* but just this once," the woman gruffly answered as she waved me off. Before I entered the forbidden bedroom, the materfamilias shouted from the couch, *"Leave the door open!"* [3]

After locating the remote control, I channel surfed and discovered that my parents' television had access to different stations than the other two rooms. Several stations offered dramas, movies, and payment plans for household items. I continued to search and gasped at a unique cartoon that captured my full attention. The illustration style differed completely from the standard Saturday-morning allotment. Images quickly flashed before my eyes and revealed painstakingly captured details. Each character's hair flowed or shifted with the wind. Beads of sweat formed a nervous trickle down someone's face. Clothing adjusted with movement, and expressive eyes mesmerized me. [4]

I had missed the beginning of the program and grew increasingly confused as I watched a glowing orb enter a stuffy business meeting where a sexual assault quickly unfolded. Out of nowhere and by happenstance, something swiftly rescued the woman and simultaneously destroyed her assailant. Without understanding a speck of the plot, the same glowing orb followed some menacing characters that suddenly emerged from a desert in the following scene. Violent and gory deaths of innocent people led to a robust and scantily clad woman's capture that caused my body to tense. Each perverse image awakened foreign sensations that were instantly recognized as *evil*, yet I watched on. Paranoia split my attention between the open door and the television screen. As the film increased in brutal carnality, I trembled and felt irrevocably tainted by what I had witnessed. [5]

The idea of being discovered terrified me. I changed the channel, shut the television off, and exited the room for an early bedtime. The connection between the stories eluded me, and I couldn't fathom how anyone could imagine such depraved events or feel the need to painstakingly illustrate them for a motion picture. [6]

Too restless to sleep, I compared my body to the sensually exaggerated woman in the illustrations. My reflection more closely resembled a starved little boy. The termagant's speeches of a cruel and vengeful God came to mind, and I became convinced that the Creator hated me *even more*. I could have changed the channel sooner, and wondered, "Is she right? Am I a demon from hell?" [7]

Looming

Something loomed, without consistent shape or form, in the corner of my bedroom. The dark figure shifted without the logical reason of candlelight or headlights passing by. As the mysterious entity grew larger, I covered my face with the sheet and waited. Desiring to breathe in cooler air, I mustered the courage and peeked. The intruder had vanished, and I questioned my sanity. When it happened again the following night, I felt validated, but it caused trips to the restroom to be considerably more terrifying. [1]

Desperate for counsel, I sought the materfamilias and informed, "Mom, I'm seeing something in my room at night. It's like a shadow, but it looks *alive*. I'm afraid to fall asleep or get up to use the bathroom."

From the couch, the woman cruelly scoffed, "You're too old for this, you *liar*."

"I'm not lying," I boldly clarified.

"Well, then… what did you do to bring a *demon* into this house?!" she accused. Her words reminded me of the adult cartoon I had stumbled upon. *"I better never catch you doing dirty things in your room! God can see through your sheets, you little demon! He's gonna get you for that!"*

"Wow. I don't even want to know what you're talking about, lady. That's not what's happening. I'm *not* doing dirty things in my room," I corrected. "I just need help to get rid of whatever that thing is, but if you don't know how, *just say so.* Talking to you was a huge mistake. I don't even know why I bother. You just make things worse. Forget I said anything."

"Well, it's not *my* fault you're seeing things in your bedroom! I know *I* didn't invite it in! I love God! I'm a good person! *You're the demon!* You brought it in here, so *you* get rid of it!" the woman aggressively added as I sighed in frustration and shook my head. "You're just being a big baby, anyway. You have no reason to be scared. It's all in your head! I've never seen anything like that. All you're doing is just trying to get attention. You want to hear something *really* scary? I used to dream that *the devil* was chasing me! It used to freak the **** out of me! Now, *that's* scary. You're just seeing shadows, so quit bothering me. I'm trying to watch my show." [2]

The school library was about to host a book fair a few days later, and Mrs. Blossom passed a thin catalog to each student. I had just enough pocket change to purchase an obscure pamphlet about ghosts. When it arrived, I studied the contents and was ready to try the ridiculous. [3]

"The worst that could happen is *nothing*," I reasoned with a shrug.

The author claimed a doorway needed to lead outside from the exterior wall, which was a technique I recognized from a popular movie. However, any *visible* mark would have led to a traumatizing spanking, so I drew an *imaginary* door and acted as though I were holding a writing utensil. I concluded that, when dealing with the spirit realm, belief held more power than the mark itself. With a firm voice, I told the spirit to leave. The imagined doorway only exacerbated my circumstances as the darkness became more pronounced and tormented me nightly, as opposed to sporadically. [4]

Another page encouraged me to inform the spirit to *go towards the light*. I said the prescribed words. That night, my fear only intensified. At dawn, the pamphlet found a proper home with the outgoing garbage. [5]

Soon after, a television special about mediums played in the living room. As the materfamilias watched on and ignored me, several mediums boasted how ghosts were simply human spirits *left behind* who needed our assistance to *cross over* from the physical realm into the spirit realm. [6]

The television program only caused more discomfort and prompted me to wonder, "Why am I even alive? What will happen to me when I die? Are *all* spirits bad? Should I listen to a spirit if it speaks to me? Could my spirit get lost and turn into a ghost that walks around with the living?" [7]

Dissatisfied in all I had read and heard, my pursuit of truth drove me to search for a real and permanent solution to my nocturnal problem. [8]

Mediums

"Sandra, it's that medium I was telling you about! Hurry up or you'll miss it!" the materfamilias shouted from the living room sofa. [1]

"Coming!" I loudly reassured from my bedroom floor, interested in witnessing a professional in action. [2]

As I sat down to watch and listen, the talk show host announced, "I want you all to welcome a very special friend of mine. She is a world renown medium who has authored several published books on spiritualism, has assisted law enforcement in hundreds of cold cases, and has helped countless people understand what lies beyond the grave. Here she is! Welcome her!" [3]

Once the audience settled, the medium pointed to someone among them and plainly stated, "The woman in purple." Wearing a loud sweater, a member of the studio audience pointed to herself to seek confirmation. "Yes, *you*. Stand up." Awestruck, the woman rose from her seat and waited for the talk show host to run the microphone up to her row. "I see two men standing beside you. One is *older* and one is *younger*. The older one is saying that his watch is inside the roll-top desk. The younger one is saying that he's sorry about burying your doll. It's in a time capsule under the old oak." The crowd stared at the audience member and waited for her response.

"Oh, my!" she gasped. As the woman in purple covered her face to weep, she continued, "The older man is my father, who died last year. I couldn't find his watch and just sat on my bed, sobbing. The younger man is my brother who died in an accident several years ago. I always wondered what happened to that doll! That's so crazy… and the tree's still there! I had forgotten all about that time capsule! I'll dig it up when I get home!" She blotted her eyes. "You can really see and hear them? *Wow.* Thank you so much! Thank you." Aghast, the crowd uproariously applauded. [4]

Another audience member stood with a transparent starvation for the medium's attention. As the host offered her the microphone, she pulled it to her face and chirped, "Hello! I have followed you on this show *for a while* and it's amazing to finally meet you!" The medium gave a sleepy and unimpressed smile as she slowly nodded for her to continue. "*Anyway*, I just wanted to know about my future. Do I need to do anything different or change anything in order to get my life *on track*?" [5]

In the manner of a stale grandmother in the presence of her exhausting progeny, the medium remarked, "I see two angels standing next to you. They are telling me you don't need to change a thing. Just keep doing what you've been doing. They're helping you." [6]

"Oh, my goodness! Wow! You see *angels*?!" the woman exclaimed as she looked around behind her. Wide eyed, she returned her gaze to the front and held back sobs before she found her seat. "That's really encouraging! Thank you!" [7]

The termagant and I made eye contact and whispered a simultaneous, *"Wow."*

Back from the base shortly after another tour, the sailor entered the house and listened to my excited words about the medium and details of the show. "Believe *half* of what you see and *none* of what you hear," my father counseled. "Not everything is as it seems. If you pay close attention, it's easy to figure out an illusionist's tricks. Assistants sit in the crowd and wait to be called on. With them in the crowd, the illusionist can easily fool a gullible and willing audience. That medium is just a glorified illusionist. A person openly presenting themselves as an illusionist is hired to entertain, and everyone knows it, but that medium tricks people to *believe* her so she can sell books and take their money. That's dishonest. She's a *fraud*." [8]

"*Sandra, come here!*" the materfamilias yelled from the living room couch the following morning.

"*Coming!*" I replied, putting down my dolls to obey.

"I had a weird dream last night. Look everything up in my dream book and interpret it for me," the woman calmly ordered, handing me the thick paperback authored by mediums. [9]

"Okay. Tell me the entire dream from beginning to end, down to the very last detail," I instructed. As the woman spoke, the interpretation of her dream seemed very obvious to me. When she finished, I asked a few clarifying questions and revealed what I understood. [10]

"Oh, *wow*. That makes a lot of sense. You're pretty good at that!" the termagant commented. "Now, use the dream book to see how close you were!"

In looking up the specifics, the separate interpretations seemed opaque, irrelevant and contradictory. She only believed the most flattering interpretations, and dismissed, "Ok. That's all I wanted. Go back to your room." [11]

Most Outstanding Student

As a fourth-grader, on the eve of Valentine's Day, I sat at my desk and carefully scribed my name onto miniature pink and red cards.

My brother spotted me, stepped into my room and interjected, "Sandra, you know what you should do? You should write mean things on the cards for the kids you don't like." [1]

Bewildered, I mentioned, "But, I *like* everyone." [2]

He shrugged and commented, "Well, *if you did it*, it would be funny." [3]

After he stepped away, I sat there for a moment in soliloquy and stated, "Well, there *are* a couple of kids that I don't like as much as the rest, but I don't want them to be singled out. To be fair, I'll write something mean on *everyone's* card." [4]

When I stirred the following morning, I had completely forgotten about the negatively altered cards, cheerfully toted the bag of ticking-time-bombs to class, and hand-delivered them to each unsuspecting child. Moments later, a student started sniffling and ran to the teacher. I knew him to be a lovely person and wondered what would make him cry.

"*Sandra. Come here, please,*" Mrs. Blossom called with a stern look. All at once, I remembered my foolish crime and stood with pangs of regret. Bearing a dry mouth, heavy feet, and a hot neck of shame, I shuffled slowly to my victim and his powerful defender. She took a knee, stared into my eyes, and inquired, *"Did you write this?"*

"Yes, I did and *totally* regret it," I admitted as I shook my head. "This was my brother's idea, and it was really dumb. I completely forgot about it." Immediately, I comforted my classmate. "I'm *so* sorry. I didn't mean a word of it. You're *awesome*."

My teacher responded, "I believe that this was your brother's idea. This behavior doesn't sound like you at all and I am *very* pleased that you told the truth. However, this cannot go unpunished. You weren't aware of this, but you had been selected to receive the Most Outstanding Student Award this year. However, after what happened today, I'm forced to withdraw your name." My mouth dropped open. "I'm sorry, but what you did today does not sound very *outstanding* to me. Look at your friend, Sandra. He's *crying*." [5]

I accepted my fate with a nod and returned to my seat. Ashamed at my own stupid behavior and livid with my vindictive sibling, I silently stewed, "How could I be so gullible?! Am I really *that* desperate for my brother's approval? I'm such an idiot! What was I thinking?! That guy had me jump off of a roof with cardboard wings, knowing it wouldn't work! What's wrong with me?! If it wasn't for him, I could have won that award three years straight! Wow. I *hate* my brother." [6]

One by one, students stood up and tearfully reported the rest of my tainted cards. Mrs. Blossom pursed her lips and conveyed, *"Sandra… I think you owe an apology to the entire class."* [7]

The woman's righteous judgement pierced my very soul. Her prophetic warning echoed in my troubled mind. I had become *the bully*. Remorseful and heavy, I solemnly made my way to the front of the room and peered into the troubled eyes of each wounded child. Expectations seemed to heighten as a hush blanketed the class. [8]

I inhaled deeply and soothed, "I am *so sorry* about those terrible cards. What I wrote in them isn't even how I actually feel. In fact, I really *like* you guys. All of you are super smart and really nice. It was wrong to write those ugly things, and *you didn't deserve any of it*. I hope you can forgive me, but if you don't, I *completely* understand. This was the dumbest thing I've ever done." [9]

Lingering before them, I winced and half-expected to be booed back to my seat with projectile school supplies bouncing off of my cowered body.

Soggy smiles emerged as Nam sweetly responded, *"It's okay, Sandra! Don't feel bad anymore! We love you!"*

Students burst into jovial applause and cheered in agreement as another shouted, *"Yeah, Sandra! We forgive you! Don't worry!"* [10]

Humbled, I wept in disbelief and peered up at Mrs. Blossom's face. Tears of joy clung to my surrogate's chin as she smiled down at me. My class replaced the shame with an undeserved robe of redemption. [11]

Goodbye

~~~~~~

As the last day of the fourth grade drew to a close, Mrs. Blossom stood before her class and warmly expressed, "It has been an *honor* to instruct each of you this year. You have been an inspiration, meaning that you have reminded me, time and time again, why I became a teacher. Watching you learn and grow, not only as students, but as individuals, has brought me incredible joy, to say the very least. I have high expectations for all of you…" [1]

"May we visit you next year? Is that *allowed*?" a classmate sweetly interrupted.

Mrs. Blossom hunched down with her hands on her knees and grinned as she softly answered, *"Yes. I would love that."* Surrounding faces lightened with the sunny news as our instructor regained her upright poise. "Visitors are welcome, *especially* when they're my former students." The woman playfully scrunched her nose at us. "Have an amazing summer, everyone. Class dismissed." [2]

The thought of moving on from two years of Mrs. Blossom's guidance, support, and kindness made me homesick for her before I ever left my seat. The foreign sensations deepened as the concept of her absence sunk in and drained the expectation of peace from my soul. Colors lost their vibrance as my breathing became shallow and filled with pain. Even if separated for years on end, the thought of missing the materfamilias, even dimly, was unfathomable to me. *Mrs. Blossom* was my mother, and I was being stripped away from her diligent care. [3]

As I struggled to bid the transcendent woman farewell, the tall heroine lowered herself and allowed me to tightly embraced her as I tearfully whispered, *"I love you."*

Mrs. Blossom refrained from parroting the sentiment, but reciprocated with a squeeze of my shoulders and her moved countenance. Many fond memories of selfless acts, wisdom, gentle correction, and abundant grace flooded my memory and robbed me of oxygen as I stepped away. [4]

Waiting just outside the door, Nam embraced me with a smile and exclaimed, "It'll be okay, Sandra! We'll see you *next* year! It's only a few months away. Summer will end and you'll be back at school with us. Just think! Maybe we'll be in the same class again!"

"Yeah!" Josh added. *"Four years in a row?* That's got to be a record for navy kids."

"Wow. Yeah. That would be awesome. That gives me some hope. You guys are making me feel better," I admitted. "Aw, man. My mom is over there watching me. I have to go. Sorry, guys. I miss you already. I love you! *See you next year!*"

My face warmed in the sun on the walk home as a soft breeze whisked away the excess heat. A bubbling excitement to visit the ocean rolled over in my mind as I gazed down the sidewalk toward the house.

What I saw in the driveway tightened my chest. My father's vehicle had a rented moving trailer attached, while the termagant's car sat packed and travel ready with blankets and pillows. Panicked, I interrogated, *"What's going on? Where are we going? What's happening?"*

Shocked at my confusion, my sibling answered, "Where have you been? We're moving today. Don't you remember?"

As my brother entered the front seat of our father's vehicle, memories flashed and fell into place. Although no one ever spoke to me about what was happening or helped me prepare for what was to come, I had completely overlooked the obvious clues that had surrounded me. My father retired from the navy that year, which meant navy housing was out of the picture. For days, I spotted rolls of packing tape in every room. The walls had slowly become bare while boxes stacked up and centered in each living space. I was ashamed of my bewilderment, especially after conversing for hours with the friendly mover that meticulously wrapped items with packing paper the night before. [5]

"How could I be so completely unaware? What's wrong with me? It's too late," I frantically murmured, wide-eyed and trembling. "*I didn't get anyone's phone number or address. I didn't give Josh or Nam enough hugs or take the time to say more meaningful goodbyes to anyone. They all think I'll be back next year, but I won't. I'll never see them again.*" [6]

The materfamilias opened the rear passenger door and added the final preparations for another unbearable road trip. Already irritated, she ordered, "Get in the car, Sandra. We're leaving. *Let's go.*"

Earth seemed to tilt as I frantically asked, "Right now?! Are we leaving this second?!"

"Yes! Now!" the termagant loudly confirmed. "*Sandra, look at the moving trailer! We're ready to leave! Let's go! You're holding us up! Move it!*"

I gasped with a sob and huffed, "Wait! I haven't said goodbye to Nancy! She doesn't know! I have to tell her!"

"*I'm right here!*" Nancy shouted as she sprinted toward our vehicles. "*You didn't tell me you were moving!*"

Her momentum collided into my weakened state and barely allowed me to utter, "I didn't know!" We wrapped our arms around one another as if our bond could somehow stop our worlds from splitting. I whispered through her thick black hair, *"What am I going to do without you? You're my best friend. I'm going to miss you so much. I can't handle this."* [7]

"I have an idea. Give me a second," Nancy requested as she reached into her backpack and shoved some scribbled information into my pocket. "That's my phone number and address. We can stay in-touch this way. If you write letters, *I'll write you back*. It's the best way. Long-distance phone calls are expensive."

I nodded vigorously and added, "Yes. That's a *great* idea, Nancy. I love to write."

"*I know*," Nancy tearfully whispered through a forced smile while she grabbed my hands.

Staring at my friend, I solemnly informed, "After we graduate from high school, *I'm coming back to you*. I promise. They can't keep us apart forever. I'll save my money and buy a plane ticket. We *will* see each other again." [8]

Nancy pulled me in for one last embrace and whispered, *"I believe you, Sandra. I love you."*

"*I love you, too, Nancy*," I softly reassured with an extra squeeze.

Quite finished with the drama, the former sailor climbed into his driver's seat and grumbled, *"We don't have time for this,"* before slamming the door.

The materfamilias grabbed my wrist and quickly added, "I'm sorry, Nancy. Sandra has to go now." When I peered upward, I couldn't have been more shocked to discover tears in the materfamilias' eyes.

As she backed away, Nancy continuously sobbed and waved until she was no longer in view. In complete silence, I wondered why I had to figure everything out on my own. There was no last hurrah at the beach or a moment in the tree with Nancy to process the transition. Without Mrs. Blossom's consistency or my trusted friends' encouragement, I had never felt more isolated in the dark. [9]

Alone with the materfamilias, I took a chance and queried, "Where are we moving?"

"*Texas*," the termagant answered sharply from behind the wheel.

"Texas? What about the land in *Montana*?" I wondered aloud. "Dad even showed me the stakes that marked where the house would be. At least Montana is *pretty*."

The woman humored me and replied, "We're *selling* the land in Montana to help pay for the land in Texas."

Wheels of fate had already been in motion, and the decision was irrevocable. Where outbursts traditionally came from the materfamilias, I beat her to it and released an eruption of suppressed emotions that flooded the vehicle. With gritted teeth and a howl, I imagined myself rolling down the window and jumping to a gory death on the asphalt as a ladybug crawled over my inanimate face. Bridges and overpasses were inviting each time we passed them. I was perfectly fine with being flattened, drowned, or splattered against some rocks. I wanted to choke myself with the seatbelt, but determined that I wasn't strong enough without decent leverage. Finally, I imagined an eighteen-wheeler as it barreled right for us. I welcomed a head-on collision and pictured my cheerful body launched through shattered glass to skid peacefully into a patch of wildflowers. Disappointed at our safe travels, I bawled until exhaustion silenced me. As always, any show of negative emotion was an act of utter futility that accomplished nothing. *Texas was going to happen.* [10]

SECTION 3

Texas Happened

~~~~

The most tormenting road trip in my first decade of life came to a close. Both vehicles pulled off the rolling highway and onto a quaint ranch road with winding turns. Each property we passed boasted cleared and well-kept land that showcased a beautifully sturdy home. One neighbor owned several exotic emus that thrilled me into an unexpected gasp.

"Maybe this won't be so bad," I thought. "Maybe we will make friends with the neighbors."

As he piloted the lead vehicle, my father pulled up to a closed gate. While the man exited to unlock the chain and grant us access, I focused on what lay in the distance. A rectangular log house waited for us just beyond a treacherous path for the termagant's luxury car to traverse. Labeled as a *driveway*, the obstacle course bore deep ruts in hardened mud, unforgiving rocks buried within, and tall dead grass on both sides that could hide any number of territorial critters. The woman drove slowly to avoid scraping the undercarriage, but missed and slammed the loaded vehicle into the deep tracks, which gave us a fright. [1]

We parked next to a gray situation. A neglectfully dingy log house with visible rot stayed upright while nestled within acres of thick brush, prickly vines, cactus patches, and dense Ashe juniper. Wilting oak trees cryptically reached toward the dilapidated front porch that boasted a decayed section, collapsed under its own weight. An imaginary wolf howled along with the screeching violins that played in the back of my mind.

Fresh sawdust rested on the porch planks closest to the exterior wall. I stepped forward to investigate and beheld small holes that speckled the entire length of each log. Within seconds, a dominating presence of burrowing residential insects made themselves known.

"Well, that's not good," I mumbled.

"This is a result of *laziness*," my father admitted. "The homeowner should have applied *preservative* immediately after construction. It's only fourteen years old, but wasn't maintained properly, so there's a lot to take on. The restoration of this house will be a *project*… but if we work together, we can fix it up. It's the *land* that has value." [2]

The *fixer-upper* seemed more like a *knocker-downer*, so I queried, "Dad, if it's going to require so much work to live in, why did we move here in the first place?" [3]

He sighed and answered, "Your mother wanted to live in Texas and I wanted to live in the country. Of all the available properties that we could afford, this was the best deal with the most topsoil. Topsoil makes it much easier to build on and is needed to grow the garden I intend to plant." My father's eyes seemed to stare at things unseen as he walked about and pointed. "Eventually, I intend to build a garage and workshop *here*. Over *there*, where that pigsty currently is, I will build and plant the garden." He was serious. Abandoned by the previous owners, an actual oinking pig had become my father's problem. Not long after closing on the property, he found a buyer for the animal and had them remove it. "The goat shed will eventually go right *there* and an interior fence will be built around the house about *this far out* and stopping right over *there*." [4]

As we returned to the precarious structure we were to sleep in that night, I stepped on something that felt unusual and peered down. I gasped and inquired, "Dad, why are there *bones* everywhere?"

The man pursed his lips in disapproval and commented, "I see that. It's *another* sign of laziness. The previous owner was a taxidermist by trade. Instead of dealing with the carcasses properly, he threw the remains directly onto the ground." [5]

"That wasn't very smart," I observed. "Wouldn't it attract wild animals and flies?"

"Yes, but that shouldn't worry you right now. These bones are old and dry. Whenever you see bones, pick them up and throw them away. Don't be lazy, too. More bones will surface after each rain. *Eventually,* we'll get them all." [6]

While examining the decomposing planks, I announced, "Whoa! There are entire *spines* under the porch! *Look!* That's disgusting! They *lived* like this?!" [7]

"It seems to look that way. Since it bothers you so much, rake up as much of it as you can," he assigned. [8]

"*Great,*" I moaned, followed by tightly pursed lips. [9]

The former sailor chuckled as he approached the front door and added, "You won't be able to get them *all*, but you'll get a lot of them. When you've finished *that* task, I'll fix the porch." [10]

"No, Dad! Leave the boards like that!" I pleaded, with my head cocked to the side. "It's kinda cool. Doesn't it look like the deck of an old wooden ship after a shark attack?! See how the rot *curves* like a bite?"

At that, my father rolled his eyes and walked inside, but I lingered. Amid the boneyard and rot, I stepped carefully onto sturdier portions and imagined myself evading hostile natives alongside a rugged movie hero who gingerly crossed a rickety bridge draped over snapping crocodiles. [11]

The front door squeaked open as I let myself in and shook my head in disbelief. Wide cobwebs sagged from dust in every direction. Spider egg sacs clung to each log as they led up to the vaulted ceiling that hosted more of the same. Frightening varieties of creatures, both living and dead, blanketed the blotched cement floor. Nothing seemed real, and I ached to wake up. Springy camel crickets gripped their disturbed abode, ready to pounce. Pulsing daddy long-legs congregated en masse. Centipedes nestled themselves into safer crevices while elusive silverfish weaved around and slipped under an interior wall. Perished scorpions dried up beside crumbling pill bugs. Unwilling to blink from fear of springing an ambush, I carefully avoided them with watchful steps toward the kitchen. [12]

"The previous owners didn't install central heating or air conditioning," my father continued. "Instead of buying space heaters, they just ignited the gas oven and left it open during the winter. That was laziness, too. Hopefully, the oven and stove still work for us to cook and bake with. I'm going to install a woodstove before winter rolls around, so heating shouldn't be a problem for us." [13]

"This house doesn't have air conditioning? I'm drenched in sweat," I added. "How hot does Texas get in the summer?"

He walked past me toward the other end of the house and quipped, "We're about to find out." I tagged along until the man stopped at the mouth of the hallway beside the utility room and bathroom. "Sandra, your room is at the end, *on the left*. Our bedroom is directly across the hall from you, *on the right*, and your brother's room will be upstairs in the loft." Having fulfilled his role as a tour guide, my father left and found another occupation.

"What? My brother gets the loft? Lucky..." I commented under my breath. *"Why does he get to be away from Mom?"* [14]

I proceeded and stepped inside the far-left passage to explore my cell. Subtle lights drew my eye to the exterior walls, toward the far corner of my room. I shook my head again. Gaps between the poorly kept timber led directly outside. Each interior wall of studs and sheetrock seemed to do their job nicely, but the four main exterior walls consisted entirely of exposed gray logs that expanded and contracted without chinking or caulking in between. Irony framed each closed window as the walls breathed the elements in and out.

The house was entirely void of insulation. Nothing prevented the sun's scorching heat from transferring through the sizzling roof. By high-noon, the loft's vaulted ceiling had created a sauna effect and steadily increased the temperature to be unbearable, even after our father installed a crank-operated one foot by one foot window as a vent sometime later. Although he reigned as the golden child, I pitied my brother when my father handed him a simple box fan. There was no genuine regard for my brother's health or safety when making *that* space his domain that first night. [15]

Before turning in for the evening, my father mentioned, "Sandra, when you're done changing into your pajamas, open your door and leave it that way. It helps the air circulate."

I obeyed, shut off my light, climbed into bed, and stared at the dingy popcorn ceiling. Alone in the darkness, chaos ensued. Without the sound barrier of two shut doors, I knew the exact moment when the materfamilias had fallen asleep. Each cartoonish sputter of her sow-like snore was no more pleasant than a rusty saw blade slowly drawn over my twitching nerves to pluck at each one.

Blaring over the sounds of a slumbering nemesis, as if congregated in my room for a recital, cicadas screeched from the trees in a morbid cycle of crescendo and decrescendo. All the while, Katydids projected their abrasive call while the unbalanced ceiling fan violently clinked the pull-chain after each unforgiving blade rotation. As I tossed and turned, madness and exhaustion volleyed the concept of peace over my head and played a miserable game of keep-away.

Sweat saturated the mattress as I bent the moist pillow over both ears. There was no silence or comfort to be found. Liquid secreted from my skin pooled on my chest and soaked through the sheets that clung to my irritated epidermis. Tangled in fabric, I gnashed my teeth in humid agony.

Plagued from without and within, a groan escaped my lips and morphed into a useless protest, where I quietly huffed to myself, *"I thought Dad was intelligent. Did he lose his mind at sea? What was the man thinking? Moving to Texas was the worst idea ever. California was beautiful, the weather was perfect, and we had the Pacific Ocean. Why did we ever leave? I don't understand any of this. Why are we here? What could possibly be the point of all this?"* [16]

Pale and Darkness

As it had the day prior and the day before that, the sun slowly dipped its brilliance beyond the horizon. Oak and juniper blocked its rays to welcome lengthy shadows. The first evening in the insectarium had come to a dramatic close and revealed how blind one was under a moonless sky. The absence of light is darkness, but even the simplest truths can possess more than one facet. [1]

In the days that followed, trepidation strangled me before bedtime. I peered down the hallway and trembled. To enter my room also meant I needed to pass by my parents' doorway. It wasn't the termagant's wrath that I had dreaded most in that moment. She wasn't there. Her faithful attention was on the luminescent screen in the living room. In those blood-chilling minutes, it was a pale, feminine spirit that caught my peripheral view each night, only to vanish when directly faced as if sent to prod me even closer to a breaking point.

"Mom, I keep seeing something in your bedroom at night," I confessed. "It's white, but it's not bright or pretty. I think it's a ghost or something, but it goes away when I try to get a better look. I'm scared to walk into my room because I have to pass by yours." [2]

"Quit being such a crybaby," the termagant dismissed. "You're just seeing my jackets hanging from the closet door."

"No, Mom," I rebutted. "That would be nice, but I checked it out. I'm telling you… I wouldn't be standing here if that were the issue."

"Well, if it's *white*, then maybe you're seeing an angel!" the materfamilias chirped. "Maybe it's something *good* in my room." [3]

"I'm not a ridiculous person. I know what I'm seeing," I pressed. "Angels don't just lurk around in the dark to scare children. There's something *evil* in your room." [4]

"Well, what am *I* supposed to do about it?!" the woman savagely replied. "*I've* never seen anything in there! What have *you* been doing to bring demons into this house?! You'd better repent and ask God for forgiveness! *You're the demon!* If something bad is in there, *you* put it there! *Why are you even looking in my bedroom?!* You better not be sneaking in there to do bad things! *Are you stealing from me at night?!* God's going to get you for that! Get away from me and be quiet! I have better things to do than listen to your lies! You just want attention! Get out of my face and go to bed or I'll spank you!" [5]

Determined to conquer my fears or at least slip past them, I stared at the lay-out of light switches along my path and developed a strategy. Before entering the hall, I turned its light on and raced to my bedroom to flip on the ceiling light. With eyes averted from where I knew the pale spirit was to manifest, I rushed back to the hall switch and slapped it down. Without hesitation, I pivoted to sprint back to my room and shut the door behind me. Once changed into pajamas, I folded down my covers, opened the door while staring at the floor, took a last glance at the layout of my room, flipped off the light, and blindly leaped into bed.

Although the doors remained open, I could not see my parents' doorway from my pillow, which comforted me. Since the feminine spirit had appeared nowhere else, I concluded that its jurisdiction ended outside of my parent's bedroom. With phase one complete, I temporarily relaxed my body, pulled the covers to my chin, and readied myself for phase two. [6]

The darkness that once limited itself to the corners of my California bedroom had followed me to Texas, bolder than ever, and reared its inky presence from the foot of my mattress. I wanted it to be a simple shadow that shifted with headlights, but I heard no engines or scratching gravel, nor was there an external light source being partially blocked. The absolute darkness contrasted against the natural darkness of the room and appeared to be some sort of animate abyss. It's daunting form closely resembled that of black smoke against a glass ceiling just feet above my face, spreading inchmeal to hover above my body. Terrified, I covered my damp face with the sweaty bedding. Sometimes, I peeked and the entity would be gone. Other times, its presence intensified and kept me hidden for what felt like hours. Usually, by the second glance, it had vanished. [7]

Living Hell

I nervously stood at the threshold of my bedroom to peer through my parents' open door and out their bedroom windows to await my father's arrival. As expected, the man pulled up to the mailbox and finished his commute back from a quickly attained civilian job, but I was afraid for him. My father had not been privy to all that occurred in his absence that day, so I stood watch as a credible witness for whatever was about to unfold. [1]

As the unsuspecting victim parked near the house, I wondered, "How can I warn him?"

Mirroring his pace across the porch, I snuck to the mouth of the hall and hid myself just around the corner. Our patriarch had stepped toward an unnerving scene that was brewing for over an hour.

Soaked in sweat and pacing the living room floor like a cinematic mental patient, the wild-eyed materfamilias unleashed a window-rattling ambush and roared, *"I want air conditioning in our bedroom, now!"* [2]

My father flinched, held up his hands in surrender, and tranquilly negotiated, "Calm yourself. Be patient. We're getting there. I'll buy one this weekend. I don't get paid until…" [3]

"Go buy one right now!" she interrupted, raging. *"I can't stand it anymore! If I don't get what I want today, I'm going to make your life a living hell!"* [4]

"What's new, Mom?!" I sarcastically interjected as I stepped into view from the hallway to distract her. "You've been making our lives a *living hell* for years! Why can't you just politely *ask* for air conditioning like a normal person?! Let the man breathe! He just got home! Besides, he's not the only one who has to deal with your yelling!" [5]

"Shut up!" the materfamilias snapped. "Who asked *you* anything?! I'm talking to your father! I don't care what you have to deal with! You're just a child! Get out of my face! Are you his wife?! No! *I'm* the wife! *I'm* the mother and I can talk however I want!" I bowed up and stood my ground as the materfamilias narrowed her eyes and growled, *"If you don't mind your own business, I'm going to do something to you…"* [6]

"Sandra! Stay out of this! Go to your room!" my irritated father abruptly ordered. [7]

Obeying *him*, I fled down the hall and shut my door to wrench on the floor and sob, convinced that the woman possessed untapped depths of fury and sociopathic capacity to kill him in broad daylight… over air conditioning. [8]

In pursuit of a ceasefire, my father drove away and promptly returned to set up a window AC unit for their bedroom. That weekend, he installed a miniature air duct system to run from my ceiling to the loft wall near my brother's bed that included two tiny registers and a switch for the fan. [9]

"Why did you choose to draw the air from my room?" I inquired. "Wouldn't it have been more effective to pull air from the *coolest* room, being *yours*? If you did, we could shut both our doors. I'd prefer to sweat in peace over hearing Mom's snoring."

"You don't have a say in this," the man replied as he pressed the vent into the popcorn ceiling. "Hand me the Phillip's head screwdriver."

I lifted the tool to his hand and queried, "Seriously, how do you even *sleep* next to that woman?"

My father smiled as he descended the stepladder and whispered, *"I try to fall asleep first."* I chuckled and shook my head. "Alright, that should do it. Let me go upstairs and do a test. Just remember to keep your door *open*."

As he exited, I boldly queried, "What about when you and Mom are *arguing*? Her screaming echoes down the hall and is *unbearable*. Can I close my door *then*? It would be easier to *stay out of it* if my door was shut." [10]

"*Keep your door open*," my father warned with a glare. "Don't make me tell you again." [11]

VHS

Included with the purchase of the log house was a massive television antenna that jetted up from beside the porch. Especially after a storm, the wind-blown aluminum required repositioning from the roof just to view a handful of local stations.

That television was her pacifier, a numbing agent that babysat the termagant until our patriarch pulled up. Without her choice of talk shows, I noticed an unspoken countdown. She boiled like a teapot and couldn't sit still until the pressure was released. To blow off steam, the materfamilias paced the house in search of a victim, namely *me*. [1]

In the spirit of self-preservation, I selected one of the materfamilias' favorite films and pleaded, "Is it okay if I watch this movie in the living room?" [2]

"*Fine*," the woman sighed and played the role of a selfless martyr. [3]

I feigned shock at her obvious façade and replied, "Really? Thanks." [4]

With the tape in the VCR, I rewound to the beginning and pressed play. During the film's introduction, the materfamilias dropped character and settled into her favorite sofa cushion with a large plastic cup of ice water. Before long, she blasted an abrupt, nerve rattling laugh and openly admitted, "I love this movie!"

The materfamilias informed me she already knew that cable television wouldn't be a part of life in rural Texas, so she hoarded stacks of VHS tapes to schlep across state lines. While the woman pouted and mourned the loss of her beloved cable television, she already possessed a wide assortment of blockbuster films that included hours of stand-up comedy, several music specials, and Saturday morning cartoons. As a bonus, most of the tapes fit double or triple features without commercials. Movies were a part of the plan the whole time. She just wasn't using them. [5]

The following afternoon, I waited for her last talk show to end and *requested* to watch another of her favorite movies. As the days passed, I performed an entertainment balancing act to keep the peace, occasionally inserting an action film that I craved. By re-watching those tapes, I memorized the lines of entire scenes and playfully quoted them to my sibling, who often did the same. Just like Wednesdays at the cinema, big-name stars provided our family a two-hour window of tranquility. [6]

Movie therapy only worked for a few weeks. The materfamilias grew bored with stability, reverted to her destructive idleness, and groped for reasons to be miserable. [7]

Stained

~~~~

While my father remained safely tucked away at work, the termagant paced over the living room rug and shouted, *"There's nothing out here! I'm going crazy! I feel like a lion in a cage! There's no movie theater! There's nowhere to shop! There's no noise! I hate this! Every day is monotonous! It's the same thing, over and over! I can't stand it!"*

I sat at the kitchen table to eat my sandwich quietly and tried to ignore her, but couldn't do it. "We live in the country," I coldly pointed out. "I didn't know what was going on, but no one surprised *you* with this scenario. You made a decision and knew *exactly* where you were moving. It was your idea to live in Texas to be closer to your family. Well, *we're closer now*. If you're bored, give them a call and invite them over." [1]

She lifted her hands and loudly admitted, "I don't want them coming to this *dump!*"

"Stop calling this place a dump, *especially* in front of Dad. You do that a lot. He's working hard to make everything nicer and you're not helping. It's no wonder your relationship is *shot to hell*. How can the man feel appreciated with you talking like that every day?" [2]

"*Keep it up,* little girl. Keep talking back and see what happens…" the villain warned.

I speedily finished my lunch and retreated to my room. [3]

Aunt-T called my parents to check on the well-being of our household and offered to help with home improvements. My father accepted and intended to make a day of it. The materfamilias even invited my eldest brother, sixteen years my elder and from our mother's first marriage, to join the family and stain as much dingy gray timber as he could.

That weekend, I heard the enchanting sound of vehicles pulling onto the property. Overwhelmed with excitement, I ran through the front doors and waited for each of them to exit their vehicles. Their welcoming presence was a fragrance of hope and selfless love that caused me to behave like a famished hummingbird surrounded by captivating perennials.

I rushed the termagant's sister and squealed, *"Aunt-T!"*

"Hello, *Sand-wah!*" the woman playfully greeted with a gentle embrace.

"Uncle-M!" I chirped as the traditionally stoic man grinned to pull me in close.

"Hey, sis!" my eldest brother called out just before I tackled him with my tiny body. "You give the best hugs, Sandra! Wow. I really miss those. *Hey!* Let me introduce you to

Stained

my fiancé. I've told her a lot about you and she's been wanting to meet you!" The woman seemed so genuine and kind that I tackled her, too, as she giggled and attempted to *out-squeeze* me.

"Come on in, guys!" I beckoned. "I'm so happy you're here! With everyone together, this should be fun!" They all laughed as they followed me onto the porch and through the front doors.

"Hey-hey!" my father warmly greeted as his adoring in-laws and stepson crowded at the threshold to receive a tight hug, one by one. "And who's this?!" he queried toward the fiancé. "Well, you get a hug, too! We'll use all the help we can get! Thank you for coming!"

"Do you have to hug *everybody*?!" the materfamilias prodded conspicuously in the presence of all. The man rolled his eyes and shook his head as her kin grew silent. [4]

"Mom, they drove *all the way here* and volunteered to work *for free!* They deserve… *a million hugs!*" I cheerfully corrected with my hands in the air. The small crowd quickly disregarded the termagant's words and erupted into laughter.

With paintbrushes in hand, the workers gathered around my father for a tutorial as the homeowner instructed, "Now, make sure you get enough stain on your brush to cover the wood, but try to avoid drips. When you apply it, your brush strokes should go *with* the grain of the wood, side to side, like *this*. Spread out and stain as high and low as you're comfortable going."

Being the youngest of the adults, the fiancé took on staining the lowest logs to spare the backs of her elders. Aunt-T comfortably focused on the logs just above them, being very petite. My eldest brother and uncle, standing much taller and armed with longer wingspans, stained lumber as high as they could reach. My father took charge of the more dangerous portions and climbed the extending ladder to cover the ceiling and vaulted region of the wall. [5]

While the others focused on a task that suited their abilities, the materfamilias prepared and arranged a spread for lunch. She finished rather quickly and idly lingered near the kitchen table to observe everyone. My father ran out of wood stain and carefully descended the extension ladder to refill his plastic bucket.

Void of discretion or tact, the materfamilias jealously growled to her husband, "Who does she think she is?! Look at her! She doesn't need to bend over like *that*, sticking her butt out!"

The unbuffered remark slacked my jaw. Without hesitation, I scanned the room and hoped that no one else heard her, especially my eldest brother's fiancé. Each adult continued to stare at their section of wall and stain-filled paintbrush.

"Leave her alone," the man warned as he casually poured brown liquid into his bucket.

The materfamilias continued, "*Okay... I get it.* I'm not stupid. I see what's going on here!" [6]

At a reasonable volume, my father angrily replied, "*Knock it off.* You're causing problems and being ridiculous. I'm tired of hearing it. Look around. Everyone's working except *you*. Find something to do or be quiet." [7]

Furious, I tiptoed toward the materfamilias and whispered, *"Keep your voice down. I heard you from way over there."*

My father changed the subject and cheerfully announced, "Okay, everybody! Good job! The stain is looking great. Stop where you are and let's take a break. Drinks are in the coolers, so let's eat and relax for a bit."

Uncle-M covertly motioned for me to meet him on the porch. I comprehended his subtle tactics and made my way outside while the others stayed behind to eat and keep the materfamilias distracted. As I sat on the replaced planks of treated wood, Uncle-M leaned against a nearby column and stared out.

"So, how have *you* been?" I queried upward.

"I'm more interested in how *you're* doing," he redirected with a warm grin.

With a sigh, I leaned toward the man and whispered, *"I'm doing much better now that all of you are here. I don't have any friends and Mom picks fights with Dad every day. It's hard. Plus, I'm not allowed to shut my door, so I have to hear everything they say. I'm sick of it. Then I get punished for getting in between them and telling Mom the truth. She says a lot of cuss words, but I'm not allowed to."*

Uncle-M struggled to keep a straight face and replied, "Maybe it's best for you to stay out of their fights. Your dad can handle himself." [8]

"Can he?" I tearfully wondered. *"Mom runs all over him and won't shut her mouth until I jump in. If I keep quiet, she keeps going and going... for hours. She's so loud. It's horrible. The woman is a walking nightmare. I hate her. She complains about everything. Dad can't seem to do anything right in her eyes and nothing I ever do is good enough, either. I feel so helpless."* [9]

"Well, you shouldn't concern yourself with their problems. They're adults and responsible for their own decisions. You're ten years old. You should be having fun and taking it easy. If they want to fight, let them fight," he counseled. [10]

"It's not that simple," I quietly rebutted. *"When Dad is at work, Mom comes for me. She goes crazy and has hurt me and Dad before. I'm worried she might kill him while I'm not watching. I can't just sit back and wait for bad things to happen. Forget that. If I don't stand up to her, no one will."* [11]

"I understand what you're saying, and it's important for you to know that *none of this is your fault*, nor can *you* fix it. Hang in there, kid," the man encouraged with a poker face as he kept watch and listened to me sniffle. "I'd hug you right now, but if your mother sees, she'll get suspicious and won't let your aunt and I come back. We know her better than you might think. Make sure you dry your eyes before going back inside to eat. I'll talk to your aunt and we'll see what we can do." [12]

"Okay, Uncle-M. Thanks for talking to me. I love you… a lot," I whispered as I dabbed my eyes with my shirt. *"You make me feel like a real person."* At that, my uncle stepped off of the porch and walked away to be alone. [13]

Despite the materfamilias' sabotaging behavior, Aunt-T, Uncle-M, my eldest brother, and his fiancé worked until dinner and lavished our once unkept-structure with a rich glow. Each helper was a recipient of a benevolent and jocose squeeze from my father before they departed. An intense pressure built up behind the tightly clamped jaw of the materfamilias. [14]

Although I waved and smiled as their vehicles pulled away, a crushing and insufferable weight rested on my chest as my lip ached to quiver. I returned to the freshly stained interior and braced myself for whatever was to come. [15]

The termagant aggressively approached my father and wailed, *"Were you planning on ******* her right in front of me, too! Why can't you give little hugs?! No, no, no! You have to give these big, long hugs! I'm not going to let some little **** take my place! I'm your wife! I deserve to be here! I put up with you being gone in the navy and raising these two brats by myself! I'm getting your retirement, not her!"* [16]

"Think what you want," my father replied as he retreated to the porch. [17]

When I turned to comfort him, the materfamilias growled, "You're just a *daddy's girl*. He doesn't need you pestering him! No one wants you up their ***! And how *dare* you talk back to me and correct me in front of everyone! Don't think I forgot that, *you little demon!* You wouldn't know any of them if it wasn't for *me*. And if I say something to your father, that's between *me and him!* You don't have to stick your nose into it!" [18]

I spun on my heels, faced the woman directly and boldly rebutted, "If you could keep your arguments and jealousy *private*, I wouldn't know about *any of it!* Dad hugged *a guest* who intends to be a part of this family! That *guest* stained your walls all day, even after hearing you make dirty accusations! What were you thinking?! I won't be surprised if they decide to never come back! *I wouldn't.* If that poor woman sticks around after everything you've said, she's worth keeping. I *like* my brother's fiancé, but I wouldn't wish a mother-in-law like *you* on anyone. I hope they *do* get married, just to show you that you can't dominate everyone's life. You just wait, lady. One day, I'll grow up and you'll *never* know if I've gotten married or have children. *You won't ever meet them.*" [19]

Dive-bombed

*J*ust before I took a much-needed shower, a desire to inspect my towel came over me for the first time in my life. Curled up in the absorbent material was a clingy scorpion that had crossed a very personal boundary. It didn't survive our brutal encounter, and I grew more alert than ever before.

During an evening movie, the screen's glow was the only light in the house when something prickly crawled across my hand.

"Whoa! What was that?! Everybody, get up! I think it was a scorpion!" I warned and popped upright to Sparta-kick the rapidly vacated sofa, violently sliding it back. "Where are you, you little punk?!"

The materfamilias flipped the ceiling light on and ordered, "Find it!"

Everyone in the living room urgently scanned every square inch of the furniture, cushions, and rug until it was located.

"*Where are you, you little* ****? *Move for me*," I growled. "Ha! I found you! You're dead!" I shoe-slapped the arachnid to a goopy pulp and returned the sofa to its original position.

"Good eye, Sandra!" the termagant cheered. [1]

Stinging tormentors scaled my brother's wall while he slumbered and dive-bombed from the ceiling onto his bedding. Stung in various places, including the armpit, the boy suffered through the heat and trained himself to sleep with a sheet over his face.

When our father renovated the bathroom, he intended to upgrade the old set up by installing a tub and shower combination with sliding glass doors. "Hey kids! Come here! I need your help with something and bring the dustpan with you!" the man loudly ordered. We abandoned our rooms and rushed to his side. "I'm going to lift this tub. Son, I need your help keeping it stable. Sandra, because you're the smallest, I need you to get the dustpan and sweep up anything that might be down there, so I don't trail junk behind me when I drag out the tub."

With the heavy item tilted off the concrete, I gasped and announced, "Dad! There's a scorpion down there! She's got a pile on her back, too. *That's weird.*"

"Sandra, we're holding up a cast iron tub!" my father reminded with irritation. "Just sweep it up! It's probably dead!"

"Okay..." I whimpered and touched the bristles to her body. "Oh no! She was carrying babies! They're going everywhere!"

The three of us scrambled and crushed as many underfoot as we could see before they crawled onto us or spread out to reproduce in the walls. Our Irish-dance extermination technique proved once more that *nothing* seemed to unify the members of our household quite like a common enemy. [2]

I peered around and queried, "Do you think we got most of them, Dad?"

"Nope," he replied as he navigated the cumbersome item out. "It looks like the scorpions won that round."

That night, the moon shone brightly as thunderous snores kept me awake. Even the screeching cicadas just outside my window failed to drown her out. Exasperated, I peered upward and noticed an unusually dark spot slowly traversing the popcorn ceiling. I shut my door and flipped on the light to discover another stinging intruder. I had prepared a glass jar for such an occasion. With a smirk, I stood on my chair and quietly collected the ruthless ninja *alive* as it clinked to the bottom.

"Enjoy your stay...and say hello to your little cousins for me when you see them," I quietly jeered as I agitated the contents. *"You won't be alone for long."* [3]

Die-hard

*A*fter returning from work, my father grabbed a chainsaw and granted the land an extreme face-lift around the house, which left my brother and me the chore of piling branches. On weekends, the man systematically tackled one task after another to remodel the entire house with instructions from a series of how-to books. [1]

Rather swiftly, the man demolished, reconstructed, and redirected an entire staircase to include a coat closet underneath with a light. With that being accomplished, he single-handedly installed a woodstove with a roof-penetrating ventilation stack. To pacify his wife, the man replaced portions of the rotten exterior and finally filled the gaps between each log. [2]

Guilt swallowed me over my complaints about the move, especially after listening to the termagant angrily verbalize much of what I had already thought. Since I found the woman detestable and lazy, I changed my tune and expressed appreciation for his efforts. In order to back up my change of heart, I attempted to improve my attitude toward the uncomfortable outdoor chore of dragging brush into burn piles. [3]

Occasionally, when the woman wasn't loudly accusing her husband of adultery, the materfamilias occupied herself with productivity. Since my father needed fence posts to build the exterior perimeter, the termagant sat down in a lawn chair with her favorite music playing to sip on an icy drink and strip bark from freshly cut juniper trunks.

"See?! I'm helping!" the materfamilias declared to me just after she assisted my father with the floor tile. "Look what I did! Doesn't it look nice!" [4]

I resisted rolling my eyes and quipped, "Why are *you* taking all the credit?! Dad did most of the work!"

"*She helped,*" my father firmly corrected.

After another rainstorm, the man remedied a reoccurring plumbing problem. Each time enough rain penetrated the topsoil, the ground became super-saturated and caused both toilets to overflow. Unable to afford rented machinery, my father clutched a pick-axe and thrust it deep into the topsoil and chalky caliche. He shattered rocks and removed them by hand to recreate a more efficient septic system. With a die-hard work ethic, he wielded the tool with brute force and tirelessly broke away chunks of earth, over and over. Battling the Texas heat and many bloody blisters for several weeks, the project was a tremendous success and inspired me to label him *unbreakable*. [5]

The extreme and elongated manual labor over the septic system had changed my father's entire physique. Blown away, I commented, "Dang, Dad! You're *ripped* and look ten years younger! That's awesome!"

My father leaned over with a smile and replied, "Well, having a desk job with the navy didn't do my gut any favors. This is actually how I'm *supposed* to look." [6]

Her husband's renewed appearance made the materfamilias leery of anyone who drove past the property. "Who's that?!" she questioned. "One of your *whores*?!" [7]

Logs

*B*efore my father started another day of home improvements, he directed my brother to continue the usual task of dragging brush to the burn piles. The man instructed *me* to shift my focus and gather oak logs from all around the recently cleared acreage to stack them neatly in proximity to the house.

To act in obedience, I walked outside, slid on my small work gloves, and quietly grumbled, "*I finally got my technique down with throwing branches onto burn piles. Now, I have to struggle again. This isn't fair. My brother is bigger and stronger than I am. Why does he get to do the easy stuff while I have to do the hard stuff? My arms are so weak. By the time I finish bringing over the first load of wood, I'll be exhausted! Branches go into nearby burn piles, but I have to keep going back and forth across the entire property with a heavy wheelbarrow. My life sucks.*" [1]

The sun seared the back of my neck and ears. Within moments, sweat beaded on my face and soaked through my long-sleeved work shirt. Some day prior, I had forgotten to use bug spray, which left chigger bites all over my wrists, ankles and waist, and itched terribly underneath my oversized hand-me-down pants. [2]

I hoisted up the two wooden handles and complained every step of the way. The empty steel violently rolled over knuckled roots, large sticks, and protruding stumps hidden behind the tall grass. I located logs strewn about the treacherous ground, and I carefully checked each one for terrifying surprises like centipedes, spiders or snakes, and tossed it into the barrow. Scorpions validated my paranoia about being stung each time they had crawled out from the bark and boasted their pinchers at me like a gang member ready to fight. [3]

When a tick crawled near me, I panicked and threw the log against a tree. Not many days had passed when such a creature had mercilessly latched on to my flesh. I was in the restroom when I discovered it, doing what it did best. Unwilling to show vulnerability to anyone in my household, I remained silent and nearly fainted, but removed the swollen parasite from my child-body with tweezers.

Determined to make as few trips as possible to the wood stack, I *repeatedly* overloaded the barrow and hit unseen stumbling blocks that toppled the logs and my entire being over sideways. My impatience flared with the rising heat. I balled up my fists while a string of vulgarities rumbled under my breath. On the verge of tears, I begrudgingly refilled the steel wheelbarrow, only to tumble a few feet closer.

While I struggled, my brother walked over and suggested, "Sandra, don't fill it up like that. You're not strong enough to carry a big load. Make it more manageable. Take *less* wood and make more trips. You're doing a lot more work than you need to. You'd probably be done by now, if you didn't keep falling over." [4]

His many acts of sabotage screamed in my mind as I shouted back, *"Shut up! Leave me alone! I don't need you to tell me how to do anything!"* [5]

Unaffected by my outburst, the boy brushed off the aggression and went back to whatever he was doing. Feet later, the solitary tire before me located another unforgiving root, brought the full barrow to an abrupt halt, and slammed my bony hip directly into the steel. I had refused to admit it verbally, but I knew that there had been wisdom in my brother's most recent words. [6]

If my ego and hip weren't bruised enough, my father eventually added, "You know, if you actually started working right when the sun came up, you'd probably be finished with your chores before noon. Sleeping-in forces you to work during the hottest time of day. Regardless of when you get out of bed, the work is *going* to get done. You're not getting out of it. I'm not going to raise lazy children. I was working the land with my father as early as I can remember. If I could do it, so can you." [7]

As the man walked away, I furrowed my brow, pulled up on the wooden handles, and pushed the full wheel barrow forward a few more feet… until I toppled over. [8]

Phone Calls

Defended by a rusty and dilapidated barbed wire fence, the acreage of trees that surrounded our home made any rural Texas neighbor seem not only distant, but non-existent. No other children were even *seen*, much less knocked on our front door to find playmates. Outside of select relatives, no other Texas resident knew I existed. [1]

The usual way of entertaining myself had become nothing more than a memory of obsolete skills. Our two-lane ranch road, which provided no shoulder or sidewalk for safely enjoying my bicycle, scooter, or rollerblades, rendered the items useless. Isolation in the lumber-clad cuckoo's nest was unbearable and took its toll on my mind to where a ringing phone brought me comfort. A call, even from telemarketers, reassured me we weren't forgotten.

The materfamilias would answer from the landline phone near the kitchen and shout who the call was for. Sometimes my father enjoyed the opportunity to speak with his beloved mother, one of his sisters, or a co-worker. Once the termagant placed the receiver in her husband's hand, she skulked to her bedroom, where I often followed and openly observed from their doorway. I stared and shook my head. The termagant scowled at me, sternly placing a finger to her lips to hush me unnecessarily. She gently lifted the bedroom receiver, covered it with her hand, and listened intently until her husband hung up.

Little did she know, we could easily detect when a third party had intruded on the conversation, as the sound quality would immediately diminish. Deluded and believing herself to be exceedingly clever, the materfamilias had ultimately fooled *no one* but herself. [2]

With a wife that eavesdropped, my father's responses to standard inquiries about his wellbeing became shallow and discreet. Right after he hung up, the termagant accused her husband of speaking *in code* and unleashed her unchecked paranoia and retribution upon him. However, when the hypocrite's siblings or childhood friend called, the materfamilias switched to her second language that the rest of us weren't fluent in. [3]

That summer, it was finally Nancy on the line who chirped, "Hello, Sandra! We have to talk quickly. Nothing has changed here, so don't waste time asking about me. *I'm fine.* How are you doing in *Texas*?" [4]

"It's very hot," I remarked, to avoid the question entirely. "Sometimes, it gets over one hundred degrees! Dad started cutting down a bunch of cedar branches and I have to drag them to the burn pile and throw them on top. Those piles get *really big*, so I'm learning how to throw them *really high*. Oh! *This* is cool. Dad installed a woodstove to keep the house warm in the winter. It's kind of like a fireplace, but not built into the walls. The smoke will go up through the long black pipe and out of a chimney! *I'm actually looking forward to that.* It's like camping, but better. Oh, dude! I don't have a problem eating anymore because of all this work! I eat a lot now!"

"Oh, wow!" Nancy encouraged. "You're learning how to be a country girl! I bet you're getting really strong! That's so cool! Are you having any fun out there?" [5]

"*Well,* if I'm not working outside, I stay in my room and listen to the radio or read my adventure books," I carefully answered, noticing that the termagant was no longer seated on the sofa. Suddenly, a wave of emotion crash over me with a sob. "I don't have any friends out here… and there isn't anyone to talk to at all. No one in the house listens to me. It's horrible. This is the saddest I've ever been. I love you and miss you a lot. You're my only friend." [6]

Nancy's voice constricted as she cleaved to positivity and tearfully replied, "I love and miss you, too. Keep your chin up, Sandra. Everything's gonna be okay." Nancy briefly shifted her attention away from the conversation, causing a sudden pause in her empathy. Exceedingly more rushed, she returned and relayed, "Oh… sorry, Sandra. My mom is telling me we've been on the phone too long. You'll have to call *me* next time so our families can share the long-distance bill. Don't forget to write. It's cheaper and we can say more. I love you so much. I have to go. Bye." [7]

The materfamilias stormed to where I was standing, violently spanked me without warning, and shouted, *"No one needs to know our business! No one wants to talk to you because you're just an ungrateful brat, you little demon! If you say anything like that again, the next time Nancy calls, I'll tell her you're busy and just hang up! Those calls are expensive! You're not making any phone calls to California! Are you paying the phone bills?! No! I allow you to talk on the phone and this is the thanks I get?! If you talk to anyone at all, it's because I let you! Remember that! I'll take everything away from you! Now, go to your room and stay there until I say you can come out!"* [8]

Letters

The materfamilias' irksome voice, erratic behavior, and poisonous speeches painfully burrowed through my soul like gnawing worms. So did her threats. I ruled out running to an unknown neighbor for protection and assumed they would simply notify the police, who might have separated me from my father, too. To dial a telephone without being noticed seemed impossible. Every sound traveled unhindered thanks to the mandatory *open-door* policy, and any unauthorized call would only put me in imminent danger. My aunt and uncle lived too far away to rescue me in an emergency, and any overheard call for help might have resulted in revoked access to them. I saw myself as a long-term hostage for the next eight years, unless I committed suicide to escape the tyrant's rage, paranoia, and violence. [1]

I didn't know my future, but radically accepted my imminent demise, either by my hand or the termagant's. In several movies, letters and diaries of the victims recorded brutal realities that police or attorneys used as evidence. Thanks to Mrs. Blossom and her author friend, I believed in details. Were I to keep a daily record of events, the contents would unearth times, dates, and incriminating stories about our depraved monocracy. The limits to the termagant's sadism were unfathomable, who had already ruthlessly concealed her crimes against me through attrition and gaslighting.

Because of her snooping villainy, I rejected the idea of hiding a diary in the house, thinking, "She'd eventually find it and kill me. Even if I were to survive her locating a tell-all diary, the woman would immediately destroy each page. There must be a better way." I therefore scripted a message to Nancy with brightly colored gel pens and a disguised outgoing envelope, covered in girlish stickers, to convince my captor that I delightfully heeded her warning and didn't breach security. The tactic worked. [2]

Dear Nancy,

Please keep this letter in a safe place as evidence in case something bad happens to me. I purposefully made everything appear cheerful as a disguise so that my mother would actually mail this. It would be good for you to do the same.

I don't know how much longer I can survive my situation. My mom was listening to our conversation on the other line. Immediately after our phone call, I was spanked very badly for talking about my feelings and was sent to my room. No one was supposed to know about all the bad things that happen in our house. [3]

My mom has no idea how much I've already told you, so let's keep it that way. If you ever call again, we'll need to be satisfied with hearing each other's voices and come up with some boring small talk. The truth will be in my letters. You may be the only person alive that knows about who my mom really is and what happens when no one else is watching. My aunt and uncle seem to have an idea, but I hardly see them. When I do, they're careful not to blow our cover, since my mom could be watching. Nothing is safe with her listening and I couldn't feel more alone. [4]

My parents still fight every day and it's getting worse, if that's possible to imagine. I'm forced to listen to every swear word that my mom screams. Since I can't avoid their shouting, I pay attention to everything being said. Dad told Mom that he makes just enough money to pay all our bills and save a little, but she won't stop spending and going over budget. That's nothing new. She keeps saying that she has to get out of the house or she'll go crazy. Well, she's been the mayor of Crazy Town for as long as I can remember! How crazy can she get?! [5]

The poor man works at his new civilian job all day and then comes home to a hateful woman. Dad just changes his clothes and runs the chainsaw outside until the sun goes down. He mostly comes inside the house to just shower, eat, and sleep, and I don't blame him. I really hate my mom. She's mean and loud, which is a bad combination. Mom keeps calling our house 'a dump' to his face and in front of guests, even though he's already fixed so much! She complains about the house that she CHOSE TO LIVE IN, accuses Dad of cheating on her as soon as he walks in the door, and is angry about how he stays outside to avoid her. I would do the exact same thing if I were him, but divorce would be better. If he's going to keep 'living in the doghouse', then he needs to build a really nice one so I can live there, too! Hahaha! I'd rather live in a cardboard box under a bridge than be around her. Maybe I can re-stack our oak logs and make a big wooden igloo in the yard! Hahaha! [6]

I'm sorry you have to hear all of this, but someone needs to know what's going on over here and I don't know what else to do. Thank you for not letting go of me. I won't let go of you either.

Say hello to the ocean for me. I hope you're having fun in the cool weather. I miss you and California more each day. After we graduate high school, if I can survive that long, I intend to see you both! Hahaha! I love you. Keep being awesome.

Your best friend,
Sandra

Nancy's letter caused me to pogo up and down. I ran to my room and opened the decorated envelope to discover a homemade friendship bracelet and a school portrait to help cheer me up. I tearfully squeezed the letter and its contents to my chest with a tearful smile.[7]

Dear Sandra,

I hope you like the jewelry I made for you! I didn't have any photos of us together, so I sent you a photo of me so you don't forget what I look like! Hahaha! If you can send me some photos of you, that would be great, not that I could forget what you look like. I just miss you a lot.[8]

I'm sorry that your mom is still being mean. Try not to worry. Remember that school will start soon and you'll be out of the house for most of the day. She can't get to you while you're there. Also, you'll make friends really fast, so you won't be alone anymore. You're awesome, so making friends will be easy for you! Hahaha! Just don't forget about me when you're popular![9]

I really miss roller blading with you and playing spy in your tree. I even get sad riding past your house on my bike. It's not the same without you. When you get really sad, do what I do. Just remember that, after we graduate high school, we will see each other again. Until that day, hopefully a miracle will happen and we can trade-off calling one another! If we can't talk for very long or about anything important, it's still better than nothing! Hahaha! Keep your chin up, Sandra. Everything will be okay. I love you. Write back soon![10]

Your best friend,
Nancy

Toothbrush

~~~

*A*unt-T and Uncle-M gifted our family with a puppy who resembled a polar bear cub, and proved to be as swift as he was mischievous. Bear often found ways over, under, or straight through the exterior fence to enjoy whatever freedoms he desired. [1]

Each day, a handful of vehicles slowly made their way down the rough caliche road that paralleled one full side of my parent's property. Addicted to adrenaline, Bear played a thrilling game of chase each time he saw those vehicles approaching. The agile dog zoomed forward at top speed and darted between their tires, perfectly unscathed each time. We soon acquired a larger puppy that was more loving than he was quick or bright and tromped behind Bear wherever he roamed. [2]

One afternoon, a stranger located my father by the sound of his running chainsaw to gain his attention while remaining on the other side of our fence. Bear suddenly found my father making his way toward the neighbor and ran ahead of him, wagging his tail vigorously. [3]

The man grievously stated, "I am so sorry to disturb you while you're working. We haven't met. I live just down the road and was almost to my driveway when two dogs started chasing my tires." He pointed. "*That* dog was one of them, but I rolled over the other one and he isn't looking good. He's right over there. Please, tell me this isn't your dog."

"It probably is. Let me see," my father affably replied. He calmly stepped to the nearest gate and over to his neighbor. As assumed, Bear's companion was on the road and took his last breath. "Yup, he's ours. Thank you for letting me know about it right away. I'll take it from here. Just know that none of this is your fault. I've been trying to stop the dogs from digging under the fence and escaping, but haven't been successful. They have a tendency to chase cars, so it was only a matter of time before one of them was going to get hit." [4]

"I'm so sorry about all of this. I love dogs, so this is really bothering me… *but I have an idea*," the neighbor offered. "*My* dog is about to have puppies, and I would feel much better if you had the first pick of the litter. This won't make up for what happened, but it might help ease your family's pain and my guilt."

"Well, thank you for the offer. It really isn't necessary. However, if it will make *you* feel better, we'll go ahead and pick out a puppy. Just let us know when they're weened and we'll take one off your hands," my father replied with a warm smile and a firm handshake.

When the time came, my father asked *me* to select a squatty puppy to take home. After stepping into their pin, I sat on the ground to observe their temperaments. Right away, a puppy broke away from the pack, scampered over, crawled into my lap, and fell asleep. The brown and white female bore a light tipped tail with a pink belly that fared low on the ground.

I rose to my feet with the tender creature cradled in my arms and announced, "This one, Daddy. She's special. She chose *me*." [5]

The following morning was sweltering, but Tippy failed to notice. She giddily raced back and forth in the yard, over and over. At once, as if hitting a wall, she abruptly stopped and whimpered.

"What's wrong, girl?" I queried as I lifted the puppy from the ground to snuggle her soft fur and kiss her head. To inspect the situation, I carried my friend to the stacked logs, set her down on the shaded dirt, and discovered crimson smeared on my hands. "Oh no, Tippy! Your belly's bleeding! You're too short to play in that dry grass. Now you're all cut up. You'll eventually grow, but for now, you need to play right here, where it's safer for you." Immediately, the puppy gadded toward the sharp grass and found herself in the same predicament. The puppy stopped and whimpered. "No, Tippy! Don't you remember! You just hurt your belly… but it's okay. I'll keep you safe." [6]

Shaking my head, I scooped the tiny canine into my arms to kiss her once more. Right then, the screen door slammed in the distance, followed by a familiar trod. The materfamilias stormed out of the house and screeched, *"Sandra!"*

*"Oh, ****,"* I whispered. *"Now what?"*

"Sandra!" the termagant howled. She quickly approached with sopping wet hair, soulless eyes, and a wretched scowl. All were distinct harbingers of a vicious beating. It was as though Satan himself approached and wore the depraved woman as a costume. [7]

I panicked and muttered, *"Oh, ****. She's coming. What the **** do I do? This better not be about Tippy."* I pressed the furry bundle to my chest and whispered, *"Don't worry, girl. I won't let her touch you."* [8]

Sadistically vacant, the demonic marionette stood right before me. I protectively cowered my body over Tippy and kept her wrapped in my arms as a human shield. The nefarious woman reached out, grabbed a handful of my hair at the scalp, and violently pressed my head farther down to knee-level. She had a devastating amount of control and kept me off-balance as I cried out in pain. [9]

"*Shut up,*" the materfamilias growled and awkwardly hesitated, as if unsure on how to proceed.

"Why are you doing this?!" I loudly moaned while I stared down at dead grass. To create room for Tippy, I forced my diaphragm up and inward to create a concave space between my torso and thighs. Near suffocation, I lowered my knees to the ground and breathed. "What did I do?! I don't understand what's happening! What's going on?!"

"*What did you do to my toothbrush, you little demon?!*" the villain accused with a despotic yank, and used my scalp to lift me to my feet. [10]

I squirmed with a wince to catch one more breath and aggressively queried, "What?! Your *toothbrush?!* What the hell are you even talking about?! I was out here, playing with Tippy! Don't you see that you're *obviously* wrong?! Stop and think!" [11]

The woman dominated me with her hair-filled fist, hoisted up my boney body, and growled, *"I'll show you what you did."* [12]

Forced back down and pulled in subjugation, I waddled forward with the puppy for approximately thirty yards. Once over the porch, I gently released Tippy to spare her from things far worse than sharp grass. [13]

The materfamilias used her free hand to throw the screen and front doors open. The woman yanked me through the threshold, swiftly maneuvered my body past the living room, and led my all but squatting body straight into the bathroom to be thrown down onto the damp tile floor. [14]

I breathed in deeply and loudly snapped, "What the hell is wrong with you, lady?! Are you ******* nuts?!" My head throbbed as I rubbed my scalp and peered down at my hand to check it for blood. [15]

"Explain to me why you stuck my toothbrush in the toilet!" the lunatic interrogated. [16]

My mind buzzed with sarcasm. With the floodgates open, I hoped to be murdered and that my death would lead directly to the termagant's incarceration. With boldness, I aggressively sneered upward from the bathmat and provoked, "Are you ******* *serious?!* You've got to be the dumbest ***** that ever lived! How could I have possibly done that?! I was outside! How the **** did I manage to stick your toothbrush in the toilet with you still in the bathroom?! The shower doors are clear glass, you ******* idiot! If you were in the shower this entire time, and I walked in to do something stupid like that, how could you not see me?! Does that make any sense to you?!" [17]

In the manner of a tattling child, the materfamilias accused, "My toothbrush is *wet…* and *you* stuck it in the toilet! Then, you peeled up the wallpaper! Look!" [18]

I palmed my face and marveled at her glaring ignorance. A radiating and merciless condescension filled me as I deduced, "Your hair is *wet*, isn't it? The walls are *wet*, aren't they? The mirror is *fogged up*... and so are the glass shower doors. In fact, even with the door open, it's still very humid in here. All evidence dictates that you have just taken *a hot shower* behind a *shut door*. Did you not?"

"Yes," the woman replied with a quizzical nod, surprised at my accuracy.

"If you would, allow me to educate you on... *the water cycle*," I arrogantly continued. "Hot water produces *steam*. Steam is a gas, also known as *water vapor*, that fills its container. In this particular instance, the container was *a bathroom*. Once the water vapor touched something cooler than itself, such as your toothbrush, it *condensed*. Condensation is when water vapor returns to a liquid state. Now, I remember when *you* had selected and installed this ugly wallpaper. *You* decided to skip the step of using *primer* because you were too lazy. Due to your own actions, water vapor easily became trapped *underneath* it and condensed. Each time you took a hot shower, the water molecules expanded into a gas and then cooled, over and over again, until they finally forced the paper from the wall. If you'll look closely, it isn't even torn."

Observing for herself, the woman murmured, *"Huh."*

"That being said, water vapor, *not toilet water*, condensed on your toothbrush to make it wet... wet like *everything else* in here. How could I stick *the toilet* in the toilet? *It's wet.* How could I stick *the sink* in the toilet? *It's wet.* How could I stick *the mirror* in the toilet? *It's wet, too.* In conclusion, you decided to drag me all the way from the woodpile... *by my hair...* because you poorly installed wall paper and are crazy enough to take a *hot* shower in one-hundred-degree heat."

The materfamilias blankly stared down from the threshold and blocked my only exit. I defiantly locked eyes with my oppressor and braced myself for homicidal tendencies. In complete contrast, as if a switch had been flipped, the termagant cocked her demented head toward her shoulder and eerily complimented, "You're so smart."

Without contrition, my assailant calmly walked away and plopped onto the sofa to watch television. Too stunned to stand on my feet, I stared at the drying tile in disbelief. [19]

"What the **** just happened?" I silently wondered. "Did I imagine that entire interaction? Am I losing my mind? Do crazy people know they're crazy? Is this real?" I rubbed my burning scalp. "That *was* real. It happened. Wow. I hate that stupid *****." [20]

Using the damp sink, I lifted myself from the floor and silently retreated to my room. When the adrenaline and shock receded, hot tears streamed down my burdened face. I concluded my father had dealt with enough, and kept the incident to myself. [21]

Post Holes

~~~

The barbed wire that looped around my parent's acreage had dilapidated and became worthless, being not much more than drooped wires sparingly tied to leaning T-posts. It was time to secure the perimeter. [1]

"Sandra, put your work gloves on and grab the shovels from the porch," my father ordered as he stepped outside that morning. I obeyed and caught up to him while he shouldered a stripped juniper post and steel tamping bar to the front of the property. "We'll take turns digging post holes." [2]

Daunted, I scanned the fourteen acres with a sigh and mentioned, "*Dang.* There's a lot of fence to replace. This'll take *forever*. Are you wanting to do all of it *today*?" [3]

"No," he answered. "We won't finish today, but we will do as much as we can each time we come out. There are machines that can expedite the process, but they're expensive. We're going to do it by hand. Besides that, you need to learn how to work. I know this seems overwhelming, but projects like this are finished like sandwiches… *one bite at a time*. First, we're going to snip all the wires and remove this rotten wood." [4]

The former sailor grabbed the brittle excuse for a corner post and manhandled it loose. Once he tossed the timber aside, he jabbed the post hole diggers into the earth to make the cavity wider and deeper. I observed as he forcefully spread the two handles apart, pinching the dirt and clay, and hoisted out the contents to create a pile at our feet.

"That looks kinda fun. Can I try?" I offered. The man had made the job look easy, but it wasn't. I felt pathetic as I struggled beside him with my bony arms and weak hands. [5]

My father took a sip of water from a canteen and coached, "You'll have to use all of your strength, Sandra. If it were easy, they wouldn't call it work."

That post needed to be set deep enough to stand against the pressures of taut barbed wire and wind. To cut into soil and clang against stubborn rocks was the hardest work I had done and forced me to use muscles never strengthened before. [6]

Vigorously wiggled, he removed the rusted t-posts to reset the distances and instructed, "Line up the new T-post with the rest of the fence. Make sure to hold it upright for me and keep it straight." He grabbed the cylindrical steel driver by both handles, slid it over the top of the T-post, and slammed it back down, over and over, to force the piercing metal tightly down into the land. "Try it," he gently commanded as he took another water break. [7]

I laboriously slid the cumbersome steel upward and released it. Although the apparatus was heavy to *me*, its dense weight and gravity's pull were not enough to overpower the unforgiving terrain and appeared to leave the T-post stuck at surface depth.

The grueling task felt impossible for me to conquer, so I paused my effort and reported, "Dad, this is super heavy... and I'm not as tall or strong as you are. Is this thing even going down? Me continuing to do this feels like a waste of time. I'm not actually *helping* you or making any progress." [8]

"Keep going. You can work while I talk," the man informed as I continued my awkward toil. "The driver *needs* to be heavy. That's what helps you *drive* down the T-post. I know it's hard for you to lift, but you'll get stronger. None of this is easy, but it's not impossible, either. It just takes *effort*. Not many people know how to stick to something until it's finished, especially when it becomes difficult. In my experience with people, I've witnessed co-workers and those I commanded mostly sit to watch the clock, expecting to receive a paycheck for just showing up. You're doing all of this work *without being paid*. After you get good at it, anything else you do will seem easy by comparison, *especially* if they're paying you to complete it." [9]

"Dad, it's not budging," I declared in my frustration. "What am I doing wrong?"

"With work like this, don't waste your energy by saving it. Bring that driver down as hard as you can. Just pay attention to what you're doing," my father guided. [10]

I drew in a deep breath, choked back tears, and conceded, *"Okay."* I fought past pain and exhaustion, and obeyed my father wholeheartedly to please him. [11]

"That was a good one. It went down. Do it again," he encouraged. "Perfect. Stop there. Let's break for lunch and then we'll dig the next post hole." [12]

I stretched to match my father's stride all the way back to the house and yearned to be as strong and useful as the man beside me. [13]

My arms tingled as I ate, which brought my father's words to mind. Each bite I took made the sandwich in my hands smaller until I fully consumed it. Full, hydrated, and rested, we stepped back into the heat. The man and I dug another post hole, dropped a juniper trunk inside, and poured dirt around its base. [14]

"Is this straight, Dad?" I inquired as I braced the post with my gloved hands.

He backed away to inspect and critiqued, "Tip it more to your left. Okay, *stop*. Keep it straight." I tensed my arms and body to steady the post as my father smashed down all the surrounding dirt with the tamping rod. To rest, the man ordered, "You try." I immediately learned there was no way I could complete the task with only my upper body, as my father did. My child-hands firmly gripped the heavy steel as I bent my knees. Using my legs, I lifted the tamping rod and thrust it downward. My hands left the bar too early, and it tapped my eyebrow to make it throb. The next time, I refused to let go and kept my head at a distance. Thankfully, dirt was far more agreeable to smash down than to remove. [15]

A neighbor from across the ranch road slowed down her vehicle, waved to us, and pulled into her driveway. As dinner time approached, we put the tools in the shed and returned to the house. All I wanted was a shower, a meal, and some music in bed, and it was just within reach.

Clean and with a full tummy, I bobbed my head to a quiet tune and suddenly heard my father's wife erupt. Her irksome voice echoed down the hall through my open door and pierced my skull as she shouted, "So, who were you waving at?! Don't think I didn't see you! I know what's going on here! You're ******* that old bag across the street, aren't you?! Look at me! I'm beautiful and she's all dried up! Is that what you want, some dried up old prune?!" [16]

Already livid, I stood to my feet, marched into the living room and interjected, "Stop picking fights with Dad! I was ******* there! I know what happened! The neighbor slowed down to pull into her driveway and waved to be nice! We've been working hard all day and I'm too tired to put up with your ****, so give it a rest, lady!" [17]

"Shut up! How dare you talk to me like that! You're just a kid! What do you know?! You just wait until your husband cheats on *you*. Then you'll understand," the woman foolishly declared. [18]

"*Really?* Show me some proof and I'll stop defending him. Since you've beaten *me* over things that never happened, I don't believe a **** thing you say," I caustically rebutted. "If you really want to shut me up, you'll just have to kill me because I really don't care anymore. Until that day comes, all you're doing is pissing me off and looking stupid in the process. Just so you know, I can't be cheated on if I never get married. Why the hell would I want a husband if I risk ending up with someone like you?! You make dying an old maid look better every day!" I turned to leave before my father could correct me, but paused and added, "If you're going to continue arguing, keep your voice down. I'm trying to relax. You aren't the only one in this house. You know?" [19]

If You're There

⸺

*A*s I threw brush onto a distant pile, I heard the circular saw squeal and relax, over and over, beside the house. Hungry, I broke for lunch to examine my father's latest building project on my way inside. I smirked as the distinct scent of freshly cut planks wafted past my nostrils. Construction offered an inviting aroma. I rounded the corner of the log house and came upon a relatively disturbing scene in our front yard. While she listened to music and sipped an icy drink in direct sunlight, the materfamilias perched her body on a lawn chair ten feet away from the saw and abrasively eyed my industrious father.

Sweat beaded and rolled down the woman's face, soaking through her altered t-shirt. As far back as I could remember, she had removed and hemmed every standard neck hole from such garments to expose her shoulders. She found the original design to be too *confining*.

"Mom, why are you sitting outside in the heat, acting weird?" I inquired, linked to the hope that if she heard descriptions of her odd behavior out loud, she would eventually recognize their absurdity and abandon them. [1]

The woman flung her hands into the air and informed, "I'm not gonna let your father be out here by himself! *Ha!* Who knows what he'd be doing if I wasn't here?! He'd probably be ******* the neighbor across the street!" [2]

"Wow. Mom, this is dumb. If you'll take notice, the house has lots of windows," I stated dryly. With a switched tone to that of a game-show announcer, I energetically continued, "Just think! You could be paranoid *and comfortable* by spying on him from your very own *air-conditioned room*!" I laughed and stepped onto the porch.

Before I could refresh myself, the termagant returned her attention to her husband and antagonized, "Hey! What are you doing?! That's not right!" The stoic man completely ignored the materfamilias and measured the next length to cut. "Are you…" she began, only to be interrupted by the abrupt squeal of his strategically timed saw. "Are you *listening* to me?!" the woman prodded, agitated by his consistent passivity. "Old man, are you deaf?! Hey! You're messing everything up!" [3]

Her irritated husband replied, "Do *you* want to finish this? Since you know so much, get off your butt and come do it yourself." With a backward step, he wiped away forehead sweat, removed his work gloves, and sipped water.

"Are you crazy?!" the woman protested. "I don't know how to do that! I'll cut my own head off if I run that thing!" [4]

"*Exactly!*" he exclaimed. "So, if you're going to sit there, then just sit there and *shut your friggin' mouth!* I'm sick of hearing it! You don't even know what you're talking about!"

Days later, the termagant spotted an obscure vehicle through the living room picture window. They slowed down near our driveway without turning or stopping and drove away.

"I see what's going on here!" the materfamilias roared, shattering the afternoon's blissful tranquility. My fully reclined father pretended to be asleep as she glared. "Why are your whores driving by this house?! Can't they just wait for you to go back to work?! Do they need to drive by our house, right in front of me?!" Badgering him for some time and getting no response, she got up and closed the gap. Sensing the shift in her proximity, my father brought down his footrest, stood up from his recliner and smoothly made his way outside. In a fit, his jealous wife followed him and shouted, "Are you going to meet her?! Was that some kind of signal?! I'm not stupid! I pay attention to everything! I'm not letting those ***** take my land and my house! If you think I'll let you run off with her, think again!" [5]

It was entirely possible that the driver was a nosey neighbor or some regular passerby that was simply in awe over the land's rapid and unexpected progress. Maybe it was the updated fence and entrance or the expedited beautification of the log house's exterior that so drastically captivated the individual's attention. Regardless of the driver's intent, the materfamilias' temper flared and ripped away what sliver of peace our household had tasted.

Nervous, I tracked my parents' outdoor movements. After I strolled down the hall, I leaned against their bedroom doorframe and watched through their windows as I often did. Even from the front yard, the woman's chronic mayhem thundered through the windows and exterior walls. A moment later, my father gave up on evading his wife, only to boomerang back through the threshold as she stomped in behind him.

The materfamilias' unyielding chaos snapped my father's lasting resolve to remain silent and provoked him to yawp, "*Shut your filthy mouth!* Don't you have anything better to do than pick, pick, pick?! You have the most disgusting mind! Everything you say is perverted! I'm not going to listen to it anymore!" [6]

"Or what?! What are you going to do?! Leave?! Go ahead! *Run to your whores!* Don't think for a second that I won't take this house, the kids, and all your money! That's *my* navy retirement! I'm not letting some other woman spend what I earned by raising these brats all by myself! Do you think you can just walk all over me and do whatever you want?! No way! You don't run things here! I do! You do what *I* say!" the woman vindictively boasted. [7]

Aghast and furious at her megalomaniacal threats, I stepped forward from the hallway and advocated, "If he leaves, I'm going with him… and don't *you* think for a second that he's alone in this! I'm a witness! I've been listening to every word and I'm willing to stand before a judge just to let everyone know how evil you *really* are! I'm not afraid of you!" [8]

"*Sandra, stay out of it!*" my father brutally corrected. [9]

Like a wiggling earthworm tossed over a fire ant bed, I futilely resisted an insatiable madness that sought to consume me alive. I despised my helplessness and winced at the familiar sting of betrayal. With nowhere else to go, I fled to my room and stared into the mirror above my dresser. Tear-filled eyes made me grimace and gnash my teeth at a burdensome wretch with no way out, a blindfolded and shoeless child, left to navigate an ever-changing maze of shattered glass. [10]

Acutely visceral anxiety throbbed within my skull and spine to swirl amid a torrent of suicidal desires. I imagined myself standing in the middle of the ranch road with my arms spread wide to absorb the impact of an approaching vehicle, but facts let the air out of my balloon. My father had recently mowed the tall grass along the shoulder, culverts, and ditches. As the scorching sun blazed my side of earth, there was nowhere to hide to complete the roadside ambush during daylight. I resolved to wait for the cover of night to execute my plan, which terrified me. Although I thought about it nearly every day of my life, I had never snuck out of the house before.

Intrusively, empathy pricked my heart and overwhelmed me with pity for the unfortunate soul behind the wheel who would never understand my dire situation or reasoning. Forced to bear a misappropriated sentence, the innocent driver would carry the immense weight of a child's untimely death, perhaps for the rest of their days.

Overtaken by a tsunami of desolation, I collapsed on my bedroom floor and struggled to breathe. Unexpectedly, a trusted image of the Messiah clearly emerged in my thoughts and stilled the once rolling tempest. [11]

Throughout my childhood, I had carefully pored over the various pictures inside of a collection of books in my room. One such image spread across the inside back cover of a children's storybook. The captivating painting portrayed an authoritative Messiah standing between a young girl and a fleeing Satan, which had deeply fascinated me.

Each time I had set my eyes on that scene, I calmed and sensed that He was *my* hero, and *I* was the young girl in need of rescue. [12]

That image conflicted with all I had seen or heard from my parents, which confused me. The tempest brewed again. Severe cruelty and neglect took its toll on my wounded heart as I sobbed on the floor with a clenched jaw while the termagant continued to shout in the distance.

Before we ever moved to California, I sat beside my parents during many Methodist sermons. My parents regularly relaxed and vacationed with a group of couples from the congregation who had children my age. In all that time, I had not witnessed *either* of my parents sincerely speak to the Messiah from a stance of genuine contrition. [13]

Instead, I recalled the termagant's infamously manipulative and conveniently selective tongue lashings that weaponized God and His commandments. [14]

When she hosted holiday dinners with relatives, the woman blathered her long and pretentious prayers that fueled multiple eye-rolls and sighs from underwhelmed guests who abhorred her glittering hypocrisy. That same individual, who relentlessly submerged me in physical, emotional, and spiritual abuse, had repeatedly claimed to love Jesus. As for my trusted father, he didn't speak of Him at all. [15]

No matter how much I pleaded, argued, or obeyed, I couldn't fix my family, and I couldn't stop the pain. Inspired by the vivid memory of His captivating image, I turned to the Messiah as a *last resort*. [16]

Already on my knees and with palms to the floor, I sobbed and desperately pleaded, "Jesus, I don't even know if You're real or would listen to someone like me. My Mom talks about You, but she's *a liar* and I don't know what to believe. If You're *really* all-powerful, then You'd better *show up*. I can't go on being sad and afraid every day. If You're *really* all-knowing and all-seeing, then You've been watching my parents this whole time and I refuse to be like them. There has to be more to this existence than clocking-in and out of life or being miserable. If that's all there is, then I choose *death*. Make my life worth living or just… *kill me*. If the same evil inside of my mother has been passed-on to me, then I refuse to have children. I'll only ruin *their* lives like she's ruining mine. *I won't do it*. You'd better step in, because I'm done living like this. I need Your help. Please… *help me*. Rescue me. Save me. Amen." [17]

SECTION 4

Golden Plates

*A*s I stirred, my prayer from the night before sat on the front of my mind. I stretched with a smile and sprung out of bed with great expectations, seeking to inspect the temperament of the materfamilias. I believed that *any* kindness from the termagant, especially after our last heated interaction, was indisputable evidence that the Messiah had heard my plea. [1]

My feet carefully transported my being into the living room. As to not interrupt her regularly scheduled programming, I silently joined the materfamilias to watch television. During the commercial break, a loving and peaceful family appeared on the screen, bathed in sunlight. The advertisement showed how well the children handled temptation. The mother held up a Book of Mormon and claimed that it helped their lives when they added its writings to that of the Bible.

I compared the idealized Mormon family to my own and silently wondered, "Is *this* my sign? Does Jesus want me to be *Mormon*?" Unsure, I turned and cleverly petitioned, "Mom, may I please I call that *toll-free* number to get a *free* Book of Mormon?" [2]

The termagant blankly stared at the screen and casually replied with a shrug, "*Sure.* I used to be Mormon when I was little."

I gasped. During my scramble to the landline, I blindly assumed the woman's permission to make a phone call was another sign from the Messiah. [3]

Just after lunch the following day, an unknown vehicle rolled into our driveway and captured the termagant's full attention. We rarely had visitors, especially the unexpected variety. Two youthful, neatly dressed, and clean-cut males stepped out of their car and towards our porch.

Confused, I asked the materfamilias, "Who are they?"

"I don't know, but I don't want to be bothered. They have nametags, so they must be Mormon missionaries. *You* called them yesterday and told them our address, so *you're* answering the door," she commanded, plopping back down in a huff. "If I knew they were going to send people, I *never* would've let you call them! I don't want to talk to them! Don't let them inside or I'll *spank* you!"

Those tidy strangers paved the way for me to answer the door for the first time. My mouth curled upward. That was my third sign. I waited for a firm knock on the latched screen door. With eagerness, I opened the interior door of wood and glass and bubbly greeted, "Hello!"

To reciprocate my enthusiasm, the young men introduced themselves and chirped, "Hello! This is Elder Joseph and I'm Elder Smith. What's *your* name?"

"My name is Sandra!" I divulged. "It's nice to meet you!" Unable to diminish my smile, I carefully read their nametags. "The Church of Jesus Christ of Latter-Day Saints? Oh. I'm so sorry. I was led to believe that you were Mormons."

"We *are* Mormons!" they giddily clarified. "LDS is the same thing!"

My brow furrowed as I wondered aloud, "LDS? *Oh! Latter-Day Saints!* Got it. Wow! You guys sure are fast! I just called and ordered a Book of Mormon *yesterday*. That's why you're here, isn't it? Did you bring my free copy with you?"

They glanced at one another and shrugged as Elder Smith admitted, "*That's very interesting*, but neither of us knew you called! We just happened to be in the area and decided to stop by! Wow! God sure works in mysterious ways!"

"So, you *don't* have my copy with you?" I sighed.

Reaching down into his black satchel, Elder Joseph added, "We don't have the copy you ordered, but I *do* have an extra copy that you can keep! Here you go." I unlatched the screen door to retrieve it and removed the last barrier between us. "Sandra, is your mother home?"

I peered over at the irritated materfamilias, who had plastered on her notoriously fake smile as they peered inside. Since they had already spotted her, I commented, "She's right there."

"May we come inside?" they pleaded.

Unwilling to seem like a religious heretic, the materfamilias caved under the slightest pressure and murmured, "*Okay*. Let me call my son to come down, too."

Elder Joseph was nineteen years of age and a few months into his two-year mission. Elder Smith was twenty-one and nearing the return to his family. I found their Mormon titles confusing and commented, "I think it's funny that you're called *elders*, when you're both so young." [4]

"You're right! That *is* funny! I've been Mormon my entire life and never really thought about it that way," Elder Joseph enthusiastically admitted. "I'm curious, Sandra. What prompted you to order a Book of Mormon?"

"Well, let's just say that I prayed and asked Jesus to do something *good* with my life," I carefully divulged. "The next morning, I saw the advertisement about the Book of Mormon and called."

He nodded and continued, "Do you feel or *believe* that our being here today is by divine appointment, meaning that Jesus made it happen?"

"Yeah!" I chirped with a grin as both missionaries chortled.

Elder Joseph turned to the materfamilias and inquired, "So, Sister Lawson, what made you feel so comfortable in allowing your daughter to make that phone call?"

Taken aback by the direct question, the termagant's face grew crimson before she timidly admitted, "Well, my mother always loved God and searched for a religion that she felt was closest to God, but I was still a little girl when she chose to be Mormon. She believes Mormonism is the *one true church* and always liked that Mormon's were polite and didn't drink alcohol." [5]

"Yes," Elder Joseph continued. "Both the Bible and the Book of Mormon states that we are to take care of our bodies. That's wonderful. The Church of Jesus Christ of Latter-Day Saints *is* the one true church. *She's right.* So, if you're not currently a member, what drew you away from the church?" The woman tightened her lips and shrugged. Elder Joseph allowed the question to hang in the air before he added, "That's okay, Mrs. Lawson. You don't have to answer." [6]

"Wow, Mrs. Lawson! So, your mother chose Mormonism and then your daughter followed in her footsteps. That's *beautiful*," Elder Smith commented. "That's a great transition for us to begin our lesson. Elder Joseph, would you like to pray over the lesson before we begin?"

"I would," Elder Joseph gently replied. "Father in Heaven, I am grateful to Thee for all of Thine blessings and for the gift of Thine Son, our Savior and Redeemer, Jesus Christ. I humbly come before Thee seeking for wisdom to teach Thine restored gospel, the Book of Mormon, according to Thine pleasure. We thank Thee for bringing us to this house and introducing us to Sandra and Sister Lawson. Bless them and keep them. Be with Elder Smith and I as we teach and discuss Thine ways. In the name of Jesus Christ. Amen."

Although the Old English distracted me, I smiled when Elder Joseph mentioned me by name in his prayer. Once the lesson from the Book of Mormon had ended, they conversed with the materfamilias and I.

My father's vehicle pulled into the driveway. Once inside, the man assessed the situation, politely greeted the two strangers who had commandeered his living room, left their presence, and quickly exited upstairs. The entire scenario was painfully odd after witnessing the indifference he had exhibited to our guests. I sensed that, although he had not asked them to leave, they weren't individuals my father sought to know or entertain. My hunch was confirmed after another hour, when the man refused to even go downstairs to find himself something to eat. [7]

Traditionally, evening meals were ready to consume by the time my father returned home from work. However, nothing of the sort had occurred since lunch. Delayed dinners were a tactic the materfamilias used out of protest to punish her household, which had yet to work. Her husband had culinary skills and was self-sufficient in the kitchen. With a shrug of his shoulders, he lit the stove and prepared a tasty meal from scratch. It was clear the man preferred to go hungry than risk a Mormon interaction.

"Why do Mormons teach from the Bible *and* the Book of Mormon?" I queried.

"Well, Sandra, Mormons believe that the Bible and the Book of Mormon are true and inspired by God, as well as *Doctrine and Covenants*, and *Pearl of Great Price*," Elder Joseph answered.

"What?!" I exclaimed. "There are even more books than the Bible and the Book of Mormon?!"

"*Yes*, but let's not get ahead of ourselves. If you would, allow me to answer your first question about why we teach from the Bible *and* the Book of Mormon. The Bible includes the Old and New Testament, right? Well, the Book of Mormon is simply *another* testament of Jesus Christ," Elder Joseph added. "After Jesus Christ was crucified, as the Bible states, He appeared to many people before ascending into heaven, which *proved* that He had resurrected or *rose from the dead*. However, what the Bible *doesn't* tell you is that Jesus Christ *also* appeared in the Americas." [8]

I gasped and questioned frantically, "What?! Jesus appeared to people in *America*?! If that's true, how do we know that He didn't appear physically in *other* countries, too?! What if He did?! Couldn't they have written their own books?! What if we're missing out on more information?!"

Elder Joseph sweetly chuckled and continued, "I'll tell you the *short* version of the story about how the Book of Mormon came to be. Maybe this will help clear things up. There was a seventeen-year-old boy named Joseph Smith, who was visited by the angel Moroni in a vision. That angel, who was *also* a former prophet, showed Joseph Smith where to dig for hidden scriptures that were inscribed onto secret golden plates." [9]

"Cool! Where were they discovered?!" I interrupted with a forward lean.

"They were buried somewhere in modern day New York state, but I can't recall the exact city right now. *I can look that up for you.* Since the writing on the golden tablets wasn't in English, the angel Moroni commissioned the prophet, Joseph Smith, to translate the golden tablets by the gift and power of God through the enclosed seeing stones or spectacles called Nephite Interpreters. However, Joseph Smith was ordered to not let anyone else see the golden tablets without divine permission. Those interpreted scriptures make up the Book of Mormon and revealed that Jesus Christ had appeared in the Americas shortly after His resurrection."[10]

"Wow. *Wait a second.* So, no one but *Joseph Smith* ever saw those golden plates?" I wondered aloud.

"Actually, eleven others saw the golden plates," Elder Joseph clarified. "They're called the Book of Mormon witnesses." [11]

"Oh! Nice!" I exclaimed. "So, did they help Joseph Smith interpret the golden plates?"

"No. Joseph Smith was the *only one* to interpret the golden plates," he admitted.

"*Huh.* So, what happened to the golden plates?" I inquired.

Elder Joseph patiently explained, "After the translation was complete, Joseph Smith returned the plates to the angel Moroni."

"*Oh.*" I scrunched my nose, cocked my head to the side and asked, "So, did anyone *else* see the angel Moroni… besides Joseph Smith?"

"Three of those witnesses *did* see the angel Moroni, known as *special witnesses*," Elder Joseph specified. "You see, Sandra, just like with the events of the Bible, believing the Book of Mormon takes *faith*." [12]

"*Ha!*" my father blasted from the loft as he maintained his gaze at the upstairs television. After a brief pause, the missionaries and I continued our conversation.

Desperate to escape tyrannical control, I inquired, "In the Mormon religion, can *girls* be missionaries, too, and do missionaries *earn* money while on their mission or does the church provide for everything? How does all of that work?"

The termagant chimed in and pejoratively corrected, "Sandra, haven't I taught you anything?! Don't ask about money! That's rude!" I ignored her hypocrisy. [13]

"No, Mrs. Lawson. *It's fine.* Sandra asks *very good questions* that I am happy to answer!" Elder Joseph overruled. "Mormon missionaries are usually male, but more females are going on missions now… and *encouraged* to do so. However, all LDS missionaries are *volunteers* and do not get paid. Missionaries are primarily funded through their own life-savings, starting from childhood. Sometimes they're helped by family members and are often blessed by the generosity of local branch or ward members." [14]

"So, are you *not allowed* to have a job while you're on your mission?" I probed further.

Elder Joseph paused for a moment and replied, "We *work* every day, but not for money. Our *job* is to teach people like you about God, which is what we're doing right now. Let's just say that, if our funds run out, our Heavenly Father provides for us in whatever way He sees fit."

My hunger pains steadily escalated in their intensity, but I refused to mention it. The termagant punished any unpermitted offers of hospitality and felt they put her *on the spot*. Since they had made no dinner preparations, *both* parents were withholding a meal from the uninvited guests. Perhaps the materfamilias believed the missionaries

Beyond Recognition

to be like seagulls. If we fed even one, an aggressively squawking multitude might chase us. [15]

The missionaries extended their lingering, making it increasingly awkward, as if they had received special training in guilt and attrition tactics for feeding. The encounter was a religiously inverted Mexican standoff, where the assuming missionaries patiently awaited a dinner invitation and the deceptive hostess refrained from an overt dismissal. Accustomed to regular mealtimes, my opinionated stomach betrayed me and growled loudly for immediate attention. The gastric symphony was too clear to ignore. [16]

Elder Smith stood to acquiesce defeat with a simple smile and mentioned, "Well, Sister Lawson, it's getting late and we'd better get going. I'm sorry we've kept you for so long. I'm sure your family is ready for dinner." The woman sheepishly offered a closed-lip smile, stood to her feet, and ushered the missionaries out the door. "Would it be alright if we visited you *next week* at around the same time?" [17]

Unwilling to be clear and honest about boundaries or her obsession with privacy, the materfamilias painfully conceded, *"Sure."* [18]

"Excellent! Thank you for having us, Mrs. Lawson," Elder Joseph pleasantly added. "Sandra, I'm really glad I met you. It's clear that you're *hungry* to learn about God, and that's a good thing." He chuckled to himself. "Keep thinking of questions to ask and we'll see you next week to answer them." [19]

Although Elder Joseph was nearly twice my age, I pined for him as he walked away. [20]

Filled with enthusiasm, I ran to my room and quietly prayed, "Jesus, thank You. I asked for You to help me and make something of my life… and You're doing it. I ordered a Book of Mormon and You added two new friends that love You! They didn't even know I had called! *You* set that up, didn't You?! I hope they come back. My mother was actually *nice* to me while they were here. *Please,* bring them back. Elder Joseph and Elder Smith let me talk and actually *listen* to what I'm saying. I like that. I want to learn all about You. Those guys answer my questions and make me feel like I actually *matter*. Please bless both of them and make a way for them to *keep* coming back. In the name of Jesus Christ, I pray. Amen."

Questions

~~~~~~~~~~~~~~

*C*urious why my father had lingered upstairs during the missionaries' extended visit, I waited for an appropriate time the following day and inquired, "Why don't you like Elder Joseph and Elder Smith? Is it because they're Mormon? They're *really* nice."

"I don't want anything to do with whatever *they* have to say. I was listening from upstairs. According to their own words, Mormons blindly believe a random man who claimed to have been visited by *some angel*… that told him to use some *contraption* to translate *secret golden plates*… that no one else saw except some *other* random people. That has got to be one of the most asinine fabrications I've ever heard! When you questioned what they said, they told you to *just have faith!* Joseph Smith was a con-man that made up a bunch of *garbage* to take people's money… and gullible people believed him without even stopping to think! You're doing the same thing! You can't believe everything people tell you, even if they seem *nice*. The Mormon religion is an obvious *scam*. You should stay away from it." [1]

Aghast, I exclaimed, "Dad, it takes faith to believe just about anything anyone says, even in history books, because neither one of us was there! You at least believe in Jesus and the Bible, don't you?"

"*I don't know,*" the man sheepishly mumbled as he shook his head in doubt. [2]

My eyes widened in awe as I rebutted, "Wow. Well, that's good to know. If you don't even believe in *Jesus*, then why should I believe what *you're* saying?" [3]

Elder Joseph and Elder Smith returned cheerful and bubbly, as though I had imagined the awkwardness of their dinnerless departure.

"Sandra," Elder Joseph chirped as I smiled. "You remind me *so much* of my little sister back home! Come here!" I stood up and approached him. As if I was experiencing some wonderful dream, the young man snatched me into his arms, flipped me sideways, and tickled my ribs and underarms to make me squeal in playful delight. I had precious few memories of being touched or enjoyed in that way and felt delighted in and affectionately cared for. Emotionally starved, whatever positive attention Elder Joseph had offered was enough to win my trust. Right then, he flipped me upward, bounced me on his knee, and lightheartedly mentioned, "Ouch! You're *so thin*, I can feel your bones on my leg!" He pinched both sides of my neck, pulled outward, and teased, "Look! It's an Ethiopian choking on a grain of rice!" [4]

The termagant and her son burst into hysterics as my wounded insecurities internally hemorrhaged. Unwilling to cause discomfort for Elder Joseph, I smiled silently through their sport until Elder Joseph and Elder Smith led the family through another prayer in Old English and taught more about the Book of Mormon, specifically the *additional* commandments and rules.

"Where in the Bible does it say that drinking caffeine is bad?" I inquired. [5]

"We believe the prophet Joseph Smith received revelation from God to follow a specific diet called *the law of health*," Elder Joseph calmly replied. [6]

"Oh, okay. So that *isn't* in the Bible. *Cool*. I like tea," I casually remarked. [7]

"Just so you know," Elder Joseph added, "tea turns your stomach into boot leather." [8]

"*Whoa! Really?!*" my brother exclaimed. "What's in tea, *exactly*, that turns your stomach to boot leather?" Stumped, the missionaries didn't respond. "I know alcohol is bad for your liver, but do Mormons believe that drinking *alcohol* will send you to hell?" [9]

"I have *another* question about today's lesson," I chimed and interrupted Elder Joseph's embarrassing hesitation. "*I'm confused*. So, if a person's already *dead* and didn't make the choice to accept Jesus while *alive*, why would God acknowledge *anyone's* baptism on that person's behalf? That doesn't make any sense to me. *If that actually works*, then what's the point in doing *anything* that Jesus says, if *someone else* could just get me out of hell later?" [10]

Elder Joseph inquired, "Isn't that good news for the dead? You could help the deceased gain full access to heaven. Don't you want *all* of your family and ancestors to be in heaven with you? Besides, you're wrong about something. Not just *anyone* can go through baptism for the deceased. It has to happen in a Mormon temple and there are *qualifications* that a person has to meet to even be *allowed* into the temple." [11]

"*What?!* Why are only *certain* people allowed into a Mormon temple? Even *I* know that Jesus loves *everybody*. So, since you believe Mormonism is the *one true church*, do you believe that all non-Mormons are going to *hell*?" [12]

"I'm not their judge," Elder Joseph gently replied, sidestepping the question. "Let's just say that following *the commandments* and *law of health*, as delivered through Joseph Smith, couldn't hurt anyone." [13]

"Yes, but you had even mentioned not being allowed to go swimming while on your mission, even if it's really hot! That's terrible!" I exclaimed. "Why are you not allowed to go swimming *while you're on your mission*, but allowed to swim before and after?"

Elder Joseph informed, "Satan has dominion over bodies of water, according to Doctrine and Covenants 61." [14]

"*What?!* If that is where Satan lives, is it dangerous to take *baths*?!" I fretted.

"No, Sandra. Satan lives in *large* bodies of water," Elder Joseph corrected.

Elder Smith added with a smile, "Don't worry, Sandra. You can still take baths."

"Well, I certainly hope so… but *you* two can't go swimming while on your mission! I mean, what's the cut-off size *for Satan*, anything smaller than a bathtub?!" I frantically queried as they chuckled. "It seems like the more I know about Mormonism… the more questions I have. This is confusing." [15]

"Well, you're not on your mission yet, so you don't have to worry about that right now," Elder Joseph sweetly dismissed.

Battlefield

~~~

Shortly after I first cried out to the Messiah, I suffered from vivid nightmares that were difficult to recover from once stirred.

"Fox One to Gray Wolf! Mayday, mayday! We're taking on suppressive fire! Requesting air support! Over!" the camouflaged officer shouted beside me. I hoped his communication with our command center was still operative as he rattled off our coordinates. Moments later, as the battlefield hummed with tanks and zinged with ricocheted bullets, a Huey approached in the distance. Command had answered. Growing larger as it drew near, our reinforcement's windy descent pushed against the palm trees and forced them to bow into submission. The chopping of powerful blades was a welcomed distraction from the screams and barrage of bombs that exploded all around. *"Lawson, move out!"* [1]

Adrenaline surged through my body. Obeying, I clutched my weapon and evacuated the mound of earth that had successfully shielded us. Without warning, an explosion blasted me forward and slammed my body to the ground as my ears rung with a swirling equilibrium that kept me stationary. I pulled my face from the dirt and glanced back at my trusted captain, who lay dead beside our former haven. Artillery mowed down troops all around me as I low crawled through casualties toward hope in the form of a helicopter. [2]

I woke up panting under sweaty sheets, already exhausted, and readied myself for the day, wondering where those images had come from and why they had arrived. [3]

After another grueling day of work and more of the materfamilias' cruelty, I avoided the pale spirit at my parent's doorway and hid from the looming darkness until I fell asleep.

I hiked alone in a desert wilderness, and peered over the crumbling edge of a deep canyon, vast and glorious to behold. My grueling voyage, if nothing else, was worth the ocular feast of brilliant splendor that greeted me as I peered over the edge of the deep canyon, carved out long before my arrival. Drawn to linger, I recalled the truth. The trail did not end where I stood. The journey was longer still. [4]

My canteen touched my cracking lips once more. Lukewarm water revived me as I wiped the sweat from my brow and cinched up the stocked pack that burdened my shoulders with vital essentials. I peered downward, convinced to adjust my socks, and sprung upward with a satisfying grunt to stretch my hips. It was then that movement caught my eye. Through binoculars, a creature was spotted barreling towards me, rapidly covering a great distance with supernatural speed. I had never witnessed a beast progress with such single-mindedness and drive. [5]

A Caucasian Shepherd, whose thick coat matched the trail of waking dust that followed behind as it charged, closed the gap between us with eyes fixed upon mine. I abandoned the urge to flee. The predator's enduring pace was far swifter than my best sprint could hope to be. Tarrying meant one of two options: submit to fear and embrace a brutal death or resist a seemingly inexorable adversary with my bare hands. I grit my teeth and widened my stance with fists set in defiant readiness. The beast would know opposition, come what may. [6]

The vicious projectile snarled and lunged, only to be struck with a mighty right hook that rendered his airborne spin. Four massive paws stuck their landing with a scraping slide. The beast launched another assault, only to be sidestepped like a raging bull against a seasoned matador. Gripping some thick scruff as it passed, I spun the carnivore outward and tossed its furry mass onto the unforgiving ground with a thud. It scrambled upright and leaped, pressing two oversized paws onto my chest that drove me backward and off the cliff's edge. Weightless, I observed the canyon walls as they blurred past. The once-open sky slimmed down, beset by rock and dust. The backpack broke my landing with a thump. Coherent and alive, I was stunned to discover the beast's body draped lifelessly over mine. [7]

I opened my eyes to feel my head cradled by a familiar pillow. It was another dream. As I lay wide awake, I could still sense the dense weight and thick coat of the creature on my chest and skin for over a minute before it dissipated upon my movement.

With daily tasks completed, the materfamilias' wrath echoed down the hall that evening as I remained in my room. I evaded the pale spirit and endured the darkness another time before sleep found my eyes.

As I exited my bedroom, I discovered the bodies of my brother, father, and the materfamilias gunned down on our tile floor. The red dot of a sniper's laser tracked me from outside through a window and centered its glow on my chest. To avoid my family's gory fate, I dove to crawl for cover behind the living room furniture as stuffing burst through the back of the sofa. [8]

My eyes shot open as I gasped for air and ripped off my sweaty sheets before searching for signs of life that morning. I peeked around the wall near the woodstove

Beyond Recognition

and observed the woman as she casually sprawled over the very sofa that had been destroyed a moment prior. It was another dream.

I filled the wheelbarrow and stacked all the logs before I witnessed yet another domestic feud. I consciously looked away from the pale spirit, only to be confronted by the menacing darkness. Once in solitude, my eyes finally gave way to slumber.

Several men donning fashionable hats and designer suits each possessed a tommy gun in one hand and a briefcase in the other. I covertly monitored from behind cover and watched as they exited an exemplary estate to walk across the courtyard and enter a classic luxury vehicle donning stylish whitewall tires. Suddenly, I appeared face-down underneath their vehicle, and listened to their diabolical plans of chaos and destruction for profit. Assuming that the mission was to be carried out immediately, I fully expected the members of the violent syndicate to vacate the premises, yet the running vehicle that cloaked my body remained stationary. [9]

In a precarious location, I endeavored to scoot out and slip away unnoticed. With my back exposed, the cold barrel of a weapon met my crown, followed by a merciless pull of a trigger. Crimson poured down and blanketed my entire view, accompanied by two words in bold print: GAME OVER. [10]

Of the multifarious nightmares I had endured, that experience was unique, being the only to end in my demise… while subtly offering solace to someone familiar with gaming. Players had the potential to *respawn*. [11]

The Holy Ghost

Elder Joseph and Elder Smith taught a lesson from the Book of Mormon about the need for baptism, even adding some Bible scriptures to back up their points. As I read along from my Bible, I saw the words myself, and knew that baptism was a *must*. Even my brother expressed an openness to the experience. [1]

"Sister Lawson, since you were Mormon as a child, is it safe to assume that you're baptized?" Elder Joseph asked.

"Yes, I am. I've *always* loved Jesus," the materfamilias proudly replied, piously folding her hands to peer upward as if posing for a medieval portrait of sainthood. [2]

"*Excellent*," Elder Joseph remarked. "So, Sister Lawson, already knowing how vital it is for salvation, do you have any objections to bringing your children to the local ward this Sunday in order for them to become baptized as well?" [3]

Aware of how acutely the materfamilias abhorred *any* inconvenience, her stunned face was *priceless*. They exploited her self-righteousness. Declining such an invitation would irrevocably reveal her warped beliefs, interchangeable convictions, and distorted priorities to all present parties. To avoid exposure, the materfamilias went along with the narrative, and allowed us to be scheduled for baptism. [4]

Upon entering the ward for the first time, someone handed a bright white baptismal jumpsuit to me. They instructed me to remove all of my clothes in private, and come out wearing *only* the provided white garments. As I scurried toward the ladies' room, unspoken doubts screamed within me. I silently fretted, "I won't have anything on under this. That means *no underwear*. Doesn't white material become *see-through* when wet? This is uncomfortable. It feels weird." Right then, I stopped myself and concluded, "*Of course* it feels weird, Sandra! Satan doesn't want you to get baptized!" I cocked my head back and whispered into the air, "Ha-ha, *loser!* I'm doing it!" [5]

With convincing, my father begrudgingly attended the ceremony and joined the materfamilias beside several gathered ward members.

Elder Smith and their bishop stood beside Elder Joseph, who queried, "Sandra, since you were the one that we first spoke to, we think it's fair that you should have the first choice of who baptizes you."

I learned that Elder Smith had attended *many* baptisms, but had yet to submerge anyone *himself*. Although I pined for Elder Joseph, my competitive nature overruled adoration.

Desiring to be *first*, I answered, "Since Elder Smith hasn't baptized anyone before, I choose *him*."

Elder Smith seemed pleasantly surprised and chirped, "Oh, *me?!* Thank you! Wow!" As a result, my brother, who had expressed favor toward Elder Smith from the beginning of our lessons, politely chose Elder Joseph instead and stood with our parents to wait.

Before the baptisms began, I noticed Elder Joseph standing alone.

Wearing only the white jumpsuit, I walked barefoot over to the white-clad young man and whispered, *"I wanted to choose you, but Elder Smith hasn't baptized anyone yet."*

Elder Joseph smiled and softly replied, *"You should have followed your heart."* [6]

I stepped away troubled and heavy with guilt, but refused to inform Elder Smith that I had second-guessed my selection. [7]

We stepped into the heated baptismal water together where Elder Smith prayed in Old English and finally announced, "Sandra Lawson, having been commissioned of Jesus Christ, I baptize you in the name of the Father, the Son, and the Holy Ghost. Amen." After being completely submerged backwards and raised forward to the surface, I grinned at the soggy missionary and caused him to crack a smile. Gently placing his hands on my head, he continued, "Sandra Lawson, you are now a confirmed member of the Church and will receive the gift of the Holy Ghost. This ordinance is performed by the authority of the Melchizedek Priesthood. *Receive the Holy Ghost.*" [8]

After briefly waiting in silence, I felt confusing tension and whispered, *"So, when do I get the Holy Ghost?"* [9]

Elder Smith struggled to keep a straight face and softly informed, *"It happens automatically."*

"Oh, nice. Okay," I softy replied. As we lingered in the water, I lifted my chin and hoped to feel a shift in my surroundings or some sort of glow to occur. Remembering the baptism lesson, I fully expected a beam of light to shine down on me or a voice to speak from heaven, but nothing seemed to change. Disappointed by the standard lighting and the silence of our aquatic setting, I pursed my lips and plainly stated, "Elder Smith, something went *wrong*. I'm not sure I received the Holy Ghost. I don't feel anything." With a glance toward the onlookers, I quipped, "Sorry, guys. I got nothing." [10]

Unable to maintain their faces of chiseled stone, several ward members covered their mouths to chuckle or hid behind their spouses to collect themselves.

Elder Smith grinned at me and whispered, *"That's okay, Sandra. I'm going to pray now."*

"Oh. Wow. I'm sorry," I murmured as more smiles and endearing giggles broke out. *"I'm holding you up. I'll be quiet."*

Elder Smith abandoned his serious demeanor and concluded, "May God bless you. May His promised peace be with you now and always in the name of Jesus Christ, our Savior and Redeemer and our Advocate with the Father. Amen." [11]

With the ceremony being completed, ward members passed compliments to my parents about my quirky personality as the missionary and I finally exited the water.

Obedience

~~~~

The Young Women President of the LDS ward graciously invited me to join the girls for an outing at a local lake. It was odd. The missionaries refrained from entering large bodies of water because they believed in Satan's dominion over them. Certain that they wouldn't subject young girls to such a threat, I assumed we would hike around in the scorching heat and enjoy a view of the lake among the wide selection of stinging bugs. [1]

"Wow! You're inviting me?! Sweet! I'll have to convince my mom to let me go, but I'd *love* to come with you guys," I chirped, preferring to bake outdoors than remain with the materfamilias.

"Great! Now, don't forget to bring your bathing suit and a towel," she casually added.

"Really?" I inquired with a scrunched nose. "You guys are going swimming?"

"Yes," the woman clarified. "It will be fun! Do you know how to swim?"

Ignoring the hypocrisy of LDS beliefs, I chirped, "I sure can! Even if I'm not allowed to go, thank you for inviting me."

Although there was a high probability of my attendance being denied, I deemed the situation worthy of the risk. I waited for the most opportune moment, beseeched permission from the materfamilias, and actually attained it. Shocked, I backed away from her and celebrated quietly in my room. As a resident of the Lone Star State, a swim with LDS Young Women would be the first time the materfamilias had permitted me to go anywhere without her. [2]

I waited by the lake in my bathing suit and observed as the other children rushed in to frolic and aggressively splash one another in the face. I preferred to swim in solitude to avoid their tumult and hoped the LDS girls would calm down or exit the water. Their youthful stamina proved disappointing as they continued to disturb what could have been a tranquil setting. Time slipped past me as perspiration trailed down my face and spine. The inviting water glistened in the sunlight. It prevailed against my sweaty abstinence and convinced me to relent. Although quite turbid from the playful thrashing, the water was cool and invigorating.

Obedience

A handful of minutes had passed when the ward's Young Women President quickly stood to her feet and announced, "Okay, ladies! Everyone out of the water, please!"

My mind buzzed with indignation as I thought, "What?! She should have stopped me before I got all wet, if she knew we were just going to turn around and leave!"

Unwilling to comply, I paddled quietly and hoped she would forget about me.

"*Sandra*, get out of the water, please," the woman repeated from the water's edge.

I sighed and pleaded, "Five more minutes? *Please*. I just got in." [3]

Speaking with authority, she firmly ordered, "Sandra, I need you to be obedient and get out of the water, *immediately*." [4]

"*Yes, ma'am*," I mumbled, sobered by the sudden change of tone and worried that I might have irritated the woman who had shown me such kindness.

I swam to the shore, climbed out of the lake, and fearfully approached the woman. I was mistaken. Her expression radiated love, not irritation, as she met me with my towel. Just then, her gentle hands squeezed my shoulders and turned my body to face the water. [5]

The woman quietly ordered, *"Look."*

"What am I looking for?" I whispered back, squinting.

After putting on my glasses, I gasped. Laterally undulating across the small inlet, right where we were swimming, were three stealthy water moccasins, known for their painfully venomous and deadly bites. [6]

"Sometimes, others have a clearer view of your situation than you do. So, it's important to be obedient right away. If I had told you that there were snakes behind you, you might have panicked and gotten bitten. I realize that you hardly swam and I'm sorry about that. I'm just glad that you *did* listen in time to escape. You're safe, now." [7]

Reinvent Yourself

At long last, summer captivity marched toward a swift close and signified the beginning of middle school and the fifth grade. I reminisced about Nancy, Nam, Josh, Mrs. Blossom, and my beloved classmates from the GATE program, and hoped that my positive experiences in California wouldn't contrast too greatly with a rural Texas school district. [1]

"I already picked out what you're wearing tomorrow for your first day," the materfamilias announced as she placed new clothing on my bed. Everything she displayed starkly represented her atrocious fashion sense. I abhorred my ridiculous wardrobe, but remained quiet. Anytime I offered any negative input about her tacky purchases for me, I received no clothing at all. My face betrayed my silence and revealed intense disapproval. "*I* buy your clothes and you'll wear what *I* tell you to wear! I don't want to hear anything about it! Look at you and that ugly ponytail! Find something to do with that hair of yours! You look like a *scarecrow*. I try to make you look nice, but I don't know what to do with you! You're so *thin*. You look like a *skeleton*." [2]

After the materfamilias vacated my bedroom, I stared at the mirror and noted my large glasses, gaunt face, protruding collarbones, boney shoulders and scrawny... *everything*. Tears filled my eyes as I observed my regrettable features in the mirror. Long and perfectly straight brunette hair pulled back into the abhorred ponytail only emphasized them. [3]

A repeated concept from children's programming flooded into my mind as I whispered, "Tomorrow, I will just be *myself*. I can't be anyone else but *me*. I'm smart. I'm funny. I'm brave. I'm a good friend and I'm a good student. I've even won awards. My teachers and classmates loved me. If *these* kids don't like me, then *they're* the ones missing out. Sandra, *just be yourself*. Be yourself. Be yourself." [4]

With wiped away tears, I took a deep breath and stepped into the hallway for lunch.

My father intercepted me before I entered the living room and explained, "When I was a kid, my dad would work somewhere until he got mad and quit. Instead of making things right or paying off his debts, he would simply uproot the entire family and move far away to work at another farm where no one knew him. Moving became expected.

I chose to save myself the grief and didn't bother making any friends. There wasn't a point in getting attached to anyone, since we moved every few months. When I was old enough, I joined the navy and focused on my work… and there wasn't any point in making friends there either." [5]

"Wow. I'm sorry, Dad. That's messed up. You must have been a lonely kid," I empathized, tearing up again. "So, you've *never* had a friend?" [6]

"My point is…" the man continued as he brushed off my words, "I know what it's like to be *the new kid*. Tomorrow, stepping foot into a new school and seeing new faces might be overwhelming, but it won't last long. I want to plant roots here and don't intend to move us again. Now, small towns aren't like the city where no one knows you. Here, everyone already knows everyone else. You're an outsider. Whatever impression you make… whatever you say and do… will follow you until you graduate high school. You're stuck with these people, so be on your best behavior. Think of this as an opportunity for a fresh start. No one knows anything about you. You can *reinvent yourself* and be anyone you want to be."

Confused and somewhat deflated, I politely responded, "Thanks, Dad." [7]

Although my father may have intended to offer understanding and wisdom, his words introduced anxieties that had yet to be considered. I ate a sandwich and wondered what portion he hoped I would *reinvent*. If I could change my appearance, I would have done it already. As for my personality, it took me ten years to grow into the person I already was. If I was to change *anything*, I would try not to fight. [8]

"Tomorrow, you both will start riding a bus to school and back," the materfamilias announced coldly to my brother and me as if we were inmates on parole. "If you're late for the bus, *it will leave you*, so you'll need to be ready and stand at the end of the driveway *before* the bus gets there. *You're not babies.* Don't force me to take you to school or pick you up. If you miss the bus because you're not being responsible, *I'm going to spank you.* You're not stupid. Catching the bus isn't that hard." [9]

Even with her cruel delivery, the news was quite *good*. Riding the school bus meant a welcomed and consistent escape from life's pressures, even if for only a few minutes each way. After all I had endured, *any* experiences at school had to be better than spending my days with the termagant. Even if the students or teachers were to be mean, the pain would at least be originating from *strangers* and not from those of my household. I didn't know what to expect, but I was excited to venture across the scholastic tundra of the unknown. [10]

Short-alls

⁓

The materfamilias flipped on my bedroom light to stir me from sleep and abrasively ordered, "Get up!" [1]

My eyes burned as I quietly groaned, *"Stop yelling."*

Once bathed, I carefully combed my brunette strands until they were air dried, sleek, and straight. Without protest or grimace, I donned the outfit my mother had pre-selected, which included a ribbon that matched my socks.

While my brother and I exited the house *on time* to wait for the school bus, the materfamilias warned, "Sandra, don't embarrass me." [2]

Her words were as comforting as ice water to the face in winter. Each step toward the mouth of our driveway closed the gap between me and freedom. More than motivated to flee the premises, I impatiently waited for my yellow chariot to crest the hill. [3]

The getaway vehicle emerged and boasted air brakes that hissed and squeaked, stopping the monstrosity before us. Our driver folded open the door with the pull of a lever, which captivated me. I felt like a film star with my very own chauffeur.

"Wow," I marveled. Running my fingertips over the faux leather seats, I embraced every detail of the experience before selecting a padded bench near the front. I searched the seat and pondered, "What? No seatbelts in a vehicle made for *children*? That's odd."

The driver's massive rearview mirror revealed movement and drew my attention to the rear seats without the need to move my body.

A spritely girl with large blue eyes and a bouncing blonde ponytail speedily walked forward, plopped down beside me, and greeted, "Hi! I see that you're new. We know *everybody* around here and I've never seen you before. See the bus driver up front? Well, I'm her granddaughter. What's your name? Where are you from?" I cheerfully answered each question and found comfort in her enthusiastic curiosity. [4]

We pulled up next to the school and entered a line of busses. I carefully stepped down to exit and noticed the building labels read Band Hall and Elementary. A handful of older children separated from the younger children to cross a small parking lot. Since I was no longer in elementary, I chose not to follow the flowing stampede of younger children. Instead, I located the woman who had been herding the youth and pleaded, "I'm a new fifth-grade student and have no idea where I'm supposed to go. Will you please help me? I don't see a building labeled Middle School."

Several inconvenienced staff members begrudgingly discovered my assigned classroom using terms such as homeroom, or A-day and B-day. I became a source of stress for the surrounding women who held back none of their frustration while they flipped through paperwork. As irritated as they were at my ignorance, they dispensed kindness towards familiar faces that strolled past the large windows that allowed a view of the hall. Elementary students bore strange expressions of disgust when they noticed me standing near the office counter, as though I were a space alien making first contact. [5]

Office staff spoke down to a man in spectacles and placed me in his care as they growled specifics at him about where to guide me. He humbly brushed off their foul manners, as if immune to their spikey tone. [6]

While we strolled together, he graciously broke the ice, and stated, "It's hard being new. I'm Mr. Alden. What's your name?"

"My name is *Sandra*," I confidently answered. "It's a pleasure to meet you, Mr. Alden, and thank you for taking the time to help me. I'm sure you have far better things to do."

After a brief chuckle, he warmly replied, "Oh. I don't know about that. I'm actually the janitor, but I'm glad I could help you. I'm not important like a teacher." [7]

"You're helping a child find their way! That sounds pretty important to *me*," I added, peering upward at him to enjoy the pleasant contrast between his coffee brown skin and graying curly hair. [8]

"I suppose you're right," Mr. Alden sweetly conceded. "I stand corrected."

As we navigated the hallways, I inquired, "How does middle school work and what's a homeroom? I don't understand. My parents didn't explain any of this to me. I'm poorly informed."

"Well, in middle school, you won't have just one classroom or teacher throughout the day anymore," the man answered gently. "You'll move around from class to class."

In my irritated heart, I blamed the materfamilias and wondered what important meeting the woman had neglected to attend or what enrollment paperwork she ignored that resulted in such a first-day twist. We exited the air-conditioned hall as heat pressed against my face from the humid, open-air walkway. Had I been alone, I would have never checked outside.

Contemplating my situation, I shook my head and silently pondered, "That was a maze. How am I supposed to remember the way back to the bus if I'm switching classes?"

Noticing my furrowed brow and burdened face, he pointed and encouraged, "Now, your homeroom class is *right there*, just ahead. Try not to worry, Sandra. You seem pretty smart. You'll get the hang of it." [9]

"*Thank you, again. You're a very nice man and I'm glad we met,*" I cheerfully whispered, secretly dreading his departure and suppressing tears.

"Well, you seem like a really nice kid. *Good luck.* I'll see you around," he reassured before stepping away.

Regaining control over my face and emotions, I walked into the classroom and waited for acknowledgement from the only adult present. Several students scanned my appearance, bearing expressions made when a stench wafts past. The instructor finally lifted her eyes and noticed my presence at the door.

The woman dryly asked, "What's your name?"

"Sandra Lawson," I informed, remaining still. "I apologize for being late and hope this is the correct classroom."

Without making eye contact, the woman peered down at a paper and lifelessly informed, "You're in the right classroom. Have a seat."

To my dismay, each chair had a tiny desk attached to it, which compelled students to hunch their backs while writing. I already missed the large folding tables and independent chairs I had grown so accustomed to. [10]

Radiating menacing temperaments, classmates skeptically tracked my movements. No chair seemed safe, which delayed my settling. Overwhelmed, but unwilling to show emotion, I clenched my jaw. [11]

"You can sit over here… *if you want.* This desk is open," a girl cheerfully announced with a smile. Breathing a sigh of relief, I sat at the tiny desk beside her with a grin. "My name is Neli. What's yours, again? I forgot." [12]

"*It's Sandra,*" I whispered. "*Well, Neli, it's nice to meet you. You're a lifesaver. You have no idea. From the way this class was staring at me, I thought they were going to eat me.*" [13]

"Hey, new girl," prodded a feminine voice from behind. I turned my seated body to encounter another blue-eyed blonde. "Stand up," she continued aggressively, postured hand to hip with a leg cocked out. "Let me take a look at you." [14]

If she was instigating a fight, standing would grant me better leverage and footing. With that in mind, I obliged her, rose to my feet, and calmly asked, "What's your name?" [15]

"*Mallory,*" the towhead dryly informed. "Spin around." Unsure of why, I obeyed, and gave a puzzled look as others laughed. Condescending in tone, Mallory viciously inquired, "Why are you dressed like that? What is this? You have on *white* shoes, *pink* frilly socks, *white* short-alls, a *pink* shirt, and a *pink* bow in your hair. *Wow.* This isn't the first day of kindergarten. You literally match from head to toe. Did your *mom* pick out your clothes for you?" I stared at her and maintained control. "Hello? Do you have anything to say for yourself?" [16]

Absolutely willing to stain my white short-alls with Mallory's blood, I hesitated further. Her verbal assault on my pride wasn't worthy of even *one* repercussion that would follow my seasoned fist. Mallory leaned forward to provoke me with a sneer, but to no avail.

With an extreme southern drawl, a boy chimed, "Where are you *from*, anyway?"

"I'm sorry. What's your name?" I inquired.

"I'm Hank," he quickly replied. "Where are you from?"

Grateful to hear a reasonable question, I calmly replied, "California."

Hank shook his head in disapproval, clicked his tongue, and jabbed, "*It figures.* Don't they have *smog* in California?" [17]

The proud Texan continued to roast me and inspire laughter from several students. Our teacher must have approved of their conduct. Her inaction screamed volumes as the pack of hyenas circled. My face was like flint and refused to reveal my hemorrhaging self-image. I wondered if the woman at the large desk was our official instructor or simply a substitute, since there was no lesson or useful information presented that day, apart from what I learned about my classmates. [18]

An abrupt bell rendered a sudden fright and signaled everyone to leave the room and flood the hallway. "Ma'am, where do I go from here?" I inquired. "I don't have a class schedule and I'm still very confused."

With her focus elsewhere, the woman coldly replied, "Just follow the crowd."

Lunch

The middle school students migrated and led me directly into the cafeteria, the shared nucleus of the elementary, middle school and high school campus. Younger children dipped their tater tots into globs of ketchup as I stepped in line to wait for my meal. The echoing bustle of clacking treys made me ache for the open-air lunch breaks in California and the soothing breeze that rustled the leaves.

My daydream ended as sizzling carbohydrates and steamed vegetables slumped on my tray, placed by morose servers who appeared as disappointed with the entire experience as I was.

Choosing optimism, I thought, "Well, eating a hot tray-lunch is better than throwing away a soggy sandwich." [1]

"What's your name?" the grumpy cashier inquired.

Bewildered, I replied, "Sandra Lawson."

The woman flipped through her stapled packet and announced, "I don't see your name on the prepaid list. Did your parents give you any lunch money for today?"

"No, ma'am," I regretfully answered. "I'm so sorry. No one informed me about the lunch situation. I'll just put the tray back and eat when I get home."

"No, no, no. You need to eat. Take your lunch," the cashier gruffly corrected. "Your parents just owe the cafeteria. I'll make a note. You can bring me the money tomorrow. Now, go on. You're holding up the line." Frustrated strangers glared as they clutched their trays. I moved on and diligently scanned the lunchroom for an unoccupied chair near some friendly faces.

Three steps later, an elementary boy lifted his arm to point at me and theatrically jeered, *"Look! She's so ugly! Medusa! Medusa! Don't look at me! I'll turn to stone!"* He bent himself backwards and forwards, holding his belly in hysterical laughter. [2]

With blood in the water, the school of voracious piranhas grew silent and clapped their eyes upon his victim. Centered in the spacious gap between two columns of tables, eyed tracked my movements as I found myself deeper in their midst. Apart from the ruthless creature I had just encountered, I discovered striking similarities between each student. Their hair, skin, eye color, and clothing blended into a pond of hateful replicas. Soulless expressions met my astonishment as if I had wandered into a horror film. Yearning for a moment of peace, I resolved to take my tray outside and preferred isolation in the baking sun over one more moment of misguided hostility. [3]

"*Sandra!*" a familiar voice called out. "*Over here!*" Two waving arms caught my attention as Neli daringly offered another timely rescue. Grinning, I all but sprinted. "Everyone, *this* is Sandra," she graciously introduced. With intense gratitude, I made eye contact with everyone at her table and sat beside her. "Sandra's *cool*. She isn't like *the other ones*. I met her this morning." [4]

A combination of girls and boys dined together in harmony on that first day of middle school. While each boisterously conversed in their mother tongue, I observed their hair, contrasting styles, and gesticulation. The girls were colorful and alive with warm and genuinely cheerful expressions. Everything about their behavior led me to believe that I was safe in their midst. All at once, they erupted into boisterous laughter, which startled me into a chuckle. [5]

Hank stood up and shouted from the neighboring table, "*Can't you people just be quiet?!*"

Neli spun around in her seat and sternly barked, "*Shut up, gringo! Mind our own business!*"

Cain, another boy from class who boasted a twang, reviled loudly, "*Go back to Mexico!*" [6]

"*Go back to Germany, you Nazi jerk!*" Neli rebutted with a casual flick of her wrist. I was slack-jawed and erupted into laughter with those at our table. My friend turned to me and gently inquired, "What *are* you, anyway? You don't look like *them*, but you don't look like *us*, either." [7]

"Your very observant. I'm actually a blend of several races. Oddly enough, two of them are Mexican and German, but I'm not offended by what you said to *the Nazi*. That was hilarious." Neli huffed with a smirk. "I'm sorry about what they said. He was way out of line and *someone* needed to shut him up. *What's wrong* with these people? The kids are so mean! I've never seen anything like this before, especially when it comes to *the adults*. That's what gets me. Men and women in this cafeteria see and hear *everything* that's going on and aren't doing anything about it! It happened in class this morning! You saw! None of it was a secret! It's in everyone's face! Leadership is *willfully* allowing bad things to happen! Is the entire school like this?" [8]

Neli nodded her head and warned, "Yeah. It's pretty bad. They're just a bunch of ignorant *racists* out here, but don't pay any attention to them." Another conversation unfolded, so I gulped down my meal. "Hey, Sandra! Since you're half Mexican, do you speak Spanish?" The table's focus politely turned toward me for confirmation. [9]

"I know *some* Spanish words, but not very many," I admitted. "My mom's side of the family speaks fluent Spanish, but she didn't teach me. Her teachers hit her when she spoke it in class." Those at the table nodded with understanding. "I may not know what you guys are saying, but your laughter is *contagious*."

Neli explained, "What those kids shouted at us earlier happens *every day*. They get annoyed by us laughing and then tell us to be quiet, but we just ignore them. Seriously, don't listen to those jerks. They make fun of what they don't understand. When we speak Spanish, those idiots think we're talking about *them*, but the truth is… they're boring and unoriginal. We don't care enough to waste our breath on them! It *is* nice to speak privately, but I'll translate for you." Neli explained their various conversations as they were occurring. Each topic was about something that happened *outside* of school, such as jokes they heard or personal stories about their families. [10]

"Thanks for including me, guys," I warmly expressed, making eye contact with each of them. "It's nice to have *good* friends to sit with… at *the fun table*!"

"*Yeah!*" they cheered in agreement, having formed a united front by being rejected *together*. [11]

My Testimony

Shortly after his baptism at the LDS ward, my brother didn't have a desire to return or take part in the mid-week lessons. Historically, that would have been enough of an excuse for the materfamilias to bring all LDS inconveniences to a full stop. However, pressured by the missionaries and several ward members, the woman drove me to Sunday School and even listened to the talks that occurred immediately after each sacrament meeting.

After one such talk had concluded, I cooperated with the termagant and quietly stood to make a stealthy retreat toward the parking lot.

Before reaching the building's exit, Elder Joseph called out, "Sister Sandra! Wait just a moment!" The materfamilias groaned, unable to evade another LDS inconvenience. Elder Joseph caught up to us and divulged, "Sandra, I wanted to share something with you. Do you remember how several ward members stood and gave their testimonies at the sacrament meeting?" I nodded. "Well, would you like to give *your* testimony at the sacrament meeting next week?"

"Well, I think I'd *enjoy* public speaking, but I don't really know what a testimony is or what to say," I admitted. "I've only been Mormon a few months." [1]

The missionary hunched over with hands on knees and whispered, *"Leave that to me. I'm not supposed to do this, so don't tell anyone, but I'll just write your testimony for you and all you'll have to do is stand up and read it aloud. How does that sound? Will you do it?"* [2]

I leaned forward with a smile and discreetly replied, *"I'm a very good reader. I'll do it."* [3]

"Okay. Just remember not to tell anyone. It's our little secret," Elder Joseph quietly reminded, still hunched beside the materfamilias. At that, the young man stood up straight and confidently announced, "Excellent! I'll have the materials we discussed ready and in hand by Sunday morning. See you then."

True to his word that following Sunday, Elder Joseph inconspicuously delivered his essay to me as we entered the sacrament meeting. The termagant witnessed as the young man slipped his secret into my tiny hand like a cinematic spy, just before I tucked the paper into my free Book of Mormon. [4]

A few adults shared their testimonies with the assembly. I sensed a pause in the flow of speakers, stood from my seat, and carried the concealed document to the front of the room. An observant LDS ward member quickly placed a carpeted box behind the podium for me to stand on.

I adjusted the microphone and boldly declaimed, "I believe the Bible is true. I believe the Book of Mormon is true…"

The second sentence disturbed me as it rolled off my tongue. It was a crowd-pleasing, ear-scratching *lie*. That document was a script presented as my personal convictions, but each sentence grew steadily farther from the truth. A dazzling fraud, my mouth regurgitated the second-hand adorations of a confusing doctrine to a credulous assembly. I might as well have stated that I fully believed Joseph Smith's claims about his encounter with Moroni and the disappearing golden tablets. I didn't. A lonely child in need of help, I was the perfect candidate to become an underage puppet, an inky deception, to appear righteous before Mormon eyes. Pangs of conviction wrenched my spirit, but I continued. Cowardice and human weakness compelled me to continue. In those moments, I learned that, under the right circumstances, I'd say anything for approval… *just like the materfamilias.* [5]

As my eyes speedily tracked each line of words, a battle raged within my soul. Conviction intensified and urged me to *stop reading* so I could address the congregation from the platform of *authenticity*. I felt led to retract the false testimony and confess the simple truth: In the months that followed my original prayer, I *still* had not read the Book of Mormon. I had relished the midweek lessons solely because of the clean-cut missionaries who regularly visited my home, paid warm attention to me, and effortlessly manipulated the materfamilias into chauffeuring me toward friendly faces each week. The missionaries' lessons, LDS Sunday School sessions, and lifeless talks had produced no noticeable, life-giving change in me or my home life. It was the unchecked *limerence* toward Elder Joseph that had altered my behavior for the worse. *Limerence* insidiously replaced my hunger for *Jesus* with an insatiable desire for Elder Joseph's charming company and smiling approval. [6]

Unwilling to expose the missionary's contrived deception and authorship of the speech, I disobeyed my fiery internal warning and followed through with his beguiling plan. I was the very sort of person who I detested the most, *a hypocrite*. [7]

In true LDS fashion, the praise of man was absent. There was no applause at the end of my well-executed performance, which saddened me. There was no reward or

My Testimony

payoff for the sacrifice of my integrity. I folded the lie, tucked it back into my free book of confusion, and returned to my seat in tormented silence.

Before the termagant and I could slip away, an unsuspecting LDS member approached us and briefly commented, "Sister Sandra, your testimony was *beautiful*."

"Thank you," I sheepishly responded, dying inside. [8]

A Bone to Pick

*T*he LDS Young Women instructor plainly stated, "Today's lesson will be focused on *purity*, which is taken very seriously. A recent example of how sinful actions can have dire consequences was provided just last week. It was revealed that an unmarried young woman in our ward had become pregnant. To make an example of her, she was told to leave the church. Her growing presence would only negatively influence those around her and cause confusion. Do you see how serious sin can be? Let *that* be a lesson for you. Now, let's move on and discuss purity as it is written in the Book of Mormon..." [1]

"What a second," I interjected with an outstretched hand. "Do you have any other information about her situation? I mean, it takes two to tango. *Right?* Where's the father of the baby? Does he belong to this ward, too? If so, what happened to him? I think we're missing some vital parts of the story here. He's just as guilty, even if his body won't reflect it. Is anyone holding him financially responsible? Seriously, what's the scenario? Help me understand, because all of this sounds pretty unfair." [2]

Clearly irritated, the instructor frigidly rebutted, "It *doesn't matter* what the scenario was. The facts are that she's *pregnant* and *unmarried*. That directly opposes the Lord's commandments." [3]

Her self-righteous tone sparked an inferno as I boldly countered, "Yes, sex outside of marriage *is* wrong, but without more information, how do we know that the girl's pregnancy was even her fault? Do you know if someone raped her? Is it possible that a family member molested her? What if someone from the ward seduced her? Things like that happen *every day* and can easily result in pregnancy. Her pregnancy doesn't necessarily mean guilt." [4]

"No. It was *nothing* like that. We know this family *very* well," she presumptuously argued.

"Are you *sure?* You don't know *what* happens behind closed doors. Was there an investigation? How did you even learn that she was pregnant? Was she ratted-out by someone? Did she come forward on her own or was she showing already and you guys simply asked about it?" [5]

"That's really none of your business," the instructor flatly dismissed. [6]

"Well, in all honesty, you made it my business when *you* brought it up as an example in today's lesson," I reminded her. The young woman's jaw flopped open. "Do you even *know* all the details of what occurred? You're *clearly* not her friend, so were you there to witness her *trial,* or did you just *hear* about it? Even if she made a terrible mistake, how could kicking her out of church be helpful? Think about it. It must be her first baby. She's probably scared out of her mind right now. *I would be.* What if she runs off and gets an abortion because of this? That would be horrible! She needs support and to feel the love of Jesus, not a bunch of pointing fingers. You know what? I'd bet her family is Mormon, too. So, w*hat happens there?* Were they pressured to kick her out… just to save face? Wow. The punishment falls on the girl and *nothing* happens to the boy. What are you teaching us?!" [7]

"Stop talking," the young woman frigidly replied. "You're interrupting the lesson."

"No!" I protested as my feet planted to the floor in a warrior stance. "This is *important* and you're not answering any of my questions! You guys kicked her out because she was pregnant! All this lesson teaches us to do is *lie* to save our own skins! Kicking her out isn't the answer! Even I know that!" [8]

"I will not discuss this any further with you," the instructor sternly concluded. "If you have a problem, take it up with the bishop. The decision was *his*."

"Fine. I *will* take it up with the bishop," I announced. *"Where is he?"*

The young instructor challenged my resolve and sneered, "He should be in his office down the hall, preparing for today's talk." Without another word, I turned on my heels, located the bishop's door, and knocked.

A muffled voice from inside cheerfully answered, "Come in!"

I turned the knob, cracked the door enough to poke my head inside, and queried, "Are you the bishop? Am I in the right place?"

"Yes! You made it! Come on in!" the man benevolently welcomed.

I quickly entered, shut the door behind me, and stepped forward to announce, "Sir, I have a bone to pick with you." His inviting expression melted to that of confusion and horror. "What is this religion teaching people? According to today's lesson, you kicked an unmarried girl out of the church last week because she was *pregnant*. Why did you do that? She needs *Jesus,* and all you showed her was the exit! Is she okay? Do you know or even care?" [9]

The bishop lifted himself from the rolling chair and leaned over the desk. With a pointed finger, he shouted, *"I will not have my judgement questioned by a child! Get out of my office!"* [10]

"Fine!" I barked. "I'm leaving!" [11]

With haste, I retraced my steps back toward Sunday School. The materfamilias intercepted me, blowing my mind as she as she exited a different classroom. Relieved that our paths crossed, the termagant grabbed my arm and whispered, *"We're leaving right now."*

"How could the instructor report me so quickly?" I internally wondered. "Man, I'm going to be in trouble when we get home. She hates being embarrassed. I'm one dead little girl." To defend myself, I thought to volunteer the entire story, but hesitated at her countenance. The woman leading me outside appeared frightened, not angry. I withheld the damning information and casually inquired, "Why are we leaving?"

"I'll tell you in the car," was her swift reply.

"Oh. Good," I thought. "There's a chance she *doesn't* know. I might live. Stupendous." Ready to see The Church of Jesus Christ of Latter-Day Saints in the rearview mirror, I leaped into the vehicle, buckled my seatbelt, and anxiously pressed, "We're in the car. Tell me."

The woman pulled out of the parking lot and confided, "You want to know why we left? Those people kept badgering me to give my testimony like *you* did, and I don't want to! Talking in front of a crowd really freaks me out and they won't stop asking me about it! I can't face them again. We *aren't* going back, and I don't want to hear a word about it."

I peered out the window and silently rejoiced, "Jesus, you really *do* see everything. Thank You for getting me out of there." [12]

SECTION 5

Magic

On the return bus ride from a class field-trip, a student peered backward from his seat about five rows ahead of me. The child's contrasting appearance caught my eye as he traveled down the aisle toward the rear seats where I was located. Alerted students all but growled as he passed them and caused my jaw to clench at their depraved behavior. [1]

To my astonishment, the distinctive boy rested himself beside *me*, having boldly approached without provocation. His careful manner of walking and timid facial expressions alluded to his extreme introversion. However, it would have been perfectly understandable if he had simply been nervous, having just traversed row after row of social hyenas. [2]

"Hi!" I greeted, positioning myself closer to the window to make space for him. "I'm Sandra."

"I know who you are," he clarified plainly, on the cusp of sounding rude. "You're the new kid." Wondering what the cut-off time was for *that* title, I confirmed his statement with a gentle smile and nod. He shifted a bit in the faux-leather seat, leaned toward me with unexpected familiarity, and continued under his breath, *"You seem like a nice person, so I will take a chance with you. I don't think you'll laugh or make fun of me."*

Ready to submerge into the deeper waters of conversation, I whispered back, "I won't."

"I believe you," the boy discreetly confided with a forward lean into my personal space. *"Sandra, I wanted to ask you something. Do you believe in magic?"* [3]

Discomfort tightened my chest and shoulders as I briefly hesitated. My desire to be agreeable grappled with the truth as I pondered how to respond. [4]

"I believe in *Jesus*," I tenderly replied. [5]

"Oh," he murmured. The boy recoiled slightly with an air of shame and disconcertment. *"Does that mean that you want me to go away?"* [6]

My classmate's insecure behavior and words displayed much of the thoughts and emotions I had often experienced, but concealed. In a way, I admired and envied his emotional transparency. [7]

Beyond Recognition

Desiring to protect him, I gently specified, "I don't want you to *go away*. I answered your question *honestly*, but I didn't mean to hurt your feelings." [8]

His posture relaxed into a suppressed excitement as he explained, "That's okay, Sandra. I just got a little scared because most Christians are mean, but you're not like *the rest of them*. I can tell." Scooting even closer than before, he whispered, *"I came over here because I want to show you something. Now, don't be afraid, but I've been practicing Wicca and learned how to change my eye color. Do you want to see?"* [9]

My discomfort intensified as I gently inquired, "You mentioned magic earlier. Is Wicca a form of *witchcraft*?"

"No, no, no," he corrected and shook his head. "I'm not doing anything *Satanic*. I just worship *nature* and learned how to concentrate *really hard* to change my eye color. It takes a lot of concentration. I've watched myself do it in the mirror, but I want to see if I can do it in front of someone else. Will you watch my irises and tell me if they change color? I'm not going to chant or anything... just focus." [10]

Warning radiated throughout my body, despite his simple definition of the religion. Before I answered, a wave of empathy soaked my thoughts. "Well, I don't know if you should do that," I gingerly commented. "It sounds... *painful*."

"No, no, no, Sandra. I've been practicing. It doesn't hurt, but it takes a lot of energy. *Just watch*," he urged. "I really want to share this with someone. You seem friendly, so I want to show *you*. Just keep watching my eyes and don't look away."

He leaned over me toward the nearby window and allowed his eyes to catch more daylight. My classmate redirected his attention to the open space between my body and the back of the next seat. The wiccan stared out the window at the speedily passing trees and clasped his hands firmly together as one would to crack a nut. He stopped breathing. The flushed child trembled as he became rigidly tense.

With no exits, I grew increasingly concerned, but remembered the assignment and shifted my attention to his brown hazel eyes. The tiny, fibrous muscles of both irises undulated and slowly transitioned to a vibrant cerulean.

Wide-eyed and shocked, I flared my nostrils in a silent, closed-lip gasp. Within a moment, his irises undulated once more to display violet, which almost immediately morphed into emerald. The wiccan's body suddenly released tension and allowed air into his lungs as both irises to return to their original state. Regaining composure and sitting back, his vulnerable glance searched my face. [11]

As we stared at one another, I remained stoic and briefly thought, "He can't fake that. What did I just witness? How's that possible? That can't be possible, but it happened. It just happened. That *really* just happened..."

Breaking my daze, Wicca wondered aloud, "Sandra, did it work?! Did I do it?! I could feel it, but I need you to confirm. Sandra, *did it work*?"

"Yes, *it worked*," I uttered with a slow nod to satisfy his need for external validation. The wiccan inhaled deeply with a smile. Although astounded, I casually inquired, "So, how did you learn to do that? Did someone show you?"

"I'm not supposed to talk about it," the child sheepishly informed, "…but you seem really nice and I trust you." Wicca drew closer and whispered, *"I've been learning spells and trying to do things with just my mind, like the eye thing."* [12]

Overwhelmed with loving concern, I cautiously expressed, "You're worshipping nature, dealing with *spells,* and changing your eye color with your mind. That's *witchcraft*." Wicca's expression reflected that of crushing regret as he scooted away from me like a wounded animal. "Just… *be careful*. You seem really nice, too, and even though we just met, I care about you. I'm very glad you shared this with me because I don't know if anyone else has told you how dangerous this is. I wouldn't get too deeply involved." [13]

"*This was a mistake. I shouldn't have shown you,*" he quietly snapped. *"No one understands me."* At that, he left my side and speedily found another seat, leaving behind an overwhelming burden on my shoulders. [14]

I smiled and waved each day between classes to convince Wicca that I didn't hate him. The boy continuously slinked past me until I openly stated, "*Hey*. I don't care if this is one-sided or not, but I'm your friend… even if you're not mine. You can avoid me or we can be friends. We *are* different, but we don't have to believe the same thing in order for us to be kind to one another. *Do we?* Besides, we will *never* fit in with this crowd. We should probably stick together. I mean, *c'mon*. You seem like a smart guy. Don't you think that would be wise? You know… *strength in numbers…*" [15]

"Why do you want to be my friend so badly?" he aggressively probed. "Everyone else just thinks I'm *a freak*."

"They think I'm a freak, too! It's really hard living in this town," I admitted. "Why should we be concerned with the opinions of *cookie-cutter* people who look, act, and dress the same? Have you ever noticed how much they all look alike? This is a village of clones. Now, *that's* freaky."

"Wait. Cookie-cutter people? *That's funny*," Wicca admitted with a straight face. "Oddly enough, I'm *related* to a lot of people in this town, but they still treat me like I'm some kind of space alien."

"Well, I don't mean to be insulting to your *kinfolk*," I continued, "…but being warmly welcomed into a group of hateful jerks isn't necessarily a good thing. *I would know.*

In this town, I'm only related to the people in my household… and they don't like me either."

"Oh. *I'm sorry.* I didn't know that you had problems at home," he concluded with concern.

I slapped my hands to my thighs and comically proposed, "Can we be friends now?"

"Yeah," Wicca conceded with a grin. "We're friends." [16]

Mara

Hank scanned my rawboned physique as I stepped past him in the hallway. The young cowboy announced, "*Dang*, Sandra. You have the flattest chest I've ever seen. The other girls already have boobs. What's wrong with you? You probably stuff your shirt, too. Don't you, *stuffer*?" [1]

Other classmates paused in their stride and awaited my response. [2]

I peered downward toward my sternum, returned my attention to Hank, and quipped, "You'll say anything. I mean, I *am* flat chested, but calling me *stuffer* indicates that I'm attempting to appear endowed. Obviously, this isn't the case. If it were, don't you think I would have done a better job? Get more creative with your insults, or at least be more *accurate*."

Bewildered, Hank hesitated for a moment, put a cupped hand to his mouth, and shouted, *"Hey, y'all! Sandra stuffs her shirt! She's a stuffer!"* [3]

As I stepped into class, Cain abruptly commented, "Why do you wear weird clothing and those *ugly* glasses?" [4]

"Wow," I exclaimed. "You guys do the same thing every day. Will picking on me ever get old? Aren't you *bored?* Don't you have nothing else in your pathetic lives to discuss besides *me*? Am I that important to you? Your painful stupidity makes me long for California. At least *there* the other students were *clever*."

"Are you gonna *cry*, city girl?!" Hank interjected. *"I miss California! Boo-hoo! I wanna go back home!"* The boy cranked his fists near his eyes to mock me. The surrounding students laughed and howled like dingoes before a meal.

"Shut-up, *idiots!* Leave Sandra alone!" Neli warned with intense irritation. "She doesn't even *care* what you think… and you keep talking! You're too dumb to quit! It's annoying."

Cain suddenly regained his vigor and jabbed, "What do *you* know?! You're just a Mexican!" [5]

"I know a lot more than you, *white-boy*," Nelly coolly replied. [6]

Weeks later, another student moved to town and joined our class. Winifred was outgoing, bubbly, and kind. During her first lunch break, she waved vigorously to capture my attention and loudly cried, "Sandra! Hey! Come here! Come sit with me!"

Alerted children followed my movement with their eyes as I scampered over and gratefully joined the endearing soul to sit in the only open seat near Winifred. I had originally sought to rejoin Neli and the crew, but had no intention to snub the gracious offer of our newest addition.

"Hey, Winnifred!" I chirped. "Thanks for calling me over! Did you want to tell me something?"

"Nope," she clarified. "I just wanted you to sit with me." Winnifred's grin radiated life and cheer. I found comfort in her confident presence and popped a crispy tater-tot into my mouth. As Winifred sipped from her carton of milk, movement drew her gaze. "What's that girl doing? She's making everyone move so she can pass between the tables. *Look*. Someone's gonna get there *** kicked. She looks *mad*."

Intrigued, I briefly glanced to my left. A corpulent fifth-grader on a mission forced her body between my row of tables and the neighboring row behind me. "You're right," I agreed. "She *does* look mad."

"*Sandra*... do you know her?" Winifred asked.

Focused on my tray, I munched on another crisp tater-tot and replied, "Nope. Why?"

Observant students ended their conversations and grabbed those around them, which caused an expectant hush to blanket the cafeteria. Within a moment, something warm and soft had squished against my bony left shoulder. I remained seated and calmly assessed the glaring antagonist, only to coldly redirect my gaze forward. Weighing in at a whopping forty-nine pounds, I was dwarfed by comparison and potentially represented a mere third of her body mass. [7]

"*You're sitting in my seat*," the child snarled with a thrust of her soft belly, wielding herself like a battering ram to slide my occupied chair sideways with a loud screech. To be dominated by a protruding stomach was not something I was prepared to tolerate. [8]

"Well, let's investigate the situation. *Shall we?*" I inquired calmly. "What's your name?"

"*Mara*," the girl snipped as she peered down her nose to scoff with a chuckle.

I slid my tray a few inches to the side and stared down at the table. While I touched its surface with the tip of my finger, I casually remarked, "Gosh. You're right. *My mistake.* Your name's written *right here*."

"*It is?*" Mara genuinely wondered as she leaned to look.

I hauntingly turned my gaze upward and brutally corrected, "*No*. Your name *isn't* there. This *isn't* your seat. This *isn't* your table and I'm free to sit *wherever I wish*. If you're in this cafeteria to do anything other than enjoy your lunch, *do it somewhere else*. Now, I realize you might be a bit rattled after this experience, so if you've forgotten everything I just said, then remember this: *Don't touch me again*, especially with your stomach." Stupefied, the delinquent lingered. Returning to my original occupation, I popped a cold tater-tot between my molars, chewed, and swallowed. Still sensing her beside me, I dismissively waved her off and calmly added, "You may go now." [9]

Bursting with adoring pride, Winnifred brought one curled hand to her mouth, pointed at Mara with the other, and loudly jeered, *"Oh-h-h-h-h!"*

Onlookers mocked the towering bully and burst into hysterical laughter. With a quivering lip and chin to her chest, Mara fled the scene. Her hips caught chairs and accidentally pressed against her ridiculing classmates. Some students pointed while hecklers in her path quickly scooted forward to create a less-painful route for the bully's escape. [10]

After Mara's emotional exit of the cafeteria, Winnifred commented, "Sandra, for a second there, I was worried about you… *until you opened your mouth*. I've seen a lot, but *that* may have been the most amazing thing I've ever witnessed." [11]

Flowers

~~~

"*T*his is a waste of money," the termagant remarked to her husband as he handed her a fragrant bouquet of fresh flowers to celebrate their anniversary. "They're just going to die." [1]

When my defeated father walked away from his wife to occupy himself elsewhere, I interjected, "You could just thank him, Mom. You're ugly to that man every day. You're so ungrateful. I'm surprised he buys you *anything*. If he forgets an occasion, you yell and start a fight. If he remembers it, you're mean to him and complain about the gift. Do you remember what you said that time he remembered your favorite candy and gave it to you as a gift? You got mad and accused him of forgetting the occasion *and* ruining your diet. You eat that candy all year long! The man can't win!" [2]

"Shut up!" the woman snapped. "What do you know? You're just *a child*. Just wait until you're married. *Then*, you'll see." [3]

My father upgraded his civilian job to earn more money and lose the commute to the city. Hired at a local electric cooperative, the man informed his wife, "According to this holiday rotation, I'm scheduled to be *on call* the evening of Valentine's Day, and could be late coming home. It's possible that I might be called away from home to solve electrical problems."

"I don't believe you. Why does it have to be on *Valentine's Day*? Huh?" the woman growled.

"Well, you can look for your-self. It's right here. The *holiday rotation* has different employees on-call for each holiday," her husband calmly explained. "This year, I'm on call during Valentine's Day. Next year, it will be someone else… but I'll just be on call during a *different* holiday. If we lose an employee, I may have to work more than one holiday. You see?"

"*No*, I don't *see*," she huffed. [4]

The day before Valentine's Day, I heard my father's work truck pull into the driveway. Excited to see him, I stood in their bedroom doorway and peered through the windows to watch his approach. With a large item in his hands, the electrician thudded his way to the front door, entered with a smile, and exclaimed, "Happy Early Valentine's Day!"

The materfamilias eyed the vivid flowers and terracotta pot that rested in my father's calloused hands. "Why are you giving me potted flowers a day early?" the woman queried with a feigned smile.

Her husband eagerly replied, "Since I probably won't be home until *late* tomorrow, I thought ahead and wanted to give this to you *early* so you would know that I didn't forget. You've said that the bouquets I give you just wither and die, so I got you *these* flowers instead! With some water and a little sunshine, they won't die! Well, at least not for a while."

The termagant walked over to the man, stood hand-to-hip, and jabbed, "So, who gets the *real* flowers on *Valentine's Day*? *Your whore?!*"

As the words escaped her lips, she snatched the decorative pot of soil and blooms from her astounded husband, swung open both front doors, and smashed his gift over the rock entryway. [5]

Choked by the sting of her abrupt cruelty, the man announced, "That's the last time I give you *anything*." At that, he retreated to his more rewarding outdoor work. [6]

The woman calmly returned to her perch on the couch and mindlessly stared at the television, behaving as though she had merely retrieved a snack from the pantry or returned from the restroom. [7]

"Well… *that* was stupid," I informed, oozing reproof. The materfamilias flashed a venomous glance. "That man doesn't have to do anything for you, *you mean woman*. He works all day to support this family… only to come home to accusations and complaining. Everyone has a breaking point." [8]

"*Oh, no, I've sinned,*" she mocked as she piously clasped her hands together with a skyward gaze.

"I'm serious, lady. People can only take so much," I warned. "Just in case no one has told you, you don't deserve him. I know he's almost a decade younger than you, but if he dies first, I'm blaming *you*." [9]

In the manner of the Pope, the woman held her hand in the air to form a cross and condescendingly uttered, "God bless you."

Dumbfounded, I couldn't understand how an intelligent man like my father married and reproduced with such a twisted individual.

In the following weeks, a cold-shoulder and a paycheck were all that my father offered to his wife. With no regard to her surroundings, the materfamilias made several open attempts in the living room to *arouse* her husband into a desired response and used delicate touches and seductive hand-placement in my presence. Expressions of disgust and irk were the immediate outcomes from both my father and I. [10]

She repositioned herself between her target and a televised sporting event. Reused words flowed past the woman's forked-tongue as she disconcertingly pouted, "Are you still mad at me? I was *bad*. Will you forgive me?" [11]

The woman's tactics broke like water against her very own masterpiece of stone. Her husband ordered, "Move. You're in the way." Entirely void of understanding, the woman lingered motionless before his horizontal recliner. "Knock it off! You're being annoying!" [12]

Like a spoiled child denied a cookie, the woman whined, "You're being bad to me! God says that you're supposed to *forgive me*." Silence filled the air. "Well, if you're not getting it from *me*, then you're getting it from *someone*!" she accused. The family strapped in for another involuntary lap on the not-so-merry-go-round. [13]

Why?

My parents' daily interactions carved a warning into my heart about matrimony. They inspired me to develop a systematic process of elimination to avoid such a disagreeable match. It was *that* or simply forego matrimony entirely. I understood precious little of what a healthy marriage required. With my resources, I explored what *didn't* work. [1]

I lingered near the sofa, just outside of the termagant's reach, emulated a personable talk-show host, and inquired, "If you actually *believe* that Dad has been cheating on you, why don't you just divorce him and leave? Why stay if you're so miserable?" [2]

At first, the woman appeared shocked at my directness, but surprisingly admitted, "*Ha!* There's no way I'm going back to work to support myself! I could if I wanted to, but I'm his *wife* and I deserve *all* his paychecks, retirement, and military benefits, not just *half*. I'm not going to raise his brats just to share his money with another woman! Are you crazy?!" [3]

"Wait a minute. It's not because you *love* him?" I queried further. "Did you *ever* love him? I mean, why did you marry Dad in the first place?"

"I was divorced with a teenage son and I didn't want to raise him *alone*," the woman replied matter-of-factly. "Your father was intelligent and good with money. I knew he would make smart children. When I saw that he got along with my son, I decided to get remarried." Her candor verified something I already understood. My father was being used. [4]

I eventually sat down at the kitchen table with the former sailor and probed, "Why did you marry a woman like Mom? You're a smart guy. How did this happen? Where did you meet her?" [5]

"Your mother was working at the courthouse and was in the navy reserve when I first saw her," he informed. "Since I was a navy recruiter, I looked up her information and asked her out."

"*Huh*," I huffed. "Mom said she was *so beautiful* that she was asked to be on the navy's float in a parade." [6]

"Your mother was Miss Naval Reserve Queen that year. I was one of two single guys at the recruiter's office and volunteered to be her driver. She was good-looking, and I asked her out. I didn't mind that she was divorced with a teenage son, and we got married that same year. *At first*, she was pleasant. Her behavior toward me didn't change until *after* we were married." [7]

"That makes sense," I remarked. "I figured it had to be some sort of trick. You're not a stupid man. You wouldn't marry a monster *on purpose*. Did she act crazy before I was born?"

"Yes. After we got married, her son would greet me when I first walked through the door, and say, '*Good*. I'm glad you're home. Now, *you* can deal with her.'"

"What?!" I exclaimed. "Are you kidding me?! You were warned?! How could you make children with someone like that?!" [8]

"We were married, and we both wanted children," he casually replied with a shrug.

I buried my head in my hands and wondered aloud, "Fair enough, Dad. Mission accomplished. You have children. *We exist*. Why stay with her if you're so unhappy?" [9]

My father shook his head and clichéd, "It's-cheaper-to-keep-her." Life drained from my face. "She has powerful friends in the judicial system. If we ever divorced, she'd take everything. Besides, I would never be able to get away from your mother completely. She would just stalk me. After everything that's happened, meeting another woman seems too *dangerous*. I wouldn't have any way of knowing if *that* woman would become even worse than your mother. The last thing I want to do is jump out of the frying pan and into the fire. Let's just say that I'm familiar with your mother and how she operates. Besides, out of all of my siblings, I'm the only one who hasn't divorced and I want to keep it that way." [10]

The idea of perpetual singlehood shimmered as I compared it to indentured servanthood under a draconian spouse. When that military man retired from serving his country, he retired from freedom and a position of authority, too. Maniacal domination insidiously subdued him over the relentless creep of time and created a shell of the man I once knew. [11]

Broken

~~~~

On a Sunday afternoon, I grew bored in my summer solitude and sought entertainment. My parents resembled manikins as they stared at the television in the living room. Uninterested in the film they were watching, I cautiously navigated past them and up the stairs to the loft, where my brother occupied himself with a game console.

Even on the desktop computer, my sibling relished gaming. The boy discovered secret pathways, loopholes, and exploitable glitches. He even developed tricks of advancement by memorizing the automated patterns of each adversary and played often enough to beat several games in my presence.

"Wanna play?" he graciously invited as he manipulated the two-dimensional character over and under various obstacles with skillful ease.

Since my participation would have proved more embarrassing than amusing, I sat down beside my brother and replied, "No, thanks. I'll just watch." [1]

Eight-bit tunes and sporadic pouncing sounds emanated from the small television as I sat cross-legged on the coarse, looped carpeting. Minutes later, I was already uncomfortable and bored in my sibling's presence, and instigated a voluminous quarrel without cause or reason. [2]

With only railing and open space separating us from our father's ears, the man grew severely irritated with the bickering and abruptly shouted, *"Knock it off! Quit horsing around!"*

Respect and a healthy fear of our father silenced us as we returned our attention to the game where the boy transitioned from sitting upright to lying down on his back. Although it seemed laborious, my brother repeatedly lifted his head, only to tap it onto the carpeting like a metronome. Mildly annoyed, I grabbed a miniature clip from my hair, timed his movement, and slid the fragile item underneath his skull that crushed the clip into pieces. [3]

"You tried to *stab* me!" my sibling declared, outraged.

Triggered into *berserker-mode*, the boy stood to his feet, grabbed me, elevated my body as high as the ceiling rafters would allow, and threw me head-downward onto the carpet. [4]

Landing awkwardly, I crumpled under my own weight and clearly heard what closely resembled a snapping carrot. Breathless and disoriented, I settled on my back like a landed fish. Once able to inhale, a rush of excruciating pain radiated from my clavicle and resulted in an unnerving scream. [5]

Alerted into action, my brother smothered the noise with a nearby pillow and frantically whispered, *"Sh-h-h. Be quiet. We're going to get into trouble."*

"That's it! I told you two to quit horsing around!" my father angrily announced as he stomped his way up the wooden staircase. Coming to himself, my brother innocently returned the breathing obstruction to its original resting place and awaited the man's response.

The former sailor made his way over to me and reached low to clutch my body, tightly pinning my arms to my sides. He hoisted me off the carpet and held my scrawny physique away from him like a filthy puppy. My injury flared with debilitating pain as he roughly descended each unforgiving step. The man reached the threshold of my bedroom, chucked my limp, skin-covered skeleton on top of my neatly made bed, and shut the door behind him. Rejection wormed through my thoughts. Motionless and throbbing, tears cascaded into my ears and hair. [6]

Despite my initial impression of indignation and horror, I whispered to myself, *"Dad didn't mean to hurt me. I deserve this. I was wrong. I disobeyed and made my brother mad on purpose. I deserve punishment. Besides, Mom is the evil parent, not Dad. Dad is good."* Each attempt to sit up or elevate my legs caused core muscles to flex and inflict intolerable tension on the injury. I had no choice but to remain still in a sloppily supine position. *"Dad is good. He didn't mean it. He didn't mean it..."* I softly repeated as the bright glow of the afternoon sun radiated through my windows. [7]

Immobile and hungry, I waited for my father to return, check on me, discover my injury, and help me to the dinner table, but dusk was upon me and no one came. Evening's shadow slowly enveloped me. I interpreted their neglect as abhorrence and I cried myself to sleep. [8]

I stirred that Monday morning and discovered myself in the same position I had originally landed in. "Maybe everything that happened was just another nightmare," I silently hoped. In my attempt to sit up, flexed muscles reintroduced pain. I relaxed my core and murmured, *"Nope. It was real."* Emotion, pain, and vulnerability didn't serve me in the realm of my family's glaring indifference. *"Okay, Sandra,"* I quietly coached with a determined brow, *"Using your abs is clearly not an option and no one is going to help you, so think. You need to get your legs beneath you, where they belong. You can do this. Focus."* [9]

Flexing only rear leg muscles, I dug my heels into the mattress and gingerly inched them sideways, repositioning the lower half of my body to stick out over the edge. Allowing myself to slide down, I firmly touched my feet to the floor and poured my bottom half into a deep squat position, which allowed my back to rest against the side of the mattress and box spring. After standing up, I marveled at my accomplishment. The next task was to receive medical attention, but I couldn't do that alone. [10]

Since my father was already at work, I knew of no other alternative but to approach the semi-catatonic materfamilias who had already planted herself on the living room sofa. I cradled my arm to discourage its use, approached the woman, and dryly expressed, "My collarbone is broken. I need you to take me to the hospital."

With a foul countenance, the woman observed my calm disposition and scoffed, "It's not broken. You're lying."

"I'll make it worth your while. If we go to the hospital and you find out that *nothing* is broken… you can spank me," I bargained, appealing to her sadism as I had once before. "Seriously, I need a sling or something." The woman ignored my supplication and returned her focus to the television. Impatient with her rampant skepticism and gross negligence, I firmly declared, "I need an X-ray!"

"If it's not broken, you're gonna get it," the woman threatened, narrowing her eyes at me as she passed by to get ready.

I stepped aside and morbidly encouraged, "Atta girl! That's the spirit!"

Sometime later, after pulling up to the local clinic, I continued to cradle my unusable arm and shared my suspected diagnosis with the woman at the check-in counter. Almost immediately, she led me to a room to be seen by the doctor within moments.

"So, Sandra… what brings you here today?" the physician inquired.

"Well, I was horsing around with my brother, even after my dad told us to stop, and I made my brother really mad. He threw me down on the floor head first," I explained matter-of-factly. "I landed on my shoulder and heard a snap, so I know it's broken, but I need an X-Ray to see how bad it is."

"I see," he respectfully replied. "You don't seem to have much discomfort. When did this happen?"

The termagant seemed nervous as I casually disclosed, "Yesterday, midday."

"Oh, okay. You should have less inflammation by now. Let's take a better look," the doctor sweetly offered as he repositioned himself closer. "I need you to relax your arm for me."

"Okay," I chirped.

As the man placed his hand under my elbow, I tensed up involuntarily and whimpered.

"It's alright. I really need to check something, so just let your arm go limp. Pretend that it's a cooked noodle." Understanding the concept, I obeyed. The doctor cautiously elevated my bony arm to become parallel with the floor and rested it back on my leg without causing even one twinge of pain.

My mother's face revealed a renewed skepticism, so I exclaimed, "Oh, wow! You could lift it really high! Is that because I wasn't using my muscles? They pull on the injury, don't they? Is that why I can't sit up after lying down?"

"It's certainly looking that way, but we'll know for sure in a bit," he answered to the materfamilias' disappointment. "Alright, let me feel around your neck and shoulders for other injuries. Tell me if anything hurts." When he touched the tender spot on my collarbone, I gasped with a wince. "It's time for that X-Ray." Within moments, the doctor confirmed, "You were spot-on, Sandra. You have a hairline-fracture on your clavicle."

I glanced at the materfamilias and highlighted, "See Mom, I *told* you it was broken." The physician lifted a suspicious eyebrow toward the woman, but redirected his attention back to me as I requested, "Sir, could you provide me with a sling of some sort? If they're too expensive, I'll just make one at home." [11]

"Well, we can do better than *that*, young lady. I'll provide you with a sling, *free of charge*. Let me get one for you from the back so I can adjust it to your body while we're here," the doctor reassured before stepping away.

Once the materfamilias and I re-entered the vehicle, I clumsily fastened my seatbelt one-handed, faced the woman behind the wheel, and quipped, "It looks like I'm not getting spanked today."

Unkept and greasy in the climbing heat, the clothes I had worn since the morning prior clung to my traumatized body. I longed for a shower. After pulling up to the log house, I retreated to my room and effortlessly removed the fitted sling. However, in toiling with my pants and top, I repeatedly tweaked my collarbone with each accidental employment of attached muscles. Overwhelmed by pain, frustration and exhaustion, sweat beaded. A groan of defeat escaped me. Hunched on my bed, silent tears splashed upon my denim clad thighs. Tempted to request parental aid, I recalled the unnecessarily rough scrubbing during bath-time experiences, violent treatment of my broken wrist, and cruel isolation when manifesting *any* symptom of physical illness. It was clear. The woman who bore me was not to be enlisted for aid. [12]

Perceiving no other alternative, I whispered, *"Come on, Sandra. Getting frustrated only wastes precious energy and it won't get you clean. You're a smart kid, so think through this. Find a way to remove your pants and shirt by yourself."*

While sitting on my bed, I adjusted my positioning and allowed my back muscles to go limp. Gravity lowered the top half of my body toward my knees as I guided my unusable arm to dangle away from my ribcage. I gasped from delight and repositioned my body to allow gravity to do the work. I delicately removed my pants and lingered in the same position. My hand reached for the fabric behind my neck and methodically slid off my shirt.

Once in the shower, I used my teeth to pop open the shampoo and conditioner bottles, and used the previous dangling technique to wash my body and hair more effectively.

Exhausted, but clean, I stared into the mirror and concluded, "If I learn to do *everything* by myself for the rest of my life, I'll never feel helpless again." [13]

Paul

While her husband was away at work, the materfamilias met a divorced neighbor. During their conversation, he revealed that his son and daughter were fluently bilingual in both English and Spanish. Having enjoyed one another's company, they arranged a play-date for their offspring to meet. [1]

My sibling and I exited the property behind the materfamilias, strolled down the caliche road for a few minutes, and stepped onto the neighbor's stunningly developed property, decorated almost entirely with cleverly arranged rocks. The termagant knocked on the front door where our neighbor answered and introduced us to his striking progeny, Paul and Jasmine.

Handmade by the neighbor's father, stones were gathered directly from the property and formed their home in a way that was unlike anything I had ever seen. I admired its rustic charm and uniqueness. During a brief tour, I noted other stone structures as our guide led us right to the edge of a steep cliff, revealing a breathtaking view of the river below. The irregular stone masonry and mosaic tile work stoked my imagination and seemed to transport me to some mesmerizing portion of rural Mexico. As our neighbor spoke, I observed how friendly and demure the materfamilias behaved towards him. She smiled and laughed at every word. [2]

At their father's prompting, Paul and Jasmine asked my brother and me to break away and play. With the adults alone to converse, the siblings entertained us for hours with question games or by chasing us around rocky obstacles. To my great astonishment, both siblings were not only stunning in appearance, but also polite, warmhearted, and energetic.

"Okay, kids! It's time to stop playing! Let's go home!" the termagant affably announced, as though she *enjoyed* motherhood.

Unwilling to break away from Paul, on whom I had already developed a serious crush, I whined, "Aw, man! It feels like we just got here! Do we *really* have to go?"

"Well, you don't have to leave just yet if you don't want to. Why don't you all stay for dinner?" Paul and Jasmine's father cheerfully invited. "We'll cook for you!"

"Thank you, but we can't stay," the woman replied more hurriedly. "We really need to head home."

"I don't get it," I remarked. "Why do we have to leave all of a sudden? What's the rush? Isn't everyone having a good time?"

"Sandra… *we don't live here*. We have to go home," the termagant patronized with a nauseating smile, causing my eyebrow to lift. "Look at *Jasmine*." As my eyes met those of my new friend, we grinned at one another. "When Jasmine is told to do something, she doesn't *talk back*. Do you see how pretty and polite she is? You need to be more like *her*. Now, come on. Let's go." The seven-year-old's face grew flush, revealing her embarrassment at the divisive remarks. [3]

Out of earshot and nearly home, I inquired again, "Seriously, we were having a great time, and they *clearly* wanted us to stay for dinner. I really hate the idea of going back home. You actually pretend to be *nice* when they're around." The woman shot me a look of warning. "*Hey!* I have an idea! We should talk to Dad and convince him to come back with us for dinner! That would be awesome!" [4]

"Why can't you just do as I say?!" the termagant snapped. "Your father is about to be home from work and doesn't need to know that we spent the afternoon at the neighbor's house! I don't feel like explaining myself to him, so don't *ruin* everything by blabbing or we'll *never* come back." [5]

"Wow. Just so you know, *not* telling Dad about going to another man's home looks *really bad*. Why is it such a big secret that we're friends with our neighbors?" I wondered aloud. "You're such a hypocrite. You would *kill* Dad if he pulled something like this and he could really use some friends. I think Dad would get along great with Paul and Jasmine's father. Besides, it's not like you're having an affair. So, what's there to hide?" [6]

"Shut up! Your father doesn't need to know *everything* we're doing!" she huffed. "I *meant* what I said. If you tell him, I'll end *everything* and you'll never see Paul or Jasmine again." [7]

"Why do you always question Mom and start problems?" my brother coarsely interjected. "It's not *complicated*, Sandra. Just keep your mouth shut. If Mom wants to keep it a secret, she has her reasons." Unwilling to lose Paul or Jasmine's company, I didn't breathe a word to my father about the encounters we shared with the neighbors. [8]

While playing in a stone hut on the edge of the cliff, Paul discreetly took my hand and guided me into the sunshine. His captivating features shown as he confessed, "Sandra, I am really glad that we met and spend so much time together. I look forward to each visit and really enjoy our conversations. You're funny, smart, and beautiful, and I have come to like you *a lot*. Do you think we could be… *more* than friends?"

Days prior, I had imagined my hand in his while I gently kissed his face. In that moment, I wondered if his words were nothing more than the glorious details of a vivid dream. However, Paul stared at me and expectantly waited for my answer.

Struck with the reality of my good fortune, a portion of my soul shrank back to determine what could be wrong with the boy. It was far too glorious to believe that such a swoon-worthy creature could fall for a scarecrow… a praying mantis… *me*. [9]

Logic commandeered the captain's wheel of my mind and declared any romantic relationship to be impossible to maintain. As thought provoking, innocent, and refreshingly articulate the conversations had been between Paul and I, he was unaware of the termagant's dark and controlling nature. I felt trapped. I desired to share my inner world with Paul, but dreaded the loss of his company as a direct result of a romantic relationship. If the materfamilias had discovered any mutual affection between Paul and me, or any transparency about our household secrets, she would have instantly stripped the boy from my life. [10]

An internal pendulum swung between adoration and trepidation. I clumsily scrambled for an excuse to reject his transcendent proposal and gently mitigated, "Wow. You're wonderful… and I mean *wonderful*… and I really, *really* like you, but… I'm, uh… *I'm just too old for you*. You're ten and I'm eleven. The age gap of a full year just seems *inappropriate* right now." [11]

Frozen in bewilderment during my speech, Paul quickly abandoned his dumbfounded expression, collected himself, and warmly replied, "That's okay, Sandra. I hope I didn't make you feel uncomfortable or drive you away from wanting to visit." Exchanging my stoic countenance for one of tenderness, I gazed with a soft grin and reassuringly shook my head. His anxiety melted between the rocks at our feet. "Oh, good. What a relief! I don't want anything coming between us. You're an amazing person and I'm just glad we're friends." [12]

Bible Study

During another surreptitious visit to our neighbor's property, a close relative of theirs stopped by. *"Hello, everyone!"* a woman greeted, waving her hand and making her way across the rocks towards our neighbor and the materfamilias.

Upon hearing her voice, the man immediately stood, thoughtfully retrieved a third chair, and encouraged, "Take my seat!"

Witnessing her arrival, Paul paused and informed, "That's my dad's sister, Martha. She visits a lot, but I don't think you've met her yet. Come on. Let's go say hello."

Sister Martha politely explained, "I'm so sorry, brother. I didn't know you were entertaining guests! I tried calling earlier, but no one answered, and when I knocked, no one came to the door. Then, I heard the children playing. When I peeked around the house, I found you! I hope I'm not intruding!"

"No, no, no," the man graciously corrected. "*Actually*, I'm glad you're here!"

As our neighbor made introductions, I observed Sister Martha's modest, shin-length dress. She wore her salt and pepper hair softly pulled back into a large clip that showcased her natural features. As the two women stood beside one another, the visual contrast between Paul's aunt and the materfamilias became stark, highlighting the full make-up, red lipstick, gold jewelry, tight shorts, dyed hair, and off-the-shoulder t-shirt.

"You have beautiful children," Sister Martha commented, sweetly grinning at my grateful expression. "Kids, I didn't mean to spoil your fun! You four, go play! Enjoy being young!" Without hesitation, we readily obeyed and started another game.

During our departure, Sister Martha smiled at the materfamilias and gently mentioned, "My church is hosting a weekly Bible study starting this Wednesday. Would you like to join us?"

"Oh, wow!" I interjected, already standing beside the termagant. "You're inviting her to a *Bible study*?! Can I come? Will they even allow children to sit in on adult Bible studies?" [1]

"Sandra, you surprise me! How wonderful! To answer your question, *anyone* that wants to learn can come, but it needs to be okay with your mother first," Paul's aunt merrily replied and quickly returned her attention to the materfamilias. "So, should I expect to see you and Sandra there this Wednesday?"

Behaving in a sheepish and soft-spoken manner, the termagant relented, *"Okay. I guess so."*

That Wednesday at dusk, we entered what appeared to be an old school-house. Resembling a metal staple in arrangement, large folding tables and a handful of chairs provided the broad workspace that I had desperately craved during my middle school classes. At once, I separated from the termagant's hovering and claimed a seat. From my backpack, I withdrew a notebook, some markers, a ballpoint pen, and my Bible.

As I organized the items before me, a man centered himself in the room and wondered aloud, "Your name is *Sandra*, right?! Sister Martha mentioned you might come… and just look at you! *Someone* here is eager to learn!" His pleasant demeanor and observations caused me to beam. Right then, the man brought attention to a large flip chart on his flank and revealed the starting page. "The most important truth to understand is that Jesus is the Savior of the world. He is the sinless Lamb of God who atoned for our sins, once and for all, by His death. Three days later, Jesus rose from the grave, revealed Himself alive to many, and then ascended up into heaven. On the day of Pentecost, fifty days after Jesus' resurrection, was the outpouring of the Holy Ghost." [2]

Wiggling in my seat, contemplating the fiery power of the Holy Spirit being poured out, I wrote each scripture reference and thought, "That's awesome! The Holy Spirit actually *does* stuff! Wow! This is so cool!" [3]

After reading the corresponding scriptures aloud with no questions being asked, the instructor moved on, and posed, "On your Texas Driver License, does it simply address you as daughter, mother, sister, or wife? No, it doesn't, although you may be *all* of those things. Those are only *titles*. What identifies you is your *name*. With that understanding, Father and Son are also just *titles*, not names. You cannot be saved in the titles of Father or Son. You're saved in the name of *Jesus*." [4]

I smiled to myself and thought, "Yup! That's Who saved *me*! Jesus is the Man!"

The following page of the flip chart revealed three labeled images with arrows directing to the word GOD as their nucleus. Pointing to each label, the man stated, "Now, there is *God* the Father who is the Creator, also known as Jehovah or Yahweh. *Jesus* is *God*, the Son, that manifested in the flesh and died as a ransom for our sins. The Holy Ghost is another manifestation of *God* that lives inside of each born-again believer." I raised my hand. "Yes, Sandra?" [5]

"According to your diagram, are you saying that God, Jesus, and the Holy Spirit are all the same thing?" I inquired, wondering why there would be different titles *at all* if distinguishing their differences weren't an important factor.

Bible Study

"Well, yes and no," he replied. "The Father, Son, and Holy Ghost make up what's known as the *Godhead*. God the Father, Jesus, and the Holy Ghost are different manifestations of the one true God. They function as one God, named Jesus, which is known as the doctrine of Oneness." [6]

Dogmatic LDS teachings, pharisaical rhetoric from the materfamilias, and the diagram of Oneness theology formed an abrasive cacophony in my mind. [7]

Scrunching my nose, I raised my hand again and posed, "How does *that* work? I mean, how can Jesus be the Father, the Son, *and* the Holy Spirit all at the same time? I don't get it. Technically, if Jesus is *the Father* and *the Son*, wouldn't that make Jesus His own Dad?" [8]

"*Sandra!*" the materfamilias interjected, drawing attention to herself. "Be quiet! You're embarrassing me! Who invited you to this anyway?! No one! *I was invited.* You invited yourself! Why won't you just let the man speak?! How can he teach the lesson if you're constantly asking questions and interrupting?! You're just a child! Let the adults talk! You're here to listen! If you keep interrupting, I won't bring you back!" [9]

Ignoring the visceral sting of humiliation, I remained stoic and fixed my eyes on my meticulous notes as an awkward silence chilled the schoolhouse air.

A woman boasting shoulder length hair and freshly trimmed bangs opened her mouth and politely stated, "I don't mean to be contradictory, but I'm wondering the exact same thing Sandra just asked and would *really* like to hear the answer. Personally, I'm glad she spoke up because I'm not sure I would have."

Moved by her meek heroism, I offered the altruistic woman a discreet smile of gratitude, which was reciprocated in a like manner. Sister Martha joined her expressions of approval, already warmly grinning when our eyes finally met.

The instructor gently added, "Mrs. Lawson, Sandra is not distracting or off topic, and her questions are *welcomed*. In fact, it's refreshing to see a youth so enthusiastic to learn about Jesus. Her questions are *good ones*. You should be proud." The materfamilias was unanimously overruled and remained silent for the duration of the lesson. Our instructor continued the lesson and stated, "To answer Sandra's question, Jesus holds the fullness of the Godhead bodily. Jesus *is* God, the Creator, in human form. The Holy Ghost is another manifestation of God. It was the Holy Ghost that settled upon Mary, a virgin, and miraculously formed the Child, Jesus, inside of her womb. Does that clear things up a bit, Sandra?" [10]

"Not really," I admitted. "Maybe the Godhead will make more sense later in the Bible study, since I haven't actually *read* the Bible." [11]

Our instructor chuckled and consoled, "Well, Sandra, you're in the right place to learn. Fortunately for you, I already have the scriptures we'll be discussing next week.

If you read them in advance to prepare, we'll go over their meaning together. Don't worry so much about the Godhead right now. The Holy Ghost will reveal it to you in time. As long as you know and accept that Jesus is your Savior, you're on the right track."

As our vehicle pulled out of the gravel parking lot, the materfamilias growled, "I don't care what they said to you! You *embarrassed* me in there! They don't *really* like you. They're just being nice to you because you're a kid." [12]

"Oh, really?" I confidently interjected. "That lady in there said she didn't understand the Godhead either, *remember*? No one else was asking questions, including *you*. Did *you* understand everything that man was saying?"

"*Yes*," the woman snapped. [13]

Having detected the familiar odor of deception, I chirped, "*Great!* Just so you know, Dad told me that if someone can't explain a concept to a six-year-old, then they don't really know it. So, let's hear it, Mom. Explain the *Godhead* to me. Help me understand."

"*Why are you testing me?!*" the termagant roared, reeking of insecurity. "I'm not in school! I don't have to answer to you! You'd better *watch it* before I knock your head off!"

"Technically, you *are* in school because we're students of a Bible study in a classroom setting. Also, you need to understand this stuff as much as I do," I firmly informed, mentally preparing for an abrupt backhand to the mouth. "You talk about God *a lot*, saying that He sees everything, that there's no hiding from Him, and that He's going to *get me*. Even *if* you really know about God and the Bible, you just refused to teach me about Him. So, where does that leave *me*?" Keeping her eyes on the road, the woman twisted her hands on the steering wheel and grit her teeth in silence. "If you want to waste your time sitting at a table just to stare at a book while someone talks in the background, that's fine, but don't stand in my way on purpose. Don't you think God would *get you* for that?" [14]

The Name of Jesus

~~~~~

*T*he following Wednesday, our instructor stated, "According to the Bible, we must be baptized in the name of Jesus to be saved." Seeming to expect it, my raised hand caused the man to smirk. "Yes, Sandra?"

"In the Mormon church, I was baptized in the… *titles* of the Father, the Son, and the Holy Spirit. So, should I have been baptized in the name of *Jesus* instead? Does that mean that, if I died right now, I'm going to hell? Do I need to get *re-baptized* to be saved?" [1]

"Let me put it to you this way," the instructor advised. "Getting re-baptized couldn't *hurt*. Remember, the only Savior of the world has a name… and it's *Jesus*. Jesus was the One that died for all our sins, and it's the name of *Jesus* that has the power to save. His Name is above all names. Jesus also resurrected and is alive. Because of this, you can talk to Jesus wherever you are, at any time, and He will hear you." [2]

Arriving home late, treading with apprehension due to the ghastly pale spirit that dwelled in my parents' bedroom, I began my nightly ritual of systematically sprinting up and down the dark hallway between the corresponding light switches.

Finally leaping into my bed and covering myself, I soon witnessed the dreaded darkness emerge before me and hover over my vulnerable body. Covering my head in a sweaty sheet-cocoon, I attempted to wait out the intruder as I had successfully done each time before. When I finally peeked, the darkness deepened before my eyes and grew even wider, and lingered above me longer than ever before. Although it had verbalized nothing, I clearly understood that the tormentor had set its will against me for my destruction. Wrestling against crippling fear with eyes tightly shut and body trembling, a sentence from that evening's Bible lesson glowed in my mind like an unexpected firefly in an abandoned dungeon. [3]

From deep within, I felt urged to utter the Name above all names and whispered repetitively, *"Jesus, Jesus, Jesus, Jesus, Jesus, Jesus, Jesus…"* [4]

I no longer sensed my haunting oppressor and uncovered my face to discover that the tormentor had fled. All that surrounded me were walls, a ceiling, standard objects, and natural shadows from the pale moonlight that poured in my window. I tearfully thanked my Messiah for His swift rescue and eventually drifted to sleep. [5]

The following morning, I pondered over my Messiah's most recent intervention and quietly uttered, "*Jesus,* thank You for helping me last night. That thing didn't like Your name at all. Did he? You sure showed him. I love You, Jesus. I know You know everything, but I really don't like being afraid. You saw what was in here. So, since You can do *anything*, would You please make my room a fortress? I need You to keep the evil spirits out of here and make this space a sanctuary. Thank You, again. In Your name I pray. Amen." [6]

UPC

~~~~~

Focused on a concept labeled *The Rapture*, the last lesson of the Bible study drew to a close. Suppressing my regret with a gentle smile, I carefully tucked my notes, Bible, and supplies into my backpack. Unwittingly coming to my rescue, Sister Martha sparked a conversation with the further inconvenienced materfamilias. [1]

Spotting the painfully awkward interaction between the two women, I hesitated in going to the termagant and regained the instructor's attention, chirping, "Sir? Thanks for answering all of my questions. I realize the lessons stretched out a couple of weeks longer because of *me*, and I'm sorry about that."

He offered a tired smile and replied, "Oh, that's alright, Sandra. Actually, I *enjoyed* teaching this Bible study. Well, not that I *didn't* enjoy teaching the rest, but it's nice to actually see genuine interest! You're hungry for Jesus and a very good student. You certainly kept me on my toes. I've been studying before each lesson just to be ready for you!" [2]

"You know what, sir? I *like* you. You're really nice to me and I learned a lot from you," I announced, noticing the contrast between the Bible study instructor and LDS bishop. "If you don't mind my asking, what's your name and what religion have you been teaching us about?" [3]

After a muffled chuckle, he answered, "Well, I'm Pastor Dolion of the United Pentecostal Church, but I wasn't teaching you *a religion*. The lessons were straight from the Bible." [4]

"What?! You're a pastor?! No way! Well, look at you! That's so neat! Where's your church located?!" I queried. "I want to go!"

"Well, Sandra, you're already here!" Dolion informed with a cheesy grin and arms opened wide. "You're already at the United Pentecostal Church! This school house is on church property!"

"Ha! Well, *that's* good to know!" I quipped as I blushed and laughed at myself. "I didn't see a sign! Wow. I feel silly that I missed it."

"Well, there *is* a sign… but, to your credit, it's out front on the *other* side of the building. You can't see it from here," Dolion added. "Hopefully, we'll see you this Sunday!"

During the ride home, I politely requested, "Do you think you could bring me back for the Sunday morning church service? If you don't want to stay, I understand. You could just drop me off."

The materfamilias wrung the steering wheel with both hands and snapped, "Why do you always do this?! You wanted to go to this Bible study… *and we went*. You even made the study *longer* than twelve weeks because of your questions! Instead of being grateful, you're asking for even *more*! Gas is expensive, you little brat! Are you going to get a job to pay for it?" [5]

"You're being super hypocritical. You spend *a lot* of money on gas every time you force me to ride with you to the city for groceries when what we need is *in town*. Then, we go shopping for hours in boring stores while you blow through *Dad's* hard-earned cash," I boldly rebutted, risking the shape of my nose.

"You're wrong. It's not *Dad's* money, it's *our* money," she clarified condescendingly.

"*Really?* That might be true in other marriages, but you just argued with Dad last night saying that all the money he brings home is *your* money… including each paycheck *and* all of his navy retirement benefits. *I'm not stupid.* You'll say anything. Who knows what you actually believe?!" I questioned, all but igniting her head with my unforgiving glare. "I'll work if that's what it takes to get away from here and into that church. I've dragged brush and dug post holes, so any other work will be a piece of cake. You're just mad because driving me to church interrupts your time on the couch! It's not like I'm not asking for toys or video games. I'm asking for an eight-mile ride into town to learn more about the Bible and be around other people who love Jesus. I don't think that's too much to ask. I don't know why you even talk about God. A person who loves God would be excited to know that their child wants to learn more about Jesus." [6]

"It's not just eight miles, you little demon! It's *sixteen* miles, round-trip!" the termagant rebutted.

"Yup. That's true… and I appreciate that you can add *eight and eight…*" I quipped, gambling with my life, "…but you've only proven my point. The city is way farther than that *one way*… and in case you've forgotten, I'm only eleven and can't drive. I'm just asking for good things that I can't get by myself. But, don't worry. When I'm *sixteen*, I won't bother you about *anything*. I'll have a summer job and work after school. You'll see. I'll have my own car and my own money. Boy, I'd hate to be in *your* shoes on Judgement Day being the one that stopped me from going to church. Why can't you just be *honest* and say that you don't feel like taking me? Stop lying and making up lame excuses." [7]

"*Ha!* You think you're so smart and have everything figured out, don't you?! You want to know the *real* reason why I don't want to take you to that church?!" the materfamilias aggressively offered. "I'll tell you! When I was a little girl, my mother visited a Pentecostal church and took me with her. I saw a woman screaming her head off and running up and down the aisle like a crazy person. She scared the **** out of me! I don't *ever* want to go back to that! Pentecostals are weird!" [8]

"Okay. Let's break down your theory about Pentecostals. You were at that Bible study every week, *right*? So, if you were paying attention *at all*, you'd already know what Pentecostal's teach: Jesus being God in the flesh, the Oneness of God, praying and baptizing in Jesus' name, getting the Holy Ghost, speaking in tongues, and the Rapture. In over twelve weeks, did you see *anyone* scream or run around? No, they didn't. The lessons were calm, informative, and interesting," I highlighted, eyeing the materfamilias as she silently stared forward. "Based on *one* experience that happened *decades ago* in a *completely different congregation of people*, you refuse to take me? *Wow.*" [9]

"What do *you* know?" the materfamilias snarked. "You're just a child." [10]

Before falling asleep that Wednesday night, I wept and softly prayed, *"Jesus, I really want to go to that church, but I need Your help. I feel stuck. You know my mother and You see my life. I hate being a child. I want to grow up as fast as possible and get far away from this place. Please, help me. In Jesus' name I pray. Amen."* [11]

That Saturday afternoon, I was mentally escaping reality by quietly laying on the carpet near my radio and analyzing song lyrics. [12]

From the living room sofa, the materfamilias abrasively shouted, *"Sandra, get over here!"* Unnerved, I made my way down the hallway and stood just out of arm's reach. "I'll take you to that church in the morning… but if they start acting weird, *we're outta there.*"

"*Really?* Wow. Fair enough. Thank you," I replied, astonished. "Out of curiosity, what convinced you to give me a ride to church?"

"Who have you been talking to?!" the woman gruffly interrogated. "What have you been telling people about me?!"

"What planet are you on?" I wondered aloud. "What are you talking about?"

"Sister Martha called today and wouldn't leave me alone until I told her I'd go to church!" she confessed. "Why does she want me to go to church so badly? She wouldn't shut up about it! What did you say to her?!"

I huffed in amazement and shook my head, rebutting, "Blaming me again, huh? At what point during any of the Bible studies were you not in the exact same room as me? When could I ever receive or make a phone call without you knowing about it and listening in on the other line? Blame me all you want, lady, but I *like* Sister Martha. Paul's aunt has convinced you to take me to every Bible study *and* a church service! She deserves an award!" [13]

The following morning, the materfamilias attempted to enter the sanctuary covertly while the worship service was already in progress. Conspicuously adorned with a full face of makeup and bright red lipstick, her dyed hairstyle, and gold jewelry, several Pentecostal greeters swarmed the termagant. Clean-cut men with shaved faces and barefaced women donning long skirts quickly closed us in, causing the materfamilias to cringe and use my body as a plow to navigate toward an open seat. One such greeter encouraged a few UPC members to scoot their positions closer in the pew to give us room to sit.

Mrs. Dolion passionately belted out a worship song to her sister's piano playing. One of her sons, Reuben, skillfully slapped the base guitar as her nephew hammered out percussion. Standing bodies with raised hands towered around our seated position. The materfamilias nervously occupied the pew, motionless.

During the lifeless LDS talks, the Mormons crossed their arms to encourage stillness. In contrast, I enjoyed the Pentecostal's freedom of expression and even attempted to stand. The termagant tightly gripped my boney wrist, held me in place, and sternly growled, *"Stay seated or you're gonna get it when we get home."*

Emboldened, I leaned my face toward her attentive ear and voiced, "Is that a *threat*, mother? Remember your own words. *God is watching you.* Are you seriously trying to stop me from praising Jesus… in a church service… while others worship around us? What's the point of even showing up? Were you trying to seem *holy* in front of Sister Martha? You can keep sitting there if you want to, but I'm going to worship Jesus… and if *you* don't like it, you can take it up with Him. Unless you want me to cause a scene, *let me go.*" [14]

She begrudgingly granted my liberty. I scooted forward and pressed my shoes to the ground as my scrawny arms reached upward. Surrounded my music and fellow worshipers, I sang along to the brightly projected song lyrics in gratitude and adoration to Yahweh's worthy Son, Jesus the Messiah. Although *physically* deprived of a loving home, I found *spiritual* solace in Yahweh's strength and protection by humbling myself before the Messiah through authentic, heartfelt worship. [15]

The materfamilias remained seated in a cacophonous room packed with swaying Pentecostals. Obstinance had exposed the woman as starkly rigid and unassociated. Naturally resorting to subterfuge, her rear end abandoned the lonely pew as she poorly mimicked those around her.

Standing close beside me, the trepidatious woman raised her hands partway, appearing more like a freshly caught thief than someone expressing love and gratitude. Her desperate forearm pressed against my unprotected ribcage and repulsed me. I took a step to the side, unwilling to be my tormentor's shield. When the woman repeated the offense, I almost stepped into the aisle. At that, the materfamilias relented. Back in her original location, she maintained a more comfortable distance from me. [16]

More than several in the building had long been bouncing, twirling, and sobbing with chattering teeth, repeating incoherent syllables over and over. Within a few moments, a soggy-faced woman near the front of the congregation released a blood-curdling shriek, turned away from the others at the altar, and nudged several unsuspecting worshippers to the side with her forearms. Having removed her obstructions, the Pentecostal sprinted down the aisle and wildly yammered, making an awkward loop around the sanctuary's fringe as bystanders urgently made way. That lady delivered leverage on a glittering platter for the materfamilias to weasel me out of the building. [17]

Refusing to reveal my shock and confusion, I pried my focus from the accurately predicted UPC bedlam and peered upward. Even with the unchecked chaos, I had already encountered more peace and love in that one boisterous Pentecostal worship service than *any* Book of Mormon lesson, LDS talk, or day spent in isolation with the materfamilias.

Eventually stopping the music, Dolion claimed center-stage to preach a prepared message that inspired nearly everyone to quiet themselves and claim a seat. Ready to be yanked away, I imagined myself gripping the door frame with all my limbs like a house cat avoiding tub water. Fortunately, the termagant remained in the pew until the end of the service.

Jesus' Name Baptism

Alone in my bedroom, I recalled the Bible study lessons about the end of the age. The concepts of Jesus' name baptism and *the rapture* had burdened me ever since Dolion had taught about them. Having already questioned my salvation since then, I retrieved my notes and opened my Bible to read the scriptures and interpret them for myself.

Despite my gifts involving critical thinking and reading comprehension, I struggled to understand the Word printed on those delicate pages. Rereading the same lines, over and over, my eyes quickly became heavy with sleep, as though some invisible narcoleptic fog was willfully hindering my spiritual growth. No matter what I tried, I couldn't remember anything I had just read. [1]

Frustrated and embarrassed, I closed my Bible and silently reasoned, "Maybe Jesus set things up to where only really good people can understand the scriptures. Pastor Dolion is a nice man and I'm sure I can trust his interpretation. Besides, they're nice to me at that church. Pentecostals speak in tongues and follow *holiness standards*, so they probably read their Bibles, too. Why would they jump through all of those hoops without Jesus telling them to? Pastor Dolion must be teaching directly from the Bible since no one is correcting him." [2]

The very appearance of Pentecostal women made the materfamilias squirm, and I sensed the intrusively familiar ticking from the time bomb who bore me. The woman didn't sacrifice her comfort or convenience easily. I believed it would only be a matter of time before the termagant would cavalierly detonate my life into oblivion, only to have a few more hours a week on her welcoming sofa.

Because of Sister Martha's powerful influence, the materfamilias begrudgingly agreed to drive me back to the Pentecostal congregation. Immediately after the Sunday morning service, while pulling out of the parking lot, the materfamilias remarked, "This place is *weird*. Why do you like it here? The women only wear dresses and they don't cut their hair! The men look nice and clean cut, but the women look homely, especially without any make-up or jewelry. I'm *not* doing that. I feel naked without my lipstick." [3]

"Has anyone there walked up to you and told you to stop doing *anything*?" I inquired.

"*No*, but if they do, we're not coming back," she threatened.

Anxiety choked me. I frantically wondered if I would have a chance to re-submerge before the Messiah returned to earth to gather up His Bride. I didn't want to be left behind to burn with the others. [4]

During the drive to the next Sunday service, I casually shared, "I want to be baptized in Jesus' name today. I really don't think the Mormon one counted and I'm not going to hell on a technicality." [5]

The materfamilias groaned, "You always do this! First, you wanted to order a Book of Mormon. I let you and the missionaries started bugging us. I even took you to the *Mormon* church to get baptized. After that, they had us going every week! I took you to that *Bible study*, and now we're going to the *Pentecostal* church every week. Is that enough for you?! *No!* Now, you want to be baptized *again!* When does it end?! When will it be enough for you?! You know what? I'm not driving you to church anymore. This is getting ridiculous!" [6]

Teetering between paralyzing dread and uncontrollable wrath, I clenched my jaw and chose my words carefully as I coldly replied, "It costs you *nothing* to allow me to be baptized. It's not an extra trip to town and they don't charge you for the water. In fact, *Satan* wouldn't want me to get baptized in Jesus' name *either*, especially if it meant me being truly saved. Whose side are you on, anyway?" [7]

"If *you* get baptized, they'll expect *me* to get baptized. *No way!* I'm not messing up my hair!" she reasoned. [8]

Staring at the materfamilias, I posed, "Didn't you pay attention to *anything* said in the Bible study? When you're *dead*, you'll have to give an account of your words and actions. Are you going to tell Jesus that you didn't want to get baptized in His name because *your hair* was more important? I don't think that will go over very well." [9]

After the sermon, before the termagant could yank me out the front door, I broke away from her grip and approached Brother Deacon to announce my urgent desire to be baptized.

Before I could speak, the materfamilias caught up to me and theatrically interjected, "I mentioned to my daughter that I wanted to be baptized in Jesus' name and now *she* wants to!" Slack-jawed and bug-eyed, I fumed at her multifaceted lie. [10]

"Aw! Good job, Mom! Way to lead by example! I'll mention both of you to the pastor and we'll schedule it soon," Brother Deacon assured.

"Wait. *Soon?*" I aggressively parroted, startling the man. "This is *important*. I may not get another chance to be baptized. I want to be baptized *right now*."

Having his patience tested, he patronizingly rebutted, "Well, we need to warm up the water, and that takes a little while. You'll just have to wait until next week at the very earliest."

Pressing harder, I leaned toward the neatly dressed adult and informed, "It's one hundred degrees outside. I don't mind the cold water. Besides, we won't be in there very long."

Out of excuses, Brother Deacon temporarily departed to retrieve Dolion, who reiterated, "It will need to be scheduled for another time, Sandra. We need to get the water ready."

Appalled, I boldly argued, "Sir, during the Bible study you said that a person *must* be baptized in Jesus' name to be saved. If you really believe that, why would you allow *anything* to get in the way of that? I don't care that the water is cold and, quite frankly, you shouldn't either. Is there anyone else I can talk to who will do this?! Come to think of it, does someone else even need to be involved for this to happen? Can I baptize myself at home in the bathtub? I'm not going to hell because of scheduling issues." [11]

"You know what, Sandra? *You're right*," Dolion conceded. "The temperature of the water shouldn't matter. However, if I schedule you for next Sunday, it gives more people the opportunity to be here and celebrate your baptism with you. I know *Sister Martha* would love to be there for it. So, will you wait one more week?"

"*No.* This can't wait. My mother already said that we're not coming back," I revealed.

Enlightened, Dolion's attention shifted to the manipulative termagant standing beside me. He gently inquired, "Mrs. Lawson, is that true? Have you decided not to return?" [12]

The materfamilias forced a beguiling laugh and deluded, "She's just confused about our family having plans *after* church next Sunday. We'll both be here, but we have to go now. See you then!"

Once in the car, a frigidity clung to my words as I stared straight forward and brutally rebuked, "*Wow.* You lied to a deacon *and* the pastor today… in the sanctuary. What I said before is absolutely true. *You'll say anything.* You threatened me for wanting to be baptized, and on the exact same day, you took credit for it. They have no idea what you are, but *I do*. If you don't keep your word and let me get baptized next Sunday, you'll have to deal with *Jesus* Himself." [13]

Still Unsure

I believed the Messiah sent Sister Martha and Dolion, who easily prevailed over the materfamilias' tyranny where I had repeatedly failed. Sweating profusely in the car on that scorching Sunday morning, the materfamilias and I pointed cooling vents toward our faces to dry off as tension hung between us. The UPC building became an oasis in my non-air-conditioned and treacherous world. Desperation convinced me that my survival hung on weekly attendance and everything I was learning from the pulpit. [1]

We stepped through the familiar threshold to join others in a pew. I swayed in corporate worship and believed the words of every song, ecstatic about my special day. When the sermon was over, they finally made the heated waters of the baptistry available to me.

In common clothing, I made my way into the small pool where Dolion announced, "You don't have to know Sandra for very long to discover her *persistence*. I had the privilege of teaching her a Bible study not long ago, and she proved to be quite the student. This girl is hungry for Jesus and willing to follow the path He has called each of us to walk. In the second chapter of Acts, verse thirty-eight, it states, '...Repent and be baptized, every one of you, in the name of Jesus Christ for the remission of sins, and ye shall receive the gift of the Holy Ghost.'" He peered down at me and asked, "Sandra, have you repented of your sins?" [2]

Pausing before Dolion, I searched my heart and peered into the water, silently asking the Messiah to forgive me for my *many* sins. Contrition filled me as I acknowledged that willful evil was to be abhorred and avoided. When the moment had passed, I looked up, nodded with a grin, and replied, "Yes." [3]

"Baptism symbolizes the death, burial, and resurrection of our Lord and Savior, Jesus Christ. This is a covenant and you're becoming a part of His body... His family... which gives you the spiritual last name of *Jesus*. You'll be Sandra Lawson-*Jesus*!" he playfully laughed. "Sandra, on profession of your faith and obedience to the Word of God, I baptize you in the name of Jesus Christ for the remission of sin." I was fully immersed and drawn back upward, hearing shouts of celebration, clapping, and praise to the Messiah. "There's a party going on in heaven for every saved soul, and one is happening for you right now!" The surrounding people placed their hands on my soggy shoulders. "Receive the baptism of the Holy Ghost! Worship Him, Sandra! Raise your hands and worship Him! Let Him fill you with His presence and speak in tongues as the Holy Ghost gives utterance! Thank Him! Yes! Praise His name! Thank you, Jesus..." [4]

As with my baptism with the Mormons, I waited for something miraculous to happen. Those around me held my arms up, chattered, and repeat unintelligible syllables. They squeezed my wrists as if trying to milk the same thing out of me. Seeing no sign of tongues, they eventually released my arms and handed over a towel. With a forced smile, I exited the water, disappointed in myself. Dolion preached that speaking in tongues was evidence of salvation. Although freshly baptized in Jesus' name, I remained unsure of my eternal future. [5]

Beg

~~~

"*J*esus said, 'And these signs shall follow them that believe; In My Name, they shall cast out devils; they shall speak with new tongues; they shall take up serpents; and if they drink any deadly thing, it shall not hurt them; they shall lay hands on the sick, and they shall recover!'" shouted Dolion from the pulpit, red faced and sweaty as he wrapped up his aerobic style of preaching. "If you have not received the gift of the Holy Ghost *with evidence of speaking in tongues*, come up to the altar before it's too late! Jesus will come as a thief in the night! No one knows the day or the hour! So, let Jesus fill you with His awesome presence to be born again into His glorious salvation! 'For with stammering lips and another tongue will He speak to this people…'" [1]

Upon hearing Dolion's words, I quickly abandoned the termagant's side and stepped into the aisle, progressing toward the pulpit with vigor. [2]

Kneeling on the carpet, I soaked its fibers with my frightened tears and quietly begged, *"Jesus, save me from hell and allow me to speak in tongues. Show me proof that I'm saved. Save me. Don't let me burn in hell. Help me. Make me speak in tongues. Help me, please. Help me. I love You, Jesus. I love You…"* [3]

One of Mrs. Dolion's sisters, Anita, walked up behind me, bent low to touch my shoulder, and asked, "Do you have the Holy Ghost, Sandra?"

With soggy eyes, I turned my body and frantically shared, "I thought I *did*… until I heard I wasn't born again unless I've spoken in tongues! After what Pastor Dolion said, I don't know if I'm even saved?! I love *Jesus* and got re-baptized in Jesus' name, but I'm so confused! Am I still going to hell?!" [4]

"Well, you love Jesus, don't you? You're obeying His Word and following Him the best you know how, right?" she sweetly inquired. I enthusiastically nodded while pulling a tissue from the box that Dolion's daughter-in-law, Giselle, had thoughtfully offered me. "Well, if that's the case, I don't think you're going to hell because you haven't spoken in tongues," the woman clarified matter-of-factly, slowly shaking her head. With a warm smile, Anita placed her gentle hand on my boney shoulder and continued, "Sandra, if you *want* the Holy Ghost, then let's just ask Jesus to fill you. Okay?" [5]

Women and girls of various ages swarmed me, holding up my arms or simply touching me while loudly worshipping, chattering, and wailing. Some gave thanks for another thirsty soul willing to be quenched by the Creator. I sobbed, hoping my Messiah was witnessing my desperation and would hear the needs of my hungry heart. [6]

The sanctuary-full of roaring Pentecostals eventually trickled down to a still-chattering handful. Unsure of how much time had truly passed, I noticed that most of the congregation had already left. Intending to stand, it proved a healthier option to sit on the platform steps, realizing that both of my legs had fallen asleep and tingled with the rush of fresh circulation.

As the remaining intercessors rose from the carpeting, Anita's young daughter cheerfully queried, "Did you get It, Sandra? Did you get the Holy Ghost?"

"Well, I didn't *speak in tongues*. So, I guess not," I somberly replied. "Sorry about wasting your time, guys. Thanks for staying to help. That was really thoughtful." [7]

"We love you, Sandra!" Anita graciously announced. "It's our pleasure… and don't worry about not speaking in tongues yet. Keep trying. It will happen eventually. Now, you'd better head on home. I see your mother waiting for you in the foyer." [8]

During the following service, as those around me worshipped and loudly jabbered, my jaw clacked with *stammering lips* attached. Murmuring similar gibberish as I had heard, I wondered if I was truly being born again in the Spirit or had simply willed myself into mimicking the actions and sounds from those around me. [9]

In my confusion, I turned back to Anita and queried, "Was *that* the Holy Ghost? Did I get it?"

She candidly replied, "Well, honey, you're supposed to *know*." [10]

You're Doing It

~~~

Another proverbial Pentecostal service drew to a close, followed by an energized altar call. Determined to *know* that my salvation was secure, I kneeled before the pulpit and fervently prayed for the Messiah to cause me to speak in tongues. [1]

To express their shared burden for this manifestation to occur through me, women surrounded me. They lifted, squeezed, and occasionally shook my arms as though the Spirit were stuck and needed a good jostling to dislodge.

Just as I had before, I tearfully loosened my quivering lips and allowed my teeth to chatter. Several women closely observed to cheer me on, enthusiastically claiming, "That's it, Sandra! Let it happen. Don't stop! You're doing it!" [2]

Even then, I privately wondered if the physical phenomenon I was exhibiting had spiritual roots at all or was simply manifestations of self-will fueled by desperate, unrestrained emotion. As instructed by a woman beside me, I used my voice and jabbered similarly to those around me. Upon hearing some familiar sounds emanating from my eleven-year-old vocal cords, several women clapped and laughed in delight, praising Jesus. [3]

Hearing myself yammering, I rejected all intrusive doubts and internally concluded, "This *must* be the Holy Ghost… and I won't ask anyone if it is because *I'm supposed to know*. I'm finally saved."

When relaxing my body, several intercessors in my proximity released my arms and readily announced, "I heard Sandra speak in tongues! She has the Holy Ghost!" [4]

With a smile, I stepped into the foyer, interrupted the materfamilias' conversation with Sister Martha, and chirped, "I spoke in tongues today!"

Sister Martha grinned and cheerfully inhaled to respond just before the materfamilias grabbed my wrist and flatly interjected, "Oh, you're done? Okay. Let's go." [5]

I concealed my deflated heart. During our hastened retreat, I awkwardly twisted my torso to glance back. With a wave to Sister Martha, I exclaimed, "Bye!"

The driver pulled away from the waving Pentecostals and coldly jabbed, "I don't believe you."

"You don't believe me about *what*?" I queried with a curious eyebrow.

"How could *you* get the Holy Ghost before me?! *You're just a child.* I'm the one that loves God!" the termagant scoffed. "Now, everyone is going to expect me to do the same thing! *That's it.* You got what you wanted. We're not coming back. Besides, I'm not going to stop dying my hair or wearing lipstick! If they want to look like bag ladies, they can go right ahead, but I'm not doing it!" [6]

I stared at the dashboard and rebutted, "I see what's really happening. I'm actually happy with those people and it *bothers* you. Doesn't it? They're nice to me and they care about me. I've learned more about God in that church than anywhere else. Are you seriously trying to get in between me and Jesus *again*? Not only that, but do you realize just how bad it will look when you pull me from church right after I got the Holy Ghost?" [7]

"No one will miss you," the woman hissed. "They don't want to babysit a little brat. Besides, you don't sound like someone who just got the Holy Ghost. You sound like a *demon*. I wish they could see how you *really* are. If you ever talked to them the way you talk to me, they would run from you. You're a monster." [8]

"No," I replied in deadpan. "You say horrible things about the Pentecostals and then have friendly conversations with them the same day. If you ever say to them the things you say to me in private, they'd run from *you*. I'm not the monster." [9]

The following Saturday night, I was determined to make it to the worship service by any means necessary and set an early alarm. After rolling out of bed Sunday morning, I readied myself for the day and made my way toward the front door.

The materfamilias noticed my neatly dressed appearance and sneered from the sofa, "Where do you think *you're* going?"

"To church," I confidently replied, pausing my steps. "It's sixteen miles, round trip. You can drop me off yourself or let me leave on foot. Either way, *I'm going.* Since I'm a little kid, someone will probably see me and give me a ride… or they won't. It doesn't really matter. I have two legs that work." [10]

"No way! You'll get kidnapped!" she argued. "Someone could kill you, molest you or worse!"

"No one will miss me. Remember?" I boldly quipped. "If you're even remotely serious about my safety, then *let's go.* I got ready extra early, expecting to walk. Honestly, it's taking longer to talk about it than if you had just grabbed the keys and started the car. We could be there already. I don't want to miss worship and you don't want to miss your precious television. Just think of it as free babysitting. I'm serious about going with or without your help." I opened the door.

The materfamilias stood and growled, "You think you're so smart. It's not *free*, you little brat. *I'm the one* paying for the gas." She slipped a pair of sandals onto her manicured feet. "I'll drop you off and pick you up, but I'm *not* going back in there." [11]

Suppressing the depth of my satisfaction and excitement, I calmly murmured, *"Deal."*

Sister Nebiyah

During each worship service and altar call, the UPC congregation sounded like an aviary of chirping birds. I had grown so accustomed to the repetitive yammering that with my eyes closed I could discern who was around me by the idiosyncratic forms of familiar jabbering and chatter.

After hearing another red-faced sermon, I stood in the foyer and waited for the materfamilias to pick me up.

Jimmy, one of Dolion's many nephews, exited the sanctuary with some cousins, threw his hands in the air, and overtly mocked, "Mitsubishi-buy-a-Honda-Mitsubishi-buy-a-Honda…" The other boys roared with laughter.

One of his cousins added, "Ride-a-boat on da wah-tah-tah-tah…"

I gasped in horror and shifted Jimmy's countenance toward sincerity as he admitted, "I didn't see you there, Sandra. I'm sorry. You're still new. I hope I didn't burst your bubble or anything. It's just that… well… I'm not so sure if everything that happens in there is actually from the Holy Ghost. *Either way*, I should be more respectful. We'll stop joking about it." [1]

During the following worship service, I made my way to the front of the congregation to sway and sing along, thinking, "If I'm not giving Jesus everything, then Satan wins. I'm coming, Jesus."

A voice silenced the congregation unexpectedly and captured my full attention. I turned to discover that the one speaking was none other than the founding pastor of that very UPC congregation, the aging mother of Anita, Mrs. Dolion, and their other present siblings. [2]

Sister Nebiyah rose from the pew and spoke with zeal in a non-repetitive, distinct language. Immediately afterward and in the same powerful tone, she translated the message to *English*, announcing, *"Thus sayeth the LORD…"* Once having uttered a full and authoritative interpretation, Sister Nebiyah carefully resettled into her seat where she discreetly leaned toward the beloved husband of her youth and curiously whispered, *"What did I say?"* [3]

Sister Nebiyah

In the unusual stillness, a handful of men and women from various positions in the sanctuary burst into wrenching tears as if cut to the heart. Although deeply interested, I too couldn't recall what the elderly woman had articulated *so clearly*. [4]

Before the materfamilias drove up to retrieve me, regret burdened me. I hurriedly sought several familiar faces to inquire about it. Of those that I had approached, not even Dolion could remember a single sentence that Sister Nebiyah had proclaimed. [5]

Test Me

~~~~~

*E*xcited to vacate the premises that Sunday morning, I patiently waited at the door as the materfamilias brutally announced, "You're not going back to that church. I won't take you and your father won't either. We've already discussed it. It's decided." [1]

Frustrated and bewildered, I posed, "Why are you doing this? I don't understand what I did wrong."

"You're just a child and I'm the adult. I don't need to explain *anything* to you and you'll do as I say. If you keep arguing with me, you're getting a spanking. Test me, little girl," the termagant threatened as she stared blankly at the television screen. [2]

In pursuit of a reliable answer, I rushed outside to my sweaty father, plowing through another home improvement project. Waiting for his power tool to pause, I respectfully inquired, "Dad, do you know *why* you're not being allowed to give me a ride to church?"

After inhaling deeply, the man divulged, "Your mother just wanted to pick you up without being bothered. Apparently, the women from church would flag her down and try to talk her into coming back. When she told them she didn't want to, they started complimenting you and saying how quickly you've been learning. She just doesn't want to take you anymore."

Furrowing my brow, I mentioned, "Well, she didn't *want* to take me to church in the first place, but that doesn't explain why she's preventing *you* from taking me. Do you feel the same way she does? Why can't *you* take me?"

"This is between you and your mother. I'm staying out of it," he warily replied. [3]

Defeated, I tearfully returned to my room and prayed, "Jesus, what was the point of me meeting those nice people and going to church if You knew it would all end like this?! I need help! I can't keep going like this! I can't! I hate my mother! I hate her! If she wasn't here, life would be so much easier and I could go to church. Dad wouldn't have to suffer being married to her anymore, and I wouldn't be her little punching bag. Would You please get rid of her? You see how she hurts me every day. Would You kill her for me? No one could get *You* into trouble. You can do whatever You want. Just help me, please. In Jesus' name, I pray. Amen." [4]

Alice

*I*solation with the materfamilias ended as I stepped into the sixth grade, but not my insecurity. A wave of hormones had drastically altered my classmates, who matured physically and grew even taller. I had not.

"Back again, *stuffer*?" Hank jabbed, accentuating his southern drawl with dripping malice. "When are your boobs gonna come in? Why don't you do everybody a favor and take your flat chest back to California?" [1]

Having already passed Hank in the hallway as he spoke, I pivoted and loudly remarked, "Hank, I'm embarrassed for you. Over the entire summer, you *still* haven't thought of anything clever to say? Thankfully, you're in the right place to make some positive changes. I suggest you build your vocabulary." Students began to pause and listen to the cutting dialog. [2]

"Shut up, Sandra! I'm *smarter* than you," the child rebutted, growing crimson from embarrassment. "You don't even know what you're talking about."

"Really?" I challenged. "If that's the case, then prove your intellect by occupying your mind and energy on something productive. You're obsessed! Since my body is the focus of your waking hours, which is *insanely* creepy, then you shouldn't have a problem coming up with an original insult next time."

"I don't think about your body!" Hank rebutted. "Gross!"

"Well, it certainly seems to be the case! You bring up my chest each time you pass me! Hank, if you don't like what you see, stop looking," I suggested. "Next time you decide to engage in a battle of wit, *come prepared*." After snickering at Hank, the onlookers dispersed to their classes. [3]

The popular girls all but ignored me in the fifth grade. However, their leader, Alice, began speaking to me in the sixth, right after I joined the middle school band. The stunning girl's legal guardian, a doting grandmother, worked at the same elementary school I walked past each morning. The woman radiated kindness as I ran to her for a tight hug that was readily dispensed.

I was terribly jealous of Alice's beauty and carousel of attractive boyfriends. Julio, her most frequent beau, was a smooth talker, very well-groomed, sharply dressed, and exceedingly popular. It wasn't unusual to catch Alice kissing him outside or walking shoulder-to-shoulder down the hall. The more they were together, the stronger the infatuation I had with the boy. [4]

During social studies, I sat on the floor to work on my project near the back wall. Alice leaned over to me from her tiny desk, smiled, and whispered, *"Sandra, do you think Caden is cute?"*

Stumped, I whispered back, *"Who's Caden? I don't even know what he looks like."*

When Alice pointed him out, I realized that Caden, too, performed with us in the middle school band. Because he and I had never spoken before, I knew very little about him other than he had perfect hair, nice clothing, sparkling eyes, and was a very gifted musician. With his commercial-worthy smile, he could have easily landed a spot in any boy-band.

Once it became clear who Alice was referring to, I whispered back, *"Of course."*

Alice immediately stood to her feet, pointed downward at my spot on the floor, and shouted, *"Hey, everybody! Sandra's in love with Caden!"* [5]

Heat radiated from my face and neck. Focusing on my project, I continued working, hoping no one would see me if I didn't stand up. The class of sixth-graders pierced my ears with their hysterical laughter and antagonization of Caden. In a flash, the bell rang and everyone hurried to their next class.

Traumatized, I slowly put away my things while internally wondering, "Why the **** did Alice do that to me?! What a *****! I thought she was my *friend*!" [6]

Still kneeling to load up my supplies, I heard a sheepish voice from the classroom doorway that uttered, *"Sandra?"* I lifted my gaze to discover Caden staring at me.

Pushing the glasses higher on my poker face, I calmly answered, *"Yes?"*

Vulnerable and shy, he queried, *"Is it true? Do you* like *me?"*

Entertaining no delusion that he reciprocated attraction, I politely admitted, *"Alice asked me if I thought you were cute… and I do."*

"Well, the answer is yes*,"* he snapped and instantly removed himself from the door frame to proceed down the silent hallway.

Bewildered, I hustled to catch him and called out, *"Caden! Yes… to* what*?! I didn't ask a question!"*

Caden briefly poked his head out from his next classroom and shouted, *"I'll be your boyfriend!"*

Turning back to retrieve my social studies project, I furrowed my brow and pondered, "What the heck just happened?! Did Alice find out that Caden secretly *liked me* and set this whole thing up? That's a cruel way to do it. This doesn't make sense. That *can't* be what happened. Alice was pointing and laughing at me. It doesn't sound like she had planned anything but harm. Why would she even think of doing that? More importantly, what would possess Caden to like *me*? I don't get it." [7]

Caden

~~~~~

I didn't look upon Caden's handsome face again until the following morning when I smiled and greeted him for the first time just outside the Band Hall. He wore a solemn expression as he anxiously waited for my arrival and announced, "Sandra, we need to talk. I don't think it's going to work out between us."

Unwilling to show even a hint of emotion, my poker face emerged as I replied, "Oh, ok. Well, *that* was quick. I'm going to my chair now. Bye!" I opened the Band Hall door and readied myself to perform. While assembling the instrument in a side room, I internally raged, "This is so confusing! I never even said that I *liked* him or agreed to be his girlfriend! What the ****?!" After taking a deep breath, I comforted myself and murmured, "This is embarrassing, but it isn't *heartbreaking*. I'm not emotionally invested, so I'm fine." [1]

After band practice, I put my hand on the door's push bar to exit and heard my name mentioned just outside. I gently cracked the metal open enough to watch Caden confess to Julio, "I don't know what I was thinking. I was just so desperate for a girlfriend, when I heard that Sandra liked me, even *she* looked appealing." [2]

My eyebrows all but touched my scalp as I pushed the door open like a SWAT alpha leader. Caden and Julio froze in terror with slack-jawed stares as I brutally clarified, "Caden, I *never* agreed to be your girlfriend. I never told anyone that I even *liked* you, so don't flatter yourself. This whole boyfriend/girlfriend ******** was all in your head… and Alice started it. So, allow me to set the record straight. You're a self-absorbed little ***** who needs a girlfriend to feel that he has value. *Good luck with that.* Hopefully, your next *pretend-relationship* lasts longer. Stop talking about me or there will be *consequences*." [3]

Julio pointed and laughed in Caden's face as I walked away, feeling *spectacular*. [4]

At recess, Alice approached me with several other girls. One spoke up and readily informed, "Sandra! We just heard from Julio about what you said to that *******! Good job! He deserved it! Caden broke up with *us*, too! He should pay for what he did!" [5]

"Don't worry," I proudly replied. "I popped that over-inflated ego of his. I think Caden's had enough." [6]

Alice chimed in and added, "We should all grab Caden and scare the **** out of him! Look! He's right over there playing football with the guys like nothing happened! He's already moved on with his life! C'mon, Sandra… he needs to be *punished*. Caden made everyone think you were *crazy*. Let's get him!" [7]

"No," I corrected. "You guys stay here. *I'll* handle this." Intending to humiliate the boy for slandering me further, I took immediate action and marched straight through the touch-football game that Caden and Julio were taking part in. *"Caden!"*

Every boy looked up with dread and backed away from the singled-out teammate, leaving him completely exposed. Little did I know that the band of bloodthirsty girls had followed behind me. Before I realized what was occurring, they rushed Caden, grabbed him by the arms, and pinned his frame to a nearby tree.

Amid the confusion and heightened emotions, Alice gave the command, *"Kick him in the *****!"* [8]

Without hesitation and to appease Alice, I grabbed Caden's shoulders and kneed him *near* his genitalia, inspiring him to feign injury. He theatrically doubled over and moaned as if shot, selling the drama for masculine sympathy. The instigators scattered in every direction, abandoning me to face the entire touch-football crew alone.

Refusing to be intimidated, I leaned over and whispered into Caden's ear, *"That will teach you not to talk about me."* [9]

Surrounded by gawking boys, I became nervous and realized that I fought without a proper cause or an adult present. Guilty of assault, I fled the scene and sought refuge on the monkey bars. [10]

Moments later, Mr. Alden, whom I adored and spoke with frequently, approached me and politely informed, "Miss Sandra, you're wanted in the principal's office."

Hanging my head, I painfully explained, "I got in a fight with a boy."

"I heard," he calmly mentioned, slowly escorting me to my fate.

Unwilling to lose his good opinion, I explained further, "Caden was saying bad things about me. *He had it coming.*"

"He probably did," the man replied with a sigh. Before releasing me into the office building, Mr. Alden stopped and voiced, "Sandra, you're different, so I'm going to let you in on a little secret. Actually, it's not a secret at all, but you may not realize this just yet. If you aren't from this town, *they don't care about you…* but don't tell anyone I said that. They'll do a lot more to me than send me to the principal's office. Anyway, you'll survive this. *Be tough.* Take your punishment and try not to fight if you can help it. It's hard being a new kid, especially out here." Once he directed me toward the entrance, Mr. Alden waved goodbye with a thoughtful grin on his aging face. [11]

At that, I straightened my clothes and journeyed toward the dreaded principal's office where the woman offered, "Come on in and have a seat, Sandra. What happened?"

In the spirit of justice and truth, I divulged *everything* about the initial betrayal of Alice in the classroom, the confusion and chaos that her words had caused, the *break-up* at the Band Hall, Caden's words to Julio, the aggressive mob of girls that approached me, and the result of their influence.

Sitting up straight and folding her hands together, the principal authoritatively replied, "Well, Sandra, I was told *differently*, and I didn't hear about anyone else being involved. Just you." [12]

"Who reported what happened?! There were *several* girls involved… and they're just as at fault, if not more!" I rebutted, surprised that Caden wouldn't seek vengeance on *all* parties.

"No one else was mentioned," the woman coolly continued. "It's your word against his, and you just admitted to hurting Caden."

"Wait a minute," I interjected. "So, I'm the only one being punished because I refuse to lie?! Are you kidding me?! Those girls approached *me*, caused this entire thing to happen, and made sure that it did! Now, they're hanging me out to dry and you're letting them do it! This was *their* idea, and *they* grabbed him! I was completely over what Caden had done to me and was going to keep to myself! Besides, the version of the story *you believe* doesn't make sense! Compare the two of us! I weigh fifty pounds! How could I push Caden from the center of a football game and pin him to a tree all by myself? A lot of people saw what happened. Where's the investigation?! Don't you *care* about knowing the truth?!" The principal stared at me patronizingly. "Those other girls have blood on their hands. Am I really the only one being punished for this?!" [13]

"*Yes*… and, honestly, I don't care *who else* was involved. *You're* the one who hit Caden, so *you're* the one who's in trouble," the principal admitted, failing to mention that Alice's grandmother worked with her at the school. "I won't condone violence. The handbook clearly states that the punishment for fighting is *three days' suspension*… which will start tomorrow. You'll finish out today's classes and I'll be calling your parents to inform them of what has occurred. Let this be a lesson for you, Sandra. *No fighting.*" [14]

My eyes widened as I exclaimed, "Exams are this week! If I miss an exam, I'll get a *zero*! My grades are *perfect*!"

"Those are the consequences," she dismissed gruffly. "This discussion is over. We'll inform your teachers of your suspension. Go back to class, Sandra." [15]

After the school bus had dropped me off at the log house, I dragged my feet all the way to the front door, as if to my death. [16]

The materfamilias didn't break her gaze from the television when she dryly ordered, "Go to your room and wait for your father to get home."

An hour later, her husband thudded across the porch with his work-boots, opened my bedroom door and commanded, "Come to the living room." I obeyed with overwhelming trepidation. "The principal called and said that you punched a boy at school." [17]

Frustrated at the termagant's inaccuracy in relaying a simple story, I clarified, "That's not true. I am in trouble for kneeing a boy in the *****."

"That's even *worse!*" the man declared. "If you think you're going to spend your *three-day suspension* just reading in your room and listening to music, *you're wrong*. I will have a list of chores for you to finish by sundown *each day*. If you don't complete an item, you'll get a spanking. Go to your room for the rest of the evening. Your list will be waiting for you on the kitchen table in the morning."

The sun rose on a new day. I studied the list of chores and smiled. It did not differ from my summer workload, apart from the weather being significantly cooler and far more enjoyable. I completed the list by late morning each day and occupied the rest of my time reading or listening to music.

Upon returning to school, I discovered that my report card would not be as negatively affected as I had predicted. Most of my other classes had exams scheduled the day following my return. However, I missed my Social Studies exam and scored a zero, which counted as thirty percent of my final grade. Thankfully, with top scores and my overachieving extra-credit, the heavy zero couldn't sink my grade below passing. In addition, my English teacher covertly moved her exam to the day of my return.

Approaching the woman, I confidently placed the completed assignment on her desk and mouthed, "Thank you."

"Don't tell anyone," she whispered with a suppressed smile and a wink.

On the ride home in the school bus, my body relaxed as I quietly worshipped, "Jesus, you get *all* the credit for this. Thanks for showing me favor with most of my teachers and my grades… and for making my suspension somewhat enjoyable. I've learned my lesson and won't listen to Alice anymore. What I did wasn't right, and I knew better than to attack Caden. I don't want to *become the bully*. I want to be like *You*. Help me care less about what others think of me. I love you. Amen." [18]

The Conductor

Because I started playing an instrument in sixth grade instead of fifth, I was at a disadvantage compared to the other band members. During a morning rehearsal, I made an abruptly disturbing sound, became overwhelmed with embarrassment, and stopped playing altogether. The instrument remained in my lap for several measures. [1]

Noticing my inactivity and hanging head, Mr. Bach stopped conducting and conveyed, "Sandra, look at me. You're allowed to make mistakes. It's your first year and you're still learning. Now, what I *won't* allow is for you to just sit there. If you make a mistake, it's not the end of the world! *Play on.*" As would a happily devoted father, the conductor suddenly tilted his head, crossed his eyes, and stuck out his tongue to cheer me up. *It worked.* I adjusted my instrument and obeyed. Refocusing on the entire middle school band, Mr. Bach gently commanded, "Alright. Let's start back at the beginning. Remember to watch me. Follow my hands to stay together. I'm keeping the tempo." [2]

Many of us elevated our stands to observe the conductor with greater ease while still reading our music. Mr. Bach lifted his wand and prompted everyone to ready themselves for the first count. After another small reach, signaling for all to draw a deep breath, he plunged down his wand for the first count and I *played on.* [3]

"Stop, stop, stop," Mr. Bach interjected, waving his arms. "We're out of tune. Horns, please stand." [4]

Each person played the same prescribed note, one at a time, adjusting their slide to the satisfaction of the conductor until each became pitch perfect. The moaning trombones were next, followed by alert trumpets and a few booming tubas. Cheerful flutes and piccolos made their dainty corrections with the jazzy woodwinds and saxophones finishing the tuning tour.

Instruction on the meaning of music symbols, seemingly endless corrections, and copious amounts of practice proved dire for growth. I didn't feel that we were getting much better until concert season came around. Everyone dressed neatly and sat up straight, focusing intently on Mr. Bach. Playing our best and as a unit, the harmonization of notes provided a clearer scope of the composer's original intent. Within a moment, the older students filled the stage after we exited to locate our parents. [5]

"Dad, how'd we do?" I whispered to my father.

"*All of you looked pretty nervous,*" he quietly mentioned. "*I thought one kid was going to pass out.*"

"Well, I was shaking, but how did we sound?" I gently pressed, seconds before the next performance was about to begin.

"*Sandra, a lot of mistakes were made. Let's just say there's room for improvement,*" he softly replied, inspiring his wife to backhand him swiftly in the chest, creating a thud. I glared at the woman for striking my father. The man leaned toward his wife and whispered, "*Stop hitting me. If she doesn't like my opinion, she shouldn't ask for it.*" [6]

The sixth-grade performance I had once been so proud of seemed no more entertaining than gum stuck under one's shoe. The seventh and eighth-grade band performed a colorful collection of tunes, but the high school level produced booming intros and fanciful melodies that drew a wide range of emotions to the surface of my skin.

Although relatively small, the high school band had been historically competitive and performed in the state marching finals, over and over, becoming known for it. Banners, plaques, memorabilia, photos, and tall trophies blanketed the elevated interior walls of the Band Hall with honor, and Mr. Bach led each of those victories. [7]

During our rehearsal, as the man gazed upon the next generation, Mr. Bach urged his young students, "Turn and look behind you at those open cabinets. One day soon, if you stay with it, *you* will fill those marching shoes and hanging uniforms." [8]

Each child had a decision before them. We could spend that hour in the Band Hall to kill time or use it to pursue excellence. Mr. Bach had been setting the stage for each of us to offer listeners more than pleasant sounds. We could offer an *experience*. The opportunity to become more was within reach. We just needed to take it. [9]

Salad

~~~~~

"*Dinner's ready!*" the materfamilias howled from the kitchen. *"Come and eat!"* As was our daily tradition, my father, brother, and I seated ourselves at the table to choke down whatever afterthought the termagant had set before us that evening. Within moments of doing so, the woman proceeded with her very own daily tradition, beginning with reaching into the cabinets for a dramatically large bowl. An edible mountain of iceberg lettuce, sliced cold-cuts, shredded cheese, and ranch dressing peeked above the container's lip to be carted before her deified television and consumed. [1]

Indignant, I inquired boldly from my chair, "Mom, why do you eat those massive salads instead of your own cooking?"

"*Ha!* I'm not eating that ****!" the virago snapped, revealing herself to be as unimpressed with the haphazard product as we were. "Besides, I'm trying to lose weight, so I'm eating a salad. I like salads." At that, she crunched her fork down into the eight-quart plastic container and shoved a wad of processed food into her mouth. [2]

"Fair enough, but what happened to sliced vegetables?" I continued. "I watch you make the same salad every day. You cut up three slices of ham, a fifth of a brick of cheddar cheese, and use globs of ranch dressing. *Do the math.* Your salad has way more calories in it than whatever *we're* eating, so it's not helping you lose weight. Also, I'm pretty sure that if you actually ate your own cooking, you might put some more effort into making it. Did you taste this before serving it?" [3]

My father held his breath as his wife spun toward us and shouted, *"How dare you?! Do you think it's easy cooking for you ungrateful monsters?! You've never liked anything that I cooked, so why try?! If you don't like it, **** off and make it yourselves! I'm not catering to you! You'll eat whatever I serve you or you won't eat!"* [4]

"Well, if you really feel that way, can I try cooking dinner?" I calmly suggested. "It'll be less work for you. Plus, I've watched all of those Saturday morning cooking shows on TV and would like to try a few things. They look really good. Is that ok?"

"No! Stay out of my kitchen, you animal!" the termagant ordered. *"If I catch you screwing around in there, you're getting a spanking!"*

"Stop talking, Sandra," the man interjected. "Eat your food." [5]

Fishing

~~~~

I contemplated ways to spend quality time with my father that somehow separated us from the quarrelsome materfamilias. When I recalled the termagant's open disdain for the great outdoors, I smiled and boldly requested, "Dad, will you take me fishing?" [1]

Before dawn that Saturday morning, my father and I loaded tackle boxes, fishing rods, five-gallon buckets, and bug spray into the pickup truck, along with ice chests containing drinks, snacks, and live night crawlers. We traveled down the neighboring caliche road and up to a locked gate.

"Dad, are we trespassing?" I nervously inquired. "The sign says that this property is restricted for POA use *only*."

"No, we're not trespassing. POA stands for Property Owners Association. So, this land is for property owners and their guests. I'm a property owner and you're my guest. We're fine," he assured just before exiting the truck. [2]

Beyond the covered pavilion was a foot trail leading down to the river. When we settled our gear on the pristine bank, I chirped, "Look, Dad! Someone already mowed the grass! How cool is that?! This is so pretty!" [3]

"I did it yesterday with the weed whacker after I got home from work," my father clarified. "There's not enough space on the rocks for more than one person to fish, so I cleared all this out and gave the grass clippings time to float downstream. Now, we have the space to move around and not get our lines tangled." [4]

I smiled and chirped, "Good thinking. Thanks, Dad. I know that took a lot of work."

We set tiny sinker weights and two-toned bobbers on our transparent fishing lines, baiting our hooks with the feisty nightcrawlers that squirmed in our hands. Although I internally mourned each of their deaths, I soothed myself in knowing that their sacrifice was providing an untainted experience with my father. [5]

As we cast our chunks of worm upstream, we hoped to entice a large fish to take a bite. The former sailor coached, "Remember to watch your bobber. If it gets yanked down, you probably have a fish. You'll be able to feel it swimming with the tension on the line."

Minutes passed in tranquil silence, allowing us to monitor our surroundings without disturbing whatever lurked beneath the rippling surface. The line tugged at my rod, causing me to squeal, *"I got one!"*

"Set that hook or you'll just yank the bait out of its mouth!" the man warned.

"Okay!" I shouted. "I think I did it!"

"Reel the fish in slowly, but keep the line taught," he added, having caught two of his own that were already swimming in our bucket of river water. "Okay. Now, carefully lift the fish out and get it above land. You don't want it to break free and fall back into the water. I'll net it." [6]

As I attempted to crane the wriggling fish over the dry grass, the smallmouth bass threw the hook, dropped with a splash, and lived to swim another day.

"No-o-o-o-o-o-o-o!" I howled, fighting back a sob to avoid irritating my father. [7]

Hoping for a word of comfort, I received none, sat back down to hook another worm, and recast, discreetly drying a tear. I eventually snagged a lively catfish, nearly slapping my father in the chest with it just to get it away from the water. [8]

"Sandra! Set down your rod! Catfish have barbs!" the man warned, slowly approaching his tackle box. Retrieving his gloves and a pair of needle nose plyers, he snagged the fish and pointed. "See those barbs at the fins? They have poison in them. I know you were excited, but don't just sling your fish at people. You could hurt someone doing that. Be careful." [9]

"Okay. I'm sorry, Dad," I apologized. "When I lost that other fish, it broke my heart. I just didn't want to make the same mistake twice."

"Well, good job, squirt. That fish is a keeper," the man encouraged as he plopped it in the bucket.

Deer Season

~~~

After moving to Texas, my father provided our household with a year's supply of venison that fall. The man ventured out long before daybreak in freezing weather and eventually brought back a tagged and field dressed whitetail shot on Mr. Weather's land. [1]

"Daddy, why do you hang the deer upside down like that?" I queried, observing him pin cheesecloth over the beheaded and freshly skinned carcass.

"If you don't allow the meat to drain of blood, it tastes *gamey*. Since I don't have a walk-in freezer, the meat needs to cool down outside, which is why I have to wait for freezing temperatures to shoot, so it doesn't go bad while it's hanging," he patiently replied. "I'll butcher it tomorrow when it's completely cooled. That's when the *real* work starts." [2]

"Oh, yeah! You package the meat up in wax paper and label it with a black marker," I added with a grin, trying to impress the man with my interest while swallowed up in one of his thick jackets. "Are you making jerky and breakfast sausage, too?"

"Yup. I already have the pork butt in the refrigerator," he informed. "You can help me make it this year."

"Yay! I *finally* get to crank on that old-school grinder Mr. Weather gave you!" I chirped, making the man chuckle.

After walking back inside, my father took off his work boots and added, "We need to finish the rest of last year's sausage before we can cook any of the new stuff."

I pursed my lips and begrudgingly murmured, *"Okay."*

"Wash your hands! Don't touch anything in my kitchen with deer blood all over you," the materfamilias interjected. "Weren't you cold out there?! I *hate* hunting!" The woman rolled her eyes in a failed attempt to be amusing. Her husband exited toward the coat closet with our jackets in hand. "Your father took me hunting one time and I'll never do it again! Freezing out there in a deer-blind is for *the birds*, man! Forget it! If I didn't have hot coffee, I *really* would have been complaining! You have to sit on buckets and be quiet for hours! No way!"

Backing away from the woman, I muttered under my breath, *"I'd rather sit on a bucket and freeze than listen to you talk."*

The first deer season, my brother had manned several trips with our father to fill the deepfreeze with meat, but his experiences didn't seem to stir any enthusiasm. When my brother declined an offer in my presence, I dove at the rare opportunity and squeaked, "Ooh! If he doesn't want to go, I will! Take me!" The man seemed annoyed at the situation, which only spurred my resolve to prove myself worthy. [3]

"Alright, Sandra. We need to field dress this deer," the man ordered the following morning. "Hold its legs open and keep them steady. I don't want to puncture the stomach. You won't forget *that* smell." My father unsheathed a large knife. Pride and my gag reflex discreetly wrestled within me as entrails steamed in the frigid air and plopped onto the dirt. "Okay, now move over there and keep the front legs apart. You're doing good. Keep it steady."

"Okay," I chirped, deserving an award for best actress.

The man produced a gleaming hatchet and continued narrating, "I'm going to split the sternum open to get the heart and lungs out. So, pay attention and keep the legs steady. I don't want to hit you accidentally."

The cringeworthy sounds, odors, and sensations were well worth the time I spent with my favorite hunter, even if it meant that some adorable woodland creatures had to eat lead and be disemboweled.

While the materfamilias consumed another massive salad in the living room, her husband finished his evening meal and informed me, "Sandra, two deer are already packaged up in the deep-freezer, but I need one more to have enough for the year. Tomorrow morning, I'm heading out to the deer blind. If you want to shoot your first deer, this is your chance. Now, if you *miss*, it's not that big of a deal. We can try again tomorrow or next weekend. The rifle doesn't have much of a recoil, so it shouldn't hurt for you to shoot. Do you want to try?"

By then, my squeamish reactions had been deeply suppressed and replaced with a tomboyish glee as I replied, "Are you kidding me?! *Hell-yeah*, I want to shoot one!"

My alarm sounded at four o'clock on a frigid Saturday morning, hours before dawn. The small woodstove heated our non-insulated log house, but was located down the hall and left my bedroom nearly as cold as outside. Since my father grew up in the northern states, he taught me a trick to implement for the occasion. Tucked right beside me in bed was my first layer of clothing that kept warm all night under my blankets. Wearing my pre-warmed items, I sprung out of my bed with a giddy grin and finished bundling up.

I puffed out my breath like smoke on that brief moonlit hike. From the front porch, we sauntered along and exited our land, eventually crunching our feet onto the caliche road that led directly to the front gate of our trusted neighbor. [4]

"Good morning, Sandra!" Mr. Weather greeted from his threshold, warmly welcoming us inside. "Since you're both so fond of hunting, I searched for some photographs that I thought you'd like to see! Take a look!"

We flipped through the developed images while Mr. Weather told stories about his big game and travel adventures. He tracked massive bears, treacherous cats, and various other animals to shoot just for sport. If he hadn't provided indisputable photographic evidence, official documents, and preserved memorabilia displayed throughout his home, we might have dismissed the man's grandiose history as a series of tall tales.

Over the course of his life, Mr. Weather had held positions at NASA, served as a deep-sea welder for the US Navy, and became a meteorologist for the National Weather Service. Mr. Weather's deep enjoyment of my father and I was a generous compliment, since he was rarely receptive to visitors, including his own kin. Our host had a manner of speaking that was as black and white as the images in our hands. The elder smoked his tobacco pipe, cheerfully shared a pot of coffee, and became more like a grandfather than a friendly neighbor. [5]

In order to be in place and settled before sunup, we waved goodbye to our host and made our way toward his deer blind. The simple structure was just large enough to fit two grown men and held two five-gallon buckets. We flipped them over and padded the seats with deteriorating patches of frayed carpet that were tossed to the side. I stilled my chattering teeth with a clenched jaw and regretted the absence of an additional layer over my aching, bony legs.

Peeking at his wristwatch, my father loaded his rifle and poked the barrel out of the blind to check the scope. Right on schedule, a timed event broke our morning silence. Centered in view was a deer feeder spraying kernels of corn around its base as a breakfast bell to the hungry prey who awaited its call. Soon afterward, a deer stepped forward to nibble in the clearing straight ahead of us. It wasn't a hunt. It was a harvest. [6]

"Can I see?" I whispered. The man gently handed the rifle to me. I peered through its scope and wiggled in my seat. *"Can I shoot that one?"*

"No," he softly replied. *"That doe isn't by herself. See? She's with her fawn. Without milk, the fawn will die. We want a healthy deer supply in the future, so let them live."*

After a few moments, the mother and her yearling wandered off and made room for another deer to expose itself in the pre-dawn hues. *"What about that one?"* I quietly asked.

"No," the man whispered. "*It's too small and not worth the effort. We need a bigger one with more meat. Depth perception is impaired with this lighting, so measure the deer against the feeder.*" [7]

The morning rays kissed the tops of the trees as another incognizant deer made its way into view. I murmured, *"Dad, that one's a lot bigger."*

"Yup," he softly agreed, granting me a nod to make my first attempt. *"Squeeze the trigger until it fires. Don't just yank on it. If you do, the end of the barrel will move and you'll miss. The shot should surprise you. Don't anticipate it."* I targeted just behind the front leg and hoped to penetrate the lungs and heart. Trembling, I exhaled and slowly squeezed the trigger. "Well, I'll be damned, Sandra! You did it!" my father exclaimed. "Where'd you hit it?"

Embarrassed, I awkwardly stretched the corners of my bottom lip downward to expose my teeth and transparently replied, "I'm not sure. I… uh… *I closed my eyes.* I didn't know I actually dropped the deer until you told me."

My father smothered his face with his hands, remarking, "You just killed your first deer… with your eyes closed… in one shot. I don't know if I should be jealous or proud. Your brother and I both missed our first deer with our eyes *open*." He sighed and softened his face. "Since I have a choice, I'm proud of you. Well done, Sandra. Just keep your eyes open next time. There is a difference between chance and skill, so let's try to rely on *skill*." [8]

Bruises

After returning home from work, my father cleaned up, joined us for dinner, and eventually reclined in his favorite chair to relax and watch whatever ballgame was broadcasting. Where his wife and son displayed indifference, I often tracked the score, remembered highlights, and tried to memorize various key players just to have something to discuss with my father that might be of interest. [1]

The termagant, as though she had not accused her husband of adultery the evening prior, predictably snipped, "Hey! Where's my kiss?!" [2]

"Why do I have to keep repeating myself?" my father queried. "If you want a kiss, meet me at the door or come here and get one. I'm not searching the house to kiss you just to avoid a fight. I'm done doing that." [3]

"Well, you must be kissing *somebody* if you're not kissing *me*!" his wife goaded. Right then, as if another individual suddenly wore her skin, the termagant's voice and manner of speaking starkly changed to that of a pouty child. Sticking out her bottom lip, the grown woman whined, "How come you don't pay attention to me?!" [4]

Calloused by his wife's nightly routine, my father plainly requested, "Would you please be quiet? I'm trying to watch the game."

Unable to ruffle her husband's feathers, the materfamilias repositioned herself on the opposite side of the sofa in order to peer out of the large picture window. She monitored the ranch road and routinely waited for the inevitable.

The termagant glared at the man with jealous paranoia and quibbled, "Why is that car driving by so slowly?! *Huh?!* Is that another one of your *whores* checking-in?!" [5]

Her husband remained still and silent until his preferred team scored or made massive errors. Miraculously, the materfamilias lost interest, abandoned her abrasive ritual, and distracted herself quietly with her bedroom television, leaving behind an unusual tranquility. Sport commentators and an assortment of beer commercials were the only sounds emanating from the living area. Having spotted the exceedingly rare opportunity, I approached my unsuspecting father, stepped around his propped-up feet, and boldly attempted to cuddle for the first time since we had moved to Texas.

Displaying subtle indications of being pleasantly surprised, he scooted to one side and lifted his arm, silently welcoming me. I wedged myself beside the man's ribcage and received an unexpected squeeze. I was just thin enough to fit. The cushioned armrest cradled my gangly spine while I rested a twiggy arm over his upper body to hug him and allowed the side of my bony knee to drape over his thigh.

I felt most like a daughter when my head rested on my father's chest, taking in the soothing rhythm of his heartbeat and slow, deep breaths. Anxiety dissolved and released the baked-in tension from my shoulders and neck. Engulfed by wondrous contentment, I let go of tracking any more events of the game and nearly fell asleep. [6]

Discovering some common ground with the wild game that roamed nearby, I sensed a threat, almost like the pricking of needles on my skin. As the predator entered the living room space and stepped into my line of sight, my neck and shoulder muscles reengaged. Ready to react, I tracked the scowling threat with my eyes.

My father's wife scanned the scenario and pecked with a pernicious tone, "What are *you two* doing?" [7]

"We're watching the game," the irritated man remarked.

I locked eyes with my accuser as she announced, "*Sandra* isn't watching the game."

"Well, she's not bothering me, either," my father replied, keeping his focus on the screen. "Sit down and watch the game or go back to whatever you were doing. Just be quiet. If all you're wanting to do is stand there and pick a fight, leave and stop causing problems."

She stomped away.

During the next commercial break, the man rose from the chair to use the restroom. Upon his return, he prevented me from resettling in my spot and claimed, "I'm getting kind of sweaty. Find another place to sit, Sandra." [8]

Preferring voluntary solitude over the sting of rejection, I retreated to my room and closed the door to solve a large, distracting puzzle on the floor. Moments later, I heard the familiar trod, a harbinger of trauma.

As if trained by Nazi Gestapo, the materfamilias burst into my domain and interrogated, "*What's going on?! What have you been doing?! Why are you and your father so close?!*"

Lifting an eyebrow of confusion, I remained seated on the carpet and stoically reminded, "Well, he lives with us… and he raised me. I'm not sure what you're getting at."

"*Ha! I raised you, you ungrateful brat! He was always gone!*" the woman raged, stoked further by my complete lack of reaction. "*Why are you two so comfortable together?! Huh?! What business do you have laying down with a man?! Why doesn't he do that with me?! Why does he prefer you?! I'm his wife!"* In the distance, her husband turned up the volume of the televised game. [9]

"Whoa. First off, he's not just some random man. That would be super weird and inappropriate," I rebutted. "He's *my father*… and why are you saying it like that? We weren't *laying down* like whatever you're suggesting. We were relaxing on the recliner… in the living room… and if he prefers my company to yours, it's probably because I don't accuse him of the same stupid **** every day. I'm giving you gold here. You should probably write this down."

"Uh-huh. You think you're *so smart*. Well, you're not innocent. I see what's *really* going on here," the materfamilias projected with vulgar contempt. *"You're ******* him, aren't you?! You're going to hell for what you're doing, you demon! My father molested me, but you like what he's doing! Don't you, you little ****?!"* [10]

"Are you ******* serious?! What the **** are you saying that for, you twisted *****?!" I roared, reflecting her tone and manner of speaking. From behind her back, a swinging object caught my eye. My father's belt dangled from her white-knuckled hand. She sentenced me before a single word had ever escaped my lips. Since a beating was virtually inevitable, I shouted upward from the carpet, *"What the **** is wrong with you?! Get out of my room, you ******* pervert!"* [11]

"How *dare* you talk to me like that, you little animal! I'll do whatever I want! I'm your *mother*, you demon from hell!" the termagant roared. [12]

Tooled leather cracked against my back, over and over, causing me to writhe. The belt wrapped around my torso and slapped at my bony hips with the buckle. As I guarded my face, the woman aimed at my exposed legs and abdomen. Out of breath and exhausted, the materfamilias removed herself as swiftly as she had arrived, abandoning me to sting and throb beside the undisturbed puzzle. [13]

Sizzling with indignation, I whispered a tearful prayer and murmured, *"Jesus, please… please, get my mother out of our lives. Kill her, if You have to. I don't care how You do it. I just want her gone. Help me. Amen."* [14]

The following day at school, Alice joined me on the uneven bars at recess and noticed the discolored skin on my exposed legs. "Whoa! *Sandra!* What happened to you?! Get down from the bars and let me see!" she ordered. Moved by her genuine concern, I obeyed and allowed her to pull the fabric away from my body to peek. "Sandra! Your legs are all bruised up! How did this happen?! *Who did this to you?!* Let me check your back!" Alice lifted the rear portion of my shirt and exposed the discoloration on my ribcage and spine. A lengthy silence only fueled the sixth grader's concern. Lowering her voice, she entreated once more, "Sandra, who did this to you?"

"My mom," I choked out. [15]

Her eyes grew wide and quickly transitioned from shock to an outpouring of rage, announcing, *"That *****! What kind of sick person does this to a child?! Your mother is a ******* psychopath! I'm telling!"* Kicking up dust, she turned and sprinted to the principal's office.

Standing alone beside the uneven bars, I internally fretted, "What's going to happen if the police get involved? What if I'm taken away from Dad, too?! He'll have no one to defend him! She'll *kill* him!"

Alice rapidly returned and skid to a stop on the loose gravel, panting, "The principal wants to talk to you. Sandra… *seriously*… it looks really bad. *Tell the truth.*" [16]

The principal was waiting just outside of her office and invited me in. After closing the door behind us, the woman prompted, "Let me take a look." Permitting her, I turned and leaned forward for inspection. "Okay, Sandra. What happened?"

Believing she would only make things worse, I flatly replied, "I was mouthy and got spanked. I had it coming." [17]

Furrowing her brow, she motioned for me to take a seat and remarked, "This doesn't look like a normal spanking. The bruises are *very dark* and *everywhere*."

"Well, naturally, I moved around," I calmly stated as I shifted my body and fought the urge to wince. "This was my fault. I did it to myself. I deserved it."

"Alice seems to think that you are being abused at home by your mother. Is this true?" the woman bluntly probed.

"It's nothing I can't handle," I proudly stated.

The principal continued, "Does this sort of thing happen *a lot*?"

"I bow up a lot. So, *yes*," I admitted, attempting to disarm her by providing a shallow candor and a few self-incriminating facts. "However, last night's encounter *did* seem to be a bit more severe than usual." [18]

"Sandra, if you come to school like this *again*, I'm not going to ask you what happened. I will notify CPS immediately. If you *are* being abused, it doesn't have to continue… and, just so you know, Alice cares about you. She wouldn't have come to me if she didn't." I focused on the desk to wrestle against rolling my eyes. "If you have nothing else to say, you may go back to class." [19]

As I exited the building, my mind groaned, "I'm an idiot! Why did I protect that *****?! What the hell is wrong with me?! Jesus just answered my prayer! He threw me a bone to get rid of my mother… and I tossed it right back in His face! Now, if I walk back in there, the principal will *really* think I'm a liar. What a mess." [20]

Doom

~~~~~~~~~~

It was unusually peaceful within the four log walls. Each member of the household was about their own business, which left me to read and doodle for hours on end while enjoying my quietly playing radio. Startling me, the telephone rang and mysteriously continued without the materfamilias snatching it up.

I curiously walked past the living room and toward the kitchen to arrive in time to watch my brother politely greet, "Hello?" Making eye contact with me, the boy calmly ordered, "Sandra, go get Dad. It's for him."

"Oh, okay," I complied, turning on my heels to exit the house. Squeaking to an abrupt stop on the tile floor, I turned back. "Wait a second. Why are *you* allowed to answer the phone? Where's Mom?"

"Mom left this morning. She'll be back later," he informed me matter-of-factly. "Now, go get Dad. Someone wants to talk to him."

Retrieving the sweaty man from his outdoor work, I grumbled to myself, "No one tells me *anything*." Back in my bedroom, I clicked on my radio. An epiphany struck me, causing me to pause and chirp, "*Ha!* It's no wonder I'm having such a good day! That ***** isn't here!" In celebration, I turned up the music and sang the familiar lyrics, dancing around my room with an exuberant flare. [1]

"Come here, kids!" our father summoned. As we tranquilly approached the man, his demeanor became uncharacteristically gentle as he informed, "Your mother has been in a car accident and is in the hospital. I just called Uncle-M. He's on his way here to watch you while I'm at the hospital with your mother."

Suppressing my bubbling glee, I queried, "Is it bad?"

"I'm not sure," the man replied. "I don't have any more information." Peering down at his offspring, the man kneeled with opened arms to offer *comfort*.

Ignoring the irony, I readily accepted his unprecedented invitation. During the picturesque group hug, I rested my cheek on the man's warm shoulder and exhaled, allowing my face to relax into a gentle smile. I longed for his wife's tyrannical reign to arrive at an abrupt and gruesome end. [2]

That night, the phone rang once more and drew a small huddle around Uncle-M as he answered and listened intently, relaying, "Your parents are about to leave the hospital. Your mother's not injured, apart from some bruising and whiplash. Your dad is bringing her home right now."

I dramatically rolled my eyes in overt disappointment as Uncle-M tightened his lips to keep a straight face. Doom engulfed my heart with each passing moment, robbing me of whatever joy my uncle had afforded. When a set of headlights approached the house, I fought back tears. Uncle-M hugged my brother and me, shook my father's hand on the front porch, and removed himself with haste.

"So, what happened?" I wondered aloud, evaluating the termagant's condition as she casually stepped across the threshold. "What are you made of, lady?! You don't even look like you've been in an accident!"

"I know! Right?!" the woman agreed, nodding with a wide-eyed and abrasively toothy grin. "God was watching out for me! You see, Sandra? It pays to be *good*." Her passive-aggressive jab caused my jaw to clench as she occupied the chair stationed beside my father's empty recliner. "The bruise is from my seatbelt, but my blouse covers it up. I won't even need makeup! Isn't that nice?! Can you imagine what would have happened if I wasn't wearing my seatbelt?! *See?* Don't I always tell you kids to put on your seatbelts? I could have died! That seatbelt saved my life!" [3]

"Where did this happen?" I dryly queried. "Were you on the highway? I mean, you only have one bruise, so the accident must not have been that bad. What condition is the vehicle in? Can it be fixed?"

"It's totaled," the woman stated, averting her eyes.

"Well, that's unfortunate. Did it happen on the highway? Was anyone else involved?" I continued. The materfamilias opened her mouth to speak but dramatically hesitated and pursed her lips together with a tucked chin. Becoming increasingly intolerant of her vague responses and impartial answers, I pressed, "*Okay*… so, was anyone else hurt? Did they go to the same hospital as you? How are they?"

"No one else was in the accident," the materfamilias coyly revealed.

"So, if there wasn't another vehicle involved, that means that *you* were at fault. Hopefully Dad's insurance will cover the damages," I remarked as the woman glared at me. "We know the incident happened in broad daylight, so your collision was most likely with a stationary object… and it must have been something sturdy, too, like concrete… since the seatbelt *saved your life*." My father cautiously rested his hand on the front door handle as he witnessed his wife's countenance all but sizzle and melt from her skull. "How *did* you lose control of the vehicle? Did you take your eyes off the road or something? What was your speed? Did the police get involved?" [4]

*"It's none of your **** business, you little monster!"* the suspect roared. "I don't have to answer to you! You're not paying for it! Who do you think you are… questioning me?! *How dare you?!* I'm the parent and you're the child! You'd better get out of my face, little girl, or I'll spank you! Go to your room!" [5]

At bedtime that night, I struggled to determine why the termagant maintained her wretched pulse and pondered, "I know Jesus loves everybody… *even her*… and saves people all the time. He could be the reason she's still alive. On the other hand, Satan hates me and wants me to suffer for as long as possible. I could see him keeping that woman alive as a weapon to destroy me. It's a coin toss." [6]

Alice Was Right

*Q*uietly sitting in proximity to the materfamilias, I attempted to watch television without disturbing her. An advertisement caused my skin to tingle. A newly developed website provided an organized, user-friendly way to search for medical and psychological information from credible sources *at no cost.*

Only one question burned in my anxious mind, as I internally wondered, "Can someone *finally* tell me what is wrong with my mother?!"

I dreaded the woman's retribution, if she were to discover my intensions, and concealed my eagerness to diagnose her by remaining motionless until the regularly scheduled program had returned to the screen. Still leery of alerting her intense paranoia, I stalled a few minutes more and casually threw her off track by using the restroom. Pretending to play a PC game, I calmly stationed myself at the family desktop computer, leaving nothing but a few cubic yards of open space between her and I. Just to be safe, in the event she stomped over to conduct a surprise inspection, I kept a game ready on the taskbar to toggle over and play.

While the webpage loaded, a solitary word jumped to the front of my mind as a starting point for my educational journey. Alice had labeled the termagant a *psychopath* just before sprinting to the principal about my suspicious bruises. I keyed in the letters, hit enter, and waited. Dial-up internet revealed the invaluable findings inchmeal on the monitor. [1]

Poring over the details of each paragraph as they were being displayed, I grew increasingly wide-eyed and slack-jawed. According to their findings, psychopathic individuals truly believe that they are superior to others. Being void of self-control and displaying no remorse for their actions, psychopaths unscrupulously deceive and manipulate others to achieve their ultimate goals. In many cases, they charmed their victims in the beginning of relationships to draw them in, only to become controlling and violent. An alarmingly large percentage of those incarcerated meet the qualifications of psychopathy. [2]

Holding my face in my hands, I silently admitted, "Alice was right."

Exploring even further, I clicked on a link regarding *paranoid schizophrenia* and flared my nostrils, thunderstruck. The warning signs included unwarranted suspicion, delusions of a cheating spouse, not trusting neighbors, fits of rage, domestic violence, and powerfully influential hallucinations. Many times, most outbursts occurred behind closed doors, aimed at members of their immediate family or household, as opposed to public displays or with strangers. [3]

During another commercial break, my body tightened as the materfamilias quickly stood from the sofa and vacated the living room, but soon relaxed when I heard water flow from the kitchen sink. She washed her hands again and immediately returned to her seat. Her unnecessarily repetitive cleansing occurred countless times a day, regardless of the activity. It reminded me of a movie about someone diagnosed with OCD who did similarly. Upon investigation, I discovered that individuals displaying symptoms of *obsessive-compulsive disorder* commonly panic about germs and dirt, are uncomfortable touching doorknobs or using public restrooms, and are afraid to shake someone's hand, all leading to ritual hand washing and cleaning. The individuals often obsess over their own potential injury or the potential injury of others and are frequently hoarders. Many of those diagnosed with OCD constantly suspect that their spouse is being unfaithful, without reason or proof. [4]

Many doctors had completed agonizing years of education, interviews, and painstakingly documented observations to grant their findings to a world seeking answers. Their efforts were not wasted on *me*. Without ever meeting the materfamilias, brilliant strangers had delivered crucial vindication through a website. Middle school posters boasted that knowledge offered its own sort of power. With my newfound understanding, I unpacked a life-altering concept: I was *not* the cause of the woman's abusive behavior. I sat back in awe and took a deep breath, no longer drowning in confusion and self-doubt. Swelling tears streamed down my relaxed smile. [5]

The website stated that there were *no known cures* for psychopathy, paranoid schizophrenia, or obsessive-compulsive disorder, but I knew the One that made all things possible. However, at the moment, I was still being monitored by a psychopathic paranoid-schizophrenic with OCD. Covering my tracks, I exited the site, carefully deleted the browser history, shut down the computer, and calmly retreated to my room. [6]

Tears soaked the carpet beneath me as I dropped to the floor and prayed, "Jesus, I need You. You see what happens in this house because You know *everything*. It's horrible here, but I know You can fix it. Help this family. Either heal my mother of psychopathy, paranoid schizophrenia, and obsessive-compulsive disorder or take her away from us. I don't care if you have to put her in a mental institution and throw away the key. Just help us, Jesus. Help us. Amen." [7]

Loophole

The sun of summer break had all but scorched every acre of grass, leaving it itchy, brown, and brittle all over again. After dousing bug spray on my ankles, wrists, waist, and neck to combat flies, ticks, and chiggers, I tolerated the temperature and completed my chores. To finish my daily ritual, I enjoyed a cooling shower and stepped into my room to avoid the materfamilias. [1]

Writing letters remained my sole mode of communication with the outside world, but correspondence with Nancy had grown less frequent. Isolated and emotionally malnourished, I craved mental stimulation to distract me during the slow creep of time. I heavily leaned upon reading fictional adventure books, re-watching movies, solving massive jigsaw puzzles, memorizing music lyrics, and hours of daydreaming to numb the pangs of social starvation. [2]

In contrast, my sibling had made a few friends among his classmates that often called and requested his presence. Not only were they allowed to enter the house, the materfamilias even permitted her son to leave with them regularly and stay out as long as he desired.

"He's gone… *again?!*" I protested. "He gets to do whatever he wants! It's obvious that you hate me and love him, so why do you keep me here and let him leave?! I don't get it! Think about it. I could be out of your hair, but you won't let me call anyone to invite them over or have them come get me! I'm trapped! You know, forcing me to watch your son live under a completely different set of rules is *evil*. Maybe that's it. Is this some diabolical plan of yours? Do you enjoy torturing me? Well, soak it in, lady. When I'm eighteen, I'm getting the hell out of here and I'm never coming back." [3]

"*Ha!* You think you know so much?! You're just a child. You don't know *what's* out there," the materfamilias rebutted, actually breaking her gaze from the television to respond. "I don't trust *anyone* with you. You think you're safe with your friends? Well, you're not! All your friends have brothers, cousins, fathers, uncles, or little boyfriends that could just hit you on the head and do whatever they want to with you! They don't care about you! And you're so small! You could *easily* get raped, molested, or *killed!*

They could throw your body in a ditch somewhere and no one would even know! *No-no-no.* No one can protect you like *I can.*" [4]

In the spirit of self-preservation, I decided against a blinding eye-roll and fixed my gaze upon the sofa. Lingering in her abrasive presence, I calmed myself and respectfully rebutted, "Well, you trusted I was safe with the Pentecostals. Remember that? I went week after week and nothing bad happened to me there. If your son is allowed to go *anywhere* with his friends, shouldn't I *at least* be allowed to go back to church? You'll know *exactly* where I am…" [5]

"No," she snapped without hesitation. "We're not doing that again. I don't feel like dropping you off and picking you up. Your brother's friends have rides, so I don't have to do anything. Besides, your brother doesn't even have to call them. They call *him*. I don't want you bugging everybody to give you a ride to church. That's embarrassing." Boldly indignant, I glared at her, motionless. "Keep it up, little girl. You'd better get away from me, or I'll give you a spanking." [6]

Days later, I discovered my sibling using the desktop computer. Expecting him to be playing one of his favorite violent games, I approached to look on and entertain myself. Displayed on the screen was *nothing* I expected. The boy typed words into a small box and hit the enter key. Seconds later, a response appeared.

"Cool! What's this?" I queried, amazed. "Who are you talking to?"

"*A friend from school,*" he frigidly whispered, already irritated at my presence. "*Now, be quiet.*"

Confused over the secrecy, I prodded, "Does Mom know about this?"

Suddenly projecting kindness and a warm smile, he swiveled the chair to face me and quietly offered, "*Do you want me to show you how to chat with someone online? You could talk to your friends, too.*" [7]

"Wait a second," I interjected. "Is *this* how you've been able to get your friends to call the house and pick you up?" He nodded, debunking the termagant's report of her son enjoying *unprovoked* adventures. "Well, I don't know if any of my friends are even *aware* of this stuff, but it doesn't really matter. Mom won't let me go anywhere. She *hates* me."

The phone rang, causing the lounging materfamilias to quickly trod toward the kitchen landline and pick up the receiver. The call was for her beloved son. Aware of the secret, I simply huffed at his genius and shook my head, witnessing my clever brother close the text box, stand from the computer chair, and walk through another loophole in our family's broken system.

The Backslider Prayer List

~~~

The materfamilias warmed the sofa that Saturday as I approached her and posed, "If you didn't have to lift a finger, would you let me go to church?"

"Ha! How are you gonna get there?!" the woman smugly barked. "I already told you… your father isn't taking you and I'm not letting you bother people by calling them." [1]

"Is that all?" I flatly verified, bringing on a suspicious glare from the termagant. "Well, if you have no other restrictions to add, I'll just return to my room and let you get back to your show."

Early Sunday morning, I rolled out of bed, changed into a comfortable t-shirt and some jeans, tied on my tennis shoes, and snagged my backpack. I found my loophole and intended to jump right through it.

Nearly exiting, the materfamilias queried menacingly from the couch, "Where do you think you're going?!"

"To *church*… but I need to leave right now or I'll be late," I informed, resting my hand on the door handle. "Since you won't let Dad give me a ride and I'm not permitted to reach out to anyone else who would, you've left me no choice but to ride my bike. Walking takes too long. Either way, it's just like I said… *you don't have to lift a finger.* May I go now? You're making me late."

"You're gonna ride your mountain bike all the way to church… *with all of those hills*… in this heat?!" The woman tossed back her head with a cackle to ridicule, "If you think you can do it, *be my guest!* You won't even make it to the highway!" [2]

"I'll take that as permission," I deadpanned, exiting with haste and jumping on my bike. Her condescending words only added fuel to my resolve. "I'll show *you*, lady." Pedaling furiously, I traveled down our gravel driveway and turned onto the ranch road. "Okay, Sandra. The hard part is over. You made it out of the house. Now, the only thing that can stop you is *you*, so ride hard. You may not get another chance." [3]

The temperature exceeded one hundred degrees and already created incredible discomfort with streams of sweat and burning skin. I quickly lost momentum at a steep incline and nearly toppled over. It was apparent that my bodyweight alone wasn't enough for progression. However, when attempting to push the mountain bike on foot, my shin painfully clipped the protruding pedal several times as I ran.

Far too short to continue that way, I painfully remounted the stinging black seat and forced the unforgiving pedals to yield to my will, utilizing whatever strength I had in the rest of my body in conjunction with my legs. Understanding basic physics, I firmly clutched and pulled upward on the handlebars, as one might lift a set of kettlebells, thus creating the appropriate downward thrust. My hands, arms, core, and thighs burned from within as I relentlessly cranked, over and over, to conquer a daunting voyage where declines had eluded me for over two excruciating miles. Summiting yet another grueling incline that barely leveled off, I realized that my path had been nothing less than a massive asphalt staircase of winding upward slopes. [4]

Tall grass, familiar wooded areas, and manicured acreage held no beauty for me as I slogged along that baking ranch road. Grasshoppers hitched a ride on my glistening skin, only to abandon me with an explosive jump and descending flutter into the parched roadside blades. Invasive thoughts of the termagant's maligning expectations continuously drove me onward like a cracking whip until I beheld a most wondrous and life-giving view.

"Oh, my gosh. I freaking did it. It's the highway. That'll show her. *Ha!*" I huffed with a Cheshire cat grin, turning toward town. "Okay. You did good, Sandra, but you're not done. Keep pedaling. We got miles to go. *Mush!*" [5]

Just before I completely ran out of energy, a portion of highway started rolling downhill, creating a steep slope that allowed me to coast and enjoy a few moments of much-needed relief. Overjoyed, I relished the breeze that rushed over my damp clothing, cooling me as I accelerated faster than I could pedal. "This is for *You*, Jesus, and You're helping me get there! *I can feel it!* I can do all things through Christ who strengthens me! I can do it! I can do it!" [6]

Arriving at the next checkpoint, I crossed a bridge overlooking the river, which encouraged me onward until I journeyed into a residential area. I felt faint, but refused to pause or retrieve my stowed bottle of water from my backpack for fear I might not regain momentum. Instead, I quietly panted, *"You're so close. Don't quit. Don't quit. Don't quit."* At long last, my grail was within reach. [7]

The congregation's granite gravel driveway sparkled in the sunlight, radiating its heat as I pedaled onto it from the street and crunched toward the rear door of the UPC building. Deciding I was close enough, I allowed my tennis shoes to slip from both pedals and flop onto the coarse ground, soon realizing that my legs had committed a dreaded mutiny far worse than I had imagined. Too spent to dismount, I locked my legs in a silent panic as my flesh baked beneath a cloudless sky.

Ready to collapse, I hung my head and murmured, *"I have been through way too much this morning to miss worship and the sermon. Jesus, help me."*

The rear door opened from the inside of the foyer and slingshot me from despair to mortification. Showcased in that painted wooden frame was an individual bearing a masculine build and dapper attire. It was Jimmy's older brother, Rex, a hard-working, gallant, and swoon-worthy seventeen-year-old. He lifted his gaze to behold my scorched flesh and distraught countenance.

"Sandra?! *Hey! It's been ages!* What are you doing out here?! Don't you know it's over a hundred degrees?! Come inside where there's air conditioning, silly girl!" he urged, beckoning with a friendly grin.

"*I can't.* I can't move my legs. I want to go to church, but I can't get off my bike," I frantically explained, attempting to control my breathing. "I'm so embarrassed. I don't know what to do… *I'm stuck.*" Overwhelmed by being spotted in my pathetic state by such an eligible bachelor, hyperventilation begun.

"Oh-h-h… no you're not, Sandra. Calm down. *You're tough.* You can lift that leg," Rex challenged, as if calling out some childish bluff. At his word, I attempted to dismount once more without help. Having exceeded my limits, my knee buckled, causing a nervous whimper to escape from my mouth. Before I had completely spilled over, Rex rushed ahead and caught me. "*Gotcha.*" [8]

I was dead weight and swelling with the shame of exposed weakness. Neglected emotions exploded to the surface as I sobbed and repeated, *"I'm sorry. I'm sorry…"*

"Awe… It's okay, Sandra. It's hot outside and you're *really tired*. I just don't understand why you rode your bike here? What's wrong with you?" As he was speaking, Rex hoisted all fifty-five pounds of me up with one arm and relocated my limp appendage away from the metal with his free hand. At once, the apparatus toppled sideways with a crash.

I murmured, *"My bike…"*

"It'll be fine," he assured, awkwardly dragging me toward the building. While attempting to stand me up, I wobbled like a newborn giraffe and buckled once more. Frustrated, he questioned, "Why are you so *tired*? What's going on?" In parting my lips to explain, a sob burst out, melting Rex's stoic demeanor. "Come here, girl," he ordered, wrapping his protective arms around my fragility and pulling me up into his strength. The young man backed his way to the exterior wall and slid down onto the grass, keeping both of us out of view from onlookers as he held me. [9]

"My bike is in the way," I softly mentioned again, resting my head on Rex's firm chest.

"Stop worrying about it. It's fine there," Rex reiterated. "Just relax."

The teen's compassion had unleashed a long-suppressed flow of tears that rapidly soaked into his damp shirt, inspiring me to convey, "I'm sorry you had to be the one to find me like this. You were so clean and dry earlier. Now, you're all sweaty, too. I know you feel bad for me, but you really don't have to stay out here in the heat like this," I pleaded. "This is *my* mess."

"I'm not going *anywhere* until I see you smiling," the young man bargained with a gentle squeeze. Lifting my gaze, the sides of my mouth gently curled upward as our eyes met. "Seriously, Sandra, where have you been? Why have you been gone so long?" [10]

As Rex helped me to my feet, I described where my father's acreage was located and divulged, "I never *wanted* to leave church, but my mother didn't feel like bringing me anymore. She wouldn't even let *my dad* drive… and nothing I did or said changed her mind. I was eleven years old and couldn't do anything about it. Being thirteen isn't much better, either. I'm still too young to drive or get a job… and I'm not allowed to use the phone, so…"

"Wait right there," Rex interjected as he laughed. "You're not allowed to use the phone?! Come on now. Your mom can't be *that* bad. You've gotta be making this up."

"*No, I'm not*," I sternly corrected. "Think about it. Do you really believe I would ride a mountain bike all the way here in one-hundred-degree heat if I had another option? If this is what it takes for me to get to church, *I'm doing it*. Believe whatever you want."

"Okay, okay. *I'm sorry.* I believe you," he yielded, seeming rather shocked at my recovered boldness. "It's just that… at first… your situation sounded too *extreme* to be true." After pausing for a moment, Rex sighed. "Gosh, Sandra. I don't know why I thought you lived somewhere in town. You riding your bike just to get here is pretty amazing. I feel bad for giving you a hard time about it. *Dang, girl.* You're determined. I'll give you that." He laughed to himself. "Actually, come to think of it, I'm a little embarrassed. I don't think I've *ever* wanted to go to church *that* badly." [11]

"Why would you? Your parents actually *go* to church. You've *always* had a ride," I reasoned.

"Huh. That's true," Rex thoughtfully confessed. As he slapped his legs, the teen grinned and enthusiastically continued, "Well, the good thing is you're here now! So, let's get you cleaned up and into some air conditioning!" At that, he clutched my bony shoulders and guided my body toward comfort.

Cooled air whirled against my skin as he pushed the door open for me. Positioned to draw attention, something caught my eye near the far wall. On display were some photos and several names scribed thickly in black marker, with mine being nestled among them. Wondering what all of it meant, I read the title and gasped in horror. I was examining *The Backslider Prayer List*. [12]

Right away, Anita inquired, "*Sandra?* Where have you been, girl?!" Mrs. Dolion's sister bent sideways and theatrically examined my appearance as she guided me toward a bright window. "You look terrible! Why is your face all red?! Did you *run* here?!"

As my hard-fought cheer faded, Rex chimed in and energetically added, "Sandra rode her bike *all the way from her house* this morning! What a champ, right?! I'm going to take her home after tonight's service. She traveled a long way *just to be here*." [13]

Anita's expression drooped, reflecting a deep pity as she reached to play with my ponytail and consoled, "I'm sorry you had to do that, honey. For now, I'll be your mama. Go fix your hair and wash that sweat off your face."

Pivoting to comply, I took note that someone had already removed the disturbing list from sight. Once in the powder room, I caught my disheveled reflection in the mirror and better understood Anita's concern. My skin was fire-engine red, which became even more alarming when accompanied by my disheveled hair from Rex's rescue.

After fixing my ponytail, I sighed and whispered to myself, "Well, I'm not a backslider, but at least *someone* was praying for me."

When I emerged, Rex announced, "C'mon, Sandra. The service is already over. You're coming home with *me* today." I stuffed down my overwhelming joy and revealed little more than a timid smile, unwilling to annoy Rex or cause him to regret his decision to help me.

Upon watching her son and I enter her immaculate house, Rex's mother retrieved ingredients and a mixer to create a fresh batch of waffles, serving them with homemade whipped cream and freshly cut strawberries. Soon after, the woman sat down without a plate, which confused me.

Seeing no one else around, I asked, "Aren't you and the guys going to have waffles, too?"

"Oh, no. We already grabbed something to eat before you and Rex got here," she casually informed. "I don't know what Jimmy's doing. He usually does his own thing between services."

I stared at her in awe and softly questioned, "So, you went through *all that trouble* making waffles from scratch… just for *me*?" The fact pierced my heart and filled my eyes with tears. "I'm so sorry! I didn't mean to create more work for you!"

"It's no trouble, silly! I'm a married woman with two growing boys! Making waffles is *nothing*. Your mother doesn't cook for you?" My mouth pursed as I fretted about my reality at home. "Never mind, Sandra. Eat up. Enjoy." [14]

"Thank you for all of this," I replied. "It was very thoughtful."

After savoring every bite and refraining from licking the plate, the woman suggested, "Why don't you go ahead and take a shower downstairs in Rex and Jimmy's bathroom? They should be long gone by now." I panicked and remained motionless, unwilling to use any more of their valuable resources or disturb one item that belonged to Rex or Jimmy. "Go downstairs, Sandra. No one should bother you there."

I descended the carpeted steps and realized that I didn't pack clean clothes to replace the sweaty ones I had on. Figuring that Rex's mother was merely tired of my company and desired to relax for a bit, I stood downstairs in the hallway for about an hour until she peered down to check on me and queried, "Sandra, why haven't you showered?! Have you just been *standing there* this whole time?!"

"*Yes*," I answered sheepishly. "I wasn't sure what to do, since I don't have any clean clothes. You've already done so much for me. I didn't want to bother you."

"Sandra, don't be ridiculous! I could have just washed them!" she replied, growing irritated. "I mean, you're just standing there! What's the deal here?!"

"Well..." I began, choking back tears of humiliation, "I just figured, since you weren't expecting company today, that you'd like to relax without catering to anyone. *I'm sorry*." Horrified at my awkward behavior and being called *ridiculous*, I trembled with shame.

At once, the woman fetched her husband from another part of the house. One of Dolion's brothers peered down the stairway at me, offered a friendly smile, and suggested, "Sandra, why don't you come back upstairs and sit with us at the kitchen table?" Rex's personable father inquired about my morning and what brought me to their home that day. Having already tearfully revealed a few details about my life to Rex, I merely displayed my poker face, gently smiled back, and calmly repeated all that I had expressed earlier. Neither of them seemed very satisfied with my sterile responses. "Sandra, these chairs are a little too stiff for me. Why don't we sit a bit more comfortably in the living room?" It was then that I noticed their plush common area and captivating decorations in various shades of white.

Trained by the materfamilias to *never* sit on her sofa with dirty clothing, I commented, "I'm pretty filthy and I don't want to stain your beautiful furniture." [15]

"*Seriously?*" the mother sharply remarked, removing herself from the room as the father furrowed his brow at her insensitive behavior. [16]

Noticing my increasing discomfort in their midst, the man soothed, "It's alright, Sandra. It'll be fine. Have a seat right there. *Let's talk.* You're pretty interesting and I enjoy hearing the things you have to say." [17]

After engaging in deep conversation over various topics, including my love for our Messiah, the time had finally come to enjoy the evening's worship service and Dolion's second sermon. Rex's father chauffeured his wife and me into town, driving their luxury SUV. Watching the trees speed past the windows, I silently assumed full responsibility for my ignorant behavior and the mother's soured temperament, picturing what life would have been like if the couple in the two front seats had been *my* parents. When I compared our starkly different lives, it was painfully obvious that the husband and wife dearly loved their two sons and willingly provided all that they could offer them. [18]

In truth, the only way to be their daughter was to marry one of their sons. Even if Rex or Jimmy had a bizarre affinity toward socially awkward stick figures on mountain bikes, I refused to pollute their sterling class, caliber, or pedigree with that of *mine*. The very thought of the materfamilias being permanently involved in their lives made my heart heavy. I pushed the idea of marriage out of my mind and admired their splendor from a distance.

Once the preaching and altar call had drawn to a close, Rex effortlessly loaded my mountain bike into the bed of his truck and was ready to take me home. As we neared my residence, I gently mentioned, "You can start to slow down now. That's my gate coming up. Just drop me off by the mailbox. I can walk the rest of the way."

Rex furrowed his brow at my request and firmly stated, "I'm driving you up to your house, Sandra. Just sit right there. I'll open the gate." [19]

My pulse raced as I winced, expecting the psychotic termagant to rush toward Rex's headlights and vulgarly accuse him of perversion. It was a pleasant surprise to see the front door remain closed, and I found myself breathing again. Rex unloaded my previous form of transportation and set it on the grass, as I sheepishly thanked him for his help and waved goodbye.

With my bike put away, I stepped onto the porch and knocked. There were more convenient ways of doing things, but a key to the house was not something I ever expected to possess. I casually glanced backward toward the night air and listened to the katydids, and was shocked to see Rex's truck was still parked in the driveway. Swiftly facing forward again, I peered through the screen, glass panels, and lacey window curtains, only to realize that the materfamilias hadn't budged from her lounging spot. In that moment, Rex's friendship outweighed any fear of the materfamilias.

I firmly knocked again and quietly prayed, *"Please, Jesus, help me. Don't let my mom take too long or yell at me in front of Rex."* Eventually, the materfamilias lifted herself from the sofa, unlocked the door, and immediately returned to her seat. At that, Rex started his truck and pulled away.

As I secured both doors, the woman coldly stared at the glowing television. I escaped to my bedroom without incident. My stomach growled without dinner, but I had proven the materfamilias wrong that day and it filled me up enough. Stepping past that woman to enter the kitchen wasn't worth an altercation, and breakfast was one night's sleep away. I tucked myself into bed and thanked my Messiah for granting me parole. [20]

Spunky

The following Sunday morning, I set my alarm even earlier than the week prior and readied myself for an encore voyage on my mountain bike. Besides snagging water, I packed a full change of clothes and prayed nothing hindered my escape. While doing so, the fifth Commandment burned in my mind and convicted me of a detail in my covert plans. If I truly desired to please my Messiah in assembling for worship, I was required to show respect to the woman who bore me by requesting her consent. [1]

Unsure of what to expect, I bravely and politely queried, "Mom, is it alright if ride my bike to church again?" The frigid woman ignored my words and stared blankly at the television screen without comment. "Okay! I'll take your silence as permission."

Without hesitation, I briskly pedaled away before the termagant could yank my leash out of spite. Determined to be on time, I urged myself to ascend to the highest point of my journey faster than the mercury that filled our outdoor thermometer. Despite my efforts, the Texas sun and pitiless humidity caused streams of sweat to navigate downward as I panted out each breath, vigorously attacking hills with the same grueling technique I developed seven days earlier. It took my entire engaged body to move forward.

Although my effort was being expensed to full capacity and the path had not miraculously relaxed its slope nor shifted its course to locate shade, the journey seemed less taxing than I had recalled. The unknown no longer rested its heavy haunches on my shoulders. I had already conquered each obstacle and violently evicted the fear of failure from my mind. No longer could anyone presume that my reaching the highway was impossible, not even the termagant. My success was historical, expected… and accomplished once more. I pedaled toward town inchmeal with grunts and a seasoned smile of confidence.

Before I could pick up speed at the first downward slope, a truck slowed down beside me. Alarmed, I remembered the warnings about kidnappers, cranked on, and was determined not to let go of my bike. A familiar voice called out, *"Sandra?! Is that you?!"*

"Yeah!" I cheerfully shouted with a grin before noticing Rhett's perturbed expression.

Pulling his truck over just a few yards ahead of me, the young man opened his driver side door and loudly scolded, *"Girl, are you crazy?! You can't ride your bike on the highway like that! What are you thinking?! You could get hit!"*

Being in his twenties and one of Dolion's many nephews, Rhett's heightened concern for my wellbeing took me aback. His speech usually included little more than quips and sarcastic remarks towards his younger, more rambunctious cousins. Without being told, I promptly dismounted at his approach and allowed Rhett to load my bike aggressively into his truck bed. My expression had frozen somewhere between dread and surprise as I opened the cab and loaded myself into the open passenger side.

Angrily shaking his head, the tall, slender man drove on and continued more calmly to convey, "I'm sorry, Sandra. I know you don't have a ride to church, but you need to call someone or something. If you keep this up, you could get yourself killed. Isn't there *anyone* that will come get you?" [2]

"My mother won't let me use the phone and thinks that if I call someone to ask for a ride, she will look bad," I explained. "Well, her plan isn't working because she already looks bad. The woman really *could* take me. She just doesn't want to… and she won't let my dad take me, either. It's a big mess. This is the only way, Rhett. I either need to stay home or ride my bike to church, and I refuse to stay in that *hellhole*." [3]

"There's got to be another way," he persisted.

"Well, *there isn't*. I already feel like a burden to my family every day. Even if I could call someone for a ride, why would I want to be a burden to others? It's not like I have a wide selection of relatives that go to this church," I rebutted. "I mean, since you feel so strongly about it, are *you* willing to pick me up at my house every Sunday?" [4]

The young man sighed and humbly admitted, "No." [5]

"That's what I thought," I remarked. "If someone sees me on the road, they can pick me up like *you* did… and *thank you for that*, by the way." Rhett smirked with a nod. "If *no one* picks me up and I don't become a tiny splat on the highway, I'll be that much stronger when I arrive. Either way, *I'm going to church*. I don't know how to say it any better than that." [6]

Rhett chuckled and admitted, "Okay, Sandra. Okay. You convinced me. You seem like you can handle yourself." [7]

After the morning service, Jimmy, Rex, and their father approached me with huge smiles, causing me to wonder if they had just been conversing with Rhett.

Stepping forward, Jimmy chirped, "Sandra, we've been talking about you for the past few days and found a word that *perfectly* describes you. You're *spunky*." I amusingly cocked my head to the side with a comical expression of ignorance. I didn't know what the word meant or if they were making fun of me. Jimmy sweetly laughed alongside his kin and playfully grabbed my shoulders. "Don't worry, Sandra. It's a *good* thing and we're really glad you're back. You've been missed." [8]

Checkmate

*W*hile in my bedroom one Saturday afternoon, I was lip-syncing to the radio when the muscles in my shoulders tensed at the approach of a familiar trod. The termagant menacingly occupied my doorway with narrowed eyes and skeptically informed, "Someone from *church* is on the phone for you." [1]

"Oh, my gosh! *Really?!*" I squeaked, popping up from the floor. Avoiding all physical contact, I slipped past the woman and sprinted toward the kitchen landline. Collecting myself, I formally answered, "*Hello?* This is Sandra speaking." It was Mrs. Dolion with an unexpected offer. Allowing her to finish speaking, I calmly replied, "Please excuse me for a moment. I need to ask my mom." As I gently rested the receiver on my clavicle, the eavesdropping materfamilias abandoned the bedroom receiver to avoid being *caught* and casually make her way into the living room. Acting oblivious to her notoriously habitual surveillance, I explained, "It's the pastor's wife on the line. The youth group is going to the city to ice skate tonight and eat dinner somewhere, and I'm invited. She's offering to pick me up right away and drop me back off around midnight. I know that's *really* late, but is it okay? Can I go with them?" [2]

"*Go,*" the irritated woman begrudgingly decreed.

Suppressing my immense surprise and elation, I casually lifted the receiver back to my ear and answered, "I can come, and thank you for inviting me. I'll see you when you get here." Not possessing a key to the house and very leery about the timing of my return, I proposed, "Since I won't be back until *late*, it might be a good idea for you to leave the front door unlocked for me tonight… *for your convenience.*" The woman stared at the television screen in eerie silence, as if she had somehow robotically powered off with her eyes open. "*Mom?* It'll be late when I get back and I don't want to wake you guys up tonight. Will you please leave the door unlocked for me? I'll lock it when I'm inside. *Okay?*" Motionless and silent, the woman resembled a propped-up corpse.

Making the most of my limited time to prepare, I scurried to my room for a wardrobe change. Apart from elaborate tights and the glittery ensembles showcased in televised performances, I didn't have a clue what was appropriate for indoor ice skating.

Feeling the clock ticking, I resolved to wear jeans, a gray sweater, some tennis shoes, and a jacket.

As I observed through the front door window, Dolion and his wife pulled into the gravel driveway. I hustled over, expecting a van-full of familiar faces to be with Rex and Jimmy. However, only their youngest son was present, spoiled and impish. I buried my disappointment and inquired about the location of the rest of our youth group. Mrs. Dolion clarified that they all lived in various neighboring areas and, being of age, simplified the evening by driving their own vehicles.

The van pulled up to our destination and barely rolled to a stop when their beloved child slid open the door and dashed ahead. While entering the building, Mrs. Dolion smiled at me and informed, "We have your ticket covered, Sandra. Go get your skates and have fun."

The adults left me standing in the foyer and ventured on to be reunited with their middle child and nephews, including various other teens from the congregation.

Having never been inside an ice rink before, I didn't understand the procedure or how anyone kept track of who had paid for what. Unwilling to irritate anyone by asking questions, I sat alone by some unattended lockers.

A manager eventually noticed my lingering presence and inquired, "Can I help you?" [3]

"Yes, sir. I've never ice skated before, and I'm confused. My pastor and his wife paid for me, but I don't have proof and they're already on the ice," I explained, suppressing my panic and fear. "I don't know what to do. Can I still skate?"

"Don't worry about a receipt. I trust you," the stranger soothed with a gentle smile, nearly inspiring me to tackle the fatherly man with a tearful hug. With gentle kindness, he patiently walked me toward the skate racks to make my selection. "Just tell them your shoe size and they'll set you up. Enjoy." [4]

Cheerful again, I laced up the hazardous footwear and clumsily approached Jimmy and Rex as they leaned against a half-wall to watch the other skaters.

"Oh. Hey, Sandra," Rex halfheartedly greeted, terribly distracted.

I followed the teenager's gaze to several captivating UPC maidens with hourglass forms, whirling about effortlessly over the ice. Donning flattering clothing, ankle-length skirts and long, cascading hair, I immediately grasped their appeal. Eventually, the feminine objects of desire flocked toward one another and exited the ice in unison to greet Dolion's middle son and his masculine kin. Confidence shriveled inside of my chest. Each contrast between their classic beauty and the frump of my reflection couldn't have been starker. The warm and benevolent greetings they received from Rex and Jimmy choked me with bitter jealousy. I despised myself. [5]

To conceal my envious disappointment, I retreated to a distant bench to sulk, sourly contemplating, "Well, Rex and Jimmy probably see me as a baby sister *at best*. They don't really care that I'm here and probably just feel sorry for me, which explains the sudden invitation. They'll *never* see me as anything more than a reject on a mountain bike that constantly needs charity… and why shouldn't they? That's all I am."

Jimmy discovered my slumped posture and jokingly prodded, "Why are you sitting over here by yourself, weirdo?! You're running out of time! What's wrong with you?! Get out there and skate!" [6]

I nodded with a shallow grin and meandered to an access point, silently concluding, "If I just abandon all hope of being admired, then I won't be disappointed anymore. I can't compete with curves or fashion, but being upset over it is *stupid*. Hard-earned money was spent for me to be here, and I may never have the opportunity to ice skate again. I'll just pretend that I don't know anyone and skate by myself." [7]

Swallowing the shame of my homely appearance, I stepped onto the slick surface and skated awkwardly for a moment, carefully maneuvering myself toward the center of the ice. Maintaining a steady pace, I gradually became less rigid and confidently explored turns at various speeds, recalling my love for rollerblading. A smile emerged on my face with the newly developing skill… until the protruding elbow of Dolion's youngest son brutally clipped my ribcage, leaving a painfully deep impression of cruelty and malice in his wake. [8]

I imagined myself tripping the assailant just to savor his smug face grating against the scratched ice at top speed. However, unwilling to compromise my precocious reputation, I refrained from executing vengeance and pretended not to notice each stinging round of his covert hostility. [9]

To cap off the evening, the UPC youth reassembled inside a classic malt-shop-style diner that boasted creamy milkshakes, deliciously aromatic burgers, and crispy shoestring potatoes. While the order lines formed, I made my way to an unoccupied table with a frosty cup of water, staring at the shifting ice cubes as they slowly melted.

Tristan, another UPC female who often contrasted against the others, waited in line and boldly jested, "I'm so hungry, my big guts are eating my little guts!" Having never heard the cliché before, I huffed and smiled in amusement, although no one else seemed to acknowledge her comical statement. Frigid silence lingered until one of the other girls changed the subject and diverted all male attention to herself. [10]

"Sandra, aren't you gonna eat?" Rex openly queried, being the last person in line and delaying his own order with a scrunched brow and confused grin. "You must be starving after all that skating! Let me buy you a burger. Get over here and pick out what you want. I'm not gonna let you wither away over there by yourself. Come on." [11]

The youth silenced one another to listen as my soul gasped for breath, drowning in a torrent of public humiliation. Having no spending money, I had evoked pity from the very generous Rex once more. [12]

"Oh. It's okay, Rex. That's really nice of you, but I'm fine. Thank you for offering," I politely replied, finding myself immediately betrayed as my stomach growled loudly. Rex shook his head in disappointment and made his order.

A few moments later, Tristan beckoned to me and asked, "Sandra, do you think you might be interested in eating my extra burger? I bought two, assuming I could eat them both, but I can't… not with all these fries. Will you eat it for me? If you don't, I'll just have to throw it away. I'd hate for it to go to waste since everyone else is already full. Will you take it? Do you mind?" [13]

Locking eyes with her, I shyly smirked and shook my head. Her cleverness had maneuvered my pride into checkmate. Breaking the tension, I playfully quipped, "Well, I can't let you throw away a *perfectly good burger*. That would be wrong. I'll just have to help you eat it."

"Good," Tristen added, observing my collection of the item before pivoting back. "Oh. You don't want to sit with me?"

Noticing the empty chair beside her, I beamed and replied, "I sure do," offering a discreet nod of gratitude as I sat beside her.

Keeping their word, Pastor Dolion and his wife dropped me off at the log house around midnight. Their bright headlights gripped my body with anxiety and prompted me to request, "Would you please leave me at the gate so the light won't wake up my parents?" They accommodated me and immediately made their way home.

The gravel driveway noisily crunched under my feet, scrunching my shoulders with palpable trepidation as I drew nearer to my prison of timber and glass. I silently rolled each progressive step across the porch and grabbed the weathered knob, locked in place.

"Oh, no," I softly fretted. To avoid a debilitating panic, I silently wondered, "Maybe she unlocked the *back* door for me instead." Continuing my stealth technique, I vacated the porch and tip-toed through the crunching grass to the far side of the house and checked that knob. It didn't budge. "*What the **** is wrong with this woman? Does she enjoy being angry? Was unlocking a ******* door too complicated?*" I grumbled, retracing my steps to reach the front porch once more. Expecting a severe beating just for waking the termagant, dread rendered me frozen on the porch for well over an hour. [14]

Weary and knowing no other alternative but to knock on my parent's bedroom window, I pleaded for protection under my breath, praying, "*Jesus, I'm terrified. You know how my mother is. Will you help me wake up my mom so that Dad can stay asleep? Will you keep her calm? Thank You. I love You. In Your name, I pray. Amen.*" [15]

I rapped gently on the dusty glass, stirring no movement from either parent. I tried once more with a miniscule increase of force. Nothing happened. My heartbeat throbbed in my ears as I held my breath and knocked more firmly. The materfamilias rolled herself out of bed, trod toward the front door, unlocked it, and returned to her lair without breathing a word. [16]

Two Storms

*M*y Sunday morning alarm chimed, even though it had only been five hours since I entered the house after ice skating. Rolling out of bed, I readied myself to mountain-bike to the service and arrive *on time*.

As I exited the bathroom, the soulless glare of the materfamilias startled me. She twistedly accused, "Do you think you're gonna get away with staying out so late last night?! *Where were you?!* Were you ******* the *entire* youth group?!" [1]

My wrath overpowered all fear as I leaned forward and growled, "First, *psycho*, I told you I wouldn't be home until midnight. Second, *pervert*, Pastor Dolion and his wife were there the *entire time*. I was always in plain sight! They even dropped me off! Call the pastor and ask him yourself!" [2]

"I'm not calling *anybody*," she viciously replied. "You're probably ******* him, *too*, for all I know!" [3]

"Yeah, Mom… with his wife and sons there?!" I rebutted. "You're *unbelievable*. How do you even come up with this ****?! Do you sit at home *all day*, just dreaming up warped scenarios… inventing disgusting and perverted ways for us to spend our time away from you?! What amazes me the most is that you won't even try to collect evidence or investigate! What if you're proven *wrong*?! For a healthy person, that would be a good thing, but you'd rather believe your own filthy lie than know the truth!" I placed my hand on the door and concluded, "You can think whatever the **** you want, but leave me out of it. You're a terrible mother and an absolute horror of a human being. I'm going to church today, with or without your consent." [4]

"And all of that coming from a good Christian girl?!" the termagant mocked as I exited. [5]

I rolled my eyes, marched off the porch, and muttered to myself, "This ******* hypocrite accuses her thirteen-year-old daughter of having sex with the pastor and the entire youth group *in front of his wife*… and I'm supposed to just let her?! **** that *****! Even with doing everything right, I set off a bomb of perversion! There's no pleasing her! It doesn't matter how I act or what I say! She actually *wants* to be angry! She *wants* to torture me! How can anyone go on living like this?! I can't take this anymore…" Tears of rage streamed down my face as I mounted my bike and pedaled in pursuit of safety and peace. It was nearing the end of the service when I slipped into the sanctuary and settled into an available seat. I only was present for Dolion's grand finale, punctuated by shouting. [6]

For the evening service, Jimmy's father introduced a guest speaker. An evangelist humbly occupied the pulpit. [7]

The stranger didn't stomp, clap or raise his voice, but spoke with confidant authority, declaring, "Through the Holy Spirit and however else He sees fit, Jesus can and will speak to *all* who seek Him… and even to some who don't. *Don't be fooled.* Jesus wants you to *know* Him… personally… intimately. Stop riding on the coattails of your family, pastor, or leadership for a 'spiritual fix' to make you feel good or get you through the week. Their prayers might help you, but they won't save you. Only Jesus can do that. [8]

"Worship Jesus, not man's approval. The movement of the Holy Spirit isn't to be confused with or measured by mere sensations or a specific mold of behavior patterns. *Beware.* God is not mocked without dire consequences. Don't fall into the rut of crying and wailing at the altar and then live your life as you please when you leave, as though God closes His eyes at your sin. The way you live your life will prove you've chosen to love and serve Jesus. [9]

"*Don't be fooled.* You *will* face the Lord, and those whom you see around you today, no matter how *spiritual*, can't save you. Only Jesus can do that. Those around you are fallible humans, just like you. Don't compare yourself to them. Compare yourself to Jesus. See your own depravity and need for a Savior. Your name will either be written in the Lamb's Book of Life through faith in the saving blood of Jesus… or it won't be. Read the scriptures and discover for yourself that salvation is so much more than a choice or an event. It's a path. Walk in it." [10]

With a turnout of about thirty people for that service, the evangelist pointed to certain individuals in the assembly and addressed a detail about their lives, causing them to burst into tears or drop their jaw from shock. They acknowledged the timeliness and accuracy of what he said and received whatever word, warning, message, or prophecy that followed. [11]

As he scanned the faces in the room, the evangelist asked, "Someone here is having *reoccurring dreams*. Who are you? You'll need to raise your hand. The Holy Spirit isn't showing me who you are."

Startled, my eyebrows jumped. I turned and peered behind me like the rest of the congregation to see if anyone was making themselves known.

"Do my violent dreams qualify as *reoccurring*?" I silently wondered. "They happen every night, but they aren't the same."

"I need you to raise your hand," the man urged. "The Lord wants you to speak up. I *know* you're here and under the sound of my voice."

"There's no way it's me. I'm a nobody," I thought, "but no one else is raising their hand. Maybe it *is* me. I don't want to miss out on hearing from Jesus. What's the worst that could happen?" Sloth-like in speed and awkwardness, my hand slowly raised above my head.

"Thank you, young lady," he acknowledged. "Tell me about your dreams."

"Well, I don't know if my dreams count, because I've never had the same dream *twice*. I've had dreams about combat in Vietnam, escaping captivity, evading kidnappers, being attacked by repelling assassins, and dodging the shots of a laser-guided sniper rifle. In one of them, a huge dog attacked and forced both of us off a cliff into a canyon. I survived the landing, but the dog didn't. I've had very violent dreams *every night* for about three years."

"Yes. That's *definitely* reoccurring," the evangelist insisted. "How old are you?"

"Thirteen, sir," I replied.

"In your dreams, do you ever get caught or killed?" he asked.

Avoiding death in all but the mafia dream that ended with the words GAME OVER, I shook my head and answered, "No, sir. I survive."

"You're a *warrior*," the evangelist announced firmly before moving on to speak to several others.

"I'm a *warrior*?" I pondered in silence. "But I'm not equipped for that kind of calling! I'm just a weak, skinny little kid! Who will train me? Does that mean I need to join the military?" After the service drew to a close, I lingered in the pew, awestruck. [12]

A gentle touch on my shoulder caused me to look back. A total stranger bearing a sweet smile introduced herself and nervously greeted, "*Hi.* I'm Aliza. You don't know me, and I don't mean to be *weird* or anything, but does your name happen to be *Sandra*?"

With a head tilt, I politely answered, "Yes, my name is Sandra."

Clearly uncomfortable with the entire scenario, Aliza continued, "I *really* don't mean to freak you out, but my husband, Kirk, had a dream about you last night. We don't know you or anything, but *in the dream*, your name was revealed to him. He would like to tell you about it if you're willing to hear, but you don't have to. I'm so sorry. I *really* don't mean to scare you."

Taken aback, I smiled myself into a chuckle at her endearing awkwardness and quipped, "Lady, this has already been a *very* strange day. Whatever your husband has to tell me won't change that. Where is he? I want to hear about the dream."

"Follow me," the woman beckoned, leading me out of the sanctuary. "He's waiting in the hall." The man maintained a stoic posture and somber face as our eyes met. "This is my husband, Kirk. I'll let him take it from here."

"Is your name *Sandra*?" he quickly asked. I soberly confirmed. At that, Kirk took a knee and plainly stated, "I am going to tell you the dream *in full*. Afterward, I am going to tell you it's *interpretation*. You were standing alone in a large open field. Two storms were approaching from opposite directions, but they weren't your average storms. They were *super* storms. The winds grew stronger as the storms approached one other and *you* were caught in between them. The wind should have carried you off or knocked you down, but you withstood the brutality of the storm for *ages*. Sandra, it's important for me to tell you that this was the *longest* dream I've ever had… I mean, *hours* in length. The storms raged *that long*, but you remained. Here's the interpretation of your dream as it was revealed to me. The two storms are *your parents*." [13]

My knees buckled under the weight of my circumstances. Someone finally understood what it was like to be me. I collapsed into Kirk's arms and sobbed, burying my face in his shoulder. Without hesitation, Kirk firmly stood my emaciated body back up, stabilized me and proceeded, underlining the urgency and importance of the message. [14]

Kirk continued, "There's more to tell you, and I need you to focus. I'm so sorry, Sandra, but it's going to get *a lot worse* before it gets any better." I wrenched over and moaned, as if punched in the stomach. "*Sandra*, I need you to calm yourself. Look at me, sweetie. I need you to pay attention. This is very important. I was told that the *only* reason you endure all of this is because you *never* let go of Jesus' hand. It was then that God told me that your name was *Sandra*." [15]

Quivering, I stammered, "G-God knows *my name*?"

"Yes, Sandra. God knows your name," the man confirmed. "In the middle of the night, He woke me up and told me to tell you the dream *today*. I knew that if the dream really *was* from God, you would be here tonight. We've never met or seen each other before, and *here you are*. He *sees you*, Sandra. You have *never* been alone." [16]

Sensing the immense weight of Kirk's burden, I put my hand on his shoulder and mentioned, "Thank you for telling me all of this. That must have been really hard."

Astonished, the man shifted my focus back to the situation at hand and added, "Don't worry about *me*, kid. You just stick with Jesus. He'll help you… and you *need* it." After Kirk stood to his feet, I hugged him and his wife, Aliza, who had remained by my side.

That night, I crawled into bed and fell asleep with a grin, whispering, *"God knows my name."* [17]

SECTION 6

Fire

~~~

In the fall of my eight-grade year, the longed-for northern winds steadily relaxed the sweltering heat and brought comfort to my frazzled nerves, especially by permitting me to keep my bedroom door *shut*. In my keep, I laid low until my father pulled into the driveway and thudded across the porch.

Having finished the home cooked meal that was waiting for him, the man stepped away from his children at the table and into the living room where the materfamilias had been lounging with her salad. Just before settling into his favorite recliner near the wall to watch a televised ballgame, the man lifted his arms and bowed slightly backwards with a grunt.

His wife spewed verbal dysentery into the air, loudly accusing, *"Why did you stretch like that by the window?! Huh?! Are you letting your whores know that you're ready for them?!"* Within seconds, her son put his plate into the sink and retreated upstairs to his game console. *"I see what's going on here! I'm not stupid! That's a sign to the whore across the street, isn't it?! Is she going to meet you outside, so you can **** her?! Is that why you're always clearing the land, so you can **** her without me knowing?!"* [1]

Indignation brewed behind my clenched teeth. The hypocrite had ritually completed her aerobics in front of the same picture window each morning, usually clad with nothing more than a sports bra and some tights. Unwilling to abandon my father to her psychotic tyranny, I calmly retreated to my observation post in the hallway and remained out of sight. Although only a moment had passed, the man simply feigned sleep and allowed the voluminous, echoing foulness to break against his ever-hardening emotional shell. [2]

"You think you're so smart!" she continued. *"I'm watching you! Keep testing me, mister! I'm going to catch you one of these days! Then, you'll be sorry! I'll take your retirement, the kids, the land… everything!"* [3]

"Just try it, lady! I'll testify against you!" I loudly interjected. Unable to hold myself back from injustice, I defiantly marched into her view. "I saw everything and heard every word you said! You won't get away with it! I'll tell everyone what you are. You're a disgusting liar and a bully! I'll *never* go with you!" [4]

"Stay out of it, Sandra!" my father corrected with his eyes closed, still reclined. Stabbed by the barbs of paternal rejection, I tearfully retreated to my room.

In the darkest moments of the woman's perverted madness, I fought to meditate on the comforting messages from my Messiah. I rocked back and forth, mumbling, *"God knows my name and I'm holding Jesus' hand. I can't let go. Things are going to get worse, but I'll survive it and I'm gonna be okay. I can survive anything with Jesus. I'm a warrior, but I can't let go of Jesus' hand. I can't let go. He's my only hope. I can't let go..."* [5]

Days later, the materfamilias crunched on another belt-busting calorie-salad in front of the television while her household gnawed through another round of under-seasoned, overcooked venison pucks. In her inept hands, the poor deer somehow managed to die a second time.

After finishing his plate, the man cheerfully mentioned, "That pile of branches in the front pasture has been sitting there for a while and needs to be burned. Since it rained the other day and there's little to no wind, would you guys like to sit around a fire tonight?"

"*Yeah!*" I cheered, hurrying to choke down the portion left on my plate.

Entering the brisk air, my brother and I schlepped four wooden folding chairs from the porch and arranged them neatly before the burn pile. We looked on as our father ignited the bottom layer of limbs and brush, releasing the inviting fragrance of burning evergreens to settle around us. Adjusting to a more comfortable distance, the three of us strategically claimed our seats to enjoy mugs of hot cocoa in the ambiance of roaring flames and popping timber.

My shoulders tightened at a familiar trod that headed our way, causing me to look back and observe the termagant emerge toting a full case of beer, playfully announcing in the distance, "Now, it's a party!"

The scenario struck me as amiss, especially when I noticed my father's expression of disapproval and shaking head. On many weekends, during a televised ballgame, the man enjoyed two bottles of lager, but nothing more. However, prior to that evening, I had never witnessed the woman openly consume alcohol in my presence. The termagant noisily claimed the remaining seat stationed between her husband and son and positioned the adult beverages on the ground between her and her husband's ankles. Without delay, the termagant's fingers penetrated the cardboard box, ripped back the rectangular top, and wrapped around a chilled can to crack it open. Appreciating her sudden silence, I resettled in my seat and sipped from my cooled mug.

Flames glowed all the more brightly as the sun's rays began to diminish and filter through the remaining oak trees. Mesmerized by fizzing sap and crumbling embers, twilight faded and opened my view to the glittering stars above. The pile eventually condensed and radiated a more tolerable heat, inspiring me to scoot closer to its glow for warmth. It was then that I noticed the termagant's unusual behavior.

Resembling a tavern strumpet, slurred erotic speech tumbled from the woman's mouth as she palmed my father's genitalia in plain view of his children. The man pushed away her exploring hand, scolding, "Knock it off." [6]

Shocked, the termagant brazenly corrected, *"Hey... I-can-do-what-I-want... I'm-yo-wife."*

Radiating discomfort, her son immediately abandoned his chair and retreated into the darkness toward the house. With a furrowed brow of repugnance, the man quickly stood to convey, "If you only want to be nice to me when you're drunk, *keep to yourself*. I'm going inside." At once, my father snatched up his seat and vanished amid the shifting shadows behind our chairs. [7]

Robbed of my escort, fear overwhelmed me as I continued to peer backward, straining to discern what famished nocturnal creatures potentially lurked in the darkness. Unwilling to traverse the unknown, I focused on the dancing flames before me and embraced the symphony of sensations that a glowing fire offered.

The materfamilias bent over sideways and startled me, noisily fumbling her hand around the crushed aluminum at her feet. Spastically palming inside the empty case, she groaned, "*Aw, man!* He drank all th'beer!"

In mid eye-roll, a sobering concept stuck me as I recalled disturbing stories of her father's alcohol-induced domestic violence. I wondered what the slumping villainess might do to an abhorred daughter while in her drunken stupor. Seeking a lit path of escape, I hastily stepped in front of the termagant and eclipsed the crackling fire, instantly reminding her of my presence.

"Sandra... C'mere. C'm-sit-on-m'lap," she sloppily ordered.

Wide-eyed and visibly confused, I paused. Although I could not recall a time where I happily and willfully sat on my mother's lap, I wondered if alcohol released suppressed maternal affections in women.

Recalling Kirk's dream and the harrowing interpretation, I snapped out of my stupor and sharply replied, "Nope! I'm outta here. *You're drunk.*"

Like a striking snake, the materfamilias snatched my bony wrist, jerked me toward her, and commanded, *"C'mere."*

Awkwardly repositioned onto her thighs with unforgiving dominance, the sloshed female wrapped her left arm around my emaciated torso to slide me close and press my back against her breasts and stomach rolls. I sat rigidly with my palms pressed to my legs as the woman's fingers slithered, tracing over the back of my right hand toward my hips. She suddenly wedged her hand between my legs and pressed it against my vagina. Waves of confusion crashed over me as reality solidified, filling my face with horror as I twisted and bucked myself free.

Standing away from her, I shouted, "*What the **** do you think you're doing?!* What *the **** just happened?!*" I backed up further, positioning the fire between us. "What have you *done*?! What the **** just happened to me?!"

With unadjusted eyes, I sprinted blindly toward the house and barricaded myself in my bedroom behind a lockless door. Inaudible sobs wrenched me as my twitching body pulsed with rage, filling my darkened mind with brutal judgement. I imagined the termagant's body drunkenly collapsing into the flaming embers as she screamed until her last breath, sentenced to live out eternity in a similar fashion. [8]

I wept in the dark, brutally whispering, "*That ***** accuses me of everything. Now she's a drunk lesbian tramp that molested her own daughter. How dare that ***** force me to sit through that? Why didn't I leave when my brother did? I'm so stupid. I should have asked Dad to wait for me. That was so dumb. I walked right in front of her. Why did I allow myself to get that close to her? Women are gross. I feel sorry for men. I'll never get married or have kids if that **** is in my blood. Being a girl sucks. My life is a ******* nightmare.*" [9]

The following morning, I awoke to discover my eyelids glued shut from dried tears. Groping the nightstand to retrieve my glasses, I carefully navigated by touch to the bathroom sink and rinsed off my face. Upon exiting, I sensed the pedophile standing up from her spot in the living room, causing my temples to throb at her approach. My body tensed while she maneuvered herself around the woodstove's wall and into my view.

Stifling my steaming wrath, I mustered an eerie tone to inquire, "Do you know what *happened* last night?"

"Well, I don't remember much," the hungover woman calmly replied. "Just that I peed, threw up, and went to bed." [10]

"Well, that's not *all* that happened," I snarled, growing more intense as I spoke. "After drinking nearly an entire case of beer *by yourself*, you forced me onto your lap, slid your hand up my leg, and grabbed *my crotch!* What the **** is wrong with you?! First, you *hate* me. Then you get wasted and do some perverted lesbian **** like *that*?!"

Her skin glowed crimson. She self-righteously projected, "*I did not, you little liar! How dare you accuse me of something like that! You're the pervert! You probably put my hand there, you demon from hell! Where did you learn that?! Huh?! What else have you been doing?!*" [11]

"Wow. You're not getting out of this, lady. Do you really think I put *your* hand on *my* crotch? I'm the problem, right? Well, go ahead, pervert! Blame *the child* and not the drunk, child-molesting adult," I scoffed. "For your information, you not remembering your own actions doesn't make you innocent. It doesn't mean that they *didn't happen*. The memory doesn't just go away. *I wish I could forget it!* Regardless, you and I are about to get one thing straight *right now*. I've *never* trusted you. You burned that bridge a long time ago, and this incident settles it *forever*. Don't you *ever* touch me again. Just looking at you makes me sick. *Stay away from me.* I don't want you communicating with me unless it's absolutely necessary. Have I made myself perfectly clear or do I need to use smaller words?" [12]

Although I readied my body for a life-altering beating, all the woman did was glare. [13]

First Bedroom to the Left

The materfamilias shouted from the living room, *"Sandra! Come here!"*

From the floor of my bedroom, I snapped out of a fascinating daydream and begrudgingly made my way into the warden's view. Keeping my distance, I cautiously answered, "Yes?"

She tapped an open envelope onto her palm before handing it to me, and ordered, "Read it."

It was a high-quality, custom printed card that read, "You're invited to a Halloween party! No children are permitted." A handwritten amendment stated, *"Sandra is the only exception to the rule and is always welcome in our home."*

"Whoa! Do I even know these people? Why am I invited… specifically?" I queried.

"Does it matter? Just look at the invitation! *They're rich*… and you should see their house! It's beautiful," she gushed. "Do you want to come with me?"

"Wait. I don't understand who these people even are," I commented, pressing the woman. "How do *you* know what their house looks like? You accuse Dad of cheating just by going to work and being outside, but you must see these people while we're all gone! Why wasn't Dad invited? Huh? It only has *your* name on here."

"Do you want to go to a party or not? If you keep asking questions, I'm going to leave you here," she weaseled with a side-eye.

Flattered by seeing my name in ink and curious about who the termagant had been visiting, I answered, "Alright. I'll go with you." [1]

"Good. We're spending the night, too, so pack a bag," she added, causing me to wince.

Beset by a manicured lawn, we pulled into an aesthetically landscaped driveway that guided my view to the pristine masonry and elegant exterior fixtures of our host's residence.

"Thank you for inviting me! You have a *beautiful* home," I raved with a smile, hugging the woman who greeted us at the door.

"Awe! Thank you, Sandra! You're so sweet!" our hostess replied. "Come inside! We're all sitting in the backyard, relaxing. Drinks and food are plenty, so please help yourself!" I found an unclaimed folding chair amid several adults and quietly consumed my plate of barbecue. A handful of individuals discussed politics, freedom of religion, and the separation of church and state. "Sandra, you seem to be intently listening, and it looks like you might have something to say. What do you think about all of this?" the hostess warmly queried.

"Well, someone mentioned earlier about prayer being taken out of public schools. In my opinion, that decision was a huge mistake. I agree that an atheist shouldn't be required to participate in prayer if they don't want to. It's not really prayer if it's *forced*. However, allowing the atheist minority to prevail in removing or discouraging the only unifying moral compass of a predominately Christian nation only *deteriorates* the core values that our stable society was founded upon. Children are the future and we need to be encouraged to follow a healthy and productive path into adulthood. Who better to guide impressionable youth than Jesus Himself, especially during unified daily prayer at school?" [2]

"What an orator! Well said, Sandra! You have a bright future!" the hostess cheered. Just then, the materfamilias exited the sliding glass doors and passed us by, gulping down a freshly poured mixed drink. Attempting to capture her attention, the hostess called out, "Hey, girl! Your daughter is *brilliant!* You should sit down with us and hear her solve the world's problems!"

"These pina coladas are *good*," the termagant announced, rapidly finishing her beverage as she noisily sucked the last portions into her face. "I'm getting another one."

As the lush returned inside, I shook my head, muttering, *"Great."*

"Don't worry about your mom," the hostess consoled. "She's having a good time, so we'll leave her alone. Would you like a beer or cocktail, Sandra?"

"No, thank you," I politely answered, recalling the disturbing testimonies of several middle-school classmates who already had run-ins with local law enforcement. "I know I *seem* older, but I'm only thirteen. It's illegal for a minor to drink or be served alcohol." [3]

"You're mature, Sandra. You can clearly handle yourself," the woman urged. "I won't tell anyone if you have a drink." [4]

"Thank you for the offer, but I'll just stick with soda," I chirped, concealing my irritation at her persistence. [5]

By nightfall, the number of remaining guests had dwindled and left the backyard in disarray. Not knowing what else to do, I gathered some trash and walked inside to find a receptacle when the hostess saw me and whispered, "Sandra, why are you cleaning? That's sweet, but it's not your responsibility. You're my guest and I'll take care of that in the morning. I'm glad I found you. I need to tell you something. Your mother drank *a lot* and will need to sleep it off. She's in the first bedroom to the left."

"Thank you," I chirped, finding the specified door to step inside.

"Sandra, come in here. I'm just brushing my teeth," the materfamilias informed from the open restroom, white-knuckling the granite counter to remain upright.

"That's okay," I replied, lingering near the exit. "I'll just make a pallet on the floor while I wait for you to finish up."

"*No,*" the woman corrected, speaking through toothpaste foam. "You're sleeping on the bed… with *me.*"

"*No,*" I firmly rebutted. "I'm either sleeping on the bedroom floor or on the living room couch. Those are the options."

While she finished up, I claimed one fluffy pillow and the disregarded comforter from the side of the bed, and arranged the items neatly on the plush carpet. By then, the termagant burped with a faint moan as she exited the restroom. Seeking safety, I immediately clutched my overnight bag and approached the bathroom sink, locking the door behind me.

Ready to sleep and donning warm pajamas, I exited the bathroom and gasped. While averting my eyes, I battled the urge to regurgitate my barbecue and soda. The materfamilias exposed her entire body, brazenly sprawled out like a chloroformed prostitute. She had removed the comfortable arrangement from the floor in my brief absence and needlessly trapped it underneath her limp flesh. Enraged and unwilling to endure another moment of her repulsive state, I shut off the lights, left the pervert behind, and fled into the living room. [6]

Mortified and twitching, I silently concluded, "If I can't trust my own *mother* when she's drunk, how can I trust drunk strangers?" Resolving to stay awake all night, I lowered the volume to barely audible and distracted myself with television until midmorning. [7]

A fully clothed and paranoid materfamilias opened her door and scanned the surrounding area, forcefully whispering, *"Grab your stuff. We're leaving."* While pulling out of the driveway, the termagant scolded, "Why did you disobey me and sleep in the living room?! Anyone could have taken you and done anything to you out there!" [8]

I blankly stared through the windshield as I spoke in a monotone and frigidly replied, "You drank yourself into a stupor, removed my floor pallet, and passed out naked right on top of the very comforter I intended to use. Considering that you exposed your entire naked body to me, facing upward with open legs, I think I handled the situation fairly well. I promise you, woman, what laid on that bed was far more dangerous and disturbing than *anything else* in that house. I will never go to a party with you again. Don't even ask."

Just a Game

"I've been thinking about what you've been telling me about your mom, how she accuses your dad of cheating all the time," Neli casually stated as we sat together at lunch. "I think your mom is cheating on your dad. People who cheat usually accuse others of cheating. I've seen it before."

"I wouldn't put it past her," I replied. "She has all the time in the world while we're all at work and school. It's funny you say that. She knows people I've never met or heard of before... and knows where they live, too. You might be right. I just don't have any proof."

"Oh! I was thinking about something else, too! Are you joining the basketball team this year?" Neli queried with a hopeful tone.

"Nope," I promptly replied. "Don't you remember when I asked my mother for permission to go to that basketball training camp with you two summers ago? She freaked out and told me she wasn't gonna spend money just to drive me to and from practices. She even threatened to spank me if I asked her again... and that was just a week-long camp. That woman will not let me play a sport for an *entire season*. That's even more driving. It's useless to ask. Besides, apart from what I've learned by watching sports with my dad, I don't know the first thing about playing basketball. I can't make a basket to save my life. I'm not even good at playing HORSE."

Neli pursed her lips and rebutted, "So, what? I'll teach you and give you pointers. *Just ask her*. Didn't you tell me that your mom likes me? *Use that*. What's the worst that could happen? If she says no, then you can't play. I get that you're on a tight leash, but I want to hang out with you *outside of school,* and this is the only way we'll be able to do that. Come on. You hate being home, *right?* Well, playing basketball will get you out of the house."

I admitted with a nod, "Good point. That *alone* is worth the risk."

After dinner, I approached the lounging termagant and cleverly mentioned, "Neli wants me to join the basketball team with her this year. Since it's *free*, can I play?"

"*Ha!* Are you kidding?! It's not free! Don't you know anything?! You'll need basketball shoes and special glasses that won't break... and those are expensive!" the woman emphasized. "Even though you're a demon that talks back to her mother, I'll let you play, but *only* because Neli is a good influence. I want you to be a good little girl like Neli." [1]

Stinging from her malicious words, I bit my tongue, retreated to my bedroom, and shut the door. The wall-mounted mirror took the place of the materfamilias as I leaned forward, stared into my own eyes, and growled, "I *am* a good little girl, *you twisted jerk*... and Neli's *the best* little girl. *You* only like her because she's Mexican." [2]

That weekend, during a trip to the city, the materfamilias purchased a pair of basketball shoes and some prescription sport goggles for me to wear, remarking, "Do you see how much I love you? I buy you things and let you play basketball. I never had new shoes when I was a little girl, but my parents were *super* poor. We lived in the projects." Having heard the same story countless times, I remained silent and stared out the window without responding. "*Man!* You ungrateful little demon from hell! You have it way better than I ever did! I never had the things you have and just look at how bad you are! You even talk back to me! I should take back everything I just bought you! God doesn't like spoiled little girls! He's gonna get you for that!" [3]

Remaining motionless, I internally rebutted, "Yeah, Mom? What happens to violent, child molesting mothers? Get ready for flames, lady."

To keep my new corrective lenses in place, I strapped them directly over my hair, just above a lifeless ponytail. Proving to be just as helpful as they were stylish, the translucent plastic frame and boxy design warped my depth perception and eliminated all peripheral vision. While wearing them, I often stumbled over stairs and experienced reoccurring head trauma when basketballs repeatedly slammed against my face during practice and games alike. Basketballs often bashed against my skull and face with misjudged passes, but most of the blows were deliberate while I wasn't looking and *always* by teammates. The laughter at my expense rang in my ears as I suppressed tears and swelling rage. [4]

Since Kirk's dream, I knew the Messiah was real and witnessed my every struggle. With that in mind, each night I prayed, "Jesus, would you please heal my eyes so I can see clearly without glasses? Amen." Fully expecting a miracle to await me by morning, I consistently opened my eyes to the same blurred vision. In response, I prayerfully reassured, "It's okay, Jesus. I love You anyway." [5]

It was more than evident that I was the weakest player on the basketball team. Nevertheless, our coach positioned me as point guard and I remained there. No matter how hard I studied each play, I couldn't remember who to look for or when to pass. Little of what occurred on the court, legal or illegal, made sense to me. On several occasions, I lost track of the half-time switch and couldn't recall which basket was ours. When dribbling, the opposing team repeatedly stole the ball from me or violently stripped it from my hands without a foul ever being called. Our coach never explained the rules to me. Completely ignorant of proper defensive techniques, I came near fouling-out of each game. [6]

During weekday practices or while playing before a small crowd of parents, my only joy was observing Neli navigate the court with absolute confidence, being as talented with a basketball as I was inept. The athlete often regained possession of the ball that I had just lost and dribbled skillfully around the competition to score. Swishing nearly every shot she attempted, my friend was our team's MVP.

Regardless of my many errors or how drastically we lost, Neli cheerfully sat beside my despondent frame for the bus ride home and chirped, "Don't worry, Sandra. It's not a big deal. It's just a game." [7]

Completely disheartened by my dreadful performance, I approached my father at home and explained my plight. Growing stern, the man coached, "Sandra, if you start something, you need to finish it. That's called *commitment*. If you see quitting as an option, you'll grow comfortable quitting *everything* and end up making a lifestyle of it. *Don't be a quitter.* After the season is over, if you still don't want to play basketball, remember that and don't sign-up for it next year, but I won't allow quitting. *Finish out the season* and I don't want to hear any more about it." [8]

"Sandra, you *really* suck at basketball," a teammate openly commented during practice.

Theatrically nodding in agreement, I wholeheartedly admitted, "That's true. I *hate* this sport."

"Then why don't you just quit?" the girl suggested. "You're dragging the entire team down."

"You're right," I replied. "I'd *love* to quit, but my dad won't let me. It looks like we're stuck with each other for the rest of the season. I've asked the coach to bench me, but he said that our team is too small."

After a few hours into our only tournament, we lost two back-to-back games, which eliminated us early on. While the rest of the team exited to the bleachers, I took my time in the locker room to enjoy the solitude. Within a moment, I heard some heavy footsteps and glanced up to see who had come in.

Mara, our largest teammate, approached me with a menacing scowl, blocking the only way out as she ridiculed, "You lost us the tournament, *pipsqueak*… and you're gonna pay for it." [9]

Concealing my fear, I quipped, "You know, if I was the *only one* who made mistakes today, I'd agree with you, but you're not very good at this sport either… or anything else, *as far as I know*. Can you sing?" [10]

"Well, not really…" she began, scratching her head. After a brief pause, Mara raged, *"Hey! Are you ******* kidding me, right now?! Shut you're ******* mouth, Sandra! I'm not stupid! You want to talk **** to me?! I can destroy you with one punch! I'll mop the floor with you, toothpick! I can snap you in half!"*

The verbal altercation piqued the interest of other teammates who rallied around the developing drama. Several were directly involved with pinning Caden to that tree in the sixth-grade. [11]

"It sounds like you've been running your mouth again, Sandra," a teammate prodded. "It's going to get you into trouble, you know. It's not like you help us on the court."

"Is this your idea of small-town entertainment?" I queried with an elevated brow. "You'll probably lie about this incident, too. It makes sense, really… all of you banding together. Strength in numbers, right? In a way, I feel sorry for you. I mean, think about it. I weigh sixty pounds. Are you so afraid of me that *ganging-up* is the only way you feel confident and secure? While you're at it, why don't you guys have a meeting and elect a spokesperson to represent you? Who knows? If you put your heads together, maybe you'll actually come up with something worth saying." [12]

"That's it, toothpick! You're dead meat! Let's get her!" Mara ordered.

The matching jerseys herded my frame toward the showerheads. Taking the lead, Mara stomped toward me and reached forward, twisting the valve beside me. Icy water poured down my scalp, soaking my uniform and only pair of athletic shoes. Shocked by the cold, I shrieked, slammed my back to the tile and slid down to the floor in torment, inspiring sadistic laughter from my peers. To shut off the frigid shower, I reached upward and mistakenly turned the knob to full blast. Their cackles echoed as one held another upright, doubled over in triumphant hysterics. [13]

Spinning with emotions, I broke character and sobbed in their presence, screaming, "Get away from me! Get away!"

"Get away! Get away!" they mocked.

"Who's screaming?! Why are you guys laughing?! Where's Sandra?!" a familiar voice shouted, storming the locker room. "Sandra, is that you?! What's going on in here?! Get away from her, you *******!" Lunging to my aid, Neli grabbed the shower head and sprayed my assailants with one steady stream, landing a solid streak of water across their shorts and tops. "I'm telling the coach what you guys did! You think you're so tough?! You'd better get the hell out of here before I kick your ***!" Shutting off the shower and grabbing my shaking hands with a gentle tug, Neli encouraged, "Get up, Sandra. Come on." [14]

True to her word, the whistleblower led me straight to our oblivious coach, who cheerfully greeted, "Hey, girls! What's up?"

"Coach! Where the hell were you just now?! Look at what our team did to Sandra! Didn't you hear her screaming?! I could hear her from the bleachers!" Neli challenged. "I ran toward the screams and found the team cornering Sandra in the showers, soaking her with water! Now she's going to be *cold and wet* the entire bus ride home!"

"I'm sorry that happened to you, Sandra. What can I do to help?" the man replied.

"Are you kidding me right now?!" Neli continued, radiating frustration. "Do something about it! You're the coach! Make yourself useful and get them into trouble! Punish them! Who's the adult here?!" [15]

The rest of the team was easily located, huddled together on the bleachers with masks of innocence as the coach called out, "Girls! Get over here!"

A teammate chirped, "What do you want *us* for? Did something happen?"

"Why is Sandra all wet?" Mara asked, instinctively lining up shoulder-to-shoulder with the others.

"Good question," the coach commented. "Were any of you involved in an incident with Sandra in the locker room today?"

"*No,*" they sharply answered in unison.

The man pursed his lips and questioned, "Are you *sure* you weren't there, ladies? Why don't you take a look at your jerseys?" The damp streaks on each of their uniforms lined up and betrayed them.

"It was all *Sandra's* fault!" Mara accused. [16]

"Yeah!" the rest agreed. "*She* started everything!"

Another noted, "She wouldn't stop insulting us!"

"They're *obviously* lying!" Neli rebutted. "Just a second ago, they said they weren't even involved! Now, they're crying about who started it! What a bunch of idiots! They can't keep their story straight!"

"We're all innocent! Sandra turned the shower on herself! Just ask her!" Mara gaslighted.

Appearing confused, the coach inquired, "Sandra, is that *true*?"

"No!" I boldly replied, watching the team feign shock. "I did *not* turn the water on. I was alone in the locker room when Mara stepped up to me… trying to pick a fight with her pathetic name-calling and lame insults. She made idiotic comments that reflected her lack of intelligence, and I made her painfully *aware* of it. Once she finally grasped what I was saying, Mara starting shouting more threats. *These guys* must have heard Mara's voice and came running to see what was going on. That's when they all cornered me in the locker room showers. *Mara* walked up to me and turned on the shower right above my head. I started screaming and was so disoriented from the cold water that when I tried to shut it off, I turned the knob the wrong way and made it even *worse*. That's when Neli found me and stopped them."

"I see," he murmured.

"Mara is twisting what happened to make herself look innocent, but she's not. *She* started everything," I clarified. "Why would I turn the shower on myself?! That's the dumbest lie I've ever heard! Coach, you don't actually *believe* that, do you?"

The man spoke up and said, "It sounds like *everyone* is at fault here." [17]

"How can you say that?!" Neli rebuked. "I didn't see how it started, but I *did* see this wolf pack huddled around Sandra, laughing as they kept her cornered under a *running shower*. That's when I grabbed the shower head and tagged them with water… just to prove that these cowards were there. It's a good thing I did, too! They're just a bunch of lying bullies!" [18]

Appearing nervous, the coach concluded, "I'll announce my decision at the next practice and I don't want to hear any more about it until then."

That Monday, Neli grabbed my hand and exhorted, "Time's up. *C'mon, Sandra.* Let's go find out what the coach decided."

"Wait a second. Maybe we should just forget about it," I reasoned, preventing her from pulling me forward. "*He doesn't care,* and they'll just keep lying to protect each other. It's what they do. They pick fights and lie, and I'm the one that gets into trouble."

"What are you saying?! If you let those ******* get away with this, they'll *never* stop," Neli warned. "Either stand up for yourself or I won't help you anymore. I'll let them do whatever they want. Why should I stick my neck out for you if you're not willing to stand your ground? Do you want me to stop helping you?" I shook my head. "Then, back me up! Let's go!" Neli spotted the man and followed him right into his office, scolding, "Coach, you're *not* getting out of this! What are you going to do about what happened at the tournament? Sandra was *alone* and got attacked in a locker room by her own teammates! If I hadn't of shown up, who knows how far it would've gone! What *more* do they need to do to her?! Kill her?!"

"Just let it go, Neli," the man urged. "*Everybody* was involved. If I have to deal out discipline, it will be for the *entire team,* and I don't want to punish the two of you."

"You're the coach and you *know* they're guilty! If you don't want to punish us, then don't!" Neli insisted. "This isn't that complicated!" [19]

Silently signaling with her head, my friend urged me to speak, so I gently added, "Neli told me that if nothing happens to them, they'll just keep doing this to me. *She's right.* Whatever punishment you come up with, even if it's for the *entire team,* will be easy for us and really hard for them. I know I suck at basketball, but at least I put forth an effort every day. They're lazy."

The coach walked Neli and I out of his office and onto the court as he shouted, *"For the events at the tournament, everyone is running twenty laps around the gym! Get started!"*

Neli exclaimed, *"What?! That's it?! What a joke!"* At that, the man pivoted and immediately returned to his office. Shaking our heads, Neli and I lapped the others, over and over, and finished what felt like a warmup. When the adult returned to the court, he came upon the two of us resting together on a bench and watching the others sweat.

Mara shouted, *"They cheated and didn't run all the laps! See, we're still running!"* The jogging girls huffed and squawked in agreement as the man painfully stared at us, seeming helpless and stuck.

"*Wow.* You know what, coach?! I have a brilliant idea that can get you out of this mess!" I announced, standing with a smirk and glancing back at Neli. "Let's start this whole thing over *from the beginning*, but this time, *you* have to stay and watch!" The conspirators groaned, having almost finished their punishment.

As we sprinted to the starting point, Neli jeered openly, "They're obviously lying, *just like last time…* but don't worry about us! We can take it! We know you're just afraid of their parents! Good ole' small town politics!"

Oozing shame, the man stared down at the polished court with a pitiful sigh. Neli and I boisterously numbered each of our twenty additional loops around the court and returned to our original resting spot, victoriously relaxing with our feet up. Huffing as they passed, the liars glared at us with a snarl, enduring one monitored lap at a time.[20]

A Second Generation

"*M*om, will you *please* let me stay home this time?" I begged.

"No!" the materfamilias snapped. "I'm not leaving you here to do God-knows-what! *No way!* You're coming with me… and if you ask me again, I'm gonna spank you. Get dressed and wear something *nice*. Let's go! Move it!" [1]

"Wait a second, lady. What do you mean by *wear something nice*?" I wondered aloud. "We always dress *nice* when we go to the city. Do you mean *nicer-than-usual*? What's the occasion?"

"Stop asking questions! You don't need to know *why*," she growled with volatile eyes. "You're just a child and I'm an adult. *Do as I say.*" [2]

As expected, after traveling a few miles down the road, the termagant began the ritual of raising her voice over the music and aggressively rambling, "Your father thinks he can just do whatever he wants and screw every woman in town without me knowing! He's not getting away with anything! I'm not stupid!" [3]

Tuning her out, I peered at the trees through the passenger window, unable to sing along to the radio as a positive distraction. Her music selection had recently changed. With speakers blaring, unintelligible singing voices raked my spine as abrasive instruments cawed against repetitive two-note thuds, over and over and over.

"Mom, could you please turn the radio back to oldies music?" I politely requested.

"No! I'll listen to whatever I want! Just sit there and be quiet," she dismissed.

I sighed and pressed, "Well, could you at least turn down the volume? It's really loud."

"No! Shut up and stop complaining!" the woman ordered. "I'm not hurting anyone listening to this! Now, reach into the back seat and hand me one of my waters! I'm thirsty!"

Obeying, I snagged one of the plastic bottles rolling around on the floorboards and scrunched my shoulders, bracing myself for what *always* occurred. While steering, the materfamilias twisted off the cap and latched her lipstick-plastered orifice around the opening of the perpendicularly flipped bottle. Forced out with unnecessary squeezes, tepid liquid rushed from the weak container with an awful crunch. Aggressive glugging accompanied a steady trickle of liquid from the corners of her lips that flowed down her neck and soaked into her blouse.

Oblivious to my cringed posture and gagging, as if attempting to entertain me with her satisfaction, she repulsively smacked her lips and capped off her nauseating habit with a loud and elongated, *"Ahh!"* The hem and haw of her music reminded me of MK Ultra tactics and nearly brought me to tears when she added, "Grab me another water."

I obeyed and immediately stared through the passenger window, feeling my attention being drawn down toward the gently weaving yellow lane marker outside. Once more, I pled, "Mom, can we *please* listen to something else?"

Staring forward, she frigidly replied, "No. If you ask me again, I'm gonna spank you."

Desperate for it all to be over, I unbuckled my seatbelt and slammed my body against the opening passenger door, leaning against the wind resistance and aching to rest in a bloody heap on the asphalt below. [4]

The materfamilias slowed her speed to a halt, screaming, *"Sandra! Are you crazy! Close the door!"* Taking my opportunity, I exited the vehicle. *"What are you doing?! Get back in this car right now!"*

I shouted over the blaring radio and declared, "I can't take it anymore! Everything is all about *you!* Change the ******* station and turn the volume down *right now* or I'll jump off this ******* bridge! I'd rather *die* than be stuck with you for another minute, listening to this ****!"

The materfamilias blandly acquiesced, *"Fine.* I'll change the music. Just get inside the car." [5]

With one gentle press of a pre-programmed button, a familiar tune filled the atmosphere before returning to a reasonable volume. Quite stunned that the woman caved to my demands, I re-entered the vehicle. [6]

We eventually pulled up to a large judicial building located downtown. Reading the official signs and labels on the stone walls and tidy parking spaces, my mind cranked to put the puzzle pieces together. For years, the materfamilias had compulsively recanted stories about working in the city for the county's district court.

According to her testimony, while still employed as a court clerk, a prisoner in the bailiff's custody had broken free and bolted down the hall towards the materfamilias' workspace. Understanding the situation, she quickly approached the runner, cold cocked him to the ground, and punched her way into legend.

"Why didn't you just tell me we were visiting the courthouse?" I inquired. "You've talked about this place a million times. Why were you keeping it a secret? Why are we here? Is someone expecting us? Don't they have important work to do? Won't we be interrupting them?"

"Be quiet! Stop asking questions!" the woman ordered. "Listen to me, Sandra. I need you to *behave* in there. Don't embarrass me."

Theatrically feigning adoration, I opened the car door and boasted an exaggerated grin, spoofing, "I'll smile for your former co-workers and make you look *really good*, Mommy. Don't you worry. I'll be *extra* fake. Believe me. They'll have no idea how miserable we all *really* are." After batting my eyelashes at her, the materfamilias looked on as my grandiose cheer melted to a piercing scowl.

We climbed the courthouse steps and made our way inside. A handful of people in suits and dressy business attire immediately recognized the woman next to me and came near to greet her with warm hugs. "This is my daughter, Sandra," the materfamilias announced, proudly displaying me as though she were pleased with my appearance and development.

"It's nice to meet you, Sandra! You're such a pretty girl!" each clerk and attorney enthusiastically cooed. Even the district court judge said so as we entered his modest office.

After visiting briefly with each individual, the woman guided me further along our trajectory. Once we rounded the corner, she whispered, *"We're almost done. I just have one more person to visit."* Before knocking on a door, the materfamilias hesitated and discreetly added, *"Don't mention anything that I told you about him. He'll get upset."* Getting the impression that the person's identity was important, I scanned the overstated mahogany door and surrounding wall for a nameplate. Upon discovering it, my jaw went limp.

According to the materfamilias' claims, which I had assumed were completely fabricated, at least one clerk and several attorneys who frequented those same halls had romantically approached her. However, a particular story savored strongly of *omission*.

Soon after accepting my father's marriage proposal, the materfamilias intended to leave her position at the courthouse and follow her military husband to his next station. Upon making her announcement to several colleagues, nearly everyone clapped and offered their congratulations, except for one man. A fellow clerk became enraged and hurled out vulgar accusations with obscene insults. Having scolded her in the sight and earshot of all, uncontrollable rage took over her body and propelled the termagant's fist into the clerk's spouting face.

Recognizing the name and reading the title District Clerk *Supervisor*, I interrogated, "What the hell are we doing here?! I thought you hated this guy?! Didn't you punch him in the face the last time you saw him?!"

The materfamilias hushed me frantically by waving her hand, causing golden bangles on her wrist to clink. She furrowed her brow and aggressively whispered, *"Shh. Be quiet. I told you not to bring that up. Don't say anything."*

Without further ado, her knuckles rapped against the mahogany surface that offered a luxuriously dense knock. The decorative knob turned just before his door swung open. The whoosh of air pulled my dress forward, surprising me. I curiously peered upward to pin a face to the name. The individual appeared exactly as the woman had disdainfully painted him so many times before. An aging dork in a nice suit stood before us, awestruck at the woman who darkened his doorway.

"*It's you*," he faintly uttered, smitten. Remembering himself, the man cleared his throat and proceeded in the manner of a used car salesman. "How unexpected! Welcome! Please, come in!" A sly hand reached backwards toward his mahogany desk to clasp a proudly displayed family portrait, only to set it face-down. Unwilling to alarm the beguiled stranger, I maintained an appearance of childlike naivety. However, having spotted his breathtaking spouse and remarkably beautiful children in the photograph, I found it bizarre that the victim still longed for his assailant.

The man's wandering eyes peered down his nose at my person, followed by a feigned enthusiasm to coo, "And who is this?! Is this your daughter?! She's beautiful, just like you!"[7]

While the two adults shallowly conversed and reacquainted, I visually explored the mahogany bookshelves filled with official binders, various leather-bound reading materials, and ostentatious décor.

Still gazing at the woman, the host pulled out a chair for her and opened his other arm wide, inviting, "Please, have a seat! Let's talk!"

Her performance was magnificent as she disguised herself as demure and temperate. The coquette gently accepted his offer and settled herself in the chair before his luxurious desk, being positioned opposite and noticeably lower than the previously scorned clerk.

Since the District Clerk Supervisor had already nestled himself in his leather rolling chair, the termagant placed her hand on the back of the empty seat beside her and suggested, "Sandra, would you like to sit down over here?"

"No, thank you," I plainly stated, testing her portrayal of feminine perfection.

Virtually unoccupied space opened up to the right, drawing my gaze to a solitary wingback tufted-leather chair offering lavish support. Seating myself, I imagined I was a princess inheriting a throne as I slid myself to the back of the leather seat cushion. Its grandiosity dwarfed my petite stature, possessing high arm rests that kept my appendages aloft when used. The decorative piece tied the vast office together, providing a profile view of the two gravitating adults, separated only by wide office furniture.

After a long while, a sudden silence drew my full attention to the scene unfolding before me. Appearing flush, the District Clerk Supervisor's tone drastically changed as he clasped his desk and passionately urged, *"Run away with me. I'll abandon my wife and kids. I don't care. If you're unhappy, leave your husband! Let's get away so we can finally be together! Let's leave and never come back! As you can clearly see, I've done very well. You'll want for nothing."* [8]

The materfamilias cocked her head to the side and down, flirtatiously withholding her obvious desire to yield to his brazenly evil supplication. Playing a game of cat and mouse, she gave a blushing smile and shifted her feet, sheepishly whispering, *"Well... I don't know..."* [9]

Without hesitation, I boldly arose and marched directly into their line of sight, stomping their fantasy into the pristine carpet with each approaching step. *"You don't know, huh?! What the **** is going on here?!"* I furiously inquired. The two conspirators turned as pale as death, staring in horror. To the cajoled egomaniac, I shouted, "You want to run away with my mother... my father's wife?! That's my dad you're talking about! Listen to me, you piece of ****! You're about to get your *** kicked by a *second generation!*" Fuming from the hypocritical betrayal, I addressed the quivering femme fatale and coldly stated, "As for *you*, we're leaving." [10]

At that, I threw open the office door and made my way down the hall.

Caught in the act and abruptly abandoned, the temptress murmured, *"Bye,"* just before sprinting to catch me. For the entire length of the courthouse and all the way to the car, I remained several steps ahead of the adulteress, leaving her to trail behind me awkwardly in a poorly concealed panic. [11]

I soaked in the blissful silence that lingered in the air during our retreat to the log house. No scolding flew past the materfamilias' teeth. No spanking lurked around the corner. After what I had endured under her abusive dictatorship, the tables had finally turned. She was at *my* mercy. [12]

With time to consider my next move, I believed myself to be ultimately responsible for any long-term damage that the information might cause and concluded it better to hold my tongue on the subject, deeming that no good would come of my father's awareness. The man already convinced me he'd never leave her. Within a week, the termagant resumed her vexatious habits of suspicion and accusation towards the very spouse that she, herself, had entertained abandoning. [13]

Goody-Goody

Abandoning the jealousy over Alice's rapidly developing beauty, I approached her in the hall and asked, "Do you remember in the sixth-grade when you saw me all bruised up and called my mom a psychopath?"

"Yeah," she replied. "That ***** should *die* for what she did to you." [1]

"I agree, but how did you learn so much about psychopaths?" I queried. "I had to look up what psychopath really meant and found out that you were actually *right*."

"Let's just say… I'm *educated* on the subject of psychopaths. I *lived* with psychopaths. I mean, look at my life. My grandmother has to raise me and it's not like I'm an orphan or anything. She became my legal guardian because I wasn't safe at home. Listen, Sandra. I don't really want to talk about my past anymore. I just know child abuse when I see it. Okay?"

"Dang. I didn't know about your parents," I confessed with concern. "I'm sorry if I upset you."

"Like hell you didn't know!" Alice scoffed. "It's a small town! Everybody knows everything about everyone!"

"Well, in case you didn't notice, people don't really talk to me," I rebutted. "I was just curious about your diagnosis of my mother. It was accurate."

Alice softened, teasing, "You have a point, Sandra. I forget you're a *troll* that no one likes. *Haha!* Seriously, I'm sorry for thinking you were a liar. You're probably the only person I can trust." Pulling me to the side, she whispered, *"I have to tell you something. I'm dating a junior."*

I blurted, "In high school?!"

Alice covered my mouth, frantically hushing, *"Shh! Keep your voice down. Yes! What other kind of junior is there?"*

"That doesn't seem right," I commented. "Isn't that child molestation? You're only thirteen."

"No, Sandra, *it's not*. Besides, it's legal. He's only seventeen, not *eighteen*. I'm older than you. Remember? I'm almost fourteen. *Anyway*, I have been sneaking out of the house to see him."

"Alice! No, ma'am!" I scolded. Leaning in, I whispered, *"You're not having sex with him, are you?"*

"Well, no. *Not yet.* I'm technically still a virgin, but I've fooled around before, you know… like *heavy-petting*… and I've made out with boys, but I really like this guy and I want to have sex with him." [2]

Fantastically sheltered, I didn't know there was a difference between 'fooling around' and sex. I also didn't understand what *heavy petting* was. It sounded painful, even for a dog.

"Alice, don't do it!" I pleaded. "That will break your grandmother's heart if she ever found out! You need to stop! What kind of high school upper-classmen goes after an *eighth-grader*, anyway?! We're little girls! Think about it, Alice. He's a ******* *pedophile*."

"You're so *naïve*, Sandra. He's hot and I like him. He's not doing anything that I don't want him to do. Besides, I'm not an idiot. I've snuck out a bunch of times and my grandmother has *never* found out. And she *won't* find out, either, unless *you* tell her."

I shook my head and urged, "I won't say anything to her, but I don't like this and it needs to stop." [3]

"Oh my gosh, Sandra. You're such a *goody-goody*," Alice scoffed. "I shouldn't have said anything."

Days later, Alice was crying and very nauseous. Concerned, I followed her into the restroom to hold back her hair as she vomited inside a stall. "Are you sick?" I wondered, feeling her forehead. "You don't have a fever." [4]

Smearing her mascara as she swiped at her tears, Alice moaned, *"I'm so sore."*

"Oh! Did you get sick from running too hard in athletics?" I queried.

"My *legs* aren't sore, idiot! I'm sore *between* my legs! ****, Sandra! Do I have to spell *everything* out for you?! We had *sex* last night!" She vomited once more and stood to rinse her mouth at a sink. "Everything is just really tender right now, but it was all my idea. I set everything up and snuck out. It was really romantic and *forbidden*. We did it on a blanket, just outside of my bedroom window. It was my first time, so he broke the seal. It was fun *at first*, but then he got really rough with me. Since I pursued *him*, I felt guilty and didn't tell him to stop, but he *really* hurt me. I better not be pregnant." [5]

"What if you are?" I posed, still wondering what *breaking the seal* meant.

Alice sliced, "I wouldn't have morning sickness *the day after*, stupid." Pausing, she seemed to question herself for a moment and then shook her head. "No. I'm not pregnant." Cruelly brushing past me, she exited the middle school bathroom. [6]

That same day, I walked toward the high school portion of campus and stood before our library, calmly asking an approaching student where I could find the popular junior.

She turned and pointed out Alice's boyfriend, having just strolled past him a moment prior. Once politely thanked, she continued away from me and into the Band Hall.

"*Hey, pedophile!*" I shouted, marching down the sidewalk toward the unsuspecting junior as he slouched near the high school building. His friend snagged his attention and pointed at me. "I'm sorry about the confusion. When I said *pedophile*, I was talking to you. Alice is *thirteen*. Are you unable to hook any more of your own slutty classmates? Are you so desperate you decided to seduce a child? Listen, *******. I'm paying attention. *Stay away from Alice.* You wouldn't want the police to get wind of this, would you? How long do you plan to keep this up? When you're eighteen, she'll only be fourteen and still a minor. Do you think a pervert like you will be able to stop? Back off or there will be consequences." [7]

"You don't know what you're talking about. *She* came to *me*," he clarified with stinging arrogance. "I don't have to listen to you." [8]

"Well, you should. If a pretty girl in *elementary* had a crush on you and wanted to have sex, would you **** her, too?!" Understanding my point, his friend raised an eyebrow and glanced over at his peer as I continued, "If you can't keep your pants up, at least stick with girls your own age. This is your one and only warning." [9]

Defend Yourself

Alice and I joined the middle school track team, practicing various races and field events. A gravel track circumnavigated our poorly maintained football field and produced greener creeping grass than the perishing blades under the gridiron. With each race, sprinters often slipped at the start and finished with a slide, spraying loose granite endlessly. Because of unsafe conditions, our under-funded school couldn't host track meets.

Being bussed to another school meant extended time away from my family. Grateful for a change of scenery and better weather, I strolled around, admiring the synthetic rubber and eight pristinely painted lanes that felt so Olympic and official underneath my cleats.

The energy and hum of athletes warming up, coaches shouting directions, and student conversations filled the air. After each crack of a starter pistol, local families and those that traveled cheered from the stands with vigorous applause as various teammates shouted encouragement from the field.

Agreeable and willing to please, I competed in the least desired events of track and field, such as the two-mile run. While huffing through eight grueling loops around the track, I whispered to myself, *"If you can ride a mountain bike to church in one-hundred-degree weather, this should be easy. Suck it up, Sandra. Keep going. This will end."* [1]

Strategizing, I placed myself just a few strides behind the lead runner until the very last lap and sprinted past on the final straightaway. Enjoying the adrenaline of my approaching victory, I rushed across the finish line with a howling war cry, amusing the track coach and several onlookers.

The coach announced, "Our high school doesn't have enough students on the varsity *and* JV track team to compete in every event. Another coach suggested that you eight-graders should fill in those missing spots. We agreed it will be good for all of you, but we're not expecting miracles here. Just do your best. Next year, you'll have an advantage over the other freshmen by having stiffer competition already under your belt."

Even against junior varsity, it became abundantly clear that I was entirely out of my league. The other runners dwarfed me and were far more developed physically, able to maintain long and powerful strides from start to finish. My gaunt and petite frame couldn't keep their pace and I finished last in all of my events.

Losing my last race for the evening, I traversed the densely populated field and observed our competition. Several teams tranquilly positioned themselves into massive stretching circles. Other students read books, finished homework, listened to music, threw a football around or peacefully napped. [2]

As I navigated between the factions of our team, I noticed lingering grimaces accompanied by whispers and snickering. It was then that I remembered something a few eighth-grade girls had mentioned in the hall. My classmates and their older siblings had frequented local dance halls with their parents and attended underaged drinking parties, becoming well acquainted with one another long before the teams had merged. [3]

A high school student peered upward from her seat on the grass and inquired, "Your name is Sandra, isn't it?"

"Yes," I confirmed.

"Sandra," she casually continued, "Why are you even here? I thought your job was to help us win team points, but you didn't win *any*. That makes you dead weight, doesn't it? You should quit and stay home." [4]

A girl sitting beside her changed the subject, wincing and rubbing her calf to interject, "Aw, man! I have another leg cramp."

Intending to be helpful, I cheerfully relayed some overheard advice from our coach, mentioning, "Start taking potassium glucosonate. That should help." [5]

"It's potassium *gluc*o*na*te, not gluco*so*nate," another high school student spitefully corrected. "Glucosonate isn't a word."

"It's glucosonate," I insisted.

"No, *it's not*. I take potassium gluconate every day," she confidently rebutted, reaching into her athletic bag. In a flash, the athlete tossed a clearly labeled bottle of potassium gluconate toward me. [6]

Catching it, I quickly glanced at the spelling. I was wrong. However, with my pride wounded and flaring, I tossed back the vitamins and condescended, "I'm not the one cramping. Maybe you should hand this to your friend." [7]

Unwilling to expose myself to further humiliation, I located my belongings, separated myself from the team, and nestled into the sleeping bag I toted with me, remaining still until drifting to sleep.

The distinct sensation of being hoisted off the ground snapped me awake. Wondering what was happening, I leaned forward and peeked at the two high school boys responsible. Realizing that it was the closest thing to a hug that I had received in some time,

I deciding not to resist and was dumped head-first into a metal trash barrel near centerfield. Laughter erupted as I awkwardly wriggled my way out. [8]

The cramping teen approached me and confessed, "I went ahead of them and made sure there wasn't any food trash in there."

Astonished, I faced her and questioned, "So you knew and you didn't *stop* them?"

That following practice, Alice and I jogged laps around the gravel track and chatted as we had many times before. She peered backward to see who was jogging behind us and instantly pushed me onto the itchy grass, repeatedly smacking me with the plastic soda bottle in her hand.

Laughing, she sadistically shouted, *"What are you going to do?! Nothing! Get up! Defend yourself! Hahaha! Defend yourself, you weakling!"* [9]

Free of physical injury, it was shock and confusion that rendered me immobile as I cried out, *"Alice! Stop! Why are you doing this?! I don't understand!"*

It was then that I noticed the three high school boys jogging past, who chuckled with each blow to my curled-up body while they admired Alice's legs. [10]

Red

~~~~~~

After finishing final exams, the teacher let us leave class hours before the busses were scheduled to depart. I contemplated how I would spend my stolen time and pushed open the middle school exit with an urgent single-mindedness.

Down the hill, standing just before the football field, was a rundown mobile home I ached to enter and explore, having only seen male athletes and their coaches in and around it. Years prior, the school converted the precarious structure into a weight room. The solitary entrance remained open when occupied and allowed passersby to hear and smell weakness leaving the human body. Our coaches did not provide me an opportunity for strength training, and I winced with indignation.

The shut door of the sacred masculine layer made me grin as I concluded, "Oh, sweet. No one's in there." Unaware of any hours of operation or protocol, I prayed, "Jesus, if you want me to lift weights, let me in. If not, have the door be locked. Amen." [1]

I climbed its three steps and twisted the knob. As the door opened, I gasped with delight and stepped past the threshold. Unwilling to attract negative attention from peers or high schoolers, I quickly shut the door behind me and ignored the light switch. Stepping into shadow, I allowed time for my vision to adjust and inhaled the sour pungency of excellence.

Dingy windows poured forth glowing shafts of light, illuminating dust particles to create a sense of reverence as stained glass would a sanctuary. Filled with wonder, I traced my fingers along the rusty artifacts of the warriors that had gone before me. [2]

Mounted mirrors lined an entire wall to cultivate the illusion of twice the space. Startled into sobriety, I shrank back from my own spindly reflection and recalled my mission. I grabbed two rusty plates and slid them onto a racked bench bar. Lying down beneath it, I attempted to press with a grunt. [3]

"Sandra, what are you doing?" a voice queried, startling me into a scream. Red, a strapping boy from my class, slowly emerged into the light. "I'm so sorry, Sandra. I really thought you saw me in here. *Honest.* I didn't mean to scare you. I was just trying to tell you that you have *way* too much weight on that bar. You could hurt really yourself. Let me help you." [4]

"No. It's fine, Red. I want to do this alone," I confessed, clinging to pride. "I'm sorry if I interrupted your workout. When I saw the shut door, I assumed no one was in here. I'm not even sure if girls are allowed in the weight room at all."

"Why wouldn't you be? You go to school here, don't you? I don't know why girls' athletics doesn't schedule time for the weight room. Anyway, if you want to become stronger, you'll have to start small and work your way up," he continued, cautiously drawing nearer. "Seriously, Sandra, let me help you." His pity only fueled my unyielding determination, causing my eyes to narrow and lips to purse. Stubborn, I laid down once more and pressed again, moving nothing. Lunging toward me, he exclaimed, "Stop! You're going to hurt yourself!"

"*I don't care!*" I shouted, bursting into tears. *"I'm tired of being a pathetic weakling that gets picked-on all the time! I'm hated at school and I'm hated at home! There's no escape! I'm tired of people hurting me! I can't take it anymore! I can't take it!"* I white-knuckled the bar and futilely pushed with tears pooling in my ears. [5]

Rushing to my side without touching me, Red patiently warned, "Stop, stop, stop. You can't lift that much. Sandra, take your hands off the bar."

"No! I'm not letting you or anyone else stop me! I'm doing this! Either help me or get out of my way!" I announced through my teeth, straining to separate the bar from the rack.

Drawing closer, Red gently smiled down at me and soothed, "I'm *trying* to help you, but you have to listen to me. *Let go.*" [6]

Realizing the foolishness of my own methods, I abandoned the heavy chip on my shoulder and obeyed my brawny classmate, murmuring, *"Fine."* Maneuvering around the bar, he carefully removed and racked each plate.

The young man was intimidating to behold, especially viewing him from beneath and upside-down. From his new position, Red peered downward and posed, "Sandra, can you eat an entire steak in just one bite?"

Confused, I sheepishly responded, "Well, no."

"No. That's right. You need to cut it into pieces and take smaller bites or you'll choke," he coached, causing me to smirk. "Like I said before, you have to work your way up. Let's just start with the forty-five-pound bench bar and see where you're at. Try again." I lifted it from the rack and struggled to press it. Embarrassed, I wrestled back a sob. "Hold on," Red interjected, setting the bar away from us before slipping away. "Okay. Let's use this twenty-five-pound curl bar instead. When you're stronger, we'll upgrade you." [7]

By the time my school bus cranked its noisy engine, I had already bench pressed a full set, learned proper form on squats and calf raises, effectively operated a butterfly press machine, and only struggled to control my grin. [8]

Opportunity

~~~

I overheard several classmates chattering about vacation destinations, sleep-overs, and various activities that they intended to enjoy during their summer break. I compared my wretched life to their plans and allowed depression to settle within me. All I could foresee for myself was isolation and manual labor assignments in the heat.

Before retreating from the presence of my peers, the most Herculean man I had ever beheld, outside of movies and televised wrestling matches, stepped into the hall from outside. It took a moment to realize that he was walking my way. I recognized him as a boys' athletics coach and instinctually stepped aside. When I did, his eyes tracked my movement, and he shifted his trajectory towards me again. Mortified, I assumed the worst for being in the weight room the day before and braced myself.

"Sandra!" Coach Burley called out, causing my heart to sink. "I've been searching for you! Red said that you're interested in the weight lifting program this summer. Are you wanting to sign up?"

"Red said that?" I replied, floored that someone, especially a boy, had spoken about me favorably. "That was really nice of him, but I don't understand what you're talking about. What program?" [1]

"Oh. I must have misunderstood him. That's okay," Coach Burley continued. "This summer, an athletic camp is being hosted by the school to develop agility and teach proper weight training techniques in a Christian setting. Are you interested in joining us? Red will be there."

While he was describing the concept, my eyes widened with enthusiasm. The concept sounded like a glorious dream. However, my bubble burst when I remembered the totalitarian grip of the materfamilias, causing me to convey, "I would *love* to, but my parents would *never* do that for me. It costs money, doesn't it?"

After thoughtfully crossing his massive arms to rest his thick fingers on his chin, Coach Burley softly mentioned, "If your parents will sign the waiver, I will grant you a *scholarship*. It would be completely free for you. How does that sound?" [2]

Peering upward at Coach Burley's gentle smile, I fought back tears. Gathering myself, I answered, "Wow. That's amazing. I will ask… but if they say no, I just want to thank you for the opportunity, sir."

While riding the school bus back to solitary confinement, I prayed, "Jesus, thank you for sending me Red. Because of him and Coach Burley, I might join a weight-lifting program that revolves around You. My parents won't have to pay for it, but I still need permission to attend. Would You please melt my mother's heart and get me into that program? It will take a miracle and I can't do it without You. Thank You for helping me. Amen." [3]

Once her favorite shows were over and she had eaten, I approached the materfamilias and campaigned, "I was invited to attend a local athletic camp. It's completely *free* and I'll be there *all day*. Can I go?" [4]

Side-eyeing, the woman bloodlessly murmured, *"Fine."* [5]

"I would ride my bike there, but that would leave me exhausted before the program even started," I added. "So, can I have a ride to school and back each day?"

The boiling termagant threw her arms in the air and raged, *"Okay, Sandra! What else do you want from me?!"* [6]

Encourage

Athletes received a t-shirt and coordinating pair of shorts from the school, which were then collected at the end of the year. Since summer break had already started, I needed to use my limited apparel and was too afraid to request anything further from the materfamilias.

Eager for the first day of camp, I rummaged through my dresser drawers and located articles of clothing from my elementary days that still fit my seemingly anorexic frame. I slipped on a bright pink tank top, faded black and purple bicycling shorts, and a pair of pink socks.

Peering into the mirror at my wet-willie to fashion, I gave myself a forbearing shrug and murmured, "**** *it. It is what it is.*" [1]

Being among the first dropped off near the weight room, I sat on the ground and observed others as they arrived. A few male upper-classmen parked their vehicles and sat beside one another a few yards away. Red walked up, greeted Coach Burley, and stretched in the nearby grass. Carpooling vans came and went, unloading more boys until the start time had arrived.

Realizing I was the only female present, I stepped up to Coach Burley and inquired, "Are any other girls coming? I'm a little confused. Am I in the right spot? Is there a separate girl's program that's meeting somewhere else?"

The colossal man replied, "This is it. You're exactly where you should be."

With that, I returned to my previous spot and silently prayed, "Jesus, *I'm afraid. Please don't let my mother find out that I'm the only girl here. She'll just accuse me of sleeping with everyone and won't let me come back. I need Your help to keep up and not be a burden. Help me do well and not embarrass myself. Amen.*"

Moments later, two dashing men in baseball caps walked towards us. Coach Burley introduced Brock and Stanley as our instructors. I wrestled to keep my jaw up and eyebrows down, wondering why those hunks were leading a bunch of kids and not starring in blockbuster films as action heroes.

"Alright, everyone. Huddle up and take a knee," Brock ordered, receiving immediate compliance. "Very good. Thanks. We have a tradition in this program that we do each morning before we begin. Who would like to be the first to volunteer and lead all of us in prayer?"

The three men patiently scanned the faces of the motionless teens. Off to the far side of the group, I slowly raised my hand. Brock smirked and acknowledged the gesture with a nod, signaling for me to begin. [2]

Blankly staring at the ground, I focused my thoughts on the One who knew my name and began praying aloud, "Jesus, thank You for the opportunity for me to even be here. *I know that was You.* Please help each of us to get stronger, faster, and better at sports. Help us grow in every way and not become discouraged when we fail. Help us get along and support each other, and please protect us from getting hurt or injured. Thank You for our coach and trainers. Please bless them and help them teach us what we need to learn as they guide us closer to You. In Jesus' name, I pray. Amen."

Silence followed.

Expecting my body to swiftly occupy another trashcan, I lifted my head to gauge my immediate surroundings. Brock, Stanley, and the massive human swiped moisture from their faces as the boys fixed their eyes in my direction. [3]

Coach Burley took a quivering deep breath to express, "Sandra, that was a *beautiful* prayer."

Brock handed each student a personalized workbook that provided an organized way to keep track of our progress. Stanley set up a scale to begin weigh-ins and mentioned to me, "Sixty pounds, Sandra. Write that on the first page." Meanwhile, Brock determined everyone's maximum lift in bench-press, squat and dead-lift, monitoring us closely.

While I patiently waited for a bench to open up, older boys clinked plates onto bars and began pressing. Spotting another athlete near the far wall racking his weights, I attempted to intercept the recently unoccupied bench. At once, Stanley located a curling-bar to replace the former. Spotting Red, I snuck a knowing smile, remembering our first day of training. Before I could thank the man for preparing my station, Wire nervously straddled the bench to lie down, being a boy of similar build to my own. Athletes standing nearby quietly witnessed his spindly arms press upward and awkwardly tremble under the weight. [4]

"Hold it," Brock interjected with authority. "Rack it. Your hands are too far apart. Adjust your grip… and bring your elbows in."

"Okay," Wire nervously murmured, pressing the bar.

"Very good. Now, keep your feet planted on the ground and don't arch your back when you press. Lay flat," Brock added, watching Wire's face grow troubled and crimson as tears swelled. "Stop. Rack the bar."

Encourage

The youth held back a sob to choked out, *"Okay."*

"Sit up for me," Brock urged as he maintained eye-contact with the boy. "When you're corrected, it's not to insult you. It's for your *protection*. If you practice incorrectly, you'll lift incorrectly and create bad habits… or worse. With enough weight, bad form could cause serious injuries to yourself and those around you, so practice *correctly*. A proper lift is when power merges with alignment and control. *Think before you lift.* Remember how proper form feels, and then replicate that each time… or you'll get corrected. Now, lay back down and try again." Wire obeyed his trainer and pressed the weight. "Good. Remember where your hands are located and how that felt. Your elbows were in, your back was straight, and your feet were planted. *Excellent. Again.*" [5]

Stanley prodded a passively observing upperclassman, whispering, *"Encourage him."* [6]

"C'mon, man! You've got this!" the teen cheered.

Before Wire completed his set, others joined in and roared in applause. Several athletes offered smiles, high-fives and fist bumps, grabbing Wire's shoulders as he cheerfully sat up from the bench. [7]

That following Sunday, Paul's *other* aunt, Ms. Bondad, approached me in the UPC hallway after the worship service, chirping, "Sandra! My son is in the same program as you! He doesn't speak English very well yet, but he understands it. He just moved here from Mexico and is still too nervous to pray in front of other people. After the first day, he ran into the house so excited! He told me all about your prayer and said that it made him cry! He thought it was *really* brave. I also heard that the boys started volunteering to lead morning prayer after that!" The bright-eyed woman embraced me and peered down at my smiling face. "Do you see what happened? People are watching how much you love *Jesus* and they want what you have! You're a good influence on them. I'm so proud of you. Keep going!" [8]

Female

$\mathcal{A}$s Red accomplished days prior, Brock and Stan earned my confidence in their instruction. Each nugget of guidance concerning hand positioning, foot placement, and proper form echoed in my mind. Pursuing explosive strength and the ability to control my body with precision, I willed my developing limbs to the point of exhaustion in every lifting circuit and outdoor training exercise. Weighing in once more, I giddily noted ninety-five pounds. [1]

The athletes tossed around a football to cap off each day of training. During the last week of the program, an upperclassman passed the ball in my direction, playfully welcoming me to the game. Having snatched it, my hands gleefully remembered all that my father had shown me, rolling the ball into a powerful spiral pass to the teen's chest.

"Uh-oh! I think Sandra wants to play! C'mon, girl! Let's see what you've got! Go long!" he urged.

Adrenaline pulsed through my body as I sprinted down the field, propelling myself faster than I had ever realized was possible. I glanced over my shoulder, gauging the football's trajectory as it peaked and adjusting my stride accordingly. I grasped the prize and secured it in my arms before slowing to a stop and launching it back down the field.

As the final day of training came to a close and everyone had their maximum lifts notated, Brock announced, "While you walk with Jesus and live out your life, it's important to understand that the only person you should ever compare yourself to is who you used to be. Our mission was to inspire personal growth in each of you. In this program, we don't honor the strongest, but the most improved. Stanley and I agree that *two* athletes were outstanding in this area and both deserve our recognition. Wire and Sandra, please stand and receive your awards for Most Improved Male and Female!" [2]

While Brock and Stanley were packing up to leave for the last time, I approached them to express, "Thank you for everything you've taught us. After training with you guys, I feel like a completely different person now… like I can do *anything*." [3]

Minutes later, Coach Burley approached our after-program football game and called out, "Sandra! Come here for a sec!" Complying, he escorted me to another man. "This is the head coach of our high school football team. I originally intended to make this introduction and *linger*, but something has come up and I'm needed elsewhere. I'll just leave you two to talk." [4]

"Well, Sandra, it's nice to finally meet you. I bet you're wondering why I'm here," the man correctly speculated. "Amazed at your metamorphosis, Coach Burley brought your developing athleticism to my attention. To be honest, *I didn't believe it*, but curiosity got the best of me and I came here to see this for myself. After a bit of scouting, I am pleasantly surprised to discover that he was right. You *do* show promise. Would you be interested in joining the freshman football team this coming season?"

Internally pogo-jumping with girlish enthusiasm, I stoically replied, "Yes, sir. I *am* interested. My father taught me how to throw and catch a football when I was very young. However, it's important for you to know upfront that I don't know all the technical rules. I'd be *really* behind."

"I'm willing to train you and teach you the rest of the game. *You can do this*. You're fast enough to avoid tackles, and more importantly, you can *catch*. I have confidence in your ability and want to turn you into a *wide receiver*. If nothing else, just you suiting-up may give our boys a healthy *competitive spirit* that will light a fire under their ***** to train harder. No one wants to be replaced by a *girl* and you're already better than a few. How does that sound, Lawson? Do you want to play some football?" [5]

Suddenly dispirited, I replied, "I would love to, and thank you for the opportunity to play, but I'll have to ask my parents. My dad *should* say yes, since he was the one that introduced me to football, but it's my mom that I'm worried about."

"I understand. Let me know as soon as you can and we'll go from there," he concluded.

A moment after the head coach pulled away in his vehicle, my father's pickup truck rolled into view. I readily loaded into the cab and buckled my seatbelt, excitedly summarizing, "Dad, this program was amazing! It really worked! I mean, just look at me! I'm so much stronger and faster! Other people noticed, too! Check this out! We've been playing football while waiting to get picked up and the coaches were watching us. They talked about *me* and want to train me as their newest wide receiver for the freshman team! Can you believe it?! It would never have happened if you hadn't of shown me how to play. So, thank you for that. Anyway, I know we'll have to convince Mom to let me join, but I wanted you to hear the good news before she spoils everything. I'm pretty sure I already know your answer, but I'll ask anyway. Can I play football?"

"Nope," the man leisurely answered without hesitation. "There's no *ladies' section* in football locker rooms, Sandra. What's the coach planning for you to do? You'd have to change somewhere else entirely. Are you going to suit up in the girl's restroom, walk all the way back in your pads and stand in the locker room to hear the pep-talks and plays while the boys are *still changing*? What about the long bus rides to and from the away games? I've seen what football players are like after a win. You'd be the only girl with a bunch of testosterone-driven teenage boys." He paused and shook his head. "You'd be the smallest person on the field and the *only* girl. I know you think you're tough, but once you get hit by someone that outweighs you by fifty-plus pounds, you'll want to quit. Those guys will single you out and come at you with *full force,* just to show you that you don't belong." [6]

Although he brought to light incredibly valid points, I stuffed down all emotion and rebutted, "Dad, I'm fast… *really* fast. They won't catch me. I won't get hit."

"Ha! *Everyone* gets hit," he corrected. "Injuries happen all the time and some can become debilitating. *You can't play football.* Don't ask me about it again. Just stick with volleyball. You're good at it." [7]

SECTION 7

Good Eye

I had a rare encounter with Aunt-T while no one else was around and quickly mentioned, "Mom's been acting weirder than usual. She opened my bedroom door without knocking while I was changing my clothes and commented on how I was growing a butt. It was uncomfortable. She sounded like she was upset about it, even though it was a compliment. Now, Mom suspiciously follows me with her eyes while I'm working outside with Dad as if we're going to do something dirty. She's already accused me and Dad of doing some messed up things just because I relaxed with him on his recliner. He won't even let me sit with him anymore. I've done *nothing* like what she's suggesting with anyone, especially with him. That's disgusting. Why does she think that? I don't understand her at all." [1]

Exasperated with the subject, Aunt-T rolled her eyes and explained, "When you were just a baby, your mother had accused your father of molesting you, even after a pediatrician had examined you and found no evidence of molestation. He *did* say that you had a very bad diaper rash. Your mother told me that she didn't believe anything the navy doctor said because they all lied to protect each other. Sandra, I know my sister very well. She's a sick person with a sick mind that's always thinking about *sex*. Your mother has always been *crazy* and belongs in the loony bin, so don't listen to the ugly things she tells you. The *truth* is what matters." [2]

"Wait a second. If she believed I was being molested, why did she stay with Dad? What kind of mother would do that?" I wondered aloud.

"That's my point," Aunt-T continued. "Even *she* doesn't believe what she's says. She's crazy."

The intense weight training that summer bulked up my legs to where the pants and shorts from my elementary days became impossible to slip over my growing thighs. To avoid the stinging thought of financially burdening my father or stirring up the wrath of the materfamilias, I remained silent about my wardrobe needs and resorted to wearing my brother's outgrown pants.

Grimacing at my appearance from the sofa, the materfamilias cruelly commented, "You look horrible. Stop dressing like a boy. What are you, a lesbian?" [3]

"Wow. Nope. I'm not a lesbian. I just can't fit into my clothes anymore," I calmly explained. "Everything is way too tight and busting at the seams. This is all I have that covers my body."

"I guess I need to take you shopping for school clothes," the woman conceded with a sigh. [4]

"It doesn't have to be an expensive experience," I added. "You could decide on a specific amount of money that you're willing to spend and I could select the clothing that I like while staying within the budget. I'll even model them for you before they're purchased. That way, none of the money will be wasted and I'll always be wearing clothes that you pre-approved. How does *that* sound?"

The face of the materfamilias unexpectedly softened as she nodded and replied, "Okay." [5]

I walked back into my room and whispered, "Jesus, thank You for convincing my mom to buy me new clothing. I know that was Your doing. Since You can do anything, I could use Your help with prices and selections. Would You please make the money stretch so that I can have several outfits for school that fit and are flattering? I'm glad I know You hear me. I love You. Amen." [6]

The materfamilias led me inside a familiar mall and navigated our course. As she did, I scanned my surroundings for advertised discounts as opposed to certain brands or trends. Drawn to a particular store, I examined the price tags and grinned. The items were not only new, but eccentric and less expensive than that of most thrift and consignment locations.

"I've never seen *this* store before," the materfamilias commented.

Biting my tongue, I maintained composure and silently thought, "That's because we've only been here to buy things for *you*." [7]

After handing me some cash, the woman sternly warned, "This is all you're getting. Don't ask for more."

Ignoring her misplaced tone, I agreed with the regurgitated suggestion I had fed her and chirped, "You got it, lady. Thank you." [8]

Cleaving to my economical standards, I snagged one clearance item after another while the termagant remarked, "That top is ugly. You *like* that?"

Unwilling to sabotage myself by verbally deflating to her ego, I remained quiet and pondered, "Her opinions don't matter. She would keep dressing me like a first grader if I let her. Who cares what she thinks? If the clothes are appealing, made of quality fabric and don't feature animated princesses, I'm trying them on."

Donning every snubbed outfit and disdained shoe selection, I stepped into better lighting for the cruel skeptic to cast her judgement. With a mild slip of astonishment, the materfamilias admitted, "They were ugly on the hanger, but look very nice on you. I like everything you tried on. You have a good eye for fashion. Which outfits are you going to pick?"

"All of them," I confidently informed, having kept a running total in my mind.

No longer concerned about standing out, even to the envious materfamilias, I carried two bulging sacks of eclectic styles and vibrant colors back to the vehicle with pennies to spare. [9]

Fish

On the last day of the eighth-grade, Mr. Bach played a VHS of the marching performance that won the state championship in our division. His intricately choreographed routine was a living work of art. Abstract designs cascaded over a gridiron canvas and morphed into various images while emanating skillfully played music. With unwavering focus, self-awareness, and intense practice, each individual executed their assigned path and movements with precision to the drum major's tempo and brought home the highly coveted trophy that year.

About three months had passed since then. Although summer break drew to a close and the temperatures continued to climb, Mr. Bach had a tradition and pre-arranged our high school band camp to operate inside a local state park in the open air.

"During each competition, judges will grade us based on appearance, balance and clarity of sound, overall performance, marching execution, and the level of difficulty," the beloved man instructed. "If anyone marches out of step or isn't performing well, the judges *will* notice and hit us with penalties. Thankfully, that will be some time from now, so don't panic." He made me smirk. I had panicked. "Memorize your music and remember your assigned number. Wherever that number is in the packet, that's your spot on the field. Now, I'm not expecting miracles this week. Many of you are doing this for the first time and will learn as you go, so just do your best. For now, I'll hand you over to your section leaders. See you in a bit."

Segregated by instrument, section leaders handed out sheets of music and the marching routine packets to those directly under their authority, eventually leading us to a dusty field marked with chalk lines. [1]

"What the **** are you doing?! Don't walk to the practice field! Move your ***, fish!" a senior abruptly ordered, causing me to cringe. Once our section lined up, she abrasively shouted, "*March heel-toe! Roll your foot forward! Get it right! Your movements need to be sharp! When you flank or kick, make it snappy! Point that toe! That looked like ****! Do it again, fish! What the **** is this ****?! A straight line isn't that complicated, fish! You should only see whoever is next to you! If you see the rest of the line, you're not in it!*

Always start with your left foot when you kick! I said left! Do you know your left from your right, fish?! Am I your mommy now?!" [2]

Triggered into rage, I bit my tongue and robotically concealed my emotions. To avoid a fight, I simply avoided that teenage girl at all costs. The only way of escaping her wrath was to improve immediately and meet her every expectation… or quit.

Just after our lunch break, an observant sophomore in our section noticed my packed instrument and troubled face. She sat beside me and inquired, "What's up?"

Holding back a sob, I vehemently confessed, "I can't stand that ******* girl yelling at us and calling us names! I deal with that **** all day at home! Why stay and fry in the sun?! I might not be able to escape my mother, but I *can* escape this." [3]

The student gently placed her hand on my shoulder and explained, "The Band Hall walls are lined with many years' worth of hard-earned trophies. You've seen them. Mr. Bach has been *repeatedly* leading this band to state competitions and into the finals, actually *winning* state before. The seniors are nervous because this is their last chance to win state and they refuse to allow the tradition of excellence to die under their leadership. I agree that some could be more patient, but a legacy is at stake and this band is all our town really has to be proud of. They yell because… *they're passionate*. None of it is personal. Please, don't quit."

"You keep saying things in plural, like some and they, but there's only *one*. That ***** is a dictator on a power trip just like my mother," I rebutted, tearing up in frustration. "We don't know what we're doing because we're just blindly following her orders instead of having things calmly explained to us. She just yells and gets in our faces! I can't take this **** anymore, especially in this heat! My mother is the same way! Nothing is ever good enough! There's no amount of effort that will satisfy them! It's only the first day and I'm just trying not to punch that chick in the face! And what's up with calling us fish?! What is that?!"

"If you need help, just come to me, and don't worry about being called a fish. Fish is just a dumb nickname for freshmen," the sophomore clarified. "I don't know your mom, but if she's that bad, wouldn't you be better off staying here with us? You won't always feel as lost or confused as you do today. Band camp will end soon and so will the yelling, but early morning practices, late football games, and all-day competitions are throughout the year… and they're fun," she sweetly reasoned. "What's more tolerable, sticking out band camp or being at home with your mom?" [4]

I sighed and reassembled my instrument. [5]

Cool It

Immediately following band camp were the high school volleyball two-a-days. In a non-air-conditioned metal-roof gymnasium, the heat intensified as freshman, junior varsity, and varsity teams all practiced simultaneously. Even in a cramped setting, it seemed advantageous to observe the upperclassmen and learn their techniques.

During varsity drills, viciously spiked volleyballs slammed down on the opponent's side, causing me to smirk. Closely observing their various approach patterns, I endeavored to replicate their success.

While the freshman and JV teams peppered off to the side of the court, the varsity setter slipped up before the approaching Fera and caused her to rage, "What the hell was that?! Are you blind?! That wasn't anywhere near me! Do it again and get it right!" [1]

"Shut up!" the setter quickly snapped. "Learn to adjust, brat! Go to the end of the line!"

Fera stepped toward the girl and leaned in, rebutting, "Don't tell me what to do! You have one job, so *do it* and quit wasting my time!"

"Get out of my face, Fera!" the setter warned.

Distracted by the verbal altercation, I whispered, *"I'm glad I don't have to train with them."*

Presumptuously readying herself for a second attempt to spike, Fera noticed the stunned freshman team and viciously shouted, *"What are you looking at?! Don't just stand there like idiots! Shag the balls, fish!"*

After enduring band camp, the command didn't seem so horrible. Without a word, I respectfully stepped forward and collected stray balls from the court.

"No, Sandra! Stop! Don't listen to her!" a freshman loudly ordered. "Let them shag their own balls!"

I turned and calmly replied, "We're starting at the bottom and need to earn our stripes. Besides, the balls need to be shagged. They're in the way. Someone could get hurt." [2]

"If you want to be their ***** for the rest of the year, be my guest, but *I'm* not doing it," the freshman added as she returned to the peppering drill. [3]

With arms fully loaded, I dropped the collected volleyballs into the portable cart and exchanged a few smiles with some upperclassmen who graciously voiced, "Thank you, Sandra."

"Don't thank them!" Fera ordered. "That's their *job*." [4]

Bearing a disapproving brow, another senior openly rebuked, "Hey! You're not being very nice, Fera. She doesn't have to listen to you. So, cool it." [5]

Nicki

~~~

*R*egular classes were about to start in a few hours, so I slipped on pink pleather pants and a bright floral blouse to wear with my new platform wedges. After strutting down our gravel driveway, I waited beside my sibling for the school bus.

As it always had, the yellow transport eventually pulled up near the Band Hall where I needed to be that morning. After smoothly stepping down to exit, I made my way across the undersized parking lot and maneuvered past a circle of freshmen who seemed shocked and confused at my approach, as though I were a total stranger. Deliberating on whether to greet the girls, recalling how most of them tormented me throughout middle school, I forgave to grant the classmates *and myself* a fresh start. [1]

Without slowing my casual pace, I offered a friendly smile to the small congregation and chirped, "Hey, guys!" [2]

"Hey…" they sheepishly acknowledged, following me with their eyes as I continued past them.

Before I had escaped earshot of them, I heard the familiar voice of Sadie remarking to her friends, "Holy ****! Was that Sandra?!" [3]

The Band Hall door loudly closed behind me, alerting others that someone else had arrived early for practice. A few of the volleyball upperclassman were also in the marching band and paused their conversation with some male musicians.

Nicki sweetly called out, "Hey, Sandra! Come over here and meet the crew!" Pleasantly surprised at the warm invitation, I grinned and speedily made my way to them.

"Hey, guys!" I replied, scanning everyone's faces to remember them as they were being introduced.

"Let me tell you about my girl, *Sandra*, since you boys haven't met her yet…" Nicki cheerfully began, putting her arm around me. "A couple of weeks ago, this chick showed up to volleyball two-a-days with the other freshmen. Eventually, Fera started throwing one of her famous tantrums to begin another time-wasting varsity fight. JV is used to her ****, so we ignored it all and kept practicing, but the freshmen didn't know any better. Fera noticed them staring at her and went on a power trip, ordering the fish to shag the spiked balls. *This girl*, without sass, immediately picks up all the volleyballs.

Fera tried to keep running her mouth, but no one wanted to put up with her being mean to *Sandra*. When I saw the other freshmen turn up their noses while *this girl* was doing all the work, I knew she was different." Nicki looked at me and continued, "Sandra, I'm impressed with you. High school can be tough, but I want you to know that everyone you're looking at here will help you whenever we can. Just so you know, you already have friends in volleyball that will look after you. The entire JV team and some of the varsity players discussed what we saw that first day. You're winning people over pretty quickly! Good job!" [4]

Unable to hide my overwhelming joy, I tearfully murmured, *"Thank you."* Moved by my response, as I presumed a loving mother would, Nicki pulled my body around to hug me while the others patted and rubbed my shoulders, accompanied with endeared chuckles.

After the closing bell rang, the band students burst through the doors and scattered. I asked an adult for directions to find the only unfamiliar hallway I had left to explore on campus and single-mindedly navigated up a few steps to the social studies classroom. A few athletes from the summer training program were standing by their lockers and waved to capture my attention. Upon glancing up at them, I waved back with a smile and kept my pace. They all grinned, including Red. [5]

Varsity

During our first freshmen game, we focused on our training, remembered to *call the ball*, and aggressively committed to our designated positions. Despite the jitters and restlessness prior to the game, we strengthened one another after errors, cheered with each successful play, and sealed the match with victory. [1]

Up next was the JV team, who practiced a steady rhythm and clockwork manner of playing. By slowing down and minimizing their mistakes, the opposing team grew impatient for some excitement and crumbled under the self-induced pressure to impress the crowd. They missed several serves and fumbled their spikes. As a result, JV chased our win with one of their own.

I expected varsity to be the grand finale in exhibiting to the freshmen what *real* volleyball was about. Exiting from the girls' locker room in a uniformed line were several players who trotted around the court with constipated, moody faces. In response, a few JV team members rolled their eyes at one another from the stands, leading me to believe that a varsity locker room fight had occurred behind closed doors moments prior.

A tweeting whistle started the game. The opposing team served and launched the spinning orb over the net, being cleanly dug up by the back row to the readied setter. The volleyball popped upward toward Fera, who thunderously spiked it down onto an opposing player's feet, winning the first point. A barbaric chant erupted, urging me to smile and clap.

Our player forced a zipping serve just over the net and rapidly transitioned to defend her portion of the court. The opposition rallied, eventually feather-touching the ball in a quick-set to align with their teammate's dominating approach pattern. Creating that visceral sound of eminent doom, the skillful attacker struck the unsuspecting globe and crushed it downward.

In a flash, a member of our varsity team dove flat-handed to save the ball, skillfully providing a stable trajectory for the setter to step underneath. As onlookers gasped, the setter returned the ball directly back toward the floored warrior as she was regaining her footing. Surprised and unable to approach, the player feebly slapped the ball directly into the opposing team's readied forces. Deflected by a human wall, the ball barreled back toward the ground. Although the setter was the closest, she failed to drop fast enough to save the volley.

Varsity's lofty superiority shattered on the polyurethane finish as the setter raged toward her back-row teammate, *"Where the hell were you?! That was right in front of you! You're making us look stupid!"* [2]

Wide-eyed, the targeted player spitefully rebutted, *"Are you ******* kidding me?! What were you thinking?! I was still getting up from the ground, idiot! That's what front row hitters are for!"* [3]

The setter flippantly shrugged, meeting the detail with a chilled insolence as she added, "Well, maybe you just need to *keep up.*" [4]

The rest of the match was a downward spiral of vicious critiques and deflected accountability, resulting in the only loss of the evening and a stifling bus ride home. Fear seemed to settle upon those in proximity as the varsity players stewed over their embarrassing civil war. Suppressing our voices and personal excitement, many JV and freshmen teammates chose the safety of silence. [5]

Ruby

Coach Gather abrasively called out, *"Sandra! Get over here!"*

Unsure of what I did to be in trouble, I abandoned the metal-box pouncing exercises and trotted to the coach, politely answering, "Yes, ma'am?"

"I want to talk to you," the woman proceeded casually. "I paid close attention to your performance the other night and noticed something special about you. You kept your head during your first game and it was impressive. *Well done.* Even though you're a freshman, you don't seem to be very bothered or intimidated by much, so I think you can handle the pressure of being on the *varsity* team. What do you say? Are you up for the challenge?"

Shocked by her invitation, I took a deep breath and paused. Although I wanted to advance and bask in the esteem of being the youngest varsity player, I could foresee the hefty price. [1]

Lowering my eyebrows back to a rested state, I respectfully replied, "Well, I'm always up for a challenge, but I don't *willingly* sign up for punishment. Some of the varsity seniors are *hateful* and remain unchecked. If I had a choice, I'd much rather play on the JV team than ride-the-pine with varsity. Volleyball is supposed to be *fun* and no self-respecting athlete would choose a team that argued more than they trained. I appreciate the offer, but I'll just wait another year for these *she-wolves* to graduate." [2]

Muffling her chuckle, Coach Gather cleared her throat and continued, "Well, I'm disappointed… but after hearing your reasoning, I feel that you've made a wise choice. I have another idea. *If you're willing*, I'd like to bump you up to JV and make you their new lead setter. Is *that* something you might be interested in?"

"Uh… *yes*," I emphatically replied, offering the woman a firm handshake. "I'd love that. I accept."

Coach Gather clasped her hands together, happily announcing, "Very good! This is effective *immediately*, so go on and start practicing with your new team."

JV paused their drill at my rapid approach as one asked excitedly, "Are you with *us* now?!"

"Yes," I replied, stifling my enthusiasm with another deep breath. "I'm your new lead setter."

Nicki cheered and pogo-jumped, gushing, "Yes! This is awesome! Oh, my gosh! Okay. Sweet. Let me introduce you to the team…" [3]

A foul-tempered player recoiled as we were being acquainted, leaving the group entirely. I leaned toward a fellow teammate and discreetly inquired, *"So, is she upset about me joining the team… or is she just antisocial?"*

"Oh, Ruby? *Yeah.* She's angry," the sophomore clarified. "You just took over her position, so she won't play as much now… but don't worry about her, Sandra. Just keep up your game."

After Coach Gather released us from practice, each team entered the girls' locker room to change clothes and disperse.

"Hey, fish!" an aggressive voice blurted from somewhere behind me, muting the hum of girlish chatter. Sensing a developing brawl between players, I kept my back to the tantrum and changed out of my sweaty clothing. [4]

As I pulled up my jeans with a wiggle, a freshman classmate caught my attention, pointed directly behind me, and whispered, *"Be careful, Sandra. She's a mean one."* [5]

Curious why *I* was the one being warned, I followed the freshman's concerned gaze to Ruby's seething face, having awkwardly maintained her tactic of intimidation throughout my oblivious delay of response. Unwilling to engage, I packed my duffle bag with my back to her and greeted, "Hello, Ruby. Is there something I can help you with?" [6]

"Listen here, *fish*. I worked really hard to get that spot… and then some freshman comes in after just one game and takes it from me. *I don't think so.* Step down, fish, or I will *make* you step down."

No longer willing to tolerate the scenario, I remained silent, flipped the zipped duffle bag over my shoulder, and turned to slip between her and some lockers to the exit.

The presumptuous sophomore snatched my arm and violently spun my body around to face her, leaning in to growl, "Are you ignoring me, *fish*?" [7]

I closed the gap with a stare and firmly rebuked, "It's *your* turn to listen. If you want that position, then you'd better out-work me, out-train me and develop a better attitude, because I'm not giving you *a damn thing*. You want a war? Let's battle on the court, but allow me to make myself perfectly clear. Don't you *ever* touch me again. Let… me… go." [8]

Overwhelmed, Ruby released my arm and fled. [9]

The following morning, a freshman excitedly approached me in the hall and informed, "Sandra, I heard all about what happened in the locker room yesterday. Do you realize how big of a deal this is?! Ruby gets into fights all the time! You stood up to one of the *meanest* bullies in school! Girl, she *cried in the hall* after she ran away from you… and what you said to her… *wow.* That was really cool. Everyone heard about it."

Moments later, Red caught up to me and privately divulged, "I'm really sorry about my sister giving you problems yesterday."

"Awe. It's okay. Bullies don't scare me anymore…" I began, suddenly hesitating. "Wait. *What?!* Ruby's your sister?!"

"Oh… uh…" Red stuttered, embarrassed. "I thought you knew that."

"No!" I exclaimed. "I had no idea! I'm so sorry that I upset your sister! If I knew…"

"Whoa. Let me stop you right there, Sandra," Red interjected. "I heard all about what she *and* you said to each other. You were right, and she was wrong. *Plain and simple.* You don't have to apologize to me about anything." [10]

Within days, Ruby transferred to another school. [11]

Not Stupid

The math instructor, Mrs. Cerulean, finished another Algebra II lesson and gave us our assignment, stating, "Let me know if you have questions."

I completed my work, turned it in, and peered around the room. A junior furrowed his brow and stared at his paper in desperate frustration. Moved with compassion, I discreetly walked over and inquired, "What's up? You look confused."

Emotions continued to surface as the junior confessed, "I hate being *stupid*. It's my third time taking this class and I'm *still* failing. I hate math. I don't understand it *at all*." Ashamed, he buried his face in his hands. [1]

I sat down beside the upperclassman and gently prodded, "Look at me." Calming himself, he obeyed and peered upward through his pain. "You're not *stupid*. You're struggling. There's a huge difference. Just so you know, struggling is a good sign. That tells me you haven't given up yet and you still want to learn. Is that true?" He nodded, wiping his eyes with the collar of his shirt. "Groovy. Let me get my stuff." [2]

"*Okay,*" he murmured.

Sitting beside him with my notebook paper, I explained the method while labeling each step for his notes. "Stick that in your binder. That's yours. Now, I want *you* to work on the next problem using those exact steps." Without abandoning my classmate, I observed his problem solving. "Very good! Now, do the next one. If you keep this pace, you'll be done with your homework before we switch classes!" He smiled and continued working. "*Uh oh…* I think someone gets it. What do *you* think?" [3]

Nodding with a gentle smile, he softly admitted, *"I get it. Seriously, thank you."* A sophomore moaned angrily from a nearby table and threw down her pencil. The junior to turned toward his frustrated classmate and suggested, "If you need help, ask Sandra." [4]

After that class period, several students requested my help each time the lesson ended.

During another class period, Mrs. Cerulean approached me and sweetly offered, "Why don't you let me run to the office to make extra copies of your notes? That might save you some time and work."

Relieved that I wasn't being reprimanded, I sheepishly smiled and replied, "Oh, wow. That's a *great* idea. Thank you."

Since I was the last to leave her classroom, our instructor stood beside me and conveyed, "Sandra, other teachers might get jealous while watching someone succeed where they have failed, but *I don't*. I'm excited. I don't care how my students learn or who teaches them, as long as they move forward with *confidence*. You have my full support. They're *passing tests* in a subject that has plagued them for years. *They're learning.* It's all a teacher could hope for." Overwhelmed, I gave her a tearful hug. [5]

"For the record," I began, pulling away, "your lessons are amazing. I understand everything the first time you show us. *You're my favorite teacher*, so I want you to cut yourself some slack. There's only *one* of you and you're dealing with several students that need extra help. You know what? I discovered something about myself in your class. I actually *enjoy* teaching." [6]

"I see that… and I want to *reward* you for it. Since you're spending your class time helping others, you are hereby *exempt* from homework! This is the closest I can get to paying you. How does our little arrangement sound?" [7]

Taking her hand to shake it, I cheerfully confirmed, "It's a deal."

Mammon

*J*ust before a geometry quiz, Mrs. Cerulean walked out of the classroom for a moment.

Seconds later, Julio abandoned his seat, laid his forearms on my desk, and slid close beside me, slyly whispering, "*Sandra, I will pay you ten dollars for the answers to this test.*" [1]

Traditionally, when other students had attempted to cheat, I covered my paper or blocked their view with my shoulder. However, Julio's winsome countenance, sharp attire, and developing muscles had never been that close to my face.

I silently reasoned, "If I help him, maybe he'll appreciate my intelligence and *like* me. Besides, how else am I supposed to save up to visit Nancy? Flights to California can't be cheap." [2]

Smelling like the fragrance fold of a magazine advertisement, Julio put his warm hand over my icy, pencil-wielding fist, and begged, "Sandra, I *need* you. Please. *Please.*" [3]

In the calloused manner of most cinematic drug dealers, I pushed up my glasses and quietly demanded, "*Give me the money upfront. Fold it up and hand it to me inside of your graphing calculator.*" After patting my desk, the teen obeyed with a smirk. [4]

Covertly using my thumb to slide its cover open, I slipped the payment into my pocket and inserted my test answers. After sliding the cover shut, I placed the object beside me on the desk and turned in my quiz. Eerily flawless in his execution, Julio strolled to Mrs. Cerulean's desk and charmingly asked for help with a problem, only to retrieve the calculator discretely during the return trip to his seat.

After that lucrative incident, I sedated my integrity and prostituted my intellect to desperate students. Even Red heard rumors of my *change of heart*. In biology, he kneeled beside me and asked, "Sandra, I *really* need you on today's quiz. Same price as last time?"

"Sure. Just slip the money under my folder," I replied. [5]

Just before geometry, another student pleaded in the hall, "Sandra, I don't have the money *on me*, but will you still help me on this quiz today, *please*? I'll pay you back."

"*No,*" I sharply replied, leaving the teen stupefied. "I'm not chasing people around for payment. Would you like to know what will help you? It's completely *free…*"

Their eyes lit up, wondering, "What?"

"*Studying,*" I whispered.

Moments later, Julio produced the fee for himself and our classmate. [6]

"Okay, Sandra," a teen expressed in the hall. "I need you to write my report for me, but it needs to be a *C-paper*. If it's *too good*, I'm worried that the teacher will figure out that I didn't write it."

"This is a tall order. I write *A-papers*. Do you know how hard it is for me to write a *C-paper?* I'll have to write the first draft *my way* and then edit it down. That will cost extra," I warned.

"That's alright," they eagerly replied. "I have the money right here."

"Don't get lazy and just turn in whatever I hand you," I added. "Rewrite the report in your own handwriting."

In Biology, the teacher narrowed his eyes at my peers and announced, "I didn't just fall off the turnip truck. I have long suspected that this class is somehow cheating off of Sandra's work. Some of you have very high grades, but can't answer *any* questions during class when she *can*, but I'm gonna fix your wagons. During today's multiple-choice exam, I'm having Sandra sit alone, all the way over here at the very front of the classroom. Let's see if y'all can pass *this* time without being able to peek at her paper." The man smiled to himself and took a restroom break just before the quiz began. [7]

Red whispered, "*Sandra, we're lost and need help on this test.*"

"*What's it worth to you?*" I softly queried, watching students shrug at one another.

Red quickly placed a twenty-dollar bill in my hand, openly wondering, "Is that enough?"

Tucking the currency into my pocket, I quietly continued, "*When I stretch out my arms, get ready for the hand signals. One is A. Two is B. Three is C. Four is D. I'll stretch again and then repeat them so you can double check your answers. Change random letters for believable grades and stagger your timing when you turn in your tests.*" [8]

By the end of class, our biology instructor was stunned to see nothing but passing scores as he audibly grumbled, "I just don't understand it. How is this possible?" [9]

Sadie

~~~

The alarm beside my bed sounded, waking me from a vivid dream that left me with a sense of urgency for a classmate I had barely spoken to. Although I didn't understand what I had observed, I felt the details were a warning from the Messiah and specifically for Sadie. [1]

While brushing my teeth that morning, I silently fretted, "What if I'm laughed at for saying that it is a message from Jesus? What if I look crazy… *or worse?* What if I'm *wrong* and it doesn't mean anything at all?" As I rinsed out my mouth, another set of questions filled my mind. "What will happen if I *don't* deliver the message? In Kirk's dream, Jesus told him *my name*. If Kirk had decided to stay quiet, where would I be?" [2]

In World Geography, I sat down at an unoccupied desk before the unsuspecting student who was chatting with her friends. With class about to start and urgency weighing on me, I slowly spun around and earnestly whispered, *"Sadie."*

"What do you want, *freak?*" Sadie all but shouted, irritated at my interruption. "Why are you whispering like a weirdo?" The surrounding girls to laughed at my expense. [3]

Undeterred, I kept my voice low, proceeding, *"I need to talk to you alone after class. I had a dream that I am supposed to tell you about, but I don't know what it means."* [4]

At full volume, Sadie smugly replied, "Anything you want to say to me can be said in front of my friends." Oozing with contempt, the others stared in arrogant silence, anticipating amusement.

"No. You don't know what I'm going to say," I softly rebutted. *"I'll just tell you later. Class is about to start."*

The freshman demanded, "Tell me now or not at all." By then, the entire class became alerted and listened intently.

I softly began, *"The dream…"*

"Speak up, Sandra!" Sadie barked with impudent laughter. [5]

"Fair enough," I replied confidently. "The dream was in black and white, *for the most part*. I was inside of a chilled garage, cold enough for my breath to be seen. Looking down, I discovered I was an adult dressed in very formal funeral attire, including a hat, matching veil, and long black gloves. I slid the glove off of my right hand and approached a black hearse that was parked inside. With the tip of my finger, I drew capital letters on the fogged window, spelling out SADIE. I looked through the *A* and saw the only color in the entire dream. Inside the hearse was a dead human fetus, curled up and highlighted *green*. Does this mean anything to you?" [6]

At that very moment, Sadie balled up her fist and screamed, *"You *****!"* [7]

"Whoa!" I exclaimed, awkwardly bending backward to dodge a right hook. [8]

Untwisting my body to flee the desk-chair combo, I scrambled to stand. Sadie cocked back her arm once more, only to be restrained by the girls closest to her.

At once, she shifted her aggression towards those very friends and beat their arms while shrieking, *"I can't trust anybody! You bunch of loud-mouthed *******!"* Sadie stood with a roar, preparing to lunge towards her horrified and painfully confused classmates. [9]

"Girls, settle! *Girls!*" our teacher sternly warned, wielding an icy squirt bottle from her mini-fridge that was originally intended for sleepy students. Before further damage could be done, our quick-draw instructor unleashed the aquatic sidearm onto Sadie's profile and right shoulder.

Scrunching back her neck and contorting her body, Sadie loudly shrieked and begged, *"Stop! It's cold! Okay! Okay! Stop! I'm done!"* [10]

The feisty comedian squinted one eye and feigned holstering her weapon, warning once more, "Try it again and I'll tag you in the ear. Test me, woman. I'm a pretty good shot. I've had lots of practice." Blown away with the gunslinger's clever approach to drama, the class surged with jovial laugher, including the once-furious Sadie. Glancing at me with an elevated eyebrow and a slight smirk, the woman continued, "Sandra, for your safety, I suggest you sit on the *other* side of the room." [11]

The freshmen class audibly acknowledged the relevance of the teacher's statement as I cheerfully grabbed my books and obeyed with a chuckle. A freshman boy offered an inviting grin and patted the back of the empty chair beside him. [12]

I Said It

Just before volleyball season had come to an official close, Coach Gather announced, "For those of you desiring to join the track team this year, a new mandatory prerequisite is being enforced as of today. Going forward, all future track athletes must also participate in basketball." [1]

"*No!* Coach, are you serious?!" I complained openly. "You *know* I hate basketball! I was looking forward to not playing this year! I drag everybody down! Is there anything that can be done?!"

She shrugged, reiterating, "Those are the rules… *if* you want to run track."

Despite maximum effort during practices, studying the plays at home and my ever-growing muscles, I remained the worst player on the basketball court.

While briefly resting on the bench during a game, I approached Coach Gather once more, pleading, "This isn't volleyball, so I would *love* to ride the pine all season long. Please bench me. I *suck* at shooting and can't remember a single play, no matter how hard I study. I'm not helping anyone by playing. Seriously, I care more about the team than I do about court time. Everyone else is so much better! Replace me! Let me be the manager to hand out water bottles and towels! Don't you want to *win* games?!" [2]

"I don't care. Stop complaining," she ordered, watching our team get pummeled by the competition. "You're a natural athlete and I'm playing you. Besides that, *you're wrong*. You *are* helping."

After a skeptic eye-roll, I peered over to inquire, "How could I *possibly* be helping?"

"You have a good attitude, *apart from this moment*," Coach Gather replied. "You simply *being here* makes things better." [3]

Her unexpected compliment silenced me just before she ushered me back onto the court to stumble, blunder, and look perfectly ridiculous.

Among those that wore a basketball jersey that season was the notorious Fera. Her toxic presence followed me during each practice with a ruthlessly violent defense strategy and cruel remarks about my ineptness.

In the locker room, Laura, a freshman teammate, loudly ranted, "I can't stand Fera! She makes me so mad! I just want to punch her in the face! Why does she have to be so mean and hateful?! Who does she think she is, running over people and pushing them around?! Seriously, Fera is a complete *****." [4]

A universal gasp occurred as Fera stepped forward into view from behind the privacy wall. Bearing wild eyes filled with wrath, the senior fiercely interrogated, *"Who said that?! Who's talking **** about me?!"*

Discreetly, I glanced at Laura, whose lips quivered in tearful angst. Overwhelmed with compassion, I quickly chimed in and lied, "I said it." [5]

Fera narrowed her eyes at me and slowly advanced in my direction with a menacing tone, slithering, *"Now, why would you do a stupid thing like that, fish? I should kick your *** right now. Do you realize how easily I could crush you?"* [6]

With a clenched my jaw to prevent my teeth from chattering, I bluffed with unwavering eyes. With a comically mordant tone, I retorted, *"Crush me, huh? What are you threatening me with, Fera? Are you gonna sit on me? Whatever you do, do it quickly. Some of us have places to be."* [7]

Teammates covered their mouths at my words, causing my right hand to tremble. Unwilling to allow my limb to betray the façade, I slowly pressed it to the side of my leg, palm to thigh, and maintained a stoic gaze. The lioness leaned forward and created inches of sliceable tension between our faces. A sudden wave of concern for my very life seemed to overcome a few witnesses as they cleaved to their peers in fright. [8]

Confusing me, Fera suddenly backed away casually and awkwardly threatened, "See you on the court, *fish*." With a hair-flick, she rapidly vacated the scene. [9]

Lightheaded, I sat down and murmured to myself, *"What the **** just happened?"*

Before following Fera out the door, a varsity sophomore replied, "You just *ruined* your high school career." [10]

"Why did you stick your neck out for Laura like that?" a perturbed teammate, Diane, questioned. "Fera isn't small time like Ruby. She's a *monster*, and you're gonna get your *** kicked for *nothing*." [11]

Without further hesitation, Laura ran to me and threw her arms around my tense body in gratitude, crying, "Oh my gosh, Sandra! Thank you for speaking up and taking my place! I hope she doesn't hurt you! I was so afraid, I froze. She's *terrifying*. I'm so sorry I got you into this. I don't know how, but I'll try to make it up to you." [12]

"For the record, *you* didn't get me into trouble. *I made a choice.* It may not have been the *smartest* decision I've ever made, but I don't regret doing it… *yet*," I jested with a smile. "Come to think of it, Laura, there *is* something you can do for me."

Wide eyed, Laura readily queried, "What is it?! I'll do anything!"

I rested my hand on her delicate shoulder and plainly stated, *"Stop running your mouth.* I don't intend to tempt God *twice*." Laura chuckled and agreed. [13]

Ignoring the lighthearted banter as if getting one last look, Diane squared up with me and squeezed both of my arms, concluding, "You're an *idiot*, but you're brave. I hope I see you tomorrow *at school* and not in the hospital."

As we all vacated the locker room and parted ways for home, I walked faster than usual, hoping Fera wasn't waiting for me around some corner. With light feet, I made my way through the gym, trying not to give away my position or trigger an ambush. [14]

While entering the unlit foyer toward the exit, I heard voices emitting from the darkness that caused me to stop in my tracks. The wretched Fera, still breathing heavily, stood before a blood-soaked Sadie who had both hands folded over her own nose. Noticing my silhouette, they glanced over.

Spotted, I did an immediate about-face and sprinted toward the alternate exit, taking the long way around the building. [15]

The following morning, before classes began, someone softly touched my shoulder and gently uttered, "Sandra?" I turned to discover Sadie with two black eyes and a shaped bar of metal taped to her face.

Gasping, I inquired, "Oh, my gosh, *Sadie!* Are you alright?!" [16]

"Fera broke my nose," the girl sheepishly admitted, "but I'm okay."

Staring at the damage, I wrestled with *guilt* and confessed, "I'm *so* sorry I bolted. I…"

"It wasn't your fight," Sadie interjected. "I did this to myself. Fera has been getting into a lot of trouble for fighting at school and I heard that the principal had finally put his foot down, telling her that if she got into one more fight, she would be *expelled*. I walked up to Fera and said everything I hated about her, thinking she wouldn't do anything about it… like a bulldog on a leash. Well, I was wrong." [17]

"There's something you need to know," I added. "Your timing couldn't have been *worse*. You poked the bear immediately after *my* encounter with Fera. She was a ticking time-bomb after basketball practice."

"Yeah… I heard about you helping Laura in the locker room. She *loves* you, by the way," Sadie sweetly informed. "I don't know if you know this, but Laura is my cousin. *Everybody's related around here.* Anyway, we talked about all of it last night on the phone and it caused me to think about what happened between us in world history class. I'm not sure if I believe you… if you really had a dream about me or you were just lying to cover up gossip, but it doesn't really matter. The way I see it is… my enemy's enemy is my friend. We're cool, Sandra." [18]

You'll Learn

~~~

Mr. Weather offered, "How would you like to earn some extra money this summer, young lady?"

"I would love to! What do you want me to do?!" I chirped.

"Sandra, you're a *terrible* business woman! You said yes before we discussed pay! *You'll learn.* Anyway, I have a metal trailer that needs a wash and some waxing, the grass around the house needs to be mowed, my garden could use some weeding, and the house needs to be dusted and cleaned. I'll pay you two dollars an hour. If I like your work, I'll hire you again. How does that sound?" [1]

Ready to be out of the house, I held out my hand to shake on it and exclaimed, "It's a deal!"

My seasoned neighbor guided me through each task. Once he provided the equipment and supplies to accomplish the work, he stayed out of sight. I remained alone until I retrieved him for inspection four hours later, having exhausted his list.

The man shook his head once more and commented, "Done already?! You're a hard-little-worker! This looks excellent, but do the math. You only made eight dollars today. When you work that fast by the hour, you don't get paid as much. With your speed, you should charge per task. *You'll learn.*" [2]

Willing to shave a rabid wombat for *free* if it meant escaping the materfamilias for the day, I gently smiled and replied, "Thank you for the opportunity to work, Mr. Weather." [3]

"Awe. You're a good kid, Sandra… a bad businesswoman, but a good kid. *Now*, come back inside. My wife enjoys spending time with you and wants you to have lunch with us."

Mrs. Weather had prepared a southern-style meal of pan-fried chicken, mashed potatoes, freshly baked bread, and fried okra that was handpicked from the garden I had just weeded. The presentation, aroma, and flavors nearly brought me to tears.

"Mrs. Weather, thank you for inviting me to have lunch with you!" I expressed, refraining from serving myself thirds and licking the plate. "You're an amazing cook, but watch out. If you keep *this* up, I may decide to stay on the property and become a troll under your porch!" [4]

The woman's face lit up to cried out, *"Oh, my! Not a troll!"* Belly laughing, she touched a napkin to her eyes and attempted to calm herself. "You're so very welcome. I'm glad you enjoyed it. I must say… you're a breath of fresh air! Goodness, girl. I haven't laughed that hard in ages." While collecting the empty dishes from the table, Mrs. Weather sweetly added, "Oh, Sandra? While you're playing under the porch, dear… *kill any mice you find.*" [5]

Mrs. Weather

*I*nvited back to the Weather's home for weekly work, I dusted their furniture, knick-knacks, and antique crystal before devouring another satisfying lunch and laughing hysterically at the clever banter. [1]

Leading us from the dining table to the living room, Mr. Weather helped his wife to her favorite chair and mentioned, "Sandra, each week, when you're finished working, you're welcome to stay and talk as long as you like. You should feel special. If you don't know this already, few people receive such an invitation, *at least from me*. I'll leave you two ladies to chat." Laughing to himself, he slipped into his work galoshes and tromped outside, closing the door behind him.

"Sandra, would you please help me with something?" Mrs. Weather requested. "I feel chin hairs, but I can't see them. Macular degeneration has done a number on me and my husband always pinches my skin when he tries to pluck them. Could I borrow your young eyes and steady hand so I don't grow a full beard?" [2]

"You got it," I cheerfully replied, immediately heading down the hallway as she shouted out the location of the tweezers. Kneeling before her, I continued, "This makes me kind of sad."

"Why? Is it because I'm going blind?" she guessed, scooting forward and sticking out her chin.

"No. Nothing like that," I corrected softly, swiftly removing the targeted hairs. "I just think you'd look really *nice* with a beard." [3]

"Oh, no!" Mrs. Weather chuckled. "Don't make me laugh!"

"Yeah. You're probably right," I deadpanned. "I'd hate to accidentally pluck out a tooth."

With a naked chin and full set of teeth, the woman relaxed back in her chair and encouraged, "Sit with me and rest for a while. It's nice to have someone to talk to."

After chatting about politics, historical figures and her passion for literature, I inquired, "Mrs. Weather, do you have any regrets? Are there some things you wish you had or hadn't done?" [4]

Furrowing her thinning eyebrows, the woman confided, "Yes, I *do* have regrets, and I feel very strongly on the subject. Don't ever get married, Sandra… at least, not at a *young age*. Wait as long as you can. When I was single, I did all the things I wanted to do. I educated myself and followed a career that only men were doing. I had my freedom, made my own money, paid my own bills, and experienced anything I wished. In those days, I was a pioneer of sorts, doing what was rarely done by women, if ever before. I was a meteorologist and a good one, too. Furious, I complained to those in charge when I received less pay for the same work. Things were different then. They told me that the men had families to feed and were paid more so they could provide for them. I told them I had a mouth to feed, too… my own! They wouldn't budge and said that I could either accept my wages or quit. Things seem to have gotten better, so maybe you'll have better luck than I did." [5]

"Were you afraid to live alone when you were single?" I queried. [6]

"No. I could take care of myself," she proudly explained. "I was a country girl that grew up during The Great Depression and raised to be tough. Women needed to be strong to survive in those days, especially when choosing a career in a male-dominated field."

Cocking my head to the side, I wondered, "How did you meet Mr. Weather? He must have been pretty impressive for you to walk away from your single life."

"He was. We met through the weather service. The very qualities that set me apart from other women made up my *allure*," she boasted with a giggle. "I was very much alive… and passionate about everything, especially the work that we were both involved in. I found the science behind it all *thrilling*. He adored me and whisked me away to see the sights. We wined and dined and explored wild lands. I fell in love with his vigor and adventurous spirit that mirrored my own. He was divorced, but I had never been married before. When that handsome man proposed to me, I felt *so* lucky." [7]

"If you're warning me about marriage, something must have changed. What happened? Is that too personal of a question?" I wondered aloud with a wince.

"I don't mind answering that," the former meteorologist replied. "After I wore his wedding ring and took his last name, *everything changed*. He became controlling. It felt as though being his wife was a *demotion* in his eyes and I was no longer seen as an equal. We continued to travel, but in a different manner than I had previously experienced. He expected me to hang back with the other wives while the husbands were gone. Even though they had all the fun, we served the men when they returned. Those evenings, the husbands would drink beer or sip cognac with their cigars and loudly relive their excursions. I really struggled with the whole idea of being left behind. It's been a lonely existence in this cage dubbed *marriage*." [8]

"You hide your feelings very well," I admitted. "I thought you two were *happy*."

My friend leaned forward and advised, "Live your life, Sandra. Don't hold your breath, waiting for some man to guide you through your days. *Think for yourself.* Find out what you want to do and *go do it*. Educate yourself. Learn everything you can… and if things change… learn that, too. If you ever stop learning, you're dead already." [9]

Scouts

*A*fter becoming an honorary scout master for my brother's troop, our father ensured that all the boys would have plenty of opportunities to sharpen their skills and earn merit badges. He organized camp-outs, hikes, and excursions for my brother and invited the troop to join them each time. Several patriarchs declined to be involved with the troop, but agreed to send their disappointed sons ahead. In time, those neglected boys floundered and phased themselves out of the troop altogether. [1]

In contrast, a few fathers found inspiration to be more hands-on than their failing peers and accompanied their male offspring to various outings, actively encouraging the steady accumulation of merit badges to achieve the top status of Eagle Scout.

"Hey! What's going on here?" our father scolded in our direction after coming inside from work. "If you have time to play games on the computer, you have time to work on your Eagle Scout project! Is it done?" My sibling shook his head as I somberly put away the folding-chair I had pulled up beside him. It was fun watching his character shoot Nazis. "I want to see an organized list of tasks for your project and at least *one* of those tasks needs to be completed before you do anything else today. Show me everything that needs to be accomplished to finish the work and what businesses you're going to call for sponsorship. You wanted to be in scouting, remember? Show some initiative! When you start something, finish it!" [2]

With his focus on the PC monitor, my sibling replied, "Okay."

"Now, son! Get on it or I'm gonna put my boot up your ***!" the man assured. [3]

"Okay. I'm just shutting down the computer," the boy clarified.

"Hey, Dad?" I interjected. "I heard you guys were going on another camping trip. Can I go, too?"

"Well, we actually have a mountain climbing trip scheduled on the weekend of your birthday. You can go on *that* one," he said with a smile.

"What?! You mean I can *actually* go?!" I squealed. "Oh, my gosh! I can't believe it! Yes! Thank you, Daddy! This'll be the best birthday ever! I need to make sure I have all my gear!"

"She can't go!" the materfamilias objected from the sofa, stopping me like a sucker punch to the stomach. "I don't want her out there with all those boys!"

Palms up in protest, I plainly stated, "That doesn't make sense. You send me to school, don't you? Neither of you are there for that. If I'm not safe with my brother and father on a scout camping trip, I'm not safe *anywhere*. You surprise me, lady. Why would you sabotage yourself like that?"

The woman appeared confused and quickly snarled, "What do you mean… *sabotage* myself?! I'm not sabotaging myself!"

"Yes, you are," I calmly rebutted. "You always complain about being a wife and mom. Having children *ruined your life*, right? When Dad comes home, all you want to do is argue with him. You *hate* us… and if you don't, you sure act like it. *Think about it.* If you let me go camping with them, everyone will be out of your hair for *days*. No one will bother you or ask questions. You won't have to cook or have your shows interrupted. Do you really want to throw all of that away?" [4]

Scowling, the woman returned her gaze to the television screen and huffed, "Fine. Go."

It was the day before my birthday when we loaded our gear into the bed of the pickup truck. I was so relieved when my father pulled out of the driveway and closed the gate behind us without being hindered by his wife. Feeling safe, I let down my guard and relaxed in my seat, expecting our adventure to be cradled within some much-needed peace. [5]

We pulled into the campsite and set up our tents beside the wooden chuck box my father helped my brother design and build. Stored inside were canned goods, dry ingredients, spices, cooking gear, and a fold-out prep area. Other boys dug holes with their fathers and lit charcoal briquettes to cook with cast-iron Dutch ovens.

"How do you not burn everything?" I wondered aloud, accustomed to propane cooking.

"Come over here, Sandra. I'll show you," invited one of the scout fathers. "We dug a hole deep and wide enough for this size Dutch oven. By placing the right number of coals underneath and on top of the lid, you achieve the proper temperature for it to cook. After that, all we have to do is wait! The trick is to put the same number of coals on top as underneath. Do you see what we're doing? Right now, we're lining the pan with bacon, which provides grease so things won't stick. Then we'll add hash browns, sausage, cheese, eggs, and seasonings." He reached for something and handed it to me. "Check out this Dutch oven recipe book. Everything you need to know for each meal is all spelled out in there."

"Wow. How cool is that?!" I chirped, flipping through the pages. "I bet this'll taste *amazing*. Good job, guys."

"Find out for yourself, Sandra! I'll call you over when it's ready!" the man cheerfully offered. "We always make more than we need, so there'll be plenty to share."

"For *me*? Wow! Thank you!" I gasped, fighting back tears. To control my emotions, I meandered to the neighboring fire pit to distract myself. "Is that peach cobbler?! Oh my gosh! Are you kidding me?! You can *bake* in those things, too?!"

"Yup! You sure can!" the father warmly replied, scooping some contents into a bowl. "Here! Have some!"

"What?! Thank you so much," I murmured, allowing a tear to be seen accidentally.

With full stomachs, we began our hike up the trail and encountered switch-backs that lead to the towering peak. During each water and snack break, I climbed boulders, snapped photos with my disposable camera, and explored the area.

"My feet hurt, Dad. I don't want to do this anymore," a scout whined, munching on some trail mix with a sour face. "Can we go back?"

"Oh, yeah! Sure!" his father jested, exciting the scouts. "You know what? I have an idea. Why don't you boys just let *Sandra* describe it all to you after she gets back from reaching the summit?" His child glanced at his sweaty friend with a nod and shrug, as if to consider it. "Aw! C'mon boys! Don't be like that! The pain is temporary. Just keep putting one foot in front of the other. Sandra can't earn your merit badges for you… and this climb might even earn some of you more than one. Just *keep going*. Don't quit." [6]

Lessons

~~~~

Although I was much younger than the majority, Rhett invited me to attend his college-and-career group composed of youthful singles from our UPC congregation. Each Wednesday, a member from the group provided dinner and hosted us in a comfortable setting for Rhett to teach a Bible lesson Dolion had written or approved of. Afterward, we openly discussed how to live out those principles in our daily lives. [1]

Just before starting time, Rhett arrived and loudly knocked on his cousin's door as several of us waited behind him. Jimmy cracked open the entrance of his newly constructed home and greeted, "Hey, guys! Give me one second. I just need to tidy up a bit."

After waiting more than a few minutes, Rhett grew impatient and announced, "This is ridiculous, Jimmy! You've known about this for weeks! I'm coming in!" Pushing open the door, Rhett exposed our young host bearing an armful of wadded clothing as he frantically relocated *mounds* of garments out of sight.

Jimmy sheepishly admitted, "Oh… uh… Y'all weren't supposed to see this." [2]

Without hesitating, I reached toward the largest mound on his living room rug and consoled, "It's okay, Jimmy. I'll help you." [3]

"No, Sandra! Don't touch it!" Jimmy abruptly warned, causing me to back away cautiously. "I'm sorry. I didn't mean to yell. It's just that I don't want to waste any more time on this. Those clothes are filthy and smelly. They've been sitting there for *a while* and it's gross. Please, don't touch them."

"Wow," Rhett commented, shaking his head and seeming to grow more perturbed by the second. "That's *disgusting*. I can't believe you even *own* this much clothing. You *live* like this?"

"I know. I know. It's pretty bad," Jimmy confessed, red-faced. "Just ignore the piles and have a seat at the table while I try to find something for y'all to eat."

We obeyed as our host scrambled through his neglected pantry and state-of-the-art refrigerator, nervously conveying, "I'm so sorry, y'all. I totally forgot to shop for this. All I have is blackberry pie and some pizza snacks from the freezer." After sliding them into the matching stainless-steel oven, Jimmy cranked opened a tin of sardines and centered them on the tabletop with a paper plate of saltine crackers. "Here's something to stave off starvation." Scratching his head, the young man mentioned, "Gosh, guys. I hope those are still good. I've had them a *long* time."

Rhett commented openly, "Jimmy, you're actually *serving* this to us?! I think I see some green in there!" [4]

Overwhelmed with compassion, adoration, and a painful hunger, I chirped, "I've never eaten *sardines* before! Neat! I'll try one, Jimmy!"

"No, Sandra! Don't eat that!" Rhett cautioned. "You'll get sick!"

Disregarding the man as cruelly snobbish, I plucked a very slick sardine from the questionable tin, set it on a stale cracker, and enthusiastically shoved the contents into my mouth, inspiring several gags from those around me. As I boldly chewed, Jimmy's gaze met mine as an endeared smile emerged on his face.

"Jimmy, get rid of this before Sandra eats the whole thing and gets food poisoning!" Rhett ordered, convincing our host to comply while we proceeded with the lesson. [5]

Tristan eventually sniffed the air and mentioned, "I think something's burning."

Jimmy scrambled to the forgotten appliance and removed the charred goods, releasing a billowing black cloud into the air. Our host served *smoked* blackberry pie and charred pizza snacks, admitting, "I forgot to set an alarm. Wow, guys. I'm *really* sorry. This evening isn't going very well."

"Where's your head today?" Rhett posed. "We need plates, utensils and napkins… and you'd better cut and serve this pie. Wake up, Jimmy!"

"Well, the Bible lesson should be our primary concern, *not the food*," I interjected. "Thank you for sharing what you have, Jimmy. This is *great*." [6]

Jimmy lightheartedly contradicted, "This is *a sad spread*, but it's the best I have to offer for now."

"That's the thing, Jimmy," Rhett scolded as he watched members of the group cautiously reach for something edible. "This *wasn't* the best you had to offer." [7]

We picked apart and nibbled on sliced carbonization. As the lingering items grew cold, I steadily consumed what remained. Rhett finished the lesson and led us outside.

As we were dispersing to head home, Jimmy stood alone near the doorway. I approached and whispered, *"Are you okay? Is your washing machine broken? Do you need some help cleaning up?"* [8]

Jimmy gave a heavy sigh and casually explained, "Okay. Okay. My habits are pretty bad, but I work really hard, make a comfortable living, and just built a new house. So, if you think about it, that's pretty good for someone my age. The thing is, I work all day in the heat and I'm too tired to cook, so I usually eat takeout. That's why I didn't have any food in the house." [9]

"I'm not buying it," Rhett chided from beside his truck. "Stop sugar-coating what happened today. We obviously weren't a priority to you, Jimmy. If you were too tired to cook, you could have picked something up for us on your way home, just like you do for *yourself*. There's no excuse you could give me to make me feel sorry for you. I work hard, too, Jimmy. You're ready to eat what everyone else prepares… and they can't afford what you can. Stop lying. You didn't *run out of time*. You probably ate before coming home and forgot all about us… and I don't know what you're doing with those piles of dirty clothes all over your house." [10]

"You're right, Rhett. You're right. I'll admit… I forgot it was Wednesday, and that I was hosting today… and I really don't have an excuse for the clothes either," Jimmy continued. "It really comes down to poor time-management and flat *laziness*. I usually make after-work plans on the fly, so instead of driving all the way home to clean up, I just buy *new* clothes, change in the truck, spray on some cologne, and go. As you can clearly see, my bad habit has really added up. The neglect is inexcusable and I really need to take care of things. I'll start making time for it." [11]

"Ha! No, you won't! I know what the *real* problem is. You're too busy chasing girls!" Rhett divulged, bursting into a cackle as he entered his truck. [12]

After leaving Jimmy's house, a thoughtful member of the group dropped me off at my parent's gate. The materfamilias allowed me inside without a word. I pondered Jimmy's strange lifestyle and Rex's scolding until I drifted to sleep.

My eyes popped open as an unsettling sensation stirred me awake. I panted and was clammy to the touch when a metallic taste and tingling sensation swirled in my mouth. At that, I flicked the bed sheets off my body and fled to the nearest toilet. As foretold by Rhett, one wave of nausea lapped on top of the other, wrenching my abdomen over and over. When the rotten sardines, stale crackers, blackened pizza snacks, and burned blackberry pie had finally vacated my system, I white-knuckled the commode and continued to dry heave. [13]

While I moaned and stared down at my ghastly reflection in the toilet water, the materfamilias opened the door and observed my condition with condescension, viciously accusing, "You're *pregnant*, aren't you?" [14]

"You don't know what you're talking about," I rebutted. "It's food poisoning. I *can't* be pregnant. I'm a virgin. Since the only virgin birth has already occurred and Jesus is already on the scene, I seriously *doubt* that I am pregnant." [15]

"Ha! *I don't believe you*," the termagant hissed. "If you think I'm watching anymore *brats*, you're crazy. We're not going to help you. You're on your own." [16]

I rolled my eyes, wheezing out, "Don't flatter yourself, woman. I wouldn't place a library book in your care, much less the lives of defenseless children. Trust me. If I ever *do* raise a family, *you'll never meet them*."

"Ha! We'll see. You'll be *begging* for my help," the woman boasted.

Anxiety and wrath inflamed the intensity of my regurgitative ailment, no longer permitting verbal warfare. To express my sentiments, I erected a solitary finger of infamy between us. [17]

With a hand over her chest, the termagant lorded, "And you call yourself a *Christian!* Ha!" At once, my accuser turned on her heels and exited my peripheral view. [18]

Having lost five pounds that night, I laboriously prepared soft foods and various liquids for myself the following day as the woman sat motionless on the couch.

Mack

～

The gap of time between UPC morning and evening services became increasingly difficult to navigate. Those who had helped me the most eventually passed by without a glance or greeting. I felt stuck and knew that if I were to call home and request to be picked up, it would only result in not returning that evening for the second service.

Willing to spend hours by myself and forego eating all day, I removed my presence early to circumnavigate the uneasiness I inflicted upon the most generous of UPC members. "I don't blame them for avoiding me," I silently concluded. "They have taken me out to eat so many times. I bet they're tired of doing it. I'm an expensive burden each week, even to my own parents. The money adds up. It's not their fault." [1]

While lying on the shaded picnic table a few yards from the building, I heard a masculine voice call out, "Who's over there by the tree?! Hey!"

Immediately assuming I was in trouble for trespassing, I sat up to discover the source of the voice and responded respectfully, "It's me, Sandra Lawson! I go to church here! I'm sorry for staying after the service! I'll leave!"

"No, no! Stop! You're not in trouble! Stay right there!" the young man shouted with a friendly wave. As he walked toward the table, I shrank back and winced. Noticing my adverse reaction to his approach, he quickly introduced himself, chirping, "Hey! I'm Mack. I don't think we've met, but I recognize you. Brother Deacon is my dad. You know *him*, right?"

"Uh, yeah. I know him. He's a nice man, but I chewed him out one time because he wouldn't let me get baptized when I wanted to. It's a long story, but… we're cool now," I reassured.

"Huh. I didn't think my dad would stop *anyone* from being baptized, but I've been wrong before," Mack admitted, wearing stylish sunglasses and a loud Hawaiian shirt. "Did you ever end up getting baptized?"

"Yeah… *the following week*… but only because I called out my mother to Pastor Dolion. While we were leaving, she said we weren't coming back to church anymore, so I broke away from her and ran to your dad and asked to be baptized right then," I divulged. "After that, my mom felt *obligated* to bring me back, just to save face. When she stopped driving me to church, I rode my bike all the way here, even getting on the highway. It made my parents look really bad, so they're giving me rides again… *for now*."

"Ha! You're feisty!" the young man laughed. "That's super cool. You're alright, Sandra. *Hey*. You weren't planning on sitting out here alone until the next service, were you?"

"Yes," I replied, embarrassed. "It's okay. I can take care of myself. I lift weights. This isn't the first time I've done this. People have things to do."

"Well, not that I don't think you're strong… I just don't think it's safe for a young girl to be out here by herself. This world has strange people in it and they might sneak up on you while you're relaxing. You're hanging out with *me* today. Come on," Mack urged, inviting me to walk back with him toward an older muscle car. [2]

As we vacated the picnic table, I wondered if Mack was as kind as he seemed, understanding how easily the materfamilias could win people over with a counterfeit smile and manipulative laugh. However, having trust in Brother Deacon's parenting and seeing no better alternative, I entered the vehicle shortly before Mack hit the gas.

"This is a small church. How come we've never met?" I wondered aloud, buckled in and enjoying the quick acceleration of his manual transmission.

"Well…" Mack hesitated, seeming apprehensive, "I sit in the back. Let's just say that I try to get out of there as fast as possible."

"Why? You don't like being Pentecostal?" I probed.

"No, no. Nothing like that…" he corrected, pausing once more to glance at me. "Alright. I'll tell you. You seem trustworthy. The thing is, I'm from my dad's first marriage, so I was already around when my he married Sister Deacon. Let's just say she hasn't been very kind to me. After they were married, they had my younger brother. I love the guy, but she dotes on him… a lot. My brother and I were raised so differently… like night and day."

"I know what *that's* like… except I'm the youngest and the only girl. My eldest brother is from my mom's first marriage and my other brother and I are from her second marriage. She adores both her sons and *hates* me. I don't mean to pry, but has your step mom ever *hurt* you?" I inquired.

"That's intuitive. You must understand pain to ask a question like that. *Yes*. However, saying that *she hurt me* is putting it lightly. To give you an idea of what it was like when I was a kid, the woman hit me in the head with a two-by-four one time. I bled a lot… and she accused *me* of being the spoiled one," Mack confided. "Has someone hurt *you*? You wouldn't have asked if you hadn't experienced it yourself."

Staring forward at the road, I growled, "Yes. My *biological* mother does. Thanks to her, I'm no stranger to pain. That's why I don't go home between services. I try to stay out of the house. Does Sister Deacon *still* hurt you?"

Mack laughed, "Not anymore, at least not physically. I'm too big and I got out of the house as fast as I could. Wait. Your mom is *still* hurting you?"

I took a deep breath and choked out, "*Yes…* but it was physically worse in elementary and middle school. I guess I'm getting too big to beat on, but it's not getting any better *psychologically*. That's so funny. They use the same words. My mom thinks *I'm* spoiled, too, but the woman is evil. When I was ten, she dragged me into the house from outside *by my hair* because she thought I stuck her toothbrush in the toilet while she was in the restroom using the glass shower! She didn't see me do anything… because I wasn't there! She's nuts! Regardless of facts, she grabbed my scalp, dragged me, and threw me down on the bathroom floor! I had to explain condensation to her while lying on the wet tile! One time, she beat me to the ground with a belt and accused me of stealing her earrings. While she was still hitting me, I screamed for her to tell me what they looked like. I told the woman to look in the mirror. *She was wearing them!* The woman just walked away and *never apologized*. She doesn't apologize for *anything*. She beat me for relaxing next to my dad in his recliner. Mack, she thought I was sleeping with him! That woman's a ******* psycho and I hate her! I want her to die! I'm not the pervert! *She* is!" Unable to maintain self-control, I burst into sobs as tears dripped onto my lap. [3]

Mack quickly pulled the car into a roadside clearing, exited the driver's side, and opened my door, snagging me into a comforting hug. The young man softly encouraged, *"It's okay. She's not here right now and you're safe. I'm so sorry this is happening to you. What a nightmare, Sandra. I'm so sorry. You're okay. It's okay."* [4]

After I calmed down, we sat together on the remarkably durable hood of his ride. Over some shared snacks, we discussed the gruesome details of our childhoods that revealed more truth about the diabolical women our fathers had married. [5]

"Sister Deacon seems so *calm* at church," I commented. "She's just like my mom. The woman puts on a good front, doesn't she? That lady must have really duped your dad, like my mom duped mine. Sister Deacon… what a *****."

"*Hey…* I've forgiven her, Sandra. I don't want you to pick up what took me years to unload. I gave that to Jesus," Mack reproved. "I just stay away from her and figure that if I avoid her, I won't have to *keep* forgiving her for new things. As for your mom, you'll be out of the house and free soon enough. What are your plans after high school?" [6]

"Well, hopefully I'll get a scholarship to college and become a writer or a marine biologist," I shared, staring at the clouds. "Jesus told an evangelist that I was a warrior, so maybe I'll be a navy seal or an army ranger. I'm getting stronger and stronger every year. The military has a good retirement plan and my medical needs would be covered. *It's possible.* I know I'm a girl, but I could do it. If I can survive my mother, I can survive *anything*. What about you?"

"Wow. You have big dreams. *That's good.* For me, I want to be a husband and a father. I want to have a *real* family that loves each other and isn't completely nuts," Mack warmly stated, causing me to scrunch my nose.

"After all *I've* experienced, marriage and having kids are the *last* things on my mind. I may never do *either*," I revealed. "If I'm anything like my mother, I'd rather just stay single and not pass that garbage on to the unborn. She's not human. The woman is a *monster*." [7]

"Jesus has helped me see my step mom as just another *flawed person* and I've chosen to forgive her. I had to let it go… *for me*. Her sin is between her and Jesus. I know you're angry, but you'll continue to age and eventually get away from her. If you stick with Jesus, you'll forgive your mother, too… *someday*." [8]

"That ***** doesn't *deserve* forgiveness," I snipped. [9]

"Sandra, *none* of us do," he gently reminded. [10]

"You're right. I'm just… *dealing with it*," I conceded with a sigh. "So, Mack, tell me something interesting about yourself, besides testing the durability of two-by-fours."

"Hey! That really hurt! Hmmm… let me think… I was in a really, really bad car wreck," the young man revealed, shifting his body to remove the wallet tucked into his back pocket. Mack flipped it open and handed me his old driver's license. "See? That's what I looked like *before* the accident."

"Huh. You know, if you hadn't told me, I would've never have guessed that you'd been in a wreck. *Hold on.* Sit up," I urged, comparing the photo with that of the winsome creature beside me. Suddenly, I noticed one *major* change which caused my eyes to flick back and forth between the identification and his actual face. "You don't have any noticeable scarring, but…"

"But, what? What's *that* look for? What?" he pressed as I chuckled and silently shook my head. "Seriously, Sandra. What are you thinking? You're making me super paranoid right now! Tell me!" he entreated, nudging me off balance as I laughed and stopped myself from falling off the vehicle.

Cracking up, I resettled and leaned back on the windshield, beginning, "Well, you *do* look a little different. You've become more masculine with age. That's probably what I'm noticing."

"No, Sandra. *I look different.* My jaw snapped in two places and they had to wire it back together! Tell me what you're thinking," Mack playfully interrogated.

"Fine," I conceded, folding my legs and spinning to face him. "Don't get a big head about it, but... I think... personally... that you look even *better* than before."

Mack gasped, laughing, "Are you saying that my injuries are an *improvement?!* You're so mean!"

"What?! I'm not being mean! You were never *ugly*, goober! *Think about it.* People pay a lot of money for a square jaw and auto insurance happened to cover yours." Doubling over, Mack's laughter became silent and ended in a loud gasp, only to repeat as he wiped streaming tears from his flush face. I chuckled with him and added, "Seriously, you look good!" Suddenly, I become perfectly still.

"What?" Mack wondered, lifting an eyebrow.

"I'm not gonna do it," I soberly stated, shaking my head and looking away.

"You're not gonna do *what*?" the young man questioned, waiting with a forward lean.

"I'm not gonna feel sorry for you, Mack. You have blue eyes, blonde hair, and received a *free* face-lift," I deadpanned. "You're just so... *spoiled.*" Our eyes finally met, slaying the other in explosive hysterics. [11]

Sweet Sixteen

Before our freshman year, Neli invited me to a quinceañera as a member of her female entourage, while politely and strategically including my mother in the celebration so I could attend. Escorted by her brother and male cousins, a choreographed and rehearsed march and waltz was mandatory for maids of honor or *damas* to perform while donning the dresses Neli selected. Family gifted the birthday girl with a customary doll wearing a miniature replica of her extravagant dress to represent the childhood that Neli was leaving behind. Savory food, rich desserts, and various forms of alcohol were plenty, with dancing highly encouraged for all.

After our exposure to this event, the materfamilias graciously inquired, "Sandra, would you like to have a quinceañera or a sweet sixteen for your birthday?"

"For me?! What?!" I wondered aloud, amazed at her sudden generosity. "Well, we're not Catholic and Neli's party seemed to be as expensive and complicated as a wedding. I don't need all of that. I'd rather just relax with some friends, so I'll wait for a sweet sixteen. Thank you for even being willing to throw a quinceañera. That was thoughtful of you."

Time passed, and the sixteenth anniversary of my birth grew neigh.

Although I was already approaching the materfamilias, she abrasively shouted, *"Dinner's ready! Come and eat!"*

"Wow. That was loud. Hey, Mom? Do you remember when you had me choose between a quinceañera and a sweet sixteen?" I nervously inquired, having heard nothing more about it in well over a year. "Well, I'm turning sixteen in a week and was wondering if I could invite a few friends over to spend the night and celebrate with me, since we don't have to go to school the next day. I don't need a cake or decorations or anything like that. I just want a quiet sleepover."

"Fine, but don't invite more than five… *four*," she acquiesced with irritation. "I don't need a bunch of people tromping around and touching everything. I'm not cleaning up a huge mess."

Obsequious in attitude, I bowed before the termagant and uttered, "Thank you."

At once, I meticulously created invitations on our PC and printed them out in color, eventually dispersing them to Neli, Nicki and two other close friends, receiving the most enthusiastic of confirmations from each girl.

The long-awaited morning arrived and began with the sound of an alarm. My eyes opened. As I stretched, I suddenly remembered the glorious occasion. Gasping, I cheered, "Today's the day! I'm *sixteen!* Oh-my-gosh-oh-my-gosh-oh-my-gosh!" After cleaning up and putting on my favorite outfit, I grinned and enthusiastically clutched my backpack to catch the bus. Passing the lounging materfamilias, I smiled in her direction and chirped, "Mom, I'm so excited! I can't believe I'm sixteen! We're going to have so much fun today! Seriously, thank you for wanting to do this for me."

"I don't feel like dealing with it. The party is off," the woman casually stated, still staring at the television. "It's too much work." [1]

"What?" I uttered, somehow shocked and winded by her flippant cruelty. "Too much work? Wow. I verified this with you *days* ago. This was *your* idea… *remember?* I wouldn't have dared to even *think* of a sweet sixteen, much less *ask* for it! It's *cheap* and hardly any work at all! Listen, I've really been looking forward to this. You don't even need to decorate or cook. My friends and I can just go out to eat and quietly pile into my room. We'll be completely out of sight. Why would you let me hand out invitations to just take it all away? *Please,* let them come! I…" [2]

"I don't care," the termagant coldly interjected, watching another commercial. "The party is off and that's *final.* After school, come straight home. You're not going out to eat. I mean it. *Come straight home.* If you say anything else to me about it, you're getting a spanking. *Go to school and get out of my face.* If you miss the bus, I'm not driving you… and if *that* happens, you won't even *see* your friends… and they better not show up here. If they come, I'm not answering the door." [3]

Once at school, Nicki rushed me with an enthusiastic pogo-hug as she shouted, *"Happy birthday, Sandra! Yay! Woo-hoo! You're sixteen! You're sixteen!"* Feeling dead weight within her embrace, she stopped bouncing and queried, "Hey, you should be happy today! What's wrong, bud? What's going on with you? It's a little early for something to have already happened."

"I… uh… I'm not allowed to have anyone over anymore. So, what's *nice* is… if you bought a gift… you can take it back and keep your money," I murmured, staring off.

"Uh, *that's dumb.* I'm giving you my gift, so we'll have enough of *that,*" she playfully replied. "Wait. *What?* Your mom canceled your party?! When did she do that?"

"This morning… before I got on the bus," I robotically informed. "She said that I can't have anyone over and that if anybody shows up, they're not allowed in the house.

I'm really sorry for any inconvenience, but now your afternoon is free to spend with your friends."

"Uh… *you're* my friend," she corrected, staring at me. Bearing the most concerned brow, Nicki touched my shoulder with one hand and guided my gaze back to hers with the other, inquiring, "Sandra, are you okay?"

Like a freshly uncorked bottle of champagne, my emotions gushed and spilled, prompting Nicki to catch my wrenching body and soothe me into stability. [4]

Running Your Mouth

"Sandra, there's a call for you. It's a *boy* from church," the materfamilias announced, narrowing her eyes at me with an air of suspicion.

I rushed to the kitchen with hopes for Mack, Jimmy, or Rex to be on the line and answered, "Hello? This is Sandra."

"Hello… *Sandra?* This is Oliver from church. We go to high school together," the boy informed. "I looked up your phone number from the church directory. *I hope that's okay.* Anyway, I don't know if you're already going to prom, but you seem like a fun girl and I wanted to know if you wanted to be my date."

Stumped, I couldn't recall who he was, nor did I recognize his name or voice, which was unusual for a student body of merely two hundred individuals and a congregation of far less. Undeterred by those details, I imagined myself dining and dancing in a stunning dress at an event created primarily for juniors and seniors.

"Let me ask my mother if I can go. Hold on," I replied, desperately trying to picture who was on the other end of the call. Assuming that the materfamilias was listening-in, I scurried to her bedroom and bluntly sought permission. I attained it. Rushing back and lifting the receiver from the kitchen table, I continued, "I can go! Thank you for inviting me! See you at school… or church! Bye!"

After the service that Sunday, a boy I instantly recognized approached me, chirping, "Hey, Sandra! Are you ready for prom?!"

Oliver had never presented himself as bold, nor had he spoken to me in person before. Humble and kind in demeanor, he had somehow faded into the background of many memories. His appearance was modest, but tidy, and I rarely observed his face not hosting a smile. I witnessed his mother frequently scream and tearfully run up and down the UPC aisles with flailing arms, which included my first day. Based on the body language of many congregation members, they considered Oliver's family as outcasts. [1]

Wondering what Jimmy, Rex, or Mack might assume about the situation, a dark arrogance flooded my thoughts with shame as I searched for words during Oliver's approach. With a forced a smile, I replied, "Prom should be a fun experience. I mean, you can't go wrong with food and dancing, right?"

"Yeah!" the boy graciously agreed. "Well, I'm headed home. I'll see you later, Sandra!"

Still lingering near the back door of the building, I noticed the upperclassmen UPC females standing in a group and chatting quietly. Having observed several of their conversations with Jimmy and Rex, I concluded that presenting some cleverly selected words to them might snuff out any *romantic* rumors revolving around my prom attendance. [2]

Assuming that they already gossiped about me or would soon do so, I walked over and interrupted their private conversation, inquiring, "Are you guys going to prom this year?" [3]

"Yes," answered one of the radiating beauties, humoring me. "Are you?"

"*Yes*," I informed. "Oliver got my number from the church directory and invited me, but he had better keep his hands to himself. I'm not that kind of girl. If he tries anything funny, he'll regret it immediately."

That same evening, my father poked his head into my room and informed, "Sandra, a woman from church called and wants to talk to you. Take it in the kitchen."

Confused, I answered, "Hello? This is Sandra."

"*Sandra?* Hello. This is Oliver's mother," the woman sweetly began, causing my soul to shrink. "I just wanted to know if my son has said or done *anything* to discourage you from going to the prom with him. Someone came up to me and told me you had some *concerns* and I wanted to make sure that everything was okay. Do you still want to go? You really don't have to." [4]

"I am *so* sorry," I back-peddled, ashamed of my behavior. "Oliver is a very nice person and has *always* been kind to me. Yes, I still want to go. Thank you for checking." [5]

"Well, *good*. He's excited about it. Oliver doesn't know very many *nice* girls, and he thought you'd be fun. I'm very glad you still want to go. I'll tell him. If you feel nervous about anything, come talk to me right away. Have a good night." [6]

After I hung up the receiver, my amused father appeared from around the corner and chided, "Well, Sandra… I talked to Oliver's mother before you did. It sounds like you were running your mouth at church and got caught! Someone's little sister overheard you talking to some girls and told the woman everything you said. Next time, keep your trap *shut*. You got off easy this time. I bet you won't make *that* mistake again." [7]

Oliver

The materfamilias zipped up the back of my sky blue ballgown she had selected for me and curled my hair before pinning it into a traditional up-do. The more time I spent in the bathroom with the woman, the more my excitement grew. I longed to be surrounded by something glamorous and exclusive, far away from home.

"Sandra, you can't go to prom looking so plain! Yuck! Do something with that face! Put on some make-up!" the termagant gruffly insisted. [1]

Possessing nothing that remotely blended with my tanned skin tone, all that I had at my exposal were cosmetic scraps that the termagant had discarded and allowed me to keep. At a loss for what to do, I applied a pale powder over my entire face, awkwardly layered on some caking mascara, and selected lipstick from some rejected colors.

While staring into my bedroom mirror, I didn't recognize myself, which I considered a *good* thing. I didn't want to be recognized. Nothing I wore reflected my personality. I felt like a warped parody of the termagant's favorite animated princess.

I stepped before the occupied recliner and queried with a twirl, "How do I look, Daddy?"

"Ask your mother," the man dryly replied, bearing a blended expression of disinterest, confusion, and disgust. "I don't know anything about fashion."

My face remained stonelike through the piercing sting. I regretted having the unreasonable expectation of a teary-eyed response or one of those loving father-daughter moments from television. In my heart, I resolved to never inquire about my appearance again. [2]

A vehicle pulled into our gravel driveway and added pressure to my increasingly tense shoulders. Oliver approached the front porch wearing a suit and neatly pinned boutonniere. In his hand was a fragrant corsage with a ribbon that perfectly matched my dress.

Gently handing the floral gift to me, Oliver sweetly greeted, "Hey, Sandra! This is for *you*. Thanks for wanting to go to prom with me." [3]

Completely ignorant of the formal custom, I was further humbled by his generosity while accepting the unexpected gift, and exclaimed, "Wow, Oliver. This is *beautiful*. Thank you." [4]

"You're welcome," he quietly replied with a large, nervous grin.

With fresh flowers resting on my wrist, the materfamilias rapidly stepped out of view. I playfully nudged Oliver and whispered from the corner of my mouth, *"Let's get out of here before she comes back."* Without hesitation, he reached for the door.

"Hold on! Wait!" the materfamilias ordered, causing us to linger awkwardly as she snapped unflattering photos that blinded us with each flash.

"Let's make a break for it," I covertly guided, having my fill of her mother-of-the-year act.

Just as we were closing the door, the termagant shouted, "Sandra, don't act like a boy!"

Expressing the utmost respect and chivalry for the occasion, the junior hurried ahead of me to open the passenger door and turned in time to witness the shame and anger that covered my face. I quickly entered his vehicle and fought back tears. The teen thoughtfully tucked my dress inside the vehicle with a gentle smile before closing the door and sliding into the driver's seat. Breaking the silence, Oliver turned toward me and delicately prodded, "Sandra? Are you okay?"

"I'm sorry. I don't mean to drag things down. It's just… she didn't have to say that. It was really mean. She ruins *everything*," I replied, choking back tears and forcing another smile.

Pausing for a moment, Oliver added, "Well, you look *beautiful*, Sandra. Don't worry about what your mom said." [5]

Surprising me again, his unsolicited kindness soothed me and drew up my gaze as I boldly chirped, "You know what, Oliver? *You're right*. We *do* look great… and we have a car! Let's go eat some free food and dance our socks off!" [6]

"*Yeah!*" Oliver laughed. At that, he started the engine and rescued me from captivity. [7]

Dance

$\mathcal{A}$s soon as Oliver and I stepped inside the venue, an upperclassman from volleyball spotted me. Cascading over, she whispered, "Come with me to the restroom and let me blend your makeup. You look like you're from eighteenth century England." In proper lighting, she determined I didn't need powder *at all* and gently removed it. "There. All better. Now, go have some fun." [1]

My date and I stood together for professional prom photos with matching enthusiasm. Candlelit tables glowed under tulle-filtered twinkle lights. A rotating disco ball speckled suits and dresses with radiance as pairs of teenagers formed a carousel that swirled to a romantic country song.

Knowing the familiar tune, Oliver leaned in and inquired, "Sandra, would you like to dance?"

"Yeah!" I chirped. "Let's go!" [2]

The young man sheepishly swayed from side to side, cheerfully out of rhythm. I gently tugged his lead hand and applied pressure to his shoulder, covertly guiding the junior around the dance floor while navigating the flow of polished students.

"I'm sorry, Sandra," Oliver admitted as he stepped on my toe. "I don't really know what I'm doing."

I chuckled and encouraged, "Don't worry about it. You're doing great." When the boy awkwardly kicked my shoe, I smirked. "No one saw. You've got this. Just feel the music and keep dancing." [3]

The DJ switched the tune and a line-dance broke out with rows of students stepping together in energetic formation. A girlish power ballad caused the boys to roll their eyes and retreat as the glamorous belles lingered to sing along. Pop music exploded from the speakers, reeling the lads back onto the floor. Rap ushered in the most hilarious moves where a dance-off caused on-lookers to circle and cheer, entertained by the hidden talents of their classmates.

"Are you having a good time, Oliver?!" I shouted over the music, having returned to the table for a break. *"They stopped playing slow songs, didn't they?!"*

"*Yeah… but that's okay!*" he assured loudly with a grin. "*I like watching! I'm having a good time! This is great!*"

A hush from the speakers prompted each student to return to their seat with the expectation of an announcement. As though the room had needed a deep breath to prepare for what came next, a salsa rhythm broke the silence and animated my foot to tap. Not a soul was returning to the dance floor, which confused me. Brass swelled as a Latin riff of acoustic guitar accompanied rattling maracas and rhythmic percussion. Compelled, I stood and danced alone.

Shimmying my shoulders, I strutted away from the shadowy table and sashayed across the carpet onto the abandoned hardwood space. A spotlight heated my skin with cinematic timing. [4]

The sharply dressed DJ removed his formal jacket and abandoned the lighting equipment to clasp my hand. The invitation needed no words. With swirling excitement and daring confidence, the slightest pressure from his fingertips instantly led me into a terpsichorean exhibition. The massive crescendos and a booming beat cued perfectly synced transitions of rapid spins and exaggerated movements. Snapped into a deep embrace, I submitted to a thrilling dip and laughed from delight as my head flipped back with complete trust in his strength.

Applause erupted from all around us as he pulled my body upright and tightly to his chest. Breathing heavily from his vibrant performance, the professional stared at me with a grin and slowly spun by body outward to behold a roaring audience standing to their feet. [5]

Moving in close behind me, the handsome stranger informed, "They're clapping for *you*." As we moved into position and simultaneously bowed, nothing seemed real. I felt adept and desirable. Before allowing me to withdraw, the young man guided me to himself and added, "You're amazing. I'll salsa with you *anytime*." At that, my partner withdrew to his vocation as I stepped away, stunned, overjoyed that the Creator had made me female. [6]

SECTION 8

Deleted

~~~~~~~~

While our father was away at work and the materfamilias entertained herself in the city, I grew bored. No longer satisfied by watching my brother conquer levels on his video game console, I went downstairs to use the PC.

Lacking the patience and determination to surf the web with our dial-up internet connection, I snooped through saved documents and found my brother's private file. When I clicked on one of the photo icons, a pornographic image filled the screen. Assuming that I clicked on the wrong thing, I frantically selected another photo icon and beheld more of the same filth.

After closing down the images, shame and fear slapped me, causing me to tremble and internally conclude, "If Mom comes home and finds this on the computer, she'll just say that it's all *mine* and call me a lesbian!" Unwilling to burn for my brother's sin, I deleted the entire file and emptied the desktop's Recycle Bin. [1]

Still disturbed with the images that branded my mind, I furiously marched to the foot of the stairs and shouted toward the loft, *"I found all your dirty pictures of naked girls and deleted them! That's disgusting! They shouldn't be on the family computer!"* [2]

"You did what?!" my brother roared, storming down the wooden staircase. The teen sprinted past me and over to the computer, sliding into the swivel chair to verify my claim. "No! You deleted all of them! I sell that stuff to the idiots at school! Do you know how long it took to download all of that?! I'm gonna kill you!" [3]

Enraged, my brother tackled me. Unable to run, I grappled with him, but with his height and bodyweight, the senior used his leverage and quickly overpowered me. My sibling straddled my legs and sat on them, rendering their strength useless.

Void of mercy or restraint, my sibling strangled me. I thought to smash my fist into his face, but refused to chance breaking his glasses. When my sibling removed his right hand from my neck to punch me in the head, I unleashed fury on his ribcage, over and over.

Shifting his mount, the senior slipped his knee over my throat to free his hands and catch my swings, forcing both wrists to the tile floor. Defenseless and completely pinned, I nearly blacked out. My brother leaned forward with a daunting sneer as I squirmed in wild-eyed silence, crushed and suffocating. [4]

"*What's going on?!*" our father shouted, grabbing his son by the shoulders and tossing the teen sideways. Stunned by the rescue, I stared at my father as if he were a caped superhero. At no time did I hear the man's approach on the porch or the turn of his noisy key in the lock. As the teen stood to his feet, the man gruffly ordered, "Both of you stay where you are! What happened?"

"*Sandra deleted my homework!*" the teen loudly accused. [5]

Slack-jaw with a gasp, I fiercely rebutted, "*That's a lie! I deleted your pornography, you disgusting pervert! You even admitted that you sell porn to the idiots at school! You'll say anything to get out of trouble!*" [6]

"*That's enough!*" our father shouted, stopping himself and taking a deep breath. "Son, if your homework has been deleted, then I suggest you sit down and start working on it. Sandra, that's what you get for messing with your brother's stuff. Stay away from his things and go to your room. I think you've been punished enough." [7]

Ditch the Girl

"Sandra, I can't take it here anymore. I'm going insane," Mack expressed, reclining on the windshield of his muscle car. "My life is the *definition* of insanity. It's the same every day. Things can't keep going on like this. I want to leave this town and change my life completely."

"Yup. I know *exactly* what you mean," I sighed, relaxing beside him after the worship service to stare at the clouds. "The sooner I graduate, *the better*. I'm gonna leave this town and never look back." [1]

The following Sunday, Mack approached me after worship as I waited for him in the foyer. He excitedly informed, "I can't wait to tell you this. I met someone! Get this. A Pentecostal family was visiting some relatives, and they refused to miss a Sunday service. Since they noticed our UPC sign from the road, they came back to worship with us today before heading home. Their eldest daughter is *so beautiful* and I think she likes me too. I have to see where this'll go. I'm headed to lunch with their family right now, so I won't be able to spend time with you today. She might be the one, Sandra! Wouldn't that be awesome?! They're waiting for me, so I have to leave, but I wanted to let you know where I was so you wouldn't wait up for me. We'll talk later."

Laying on the picnic table outside of the building, I silently concluded, "Wow. Mack must be *desperate* for a wife to be interested in someone like *her*. What do they have in common, anyway? *Age?* It won't work out between them. How could Mack choose that chick over me? We're alike in all the ways that matter. We love Jesus, laugh until it hurts, relax together, and care about each other. What more could a person want? After all the fun he's had with me, he'll grow bored, ditch the girl, and tell me *all about it* later. In two more years, I'll be eighteen and finally graduate. *Then*, we can be together." [2]

That winter, the UPC held a holiday party at a rented venue. Caterers served a delicious meal as our entertainment stepped into view. A cross-dressed comedian presented himself as a stereotypical religious southern woman, walking around to each table in a curled wig and making sassy comments to various individuals. Shocked, I wondered why Dolion used tithe money to hire someone with a comedy act that defied the focal points of Pentecostal beliefs. Although many refused to laugh at the performer's accurate depiction of passive-aggressive catty women, no one ushered him out before he finished his set and ate a plate of food. [3]

Seasonal decorations and the twinkling lights were beautiful, but even a man in a dress couldn't distract me from the agony of sitting alone among clumps of families. I peered over and discovered Mack holding hands with the same young woman he left me for. Although I couldn't hear what was being said, I knew he was formally presenting her to various members of the congregation.

My chest tightened with jealousy and despair. Refusing to draw attention to myself, I discreetly retreated through the glass exit to sit outside of view on the sidewalk. Tears soaked into the fabric of my dress as a change in hue caught my eye. Shades of brilliant tangerine and coral illuminated the sky above the treetops, but even they didn't soothe me. I knew those shooting rays would soon fade into darkness alongside my relationship with Mack. [4]

A breeze brushed past my ears and carried with it a familiar voice, inquiring, "Sandra? Are you *crying*?" Mack had spotted me and walked in my direction. Shame rushed up my neck, causing me to hide my tormented face. Offering his hand, he gently ordered, "Stand up." [5]

"Why are you pretending to care about me?" I bitterly snapped with a quivering lip, rising to my feet. "Isn't your *girlfriend* wondering where you are?" [6]

"Okay, Sandra. We need to talk," Mack announced. "Come on." The young man confidently led me into the parking lot to position himself on the hood of his car. As he patted the space beside him, the sun slowly dipped over the horizon and set his platinum blonde hair ablaze with crimson light. "Sandra, you *are* my friend and our friendship *is* real. I miss talking to you and hanging out. You're the coolest chick I know."

"Then why are you with *her* and not *me*?" I divulged, dreading that I might have just pushed him away forever.

"Sandra, you're still in *high school* and I've been out for a while. You'll find this out for yourself, but there's way more to life than just having fun. Don't get me wrong. You're *super* fun and I hope that never changes, but I want to get away from this hopeless town and have a family of my own. *I want children*, Sandra. I love this woman very much and I want her to be *my wife*. In a few months, we'll be married." The finality of his statement shattered my hardened exterior into a wrenching sob. Mack placed his arm around my shoulders and pulled me close. "Sandra, *please* don't cry. You're like my baby sister. This is *killing* me." [7]

His pity added salt to my wounds. "I'll be fine. Don't worry," I coldly replied, wiping tears away as I embraced the demise of our future. "Thank you for giving me the news yourself instead of letting me hear about it later from somebody else. Also, thank you for your friendship. You certainly deserve to be free and happy. I wish you and your fiancé the very best. Goodbye, Mack." Unable to linger further in his presence, I slid down from his hood and abandoned the young man in the twilight, walking towards the soft glow of the party.

That Sunday, after the morning church service had ended, someone touched both my shoulders. It was Mack's fiancé, whom I had never spoken to before. I fought an eye roll and mild gag reflex as she sat down beside me and whispered, *"Sandra, are you okay? I was told that you were a little upset at our news?"* [8]

Livid at her presumptuous approach, my body tensed as I vividly imagined myself gripping her by the blouse and catapulting her delicate body into the platform's drum set. For Mack's sake, I remained still and casually replied, "Thank you for your concern, but I'm just fine. I wish you both well." [9]

"Okay," she added as she stood up to leave. "I just wanted to check on you." Unable to leave well enough alone, as if speaking to a sickly puppy through a frosty pet shop window, she peered down at my seated frame and patronizingly coached, "Don't worry, Sandra. You'll find *somebody* that will love you." [10]

Launched

～∞～

The school district replaced that dusty trailer Red and I were so fond of. A large metal building with huge roll-up doors stood in its place. Our new weight room smelled of fresh rubber flooring and bore plenty of equipment with room to house it. New machines, weight racks, dumbbells, bumper plates, bars, and padded benches lined the corrugated walls. When I discovered Coach Gather had scheduled the girls' athletic teams to lift several times a week, I couldn't stop grinning.

As the team was weight training, Coach Gather called out, "Sandra, would you come here, please?" Obeying, I carefully set down the stacked dead lift bar I was gripping and walked over to the woman as the boys' head coach stood beside her. "Sandra, I need you to max out on squats as a demonstration. This man doesn't believe that you can lift more than most of his boys." [1]

"Oh. Okay," I replied with a brief shrug, beginning at my last recalled max.

Bearing the loaded bar on my shoulders, I lowered myself as the critic watched me closely, even squatting beside me to ensure proper form. He nudged, "Can you drop lower?"

"No, sir. My thighs are resting on my calves as it is. There's no more space," I ensured. "May I lift now?"

The man nodded, and replied, "*Lift.*" Standing up, he crossed his arms and inquired, "How much do you weigh, if I may ask?"

On my way up to rack the bar, I grunted, "One-hundred and twenty pounds, sir."

I added plates, lifted, and then added more, repeating the process until Coach Gather interjected, "That's enough, Sandra. Do you even know how much you're lifting right now?"

"No ma'am. *It's a mental thing.* I don't add it until I'm finished maxing-out. What is it?" I queried, coming out from under the machine to do the math.

"Don't bother. I kept track. You just lifted *three-hundred and sixty-five pounds*," she boasted, playfully rolling onto her tip-toes. "Well done, young lady."

"What?! *Wow!* Am I allowed to keep going?!" I cheerfully petitioned, springing up and down. "I want to see how much I can do!"

Coach Gather smiled at her frustrated male counterpart and replied, "No, Sandra. I think you've proven my point. We don't want you to blow out your knees. Go ahead and rack those plates, though. I don't want *the boys* to hurt themselves taking all of that off." 2

The following week, the materfamilias scanned my body with narrowed eyes and jabbed, "What have *you* been up to? Why do you want to build muscle like that? Do you want to look *like a boy?* Are you a lesbian now?! Is *that* why you don't have any boyfriends?!"

"What?! *No!* I don't have a boyfriend because you told me I *couldn't* have one! Besides, if I really cared about a guy, I wouldn't date him! Someone has to keep these people safe from you! If you're acting this aggressively while I'm *single*, I'd hate to see what you'd do if I was actually in a relationship," I defended, only to stop myself. "Wow. *Never mind.* You just want to fight. I hate to disappoint you, lady, but I have to catch the school bus." 3

"Don't act so *innocent*. Who knows *what* you've been doing while I'm not watching you? Do you *really* spend all that time at church?" she probed menacingly. "What happens between services?! You could be doing *God-knows-what!* I bet you've slept with all the boys there! You want to stay late after school, too! *Track practice.* Ha! You've probably ****** them all!"

Shaking my head with an eye roll, I calmly replied, "First, you called me *a lesbian*. Now, you're saying that I'm sleeping with *all the boys*. Make up your mind. How do I keep my grades up and do so well in sports if I'm *that* busy having sex with everyone? For your information, I'm *still a virgin* and waiting until I'm married… and with the way things are going around here, fat chance at that happening. It's a small town and no one will want *you* for a mother-in-law, so I'll probably *die* a virgin. As pleasant as this conversation has been, I really need to go."

"Ha! *You're not a virgin*," the materfamilias sneered, blocking the door. "You're just another *whore*… like that woman across the street! She's always driving slow in front of our house while your father is working outside… just waving! *Why does she have to wave to him?!* Why does he have to wave back at her?! I know he's having an affair with her! And don't think I don't know what's going on in here! I see how close you and your father are! Why are you so comfortable with him?! You're probably ******* him, too!" 4

Taking a step toward her, I shouted, "*That's it, *****! Shut your ******* mouth!* I don't even get to *sit* with my father anymore because of you! You're nothing more than a fantastically horrific *psychopath* with a forked tongue! All you ever do is sit on your *** and pick fights! Do you wake up each morning and lie there, contemplating just how far you'll drive your family into madness that day… *or do you just wing it?!* You should be locked up! No family should have to endure your level of crazy!" [5]

With gnashed teeth, the termagant rushed me, shrieking, *"Nobody calls me crazy!"*

My eyes widened as I instinctively dropped to my back in a cat-like manner and pulled my knees to my chest. The raging woman threw her entire bodyweight over my feet, growling at me as I grabbed both of her fists. With my heels firmly placed against her hips, I leg-pressed with fury, launching my vicious assailant airborne and backward. The shocked termagant failed to catch herself and bounced on her pronounced rear-end like a stone skipping across a pond. [6]

Observing her disorientation, I snagged my backpack and fled. Sprinting toward the end of the driveway, I fretted over the retribution that would await me after school. Wondering what she might do, I quickly slid to a stop by the mailbox and replayed the scene in my mind.

Standing alone, my mouth curled upward. *I laughed.* I laughed so hard my knees buckled. "I sure shocked the **** out of *her!* That psycho has no idea what I'm capable of. Man, that felt good," I admitted. "Oh, my gosh! I should challenge that ***** to a fight and sell tickets!" Doubled over in hysterics until the school bus came into view, I wiped my eyes, calmed myself, and concluded, "Nah. She won't try *that* again… not after this morning. Bounce, bounce, bounce!" [7]

What's Your Emergency?

With my father in his recliner and me on the sofa, we peacefully lounged in the living room and watched a televised football game. Snack, beer, and soda commercials made me laugh the first few times I had seen them, but quickly lost their luster as they looped between plays, over and over.

The materfamilias wrathfully trod toward us. Between my father and the television screen, the woman abrasively prodded, "Don't act so innocent over here! I know why you want your chair by the window! It's so that **** across the street can see you get up and know where you are! I'm not stupid!" The man remained silent and stared straight through her. "Are you ignoring me?! I'm your wife! Explain to me why you put your chair by the window if you're not signaling to her!" Not so much as a throat clearing came from her husband. "How come you don't touch me anymore?! You *must* be giving it to somebody else! Look at you! You're ugly and already have gray hair! I'm beautiful and can get any man I want! Why am I over here chasing you?! You should be kissing my feet and begging me to be with you!" At that, my father closed his eyes. "You're not asleep! Why don't you pay attention to me?! You're ******* all the woman at work, aren't you?! Is that why you're so exhausted?! Huh?! You're probably doing all the men, too! That's it, isn't it?! You'd have to be *gay* not to want me! Look at me! I'm older than you and *you're the one* that looks like a dried-up old man!" [1]

Closing in on his face, her verbal diarrhea continued for another forty-five minutes, having nothing new to say that she hadn't abrasively declared hundreds, if not thousands, of times before.

The man suddenly sprang the backrest up from its reclined position and startled me. The termagant stepped back to pose like a heavyweight fighter, but in a fluid motion, he pivoted away from his vicious wife and stepped into the restroom. Unwilling to remain alone with the tyrant, I vacated the sofa and stationed myself in the kitchen to observe from a distance. My father strolled into view and toward the kitchen, made himself a sandwich, and sat at the table beside me, avoiding her completely. [2]

The materfamilias picked up right where she left off in the same venomous tone, and brutally continued, "Yeah! Go make a sandwich, you ******* homo! Why do you need *me* when you have everyone else to ****?! You're so ungrateful! I cook you dinner! I wash your clothes! I raised these brats while you were gone with the navy… and for what?! *To be ignored?!* I don't think so!" As she instigated, the man peacefully finished his food and canned soft drink. Narrowing her eyes, she spitefully added, "It's no wonder you're the way you are! You ignore me the way your mother ignored your father!" [3]

"Shut up! You don't know what you're talking about!" the man angrily protested, pushing back the chair and standing to his feet.

The shrew located a gap in his emotional armor, plunged the blade, and twisted the handle. Smelling blood, she laughed at his wound and pressed, "I blame your mother! No wonder you're all screwed up! It's your *whore-of-a-mother's* fault that your father killed himself!" [4]

"That's a lie! Leave my mother out of this!" the man shouted.

Without hesitation, the termagant's husband slipped his calloused hand around a flimsy souvenir-cup of water that she had compulsively filled and neglected to drink. Skillfully launching the aquatic clutter at his desired target, he rolled the flexible plastic from his fingertips and nailed her fleshy upper-arm, splashing a wave of liquid in theatric splendor over her astonished face. As it trickled to the rug under her feet, the matriarchal ticking-time-bomb peered down at her swiftly bruising appendage in bass-mouthed shock. [5]

"How dare you?!" the woman roared, gnashing her teeth as she reached for one of her dumbbells resting on the ground by the window.

As she cocked back her arm, I stepped directly between them to draw her attention and swiftly warned, "If you don't put that weight down right now, I'll call the police. Don't test me. *Put it down.*" [6]

"You won't call the police," she arrogantly scoffed.

I snatched the receiver from the mounted phone beside me and confirmed, "Yes, I will. Put the weight down. *Now.*"

"You saw what happened! He *hit* me!" the woman gaslighted, insulting my intelligence.

"Yeah… *with a cup of water*… after your disgusting forty-five-minute rant. I'm not waiting anymore. You've had your chance. I'm calling," I informed, dialing the authorities. [7]

Dispatch answered, inquiring, "What's your emergency?"

In the disarming manner of a cheerful flight attendant, I informed, "My name is Sandra Lawson and I'm sixteen years old. Please send the police. My mother has a weight in her hand and intends to kill my father with it. I'm currently standing in between them right now and she is looking right at me. Please hurry."

Dispatch skeptically questioned, "Are you being perfectly serious?"

The materfamilias conveniently barked, *"I don't believe you! You're not really on the phone with the cops!"* [8]

Dispatch instantly added, "I heard her. Good job at staying calm, Sandra. A unit is nearby." Within seconds, a squad car pulled into our gravel driveway.

Behaving like a sweepstakes winner, I chirped, "Dang, you guys are fast! I see them! Thank you! Bye!" After quickly hanging up, I urged, *"Dad! Run!"*

Everything seemed to unfold in slow motion. I sprinted past the woman to the front door, pulling it wide open for the man behind me to flee. He seamlessly pushed the screen door open as I followed him off the porch and scrambled toward the parked cruiser. At once, the termagant locked the doors behind us. [9]

Watching the stoic female officer step past me toward the house, I respectfully warned, "Ma'am, be careful. My mother's inside and she's angry."

The uniformed woman paused and queried, "Is she armed?"

My father interjected, "I have a rifle in the bedroom, but I keep the bullets in a separate location. She not familiar with guns *that I'm aware of*, but you never know."

As she proceeded on her trajectory, her partner inquired, "Are either of you injured?"

"No," I sighed, "but it was a close one."

"Sir, I need to ask you a few questions," the officer informed. "Sandra, would you please stand over there by those trees and wait for me?"

"Yes, sir," I respectfully replied.

In time, the officer joined me to interrogate, "Okay, Sandra. Tell me what happened."

I took a deep breath and quickly divulged, "My dad and I were relaxing in the living room watching a football game when mom stomped over and started yelling at him and accusing him of cheating for about forty-five minutes straight. He needed to pee after ignoring her for so long and got up from his recliner to use the bathroom. I didn't want to be alone with my mom, so I went into the kitchen to watch from there. When my dad came back, instead of going to his chair where she was standing, he made himself a sandwich and sat down at the table to eat. Mom kept yelling a bunch of perverted stuff at him. Then, she dragged my grandma's name into it by calling her a whore and other mean lies. Dad stood up, grabbed a flexi-cup of water from the table and launched it at her, hitting her in the arm. That set Mom off, so she grabbed one of her weights to throw it at him. *That's when I called you guys for help.* I had to act like I was *pretending* to call so she wouldn't throw the weight at me, or worse. When I saw you, I told Dad to run, and we sprinted outside. You were there for the rest."

"Okay. Let's go back to your dad. Come on," he replied, walking me over to my father. "I'm absolutely amazed. In my years of experience, I've *never* heard two stories match *so perfectly* without any time to collaborate. There's no way that the two of you are lying. Your stories were almost verbatim." [10]

As he finished speaking, the female officer returned to stand beside her partner and inquire, "Mr. Lawson, does your wife have a history of mental illness?"

He sighed and dropped his chin, admitting, "Yes. Before we were married, she seemed normal and pleasant, and kept that up for a few months after the wedding. For whatever reason, everything suddenly changed. She started making up extreme stories and began to falsely accuse me of cheating. I suggested we go to marriage counseling. She agreed to it, but we only went *once* because in that first session, the therapist quickly diagnosed her with paranoid schizophrenia and obsessive-compulsive disorder."

My eyes widened at the life-giving information that was revealed. I had diagnosed the materfamilias *accurately*. As my father spoke, I realized that my existence had *never* been the origin of the woman's violent and confusing madness. A trained professional had quickly perceived her mental instability before my conception. I really *didn't* ruin her life. I truly *hadn't* been the source of her daily outbursts and unprovoked rage. More importantly, I *didn't* hallucinate the random beatings. With my brother detached and occupied upstairs, and our father away at work, I often had no witnesses to the violence, but the nightmarish horrors of my upbringing had actually happened. My memories of continuous and unrestrained abuse were trustworthy and solid. Knowing sooner would have been helpful, and it took an inquiry from the *police* to hear the simple truth. Although I couldn't perceive any wisdom from my father hiding her diagnoses from his two children, I clung to a specific reality that comforted me. His wife's contagious misery was not *my fault*. [11]

Exasperated, the uniformed woman continued, "I only asked about your wife's mental history because of her erratic and irrational behavior. At first, she wouldn't open the door or acknowledge me at all, even after I knocked and repeatedly announced myself as a police officer. I had to *pound* on the door before she would unlock and open it. Once she did, she smiled and cheerfully invited me inside, as if she was expecting me over for dinner. When I started asking questions, she gave three completely different stories, none of which made any sense or matched the others. She kept contradicting herself." The female officer paused for a moment and inquired, "Mr. Lawson, has this level of violence from your wife happened before?"

Appearing ashamed, my father made eye-contact with me and diverted his gaze to the grass, replied, "Yes. Many times." [12]

"Mr. Lawson, based on your wife's behavior and mental history, and after listening to both of your matching testimonies, we can legally take your wife into custody," the male officer informed. "It seems she will not pass the psychological evaluation. The point I'm trying to make is… we can keep her away from you and your daughter. What would you like us to do?" [13]

Pausing before speaking, my father lifted his gaze, puffed out his chest, and answered, "I can handle her. We've been married a long time and I don't want to be the one that takes a mother away from her children. Ask the girl." [14]

The male officer lowered his burdened gaze to meet mine as he gently pleaded, "Sandra, you can end this *right now*. Just say the word and your mom will never lay a hand on you or your dad *ever again*. What do you want me to do?"

Surprised at myself, I actually hesitated. Having prayed so many times for that day to come, I wondered if I was willing to carry the crushing burden of her incarceration and involuntary confinement for the rest of my days.

I sighed, puffed out my chest, and replied, "I have less than two years of high school before I graduate. After that, I'm out of this house *for good*. My dad is the one who has to deal with her. If he says *he* can handle it, then *I* can handle it." [15]

The officer furrowed his brow and pursed his lips to conclude, "I understand your decision. I'm not authorized to give you advice, but I will tell you that if anything like this happens again, we won't even ask. We will take her straight into custody." Before walking away, the man added, "You're a tough kid, Sandra. Hang in there." [16]

Odd

$\mathcal{A}$t the beginning of the school year, I registered for a computer class that our instructor didn't bother to attend. When the man was absent repeatedly at the scheduled time, most of his students followed suit. By the second week, I ended up stranded with a very slim younger classmate who hadn't said a word to me. He differed completely from anyone else I had encountered in all my years of school. Along with a large spiked bracelet, the youth donned more jewelry than I owned, had gel-styled hair, wore black pants that barely clung to his hips, and a loud shirt bathed in printed flames.

Lingering together in a silent classroom felt uncharacteristically standoffish, so I broke the tension and chirped, "I'm afraid it's a bit late to worry, *but*... I hope our teacher hasn't become some sort of missing person. What if he's alone and injured somewhere? Shouldn't we look for him?" The boy cautiously peeked over his monitor in silence, so I added, "I don't like the idea that he utterly abandoned us, so I'll just pretend that he's somewhere fighting crime... *cybercrime*."

The youth casually responded, "Well, his identity is safe with me. It's been so long since I've seen him, I already forgot what he looks like." Our eyes locked just before I erupted into hysterics. His countenance softened as he broke into a relaxed chuckle.

"You know what? I *like* you... and since we live in a small town and I don't know you, I'm assuming you're a freshman. Well, allow me to introduce myself. I'm a *junior* and my name is Sandra," I formally divulged. "What's your name?"

"I *know* who you are... and I know that you're a *Christian*," he bluntly replied, "... and yes, I'm a freshman. My name is Zephaniah."

"Well, Zephaniah, it's a pleasure to make your acquaintance. If it's alright with you, I'm gonna move my stuff closer to you so I don't get a crick in my neck. It's not very often when we get to privately chat with someone in class."

Mildly shocked, the freshman murmured, *"Okay..."* Within half an hour, we practiced our foreign accents and laughed so hard the two of us almost drooled. For the next few weeks, it was more of the same until Zephaniah queried, "Sandra, don't you think it's *odd*?"

Pretending to smoke an imaginary cigarette, I raised a sassy eyebrow and wondered aloud in a Russian accent, *"Vhat is odd, dah-ling?"*

"That we're friends!" Zephaniah emphatically clarified. "Don't you think it's odd that we get along so well?"

In my normal speaking voice, I corrected, "No. You're ******* hilarious and I love you."

My colorful language caused him to explode into laughter and squeal, "I love you, too! I *never* know what you're going to say!" He calmed himself and wiped his cheerful eyes. "Seriously, when we first met, I had already heard about how conservative and *virgin* you are." [1]

"There are *levels* of virginity?" I smirked with a confused head tilt.

"In your case, *yes*," the boy playfully jabbed. "Have you ever made-out with anyone? *No*. Has a boy ever seen you naked? *No*. You're a *super virgin*, Sandra. Now, shut up." I huffed in amusement and grinned as he made his point. "In all honesty, I expected judgement from you. Everyone knows you love Jesus and won't party or sleep around. *It's no secret*… and yet… you've never made me feel like a freak or openly judged me. Every other *self-proclaimed* Christian I've encountered has been rude and hateful, either to my face or behind my back. After all this time, I need to know something. *Why are you so nice to me?*" [2]

I stared at the freshman and conveyed, "I already told you. *I love you.* When you look at me, you see who I actually am. When I see you, I see who *you* are… a person brimming with generosity, kindness, intelligence, and *biting* wit. You're one of the funniest people I know. Wait and see. In five minutes, we'll be in stitches over something random. For the record, I'm really sorry that jerks posing as *Christians* have been hateful to you. Jesus didn't teach that, and he bowed up to the people who did… the *Pharisees*. Jesus didn't just save me once, either. He saved my life, over and over. Believe me when I say that I understand where you're coming from. My mother claims to love Jesus… and yet she's a psychotically violent liar who hates seeing anyone happy. I refuse to be like her and I *certainly* never want to hurt *you*. I'm very serious when I say that I love you." [3]

"But I'm *gay*, Sandra… and you're a Christian," my friend rebutted. "You don't care?"

"Don't get me wrong. I'm not in agreement with a homosexual lifestyle, nor am I in agreement with lying, sleeping around, or alcoholism. Sin is sin, and we all need forgiveness. I side with Jesus and what He actually preached, even though I swear like a sailor and *might* have some anger issues."

"I remember your stories about schoolyard fights," he cheerfully added with a nod.

"*Exactly,*" I confirmed. "Listen. I'm not trying to justify violence or my crude mouth. What I *am* saying is that I'm not perfect. I struggle, too. People who serve Jesus are a work-in-progress until the day they die. He taught everyone to love Him *and* their neighbor. If I say I love Jesus and know how much I need Him… how could I also believe the ugly lie that I'm better than you? *I'm not.* Jesus said that *no one* is good. He came for the sick, like *me*. I'm a sinner that needs a Savior. Some people's sins are easier to spot than others. Truth be told, I'm far more comfortable in your sweet presence than wading in the murky shallows of lukewarm Christianity. *We're friends…* and if I can ever help you, I will." [4]

Zephaniah wiped away hot tears from his face and divulged, "I've been rejected by *everyone…* my family, my friends… *and all of these ******* rednecks!* But you're different. I believe you when you say that you love me." At that, he slumped forward with his hands over his face and sobbed. [5]

I swiftly approached the freshman, dropped to my knees, and pulled his gaunt frame in for a long embrace. [6]

"I really *do* love you," I repeated, backing up a bit. "Believe it or not, Jesus loves you, too… even more than I do. If it weren't for Him, I'd be *dead*. Because of the abuse at home, I've contemplated suicide several times, but Jesus always stopped me. He gave me *hope*. Our situations won't always be like this. We're gonna grow up, and we won't always feel so… *trapped*." [7]

Zephaniah sat up, wiped his nose, and concluded, "You know, Sandra, you're pretty cool… *for a Christian.*" His side glance and endearing smirk sparked a laughing-fit that lasted until the bell.

Goals

Stepping into my room as I completed my homework, my father instructed, "Have a seat with me in the kitchen."

Rarely having private conversations with the man, I followed behind him and wondered aloud, "Did someone die? Did I do something wrong? Am I in trouble?"

Sitting at the head of the table while motioning for me to join him, he inquired, "Did you do something wrong?"

"No, but that's never mattered in *this* house," I quipped, pulling out a chair for myself. "If I'm not in trouble, what *do* you want to talk about?"

"First, I feel that you're spending too much time at church. It's a distraction. I think you need to pull away from that and put all of your efforts towards athletics and your schoolwork," the man revealed, clasping his hands together as if we were in a boardroom. "You need to focus on your future."

"By going to church and learning about Jesus, *I am* focusing on my future. Eternity is a long time," I rebutted. "What brought this on? Did Mom put you up to this? Are my grades suffering? Am I not good enough at sports? Is that what this is all about?" [1]

"No. You make good grades and you're *very* good at sports," he admitted.

"If that's the case, how is going to church a distraction?" I posed. "I'm more distracted *here*, listening to you and Mom fight every day and…" [2]

"Never mind. You can keep going to church. Let's move on," he interrupted, proceeding with his agenda. "You're quickly approaching adulthood and your junior year is a crucial time in which you need to be deciding about your future and taking *purposeful steps* to achieve your goals. Before you can achieve *any* goal, you have to set one. This brings me to my first question. What career path are you intending to embark on?"

With enthusiasm, I responded, "I want to major in English and become a writer. It's been my dream since the third grade and I'm good at it. I was *born* to do it. My English teachers believe in me and I've been improving my skills. I want to write a book filled with a collection of short stories. I never told you about this, but during my freshman year, we wrote short-stories as an assignment and I read mine aloud in class.

My English teacher *loved it* and a classmate requested for me to write a new story each week to read aloud on Fridays. So, *I did*. I've been told I have *a gift* and…"

"You can't be a writer, Sandra. No one cares about *anything* you have to say," the man coldly interjected, shattering me as I remained motionless. "Most best-selling books are written by people who are already famous for something else. Other successful writers already know the right people. You have *neither* going for you and you won't make any money. A very small percentage of writers truly succeed. All you will do is struggle." [3]

"Wow. This conversation is turning out to be a terrible experience," I deadpanned.

Ignoring me, my father prodded, "What *else* have you considered?"

"Well, I'm very passionate about science, biology, and the ocean. Since you don't want me to major in English, I'll just study ocean science and become a marine biologist," I said proudly.

"In Texas, everyone and their *grandmother* wants to be a marine biologist," he sliced, shaking his head. "You won't stand out unless you gain some very large sponsors or star in a television program… which is rare."

"Fine," I deadpanned once more. "Since my interests mean nothing to you, and what I actually want to do with my life is doomed to failure before I even begin, why don't you just tell me what *you* want me to do and I'll just mindlessly follow that."

As though my words were unintelligible, my father continued, "What about engineering? You're good at math and science, and engineers make *a lot* of money."

Recalling the hours my sibling and I had spent on the floor with his plastic connecting blocks, I queried, "What kind of engineers build structures?"

"A *civil* engineer builds bridges, roads, and buildings. You should do that," he urged. "If you're considering applying for a military scholarship to pay for your education, engineering will cause them to favor *you* above other applicants. No matter what the economy is doing, civil engineers are *always* needed."

"Fine. I'll just grab a dictionary, look up civil engineering, get a degree, build things, and make enough money to meet all of your expectations. After all, that's what my life's all about, *right*… making you look good? I'm impressed, Dad. It only took thirty minutes for you to change the course of my entire future. I mean, why should I start thinking for myself now? I'm so glad you've planned out the course of my existence, so I don't have to worry," I dryly conceded, staring at his blindly satisfied face. Nothing I conveyed seemed to penetrate his understanding. Unable to remain seated without embarrassing myself further with tears, I stoically stood to conclude, "Excuse me while I mourn the demise of my dreams." [4]

Indifference

While traveling with my peers to a school-sponsored event, the bus driver paused our trip so we could purchase something to eat and enjoy a stretching break. Nestled amid female classmates, I sat down at a table to enjoy my meal.

"Hey, Sandra!" Julio called out from behind me, catching me off-guard.

Confused as to why the flippant student had desired my attention outside of class, I twisted my body and peered backward to behold a table full of grinning teenage boys. Suspicious of the motives behind Julio's smile, I pretended to be indifferent and returned my attention to the sandwich in my hands, groaning, "I'm trying to eat. What do you want?"

"Do you do *favors*?" the teenager inquired, hushing the giggling juveniles that surrounded him.

"What are you talking about?" I snipped, taking a bite, and proceeding with my mouth full of food. "I do your *homework*. What else do you want from me?" [1]

As the snickering increased, several girls at my table grew noticeably irritated and rolled their eyes. One openly rebuked, "Y'all are gross. Leave Sandra alone. She doesn't even know what y'all are talking about."

"Sandra. *Seriously*. Look at me," the boy ordered, causing me to sigh and turn back once more. "I mean *favors*… like this…" Julio opened his mouth and shifted his entire head forward and backward. [2]

"Okay, guys. Stop it," another girl pleaded. "Sandra's not like that. She doesn't understand what you're doing, but *I do*. Leave her alone." [3]

I winced and shook my head, mentioning, "You shouldn't do that, Julio. You look like a chicken."

As several boys broke out into hysterical laughter, Red leaned toward the youth and stated, "That's enough, Julio. Leave her alone." [4]

Pleasantly shocked, Julio instantly switched his focus to Red and pulled him into a razzing headlock, mocking, "Are you *protecting* her?! Are you *in love*?!" [5]

As Valentine's Day approached, I considered Julio. The frustration was overwhelming, having suffered from intrusive thoughts and a lasting crush since middle school. Against all logic, considering the teen's womanizing and questionable morals, I couldn't shake the one-sided attachment. Encouraged by Julio's unsolicited attention before our peers, I took action by baking heart-shaped cookies from scratch to be bagged and labeled with a handmade card. [6]

The following day, I opened Julio's locker, placed the gift inside and jetted to chemistry class before the tardy bell.

A concerned student popped her head into my classroom, inquiring, "Sandra, did you put some cookies in Julio's locker?"

"Yeah," I replied with mild aggression. "There shouldn't be any question where they came from. I left a card with my name on it. *Why?*"

"Well, Julio is telling people that the cookies are from a *stalker*," she divulged. "Everyone knows they're from *you*. I figured you should know what he's saying." [7]

I shook my head and replied, "Thanks for letting me know. For the record, Julio is an idiot and just destroyed his most beneficial relationship. I'm not doing his homework anymore. Spread *that* rumor." [8]

Later that day, Julio found me in an isolated branch of the hallway and stopped directly in my path. Speaking as I progressed, he admitted, "I shouldn't have called you a stalker. It was wrong and I'm sorry, Sandra. Please forgive me." [9]

"Oh, I see. You embarrass me publicly and apologize in private, huh? *What a coward*," I replied, smoothly maneuvering my body around his presence with the authentic indifference I had desired for years. As I continued my pace beyond his shocked stance, I projected my voice and sardonically added, "You should start studying, Julio. You're on your own from now on." [10]

Peacock

~~~~

The rest of the girls left the locker room as Alice waited for me to finish dressing out for track practice. Still wearing her regular clothing, she sat on the bench beside my athletic bag and inquired, "How do you do it?"

"How do I do *what*?" I wondered aloud through my track jersey, having already pulled it over my head. "What are you talking about?"

Staring at me in absolute transparency as I finished up, she continued, "How do you *not care* about what people think about you? I'm *obsessed* with it. I'm constantly afraid of what people are thinking or saying about me. I'm riddled with anxiety over it all the time. It's like I'm not in control… like I'm losing it or something. I don't want to go *crazy* like my…" Alice sobbed. [1]

"*Whoa.* Hey. Let's get some outside perspective here," I counseled, sitting beside her. "You're a cheerleader, the most popular girl in school, and *so beautiful* that you can stop traffic. Don't you realize that? Don't you *know* who you are? Everybody loves you."

"Thank you, Sandra, but you're wrong. Everyone does *not* love me," the junior corrected, hiding her face in her hands. "I wake up thinking about what others want me to *wear* or *do*." Alice gazed up at the ceiling, shaking her head as tears streamed down her neck. "I realized this morning that, after all this time, I really *don't* know who I am. I don't have my own opinions or thoughts on anything. *I hate myself*… and I don't even know why I feel this way or how to change it." Seeing an uncomfortable drip, I snagged a paper towel and handed it to her. "*Thanks.* I watched you blaze through the hall today with your pink pleather pants, platform shoes, and that contagious laugh… and I realized that you're *nothing* like the rest of us. We *conform*. We worry about *being cool* and having the right labels on our clothes. You walk in like a peacock… totally different… and you own it."

Blown away by her words, I murmured, *"Alice…"*

"No. I have to say this," she gently interrupted, grabbing my hand. "I'm so sorry for everything I've done to you. For years, I've tried to smother you, hoping that you'd somehow stop shining… that you'd be *afraid* like the rest of us. I've never been so thankful for failing in my entire life." [2]

"Hey. It's cool. Stop feeling bad about it," I urged. [3]

Alice gnashed her teeth and shouted, *"No, Sandra! Don't ever let anyone treat you the way I did!"* Calming herself, she continued, "It *amazes* me that you stuck around all this time, but I'm so glad you did. If I didn't have your consistent friendship, I'd be *lost*. You don't care what people think, say, or do. You just *are*. I love that about you. I don't know if we'll stay friends or keep up with each other after high school, but you've *changed* me. I love you."

"I love you, too. *Wow*. Your words mean a lot. Thank you," I huffed in amazement, pulling her in close. "Originally, you asked me about how I do it. Well, just so you know, I can't take credit for the positive changes that you've seen in me. Miraculous things have happened in my life that I could *never* deserve. Jesus has shown me that He really *sees* me, that I have value, and that I can grow and be a better person through *Him*. When I see something in myself that I don't like, I pray and ask Jesus for help to change it." [4]

Trembling, Alice whispered, "Sandra, *I'm pregnant…* and I don't think *Jesus* will fix that."

"First, if no one has told you yet, *congratulations*. I have no doubt your child will be gorgeous. Second, you're right. Jesus probably won't take the baby, but He *can* help you be a really good mom… if you let Him," I added with a smile. "*Wait*. You're not going through this whole thing *all by yourself*, are you? Who's the father? He's just as responsible and should help you financially. Does he go to school with us?" [5]

"I don't want him involved and I'm not telling *anyone* his name, not even *you*," she clarified. "I have to get out of here. This town is *way* too small and I don't need those hypocrites staring at me and talking **** behind my back with their judging eyes. I'm quitting school and moving away. Someone encouraged me to kill it, but I won't. I know the other girls have had abortions, but I just *can't*. I love the baby already. I'm going to raise it, but I'm so scared. I have no idea what I'm doing." [6]

Tearfully, I cupped my hands over her cheeks and declared, "Alice, I am *so* proud of you." [7]

"What?!" my friend snapped, pulling away from me. "Proud?! What are you?! How can you be so damn nice to me?! You don't sleep around! You have every right to judge me! I was hateful to you and I deserve to be punished! Why don't you?!" [8]

"Judge you? For *what*… choosing to face the music and bravely raise a baby by yourself? That's admirable. *Look at you*. Instead of listening to corrupt voices telling you to take the easy way out, you chose the hard path… the *right* path. I don't even want to know who told you to kill it." I held her hand and gripped it tightly. "I think you're right, Alice. You should get out of this town *as fast as you can*. Find a good woman that can counsel you and knows how to raise healthy babies, but remember that this is *your* child. If a person isn't actually *helping* you and just wants to make mean comments, then their opinion doesn't matter and you need to get away from them." She slowly nodded and breathed a little easier. "You'll be a *great* mom, Alice. You already love your baby. It doesn't come naturally for all women, but *we're not our mothers*. I'm preaching to myself when I say this, but just because we came from those women doesn't mean that we have to share their fate. *You can do this…* and Jesus can help. Let's pray." [9]

Furrowing her brow, she frantically questioned, "Right now? Here?!"

I grabbed her other hand and prayed, "Jesus, please help Alice get away from the people who would only hurt her and the baby. Keep my friend from bad influences and show her what she needs to do to be a good mom. Protect her baby and keep it healthy and strong. Bless my friend for her bravery and for choosing *life*. Help her to remember You when things get dark and scary. Remind her that she's *not* alone. Thank you, Jesus. Amen." [10]

Armageddon

A hunched Zephaniah dragged himself into our classroom and collapsed into a chair, beginning to sob. I kneeled down by his side with a tissue in hand and queried, "Hey, buddy. What's going on? What's wrong?"

"Sandra, I've been asked to prom by five different girls. *Five*. The first was crying and invited me because she didn't want to go to prom alone. Wanting to be a good friend, I agreed to be her date and spent all of my money on a suit. In case you haven't figured it out, *I'm not rich*. The next day, she dropped me because her *crush* invited her!"

"What?!" I exclaimed as heat traveled up my neck. "That's messed up!"

"I know! Right?! When I told one of my other friends, she got mad and said that *she* would take me. The story just keeps repeating. Each one of them went belly-up, one right after the other, as soon as a straight guy asked them to prom. I thought those girls were my friends, but I am just their emotional safety net. I…" [1]

"*That's it*," I gruffly interrupted. "You're coming to prom with *me*." [2]

Zephaniah's eyes grew wide as he wondered aloud, "Sandra? Are you *serious*? I mean, are you *sure*? You could have any guy you want."

I laughed at his flattering perception and quipped, "Well, Zephaniah… *you're* the guy I want."

The teenager clasped his hands together and cheered, "*Yay!* We're going to have so much fun! Okay. *Let's talk*. What color dress are you wearing?"

"Black with *silver glitter*," I divulged with a subtle shimmy.

"No way!" he squeaked. "My suit is black! This is perfect!" [3]

"I have your back… and don't worry about me ditching you, either. Even *if* someone else asks my virgin *** to prom, I'll just tell them *I'm already taken*."

"*E-e-e-e-e-e-e!*" He shrieked with excitement. "I love you, Sandra!"

I mimed the puff of a cigarette and replied in a Russian accent, *"Dah, dah-ling."*

The following week, Zephaniah seemed closed-off and unnerved when he stepped into the room, causing me to boast a curious brow.

"Okay. I'll tell you what's going on, Sandra, but don't get mad," he warned, which only alerted me to a more aggressive form of active listening. "Some guys from school tried to beat me up yesterday and I don't know what to do." [4]

Rage swelled within me as I hissed to myself, *"Bullies."* Popping every knuckle in my hands and neck, I inquired through my teeth, "Zephaniah… sweetheart… what are their names?"

"No, Sandra," he cautioned. "These aren't little *gangsta-wanna-be* elementary kids that you can just knock-out in some playground fight. These are really bad guys. They came with baseball bats this time, but I got away using *this*…" Zephaniah popped a razor blade out from the roof of his mouth, causing my jaw to drop as I wondered how he managed to speak or keep from swallowing it. "I know it looks *extreme*, but this wasn't the first time they've jumped me. I'm defending myself the best way that I know how, but I'm always outnumbered and I can't outrun their trucks." The teenager buried his face in his ring-filled hands as I wrapped his emaciated body in my arms. [5]

I gently pulled back to convey, "Cherished friend, *look at me.* I adore you and I know everyone in this school. You may not be aware of this, but I'm one of the strongest students here, and that includes the boys. I can handle *any* of these ******* cowards. If you don't tell me who's doing this to you, they'll only continue. Adults won't help you in this ******* redneck town. If you're forced to use your blade to protect yourself, these people won't care that you were ganged-up on. I've learned the hard way that this town is not fair when it comes to outsiders, nor do they care about the monsters that they breed. My love, give me the opportunity to speak to these jerks in a way they'll understand. *Tell me their names.*" [6]

"I'm afraid to," he admitted. "I just don't want things to get *worse.*"

"You've been doing it your way and things have already gotten worse. Look at your current situation. You carry *a razor in your mouth.* I don't know how you've been eating with that thing in there," I reasoned. "Let's try it *my* way. I need for you to trust me and give me the name of their leader. You won't have to do anything else. Just one name."

Using his shirt to dry his face, Zephaniah relented and whispered, *"Buzz."*

When the bell sounded, I stepped out of the classroom and scanned the swarming hall for my target. Spotting the identified teen's lanky frame, I shouted, *"Buzz Plaguy!"* Students turned toward me with wide eyes and parted, distancing themselves from my trajectory. I grabbed the unsuspecting sophomore by his pearl-snap shirt and lifted him to his toes, loudly slamming his tense body into the nearby lockers. His closest friends scattered like vermin, leaving the knave to dangle helplessly in my grasp. Although taller than me, he was the wiry type, making the cowboy easier to lift than I had originally assessed. With unwavering clarity, I spoke slowly for all to hear, interrogating,

"So… you think it's fun to gang-up on a little guy? Huh? You like jumping kids when they're alone, trying to walk home from school? You enjoy doing that? Is that your idea of fun?" [7]

"I've never jumped anyone!" the boy snapped, attempting to bow-up. [8]

Pinning him in place with my right hand, I slammed my free palm on the locker beside his head, and shouted, *"Liar!"* Stepping forward and leaning into his vulnerable body, I growled, *"Stop wasting my time.* You know *exactly* what I'm talking about. If you or your ******* friends touch a hair on his head again, I will permanently change the octave in which you speak. Do you understand me?! Show me you understand!" Buzz bobbed his head vigorously. "If you want to pick on someone, pick on *me*. If you little pansies like using baseball bats on a defenseless guy, then you shouldn't have a problem fighting a *girl*… right? *Well, c'mon, Buzz! Fight me, you coward!"* The sweaty young man shook his head, refusing. "I'm only warning you *once*. For your own safety and the safety of your pathetic crew, remember my words. If you plan to come against *me*, you'd better arm yourselves with a hell of a lot more than baseball bats. You can feel how strong I am, can't you? *This is nothing.* You have no idea what I'm capable of. So… are you done picking on my friend?" [9]

"Y-yes, ma'am," he murmured.

"That's a good boy," I encouraged. "You're smarter than you look. Now… use those quivering lips of yours to tell your redneck gang to lay-off… *or I will rain down on you like your own personal Armageddon.* If anyone hurts my friend again, I won't investigate or try to figure out who did it. I'm just coming after *you*. So, spread the word. Leave… him… alone." [10]

I released the bigot and straightened his crumpled shirt. While walking away, I discovered coaches, teachers, and youthful onlookers that seemed to be frozen in time. All at once, they simultaneously turned a blind eye and proceeded on their original course, as if justice had rightly been served. [11]

Days later, as Zephaniah and I hustled to the car to embark on our glamourous prom adventure, the materfamilias chased us outside and spitefully shouted, "Sandra! Don't act like a boy!" [12]

Once inside the car, I stared at the woman and offered a finger of my choosing for her to behold. To my amusement, the materfamilias gasped in horror as we pulled away.

My date laughed and proudly added, *"Yeah!* **** *that* *****! Listen, Sandra. You're young, you're beautiful, and the night is ours! Let's eat some pizza!"* [13]

Gallivanting in our elegance, we pulled up to a popular Americanized Italian buffet, scarfed all the delicious pizza we could eat, and played arcade games until each finger cramped. Using our combined stash of points, we shopped for prizes and purchased two plush sea lions in our favorite colors.

At the same venue as the year prior, Zephaniah and I enjoyed a new arrangement of elaborate decorations. We enthusiastically posed ourselves for photos, ate all the hors d'oeuvres and dessert we could fit on our plates, and danced until our feet ached.

Thrilled to spot the same DJ as before, I forgot the pain, cascaded over the dancefloor with a remember-me grin, and confidently requested, *"Salsa."*

"Yes, ma'am!" he replied with a smirk.

Lighting dimmed. The altered mood complimented the Latin rhythm pouring from every speaker that alerted my peers. With a quick hop over his station, my saucy partner placed his hand on my waist and led me into position. One smooth spin was all that it took for the students to back away and safely observe. Polished Oxfords led my stilettos into a full exhibition that spanned over the entire floor. The song ended in a stark silence that was shattered by an eruption of applause, inspiring a bow.

Out of breath, I touched my partner's arm and whispered, *"Thank you, again. See you next year."*

Back at the table, Zephaniah grinned and pressed his hand over mine to confess, "Sandra, I've never had this much fun in my entire life… and *****, girl! You can dance!"*

Amin

My brother was wrapping up his freshmen year of college as I completed my junior year of high school. When Summer break returned, it forced my sibling to haul back his belongings and some new ideas.

"Sandra, why don't you come work with me at the scout camp this summer?" the young man suggested, terrifying me with what appeared to be genuine thoughtfulness. "It's not much, but the food is decent and they'll pay you. Plus, you get to live there."

Before I hoped, I reasoned aloud, "That sounds amazing, but there's no way Mom would ever let me stay anywhere that long. The woman didn't even want me to go camping with you and Dad. *Remember?*"

"Let *me* worry about Mom," he assured, "but I don't want to talk to her about it if you don't want to go. Are you in?"

Believing that my brother could convince his mother of anything, I replied, "Sign me up." [1]

Armed with a sleeping bag and some personal items, I ventured to the secluded scout acreage and taught a merit badge class on a topic I knew absolutely nothing about. At night, I enjoyed a cot opposite a tent mate, another girl who shared residence with me. It was a challenge for me to trust co-workers and wildlife not to harm me at night, but if we slept with the flaps rolled up, we'd sometimes catch a cooling breeze. I chose the breeze.

Cold water from the shower head was the quickest way to become comfortable, especially during early mornings and late nights when no one else was around or waiting. I didn't trust many females and found very little to discuss with the handful that were employed there.

Air conditioning was available in the staff lounge, which provided us with card tables, couches, a television, a beloved VHS player, and just enough space to the play ping-pong and pool.

When I stepped inside the lounge on the first evening at camp, the activity amazed me. Unwilling to sit too close to strangers, I stood near the pool table and watched a college-aged counselor run the entire round, sinking shot after shot. It was *magnificent*.

The pool-shark noticed me, paused his break, and queried, "You're *Sandra*, right?"

Every counselor dropped what they were doing and turned to face me as if I were some alien visiting their humid planet, comprising olive shorts, testosterone, and sweat stains. Ignoring the awkward behavior of those around me, I smiled with a slight nod and casually confirmed, "That's right."

After peering around, he made a bewildered face and lightheartedly chided, "Okay, guys. *Stop staring*. You've all seen a girl before." At once, they went back to their previous activities. "I know your brother, but you two don't look much alike. *I'm sorry*. How rude of me. Please allow me to introduce myself. I'm Amin. *Give me one moment*." The fellow lowered his torso and aimed the cue stick. "Eight ball, corner pocket." The white orb tapped its black counterpart with a nudge of English to plunk it neatly into the targeted hole. His opposition groaned, finding a place on the wall to lean while handing their cue stick to the next victim. "You seem genuinely interested in the game. If you want, we can play teams. Do you want to join in?" The next player began to re-rack the colorful spheres in preparation.

"Maybe tomorrow. I *do* love the game and know the rules, but it's been a while," I admitted. "My uncle showed me the basics when I was ten, but I haven't played since."

"Sounds like it's time to get some practice in," he urged. "If you'd like, I can show you some techniques." Leaning forward, Amin jokingly whispered, *"I rarely offer my services, so you should feel special."*

"Oh, *I do*…" I politely bantered, "…and I would enjoy that. Thank you." Pausing for a moment, I observed Amin as he effortlessly banked the cue ball to accomplish a series of seemingly impossible shots. "Just so you know, I'm a navy brat and have made friends with people from all over the world, but you have an accent that I can't quite place. Where are you originally from?"

"*Eight ball, corner pocket,*" the young man confidently announced. With a wicked back-spin, the cue ball flicked the eight into its predicted destination and jerked to a sudden stop. Vulgarities spewed from the opposing team, inspiring a grin to sweep across my face as I shook my head in amusement. "That's game, boys. *I'm out*. You guys play." Handing the stick to the next in line, he continued, "My parents are from Pakistan, but I grew up in the UAE and attend university here in the United States."

After the official first week of camp, Amin and I took a break from the younger staff members to visit a local pool hall where he nonchalantly inquired, "So, Sandra… do you enjoy teaching the scouts their astronomy merit badge skills?" I smirked as my friend dropped the last stray ball into the rack, rolling the entire collection forward and backward for a tight formation. Right as he gently removed the triangular piece of carved wood, I got low on the table and shattered the familiar cluster, ignoring his probing question until I eventually missed a shot. "Sandra! Why are you just smiling and staying quiet?! I'm asking you a serious question! Do you enjoy teaching it?!"

"Oh! *Ha!* I thought you were trying to distract me by making me laugh!" Cracking up, I positioned myself on a nearby bar stool and sipped my cola through a straw to watch Amin run the table for the win. "Well, it's hardly teaching since I can't convey to the scouts what I don't know. I have no idea what I'm doing, have never been a scout, and haven't been trained. *I'm* the only one learning something and it isn't good. Regardless of the scout oath and law, those rotten mama's-boys are mouthy, spiteful, and wretched creatures. They understood way more about what was required of them than I did. Since I felt bad for not being able to teach them astronomy, they manipulated my ignorant *** into signing off on their *unmerited* merit badges. Another instructor corrected me earlier today because he overheard them making fun of me. Now, I know. If they don't know the material and can't prove that they do, don't sign their merit badge cards." [2]

"*Sandra… no-o-o-o…*" Amin groaned. "Those little con-artists! I can't believe you signed their cards!" Shaking his head, the young man watched as I hopelessly shrugged at my inexperience. "Well, I think I have a solution. If teaching astronomy doesn't suit you, what are your thoughts on working for *me*?"

"What?!" I questioned with a heavy lean in his direction. "You want me to work with you in the Trading Post?! That's an *option?!* Are you kidding me?! Uh… what I mean to say is… *yes, Amin. I accept.*"

As director of the Trading Post, Amin pulled one influential string and shifted me from being an under-informed scout-sitter to someone comfortably working behind a counter. The following day, he introduced me to his staff, instructed how to operate a cash register, and sold a plethora of merit badge materials, scouting merchandise, and tasty treats inside of a ventilated building with box fans.

"So… *Sandra*… are you happier here with us?" my boss inquired with a smirk.

"Amin…" I began, "…this is one of the coolest things anyone has ever done for me. *Thank you.* This job is *fantastic*."

After three weeks at camp, I ventured to the main office to collect an envelope that unveiled a smile no one could crush. Immediately scurrying to my tent, I retrieved my disposable camera and requested of a passing counselor, "Would you please take a photo of me and my first paycheck?"

"*Ok-a-a-ay…*" he awkwardly replied. "Sandra? What the heck? Are you actually tearing up? I don't understand how you're so damn happy. This job sucks, it's hot as hell, and we make next to nothing!" [3]

"Let me help you wrap your mind around my gratitude. Shoveling elephant **** for *free* would be just as rewarding as long as my mother was nowhere around. In this place, I don't have to hear her voice and I don't have to see her face. I don't *ever* want to go back. If I had it my way, I'd stay here permanently. Believe me. You have no idea what I've escaped, and they're *paying* me to be away from her." [4]

"Alright, alright… I get it," he remarked, winding the camera before bringing it to his face.

That evening, Amin and I sat outside to have a private conversation. My friend listened intently as I spilled about the materfamilias and the things endured at her hand, eventually concluding, "Well, I've been dominating the entire conversation. *Sorry about that*. Let's talk about *you*. What was it like for *you* growing up?"

"Well, *not to compare*, but my childhood wasn't a bed of roses either," Amin confided. "I don't want to speak ill of my father. Let's just say I used to be bitter towards the man over how he raised me. Later, after moving out and being away from him for a while, I realized my father couldn't offer what he had never received. Once I understood *why* he was so cold with me, I stopped seeing him as the enemy. *I'll give you an example*. When my father was just a boy in Kashmir, he stumbled upon a place filled with mutilated dead bodies. That was the tamest story he could share and confessed that he saw far worse many times over. How could the evils of humanity not harden his heart? It shaped the way he viewed the world. *You see?* My father wasn't an *evil* man that just wanted to torment me. I don't think he meant to be so harsh. I'm no psychologist, but I think he became hardened by his surroundings in order to *survive* them and then kept himself emotionally distant. I eventually forgave my father and let go of all the hurt. When I did, I felt… *better*. I don't know. Everybody's different. Hopefully, one day, you'll forgive your mother, too. She must have had a lot of bad experiences. You know? I mean, no one becomes *that* calloused overnight." [5]

I sighed and dropped my shoulders, conveying, "I understand what you're saying, but my experiences aren't distant memories. My mother is *actively* trying to destroy me and I have to go right back to her after camp is over. Going through scarring experiences shouldn't be an excuse to become a grown adult that fabricates disgusting lies, beats their child, and keeps them isolated. The woman *is* evil… and I refuse to sugarcoat her crimes against our family." [6]

"No one is asking you to," he sweetly replied.

"*I don't want to go back to her*," I sobbed, angry at myself for becoming vulnerable. "I'm already failing at trying not to hate her, but *forgiving* her sounds impossible. I don't want to become hardened and calloused. I don't want to be like her at all. That's why I need *Jesus* so much. He helps me, even in sending me people like *you*… a *real* friend that talks about *real* things, but you won't be there when camp is over. Jesus will be my *only* friend in that house. Without Him, I wouldn't survive." ⁷

Amin murmured, *"I'm not supposed to do this, but…"*

Pulling me directly to his chest, he wrapped his arms around my trembling body and planted a gentle kiss on my forehead as I lingered there and wept. Although he was a devout Muslim, the young man continued to hold me as he softly explained how *compelled* he felt to shatter a major rule of Islam. Except for blood relatives, an Islamic man is to never have physical contact, not even a handshake, with a woman that isn't his wife. ⁸

"Dang! I didn't know hugs were so *scandalous*… and at night, too," I lightheartedly added. "I won't tell your dad if you don't tell my mom."

"It'll be our little secret," he whispered with a smile.

Coach Gather

"*Man*, I missed volleyball!" I cheerfully commented to a fellow senior. "This will be our best season yet! The last of those evil ****** finally graduated! Woo-hoo!"

"*Lawson!* Watch your language!" Coach Gather shouted from across the court. "Fifty push-ups per swear word this year. You'd better drop and get started." [1]

Obeying, I knocked out my set, stood back up, and commented, "You know, this isn't a bad idea, coach! My foul language could help get me ready for army ROTC next year in college! *Ha!* With my mouth, I'll be able to do push-ups *all day!*" [2]

"What?! Did I hear you right?! Are you joining the *army* next year?!" a teammate inquired.

"Not *exactly*," I corrected. "The college awarded me a full army ROTC scholarship to study civil engineering with them. I'll be going to school for *free* and get paid a monthly stipend to train at the same time! According to this special contract, if I finish the program within five years, I'll graduate as a butter-bars second lieutenant in the United States army. Check this out. If I find out within that *first year* that I don't want to be an engineer anymore or even a soldier, I can walk away with no repercussions. If I stay *beyond* that first year, and *then* quit, I have to either pay it all back or enlist in the army. That's fine with me! Being shot at it is *way* better than being home. At least the people trying to kill me will be strangers and not family members. It won't be personal. This scholarship is my ticket out of that house." [3]

"*Lawson!* Stop talking and do your drills!" Coach Gather barked with a smirk.

"Yes, ma'am," I replied, staying low while peppering.

Another varsity teammate laughed and commented, "You look dumb, squatting down like that."

"Well, I dig up those spikes, don't I?" I rebutted. "Wouldn't you rather *look dumb* while saving a ball than look pretty as it hits the floor in front of you? *This* is ready position."

"Whatever. You sound just like the coach. What a teacher's pet," another senior huffed. "I'm surprised that woman doesn't just go ahead and hit you with a rolled-up newspaper."

During a spiking drill, I was at the front of the line beside Coach Gather when she playfully growled, "Don't stand *there*." Yanking my arm towards her, she continued, "Start the line *here*."

A lower-classman approached me later and whispered, *"Why do you let Coach Gather do that to you? If she did that to me, I'd tell her to **** off."* [4]

"Nah. Coach knows what she's doing," I defended. "Seriously, don't worry about it. It doesn't bother me. *I've been hit harder.* Coach Gather has *nothing* on my mom." Before the teen scurried back to her drill, I added, *"Hey.* Thanks for caring enough about me to talk about it. That was pretty cool." The girl just offered a gentle smile and went her way.

During a home game, a spiked volleyball shanked sideways from the arms of my teammate, but provided just enough height for me to gauge the arch of descent toward the spectators and shouted, *"Got it!"*

"Watch out! Here she comes!" an adult cheerfully warned, scooting away quickly.

The dense crowd of parents and students parted for me to leap onto the bleachers and pop the stray ball backwards toward our side of the court. Shocked by the entire display, my teammates had frozen completely still and allowed the ball to hit center court, right in their midst.

"What's going on?! Sandra's over there killing herself in the bleachers and you're all just standing there!" Coach shouted, radiating crimson with arms raised.

Looking back towards the crowd as I stepped from their company, I quipped, "Well, it was worth a shot. Sorry about that, guys. I really hope no one was hurt."

"Nah! We're fine! We saw you coming, sweetie!" a parent kindly shouted back. *"Great dig! Keep it up!"* [5]

The following practice, Coach Gather called out, *"Lawson!* Would you get over here, please?!" Immediately, I tossed my teammate the ball and hustled to her. The woman folded her arms and looked away from me, facing the rest of the team. Understanding her covert tactic, I did the same as she gently conveyed, "I feel the need to *express* something to you. Your attitude and natural leadership have changed the entire dynamic of our team. If you learn something new or how to do it better, you pass it on to others. The younger girls respect and follow you because you work without complaint and lead by example. *Don't think that I haven't noticed.* If I seem hard on you, it's because you can take it and do something good with it. I want you to know that." [6]

As I readied myself for a weekend tournament, the materfamilias announced, "I'm gonna go watch you guys play today."

"Oh, okay. Well, it's a bit of a drive, but it should be a good show," I replied.

Hours later, our team finished warming up just prior to the second round of games and sat on the floor to hydrate as we listened to Coach Gather.

"What?! I'm gonna kill that *****! How dare she touch my daughter!" a familiar voice roared from a distance, prompting me to peer backwards and witness the materfamilias stomping down from the bleachers and onto the court, coming straight toward us.

I faced my horrified teammates and confidently reassured, "Don't panic. *I'll handle this.*"

"*No,*" Coach Gather argued. "I'm an adult and I'm the coach. This is *my* job. I've handled disgruntled parents before. I'll talk to her."

"No, you won't," I clarified. "That woman doesn't want to *talk*. She's *nuts*. She'll murder you in front of God and everybody right here on the court. You'd better let me handle this before the police show up with a body bag."

"*Sandra…*" the woman softly pleaded, reaching for my arm and missing as I removed myself to face the courtside terrorist.

Staring the charging woman down with matching determination, I boldly demanded, "Stop right there." The materfamilias obeyed, pausing center court as scores of whispering players and spectators mumbled in disbelief and confusion. Standing directly in front of her, I continued in a hushed tone, *"What are you doing? Why are you shouting profanity and threatening people during a tournament? You're in a public setting. Do you realize how crazy you look right now?"* [7]

The termagant maintained her wretched volume and shouted, "I don't care! Has your coach ever hit you?!"

"Go back to your seat," I calmly pacified. "We'll discuss this at home."

"No!" she roared again, seeming all the more irritated at my tranquil demeanor. "I heard the other moms talking! Their daughters told them that your coach hits you all the time! Is this true?!"

"*She's been a bit rough, but that's sports,*" I instructed quietly. "*Now, take a seat.*"

"That's not sports!" the shrew raged, causing her voice to echo throughout the gymnasium. "No one should be touched like that by a coach, especially not *my* daughter! I'm gonna kick her ***!" [8]

Leaning forward, I whispered through my gritting teeth, *"The hell you are. If you hit that woman in front of all these people, you're going to jail. No one is going to pay attention to your explanation. They're going to remember you screaming threats and profanity across the court, and assaulting a coach. Here's how this is gonna go down. You're going back to the bleachers and you're staying there. After the tournament, when we're home,* we'll discuss everything. Believe me. I'm doing you a favor by keeping you out of jail. So, please, if you would be so kind, keep your **** together and go sit down."

"Only if you *promise* to have a meeting with the principal," she bargained.

"*Deal. Now, have a seat*," I ordered with a growl, lingering there to monitor her movements until she sat down with the other parents. [9]

Upon my return to the sidelines, Coach Gather sweetly queried, "You okay, kid?"

"I'm fine," I replied, "but my mother's going for your *throat*."

Chuckling, she boasted, "Disgruntled parents are nothing new for me."

I huffed and shook my head, warning, "This *will be*. You have no idea what you're dealing with. She's *evil*, and I'm the only thing standing between you and her."

Unnerved from the materfamilias' outburst, the team never refocused and we quickly lost the game, knocking us out of the bracket. Before I headed for the bleachers to leave, Coach Gather held my shoulders with a light squeeze and gently added, "*Seriously*, don't worry about me. Go home with your mother and take care of *yourself*, Sandra. I'm an adult that can go wherever I want. You're the one that has to live with her."

At home, I interrogated, "Alright, woman. I'm pretty sure you lost us the tournament. So, what the hell happened that set you off?"

"I was sitting a couple of rows behind a group of mothers talking to each other," she began. "At first, I was excited about their conversation because they talked about how much they *loved you* and I was proud to hear them say that you're a good player. I like that other people notice how good you are and say nice things about you, but when I heard that your coach was hurting you, *I lost it*. That ******* woman…"

"Hold up," I interjected. "What *exactly* did you hear them say?"

"One mom talked about how hard the team has been working. The other one said that we had a really good varsity team this year and how happy her daughter was to play with you guys. The rest of the moms agreed, and they all stopped talking to watch you spike while warming up. They talked about how you sometimes run into the bleachers and entertain everyone… that you're *really good*," she recalled proudly. "Then, another mom said that *her* daughter felt bad for you because the coach *hits you* and is really rough when correcting you. A different mom said that her daughter told her *the same thing*, and that you were the only one who's treated that way! I lost it! Who does she think she is?! How dare that ***** touch you! She can't do that to you! No one hits my daughter and gets away with it! I'm calling the principal! That woman's getting *fired!* She has no business putting her hands on you!"

"That's right, mother," I deadpanned, shaking my head. "You're the *only one* that's allowed to abuse me."

"That's right! I am!" she cackled. ¹⁰

In class that Monday morning, the loud speaker cracked and announced, *"Sandra Lawson to the principal's office. Sandra Lawson to the principal's office."*

Before excusing myself, a random classmate soothed, "Don't let your mom get you down, Sandra." The small-town student body was already aware of my situation and shared their concerns.

"Wow. Word traveled fast," I replied, offering a gentle smile. "Thanks, guys."

Stepping into the meeting, I noticed Coach Gather seated with her back to the wall to face the principal's desk head on. The accuser and I had chairs already stationed along an adjacent wall by the door, intelligently positioning me between the two opposing women. Before taking my seat, I greeted Coach Gather and the principal with reassuring smiles and firm handshakes.

The principal began, "*Sandra*, please tell me in your own words why we're here today."

"We're here to address the allegations that Coach Gather has been abusing me," I confidently replied.

The man huffed with a wide-eyed smirk and commented, *"Well said. That's right.* Let's proceed, then. *Mrs. Lawson*, please repeat what you overheard from the other mothers." The woman theatrically recited their words from the bleachers and became emotional, shedding her all-too-familiar *crocodile tears* that caused my face to tighten. Noticing my obvious irritation, the principal inquired, "Sandra, what's *your* perspective of Coach Gather's treatment of you?"

After a deep breath, I admitted, "Sir, I would feel much more at ease if it were only you, Coach Gather, and myself in the room." Since the woman beside me didn't budge, I peered through her doting-mother persona with a professional touch and stated, "Mother, you're *clearly* upset. If you would, please step out into the main office and wait for me there. I'll tell the principal everything that we've discussed. This shouldn't take very long." The woman starkly dropped the act, shot me a hellish look, and removed herself without a word. ¹¹

The principal waited patiently for the termagant to leave. When she shut the door behind her, he smiled and said, "Please, Sandra, *tell me*. What is your perspective?"

"Coach Gather is an amazing teacher and an even *better* coach. *Yes*, she *has* hit me… in order to correct mistakes and enforce good habits. *Yes*, she has pushed me down into ready position and yanked me arm to relocate me on the court. *It's all true.* Coach Gather can be a bit rough," I admitted, causing the principal to stare at the instructor. "However, I do believe that it won't happen anymore after today… and I have a valid reason for believing this." Expressing interest, the principal returned his gaze to meet mine. "Coach Gather, until today, was not notified of how she's been perceived by the other players, *which is why we're here.* As for *my* perspective, the team would not be competing at such a high level if it weren't for the woman seated before you. I didn't notice anything wrong with her treatment of me, and figured it all came with the territory of being an athlete. I didn't feel *small* or *picked on*. Quite frankly, her coaching style has been *highly effective.*" I paused and leaned toward the man. "Sir, I don't mean to brag, but you've attended my games and have seen what I can do. I train hard and play harder. I live, breathe, and eat volleyball." The principal chuckled as I sat back. "Just so you know, I'm at this level because of *Coach Gather*. I strongly believe that if she were approached by one of my teammates or a concerned parent early on, her coaching tactics would have changed *immediately*. However, because of inaction and some overheard gossip, this is the *first time* Coach Gather is hearing about this. How can anyone correct a problem that they're unaware of?" The principal pursed his lips and nodded. I looked at Coach Gather, noticing her vulnerable state. "Coach, do you think you can guide me *verbally* from now on?" [12]

With tears in her eyes and a sheepish smile, her voice cracked as she answered, "*I can do that.*"

My attention returned to the principal as I added, "You see, sir, my mother's intentions were to *protect her daughter*. You clearly desire to *protect your student*. Coach Gather wants me to *excel as an athlete* and I want to play a sport that I love and *win games*. If Coach Gather makes this *one small tweak* in her coaching style, I think *everyone* will ultimately have what they want… and if I ever feel the need to come to you, *I will*."

"Sandra, I believe I already know your answer to this question, but I'm still required to ask it," the principal prefaced. "Do you feel Coach Gather should keep her job?"

"*Absolutely,*" I boldly declared. "If she were *let-go*, it would do this school, our team, and me a *great* disservice. I want her to continue teaching and coaching me." [13]

"Well, ladies, I think this was a *very* successful meeting. Sandra, you're *exceptional* and have a bright future. If you keep up the good work, I believe you'll go far." [14]

Hours later, Coach Gather got my attention during practice in the sweetest manner and motioned for me to approach her, allowing her to express, "Sandra, there were some things that I wasn't given an opportunity to say during our meeting this morning. First of all, you didn't deserve to be put in that situation. Secondly, if I've *ever* hurt you, I am *truly* sorry. In reality, you're very special and mean a great deal to me. I really can't thank you enough for what you did for me in that office. You not only saved my job, but my career and livelihood." Tears filled her eyes. "You said some really nice things in there and handled everything in a completely different way than I had expected.

I thought I was going to pack my bags today, but I'm still here because of *you*. I will never forget this." [15]

Under Coach Gather's extended leadership, our varsity team won district and competed at the regional tournament, which was the farthest our high school's volleyball team had gone in many years.

Words

〜

*A*s graduation drew closer, students and teachers freely offered me compliments, genuine smiles, hugs, and enthusiastic well wishes. Even my autograph book became riddled with heart-felt messages from friends, fellow band members, teammates, *many* lower-classmen, and even some former bullies. [1]

Spotting me in the hallway, a much healthier Zephaniah approached robotically and expressed, "Sandra, if I seem cold, I'm sorry. I'm just not very good at goodbyes, so I wrote you a four-page letter. *Here.*" I took the stapled packet from his trembling hand and peered down at the paper. "You already know how I feel about you… so… *Oh, God.* Are you reading that *now?* Uh. I can't do this. I have to go. Bye."

Although I wanted to squeeze the sophomore in front of the entire student body, I let him escape into the crowd as I entered my next class to read his printout. I swelled with bittersweet emotions. Zephaniah's loving words weren't wasted on me. They filled my thoughts with fond memories of laughter and dancing. I almost worried about the boy's wellbeing without my protection, but recalled the peace my friend enjoyed at school after my public confrontation with Buzz. I trusted and prayed that my Messiah would watch over Zephaniah for me, whether or not he believed in Him. [2]

Hours later in the girls' locker room, I was sliding my track shorts over my thighs when Winter, a wealthy junior with a prominent last name, spoke to me for the very first time, addressing, "Sandra?"

"What's up, Winter?" I casually queried, progressing to slip on my practice jersey.

The calloused teen turned to face me and sneered, "I don't really know why, but I just *don't like you.*" The team stared as their chatter faded to silence. [3]

"Dang, Winter," I deadpanned, zipping up my gym bag. "That would really hurt my feelings if your opinion actually mattered." The team's explosive laughter was in stereo as I exited the scene. [4]

Days later, our coaches voted and awarded me as The Most Outstanding Female Athlete of the Year, making me choke up and grin as students roared in cheerful applause. [5]

Thad

~~~

Three seniors approached me and wondered if I would do them a favor by bringing their favorite baby-faced freshman to prom so they could enjoy his company. I laughed and agreed, finding it sweet that they concocted such a plan for their young friend.

The long-awaited day finally arrived. Upon our entry into the building, I noticed a frustrated Winter standing beside her patient boyfriend, Thad, as she struggled to remedy her broken shoulder strap. Curiously glancing upward to see who had stepped through the door, the junior's eyes grew wide as he gazed upon my turquoise evening gown that was bathed in white glitter and fit my form like a glove.

Breaking free from his stunned posture, the teen enthusiastically gushed, "Sandra, *wow*. You look amazing. Your hair and your dress really complement you. Just… *wow*."

"Thank you," I timidly replied, taken aback by his candor.

With a bitter scowl, Winter violently jerked Thad's dashing white suit and snapped, "*Hey!* You never said that to *me!*" [1]

Gently escorting the clueless freshman away from the scene, I found the table of his upperclassmen friends and released my date into their care. One of them broke away from playfully razzing the boy and conveyed, "Seriously, Sandra… thanks for doing this. That was pretty cool."

"Well, he's *precious*. Have fun with your little buddy," I gently teased.

Within moments, Thad quickly made his way to my table and nervously explained, "Winter is *really mad* at me for complimenting you. I had to wait until she used the restroom so we could talk. *Please* save me a dance, Sandra. It's your senior year and I don't want to miss out."

"You've got it," I replied, realizing that Winter finally had her reason to dislike me. Poorly hiding a grin, heat radiated from my face. "Come find me when you're ready." [2]

Thad's affection was not something I intended to reject again. During my sophomore year, our marching band had taken an unexpected trip to the coast. Through a miracle, the materfamilias allowed me to go. I barely knew the towering freshman when he snuck up behind me and wrapped his muscular arms around my torso. Unable to see who held me, I thought an upperclassman had simply snagged the wrong girl. I panicked and pulled away from him, assuming it was a mean joke to lead me on or some passing moment of weakness one might suffer from when surrounded by scantily clad females at a sparking beach. It was Thad, and he knew exactly who he was holding. He apologized for scaring me and wished he had spoken to me first. The two years that followed, Thad offered his playful affections by romantically sweeping me off my feet to carry me from our charter bus to the sidewalk at a band competition. I couldn't believe the darling young man had truly chosen *me*, someone who viewed herself as hopelessly broken with a mother no one should encounter. Thad eventually gave up. We remained platonic as the young man focused his romantic interest elsewhere.

After I danced with nearly every male in the room, the DJ arranged for one last salsa experience. He claimed the opportunity to converse with me and expressed, "You're going to college out-of-state?! I'm sorry to hear that. You'll be *missed*, Sandra. It's a shame you won't be local anymore. I don't live very far from your town. *Dang it.* I should've said something to you a long time ago. I've had a crush on you since we first danced together. You're a total knock-out."

"What?! *Really?* I can't believe I'm hearing this right now! With the way you're built, I thought you were in your twenties and lived way out here in the city! How are you just a couple of years older than me and already running your own business? That's great! Well done, sir! *Wow…* and you *like* me. I would've never guessed that. I really just thought your salsa dancing with me was a part of being an exceptional DJ."

"It is, but with you, it was much more than that," he confessed with a sigh. "I really would've enjoyed getting to know you, but it's too late."

Near the evening's end, a slow song inspired Thad to leave Winter's side and guide me onto the dance floor. He pulled me in close. The comfort of his touch overwhelmed me as I rested my cheek on his lapel and swayed to his lead. When drawn into a twirl, a shadow on his jacket caught my eye. I gasped, "Oh no, Thad! I used dark make-up to match my track tan, and it stained your white suit! I'm so sorry!" The strapping teen examined his chest and smiled, keeping his hand on my waist to pull me back toward him.

Soothing me by the rhythm of his deep breaths, Thad whispered, "That's okay. It should come out… and if it doesn't, it'll be a nice memento to remember you by." The junior gave me a final spin with a skilled dip, nearly causing me to swoon upon my return as the song drew to a close. "Thank you for the dance. As memorable as this is, I really have to go. It's Winter's prom, too, and I don't want to keep her waiting outside in the car. Sandra… *seriously*… you look amazing, and you'll be missed. Goodnight." [3]

Degrading

After graduation, I looked forward to my second summer at scout camp, where the trading post staff became more like beloved brothers than coworkers. We conversed freely *all day* about any topic that came to mind, including probing questions about the opposite sex and my female perspective on life.

As the last scout had vacated the Trading Post for the afternoon, Amin locked up the shop and walked his loyal staff up the hill to eat dinner. My friend turned to me and casually inquired, "Sandra, what kind of pornography do you watch?"

Confused, I wondered aloud, "*Wait.* There are different kinds?"

My camp brothers chuckled as Amir clarified, "Yes, there are different kinds."

"I've never watched pornography before *and I don't want to*," I expressed with a grimace. "I think it's degrading to women. Those things should remain private between a husband and his wife." [1]

A camp brother chimed in to educate me and added, "Sandra, the women in those videos get *paid* to do those things. *They degrade themselves.* No one is forcing them to do anything. That would be *rape*. I honestly can't believe this. Seriously, Sandra, you have never seen porn?" [2]

"Should we show her one…. for *educational* purposes?" suggested another camp brother as he used his t-shirt to wipe some sweat from his eyes.

"Yeah!" the rest urged.

We ate our evening meal together as each camp brother made his case, expressing that I was *far too sheltered* and would not fare well in college with my level of innocence. They spoke of various titles of pornographic films and used a variety of phrases that were so foreign to me they might as well have been speaking in code.

Amin quietly informed, "In the staff lounge, there's a small closet with a computer hooked up to high-speed internet, so we can stream videos online. Now, I don't want to *force* you to do anything you don't want to do, but someone will eventually expose you to this, so it might as well be us. We're *safe*. Do you want to see this or not?" [3]

Unwilling to lose status in their eyes, I begrudgingly huffed, "*Fine.* Let's get this **** over with." [4]

"*Yay!*" the teenagers cheered, finishing their chicken fried steaks and mashed potatoes.

Four of us crammed into the tiny computer closet located inside the staff lounge. One sat down to operate the mouse and keyboard, while another kneeled by the desk to make room for Amir and me to stand behind them, shoulder to shoulder. The screen's glow reflected off our squinting faces and disguised my growing conviction.

One camp brother coached, "No, no, no. Scroll down. Farther. *Wait.* Go back up. *That one.* It's pretty mild." With the volume turned down, the vilest act I had ever witnessed played out on the computer screen and disgusted me, evoking a severe gag reflex.

Still staring at the screen, a camp brother whispered, "That's *nothing*, Sandra. This is just the kiddie pool. Do you want to see some more, or have you had enough?" In my silence, they turned to check on me. My eyed watered as I covered my mouth. "Uh. *Yeah.* She's seen enough. Let's get her out of here."

Thoughts raged within me as I pondered, "Why would *anyone* allow that to happen to them? Is *that* what men expect from women? Am I supposed to behave like that in order to have a romantic relationship?" We piled out of the computer closet and kept what we saw a strict secret.

"Are you okay?" Amir later inquired. "I'm starting to think we shouldn't have done that. I'm really sorry."

Pretending I was fine and nothing had changed, I sensed a great darkness growing inside of me. Heavy from guilt, I grew ashamed and paranoid about being discovered. My reputation of innocence had been officially tarnished. I tried to force the images out of my thoughts, but they were branded on my soul.

Arrested by self-loathing, I laid awake that night and pondered, "I'm such a *coward*. What have I done? The boys were right. I wasn't forced. We degrade *ourselves*." [5]

Dear Nancy

Dear Nancy,

 The time has finally come to fulfill my tear-soaked promise to you, made during our fateful last moments together. Our hands were ripped from one another's grasp, but found a way to hold on through the written word. Soon, we will be reunited and face to face again. [1]

 After eight years of separation, we both have finally graduated and are still best friends! Can you believe it?! We've come so far! What a ride, chica! I went from being a Californian beach baby to a gun slinging Texan, and it took all this time to do it! I'm so proud of your involvement in Airforce JROTC and playing high school football. You've lived-out one of my dreams to battle on the gridiron. At least one of us did it! Thanks to my dad telling me I couldn't suit-up as a wide receiver, I turned volleyball into a blood sport. With our aggression, we definitely redefined the term 'playing like a girl'. Hahaha! Hopefully, all of my channeled aggression pays off and fuels me even farther in the military. [2]

 So, you trained with the Airforce and I'm going into the Army. What must our Navy fathers think of us? Hahaha! I'm excited about experiencing Army ROTC in college. I'll train harder than anyone else and win this war! Just make sure I get that air support, girl! [3]

 The best part about going to college is that I'll be on the other side of the country, making it too expensive and inconvenient for my mother to reach me. Whatever works, right?! I'd prefer being shipped to a foreign country and risk my life for a worthy cause over staying in this hell-hole. At least my enemy won't be someone that's supposed to love and protect me.

 Thank you for sticking with me through all the ups and downs. The promise of seeing you has been my main motivation to earn money and save it. It's no secret. Everyone who knows me has heard all about you. As soon as I get details about my flight to California, I'll call you and give you the scoop. We'll have to make it a quick conversation, though. "Long-distance phone calls are expensive." Until then, enjoy your summer! I love you. Stay awesome.

Your best friend in the whole wide world,
Sandra

Welcome

"*H*i, Nancy! We can't talk long, but I bought my flight… *online*," I playfully bragged, fiddling with the telephone cord.

The teenager laughed and quipped, "Welcome to the world of technology, Sandra."

"Right?!" I chirped. "I feel like such a *big-girl*… and it's so good to hear your voice! Anyway, let's talk business. My flight number is…"

Days later, while scanning the faces in the airport baggage claim area, I spotted Nancy checking my flight status while clutching a bouquet in her trembling hand. "*Nancy!*" I shouted, waving as I dodged the rolling luggage behind the crossing passersby.

Bursting into tears, my friend sprinted forward and wrapped me up in a tight hug. Eventually becoming calm enough, she ordered, "C'mon, girl. Let's get out of here. After all this time that we've been friends, you'll *finally* get to sleep over at *my* house!"

During the trip, we used public transportation and came upon a beach with a bustling boardwalk. Carnival rides, souvenir shops, and a variety of food vendors with mouth-watering aromas caused me to tear up and exercise the freedom to do what I wished.

"Hey! Look! Let's check out this surf shop!" I squealed, having never been allowed to enter one before.

While scanning the walls, racks, and shelves for a souvenir, I heard Irish accents coming from a group of young males standing in another part of the store. Curious, I followed the sound of their voices to behold a stoic young man amongst his rowdy companions.

He sensed my lingering presence and smiled before inquiring, "Can I help you?"

"Excuse me. I didn't mean to interrupt, but… are *all of you* from Ireland?" I wondered aloud, causing his friends to cheer and playfully push each other. "That's so cool. I've never met anyone from Ireland before. Is it alright if I take a photo with you guys?" They laughed and huddled together to oblige me.

As the group dispersed, the stoic asked, "Do you want me to put an image on that shirt in your hand?"

"Oh. You work here? I didn't realize," I commented. "I'm sorry for distracting you. My name is Sandra, by the way. I flew here from Texas to visit my friend Nancy. She's standing over right there." Nancy laughed at me and waved.

While imprinting a decal onto my shirt, the young man chimed, "I'm *Ciaran*. My mates and I are going out for a drink after the shop closes. Would you join us?"

"That sounds wonderful, but we *can't*, actually. We're both eighteen," I sighed. "The legal drinking age is twenty-one in America and they won't let minors in."

"Ah, I see. We're all twenty-one here. Well, the shop closes at seven o'clock. If you come back by then, maybe we can go do something else for a while," he suggested, leading me to the cash register.

Failing to control my grin, I collected my item and giddily chirped, "Okay. See you at seven."

I rushed up behind Nancy and took her arm as we exited. She arched an eyebrow and teased, "Dang, Sandra! *You* make friends quickly!"

"Isn't he just… *wonderful*?" I rhapsodized.

"Poor Sandra. You've been stuck in a cage all these years," she commented, patting my hand. "There's so much you haven't experienced."

The boardwalk contained a contraption that astounded me as patrons sat in harnesses and bounced themselves into the air with hair-dos flying. "Look, Nancy!" I exclaimed, pogo jumping for a chance at an adrenaline rush. "Let's defy *gravity*!"

Amused at my enthusiasm, the teen cheered, "*Yeah!* Let's go!"

Trusting the equipment fully, I leaped yards above a huge trampoline just to flip backwards, over and over, until I was exhausted and light-headed. I hadn't experienced that level of elation since my elementary days on the swing set. Hungry from our acrobatic cardio, we enjoyed a meal and explored various stores. Each became pale next to the surf shop.

"Nancy!" I gasped, pointing to an outdoor clock. "Look! It's *seven!* Let's go back to the shop!"

Softening her face, my friend grabbed my hand with a squeeze and informed, "No. That's okay, Sandra. *You go.* I'm gonna keep looking around for a while. I want you to enjoy your time away from your mother." She twisted her hair and teased, "Have fun with your *Irish* boyfriend!"

"Are you *sure*? I came to California to spend time with *you*," I reasoned.

"Yeah, but this is something that you *really want* and you've been in captivity your entire life," she rebutted. "*Live a little*. Besides, it's only for a short while. Just come find me in an hour or two. I'll be in this area right here. Hurry! Go or you'll miss him!" [1]

Hugging my friend, I hustled over to the shop and found Ciaran waiting for me with a smile, greeting, "There you are! I stood around for a bit… *just in case*. Where's your mate… err… your friend? I keep forgetting that I'm supposed to say *friend* in America."

"Don't worry about it. I know what you meant. Nancy decided to give us space to talk, which was super sweet. We've been best-friends for years, even though I haven't seen her since *the fourth grade*. I promised to return to California after we both graduated high school… which has just been *fulfilled*," I divulged. "That's why I'm here."

"Wow! That's quite the story!" he commented, walking me toward the sand. "Texas must be pretty far away to not see your best-mate in *years*."

"It is. Especially for us. We were just kids and didn't have the money or freedom to see one another until now. After I return to Texas, I'll head to college for civil engineering," I shared, soaking in the ocean's roar as we dug our toes into the sand. An hour passed too quickly. The setting sun illuminated each cloud and reflected a sparkling brilliance from each rolling wave. "So, Cirian, what brought you to California?"

"I've been coming here every summer since I started university. I return to California with a work visa, summer after summer, to earn money to bring back home to Ireland to pay for school. Many of us do that," the young man explained. "I'm studying economics. Ireland's economy is dreadful and I'm hoping to learn more about how we can turn things around for the better." [2]

"Wow. I'm sorry that you need to go through so much trouble to make things work. It's a good thing there's a *silver lining* to your situation," I chirped.

"There is?" he queried. "I have to hear this."

"Your summer adventures caused *us* to meet," I flirted with a grin. "Not too shabby!"

Finding my girlish optimism endearing, Ciaran smirked to concede, "I suppose you're right." He breathed in deeply and stood to his feet, immediately helping me to mine. "Sandra, I've had an amazing time with you, but it's getting dark. We should probably move along, since you can't come to the pub with me and my mates are waiting there. Besides, it's not safe for you girls to be walking around at night without an escort." [3]

Appreciating the wisdom, I confessed, "You're right. I didn't think about that."

"Do you have paper and a pen?" he inquired. Reaching into my bag, I grabbed my t-shirt receipt and a writing utensil, and handed them over. "This is my full name and email address. You're a very interesting person and I'd like to keep in touch. Now, let's hurry and find your best-mate."

Beaming upon our approach, Nancy remained still until the young man was out of earshot. Drawing me near, she prodded, "Okay, Sandra, *spill*. Give me every juicy detail."

Help Us

That Saturday night, Nancy wondered aloud, "Is there any church in particular that you wish to visit tomorrow morning?"

"I hadn't thought about that," I replied. "I'm not familiar with any of the churches in California. Where do *you* usually go?"

"Well, my family is *Catholic*, but we aren't very religious. We rarely go to mass, *if ever*," she confessed.

"In that case, let's see if we can find a Pentecostal church," I suggested, which inspired Nancy to locate one using the internet.

That following morning, a lively congregation was already singing and worshipping when we stepped into the massive sanctuary. Nancy and I lifted our hands and sang along to the words on the projector. The preacher read scriptures and delivered a simple message of salvation.

Nancy silently wept. She eventually touched my arm and whispered, *"Sandra, I've never felt anything like this in my entire life."*

"That's the Holy Spirit," I informed with a smile. "Don't resist Him." [1]

"I feel… *dread*," she continued softly, trembling. "I don't *want* to go to hell." [2]

"We don't *have* to go to hell, Nancy. We have a choice! God made a way for us to be with Him," I explained. "He sent us His Son, *Jesus*, who willingly sacrificed Himself for us to pay for all our sins. If you accept what Jesus did for you on the cross, your sins will be forgiven, too! *It gets even better.* After Jesus resurrected from the grave and ascended into heaven, He released the Holy Spirit for us to receive. For those that are saved, the Holy Spirit lives inside of *us*, to help us." [3]

"But… the preacher said that I needed to get baptized in Jesus' name to be saved," she sobbed. "I was baptized as a baby by being sprinkled with water by a priest, but it wasn't by *choice*."

"Getting baptized *willingly* couldn't hurt," I reasoned. "I was baptized under the Father, Son, and Holy Spirit with the Mormons, but got *re-baptized* in Jesus' name with the Pentecostals later on. If you're getting baptized in *faith*, choosing to be obedient to

Jesus is what matters the most. Otherwise, it wouldn't be much more than being awkwardly dunked in front of a creepy audience." [4]

Burying her face in her hands, she groaned and added, "I don't know what to do. I don't even know if I'm actually *saved*. What I got out of his sermon is *totally different* from anything that I've ever learned in Catholicism or from my parents. I feel like I'm being pulled in two directions!" [5]

"Stop trying to pick between two *religions*," I gently corrected. "A *religion* can't save you, but Jesus *can*. If you're not sure that you're saved, I wouldn't wait any longer. Just accept the fact that Jesus came to save all of us, even *you*. Just think about it. Jesus set all of this up! For eight years, He put it on my heart to return to California. If all of this was just so He could show you He's real, *it was worth it*. Do you think it's just some coincidence that *you* asked about going to church? I wasn't even thinking about it. So, why wait? You can talk to Jesus *right here*. He hears you." [6]

Drawing in a deep breath, Nancy quietly prayed, *"Jesus, I don't want to go to hell. I believe You died for me on the cross so that I can go to heaven. I need You in my life. Thank You for saving me and for forgiving my sin. Help me know You better. I love You. Amen."*

I wrapped my arms around Nancy and added, "Do you feel better?"

"No," my friend emotionally divulged. "My parents will *never* allow me to be baptized in the name of *Jesus*. They'll be *furious* with me. You'll be in Texas and I'll have *no one* here to back me up. What do I do?! I feel hopeless!" [7]

I silently prayed, "Jesus, help us." Suddenly, my eyes grew wide as I exclaimed, "I know! Come visit *me!* You can get baptized at my church in Texas!"

Nancy dried her once troubled eyes and smiled with a nod, confidently confirming, "*Texas.*" [8]

Before my feet touched Texas soil, Nancy purchased a plane ticket to the lone star state. To my surprise, the materfamilias enthusiastically welcomed Nancy to stay in her home.

A week had not passed when I embraced my sister-in-faith at the airport, causing her to laugh and chirp, "Long time no see, girly!"

"Right?! It's been *ages*!" I laughed.

"*Nancy!* It's so good to see you again! How long has it been? *Wow!* Look at how much you've grown!" the materfamilias gushed, moving me out of the way. The woman violently grabbed Nancy into a suffocating embrace as I shook my head in irritation. "I always wanted Sandra to be a good girl like *you*."

My friend pursed her lips as the termagant squeezed, prompting me to roll my eyes. Nancy's knowing smirk put my soul to rest, reminding me that the teen had yet to be beguiled by the woman's deceptive charm and passive-aggressive ways. [9]

That Sunday, my childhood confidant came to church with me to experience baptism in Jesus' name. Giselle snapped a few photos of my best friend being submerged and then raised out of the water with hands lifted high. A grin I had never beheld stretched across Nancy's victorious face. [10]

Mascot

The college scheduled their orientation to occur mid-summer, forcing my parents and me to embark on the first of *two* out-of-state trips to campus that season. Hours of arguing, yelling, panic, complaining, and tension radiated from the termagant as it had so many times before. From our lodgings, my father and I quickly abandoned the termagant to explore the relatively small campus without her.

The following morning, the materfamilias joined us in the car and continued spouting her captious rants from the front passenger seat. My neck tightened as I imagined life away from her forever. Her virtually exanimate husband pulled the vehicle into a campus parking spot to release his offspring into the future of *his* dreams. Ready for a weekend getaway from the materfamilias, I snatched up my backpack and exited with urgency. [1]

"Do you have your orientation packet and understand what you need to do?" the man inquired dryly.

I turned, politely answering, "I do. *Thank you.* If I need help, I'll just ask someone."

"Very good," he replied before entering the vehicle. "We'll be back for you tomorrow afternoon." [2]

"Wait, Sandra," the materfamilias interjected, causing me to stop and face her. "You're not *afraid*… being all the way our here all by yourself? Do you want us to come back for you today when you're done? It's not a big deal. We would just bring you back again tomorrow. You could just stay the night with *us*." [3]

"No, thank you. This is the best route," I reassured. "If I can't make it through one weekend, I have no business going to college at all."

With that, I turned away and honed in on the cherished sound behind me. Four tires backed out, pivoted on the gravel beneath, and rolled away. As if chained to their bumper, the weight of the world ripped from my undeterred frame as I peered upward with arms spread wide. Tears swelled and rolled around my cheeks as I lifted a grin to my Creator in worship. [4]

I located the correct building, navigated the empty halls, and arrived at my destination. The push-bar double doors loudly opened to a dismal display, revealing the side profiles of my peers who submissively faced a row of rigidly somber adults. I filled the closest available seat on the outside right edge, unsure of what unfortunate mistake I had made in forgoing my *first* choice of studying literature and writing.

A suit nearly filled with a body stepped in front of the microphone and turned it on with an echoing thump. He tediously introduced administration and staff, while I simultaneously forgot them. Minutes felt like hours as information droned on in monotone and echoed in my skull as they lost all cohesiveness.

One sound stirred me. The double-doors opened, followed by the distinct clack of high-heels. Casually glancing to determine its origins, I spotted an ostentatious woman in a formfitting black dress approaching our chairs. Returning my eyes forward, I chuckled at the predominately male student body, unable to break their gaze from her sashaying hips, flowing hair, and bewitching eyes. Within seconds, the students focused their attention on *me*.

Curious, I became startled by someone whispering, *"Cadet Lawson..."* Squatting down beside me was the mysterious woman in a very late stage of pregnancy. *"Hello. I'm Captain Ladette. I'll be responsible for you during your training in ROTC. I just wanted to introduce myself to you today, since I won't have another opportunity to see you again until your return for Zero Week."*

I softly responded, *"It's a pleasure to meet you, Captain Ladette. I'm sorry you had to walk all the way over here. If I had known your intentions, I would have gotten up or met you somewhere else. Until you walked in, I numbed out and was about to fall asleep. I doubt I'll get bored in ROTC."*

"I doubt that, too, and don't worry about not getting up," she continued. *"I just came over to meet you and say hello. See you in a few weeks, Lawson."* The soldier effortlessly stood and pivoted, clacking her way to the exit and twisting so many of the necks in proximity. [5]

It was time for phase two of orientation.

Students traveled in a herd toward a carpeted room with cushioned seating. Someone switched off the overhead fluorescents and caused a hush to envelope the up-and-coming freshmen as we sat in complete darkness. Portable stage lights illuminated the temporary platform and revealed a solitary microphone. After an awkward pause, an eccentric young man with a wild expression violently pounced onto the platform, causing a boom from his firm landing. Bursting into laughter all alone, I inadvertently drew more attention to myself.

Exhibiting a kindergartener's energy with the persona of a game-show host, the young man announced, "Welcome, future engineers! I'm a sophomore here, this year's mascot, and your student Orientation Leader for the weekend!"

"*Oh, thank God,*" I praised under my breath as he continued, grateful for the demise of monotony. [6]

"Enough with the formalities," Mascot chirped. "I need some volunteers! Who in this crowd likes to dance?!" Eyes wide and pulse racing, my hand skyrocketed upward and drew his attention. "Hey! Nice! Get up here, girl!" Wearing my favorite superhero shirt and a pair of flare jeans, I confidently made my way to the spotlight. "Who else?! Don't make her dance all alone!" Hands sheepishly poked up from the herd. "Yes! All of you! *Get up here!* Once everyone is on stage, I'll tell you the details. Alright! The six of you are going to have a *dance-off*! Let's meet our contestants! Tell everyone your name, where you're from, and your major."

"My name is *Sandra*. I'm from Texas and I'll be majoring in civil engineering," I divulged, permitting Mascot to progress with the more local students.

"Excellent!" he exclaimed. "When the music starts, show us what you've got!"

The tune exploded from the speakers and filled my nervous system with rhythm. One contestant bobbed their head and snapped their fingers while the next attempted more modern and mainstream styles. Standing out, a different person executed iconic moves from pop-culture, getting a rise from the audience. I held nothing back. My exaggerated movements rocked the crowd with energy and laughter. [7]

Mascot cut the music, raised his voice over the applause, and continued, "*Wow! Okay, you guys! Let's see who made it to the next round!*" Having landed in the finals, I faced off with a talented and fearless male student. The music switched unexpectedly to different genres, allowing a sporadic change of styles. We shifted from explosively silly to smoothly thug, followed by comedically retro moves that belonged in a disco. "I don't know, guys! They're pretty good! I can't decide! It's time for *sudden death!* This round is called *Dance and Pass*. Bust a move and pass it back to your opponent. *Let's go!*"

After doing some snazzy footwork, the student quickly passed the torch to me. Immersed in full character, I transformed my actions to mimic something battery powered and executed my magnum opus through a realistic and combative version of *the robot*.

Losing composure with the rest of the student body, the contestant beside me clapped and shouted, "Is this *happening* right now?!"

The song abruptly ended, silencing the crowd's roar as they waited with expectation. Blankly peering at my opponent, I spun two pretend sidearms, slid them into their imaginary holsters, and mechanically powered off. As the engineers went wild, I dropped character and stepped forward to shake the other contestant's hand. With a lean toward my competitor, I mentioned with a smile, "You've got skills, bro."

Mascot awarded me first-place and handed over an inflatable microphone as a prize. We played various games and received all the information we needed about the following day's events. After spending the day with my future classmates, the entertainment came to a close.

While attempting to exit and find the dorms, Mascot called out, "Sandra, wait up!" Having dropped his on-stage character, he spoke calmly. "Uh, *great dancing*. Holy-moly. I was so worried that everyone would be dead in there, and then you jumped on stage like my own personal… superhero!"

Peering down at my comic book themed shirt, I laughed, "Ha! I see what-cha did there!"

"Seriously, you need to know that what happened today isn't *normal*. Engineering students don't do that. They don't cut loose in front of strangers or clap and cheer. This was surprisingly fun for me. I had reluctantly agreed to MC orientation this year, but my nightmare turned into a dream. So, *thank you*. Now, Sandra, let me tell you the *real* reason I came over here. I have two questions for you. *Are you single* and will you have dinner with me tonight? I have to get to know you." [8]

"I *am* single and I would *love* to have dinner with you tonight," I calmly replied with a smirk, internally pogo-jumping.

"I'm pretty handy in the kitchen and just bought a ton of groceries. So, is it alright if I cook for you this evening?" A flash of concern covered my face. "Whoa. It's okay, Sandra. I realize you aren't from the area… *or this state*… and will enter the home of a stranger. Just so you know, we won't be far away from here *at all*. I live nearby, right here in town."

"So, you're saying that I can sprint all the way from your place to the dorms if I needed to? *Good to know*," I jested as we lightly chuckled. "Seriously, a home-cooked meal? That sounds *great*. Thank you."

Mascot drove us to his local home within a minute, donned a frilly cooking apron, and chopped vegetables while we chatted. I enjoyed his confidence and couldn't stop smiling as I stationed myself on a barstool near the kitchen island. He asked interview-style questions in perfect deadpan until I couldn't take it anymore and erupted into laughter.

After collecting myself, I admitted, "You're *killing* me right now with that pink apron! Oh, my gosh! Okay. You have my attention, sir, and I have a question for *you*. When you're not taking engineering classes, making students dance, or dazzling women with your pink apron, how do you spend your free time?"

"I'm an entrepreneur and have two businesses. Right now, I'm a photographer and a DJ. Sometimes, I'm spread pretty thin with engineering homework and classes, so I was thinking about stepping away from being an MC for the school. Then, I met a fearless girl that did a *sick* robot for a bunch of lovable nerds, and it reminded me of why I do what I do. I had to ask her out and cook her dinner. Speaking of dinner, *it's ready.*"

The young man and I conversed for hours, sharing our dreams, favorite memories, home-lives, interests, and frustrations. Having cleaned the kitchen, we selected a movie which led to us sitting on opposite ends of Mascot's sofa. I removed the decorative pillow from the corner and wielded it like a shield in my lap.

Unsullied in manner, Mascot gently offered, "Sandra, you can come sit over here with me *if you would like to.*"

"*Hmmm...*" I stalled, feeling myself tense up. The materfamilias and all of her perverted accusations rolled through my mind, but the last thing I wanted to do was miss *another* opportunity to be close with a decent human being... the way I had with Thad. Finding Mascot to be a gentleman and attractive, I girlishly announced, "Okay. *Here I come.*"

Mascot sweetly huffed at my child-like response and lifted a welcoming arm. Relinquishing my defenses, I scooted to his side and relaxed. As I nestled into his warmth, gently rocked by his steady breathing, Mascot's arm found a resting spot over my shoulder. "Glad you could join me," he added.

While the ending credits rolled, I smiled and stretched, chirping, "Well, *this* was a pleasant evening. Thank you for letting me peek into your world."

"You're welcome to *peek into my world* anytime. You're exceptional," the young man replied. I stood up and smiled, politely giving a social cue to exit his home. "Yeah, it's getting late and we have a big day tomorrow. Let's get you back to campus." While pulling out of his driveway and cruising down the street, Mascot queried, "Sandra, do you still have your V-Card?"

"My... *what*? Did you say *V-Card*? What's that?! Do I need one of those for school?! Oh no. It wasn't in the orientation packet."

He laughed and clarified, "No, no, no. I mean... you know, your *V-Card*." I stared blankly, having absorbed copious amounts of commercials and never hearing about that method of payment or identification. "*Sandra...* I'm asking if you're still a virgin."

"Oh. Ah... yes. I'm a virgin. A friend of mine has called me a super virgin," I confessed sheepishly. "You see, I'm a child of the King, so I try to adhere to Biblical principles. Jesus said that sex is only for marriage, so I'm saving myself for my husband." [9]

Mascot warmly smiled as he pulled into the dorm parking area and stated, "Sandra... *Wow.* Again, you amaze me. I have nothing but respect for you. Virginity is very rare these days, especially among attractive people. So, *well done.* I hope you succeed in your quest. I, too, am a virgin. However, I'm just waiting until I meet *the right person* to share that amazing first experience with. I'll admit, after everything that occurred today, I hoped that this *special person* would eventually be you, but I have no intentions on shattering a dream that's so very honorable. I'm an atheist, but an advocate for adhering to many global concepts of morality. Although we disagree about what happens after death, I like that you actually *practice* what you claim to believe. In my experience, *most don't.*" [10]

Don't Look Back

After Dolion finished another Sunday morning sermon in the newly constructed building on the other side of town, he stepped down from the pulpit and allowed one of his many brothers to approach.

Jimmy's father pulled the microphone lower and announced, "Someone is going to be leaving us today. This is their last service here and we want to show our love and support. *Sandra Lawson* will leave the state for college to be an engineer and train with Army ROTC." The man cheerfully gazed down at me and continued, "You're gonna be missed, girl. *What a fireball.* The Lord broke the mold when He made you." His gracious words floored me. The man returned his gaze to the congregation and added, "A going-away party in Sandra's honor starts *right now* in the gymnasium."

I peered upward at the overhead screen. Written above an image of *me* were the words WE'LL MISS YOU. I remembered when Giselle snapped my photograph the Sunday prior. She was always thoughtful, kind, and sincere. Her husband was Dolion's eldest son, Reuben, who seemed disconnected and kept to himself.

While the gymnasium migration was in full swing, Giselle cheerfully snagged my hand and led me into the side hallway. She held my face and declared, "Sandra, your journey *should* be celebrated. All of this is for you."

"Thank you for putting it together! I feel so loved! The party was *your* idea, wasn't it?" I guessed with a smirk. [1]

"That doesn't matter. *Listen to me.* We don't have much time," Giselle urged with a determined stare, and grabbed my hands with a squeeze. "*Don't sell-out.* You're young and unattached. Do the things that are in your heart to do. Do the things that *drive* you and don't settle for what you think you know. There's so much to experience outside of this town and these people. Go to school, train with the army, and *don't look back.* I could be in the *air force* right now, but I'm tied down by the things I thought I wanted. While we were sill dating, Reuben and I fished, went on excursions, talked for hours, and said the most loving things to each other. On top of being handsome, he was very romantic and spontaneous. *I fell in love.* It all seemed like a fairytale, so I gave up my military dreams and exchanged them for a life of love and adventure with *Reuben*. My parents were furious with me. They told me to call off the wedding and get away from him, but I didn't listen. Once we were married, the fairytale ended. Every bit of passion and excitement in our relationship completely disappeared. Reuben already *had* his prize and saw no point in continuing to romance me. Now, we hardly even speak." Giselle grabbed my shoulders. "I'm telling you this for a reason, Sandra. Please, don't make the same mistakes I made. *Go.* Get away from here and *live your life*." [2]

My eyes filled with tears as I whispered, *"I didn't know you were going through all of this, Giselle. Are you alright?"*

"Don't feel sorry for me, Sandra," she sternly ordered. "Just remember what I said. *Okay?* Go and don't look back. Things aren't always what they seem." [3]

I hugged her tightly and whispered, *"I heard every word. Don't worry. I'm getting out of here."*

She pursed her lips, gave a brave nod as she fought back tears, and rushed out of sight.

A cake riddled with toy soldiers waited for me beside many familiar faces. After the party, I took the side exit, stepped into the parking lot, and discovered Jimmy sitting in his truck. Hoping for a friendly hug, I made my way toward him.

"Hey, Sandra!" Jimmy called out, causing me to quicken my pace to his driver's side window. "Are you leaving already? Hop in. Let's talk awhile." Making my way around, I climbed into his truck. "So, are you excited?!"

"*I am.* College is my ticket out of here. Do you remember when I used to ride my bike to church?" The young man nodded. "I needed to escape my horrific life, even if it was only for a few hours a week. Everything I have worked for has led up to this. *Everything.* This is the only way I know to break free."

"C'mon, *Sandra…* don't you think you're being a little dramatic?" Jimmy scoffed. "Being here can't be *that* bad."

My eyebrows reached for my scalp as I snipped, "Well, not everyone has a bright future *handed to them* on a silver platter. You work for your dad, Jimmy. He promotes you whenever he wants to and pays you as much as he desires. Don't assume that everyone has had a life as easy as *yours*." [4]

"Whoa! Wait a minute! You've got this all wrong! I work really hard for what I have. *Nothing's* been given to me. I might inherit the business someday, but it will be up to *me* to keep it going. C'mon, Sandra. Cut me some slack," he rebutted. "Why are we fighting? This is your last Sunday before shipping off. Let's make these last moments together good ones. What's really on your mind? I seriously doubt that it's my family's business." [5]

"*You're right.* I'm sorry about biting your head off. It's just that… I have been through a lot and you saying *it wasn't that bad* is insulting and makes me feel like you don't even know me. It was a ******* nightmare growing up in my house," I clarified with tears. "You have no idea what you're talking about." ⁶

"That's true, Sandra. *Actually*, I don't even know why I said that. I remember how your parents wouldn't give you a ride to church and you ended up pedaling your mountain bike all that way," he admitted. "I'm an idiot. I *completely* forgot. I'm sorry. That was a careless thing for me to say. I didn't mean to sound so dismissive. Come over here and give me a hug. I don't want us to part ways angry." Jimmy opened his arms to me, but I hesitated, unwilling to reveal my attraction to him. "*Sandra*. What are you afraid of? How long have we been friends? *Get over here.*" I awkwardly scooted a little closer on the bench seat. "Nope. You're too far away. Come here, *weirdo*." He grabbed my lower torso and pulled me right beside him, hip to hip. In the silence, my mind spun with regret and intense longing. "What is it, Sandra? You're *never* this quiet."

I breathed in deeply, as if courage was something to be inhaled, and murmured, "*I have always wanted to tell you something, but I was afraid of what it could mean. Since I'm leaving, I guess it couldn't hurt anything…*"

"C'mon, Sandra," Jimmy prodded, giving me a squeeze. "Don't leave me hanging."

Tears choked me as I confessed, "I have *always* loved you." Overwhelmingly embarrassed, I sat up and looked away.

"I wish I had known that," the young man divulged, becoming emotional and confusing me. "I love you, too, Sandra."

"Aw. You're sweet," I added, writing off even the smallest possibility of mutual affection. "I know you do. You're a great guy that sees me like a baby sister. I just mean… you know… I love you *in that way*."

"I *know* what you meant, Sandra," Jimmy boldly corrected. "You're misunderstanding me. I love you… *a lot*. I never said anything to you because you were always so *anti*-marriage and *anti*-kids. Now you're going off in a direction that I can't follow, and I don't want to hold you back."

I closed my eyes and remarked, "*Wait*. Do you mean to tell me we could've been together *this entire time*?" ⁷

"Why are you so shocked that I love you? Don't you get it? You're totally *different* from everybody else. You're beautiful, strong, have an amazing personality, and you're *smart*," he highlighted. "You're also *leaving*… and my career is *here*. I can't follow you where you're going." Covering my face, I sobbed as if ripped apart by two worlds. "Hey, don't cry. Everything happens for a reason, Sandra. You'll meet a bunch of people and experience all sorts of things. I'm not excited that you're leaving, but I am excited for *you*. Just know that you'll be missed… *a lot*."

Jimmy reached over and pulled me back towards him, guiding my head to his chest. It was then that I remembered Giselle's timely and eerily prophetic warning. I refused to make the same mistake she made and found the strength to sit upright once more. [8]

"Well, Jimmy, let's rip this band-aid off," I huffed, wiping tears away with a weak smile. "Thank you for your friendship… and for loving me. It makes a huge difference knowing that it was possible."

At that, I got out of Jimmy's truck, walked away… *and refused to look back.* [9]

Closing Thoughts and Prayer

You might think I got away from my problems scot-free, unless you've survived narcissistic abuse yourself and chuckled at the idea. If that's the case, you'll understand the next sentence better than most. *Wherever you go, there you are.*

Throughout my childhood, I endured physical abuse and gaslighting, which crippled me into remaining in dangerous situations, even when escape was possible. If you recall, Jesus answered my many cries for help. Alice discovered my extensive bruises in the sixth grade and reported it. The principal threatened to call CPS, but I covered for my abuser… my sadistic mother. When the woman toyed with adultery right in front of me, I kept the heavy secret from her husband… my father… whom she had repeatedly accused of infidelity. While my abuser was drunk, she touched me sexually. When I confronted her the following morning, she accused *me* of controlling her hands. The next time she was drunk in my presence, my mother removed her clothes and exposed her private areas to me. As much as I wanted her out of my life, I reported the traumatizing events to no one. Even when the police offered to remove my abuser from our midst, I declined their help.

The bars of my cell were invisible to me. My narcissistic mother had skillfully created a *mental* trap, installed and programmed for her benefit. *Deprogramming* was vital for me to see what was real, understand what had happened to me, and do what was necessary to stay free. To become resistant to further abuse, I needed deeper healing.

Research about psychopathy, sociopathy, and narcissism helped me understand that the abuse wasn't my fault, but it didn't heal my wounds. Conversations about my trauma helped others understand me, but it didn't undo the damage. My continual restoration is a job for *Jesus*, and His ways and thoughts are higher than our own. The Messiah patiently offers His healthy love and shows me how to recognize it in myself and others, while also revealing what isn't healthy at all.

My parents provided food, shelter, and clothing. Asylums, orphanages, and correctional facilities offer the same thing. I needed *love*. Although one parent in my childhood was *safer* than the other, neither of them reflected the love of Jesus. In all of my mistakes, vulgar thoughts, and violent behavior, I was just a kid reacting to what was happening around me. *I was a child.* When I was born, they were already adults, but my mother's needs were the priority for the household. I was ill-equipped to satisfy her ever changing whims, and I paid for it. If it wasn't for Jesus carrying me through that season, I would not have survived.

Even though my father wasn't aware of what happened in his absence, he wasn't *always* gone while abuse was occurring. My father was right down the hall from my bedroom when my mother thrashed me with his leather belt for lying next to him on his recliner. Instead of investigating the clamorous interaction between his wife and daughter, or intervening on my behalf to stop the audible abuse, the man turned up the volume on that television he was watching. Was the game more important than my safety and wellbeing? No. It *wasn't* more important. He could have helped me and he didn't.

If you recall, he overtly shifted his paternal responsibility onto me to determine if *a mental institution* was where our abuser would sleep that night and the many nights to follow. I was sixteen years old and not mature enough to make that decision. It was my father's responsibility to determine what needed to happen. It was a cowardly act to place that immense weight on my shoulders. The burden of my mother's future never should have touched me, and yet I carried it for years, wondering if I made the right choice. My passive father enabled my narcissistic mother to dominate the household and create chaos. It was *his* job to protect *me*.

It's the responsibility of adults to protect children from the evil monsters, and evil monsters come in all shapes and sizes. As soon as we think we're above abusing others, our own pride paves the way for us to become *the bully*… an evil monster… even if only temporarily. The sin behind Satan's demotion, that left him to walk back and forth on the earth, was *pride*. Disgusting pride. Jesus has a way of dethroning the proud, and my rear end hurts just thinking about all the times He removed that chair from under me.

Despite all that happened, I still needed to *forgive* my parents. Forgiveness didn't mean that I excused what happened, that it was less evil than once perceived, or that I was required to reconcile with my abusers. No. I needed to let go of the hate, bitterness, and self-righteousness, because I'm not their judge. I have done some horrible things in my life, and unforgiveness in my heart prevents me from receiving forgiveness from Yahweh, who *is* the Judge. I want nothing in the way of my forgiveness.

If you've discovered yourself being the monster, like I have, humble yourself. The first thing I try to do when I play the role of the accidental monster is talk to Jesus about it. I repeat. Talk to Jesus. I confess to Him how I've messed up royally and ask Him to forgive me. I have to forgive myself, too. If I have the opportunity, I try to make it right with the person as soon as possible. (If you have a spouse or children, humility matters even more. Your children will learn how to handle situations from you, and a healthy relationship with your spouse is a wonderful gift to them.)

You and I aren't above being the monster as along as life is in us and flesh still robes our bones, but you can break the cycles of abuse through the Holy Spirit. Ask Jesus for His Holy Spirit, ask Him for help, and read your Scriptures to be washed by the Word. If you could emotionally and psychologically heal all by yourself, you would have done it already. The words I told my young friend are true. *We're a work in progress until we're dead…* but only if we're turning to our Healer… the One on the throne… Jesus.

If we're not looking to Him, we'll do what so many others have done before us. We'll do what's right *in our own eyes.* We'll stay married to our own experiences, ideas, opinions, cycles, excuses, curses, and demons… until we've convinced ourselves that we're righteous in our own strength and our path is good.

Attaining freedom from the abuse was elating, but I didn't know what to do with it. At eighteen, I didn't know what a narcissist was or about the lingering wounds that prolonged abuse inflicted on my mind. C-PTSD symptoms followed me into adulthood and altered my decision making, crippling me as I fell in love with unattainable people and opened myself up to 'friendly' predators looking for someone just like me. C-PTSD affected every facet of my world and sabotaged me from within. I brought my trauma and demons with me wherever I went until I invited Jesus to intervene further, heal my heart, and deliver me.

Anyway, you might wonder what you should do if you're in a narcissistic situation *right now…* and it's a situation alright. A dark one. What if you're a kid reading this and you're afraid of what will happen if you open up about it? What if you're a spouse reading this and you feel stuck and too dependent to leave, or your kids are involved and at risk? What if you're at work or at school or at church or locked away in isolation and dealing with a narcissist that wants to destroy you or your reputation?

I have Good News for you. Yahweh did not create you to be a punching bag, a puppet, or a host organism for a human parasite to feed from. Jesus can work miracles if you let Him and obey what He says.

In Scripture, Moses and the Israelites escaped Pharoh and got out of Egypt, but it took some major miracles. If they obeyed Yahweh, their situations worked out for their good. However, most Israelites complained about their discomfort and preferred to remain in the wilderness or return to Egypt over fighting the giants that blocked their way to the promised land. Many ignored the years of cruel slavery, longed for the scraps that Egypt had offered, and *died* before reaching what Yahweh intended for them. We need to learn from their forty years of mistakes. We need Yahweh to take out our spiritual giants. Let's pray together and ask His Son, Jesus, to deliver you.

First, read the prayer **in your head.** If you're ready to move forward, read the prayer aloud and mean every word. I assure you. The Messiah is big enough, even for *your* problems. You're not alone in this, and freedom is *possible*. Many have escaped, received healing, and lived to tell the tale… all in Jesus' name.

Prayer:

"Abba Yahweh, in the name of Jesus, I desperately need Your help. Thank You for salvation. I believe Jesus is the Messiah and I want to learn how to be a good and faithful servant to Him. I can't escape this situation and trauma by myself, and I feel stuck, but the hole I'm in isn't deeper than Your arm is long. I trust You with my life. Would You please cover me with the blood of Jesus from the top of my head to the bottom of my feet, in the name of Jesus? Would you please fill me with Your Holy Spirit, in Jesus' name? Would You please heal my heart, layer by layer, more and more, and show Yourself strong on my behalf, in Jesus' name? Would You please rescue me from whatever is keeping me bound in my situation, in Jesus' name? Would You please deliver me from sin, abuse, suicide, oppression, depression, fear, anxiety, wrath, C-PTSD, triggers, defense mechanisms, substance abuse, a distorted self-image, addiction of every variety, all sexual sin and every perversion, coping mechanisms, generational curses, witchcraft, stubbornness, false doctrines, demonic religions, occult practice, independence from You and rebellion against You, isolation, paranoia, phobias, illness and disease, mental disorders, invisible wounds, injury, barrenness, and pride, in Jesus' name? You see everything that is happening to me and has happened to me, and You know all that I've done. Would You please forgive me of my sins and give me the ability to forgive my abusers, in Jesus' name? Would You please reveal to me Your definition of forgiveness and how to do it, in Jesus' name? Would You please reveal to me what I need to do in my life and situation, and help me accomplish it through the Holy Spirit, in Jesus' name? Would You please strengthen my hands and knees for spiritual battle the correct way, and walk me through defeating the demons that seek my destruction, in Jesus' name? Would You please break the chains of bondage in my life, in Jesus' name? Would You please reveal to me how You feel about me and show me Your love, in Jesus' name? I need Your love. Would You please take my broken heart and glue me back together with Yourself, in Jesus' name? Would You please hold me in Your hands and show me the beauty that can come from so much pain, in Jesus' name? Would You please teach me what to pray next, in Jesus' name? Satan can't defeat You, and if I trust You with my entire life, he won't defeat me, either. I give my entire life to You, Jesus, whatever that looks like, because this is what my life looks like when I do things my way. Would You please stop me from continuing on destructive paths and show me Your Way,

in Jesus' name? With child-like faith, I run into Your capable arms and rest my head on Your chest. Would You please comfort me and parent me, in Jesus' name? You love me. You made me. Jesus, You gave Yourself over to a brutal death so that the wrath of Yahweh, that I deserve, would pass over me. You resurrected to show me that death couldn't defeat You. You ascended so that I could receive Your Holy Spirit within me, a Helper, for times such as these. Thank You for everything You have done, are doing, and will do for me. I'll get out of my own way now and let You do the things I never dreamed were possible. I submit and petition all of this to You, Abba Yahweh, in Jesus' name. Amen."

Let me tell you something, fellow warrior. *I love you.* I love you for your desire to heal. I love you for accepting the *responsibility* to heal, and choosing not to perpetuate the demonic madness of abuse and victimhood by harming those around you or continuing on as a living doormat. If you prayed this prayer, it's just the beginning. You'll need to pray prayers much like this every day for the rest of your life. The more you learn from Him, the deeper your healing will go. If you don't know what to say, keep borrowing this prayer until you do. The Holy Spirit will help you.

Precious one, you're worth fighting for, but don't allow another person to fight harder for you than you're willing to fight for yourself. So, *fight*... in prayer and however else the Holy Spirit leads you into action. Put on the armor of Yahweh, pick up the sword of the Spirit, stand behind Jesus, and wage war on those demons. Don't take abuse lying down, so Satan can kick you mercilessly until you eventually die. Suicide isn't for you, honey. Satan is trying to kill you because there's a calling on your life that *scares* him. *I'm excited for you.* Satan is *not*.

Stand up, in Jesus' name. Stand up, walk out your faith in the Messiah, and send those demons packing. A life lived experiencing the power and authority of Jesus often comes from *applying* the power and authority of Jesus over and over. You'll need to be praying over and over. The demons won't quit coming for you, especially when we fall and stumble, are ignorant of open demonic doors in our lives, or when circumstances kick you *really* hard. If demons won't quit, then you can't quit praying. *Never quit praying.* Never let go of Jesus' hand. He sees you and knows *your* name. He'll get you through the storms, no matter how vicious or strung out those tempests may be. You might be a bloody mess before the clouds part, but you don't lose the war until you stop fighting.

Remember, Jesus already defeated Satan on the cross. It's a done deal, so obey Jesus and make those demons fear the Holy Spirit inside of *you*. Believe me, tag Jesus in. He hits infinitely harder than those demons ever could, and *it's fight night*. My testimony is real, and I'm telling you from experience... don't give up. Stand up.

SCRIPTURE STUDIES

Section 1

Salt Water: [1]Psalms 107:23-32 / [2]Psalms 89:5-9, 93:1-5 and Isaiah 51:10-16

The Cove: [1]Psalms 42:1-11 / [2]2 Samuel 22:31-32, Psalms 18:1-2, Proverbs 30:5, Job 1:1-10 and Matthew 6:25-34 / [3]Genesis 1:21-23 and Psalms 139:1-10 / [4]Deuteronomy 5:1-33, Proverbs 30:17, Jeremiah 17:9-10, Ephesians 6:1-4 and Colossians 3:20 / [5]Proverbs 22:6, 22:15, 29:15 and 29:17 / [6]Matthew 18:1-10, Luke 15:1-7 and Revelation 21:7-8 / [7]Proverbs 3:7-8, 21:2 and 27:12 / [8]Psalms 18:1-2, Matthew 7:1-29, Luke 19:28-40 and 1 Peter 2:1-10 / [9]Proverbs 15:1 / [10]Proverbs 18:21, 25:28, 1 Corinthians 9:24-27, Ephesians 6:4 and Philippians 2:1-4 / [11]Proverbs 29:11 and James 3:1-18 / [12]Matthew 6:1-4, 12:33-37 and 1 Corinthians 13:1-13

Dirty Hands: [1]Exodus 20:12, Ephesians 6:1-4 and Colossians 3:18-25 / [2]Psalms 34:11-16, Proverbs 3:7-8, 10:12-14, Zechariah 1:2-4, 7:8-14, Matthew 5:46-48, 18:2-7, Mark 7:1-23 and James 3:1-18 / [3]Proverbs 25:2 / [4]Luke 12:1-5 and Romans 16:17-20 / [5]Genesis 1:26-31, Psalms 103:13, Proverbs 22:6, 22:12, John 13:34-35, Acts 10:34-44, Romans 12:2-13, James 3:13-18 and 1 Peter 3:8-12 / [6]Proverbs 8:1-36 and 1 Corinthians 13:1-13 / [7]Isaiah 1:16-20, Matthew 15:1-20 and John 8:1-12

Different Stuff: [1]Jonah 1:1-17, 2:1-10, 3:1-10 and Matthew 12:38-42 / [2]John 13:1-17 / [3]Genesis 2:18-25 / [4]Galatians 3:26-29 / [5]Leviticus 18:1-30, Proverbs 10:20, 12:16, Matthew 18:1-11, Mark 7:17-23, Romans 14:10-13, 1 Corinthians 6:9-20, Galatians 6:1-10, 1 Peter 3:8-12 and 1 John 3:1-3 / [6]1 Corinthians 13:1-13 / [7]Isaiah 49:14-18, Romans 8:12-17 and Philippians 4:6-9 / [8]Genesis 3:1-24, Psalms 91:1-16 and Ephesians 2:4-10

No Hitting: [1]Isaiah 30:18-21, Matthew 18:10-14 and Philippians 4:6-7 / [2]Joshua 1:9, Psalms 9:9-10, Isaiah 49:15-16 and 2 Corinthians 1:3-4 / [3]Philippians 4:8-9 / [4]Psalms 32:8, Matthew 11:29-30 and John 10:1-16 / [5]Matthew 7:1-6 and James 4:11-12 / [6]Proverbs

26:18-19 / [7]Proverbs 3:11-12, 4:11 11:2, 12:1, 18:12, Psalms 25:8-12, Daniel 4:36-37, Philippians 4:9, Colossians 3:12-14, James 4:7-10, 1 Peter 3:3-4 and 5:6-10 / [8]Proverbs 1:7 and Ephesians 4:1-16 / [9]1 Corinthians 15:51-58 and Revelation 11:15-19 / [10]Luke 9:51-62 and Galatians 5:19-26 / [11] Romans 13:1-7 and 2 Timothy 2:19-26 / [12]Ezekiel 33:1-6, Romans 12:17-21, 2 Corinthians 10:4-6, Ephesians 2:1-10 and Hebrews 4:16

Same: [1]Daniel 2:1-49, Philippians 4:6-7 and Colossians 1:24-29 / [2]Exodus 20:12, Deuteronomy 10:12-16, Proverbs 2:1-22, 4:1-27, 9:1-18, Jeremiah 33:1-3, Matthew 7:7-12, John 15:1-17, 16:21-24, 1 Corinthians 15:33-34, James 1:2-8, 4:1-10 and 1 John 5:1-5 and 5:14-15 / [3]Luke 8:16-18, John 3:1-21 and 1 John 2:1-11 / [4]Luke 18:1-8 /[5]Psalms 133:1-3, Ephesians 4:1-6 and 1 Peter 3:8-12 / [6]Matthew 10:16-20 / [7]Psalms 109:1-5, Proverbs 18:2, Ecclesiastes 10:11-15, 1 Corinthians 13:1-13, Ephesians 5:1-7, Colossians 3:18-25 and James 3:1-18 / [8]Ephesians 5:8-17 / [9]Romans 5:6-21, 8:31-39 and 1 John 4:17-21 / [10]Matthew 10:21-36

Up Next: [1]Isaiah 49:14-16 and Jeremiah 17:5-10 / [2]Matthew 18:1-10 / [3]Matthew 7:1-5, 23:1-36, John 8:1-11 and 1 Corinthians 6:7-20 / [4]Proverbs 15:14-17, Romans 1:18-32, Ephesians 4:11-32 and 2 Timothy 4:3-4 / [5]Exodus 20:16, Deuteronomy 19:15-21, Proverbs 12:22 and Ephesians 5:8-21 / [6]Psalms 101:1-8, Matthew 13:14-30, John 8:31-47 and 2 Thessalonians 2:1-12 / [7]Proverbs 29:27 / [8]Matthew 5:27-32 and James 3:1-18 / [9]Proverbs 31:10-31, 1 Corinthians 7:1-40 and Ephesians 5:22-33 / [10]Proverbs 29:9-10, 29:20 / [11]Proverbs 29:11 and Ephesians 6:1-4 / [12]Proverbs 15:1-2, 15:12 and 28:15-16 / [13]Ephesians 6:5-9

The Highway: [1]Proverbs 18:1, 24:8-9, 24:15-20 and 24:28-29 / [2]Psalms 59:1-17 / [3]Proverbs 18:2 / [4]Proverbs 18:3 and 18:17 / [5]Joshua 5:13-15 / [6]Proverbs 12:15-23, 18:5-8, 18:21 and 2 Peter 2:1-22 / [7]Proverbs 17:6 / [8]Psalms 127:1-5, Proverbs 27:17 and 1 Corinthians 13:1-13 / [9]Philippians 4:6-9 / [10]Proverbs 16:27-30 and Ephesians 5:1-7 / [11]Matthew 7:1-6 / [12]Proverbs 16:25, 16:31-32, 26:1-12, 27:15-16 and Galatians 5:13-26 /[13]Isaiah 1:16-20 /[14]Proverbs 26:17

Tell the Truth: [1]Deuteronomy 8:1-6, Proverbs 3:11-12, 18:17, 22:6 and Hebrews 12:1-17 / [2]Proverbs 13:24, 19:18-19, 22:3 and 22:15 / [3]1 Peter 3:8-17 / [4]Psalms 37:1-40, Proverbs 4:24, Isaiah 48:22, 2 Corinthians 10:4-6 and Hebrews 10:23-31 / [5]Exodus 34:5-7, Proverbs 11:7-10, Ecclesiastes 8:10-13 and Ezekiel 18:1-32 / [6]Jeremiah 17:9-10, Luke 8:17 and 1 Corinthians 13:11-12 / [7]Isaiah 1:1-20 / [8]Proverbs 12:22, 14:5, Mark 7:14-23, John 8:42-44 and Revelation 21:5-8 / [9]Proverbs 10:9, 12:19, 23:13-16, 28:13,

Ephesians 4:17-32 and Hebrews 12:11 / [10]Psalms 32:1-11, Proverbs 13:1, 13:5-6, 13:10, Romans 3:21-26 and 1 John 1:5-10 / [11]2 Chronicles 7:12-14, Proverbs 1:20-23, 30:6-9, Matthew 3:1-12, 9:9-13, Luke 15:1-7 and Revelation 3:19-21

Get Back Up: [1]Matthew 18:1-7 / [2]Hebrews 5:12-14 and 6:1-8 / [3]Proverbs 12:4 and Philippians 4:6-9 / [4]Proverbs 15:1 and 1 Peter 3:1-7 / [5]Numbers 13:27-33 and 14:1-9 / [6]Psalms 143:10, Proverbs 28:26 and Isaiah 55:6-11 / [7]Psalms 139:23-24, Proverbs 4:23, 16:3, Mark 7:17-23 and Romans 12:1-3 / [8]Psalms 25:1-5 / [9]Jeremiah 17:5-10 / [10] Deuteronomy 31:8 and Isaiah 41:8-10 / [11]Psalms 37:23-24 / [12]Proverbs 24:16, Galatians 6:1-10 and Hebrews 12:1-11 / [13]Jeremiah 29:11-13, Romans 8:27-28 and 1 Peter 4:12-19 /[14]Genesis 19:15-26, Ecclesiastes 7:8-10, Isaiah 43:18-21, Luke 9:57-62, Philippians 3:12-14 and 2 Peter 2:1-22 / [15]Matthew 14:22-33 and 2 Corinthians 4:1-10 / [16]Proverbs 3:11-12, 10:17, 22:6, Nehemiah 1:8-9, Zechariah 1:1-3, 1 Corinthians 7:32-35 and 10:1-13 / [17]Psalms 34:1-22, John 14:1, Romans 8:12-15, 2 Timothy 1:6-7 and James 1:2-8 / [18]Psalms 25:6-12, 32:8-11 and Proverbs 4:10-13 / [19]Proverbs 1:1-7, 12:1, Matthew 24:3-51, 1 Corinthians 13:4-7, 2 Corinthians 11:22-33 and James 1:12-20 / [20]John 14:25-27 and 1 John 2:24-27 / [21]Psalms 50:12-23 and Jeremiah 33:1-3 / [22]Genesis 1:1-3, Numbers 6:22-27, Mark 2:1-12, John 5:1-15, 10:1-30, 1 Corinthians 10:24 and Hebrews 13:1-3 / [23]Psalms 119:105, Isaiah 60:1-4, John 1:1-5, 8:12 and 1 John 1:5-7 / [24]Psalms 68:5-6, James 1:21-25 and 2:14-26 / [25]Psalms 119:129-130, Matthew 5:14-16, Luke 10:25-37, John 7:37-39, 1 Corinthians 13:1-13 and 1 Thessalonians 5:1-11/ [26]Romans 3:9-26, 15:1-6 and Philippians 2:1-4 / [27]Psalms 133:1-3, Ecclesiastes 4:9-12 and 1 John 4:7-11 / [28]Matthew 7:7-12, 10:40-42, 25:31-46, John 4:1-26 and 1 John 3:16-18 / [29]1 Peter 5:1-11 / [30]Proverbs 3:29-30, 16:28, Isaiah 5:20-25, Matthew 5:10-12, 10:24-31, Luke 6:22, Romans 2:1-11, 13:8-10, 14:10-13, Galatians 5:13-15 and 1 Peter 3:8-17 / [31]Isaiah 1:15-20 and 1 Thessalonians 5:14-15 / [32]1 John 4:20-21 / [33]Matthew 5:43-48, Romans 12:9-16 and Revelation 12:7-12 / [34]Deuteronomy 32:35, Psalms 97:1-12, Luke 8:17, 12:1-3, John 2:13-17, Acts 10:1-48 and Romans 12:17-21 / [35]Proverbs 3:31-35, Matthew 3:1-12, 7:13-23, 23:1-39 and Revelation 3:14-22 / [36]2 Chronicles 30:7-9, Isaiah 49:14-16, Micah 7:8-10, Matthew 6:8-15, 18:21-35, Mark 11:25-26, Luke 6:37, Colossians 3:12-17 and Ephesians 4:25-32 / [37]Hebrews 12:12-17 / [38]Genesis 50:15-20, Psalms 51:1-13, Proverbs 4:1-27, Galatians 5:16-26 and 2 Peter 1:1-11

Double Standard: [1]Revelation 3:14-22 / [2]Proverbs 10:18, Matthew 18:10-17, Luke 11:5-13, 11:37-54 and 18:1-8 / [3]Matthew 18:1-5 / [4]Luke 16:19-31 and 18:15-17 / [5]Psalms 15:1-5, 34:1-22, 120:1-7, Proverbs 6:16-19, 8:13, 12:22, 14:5 and John 8:37-47 / [6]Ephesians 6:1-9 and Colossians 4:1 / [7]Exodus 20:1-17, Psalms 139:1-24, Proverbs 20:30,

Matthew 15:1-20, Acts 5:1-11, 1 Corinthians 6:9-11, Ephesians 4:17-28, 1 Timothy 1:3-15 and Revelation 21:6-8 / [8]Isaiah 48:22 and Philippians 4:6-7 / [9]Romans 2:1-11 / [10]Ecclesiastes 9:13-18 / [11]Proverbs 1:20-33 / [12]Matthew 18:6-9

Nancy and the Secret: [1]Psalms 12:1-8, Proverbs 27:6, 29:5-6, Romans 16:17-20 and Jude 1:1-25 / [2]Joshua 2:1-24, Ruth 2:1-18, Matthew 1:1-17 and Acts 10:1-48 / [3]Proverbs 23:1-3 and 23:6-8 / [4]Ecclesiastes 4:9-12 / [5]Luke 8:17, 1 Corinthians 13:1-13 and Hebrews 4:1-16 / [6]Proverbs 18:17 / [7]Luke 12:1-7 / [8]Proverbs 11:25, 18:24, 27:17 and 2 Corinthians 1:3-7 / [9]Matthew 5:38-48, 7:12-14, Ephesians 4:1-6 and 4:26-32 / [10]Proverbs 2:1-22, 15:4, 17:28, 27:15-16, Matthew 10:34-42 and Luke 8:19-21 / [11]Proverbs 11:29, Matthew 20:24-28, 25:31-Luke 6:43-45 and 1 John 3:10-24

The Movies: [1]Deuteronomy 24:7, Proverbs 18:17, 27:12, 1 Thessalonians 5:21-22 and 1 John 4:1-6 / [2]Proverbs 17:28, 20:3, 21:19, 27:15 and Exodus 20:12 / [3]Proverbs 27:7 / [4]Proverbs 12:2 and 14:17 / [5]Psalms 14:2-3, 52:1-9, 120:1-7, Proverbs 4:24, 10:9, 11:18, 12:15-22, 23:1-3, 23:6-8, 31:10-31, Galatians 5:19-26, Ephesians 5:1-7 and 1 Peter 3:8-12 / [6]Matthew 18:1-9 / [7]Psalms 107:1-9, John 4:1-42, 1 Corinthians 15:50-58 and Revelation 19:1-21 / [8]Matthew 6:1-4, Colossians 3:12-17 and James 1:16-18 / [9]Matthew 7:7-12 and 1 Thessalonians 5:16-18 / [10]Isaiah 55:1-13 / [11]Proverbs 4:1-27, Proverbs 8:1-36, 10:9, Matthew 10:27-31, Galatians 5:7-10, Ephesians 5:8-17 and Hebrews 10:26-39 / [12]Psalms 12:1-8, 27:1-14, Proverbs 6:16-19, 11:3, 12:17-22, Isaiah 49:14-18, Jeremiah 17:1-13, Ezekiel 18:19-32, Matthew 7:1-6, 7:13-29, 15:1-20, 18:6-7, 23:1-39, John 8:42-47, Romans 12:2, 13:1-7, 1 Corinthians 6:9-12, Galatians 5:13-18, 6:7-8, Ephesians 4:25-32, 6:1-4, 2 Timothy 4:1-5, Titus 1:10-16, 2:1-8, James 1:19-27, 1 Peter 2:1-17, 3:13-17, 2 Peter 2:1-22, 1 John 1:5-10 and Revelation 21:6-8 / [13]Proverbs 22:5-6, Matthew 10:16-26 and Romans 1:18-32

Praying Mantis, Scarecrow, and Grandma: [1]Proverbs 17:1 / [2]Exodus 16:1-21 and Philippians 4:6-9 / [3]Jeremiah 23:23-24 and Luke 12:2 / [4]Proverbs 12:20, Matthew 12:33-37 and James 3:1-12 / [5]Deuteronomy 32:28-43, Psalms 19:1-14, 34:1-22, 94:1-23, Proverbs 15:4, 16:32, Romans 8:1-21, 12:17-21, Ephesians 4:25-32, Hebrews 4:14-16, 12:12-17 and James 3:13-18 / [6]Proverbs 10:19-21, 10:31-32, 15:1, 18:6-7 and 20:2-3 / [7]Ephesians 6:4 / [8]2 Kings 2:23-24, John 19:1-3 and Acts 16:16-18 / [9]1 Samuel 16:1-7 / [10]Psalms 139:13-18 / [11]Ephesians 5:1-21 and 1 Peter 4:1-5 / [12]Psalms 82:1-4, Proverbs 17:22, 27:7 and 1 Peter 4:7-11

Hypocrite: [1]Proverbs 31:30 / [2]Proverbs 21:2 and 1 Thessalonians 5:21-22 / [3]Proverbs 4:1-27 / [4]Psalms 32:8-11, Isaiah 40:28, 55:6-11, Jeremiah 33:1-3 and Romans 11:33-36 / [5]Psalms 119:129-144, Psalms 139:1-4 and Proverbs 11:9 / [6]Proverbs 3:13-18, Matthew 6:1-18, 15:1-20, 22:15-22, 23:1-36, 24:45-51, Luke 12:1-3 and 1 Corinthians 2:1-16 / [7]Proverbs 16:31 / [8]Proverbs 9:8, 11:22, 12:1, 17:10, 27:2, Ecclesiastes 7:5-12, 1 Corinthians 13:1-13 and 1 Peter 3:1-6 / [9]1 Peter 3:7-12

No Crying: [1]Psalms 18:1-50, 25:1-22 and 144:1-15 / [2]Judges 6:1-6 / [3]Judges 6:7-22 / [4]Judges 6:23-40 / [5]Matthew 7:7-11, 21:18-22, John 15:1-11, James 1:5-8 and 1 John 3:16-23 / [6]2 Timothy 2:1-26 / [7]Judges 7:1-15 / [8]Judges 7:16-25 / [9]Judges 8:1-12 / [10]Judges 8:12-35 / [11]2 Corinthians 4:1-18

BCGs: [1]Proverbs 6:12-19, 27:15-16, Matthew 6:25-34, 10:27-31 and Romans 16:17-20 / [2]Psalms 27:1-14, 118:5-9, 119:105-120, Isaiah 60:1-2, Matthew 4:12-22, John 8:12 and James 1:16-18 / [3]Proverbs 4:23-27, 17:6 and 27:12 / [4]Proverbs 27:14 / [5]Numbers 6:22-27 and Psalms 103:6-18 / [6]Psalms 91:1-16, Matthew 23:37 and Revelation 3:20-21 / [7]Proverbs 14:1, 1 Peter 5:5-11 and Revelation 12:7-12 / [8]Psalms 38:1-22, Proverbs 14:3, 14:29 and James 1:19-20 / [9]Proverbs 12:25, 17:22, Isaiah 41:8-16, John 14:27 and Philippians 4:6-9 / [10]Deuteronomy 31:6, 2 Samuel 22:32-37, Psalms 3:1-8, 18:25-36, 46:1-3, 62:1-12, Proverbs 18:10, 29:25, Isaiah 46:3-10, Jeremiah 17:5-11, Nahum 1:2-8, Ephesians 6:10-20, 2 Timothy 1:7 and 1 John 4:18-21 / [11]Exodus 22:2-4, Proverbs 3:7-8, 6:30-31, 27:22, John 10:1-10, Luke 8:16-17 and Acts 5:1-11 / [12]Exodus 20:15-16, Proverbs 3:29-35, 27:19 and Job 1:6-22 / [13]Leviticus 19:11-18, Deuteronomy 19:15-20, Psalms 15:1-5, 55:20-23, 109:1-5, Proverbs 14:5, 14:22, 14:25, 19:9, Isaiah 54:11-17 and 1 Peter 2:1-3 / [14]Proverbs 14:15-19 and Ephesians 5:1-21 / [15]Proverbs 11:8-9, 23:23-24, Psalms 35:1-28, Ecclesiastes 1:16-18 and Jeremiah 20:10-13

Peas: [1]1 Timothy 5:8 / [2]John 6:22-40 / [3]Proverbs 21:9, 21:19, 23:9, 27:15-16, Ephesians 5:22-33 and 1 Peter 3:1-12 / [4]Proverbs 15:16-17, 16:16, 21:17, 21:20, Ecclesiastes 3:9-13, 5:9-20, Matthew 6:19-21, Luke 12:15-21 and James 1:2-8 / [5]Proverbs 28:12 / [6]Exodus 16:1-21 and Psalms 37:16-17 / [7]Psalms 127:1-5, Proverbs 13:10, 27:2 and Titus 2:1-5 / [8]Proverbs 19:22 and 30:5-9 / [9]Exodus 9:23-26, 2 Kings 1:10-12, 2:23-24, Proverbs 1:1-7, 9:1-18, 10:8, 11:4, 11:17-22, 18:2, 22:1, 28:19, 28:25-26, 31:10-31, Ecclesiastes 5:1-7, 10:11-15, Romans 11:33-35, 1 Corinthians 3:18-21, Galatians 6:7-10, 1 John 4:20-21 and Revelation 8:1-5 / [10]Proverbs 14:29, 1 Corinthians 7:10-16, 7:25-40, Ephesians 4:25-32, Colossians 3:18-19, 1 Peter 2:1-22 and 5:1-4 / [11]2 Corinthians 1:3-4 and 1 John 3:16-23 / [12]Psalms 27:10, Isaiah 49:15-18, Colossians 3:20-25 and James 3:1-18

/ [13]Proverbs 26:17 / [14]Proverbs 21:25-27, Matthew 6:25-34 and 2 Timothy 1:3-11 / [15]Leviticus 19:17-18, Proverbs 21:13, 23:20-21, 28:3, 28:15-16, Matthew 5:43-48, 1 Corinthians 13:1-13, 1 Timothy 6:1-21, Titus 1:1-16 and 1 Peter 2:1-3 / [16]Psalms 19:1-14, Proverbs 4:7-19, 11:9, 13:2-3, 13:20, 15:5, 17:27-28, 19:8, 21:10, 21:23, 22:6, 23:15-16, 23:23-24, 29:11, Isaiah 55:6-11, Matthew 5:3-10, 6:22-23, Ephesians 5:1-21, Philippians 4:5-9 and James 3:13-17 / [17]Exodus 20:12 and Matthew 10:34-39

Quiet: [1]Isaiah 55:6-9, Romans 2:1-16 and Revelation 20:11-15 / [2]1 Samuel 17:1-51, Daniel 10:1-14, Ephesians 6:10-20 and Revelation 12:1-17 / [3]1 Corinthians 9:24-27 / [4]Psalms 37:1-40 and Proverbs 27:15-16 / [5]Proverbs 29:9 / [6]Proverbs 29:10 and Matthew 10:27-31 / [7]Proverbs 29:11, 29:20, 29:22 and Matthew 12:33-37 / [8] Proverbs 4:1-27, 28:10, 29:27, Ecclesiastes 3:16-22 and 2 Peter 2:1-22 / [9]Proverbs 21:2, 21:6-12, 25:28, John 5:37-47, Romans 8:1-8, 1 Corinthians 7:1-5, Ephesians 4:17-24, Philippians 2:1-4 and 2 Timothy 3:1-9 / [10]Proverbs 9:7-18, Psalms 7:1-17 and Jeremiah 17:9-10 / [11]Proverbs 14:1, 29:25, Jeremiah 17:5-8, Matthew 7:13-27, 13:3-23 and Philippians 4:6-9 / [12]2 Chronicles 7:12-14 and Psalms 91:1-16

Heroes: [1]Psalms 107:23-32, 139:23-24, Proverbs 4:23, 14:12, 16:3, Isaiah 43:1-4, 55:6-9, 61:1-3, Matthew 8:23-27, Mark 7:20-23, Acts 12:1-10, 27:1-44, Romans 8:12-17, 12:1-2, 2 Corinthians 10:3-6, Philippians 4:6-8 and 1 Peter 1:13-16 / [2]Exodus 23:20-22, Deuteronomy 4:5-10, Joshua 23:1-13, Proverbs 12:26, Romans 1:18-32, 1 Corinthians 10:1-13, Ephesians 5:15-17, James 4:1-10 and 1 Peter 5:8-10 / [3]Leviticus 20:1-8, Deuteronomy 18:9-12, 1 Samuel 28:1-25, 2 Chronicles 7:12-14 and Ezekiel 13:1-23 / [4]Matthew 10:1, 12:43-45, 17:14-21, Acts 19:11-17, Ephesians 6:10-20 and Revelation 20:10-15 / [5]1 Corinthians 13:11-12, Ephesians 4:11-16 and 3 John 1:2-4 / [6]Hebrews 4:14-16 / [7]Matthew 19:13-15 / [8]Matthew 7:7-20, 25:31-46 and Titus 2:1-5 / [9]Matthew 23:1-39 / [10]Matthew 7:21-27, Proverbs 11:17, 31:10-31, Ezekiel 16:44-52, 2 Timothy 3:1-9 and Titus 1:10-16 / [11]Psalms 34:8-22 / [12]Proverbs 25:24 / [13]Matthew 18:1-9 / [14]Psalms 18:1-6, 97:10-12, Jeremiah 17:5-8, Zephaniah 3:14-20, John 14:1-6, 1 Peter 3:3-4, Revelation 19:6-9 and 21:1-27

Dolls: [1]Ephesians 6:10-20 / [2]Psalms 5:1-12, 12:1-8, Proverbs 26:23-28, 27:6, 28:23, 29:5, Jeremiah 17:7-11, Matthew 5:43-48 and Romans 16:17-20 / [3]Exodus 20:15, 20:17 and Proverbs 6:30-31 / [4]Genesis 2:15-22, Isaiah 61:10-11, Matthew 25:1-13, Romans 14:1-4, 1 Corinthians 16:13-18 and Galatians 5:1 / [5]Proverbs 13:20, 18:2, 26:11, 27:19 and Jeremiah 17:5-6 / [6]Proverbs 11:22 and 13:3 / [7]Psalms 42:1-11, 118:5-9, Proverbs 11:24-31, Matthew 7:6, John 4:1-42, 7:37-39, 1 Corinthians 10:12-22, Philippians 4:6-9 and

James 1:2-8 / [8]Proverbs 6:12-19 and Matthew 4:1-11 / [9]Isaiah 52:1-15, John 19:1-37 and John 20:1-31 / [10]Philippians 2:1-18, Colossians 4:2-6 and James 3:1-18 / [11]Ecclesiastes 4:1-12 / [12]Psalms 147:1-11, Proverbs 2:1-22, Isaiah 40:27-31, Matthew 23:37-39, Luke 4:16-21, Galatians 5:16-26, 1 Thessalonians 2:1-12 and Revelation 19:1-16 / [13]Luke 16:19-31, 2 Corinthians 11:1-15, 2 Timothy 2:1-26, 3:1-17, 1 Peter 5:5-11, 1 John 4:1-11, Jude 1:3-23, Revelation 12:1-17 and 20:7-15 / [14]John 10:11-30, James 4:1-10 and Revelation 21:6-8 / [15]Joshua 5:13-15, 11:1-23, Psalms 18:25-42, Proverbs 18:10 and Daniel 6:6-24 / [16]Proverbs 31:10-31 and Hebrews 4:1-13 / [17]John 3:13-20, 11:25-44, Romans 10:8-13, 1 Corinthians 13:1-13, Hebrews 11:5-6 and Revelation 3:14-22 / [18]Mark 9:14-29 / [19]Isaiah 55:1-13, Matthew 4:18-22, 16:21-28, Luke 18:18-30, John 10:1-10, 2 Corinthians 11:22-33 and 12:1-12 / [20]Isaiah 6:1-8, Luke 5:1-11 and 1 Corinthians 1:18-31 / [21]Ruth 2:1-12 and 1 Samuel 16:4-13 / [22]Isaiah 41:1-16, Jeremiah 29:11-14, Luke 12:4-7, Hebrews 4:14-16 and 1 John 4:12-19 / [23]Matthew 11:25-30, Luke 12:8-12 and John 14:15-18

Shredded: [1]Ecclesiastes 7:23-26, Galatians 5:16-26 and James 4:1-10 / [2]Proverbs 12:4 / [3]Proverbs 4:14-19, Proverbs 14:1 and Ephesians 4:25-32 / [4]Proverbs 18:6 and 24:17-18 / [5]Psalms 35:1-8 and 1 Peter 3:1-12 / [6]Proverbs 21:19 / [7]Proverbs 15:5, Matthew 6:24, 1 Timothy 6:3-10 and 1 John 2:15-16

Tomahawk: [1]Genesis 3:9-19, Judges 16:1-22, Proverbs 6:16-19, Galatians 5:7-26, Colossians 3:18-25 and 1 Peter 3:1-12 / [2]Proverbs 26:17 / [3]Luke 23:13-34 / [4]1 Kings 16:29-33, 18:7-40, 19:1-3, Proverbs 19:19, 26:20-22, 29:25, Matthew 14:3-12, 2 Timothy 1:7, 1 John 4:17-21 and Revelation 21:6-8 / [5]2 Samuel 21:15-17 and John 15:9-13 / [6]Proverbs 24:15-16, 24:19-22 and Philippians 4:6-7 / [7]Proverbs 24:17-18 and 26:18-19 / [8]Proverbs 13:20, 26:24-27, Mark 7:14-23, Ephesians 5:1-7 and James 3:1-18 / [9]Ephesians 5:8-21 and Colossians 4:5-6 / [10]Proverbs 12:16, 18:2, Ecclesiastes 10:11-15, Jeremiah 1:4-10, 1 Timothy 4:12-16 and James 5:1-11 / [11]Exodus 23:1-8 and Matthew 10:16-26 / [12]Luke 8:19-21, Ephesians 5:22-33 and 6:1-4 / [13]Psalms 62:1-12, 91:1-16 and Matthew 13:1-23

Toys: [1]Psalms 37:3-8, Philippians 4:6-7 and James 1:2-8 / [2]Psalms 119:33-40 / [3]Mark 7:20-23, Luke 12:13-21, Ephesians 5:1-7, Colossians 3:1-7, 1 Timothy 6:1-10 and Hebrews 13:5 / [4]Matthew 7:7-12 / [5]Proverbs 12:17-22, Luke 12:1-7 and 2 Timothy 2:15-26 / [6]Matthew 23:1-39, John 8:31-47 and James 2:1-13 / [7]2 Corinthians 10:1-11 and Ephesians 5:8-14 / [8]Psalms 27:7-14 and Ecclesiastes 4:9-12

Retribution: [1]Exodus 20:17, Mark 8:34-38 and James 4:1-10 / [2]Genesis 3:1-8 and Romans 13:8-14 / [3]Genesis 3:9-13 / [4]Genesis 3:14-24, Proverbs 19:18, 23:13-14 and 1 Corinthians 13:1-13 / [5]Matthew 6:19-21 / [6]Deuteronomy 32:35 and Romans 12:17-21 / [7]Romans 1:18-32 / [8]Matthew 6:1-4 / [9]Matthew 6:14-15 and 1 John 3:10-15 / [10]Genesis 49:5-7 / [11]Proverbs 29:17 / [12]1 Kings 19:1-12, Psalms 140:1-13, Jeremiah 29:11-13, Matthew 4:1-11, 24:3-14 and Revelation 21:6-8

Jump: [1]Matthew 19:16-30, 20:1-16, Mark 9:33-35 and Luke 14:1-11 / [2]Leviticus 19:14, Proverbs 12:26, 13:20 and Matthew 4:1-11 / [3]Proverbs 26:18-19 and James 3:1-18 / [4]Proverbs 26:11 / [5]Proverbs 14:15-19 and 21:10 / [6]Proverbs 6:12-19, 14:22, 26:20-26, Matthew 12:33-37 and 18:5-10 / [7]Psalms 33:13-15, Proverbs 15:3 and Hebrews 4:12-16 / [8]Ecclesiastes 11:9-10 / [9]Proverbs 21:9 / [10]Proverbs 8:1-36 and 21:23

Bite Down: [1]Psalms 133:1-3, Acts 4:32-35, Romans 12:1-13, Hebrews 10:23-25 and 1 Peter 3:8-12 / [2]1 Samuel 17:1-58 and Jeremiah 1:4-10 / [3]1 Corinthians 13:1-13 / [4]Proverbs 6:12-19, 26:20-26 and 2 Corinthians 10:7-12 / [5]Psalms 18:1-6, 34:1-18 and 121:1-8 / [6]Isaiah 49:8-18 / [7]Galatians 6:1-10 / [8]Deuteronomy 31:1-6 and Psalms 127:1-5 / [9]Proverbs 3:27-30, James 4:17 and 1 John 3:1-24 / [10]Isaiah 1:10-31 / [11]John 10:1-30 / [12]Matthew 18:1-14 and 2 Timothy 1:7 / [13]Luke 18:1-8 / [14]Romans 1:18-32 / [15]Proverbs 19:24, 26:14-16 and 1 Timothy 5:8 / [16]Proverbs 26:18-19 / [17]Ecclesiastes 4:9-12 / [18]John 15:18-27 / [19]Isaiah 41:8-20 / [20]Matthew 6:22-23, Romans 15:1-6, 2 Corinthians 1:3-4 and 2 Thessalonians 1:3-10 / [21]Psalms 9:6-10, 42:1-11, 143:1-12, Proverbs 3:5-6, Jeremiah 29:11-14, Matthew 13:1-23, 15:7-20, Mark 7:31-37, Romans 5:6-11, Philippians 4:6-9 and Revelation 21:1-4 / [22]Proverbs 12:25, 16:24, 17:22 and Isaiah 43:1-21 / [23]Proverbs 4:1-27 and Matthew 9:9-13 / [24]Hebrews 4:11-16 / [25]2 Timothy 3:1-5 / [26]Matthew 7:13-23 / [27]Psalms 54:1-7 and 124:1-8 / [28]Psalms 37:1-15 and 109:15-31 / [29] Proverbs 19:19 and Micah 7:1-10 / [30]Psalms 147:1-11 and Hosea 6:1 / [31]Romans 5:1-4

Jay: [1]1 Corinthians 13:1-13 / [2]1 Corinthians 10:1-13 / [3]Exodus 32:1-35, Daniel 12:1-4, Malachi 3:13-18, Luke 10:17-20, Ephesians 6:5-9, Revelation 3:1-5, 17:1-8 and 20:11-15 / [4]1 Corinthians 15:33-34 / [5]1 Corinthians 9:24-27 / [6]1 Timothy 4:12-16 / [7]Matthew 12:33-37, Galatians 5:16-26, and James 3:1-18 / [8]Proverbs 15:15 and 17:22 / [9]Exodus 20:16, Proverbs 6:12-19, 19:5 and Romans 13:8-10 / [10]Proverbs 19:18, Matthew 18:1-10 and Colossians 3:20-21 / [11]Deuteronomy 32:35-36, Romans 12:9-21 and Philippians 4:6-9

Now: [1]Matthew 18:15-17, 1 Corinthians 13:11 and Galatians 5:22-26 / [2]Deuteronomy 8:1-6, Proverbs 3:11-12, 15:5, 23:13-14, Hebrews 12:3-17 and Revelation 3:19 / [3]Proverbs

30:21-23, Ecclesiastes 7:25-26, Galatians 5:13-21 and 2 Timothy 1:7 / [4]Ephesians 5:1-21 / [5]Proverbs 13:20 and Colossians 3:12-15 / [6]Ephesians 5:22-33, Colossians 3:18-19, Titus 1:10-16 and 1 Peter 3:1-12 / [7]Proverbs 1:7, 18:2, Matthew 7:1-5, Romans 2:1-11 and James 1:19-26 / [8]Matthew 7:6 / [9]Proverbs 26:11, 27:15-16 James 2:14-26, 2 Peter 2:12-22 and 1 John 2:1-11

Montana: [1]Proverbs 16:9 / [2]1 Corinthians 13:11 / [3]Ephesians 6:1-3 / [4]Proverbs 27:5 / [5]Proverbs 27:7 / [6]Proverbs 4:1-27 / [7]Proverbs 9:1-12, 17:10 / [8]Proverbs 22:6 / [9]Matthew 4:19 and Luke 5:1-11 / [10]Proverbs 17:6 and Luke 11:1-13 / [11]Psalms 23:1-6 / [12]Proverbs 27:19, Philippians 4:10-13 and Jude 1:5-23 / [13]Numbers 11:1-3, 16:25-50 and 17:1-11 / [14]Numbers 15:1-10 and 2 Corinthians 2:14-17 / [15]Proverbs 9:13-18 / [16]Proverbs 17:1, 21:19, 22:10 and 26:20-21 / [17]Proverbs 17:12, 17:24 and Ecclesiastes 10:1-15

Ponytails: [1]Proverbs 3:9-10, 10:22, 15:16-17, 23:4-5, 30:7-9, Matthew 6:24, 25:14-46 and Luke 12:13-34 / [2]1 Chronicles 29:10-12 and Ecclesiastes 5:8-20 / [3]Proverbs 22:1-2 and Matthew 6:19-21 / [4]Mark 8:34-38 and Luke 12:13-21 / [5]Proverbs 16:9 / [6]1 Samuel 2:1-10, Proverbs 10:2-3, 16:8, Psalms 97:10-12, Matthew 10:7-20, 19:16-22, John 15:1-17, Romans 13:1-7, 2 Corinthians 6:1-10 and 1 Timothy 6:6-19 / [7]Isaiah 61:1-3, Matthew 11:28-30, John 8:31-47, Philippians 4:6-9 and James 4:1-10 / [8]Proverbs 18:24, 27:17, Psalms 68:1-6 and Ecclesiastes 4:9-12

The Fox: [1]James 3:1-18 / [2]Proverbs 27:17 / [3]Proverbs 3:31-35, 11:7-10, 28:15-16, Psalms 91:1-16, 1 Timothy 3:1-7 and John 10:1-16 / [4]Proverbs 18:24, Psalms 68:1-6, Ecclesiastes 4:9-12 and Matthew 18:19-20 / [5]1 Corinthians 1:10-13, Galatians 3:26-29 and 1 Peter 3:8 / [6]Proverbs 1:1-33 and 1 Corinthians 13:1-13 / [7]Proverbs 2:1-22 and 3:1-26 / [8]Job 10:12 and Proverbs 31:10-31

Promise Me: [1]Proverbs 10:12, 1 Corinthians 13:1-13, Galatians 5:13-26, 1 Peter 3:8-12 and 1 John 4:20-21 / [2]Isaiah 49:14-18 and Romans 8:38-39 / [3]James 3:1-18 / [4]Proverbs 25:2 and Ecclesiastes 4:9-12 / [5]Luke 8:16-17 and 12:2-3 / [6]Proverbs 15:4, 27:6 and 27:17 / [7]Galatians 6:1 / [8]Psalms 34:11-16, Proverbs 14:29 and Matthew 18:1-10 / [9]2 Timothy 2:15 / [10]Proverbs 31:8-9 and John 8:31-32 / [11]Psalms 19:7-14, 32:8-11, Proverbs 2:1-9, 13:10, 16:16, 19:19-21, 30:5, Isaiah 55:6-9, Matthew 5:33-37, 7:1-6, 11:28-30, Ephesians 5:15-17, Colossians 4:5-6 and James 1:2-8 / [12]Proverbs 4:20-27 and 14:5 / [13]Philippians 4:6-7 / [14]Proverbs 15:23 and Philippians 4:8-9 / [15]Matthew 25:31-46

You're Not Going: [1]Proverbs 25:2 / [2]Isaiah 55:8-9 and Matthew 18:1-10 / [3]Psalms 34:1-22, Matthew 5:1-12 and Revelation 7:9-17 / [4]John 11:1-44 / [5]Proverbs 27:5, Matthew 7:1-5 and Philippians 2:1-4 / [6]Matthew 7:7-12 and Hebrews 4:1-16 / [7]Deuteronomy 32:30, Proverbs 18:10, Ecclesiastes 4:9-12, Matthew 18:11-14, John 10:1-16, 1 Corinthians 13:1-13 and 1 Thessalonians 5:12-24 / [8]Luke 16:19-31 / [9]Proverbs 29:9-11, Matthew 5:38-48 and Ephesians 6:1-4 / [10]Proverbs 3:1-8 / [11]Proverbs 11:10 and 29:1-2 / [12]1 Kings 19:1-21, Psalms 139:1-24, Matthew 7:13-27, Philippians 4:6-9, Colossians 4:18-25 and James 3:1-18 / [13]Proverbs 11:22, Galatians 5:7-26, Ephesians 6:10-20 and 2 Timothy 3:1-16 / [14]Proverbs 18:17, Hosea 4:1-10, James 4:1-10 and 1 Peter 5:1-11 / [15]Genesis 4:1-15, Deuteronomy 32:35, Micah 7:1-7, Matthew 6:9-14, Mark 11:25-26, Romans 12:1-21 and 1 Timothy 1:5-17

Section 2

The Aquatic Abyss: [1]Exodus 20:1-6, Psalms 38:1-22, 94:1-23, John 14:26-27, 2 Corinthians 7:1-12, 10:1-6 Philippians 4:6-9 and Colossians 3:1-2 / [2]Exodus 31:1-11, Proverbs 12:25, 26:18-19, Jeremiah 33:1-3, Matthew 7:7-12, John 14:12-18, 15:1-17, 16:19-24, Ephesians 5:1-7, James 1:2-8, 1 John 3:16-23 and 5:14-21 / [3]Proverbs 7:1-27, Matthew 5:27-30, 1 Corinthians 6:9-20, 10:1-13, Galatians 5:16-26, 1 Thessalonians 4:3-8, Jude 1:1-25 and Revelation 21:6-8 / [4]Psalms 42:1-11, 107:23-32 and Mark 4:35-41 / [5]1 Samuel 3:1-21, Psalms 107:10-22, Isaiah 43:1-2, 61:1-3, Jonah 1:1-17, 2:1-10, Matthew 14:22-33 and Hebrews 13:1-3 / [6]1 Peter 5:8-11 / [7]Joshua 1:1-9, Psalms 27:1-14 and Proverbs 16:7 / [8]Psalms 144:1-4, Isaiah 35:1-10, Ephesians 6:10-20 and Hebrews 4:12-13 / [9]Psalms 18:31-42, Luke 10:17-20 and James 4:1-10 / [10]Joshua 5:13-15, 2 Kings 6:8-18 and Romans 11:33-36 / [11]Psalms 18:28-30, 119:105, Job 41:1-34, Daniel 2:22, 1 Corinthians 2:1-16 and 2 Corinthians 11:12-15 / [12]Matthew 10:34-39

Sea Bag: [1]Psalms 4:1-8, Isaiah 26:1-9, Philippians 4:6-9 and 1 John 4:12-19 / [2]Daniel 12:1-13, Matthew 24:1-51, 1 Thessalonians 4:13-18, 5:1-11, 2 Thessalonians 2:1-12 and Revelation 3:1-22 / [3]Psalms 34:1-22, Proverbs 12:12-23, 16:32, 20:3, 26:17, Matthew 5:1-16, Romans 8:1-8, 12:9-21, 2 Corinthians 13:5-11, Hebrews 12:12-17, James 3:1-18 and 1 Peter 3:1-12 / [4]John 16:5-33

GATE: [1]Psalms 44:1-8, 68:1-6, 133:1-3, Proverbs 3:1-8, 18:24, 22:1 and Ecclesiastes 4:9-12 / [2]Proverbs 8:1-36, 25:28, Matthew 7:1-5, 7:13-27, 23:1-39, 25:14-46, Romans 2:1-11, 12:1-2, 1 Corinthians 9:24-27, Galatians 5:16-26, Hebrews 5:12-14, 6:1-12, 2 Peter 1:1-11 and Revelation 21:1-8 / [3]Psalms 23:1-6, Isaiah 55:1-13 and Jeremiah 29:11-13 /

[4]1 Samuel 16:1-23 and 17:1-58 / [5]Joshua 7:1-26, Proverbs 13:20, 1 Corinthians 5:1-13 and 2 Corinthians 6:1-18 / [6]Deuteronomy 28:1-68 / [7]Exodus 14:1-31, Psalms 3:1-8, 5:1-12, 28:1-9, 91:1-16, 119:113-120, Proverbs 2:1-22, 30:1-5, Isaiah 52:11-12, Matthew 10:1-26 and Ephesians 6:10-20

Don't Become the Bully: [1]Exodus 20:1-17, Deuteronomy 19:1-21, 32:1-6, Psalms 37:1-40, 82:1-8, 139:1-24, Proverbs 21:3, Isaiah 1:15-31, Matthew 5:17-26 and 27:15-26 / [2]Jeremiah 1:4-10 / [3]Proverbs 31:8 / [4]Ecclesiastes 9:1-12 / [5]Proverbs 2:1-22, 27:17, Ecclesiastes 4:9-12 and Matthew 18:1-10 / [6]Proverbs 12:15, 15:22, 19:20-21 and 28:26 / [7]Proverbs 18:24, Psalms 133:1-3 and 1 Corinthians 13:1-13 / [8]Proverbs 10:12, 16:32, Leviticus 19:17-18 and Ephesians 4:26-32 / [9]Proverbs 14:29, 20:3 and James 1:19-20 / [10]Proverbs 18:6 and 29:11 / [11]Proverbs 4:1-27 and Philippians 2:1-4 / [12]Proverbs 8:13, 10:9 and 19:5 / [13]Deuteronomy 32:35, Isaiah 30:8-21, Matthew 7:1-5, 26:47-56 and Romans 12:9-21 / [14]Proverbs 21:12 / [15]Proverbs 9:7-9, 19:25, 21:10-11 and 22:10 / [16]Proverbs 31:9 / [17]1 Samuel 17:1-58, Proverbs 6:12-19, 21:4, 21:24 and Galatians 6:7-10 / [18]Proverbs 25:2 / [19]Proverbs 21:2 and 21:15 / [20]Proverbs 18:17 / [21]Proverbs 25:18 / [22]Psalms 33:13-15, Proverbs 12:13-14, 12:17-22, 14:5, 21:7-8, 25:11-12, Jeremiah 7:1-7, Daniel 4:1-37, Zechariah 7:8-14 and Luke 12:2-3

That's My Brother: [1]Proverbs 25:2 and Matthew 18:10-14 / [2]Hebrews 5:12-14, 6:1-8 and 12:1-11 / [3]Psalms 32:1-11, 34:1-22, 139:1-24, Isaiah 9:1-7, Jeremiah 17:5-10, Luke 6:43-45, Galatians 5:1-26, Hebrews 4:12-16 and James 1:19-20 / [4]Proverbs 1:1-7, 3:1-35, 10:20, 12:1, 13:20, 18:2, 20:3, Ecclesiastes 10:11-15, Mark 7:1-23, Colossians 3:1-17 and 1 Peter 2:1-12 / [5]Matthew 24:3-14 and 2 Timothy 3:1-17 / [6]Proverbs 12:5-7 / [7]Psalms 116:1-19, 138:1-8, Proverbs 12:2-3 and Matthew 12:22-30 / [8]Romans 5:1-11, 1 Corinthians 13:1-13 and 1 Peter 4:1-19 / [9]Deuteronomy 31:3-8, Psalms 1:1-6, Proverbs 12:8 and Hebrews 12:12-17 / [10]Proverbs 27:12, Ephesians 5:15-16 and Revelation 21:1-8 / [11]Proverbs 1:8-33, 17:15, 19:19, 26:17 and Matthew 7:6 / [12]Proverbs 12:25, 17:11-14, Matthew 5:38-48, John 2:13-17 and Romans 12:1-21 / [13]2 Corinthians 10:1-18, 12:1-10 and Ephesians 2:1-10

God is Watching You: [1]Proverbs 31:10-31 and Titus 2:1-15 / [2]Deuteronomy 28:1-68, Isaiah 52:13-15, 53:1-12, Ezekiel 5:1-17, Matthew 27:1-43, John 15:1-25, 1 Corinthians 1:18-31 and 2 Corinthians 9:1-15 / [3]Matthew 22:22-30 / [4]Matthew 7:7-27, 18:1-10, Colossians 3:18-25 and 1 Timothy 5:8 / [5]Proverbs 3:27, Luke 16:19-31, Acts 20:32-35, Philippians 2:1-4 and James 2:14-26 / [6]2 Corinthians 10:12 and Philippians 4:6-9 / [7]Matthew 25:31-46 / [8]Leviticus 19:17-18, Jeremiah 23:9-24, Matthew 5:38-48, 7:1-5,

Romans 2:1-11, 1 Corinthians 13:1-13, Galatians 5:7-26, 6:7-10, Philippians 4:10-13, 2 Timothy 3:1-9, Titus 1:10-16, Hebrews 4:12-16, James 1:19-27, 2:1-13 and 1 John 2:3-17 / [9]Luke 5:27-32, John 3:1-21, Ephesians 2:1-10, Hebrews 11:1-6, Revelation 20:11-15, 21:6-8 and 22:12-14

Run for Your Life: [1]Genesis 9:18-29, 19:1-38, 34:1-31, Deuteronomy 22:13-30, 2 Samuel 13:1-39, Psalms 72:4, 1 Corinthians 5:1-13, 6:9-20, 10:1-13, Galatians 5:1-26, Ephesians 5:1-21, 6:1-9, 1 Thessalonians 4:1-12 and Revelation 21:1-8 / [2]Psalms 107:1-9, Proverbs 27:7-8, 1 Corinthians 13:1-13 and Titus 2:1-15 / [3]Deuteronomy 24:7, Matthew 18:1-14 and Romans 12:1-21 / [4]Genesis 2:15-17, 3:1-24, Psalms 1:1-6, Proverbs 1:1-33, 6:12-19, 27:12, Jeremiah 17:5-13, Matthew 10:16, 15:1-20, John 8:31-47, 10:1-30, Romans 1:18-32, 2 Corinthians 11:1-15 and 2 Timothy 3:1-17 / [5]Proverbs 9:1-18, 10:8 and 13:20 / [6]Proverbs 4:1-27 / [7]Psalms 18:28-42, 34:1-22, 141:1-10, 144:1-2, Proverbs 8:1-36, Isaiah 41:8-13, 2 Thessalonians 3:1-3 and 1 Peter 5:8-11 / [8]Proverbs 13:10, 15:5, 20:3, Judges 6:1-40, 7:1-25, Isaiah 40:27-31, Matthew 26:1-75, Romans 13:1-7, 2 Corinthians 12:7-10, Ephesians 6:10-20 and James 4:1-10

Can I?: [1]Proverbs 23:1-3, 23:6-8, 23:19-21, 25:17, 25:24, 27:10, Ephesians 6:1-9 and James 3:1-18 / [2]Luke 12:1-3 / [3]Proverbs 12:25, 16:24 and 1 Corinthians 13:1-13 / [4]Proverbs 18:24 and Ecclesiastes 4:9-12 / [5]Psalms 5:1-12, 12:1-8, Proverbs 6:12-19, 16:28, 26:24-28, 27:6, 28:23, 29:5, Romans 16:17-20 and Jude 1:3-19 / [6]John 3:19-21 / [7]Psalms 9:1-20, 15:1-5, 34:1-22, Proverbs 4:24, 10:32, 12:17-22, 30:1-33, Matthew 12:33-37, 15:1-20, Luke 4:16-30, John 8:37-59, Galatians 5:13-26 and 1 John 1:5-10 / [8]Proverbs 26:20-23 / [9]Proverbs 18:17 and Ephesians 5:1-16 / [10]Genesis 50:15-20, Exodus 34:6-7, 2 Chronicles 7:12-22, Proverbs 26:18-19, Isaiah 55:6-13, Jeremiah 31:27-34, Ezekiel 18:1-32, Micah 7:1-20, Matthew 10:34-39, Luke 8:19-21, John 3:1-18, 14:1-18 and Romans 8:1-39

Don't Be a Burden: [1]Psalms 31:1-24, 42:1-11, 121:1-8, Isaiah 61:1-3 and Jeremiah 29:11-14 / [2]Proverbs 3:5-6, Philippians 4:4-9 and James 4:1-10 / [3]Psalms 140:1-13 and Proverbs 21:19 / [4]Jeremiah 33:1-3, Matthew 5:43-48, John 15:1-17, 2 Corinthians 10:1-6, Ephesians 6:10-20, James 1:1-6 and 1 John 3:16-24 / [5]Proverbs 13:12 and Ecclesiastes 4:9-12 / [6]John 15:18-25 / [7]Proverbs 10:28, Isaiah 54:11-17 and 1 Corinthians 13:1-13 / [8]Matthew 7:7-12, Ephesians 1:15-23 and 1 Peter 4:1-11 / [9]Proverbs 25:6-7 and Matthew 23:1-12 / [10]Matthew 5:1-16 and Romans 12:1-13 / [11]Proverbs 6:12-19 and 25:14 / [12]Psalms 15:1-5, Proverbs 12:17-22, 18:17, Colossians 3:1-11 and 1 Peter 3:8-11 / [13]Proverbs 16:24 / [14]Proverbs 11:22 and 27:15-16 / [15]Proverbs 15:1-4 and Romans 12:14-21 /

[16]Matthew 5:17-26 / [17]2 Samuel 22:26-37, Psalms 3:1-8, 28:1-9, 91:1-16, 119:113-120, Proverbs 5:1-6, Jeremiah 17:5-10, Matthew 7:13-27, 2 Timothy 1:7 and 1 John 4:17-21 / [18]Proverbs 16:27-30, John 10:27-30, Romans 5:1-4, 8:1-39 and 1 Peter 4:12-19

You Can't Go in There: [1]Psalms 42:1-11 and John 10:1-30 / [2]Luke 2:41-52 / [3]2 Samuel 6:1-23, Psalms 13:1-6, 133:1-3, Isaiah 12:1-6, Acts 16:16-40 and Revelation 19:1-10 / [4]Matthew 19:13-15 and 23:1-14 / [5]Psalms 59:1-17, 68:1-6, 71:1-24, Proverbs 20:11, Ephesians 4:1-16, Colossians 3:1-17, Hebrews 10:24-25 / [6]1 Samuel 16:1-7, Mark 9:38-41, John 7:24, Acts 10:1-48, Romans 2:1-11, 1 Corinthians 1:4-17, 12:1-31, Galatians 3:26-29, Ephesians 4:17-32, James 2:1-13, 1 John 2:1-11 and Revelation 7:9-17 / [7]1 Corinthians 1:18-31, 2 Timothy 4:1-8, 2 Peter 2:1-22 and 1 John 4:1-6 / [8]Matthew 7:13-27, 18:1-10 and 22:1-14

You're Still Gonna Get It: [1]Proverbs 13:22, 21:9, 21:19, 1 Corinthians 5:1-13 and 2 Timothy 3:1-9 / [2]John 3:16-21 / [3]Proverbs 3:31-35, 6:12-35, 7:1-27, 9:7-8, Jeremiah 23:23-24, Luke 12:1-7 and Ephesians 5:1-33 / [4]Matthew 5:43-48 and Philippians 2:1-16 / [5]Matthew 5:38-42, 2 Corinthians 4:7-18 and Romans 12:9-21 / [6]Psalms 30:1-12, 32:1-11, 121:1-8, 138:1-8 and 142:1-7 / [7]Job 1:6-7 and 1 Peter 5:8-9 / [8]2 Chronicles 7:12-20, Proverbs 12:1-3, 12:5-8, Jeremiah 17:5-10 and 1 Corinthians 15:33-34 / [9]Proverbs 1:10-19, 13:10, 20:3, Psalms 109:1-5, Mark 7:20-23 and Galatians 5:16-26 / [10]Proverbs 14:29, Titus 1:10-16 and Revelation 14:6-20 / [11]Psalms 18:1-50, 144:1-15, 2 Corinthians 10:1-6, Ephesians 6:10-20 and Revelation 21:1-8 / [12]Proverbs 25:21-22 and 1 Corinthians 13:1-13 / [13]Proverbs 1:20-33 / [14]Psalms 118:1-29, Isaiah 54:1-17, Matthew 26:47-52, Acts 4:1-31 and 1 Peter 3:8-17 / [15]Proverbs 11:13, 26:20-22, 27:2, 2 Corinthians 10:12-18 and James 1:19-27 / [16]Psalms 91:1-16 and 124:1-8

Gray Mouse: [1]Titus 2:1-5, Proverbs 10:6-7 and 21:19 / [2]Matthew 7:7-11 / [3]1 Samuel 16:1-13, Proverbs 10:19-21, 31:30-31, 1 Corinthians 5:1-13 and 15:33-34 / [4]Proverbs 10:9-11 and 10:31-32 / [5]Psalms 140:1-13, Proverbs 11:22, Isaiah 5:1-30, Matthew 7:1-5, 7:13-27, 18:1-10, Luke 6:27-49, 2 Corinthians 11:12-15, Galatians 5:1-26, Ephesians 6:10-20, 1 Timothy 4:3-17, Titus 3:1-11 and 2 Peter 2:1-22 / [6]Psalms 107:1-16, Ecclesiastes 3:9-22, Luke 4:16-21 and Ephesians 6:1-9 / [7]Proverbs 25:2 and James 1:12-20 / [8]Acts 20:25-35, Romans 16:17-20, Galatians 1:6-10, Colossians 2:1-10, 1 Timothy 6:1-21, 2 Timothy 4:1-5, James 1:21-27 and 1 John 4:1-21 / [9]Ephesians 4:1-32

Scarlet Letters: [1]2 Kings 13:20-21, Matthew 17:14-21 and 19:16-30 / [2]Daniel 2:19-22, John 1:1-13, 3:16-21, 8:1-12, 2 Corinthians 10:1-6, Ephesians 5:1-21, 6:10-20, 1

Peter 2:1-10 and 1 John 1:1-10 / [3]Proverbs 1:1-19, Luke 12:1-5 and John 10:1-10 / [4]Proverbs 1:20-33, Romans 13:1-7, 2 Corinthians 10:12-18, 1 Timothy 1:8-17 and 1 Peter 2:11-17 / [5]Matthew 18:1-10, Romans 14:10-13 and Galatians 5:7-15 / [6]Proverbs 3:1-8, Ecclesiastes 3:9-11, Isaiah 55:8-11 and 2 Peter 3:1-18 / [7]Proverbs 11:2, 15:31-33, 29:23 and Jeremiah 29:11-13 / [8]2 Chronicles 15:1-7, Isaiah 41:10, 2 Corinthians 4:1-10, Galatians 6:1-10, Philippians 4:6-9 and Hebrews 12:1-13 / [9]Isaiah 40:25-31, Romans 5:1-5, 15:1-13 and Ephesians 3:14-21 / [10]Psalms 25:1-22, 32:1-11, Proverbs 4:1-13, Matthew 7:21-27, 11:25-30 and 24:3-14 / [11]Proverbs 4:14-25, 16:3, Romans 8:1-8, Colossians 3:1-17 and 2 Timothy 2:14-26

The Surprise: [1]Matthew 24:3-51 and 25:1-13 / [2]Psalms 31:1-24 and 1 Corinthians 2:1-16 / [3]Proverbs 27:17 / [4]Proverbs 1:1-7, 2:1-22, Matthew 3:16-17 and 17:1-8 / [5]Proverbs 23:4-5, Matthew 6:19-34 and 1 Timothy 6:1-21 / [6]Proverbs 22:29, Ecclesiastes 9:10-18, Jeremiah 20:1-12, Acts 4:1-22 and 2 Timothy 4:1-5 / [7]Proverbs 29:25, Mark 10:13-45, John 12:42-43, Galatians 1:6-10 and 1 Thessalonians 2:1-12 / [8]Ezekiel 33:1-20 and 2 Timothy 3:14-17 / [9]Proverbs 13:10, 17:10 and Matthew 7:6 / [10]Psalms 25:1-22, Proverbs 4:1-13, Galatians 6:1-10 and 1 Thessalonians 5:8-15 / [11]Proverbs 16:24, Isaiah 6:1-8, 65:1-12, Matthew 22:1-14, John 15:1-17, Romans 8:18-30, 1 Corinthians 1:26-31 and 2 Timothy 1:8-14 / [12]Numbers 6:22-27, Philippians 3:8-21, Hebrews 4:12-16, 10:19-31 and 1 Peter 2:1-25 / [13]2 Corinthians 13:5 and 1 Peter 4:1-19 / [14]Deuteronomy 8:1-20, Proverbs 10:17, 12:1, 15:5, 2 Timothy 2:14-16, Hebrews 12:1-17 and Revelation 3:14-22 / [15]Psalms 139:1-24, Proverbs 3:1-26, 11:2, 18:12, 29:23, Daniel 12:1-13, Zechariah 13:7-9, Matthew 11:25-30, 25:14-30, James 4:1-10, 1 Peter 5:5-11, and 2 Peter 1:1-11 / [16]2 Corinthians 10:12-18 / [17]Mark 16:15-20 / [18]Revelation 19:6-21, 20:11-15, 21:1-27 and 22:1-21 / [19]John 14:25-26, Hebrews 5:12-14 and 6:1-8

Set It on the Table: [1]Proverbs 12:25, 13:2, 15:4, 15:23, 16:23-24, 18:20-21 and Luke 6:43-45 / [2]Proverbs 10:19-21, 13:3, 15:1, 17:27-28, 20:3, Ecclesiastes 10:11-14, Matthew 12:33-37, Ephesians 4:29-32, Colossians 4:5-6 and James 3:1-18 / [3]Proverbs 13:20, 14:1, 16:32, 18:2, 18:6 and 1 Corinthians 6:9-11 / [4]Psalms 19:1-14, Proverbs 3:7-8, 3:31-35, 8:13, 10:6, 11:2-11, 12:2-3, 16:25, Daniel 4:27-37, Mark 7:20-23, Luke 6:37-42, Romans 12:9-21, 1 Corinthians 13:1-13, 2 Corinthians 10:12-18, Ephesians 5:1-21, 6:1-20, Colossians 3:12-25, Titus 2:1-5, James 1:12-27, 4:1-17, 1 Peter 3:8-17, 1 John 2:15-17 and 3:18-24 / [5]Proverbs 29:23, Jeremiah 17:5-13, Matthew 7:6 and James 1:2-11 / [6]Proverbs 3:11-12, 10:8, 12:1, 15:5 and Hebrews 12:1-29 / [7]Jeremiah 29:11-13, Matthew 24:3-14, John 10:1-16 and 1 Corinthians 2:1-16 / [8]Proverbs 3:5-6, 1 Corinthians 1:18-30 and Ephesians 2:1-10

Leaves: [1]Luke 12:4-6 / [2]Proverbs 17:22 and 18:14 / [3]Proverbs 3:5-6 and 2 Corinthians 10:12 / [4]Ecclesiastes 4:9-12 and Romans 12:1-8 / [5]Ephesians 6:1-4 / [6]Proverbs 11:22, 22:1, Matthew 12:33-37 and Luke 12:1-3 / [7]Psalms 82:1-8, James 3:1-18 and 5:1-8 / [8]Proverbs 6:6-11, 10:4-5, 13:4, 29:15, 29:20 and Isaiah 1:10-20 / [9]Proverbs 28:1, 29:10 and 29:25 / [10]Proverbs 10:18-21, Matthew 7:13-27, John 8:31-44, 2 Corinthians 11:12-15 and Revelation 2:8-11 / [11]Proverbs 10:20, 17:7, 18:2 and 23:9 / [12]Proverbs 25:2 / [13]Psalms 34:1-22, 147:1-6, Proverbs 27:19, 29:27 and Luke 11:33-36 / [14]Psalms 41:1-13, 1 Timothy 5:8 and Titus 2:1-5 / [15]Proverbs 23:1-3 and 23:6-8 / [16]Romans 12:9-21 and 1 Peter 3:8-12 / [17]2 Kings 6:11-23, Matthew 13:10-17 and Mark 10:46-52 / [18]Proverbs 21:1-9 and 29:13

Got Tacos?: [1]Matthew 16:1-4 / [2]Proverbs 23:1-3 and 23:6-8 / [3]Luke 12:13-21 / [4]Matthew 24:3-51 / [5]Proverbs 31:9 and James 2:1-26 / [6]Proverbs 21:13, Matthew 25:31-46 and Luke 3:7-14 / [7]1 Chronicles 29:10-15, Psalms 34:1-22, Proverbs 11:24-26, 19:22, Luke 6:30-38, 1 Corinthians 13:1-13, 2 Corinthians 8:8-15 and 9:6-15 / [8]Genesis 18:1-33, 19:1-29 and Hebrews 13:1-2 / [9]Matthew 6:1-4

Tiger Cruise: [1]Hebrews 12:7-17 / [2]Proverbs 12:10 and Jeremiah 17:5-10 / [3]Ephesians 6:1-4, James 3:1-12 and 1 Peter 3:8-12 / [4]Exodus 20:1-6, 34:10-17, Proverbs 11:17, 14:30, 27:4, Job 38:1-41, 40:1-14, 42:1-17, Isaiah 55:1-13, Ezekiel 14:1-23, 33:12-20, Matthew 7:24-27, 10:34-39, 18:1-10, Luke 13:22-30, Romans 1:18-32, 13:8-14, 1 Corinthians 3:1-3, 6:9-11, 13:1-13, Galatians 5:13-26, Ephesians 4:29-32, Colossians 3:21 and James 4:1-10 / [5]Psalms 56:1-13, Isaiah 45:9-13, Jeremiah 29:11-13, Romans 8:18-30, 12:9-21, Philippians 4:6-9, James 3:13-18 and 2 Peter 3:1-9

Forbidden: [1]Proverbs 15:4, 18:21, Ecclesiastes 10:11-14, Jeremiah 17:5-10, 23:9-40, Matthew 6:1-15, 12:33-37, Mark 4:21-23, Luke 6:43-45, 12:1-3, Ephesians 5:1-21, 6:1-9 and 1 Peter 2:18-25 / [2]Psalms 91:1-16, Proverbs 9:13-18, 13:3, 13:20, 18:2, Matthew 11:25-30, 1 Corinthians 7:1-40, Ephesians 5:22-33, Philippians 4:6-9, 2 Timothy 2:14-26 and James 4:1-12 / [3]Exodus 20:1-17, Deuteronomy 19:1-13, Proverbs 4:5-13, 4:20-27, 9:1-12, 13:10, Ecclesiastes 1:12-18, Jeremiah 33:1-3, Matthew 5:21-26, Galatians 5:16-26, Ephesians 4:17-32. 2 Timothy 1:7, James 1:2-8 and 1 John 3:10-15 / [4]Judges 16:4-31 and Proverbs 4:14-19

Backwards: [1]Proverbs 21:19 and 25:24 / [2]Numbers 23:19, Jeremiah 23:1-8, Matthew 18:1-10, 19:13-15, John 14:27, 1 Corinthians 1:26-31 and James 3:1-18 / [3]Isaiah 49:14-16, Jeremiah 31:3, Romans 8:26-39, Hebrews 4:1-16 and 1 John 4:4-11 / [4]Proverbs 26:14-16, Matthew 7:7-11, 1 Timothy 5:8 and James 4:17 / [5]Luke 5:27-32 / [6]Exodus

15:22-26, 23:25, Proverbs 17:22, Matthew 9:9-13, 10:1-15, Luke 13:10-17 and James 5:13-18 / [7]Proverbs 31:10-31 / [8]1 Corinthians 13:1-13 and Titus 2:1-5 / [9]Ecclesiastes 4:9-12, Isaiah 53:1-12, Luke 4:16-21 and 2 Corinthians 1:3-7

The Cartoon: [1]Proverbs 4:1-19, 14:12, 21:9, Isaiah 49:14-16, Matthew 18:1-10, Romans 12:3 and 16:17-20 / [2]Psalms 37:5-6, 119:105, Proverbs 13:3, Matthew 5:14-16, John 1:1-5, 8:12, Ephesians 5:8-16, 1 Peter 2:1-10 and 1 John 1:5-10 / [3]Matthew 7:7-11, Luke 18:1-8 and James 1:5-8 / [4]Proverbs 27:7 / [5]Psalms 34:1-22, 55:22-23, 72:4, 97:10, 101:3-4, Proverbs 4:20-27, Song of Solomon 8:4, Romans 13:2-3, Galatians 5:7-21, 1 Thessalonians 5:21-22 and James 4:17 / [6]Proverbs 6:12-19, 28:6, Mark 7:18-23, Luke 8:16-18, 12:1-3 and Romans 1:18-32 / [7]Judges 4:1-22, 1 Samuel 16:7, Isaiah 55:6-11, Jeremiah 29:11-13, Psalms 119:1-16, 139:1-24, Proverbs 11:16, 11:22, 14:1, 16:3, 31:10-31, Luke 1:26-38, 8:1-3, Romans 8:12-30, 12:1-2, 1 Corinthians 13:1-13, 2 Corinthians 10:3-6, Philippians 4:6-9, Hebrews 4:12-16, James 3:1-18, 4:1-10 , 1 Peter 1:13-16 and 3:3-4

Looming: [1]Psalms 23:1-6, 101:1-4, Isaiah 9:1-7 and 2 Timothy 1:7 / [2]1 Corinthians 13:1-13, 2 Corinthians 1:3-4, Hebrews 5:12-14 and 6:1-12 / [3]Hosea 4:6, John 10:1-30, 1 Thessalonians 5:21-22, 1 Timothy 4:1-3, 2 Timothy 3:16-17, 4:1-5, James 1:12-18, 3:1-18, 2 Peter 2:1-22, 1 John 4:1-6 and Jude 1:3-25 / [4]Matthew 12:43-45, 17:14-21, 18:18-20 and Revelation 3:7-13 / [5]Mark 9:38-41, 16:14-18, Luke 10:17-20, Acts 16:16-40, 1 Corinthians 10:14-22 and James 4:1-10 / [6]Deuteronomy 18:9-14, 1 Samuel 28:3-25, 1 Chronicles 10:13-14, Job 1:6-7, Ezekiel 13:17-23, Acts 8:4-24, 19:11-20, 2 Corinthians 10:3-6, Galatians 5:16-26 and 1 Peter 5:6-11 / [7]Genesis 1:26-31, 19:1-26, Leviticus 20:27, Deuteronomy 10:12-22, Judges 6:11-24, 2 Kings 13:20-21, Ecclesiastes 12:9-14, Matthew 4:1-11, 13:47-50, 27:45-53, Mark 5:1-20, Luke 1:26-38, 11:14-23, 16:19-31, John 11:38-44, 20:11-18, Acts 4:8-12, 1 Corinthians 2:1-16, 3:9-17, 6:9-20, 2 Corinthians 3:12-18, 11:12-14, Ephesians 6:10-20, 1 Thessalonians 4:13-18, 2 Thessalonians 1:3-12, Titus 2:11-14, Revelation 11:15-19, 12:7-12, 14:9-20, 20:10-15 and 21:1-27 / [8]John 8:31-47

Mediums: [1]Leviticus 19:31, 20:6-8, 2 Kings 21:1-16, Proverbs 22:6, Luke 8:19-21 and 2 Timothy 4:1-5 / [2]Deuteronomy 13:1-18, Matthew 10:34-39 and 18:1-9 / [3]2 Timothy 3:1-17 / [4]2 Peter 2:1-22 / [5]1 Samuel 28:3-25, 1 Chronicles 10:13-14, Proverbs 27:7, Isaiah 8:11-22, Hosea 5:1-15 and Romans 12:1-2 / [6]Deuteronomy 18:9-14, Matthew 7:15-29, 15:7-20, 24:3-31, John 10:1-30 and 2 John 1:7-11 / [7]Revelation 22:1-17 / [8]Proverbs 18:17, John 8:31-32, Acts 20:28-31, Romans 16:17-18, 2 Corinthians 4:1-6, 11:1-15, Ephesians 5:1-17, Colossians 2:1-10, 2 Thessalonians 2:1-17, 1 Timothy 4:1-16, Revelation 12:7-12, 13:11-18, 16:12-16 and 19:11-21 / [9]Joshua 6:17-19, 7:1-26 and Acts 19:11-19 / [10]Genesis

40:1-23, 41:1-57, Daniel 1:1-21, 2:1-49, 4:1-37 and 1 Corinthians 12:1-31 / [11]1 Kings 22:1-40 and 1 Corinthians 13:1-13

Most Outstanding Student: [1]Proverbs 1:10-19, 13:20, 16:27-30, Matthew 18:1-9 and Romans 14:10-13 / [2]Proverbs 4:1-13 and 16:17 / [3]Proverbs 4:14-27, 6:12-19 and 26:18-19 / [4]Genesis 3:1-6, 1 Chronicles 21:1-6, Proverbs 26:20-28 and Galatians 5:7-26 / [5]Genesis 3:7-24, Numbers 20:1-12 and 1 Chronicles 21:7-30 / [6]Proverbs 14:15-18, 26:11, Galatians 1:6-10 and James 4:1-10 / [7]Matthew 5:17-26, 2 Corinthians 10:3-6, Ephesians 4:7-32, Titus 2:11-15 and James 5:13-20 / [8]2 Samuel 11:1-27, 12:1-15 and Proverbs 1:20-33 / [9]Colossians 3:1-17, 1 Peter 3:8-17 and 1 John 1:5-10 / [10]Psalms 103:1-22, Proverbs 16:24, 27:17, 28:13, Ecclesiastes 4:9-12, Isaiah 55:6-13, Luke 15:1-10, John 3:16-21, Ephesians 2:1-10 and Hebrews 4:12-16 / [11]Numbers 6:24-27, 2 Chronicles 30:1-12, Proverbs 13:18, Isaiah 61:1-11, Joel 2:1-14, Luke 5:11-32, Romans 3:21-26 and 1 Peter 5:5-11

Goodbye: [1]Deuteronomy 4:1-6, Matthew 10:1-16, 2 Thessalonians 1:3-10 and 2 Timothy 4:1-8 / [2]John 16:1-33 / [3]Isaiah 49:14-16 / [4]Luke 17:11-19, 1 Corinthians 13:1-13, 1 Thessalonians 5:12-15 and 1 John 3:18 / [5]Matthew 16:1-4, 24:3-51 and 2 Peter 3:1-18 / [6]Luke 9:59-62 and 12:16-21 / [7]Ecclesiastes 4:9-12 / [8]Numbers 30:1-5, Matthew 5:33-37 and James 4:13-16 / [9]Jeremiah 17:5-10, John 10:27-30, 15:1-17, Philippians 4:6-9 and 1 Thessalonians 5:1-11 / [10]Galatians 5:13-26 and Ephesians 6:1-4

Section 3

Texas Happened: [1]Psalms 25:1-22, Isaiah 35:1-10, Matthew 7:13-14, 15:1-20 and John 10:1-30 / [2]Numbers 13:1-33, Proverbs 6:6-11 and Ecclesiastes 10:18, / [3]Numbers 14:1-38 / [4]Psalms 20:1-9, Proverbs 16:2-3, 16:9, 19:21 and Matthew 13:1-43 / [5]Deuteronomy 23:9-14, Proverbs 18:9 and 19:24 / [6]Ezekiel 37:1-14 / [7]Matthew 7:1-5 / [8]Proverbs 24:30-34 and James 4:17 / [9]Proverbs 4:23 / [10]Deuteronomy 28:1-68, 2 Chronicles 7:13-14 and 2 Corinthians 10:3-6 / [11]1 Corinthians 13:11-12 / [12]Luke 10:17-20 / [13]James 2:14-26 / [14]Psalms 142:1-7 / [15]Ecclesiastes 9:1-12 / [16]Numbers 11:1-35, Isaiah 43:18-21, 55:8-13, Jeremiah 29:11-14 and Philippians 2:12-16

Pale and Darkness: [1]Matthew 5:13-16 and Luke 8:16-18 / [2]Matthew 7:6 / [3]1 Corinthians 3:18-20 and 2 Corinthians 11:1-15 / [4]1 Corinthians 12:1-31, 13:1-13 and Ephesians 5:1-21 / [5]Psalms 37:1-20, 56:1-13, Matthew 7:1-5, 10:7-8, Mark 5:1-20, 16:15-18, Luke 8:19-21, 10:1-21, John 3:16-21, Acts 19:11-20, Ephesians 6:10-20, 2 Timothy 3:1-17,

Hebrews 5:9-14, 6:1-12, James 1:19-27, 1 Peter 2:1-10 and 1 John 1:5-10 / [6]Psalms 119:105-112, John 8:1-12 and James 1:16-18 / [7]Numbers 6:24-26, Psalms 91:1-16, Proverbs 3:5-8, Isaiah 61:1-3, Daniel 2:20-22, John 1:1-5 and Colossians 1:9-18

Living Hell: [1]Exodus 20:1-17, Psalms 120:1-7, Proverbs 14:5, 14:25 and Romans 13:8-10 / [2]Proverbs 10:6-7, 12:2, 12:4-6, Proverbs 14:17, Colossians 3:1-17 and 1 Peter 5:5-11 / [3]Proverbs 8:1-36, 10:13-14 and 14:29 / [4]Genesis 3:1-19, Judges 16:4-21, Proverbs 10:27-32, 14:1, 14:12, 14:33, Mark 7:20-23, Colossians 3:18-19 and 1 John 1:5-10 / [5]Proverbs 3:5-6, 3:13-18, 15:1-2, 17:14, 17:27-28, Galatians 5:7-26, Ephesians 4:1-29, 5:1-21 and James 3:1-18 / [6]1 Kings 18:17-46, 19:1-18, 21:1-29, 2 Kings 9:30-37, Proverbs 3:7-8, 12:17-22, 14:16, 17:12, 17:16, 26:7-12, 27:3, 27:15-16, 27:19, 31:10-31, Isaiah 1:1-20, Matthew 5:21-22, Luke 6:43-49, John 8:42-47, 1 Corinthians 13:1-13, Ephesians 5:22-33 and 6:1-9 / [7]Proverbs 26:17, 27:8, 27:12 and Colossians 3:20-25 / [8]Psalms 34:1-22, 37:1-40, Proverbs 3:13-26, 6:12-19, 12:10, 14:26-27, 14:32, 17:1, 17:6, Isaiah 49:14-16, Ephesians 6:10-20, Philippians 4:6-9, 2 Timothy 3:1-17 and Hebrews 12:1-29 / [9]Romans 12:1-21, 1 Corinthians 7:1-40, 1 Thessalonians 5:14-15, 1 Timothy 5:8 and 1 Peter 3:1-12 / [10]Proverbs 15:5, 18:6, 20:3 and 26:20-22 / [11]Deuteronomy 8:1-5 and Revelation 3:14-22

VHS: [1]Psalms 9:1-20, Proverbs 1:10-33, 3:21-26, 3:29-30, 6:12-19, 25:24, Isaiah 61:1-3 and 1 Peter 5:1-11 / [2]Proverbs 1:1-7, 3:5-8, 3:31-35, 17:14, 20:3, 24:1-2, 24:15-16, 25:21-22, Romans 12:9-21, Ephesians 6:1-9 and Philippians 2:1-4 / [3]Matthew 6:1-4, 6:16-18 and 2 Corinthians 9:6-7 / [4]Proverbs 2:1-22, 11:22 and 19:11 / [5]Matthew 6:19-21 and Luke 12:13-21 / [6]Isaiah 26:1-6, John 14:25-27, Philippians 4:5-9, Hebrews 12:12-17, James 3:13-18 and 1 Peter 3:8-12 / [7]Isaiah 55:1-13, Ezekiel 18:1-32, Matthew 10:34-39, Romans 8:1-17, Ephesians 6:10-20 and James 4:1-10

Stained: [1]Psalms 19:1-14, Proverbs 13:2-3, 18:6 and 27:12 / [2]Luke 6:43-49 / [3]Ecclesiastes 4:1-3 / [4]Proverbs 27:4, 27:15-16, Ecclesiastes 10:11-14 and Galatians 5:13-26 / [5]Mark 9:38-41, 1 Corinthians 1:10 and 12:1-31 / [6]Proverbs 6:12-19, 10:32, 16:2 and Ecclesiastes 4:4-8 / [7]Proverbs 16:3, Galatians 6:1-10 and 2 Thessalonians 3:1-15 / [8]Proverbs 26:17 / [9]Numbers 22:1-33, Proverbs 29:25, Matthew 10:27-31, 2 Peter 2:1-22 and Revelation 21:1-8 / [10]Proverbs 8:1-36, Jeremiah 17:5-13, Ezekiel 18:20, Matthew 12:33-37 and Romans 14:10-13 / [11]1 Samuel 3:1-21, 17:28-58, Isaiah 6:1-13 and Jeremiah 1:4-10 / [12]Proverbs 27:21, 27:9, Ecclesiastes 4:9-12, Ezekiel 33:1-20 and Matthew 13:1-50 / [13]Psalms 34:1-22, Proverbs 16:24, 25:11-12, 27:17 and Isaiah 41:8-13 / [14]Proverbs 16:7, 25:21-22 and 1 Corinthians 13:1-13 / [15]Deuteronomy 31:6, Psalms 23:1-6 and

Ephesians 6:10-20 / [16]Proverbs 16:25-30, 25:23-24, 27:19, Ephesians 4:17-32, James 3:1-18 and 1 Peter 5:1-4 / [17]Proverbs 16:32 / [18]Proverbs 16:22, 27:22, Ephesians 6:1-9 and 1 Peter 5:5-11 / [19]Genesis 2:21-25, Proverbs 14:1, 26:20-28, Ecclesiastes 4:13-16, Matthew 10:34-39, Luke 8:19-21, Romans 16:17-20, 1 Corinthians 15:33-34, Ephesians 5:1-33 and 2 Timothy 3:1-17

Dive-bombed: [1]Psalms 68:1-3, Luke 10:17-20 and 1 Peter 5:8-11 / [2]Exodus 23:20-22, Leviticus 26:1-8, Deuteronomy 28:1-14, Joshua 23:1-13, Psalms 18:28-42, 144:1, Isaiah 35:3-4, Romans 16:17-20, Ephesians 3:8-21, 4:1-6, 6:10-20, Hebrews 12:25-29 and James 4:7 / [3]Matthew 12:43-45, 25:31-46 and Revelation 12:7-11

Die-hard: [1]Exodus 25:1-9, 31:1-11 and Revelation 11:1-19 / [2]1 Corinthians 7:32-35 and 1 Timothy 5:8 / [3]Numbers 11:1-3, Jude 1:3-25, Philippians 2:14-16 and 2 Thessalonians 3:6-15 / [4]Proverbs 27:2 and Ephesians 2:1-10 / [5]Deuteronomy 32:1-4, 2 Samuel 22:32-35, Psalms 31:1-3, Ecclesiastes 9:10, and Jeremiah 17:5-10 / [6]Genesis 3:17-19, Proverbs 13:11, Ecclesiastes 3:9-22 and 5:12-20 / [7]Exodus 20:16, Leviticus 19:15-18, Deuteronomy 19:15-20, Psalms 15:1-5, Proverbs 27:4, 1 Peter 2:1-12 and Revelation 12:7-17

Logs: [1]Proverbs 14:30, Philippians 2:14-16 and Colossians 3:22-25 / [2]Proverbs 22:3 / [3]Luke 10:1-24, 2 Timothy 1:6-7 and 1 John 4:17-19 / [4]Proverbs 2:1-22 and 16:16-20 / [5]Proverbs 10:8, 11:2, 12:1, 12:15, 13:10, 14:3, 14:33, 15:31-33, 18:1-2, 22:24-25, 22:29, Galatians 5:16-26, James 3:13-18 and 1 John 4:20-21 / [6]1 Peter 2:1-10 / [7]Proverbs 6:6-11, 10:4-5, 12:11, 12:18, 12:27, 13:1, 13:4, 15:19, 22:6, 22:15, / [8]Proverbs 14:16

Phone Calls: [1]Judges 4:1-24, 6:1-14, 1 Samuel 16:1-13, Jeremiah 1:1-10 and 1 Corinthians 1:26-31 / [2]Isaiah 47:1-15, Jeremiah 17:5-13, 1 Corinthians 3:18-23, Galatians 6:1-8 and 2 Timothy 3:1-17 / [3]Proverbs 18:1-3, Matthew 7:1-5, 23:1-39, Mark 7:20-23, John 3:16-21, Romans 2:1-11, Titus 1:10-16, James 1:21-27 and 1 John 2:1-29 / [4]Ecclesiastes 4:9-12 and Philippians 2:1-4 / [5]Exodus 1:1-14, Ecclesiastes 8:10-17, Matthew 11:11-30 and Luke 12:13-34 / [6]Psalms 6:1-10, 34:1-22, 146:1-10, Proverbs 12:25, Matthew 5:1-12, John 15:1-25, Philippians 4:6-9 and 1 Peter 5:1-11 / [7]Romans 12:1-21 and Revelation 7:9-17 / [8]Matthew 18:1-14, Luke 8:16-21, 12:1-7, 16:19-31, 1 Corinthians 13:1-13, Ephesians 6:1-9 and James 2:1-13

Letters: [1]Psalms 23:1-6, 46:1-11, Proverbs 4:5-27, 14:12, 27:3, 27:10, 27:15-16, 27:19, Jeremiah 17:5-13, Matthew 18:1-14, Luke 12:4-7, John 10:1-10, Galatians 5:7-26, Philippians 4:6-7 and James 3:1-18 / [2]Proverbs 27:12, Isaiah 26:20-21, 59:1-19, Matthew

23:1-39, Mark 4:21-25, Luke 12:1-3, John 3:16-21 and Ephesians 5:1-21 / [3]Psalms 27:1-14, Proverbs 1:1-33, 2:1-22, 8:1-36, Isaiah 26:3-6, 53:1-12, Matthew 11:28-30, 1 Corinthians 10:12-13, 2 Corinthians 11:22-33 and Galatians 6:7-8 / [4]Psalms 62:1-12, 91:1-16, 147:1-20 and 2 Timothy 4:16-18 / [5]Romans 1:18-32 / [6]Psalms 97:10-12, Proverbs 21:19, 25:24, 27:20, Matthew 5:38-48, 19:3-12, Mark 7:14-23, Luke 6:27-36, John 10:11-30, 1 Corinthians 5:1-13, 7:1-40, 13:1-13, Ephesians 5:22-33, Philippians 2:12-16, Colossians 3:1-25, James 4:1-12, 1 John 4:7-21 and 1 Peter 3:1-12 / [7]Proverbs 15:23, 17:22, 27:17, and Ecclesiastes 4:9-12 / [8]Philippians 2:1-4 / [9]Psalms 68:1-6, Proverbs 18:10 and 27:9 / [10]Genesis 50:20, Romans 8:18-39, 1 Corinthians 9:24-27 and Philippians 4:8-9

Toothbrush: [1]Job 1:1-10, Psalms 91:1-16, Ecclesiastes 9:11-12, Isaiah 59:1-8, 1 Kings 3:1-28, 11:1-13, Matthew 23:37 and Luke 15:11-32 / [2]Psalms 1:1-6, Proverbs 1:1-33, 3:1-8, 13:20, 22:24-25, 1 Corinthians 5:9-13, 15:33-34 and 2 Corinthians 6:14-18 / [3]Proverbs 18:17 / [4]Proverbs 4:1-27, Ecclesiastes 9:1-10, Mark 3:28-29, Romans 6:1-23, Hebrews 5:12-14, 6:1-8, 10:26-31 and 1 John 5:16-17 / [5]Matthew 22:1-14, 1 Corinthians 1:26-31 and 1 Peter 2:1-10 / [6]Psalms 24:1-10, Proverbs 26:11, Isaiah 1:1-20 and Ezekiel 33:1-11 / [7]Matthew 6:22-23, 18:1-10, Galatians 5:16-26 and James 1:19-20 / [8]Psalms 5:1-12, 32:1-11, Matthew 7:15-27, Luke 8:19-21, John 10:1-18, 15:9-17, 2 Corinthians 11:12-15 and Ephesians 6:10-20 / [9]Luke 12:1-7 / [10]Matthew 12:22-37 and James 1:21-27 / [11]John 15:18-25 / [12]Proverbs 18:1-2 and Luke 4:16-22 / [13]Proverbs 12:10 / [14]Colossians 3:20-25 and Titus 2:1-5 / [15]Ephesians 6:1-9 / [16]1 Kings 19:1-21 / [17]Exodus 20:12, Proverbs 20:3, 26:1-10 and James 3:1-18 / [18]Zechariah 3:1-5, 1 John 2:1-11 and Revelation 12:7-10 / [19]Proverbs 26:18-28 / [20]Jeremiah 33:1-3, Matthew 5:21-22, 5:38-44, 2 Timothy 1:7 and 1 Peter 4:1-19 / [21]Psalms 56:1-13 and Ephesians 5:1-21

Post Holes: [1]Nehemiah 2:1-20, Job 1:1-10 and Proverbs 24:30-34 / [2]Isaiah 58:1-14 / [3]Nehemiah 4:1-5 / [4]Proverbs 6:6-11 and 22:6 / [5]Nehemiah 4:6-9 / [6]Isaiah 43:1-21, Matthew 10:1-42, 14:22-33, 16:24-27, 1 Corinthians 1:18-29, 2 Corinthians 12:7-10 and Hebrews 5:12-14 / [7]John 4:1-42 and James 2:14-26 / [8]Nehemiah 4:10-12, Psalms 28:1-9, 73:1-28, Isaiah 40:25-29, 41:8-20 and John 15:1-8 / [9]Nehemiah 4:13-23, Proverbs 10:4-5, 12:24, 12:27, 13:4, 14:23 19:15, 20:4, 26:14-16, Ezekiel 36:16-36, Luke 16:1-13, Ephesians 6:10-20 and Hebrews 13:20-21 / [10]Ecclesiastes 9:10, Matthew 25:14-30, Mark 12:28-34 and Colossians 3:18-25 / [11]Nehemiah 6:1-9, Zechariah 4:1-10, Luke 5:1-11 and Ephesians 5:15-17 / [12]Ecclesiastes 8:1-17 and 9:1-9 / [13]Psalms 37:23-24, Ephesians 2:1-10, 5:1-14, 2 Thessalonians 3:1-15 and 1 Peter 2:1-25 / [14]Nehemiah 6:10-16 / [15]Psalms 18:31-36, Proverbs 15:5, Isaiah 28:16-17 and 35:1-10 / [16]Proverbs 11:22, 12:4, 21:9, 21:19,

22:10, 27:15-16 and 2 Timothy 2:1-26 / [17]Ephesians 6:1-9, James 1:12-27 and Revelation 12:7-12 / [18]James 3:1-18 and Revelation 12:13-17 / [19]Exodus 20:1-17, Proverbs 18:17, 19:5 and 2 Timothy 3:1-17

If You're There: [1]Proverbs 18:2 and 26:10-12 / [2]Proverbs 21:7-10, 27:4 and 29:11 / [3]1 Corinthians 7:32-35, Ephesians 5:22-33, Colossians 3:18-19 and 1 Peter 3:1-7 / [4]Proverbs 11:29, 26:16 and James 3:1-18 / [5]Proverbs 14:1, 21:19, 27:15-16, Matthew 15:7-19 and 1 Timothy 6:1-10 / [6]Proverbs 3:31-35, 4:23-27, 6:12-15, 8:12-13, 10:9, 10:31-32, 11:3-6, 15:4, 16:27-30 and 31:10-31 / [7]1 Kings 18:20-40, 19:1-3, Proverbs 11:12 and 1 Corinthians 6:1-11 / [8]Ecclesiastes 4:9-12, Lamentations 3:52-66, Matthew 10:16-39 and Ephesians 5:1-17 / [9]Proverbs 26:17 / [10]Psalms 37:1-40 / [11]Psalms 55:1-11, 107:23-32, Proverbs 10:23-25 and Matthew 14:22-33 / [12]Matthew 18:1-14, John 3:16-17, Acts 4:8-12, Romans 5:6-10 and 8:18-30 / [13]Hebrews 5:12-14 and 6:1-8 / [14]Exodus 20:1-17, Deuteronomy 6:1-9 and Matthew 22:34-40 / [15]Jeremiah 24:1-10, Matthew 6:1-15, 7:15-29, Luke 18:9-14, Romans 8:1-17, 1 Corinthians 15:34, Hebrews 4:1-16 and Revelation 3:14-22 / [16]Jeremiah 17:5-10 / [17]1 Chronicles 28:9, Job 38:1-18, Psalms 18:1-50, 34:1-22, 51:1-17, 62:1-12, 139:1-18, 147:1-6, Proverbs 3:5-8, 6:16-19, 15:3, Isaiah 40:25-31, Jeremiah 23:23-24, 29:11-13, Ezekiel 36:16-38, Matthew 7:7-14, Mark 8:34-38, Luke 15:1-7, John 10:1-16, Romans 10:10-13, 1 Corinthians 1:18-31, Ephesians 2:1-10, James 4:1-10, Revelation 19:6 and 21:6-8

Section 4

Golden Plates: [1]Psalms 34:1-22, 51:1-17, Proverbs 17:22, Isaiah 61:1-3, Matthew 18:1-14, Luke 4:14-21, 11:1-13, Hebrews 4:12-16, James 1:2-8 and 4:1-10 / [2]Proverbs 2:1-22, 2 Corinthians 10:3-18, Ephesians 5:1-17 and James 1:12-18 / [3]Proverbs 12:10 and 27:7 / [4]Titus 1:5-16 / [5]Psalms 12:1-8, Proverbs 29:5, Matthew 11:11-30, 15:1-20, Mark 2:13-17, John 14:1-6, Galatians 5:1-6, Colossians 2:11-17, 2:20-23, 3:1-11 and 1 Timothy 4:1-16 / [6]1 Corinthians 1:10-25 / [7]Deuteronomy 10:12-22, 1 Corinthians 13:1-13 and 1 John 4:7-21 / [8]Genesis 3:1-24, 2 Corinthians 11:1-4 and Galatians 5:7-10 / [9]2 Corinthians 11:5-15, Ephesians 6:10-20 and Colossians 2:18-19 / [10]Jeremiah 5:26-31, Galatians 1:1-24, Colossians 2:6-10, 2 Peter 2:1-22 and 1 John 4:1-6 / [11]Acts 20:28-31 / [12]Leviticus 10:1-11, Psalms 5:1-12, Isaiah 5:20-21, Romans 1:18-32, 1 Corinthians 2:1-16, Philippians 1:9-10, 2 Timothy 4:1-5 and Hebrews 5:12-14 / [13]Galatians 5:16-26 and Colossians 3:18-25 / [14]Acts 20:32-35 and 1 Thessalonians 2:1-12 / [15]Proverbs 23:6-8, 28:23, Romans 12:1-21, Galatians 5:11-15 and Colossians 3:12-17 / [16]Matthew 7:15-27 and Romans

16:17-20 / [17]Jeremiah 9:1-6 / [18]2 John 1:7-11 / [19]Isaiah 29:9-14 and Matthew 7:7-12 / [20]2 Timothy 3:1-17

Questions: [1]Proverbs 18:17, 22:6, 27:12, Ephesians 4:11-16, 5:1-14 and 1 John 4:1 / [2]Matthew 10:32-33 and Philippians 2:5-11 / [3]Proverbs 23:22-24, Matthew 10:34-39, Philippians 2:12-16, 1 Timothy 5:1-2 and 1 John 4:2-16 / [4]Proverbs 27:7, Matthew 18:1-14 and Philippians 2:1-4 / [5]Matthew 15:10-20 / [6]Galatians 5:1-18, Colossians 2:1-23 and 1 Timothy 4:1-16 / [7]Psalms 119:1-48, Daniel 1:1-21, John 8:31-47, 1 Corinthians 8:1-13 and 10:23-33 / [8]Ezekiel 47:12 / [9]Proverbs 20:1, 23:19-21, 23:29-35, 31:4-7, Isaiah 5:11-23, 28:1-8, Matthew 11:1-19, John 2:1-11, 1 Corinthians 5:1-13, 6:9-14, Galatians 5:19-26, Ephesians 5:15-21, 1 Timothy 5:23 and Titus 2:1-15 / [10]Matthew 12:31-37, 15:1-9, 22:34-40, John 14:15-27, Romans 10:1-13, 2 Timothy 2:1-26, Hebrews 4:12-13, 1 John 2:1-6 and Revelation 20:11-15 / [11]Jeremiah 17:5-13, Ezekiel 18:1-32, Matthew 27:45-54, Luke 11:37-54, 1 Corinthians 6:15-20, Hebrews 4:14-16 and 10:1-39 / [12]Matthew 11:25-30, John 3:1-21, Romans 5:1-11, 13:8-14, 1 Corinthians 3:1-23, Ephesians 2:1-22, 1 Timothy 1:3-17 and 1 Peter 1:3-25 / [13]Proverbs 3:1-8, 21:2, Romans 8:1-17 and 10:14-21 / [14]Genesis 1:9-28, Job 1:6-7, 41:1-34, Psalms 72:1-9, 74:12-17, 104:24-30, Matthew 3:1-17, 12:43-45, 14:22-33, John 21:1-14 and Romans 6:1-14 / [15]1 Corinthians 14:33, Philippians 1:3-11, 1 Peter 5:6-11 and 1 John 4:17-19

Battlefield: [1]Isaiah 9:5 / [2]Psalms 144:1-8 and 2 Timothy 2:1-26 / [3]Genesis 40:8, Jeremiah 33:3, Daniel 1:1-21 and 2:19-22 / [4]Genesis 1:1-10, Job 38:1-7, Ecclesiastes 3:9-15, John 1:1-3 and Hebrews 3:1-4 / [5]Job 1:6-7 / [6]Judges 13:1-25, 14:5-6, 15:14-20, 16:23-31, 1 Samuel 17:1-58, Psalms 119:89-128, Isaiah 11:1-5, Ezekiel 22:23-31, Matthew 4:1-11, 7:6, 7:15-27, Luke 10:1-12, John 10:1-30, Acts 20:28-35 Romans 1:18-32, Ephesians 6:10-20, Philippians 3:1-21 and James 4:1-10 / [7]Ecclesiastes 3:16-22, Isaiah 40:27-31, Matthew 16:24-27 and 2 Corinthians 4:1-18 / [8]Isaiah 54:1-17, Ezekiel 18:1-32, Daniel 4:1-37, Matthew 3:1-12, Luke 13:1-5, Acts 17:30, Romans 6:1-23, 2 Corinthians 7:1-12, 1 Peter 5:1-11 and 1 John 5:1-21 / [9]Matthew 6:19-34, 1 Timothy 6:1-10, Revelation 18:1-24 and 19:1-21 / [10]Matthew 10:16-39, 24:3-51, Mark 6:14-29, 2 Timothy 4:1-8, Hebrews 11:30-40, 12:1-29, Revelation 2:8-11, 6:1-17, 7:9-17, 12:1-17, 13:1-18, 14:6-20, 17:1-18, 20:1-15 and 22:12-21 / [11]Matthew 10:7-8, John 11:1-44 and 14:1-14

The Holy Ghost: [1]Mark 16:15-18, John 3:1-21 and 1 Peter 3:18-22 / [2]Matthew 6:1-18, John 14:12-24, 21:15-17 and 2 Corinthians 10:3-18 / [3]Acts 8:26-40 and 10:47-48 / [4]Isaiah 33:10-16, Matthew 15:1-20, 22:1-14, 23:1-39, 24:45-51, Luke 12:1-7, Romans 12:9-21, Titus 1:10-16, James 1:19-27, 2:14-26, 1 John 2:3-11, 4:1-21 and Revelation

21:6-8 / [5]Acts 22:1-16 / [6]Jeremiah 17:9-10 and James 3:1-5 / [7]James 3:6-18 / [8] Genesis 14:8-20, Psalms 110:1-7, Matthew 28:18-20, John 14:25-26, 20:19-23, Acts 2:1-47, 19:1-6, Romans 6:1-4, Galatians 3:26-29, 1 Timothy 4:1-16, Hebrews 5:1-14, 6:1-20, 7:1-28 and 8:1-13 / [9]Luke 11:5-13, Acts 4:1-31 and 10:34-46 / [10]Luke 3:1-22 and 1 Corinthians 12:1-11 / [11]John 14:1-11, 1 Corinthians 12:12-29, 13:1-13, Titus 2:11-15, 3:1-11 and 1 John 2:1-2

Obedience: [1]Job 1:6-7, Luke 10:17-20, Ephesians 2:1-10 and Revelation 12:7-12 / [2]Matthew 7:7-11, John 15:1-8, James 1:2-8, 4:1-10 and 1 John 5:14-17 / [3]Proverbs 10:17, Romans 12:1-21, 1 Corinthians 13:1-13 and Galatians 5:13-26 / [4]Hebrews 13:7-17 / [5]Luke 15:11-32 / [6]Numbers 21:4-9, Daniel 6:1-28, Luke 10:17-20, John 3:14-21, Acts 28:1-10 and 1 Corinthians 10:1-13 / [7]Genesis 2:15-17, 3:1-24, Deuteronomy 26:16-19, 27:15-26, 28:1-68, 1 Kings 2:1-4, Psalms 128:1-6, Proverbs 27:6, Isaiah 55:6-9, Jeremiah 33:1-3, Ezekiel 33:1-20, Ephesians 5:15-21 and James 1:19

Reinvent Yourself: [1]Matthew 2:1-23, Mark 6:1-6 and John 1:43-51 / [2]Numbers 11:1-34, 1 Samuel 16:1-7, Psalms 139:1-24, Proverbs 31:30-31, Ephesians 4:29-32, 5:1-21, Philippians 2:12-18, 4:10-13, Colossians 3:1-17, 1 Thessalonians 5:16-18 and 1 Peter 3:3-4 / [3]Isaiah 49:1-16 / [4]Proverbs 28:24, Matthew 22:34-40, Galatians 5:7-26 and Philippians 4:8-9 / [5]Ecclesiastes 4:1-8, Ephesians 6:5-9, 1 Corinthians 6:1-11 and Colossians 3:22-25 / [6]Proverbs 27:10, 27:17 and Ecclesiastes 4:9-12 / [7]Colossians 3:20-21 / [8]John 15:1-25, Romans 12:1-21 and Philippians 4:6-7 / [9]1 Corinthians 13:1-13 / [10]Matthew 10:16-39

Short-alls: [1]Deuteronomy 6:4-9, Proverbs 15:1-4, 31:10-31, 1 Corinthians 13:1-13 and Titus 2:1-5 / [2]Proverbs 3:1-18, 4:7-13, 17:25 and James 3:1-18 / [3]Proverbs 12:10, 15:13 and Ephesians 4:17-32 / [4]Proverbs 18:24 / [5]Deuteronomy 10:17-19 and James 2:1-13 / [6]Matthew 10:16-31 / [7]Proverbs 16:19 / [8]Psalms 25:1-22, 32:1-11, 119:129-136, Proverbs 16:31, 22:6 and John 21:15-17 / [9]Philippians 2:1-4 / [10]Genesis 19:15-29, 1 Kings 19:19-21, Luke 9:57-62 and Philippians 2:14-16 / [11]Proverbs 6:16-19 and Matthew 6:22-23 / [12]Proverbs 15:30, 29:10, Matthew 25:31-46, Luke 10:25-37, Acts 10:34-35 and Romans 12:9-16 / [13]Proverbs 16:24 and Ecclesiastes 4:9-12 / [14]Psalms 146:1-10 / [15]Proverbs 16:32, 25:28, 29:9, 29:25, Romans 12:1-3, 12:17-21, 1 Corinthians 9:19-27, 10:12-13, Galatians 5:7-26, James 1:19-20 and 2 Peter 1:2-11 / [16]Proverbs 4:14-27, 10:19-21, 12:5-6, 12:8, 12:18-21, 15:28, 16:27-30, 18:6-7, 18:21, 21:4, 29:20, 29:22, 30:12-14, 30:32-33, Ecclesiastes 10:8 and 10:11-15 / [17]Proverbs 12:12-16, 16:5, 21:2, Leviticus 19:33-34 and Ephesians 2:1-22 / [18]Proverbs 3:19-35, 29:11, 29:15-17, 29:27, 31:8-9, Romans 1:18-32 and 1 Thessalonians 5:14-15

Lunch: [1]Philippians 4:8-9 / [2]Proverbs 6:12-19 and James 3:1-18 / [3]Psalms 69:1-36, Proverbs 1:10-19, 18:14 and 27:12 / [5]Proverbs 12:25-26, 18:20, 18:24, Isaiah 43:1-2, Matthew 25:31-46 and Luke 10:25-37 / [6]Proverbs 1:20-33, 18:2, 18:21, 26:20-27, 27:19, Matthew 5:21-22, 18:1-14, Romans 16:17-20, 1 Corinthians 5:6-13, 6:9-11, Galatians 3:26-29, 5:16-26 and James 4:1-12 / [7]Romans 12:9-21 and 1 Peter 3:8-17 / [8]Genesis 19:1-29, Psalms 109:1-5, Proverbs 18:5, 22:15, 27:23-27, 31:8-9, Matthew 15:1-20, 23:1-36, 24:3-13, John 10:1-29, Romans 1:18-32, Galatians 5:13-15 and Revelation 21:1-8 / [9]Proverbs 26:10-12 and Matthew 12:1-7 / [10]Psalms 133:1-3, Proverbs 27:9, 27:17, Matthew 22:36-40, John 1:1-13 and 1 Corinthians 13:1-13 / [11]Psalms 68:6, Ecclesiastes 4:9-12, Matthew 18:18-20, Romans 12:1-8, 1 Corinthians 1:10-31, Ephesians 4:1-6 and Hebrews 10:24-25

My Testimony: [1]Daniel 4:1-2, Mark 5:18-20, Luke 21:7-15, John 4:5-42, 1 John 1:1-5 and 5:9-11 / [2]Proverbs 4:1-27, 11:9, Matthew 4:1-11, Luke 6:43-45, John 8:37-47 and Titus 2:6-8 / [3]Jeremiah 17:5-13, Matthew 18:1-14, Luke 6:46-49 and Galatians 5:7-10 / [4]Genesis 2:15-25, 3:1-6 and Romans 1:28-32 / [5]Psalms 33:4, Proverbs 12:17-22, 2 Timothy 2:1-26, 4:1-5 and 1 John 1:6-10 / [6]Psalms 19:7-14, 25:1-22, 119:1-16, Proverbs 8:1-36, 30:1-9, Matthew 13:1-43, John 8:31-36, 12:42-50, Acts 5:12-42, 2 Corinthians 1:12-14, 10:3-6, Galatians 1:1-12, 5:13-26, Ephesians 4:17-32, 5:1-21, 6:10-20, Philippians 1:3-30, 1 Thessalonians 2:1-6, 1 Peter 3:8-17, 1 John 2:15-29, 3:1-24, 5:18-21, 3 John 1:2-4 and Revelation 12:7-11 / [7]Proverbs 13:2-3, 29:25, Matthew 12:33-36, Romans 7:14-25 / [8]Proverbs 10:19-21, 15:4, Romans 10:1-21 and James 3:1-18

A Bone to Pick: [1]Leviticus 18:19-30, Proverbs 4:10-27, 1 Corinthians 6:9-20, Galatians 5:13-26, Ephesians 5:1-21, Colossians 3:1-11, 1 Thessalonians 4:1-8, Hebrews 13:4, James 1:1-18, 4:1-10 and Jude 1:3-25 / [2]Exodus 22:16-17, Proverbs 4:1-9, 18:5, 18:13, 18:15, 18:17, 25:2, Matthew 5:21-30, 18:21-35, Luke 19:1-10, 1 Corinthians 2:1-16, Galatians 6:1-10, 1 Timothy 1:3-17, 5:24-25, Hebrews 4:12-16, 12:1-17 and Revelation 21:6-8 / [3]Exodus 20:1-17, Matthew 7:1-5, 23:1-36, Mark 7:1-23, Luke 12:28-34, 18:9-14, Romans 3:9-31, 12:1-21, 1 Corinthians 7:1-9 and 7:25-40 / [4]Leviticus 18:1-18, Deuteronomy 22:23-27, 27:22, 2 Samuel 13:1-20, Psalms 25:1-22, Proverbs 12:17-22, 28:1, 28:10, Jeremiah 20:3-12 and Matthew 18:1-14 / [5]Proverbs 28:13, Isaiah 55:6-13, Luke 17:3-4, James 5:13-20 and 1 John 1:1-10 / [6]1 Thessalonians 4:9-12 / [7]Deuteronomy 22:28-29, Psalms 103:1-22, 106:34-48, Proverbs 6:16-19, 11:13, 11:22, 18:6-8, 18:14,

25:8-10, Isaiah 61:1-3, Matthew 6:14-15, 18:15-17, John 8:2-12, 9:1-41, Acts 9:1-31, 1 Corinthians 5:1-13, Ephesians 2:1-10, 2 Thessalonians 3:1-15, 2 Timothy 2:1-26, Titus 2:1-15, 3:1-11, James 3:1-18 and 4:11-12 / [8]John 4:1-42 / [9]Psalms 37:1-8, Proverbs 15:1, 15:18, 16:32, 25:15, 29:11, Ecclesiastes 7:5-9, Matthew 23:1-39, Luke 12:1-3, John 2:13-17, 2 Corinthians 10:1-6, Ephesians 4:1-32, 1 Timothy 4:1-11, 5:1-2, 5:19-21, James 1:19-20 and 1 John 4:1-21 / [10]Proverbs 11:14, 15:2-3, 18:20-21, 25:28, Matthew 7:21-28, 15:1-20, 21:14-17, Luke 6:43-45, Colossians 3:12-17, 1 Timothy 3:1-7, 4:12-16, James 1:21-27 and 2:12-13 / [11]Matthew 10:11-20 / [12]Psalms 37:9-40, Isaiah 52:1-15 and Romans 8:26-39

Section 5

Magic: [1]2 Kings 2:8-24, Psalms 97:1-12, Romans 1:16-32 and Jude 1:12-25 / [2]Proverbs 6:12-19 and James 2:1-13 / [3]Leviticus 19:31, 20:6-8, 1 Samuel 28:3-25, 1 Kings 16:30-33, 21:23 and 2 Kings 9:1-37 / [4]Acts 5:17-32, 1 Corinthians 12:1-11, Galatians 5:13-26, Hebrews 5:12-14, 6:1-12 and 1 Peter 5:6-11 / [5]Matthew 10:24-33, 1 Corinthians 10:1-33, Ephesians 6:10-20 and James 2:14-26 / [6]Matthew 9:9-13, 1 Corinthians 5:9-13 and 15:33-34 / [7]Proverbs 29:11 / [8]Galatians 6:1-10 and James 1:12-27 / [9]Matthew 15:1-20, 23:1-39, 1 Corinthians 13:1-13, Colossians 2:1-10 and 2 Timothy 3:1-17 / [10]Deuteronomy 4:15-40, 2 Corinthians 11:1-4 and 1 Timothy 4:1-16 / [11]Exodus 7:1-13, Deuteronomy 13:1-4, Mark 13:21-23, Acts 8:5-25 and 2 Thessalonians 2:9-12 / [12]Deuteronomy 18:9-14, Ezekiel 13:17-23 and Revelation 21:6-8 / [13]Isaiah 8:19-22, 47:1-15, Acts 19:11-20, Romans 12:1-2 and 1 John 4:1-6 / [14]Proverbs 23:9, 28:1, Luke 6:20-23, John 15:18-25 and Revelation 22:12-15 / [15]Ecclesiastes 4:9-12, Matthew 18:1-14, Luke 6:27-42 and 15:1-10 / [16]Romans 12:3-21 and 1 John 4:7-21

Mara: [1]1 Samuel 16:1-13, Psalms 139:1-24, Proverbs 31:30-31 and Matthew 7:1-5 / [2]1 Timothy 4:7-16, Hebrews 12:1-4 and 1 Peter 5:1-11 / [3]Exodus 20:1-17, Proverbs 6:16-19, 19:1-5, Matthew 7:6, Romans 13:8-10 and Revelation 21:6-8 / [4]Matthew 19:16-30, James 2:1-26, 4:11-12 and 1 Peter 3:3-4 / [5]Genesis 1:26-31, John 7:24, 8:37-47, 13:34-35, Acts 17:22-31, Romans 2:11, 10:10-13 and 1 John 2:3-11 / [6]Romans 12:1-21 / [7]1 Samuel 17:1-58 / [8]Proverbs 6:12-15, 21:7, 21:23, Philippians 3:17-21 and James 4:1-10 / [9]Psalms 19:7-14, Proverbs 3:31-35, 12:17-22, 18:20-21, 27:19, Jeremiah 17:5-13, Matthew 5:38-48, 6:22-23, 7:13-27, 12:33-37, Mark 7:1-23, Ephesians 2:1-10, Colossians 3:1-10, James 3:1-18, 1 Peter 3:10-17 and 1 John 1:5-7 / [10]Proverbs 12:25 and 21:11-13 / [11]John 12:37-43 and 1 Corinthians 13:1-13

Flowers: [1]Isaiah 40:1-8 and 1 Peter 1:13-25 / [2]Matthew 12:1-14 and Mark 2:1-28 / [3]Proverbs 1:10-31, John 3:19-21, 8:12 and 1 John 1:5-10 / [4]1 Corinthians 7:25-40 / [5]Psalms 103:1-22, Proverbs 6:12-19, 11:9, 13:20, 14:1, Mark 7:20-23, Colossians 3:1-25 and James 1:19-27 / [6]Deuteronomy 32:35, 1 Samuel 24:12-19, Psalms 25:1-9 and 1 Peter 3:1-12 / [7]Proverbs 13:2-3, 15:1-4, 18:20-21, Ecclesiastes 10:11-15, Matthew 12:33-37 and Romans 14:10-13 / [8]Exodus 20:12, Psalms 94:1-23, Matthew 22:36-40, Romans 12:1-21, Ephesians 4:1-32, 6:1-4, Philippians 2:1-18 and 1 Thessalonians 5:14-15 / [9]Psalms 37:1-40, Proverbs 27:19-22, Matthew 10:34-39, Luke 8:19-21, Romans 3:9-20, 1 Corinthians 13:1-13 and James 3:1-18 / [10]1 Corinthians 7:1-9 / [11]Proverbs 10:18, 12:17-22, 27:6, 28:13, Isaiah 1:1-31, 55:6-11, Joel 2:1-13, Matthew 7:13-29 and Acts 17:30-31 / [12]Psalms 120:1-7, Proverbs 18:19, 21:9, 21:19, 27:15-16, Isaiah 5:18-25, Mark 11:25-26, Luke 6:37 and 2 Corinthians 10:3-6 / [13]Psalms 34:1-22, 95:1-11, Proverbs 4:20-27, 8:1-36, Daniel 4:37, Micah 6:8, Luke 18:9-14, Ephesians 5:1-33, 2 Timothy 3:1-17, James 4:1-12 and Jude 1:3-23

Why?: [1]1 Corinthians 7:25-39 / [2]Genesis 2:21-24, Deuteronomy 24:1-5, Malachi 2:10-16, Matthew 19:3-12 and Hebrews 13:4 / [3]Proverbs 31:10-31, 1 Timothy 6:3-21, Titus 1:10-16 and 2:1-15 / [4]Proverbs 7:1-27, 30:20-23, Romans 8:1-14, 2 Peter 1:1-11, 2:1-22, 1 Peter 5:8, 1 John 2:1-11 and 4:1-21 / [5]Matthew 7:6 and 2 Corinthians 6:12-18 / [6]Proverbs 27:2 / [7]Proverbs 1:20-33, 4:7-27, 6:20-35, 8:1-36, Matthew 5:27-32 and 2 Timothy 2:1-26 / [8]Job 38:1-18, Isaiah 45:9-13 and Jeremiah 1:4-10 / [9]1 Corinthians 7:1-16 / [10]Exodus 23:1-9, Deuteronomy 16:18-20, Psalms 26:1-12, Proverbs 15:27, 17:23, 18:25-39, 20:25, 29:4, 32:1-11, 46:1-11, 59:1-17, Ecclesiastes 7:7, Isaiah 5:21-25, 33:14-16, 54:11-17, Matthew 26:14-16, 27:3-10, Luke 18:9-14 and 2 Corinthians 10:17-18 / [11]1 Corinthians 15:33

Broken: [1]James 1:21-25 / [2]Proverbs 6:12-19 and 22:15 / [3]Zechariah 7:8-12, Romans 6:11-23, Ephesians 6:1-4, Hebrews 12:1-17, 1 Peter 3:8-12, 1 John 1:5-10 and 3:4-10 / [4]1 Thessalonians 5:14-15 and James 4:1-10 / [5]Proverbs 3:1-8 / [6]Psalms 27:1-14, 139:1-24, Proverbs 11:17, 13:24, 21:2, 22:6, Matthew 18:1-10 and Galatians 6:1-10 / [7]Psalms 25:1-22, Proverbs 19:20, 19:25, Isaiah 55:1-13, 59:1-21, Jeremiah 17:5-13, Matthew 7:1-5, 9:10-13, 13:36-43, 19:16-17, Romans 2:1-11, 3:10-26, 5:1-21, 2 Corinthians 5:9-21, Revelation 20:11-15 and 21:7-8 / [8]Psalms 103:1-22, Proverbs 3:11-24, Matthew 10:34-39 and 18:11-14 / [9]Isaiah 49:14-16 and Philippians 4:6-9 / [10]Proverbs 6:6-11 and 19:15 / [11]Mark 7:20-21, Luke 6:27-36 and John 3:16-17 / [12]Ecclesiastes 4:9-12, Galatians 5:13-26 and Titus 2:1-5 / [13]Proverbs 11:2, 29:23, Ecclesiastes 4:1-3, Daniel 4:37 and 1 John 2:15-16

SCRIPTURE STUDIES

Paul: [1]Proverbs 7:1-27 and 27:7 / [2]Psalms 12:1-8, 36:1-12, Proverbs 6:20-35, 29:5, Jeremiah 9:1-6 and Jude 1:3-19 / [3]Proverbs 6:12-19, 18:17, 26:23-28 and Romans 16:17-18 / [4]Proverbs 27:6 / [5]Psalms 55:1-23, Matthew 10:27-31 and Acts 4:1-31 / [6]Proverbs 11:9, 28:23, Matthew 5:27-30, 10:34-39, 23:1-39 and Romans 13:8-14 / [7]Psalms 5:1-12, Mark 7:18-23, 1 Corinthians 6:9-20 and Hebrews 13:4 / [8]Matthew 13:24-50, Luke 12:1-7, John 3:16-21, 8:12, Galatians 5:13-21 and 1 John 1:5-10 / [9]Genesis 1:27, 1 Samuel 16:7, Isaiah 53:1-3 and 1 Corinthians 1:26-29 / [10]Philippians 4:6-9, 1 Peter 5:1-7 and 1 John 4:18 / [11]Song of Solomon 8:4 / [12]1 Corinthians 13:4-7, Galatians 5:22-26 and Philippians 2:1-4

Bible Study: [1]Psalms 42:1-11 / [2]Genesis 3:6-21, 4:1-5, 22:1-14, Leviticus 16:16-34, 17:11, Isaiah 53:1-12, Joel 2:28-32, Zechariah 12:10, Matthew 20:25-28, Luke 3:16, John 1:29, 10:11-18, 11:47-52, 16:28, Acts 1:1-11, Acts 2:1-36, 20:28, Romans 3:21-26, 5:6-11, Galatians 1:1-4, Hebrews 9:11-28, 1 John 2:1-2, Revelation 1:1-6 and 5:1-14 / [3]Mark 16:15-20, Acts 3:1-11, 4:1-13, 19:11-20, 1 Corinthians 12:1-14, Galatians 5:16-26 and Ephesians 6:10-20 / [4]Matthew 1:18-23, John 3:16-21, Philippians 2:1-11, Colossians 3:17 and 1 John 5:1-13 / [5]John 1:1-18, 3:1-8, Acts 5:29-32 and 1 Timothy 3:16 / [6]Genesis 1:26-27, Deuteronomy 6:4, Matthew 3:13-17, John 14:1-26, 1 Corinthians 15:22-28, Ephesians 4:1-6 and Colossians 2:1-10 / [7]Matthew 23:1-39, 1 Corinthians 1:1-31, 2:1-16, 1 Timothy 4:1-16, James 1:16-20 and 1 John 4:1-6 / [8]Deuteronomy 18:15-19, Isaiah 11:1-5, 42:1-8, 49:1-7, 52:13-15, 55:4-11, Daniel 7:13-14, Micah 5:2-4, Zechariah 6:11-15 and 13:7 / [9]Jeremiah 1:4-8, Matthew 18:1-5 and Luke 2:41-52 / [10]Genesis 1:1-2, Judges 6:1-34, Psalms 139:7-8, Proverbs 4:5-13, Isaiah 7:14, 9:6-7, 61:1, Ezekiel 36:23-28, Zechariah 4:6, Matthew 1:21-23, 10:16-20, 12:30-32, Luke 1:13-37, 9:46-50, John 14:15-31, 15:1-27, 16:1-16, 2 Corinthians 3:21-22, 13:14, Galatians 6:1-10, Ephesians 1:1-14, Hebrews 1:1-14, 2:1-18, 4:14-16, 5:1-11, 6:13-20, 7:1-28, 8:1-6, James 1:5-12, 1 John 3:1-5 and 4:7-15 / [11]2 Timothy 3:12-17 and Hebrews 4:12-13 / [12]Matthew 12:33-37 / [13]1 Corinthians 13:1-13 / [14]Deuteronomy 6:5-9, Matthew 18:6-14, Mark 3:31-35, Romans 14:9-13, 1 Corinthians 3:1-23, Hebrews 5:12-14, 6:1-12, James 1:21-27 and 1 Peter 3:8-17

The Name of Jesus: [1]Matthew 28:19-20, Mark 16:14-16, Luke 3:16-22, John 3:1-21, Acts 19:1-6, Titus 2:11-15, 3:1-8 and 1 Peter 3:18-22 / [2]Psalms 27:1-14, 47:1-9, Luke 5:17-26, John 4:1-42, Acts 2:1-41, 4:1-13, 26:1-29, Romans 3:19-26, Philippians 2:5-11, 1 Timothy 3:13-16, Hebrews 9:1-28, 12:1-2, James 4:1-12, 1 Peter 1:1-21 and 1 John 1:1-20 / [3]John 10:1-10, 1 Corinthians 12:1-13 and 2 Corinthians 12:7-10 / [4]Psalms 28:1-9, Proverbs 18:10, Galatians 4:1-7 and James 2:17-26 / [5]Deuteronomy 2:20-22, 31:1-13, Psalms 4:1-8, 18:1-50, 23:1-6, 91:1-16, 127:1-2, Isaiah 35:1-10, 52:1-15, Proverbs 3:1-26,

Jeremiah 33:1-3, Matthew 11:19-30, Mark 16:17-20, John 14:22-27, 1 Corinthians 1:1-31, 2 Corinthians 10:3-6, Galatians 3:1-29, Ephesians 6:10-20, Philippians 4:4-9, Hebrews 4:15-16, 13:12-16 and Revelation 19:1-16 / [6]Exodus 12:1-13, Leviticus 17:11, Jeremiah 32:26-27, Zechariah 2:3-5, John 1:29 and Hebrews 10:10-23

UPC: [1]Matthew 24:3-51, 1 Corinthians 15:51-58, Revelation 1:1-20, 2:1-29, 3:1-22 and 7:9-17 / [2]Proverbs 22:6, 2 Timothy 2:15-26, 4:1-4 and Titus 2:1-16 / [3]Matthew 7:13-27, John 10:1-30, 1 Timothy 1:3-20, 3:1-7 and Titus 1:1-16 / [4]Mark 9:38-50, 1 Corinthians 1:10-21, Hebrews 4:12-13 and James 3:1-18 / [5]Matthew 7:6, 23:1-39, 2 Timothy 3:1-17, 1 Peter 1:22-25, 2 Peter 2:1-22 and 3:1-18 / [6]Matthew 6:19-34, Ephesians 4:1-32, 5:1-33, 6:1-4, 2 Thessalonians 3:1-18, 1 Peter 1:1-21, 2:1-25, 3:1-17 and 2 Peter 1:1-21 / [7]Matthew 5:1-48, 1 Thessalonians 4:1-18 and 5:1-24 / [8]Matthew 7:1-5, Romans 1:14-32, 2:1-11, 1 Corinthians 3:1-23 and James 4:11-12 / [9]1 Corinthians 15:1-28 and 1 Timothy 2:1-7 / [10]Proverbs 1:1-33 / [11]Matthew 7:7-11, 2 Corinthians 1:3-11, Philippians 4:6-7, Hebrews 4:14-16 and James 4:1-10 / [12]Philippians 4:8-9 / [13]Proverbs 11:16-27, 22:4, 1 Corinthians 2:1-16, Galatians 6:1-10, Colossians 3:23-25 and Revelation 22:11-21 / [14]Matthew 6:1-18, 10:16-42, 18:1-14, 23:1-39 and Luke 16:1-15/ [15]Psalms 42:1-11, Isaiah 12:1-6, 51:1-12, 61:1-3, Luke 4:14-21, John 4:19-24, 14:1-17, Philippians 2:1-11, Hebrews 13:8-15, Revelation 4:1-11 and 5:1-14 / [16]Psalms 56:1-13, Matthew 7:12-27, James 1:1-27 and 2:1-26 / [17]2 Samuel 6:1-23, Mark 5:1-15, 16:15-20, Acts 2:1-40, 8:4-8, 19:1-20, Romans 12:1-16, 1 Corinthians 14:1-40, Galatians 5:1-26 and Ephesians 6:10-20

Jesus' Name Baptism: [1]Isaiah 11:1-4, Daniel 1:17, Luke 24:36-49, John 14:21-26, 1 Corinthians 2:1-16, 2 Corinthians 3:1-18, 2 Timothy 3:16-17 and 1 John 5:13-15 / [2]Matthew 4:1-11, 11:1-30, 1 Corinthians 3:1-23, 4:1-21, 13:11-12, Ephesians 4:1-32, 5:1-21, Hebrews 5:4-14, 6:1-15, James 3:1, 5:7-11, 1 Peter 1:1-21 and 1 John 4:1-6 / [3]Deuteronomy 15:12-17, 22:5-12, 1 Samuel 16:1-7, Psalms 139:13-18, Proverbs 31:10-31, 1 Corinthians 11:1-16, 1 Timothy 2:1-10, James 2:1-13, 4:11-12 and 1 Peter 3:1-17 / [4]Jeremiah 17:5-14, Ephesians 1:1-23, 2:1-22, 3:1-21 and Philippians 4:4-9 / [5]Matthew 28:1-20, Mark 16:14-20 and Acts 2:29-41 / [6]Proverbs 14:1 / [7]Proverbs 8:1-36, 17:11, Matthew 7:6, 10:7-40 and James 4:1-10 / [8]James 1:1-11 / [9]Matthew 12:30-37, 1 Corinthians 1:17-31, James 5:19-20 and Revelation 20:1-15 / [10]2 Timothy 3:1-15 / [11]Matthew 19:13-15, Acts 8:25-40, 2 Timothy 4:1-5 and James 1:12-27 / [12]Proverbs 18:17 and Luke 12:1-5 / [13]Matthew 18:1-14, James 3:2-18, 4:17 and 5:12

Still Unsure: [1]Exodus 20:12, Deuteronomy 5:22-33, 8:1-6, 1 Samuel 8:1-22, 2 Samuel 22:1-51, Psalms 19:1-14, 119:1-10, Proverbs 2:1-9, 4:1-27, 17:12, 20:3, 23:9, 27:22,

SCRIPTURE STUDIES

Romans 15:1-4, Ephesians 5:1-17, 2 Timothy 2:14-26, 2 Timothy 3:1-17, Hebrews 4:12-16, 12:18-29, James 1:1-21, 3:1-18, 4:1-12 and 1 John 2:15-29 / ²Isaiah 35:8-10, Ezekiel 36:16-27, Joel 2:11-14, 2:28-32, Matthew 7:13-27, Luke 1:1-45, John 1:29-37, Acts 2:1-41, 5:32, 10:34-48, 11:1-18, 16:22-26, 19:1-6, Colossians 3:12-17, 2 Timothy 2:1-5, Hebrews 12:1-17 and 2 Peter 1:19-21 / ³Romans 5:1-21 and Ephesians 4:17-32 / ⁴Zephaniah 3:9-20 and Luke 15:1-32 Romans 6:1-11, 1 Corinthians 12:12-27, Galatians 3:26-29 and Ephesians 2:1-22, 2 Timothy 2:6-13 and 1 Peter 3:18-22 / ⁵Matthew 24:3-13, Mark 16:15-18, John 3:1-36, Acts 4:12, 16:29-34, Romans 10:8-15, 1 Corinthians 12:1-11, 1 Thessalonians 5:8-24, Titus 2:11-15, 3:1-11 and 1 Peter 1:1-25

Beg: ¹Deuteronomy 6:16-19, Isaiah 28:1-29, Ezekiel 36:16-27, Matthew 3:1-17, 4:1-11, 24:1-51, 25:1-46, Mark 16:1-20, Acts 2:1-47, 19:1-20, 28:1-10, 1 Corinthians 13:1-13, 14:1-40, Galatians 3:1-29, 1 Thessalonians 4:1-18, 5:1-28, 2 Peter 1:1-21, 2:1-22, 3:1-18, Revelation 1:1-20, 2:1-29, 3:1-22 and 16:1-21 / ²Matthew 10:34-39 and Hebrews 4:12-16 / ³Philippians 1:1-11, 2:1-13 and James 4:6-10 / ⁴Matthew 10:32-33, Romans 3:19-31, Galatians 5:1-26, Philippians 4:4-9, 2 Timothy 1:6-11, James 3:1-18, 1 Peter 1:1-25 and 2:1-10 / ⁵Proverbs 21:2, Jeremiah 17:5-14, Matthew 15:1-20, Luke 5:27-32, John 14:1-29, 15:1-17 and James 4:17 / ⁶Psalms 38:1-22, Isaiah 55:1-13, John 4:1-42, 7:37-39, Romans 8:1-39, 1 Timothy 4:1-16 and 5:22 / ⁷1 Corinthians 12:1-31 / ⁸Psalms 34:1-22, Isaiah 58:1-14, 59:1-21, Matthew 7:7-11, 1 Timothy 6:11-16, Hebrews 12:1-29 and 1 Peter 3:8-12 / ⁹Proverbs 2:1-22, 3:1-26 and John 3:1-21 / ¹⁰John 8:31-32

You're Doing It: ¹Ezekiel 36:16-38, 37:1-14, Acts 1:1-2:1-47, 3:1-26, 5:30-32, 10:34-48, Romans 10:1-13, Ephesians 1:1-23, 2:1-22 and 1 John 5:1-21 / ²1 Thessalonians 5:14-28 / ³2 Thessalonians 2:1-17, 2 Corinthians 4:1-2 and 2 Peter 1:16-21 / ⁴Matthew 7:13-29, Mark 16:15-20 and Galatians 5:1-26 / ⁵Matthew 7:6 / ⁶Psalms 36:1-12, Matthew 7:1-5, 11:25-30, 23:1-39, Romans 14:1-23, 15:1-16, 1 Corinthians 6:9-20, 11:1-16, 1 Timothy 2:1-15, 4:1-16, Titus 1:1-16, 2:1-15, 3:1-11, 1 Peter 3:1-22, 4:1-19, 2 Peter 2:1-22 and 3:1-18 / ⁷2 Corinthians 4:3-18, 5:1-21, 6:1-18, Ephesians 6:10-20, 2 Thessalonians 1:1-12 and James 3:13-18 / ⁸Matthew 10:16-40, 11:16-24, Luke 5:27-32, James 3:1-12 and 1 Peter 5:1-11 / ⁹Psalms 5:1-12, 12:1-8, Proverbs 12:18-23, 26:18-28, 27:5-6, 28:23, Ecclesiastes 7:21-26, Romans 16:17-20, Ephesians 4:1-32, 5:1-21, Colossians 3:1-17, Jude 1:1-25 and Revelation 21:6-8 / ¹⁰Matthew 7:7-12 / ¹¹Psalms 68:1-6 and Luke 18:1-8

Sister Nebiyah: ¹Matthew 18:15-17, 1 Corinthians 1:1-31, 2:1-16, 3:1-23, Ephesians 4:29-32 and 5:1-21 / ²Judges 4:1-24, 5:1-31, Proverbs 31:10-31, Galatians 3:13-29, 1 Timothy 2:1-15, 3:1-13 and Titus 1:1-16 / ³Joel 2:28-32, Luke 2:25-38, 19:29-40, Acts

2:17-18, 1 Corinthians 12:1-31, 13:1-13 and 14:1-40 / [4]Deuteronomy 10:12-21, 30:1-8, Jeremiah 4:1-4, Romans 2:25-29, 1 Thessalonians 1:1-10, Titus 2:1-15, Hebrews 4:12-16, 1 Peter 1:1-25 and 2:1-25 / [5]Isaiah 6:1-13, 42:16-25, 44:1-28, Jeremiah 5:1-31, Ezekiel 12:1-2, Matthew 13:1-30, Acts 28:17-31 and Romans 11:1-36

Test Me: [1]Matthew 19:13-15 / [2]Exodus 20:12, Micah 7:1-20, Matthew 10:24-42, 18:1-14 and Ephesians 6:1-9 / [3]Deuteronomy 11:1-23, Joshua 24:11-29, Proverbs 14:1, 22:6, Matthew 6:19-23, Ephesians 5:1-33, Philippians 4:4-9, 1 Peter 3:1-16 and Revelation 21:1-8 / [4]Psalms 27:1-14, 68:1-6, Proverbs 3:1-8, Ecclesiastes 3:1-11, Isaiah 40:1-31, 54:1-17, 55:1-13, Lamentations 3:1-66, Matthew 5:1-48, 6:9-15, 7:1-5, 24:34-40, Romans 8:1-39, 1 Corinthians 13:1-13, 2 Corinthians 4:1-18, Philippians 1:1-30, 2:1-18, Hebrews 4:12-16, James 3:1-18, 4:1-12 and 1 Peter 5:1-11

Alice: [1]Proverbs 18:2, 18:12, 18:20-21, 21:2-4 and 21:23-24 / [2]Romans 12:1-21, 1 Corinthians 6:9-11 and James 3:1-18 / [3]Matthew 12:33-37, Luke 6:27-36, Hebrews 12:1-3 and 1 Peter 2:1-12 / [4]Exodus 20:17, Proverbs 24:1-2, 24:19-22, Matthew 5:27-30, Mark 7:20-23, 1 Corinthians 6:12-20, Galatians 5:13-26, Colossians 3:1-17, Titus 2:11-15, 2 Peter 1:1-12 and 1 John 2:15-17 / [5]Psalms 15:1-5, Proverbs 10:18-23, 11:11-22, 15:1-18, 18:6-8 and 20:19 / [6]Proverbs 19:1-5, Matthew 7:6, John 13:1-38, 18:1-27 and James 4:1-10 / [7]Proverbs 3:29-35 and 6:12-19

Caden: [1]Philippians 4:4-9 / [2]Leviticus 19:15-16, Proverbs 25:23 and 27:7 / [3]Leviticus 19:17-18, Proverbs 24:28-29, 25:21-22, Luke 6:26-37 and Ephesians 4:17-32 / [4]James 1:26-27 / [5]Matthew 7:1-5, John 8:1-12 and Romans 2:1-16 / [6]Proverbs 8:1-13, 11:2-3, 18:12, 29:23, Daniel 4:37 and 1 Corinthians 13:1-13 / [7]Proverbs 1:1-19, 4:1-27, 6:12-23, 12:26, 13:13-16, 13:19-20, 13:25, 16:28-30, 17:14, 24:1-10, Jeremiah 9:1-8, Romans 6:11-23, 1 Corinthians 15:33-34, Ephesians 5:1-21 and James 1:12-25 / [8]Proverbs 22:14, Matthew 18:1-14 and 2 Corinthians 10:1-6 / [9]Galatians 5:13-26 and Colossians 3:1-17 / [10]Proverbs 25:26 and 1 Peter 3:8-17 / [11]Leviticus 19:33-34, Psalms 1:1-6, Proverbs 9:1-12, 12:15, 13:10, 19:20-23, 24:11-14 and 28:26 and Romans 12:1-21 / [12]Exodus 20:16, Leviticus 5:1 and Proverbs 18:17 / [13]Exodus 23:1-9, Deuteronomy 19:15-21, Psalms 64:1-10, Proverbs 31:9 and Matthew 5:38-48 / [14]Proverbs 17:15, 18:5, 18:13, 21:13, 24:23-27, Isaiah 5:20-24, Jeremiah 22:3-5, Micah 7:1-4 and James 2:1-13 / [15]Romans 13:1-14 / [16]Psalms 38:1-22, 69:1-5, Proverbs 1:20-33, 18:14 and Jeremiah 17:5-10 / [17]Deuteronomy 8:5-6, Proverbs 3:11-26, 12:1, 15:5, Hebrews 12:1-14 and Revelation 3:19-22 / [18] Numbers 6:22-27, Psalms 34:1-22, 40:1-5, 124:1-8, Proverbs 5:1-14, 9:13-18,

20:19, 22:24-25, 24:15-22, 26:18-28, Micah 7:5-8, Nahum 1:1-15, Romans 8:12-39, 16:17-20, Ephesians 2:1-10, 2 Timothy 3:1-17, Titus 3:1-11

The Conductor: [1]Proverbs 11:2, 29:23 and John 15:1-8 / [2]Psalms 32:1-11, 133:1-3, Matthew 11:28-30, Romans 8:1-11, Galatians 6:1-10, Philippians 3:12-21, 4:6-9 and 1 Thessalonians 5:11-15 / [3]Psalms 25:1-22 and Isaiah 41:8-16 / [4]Deuteronomy 8:5-6 and Proverbs 3:11-12 / [5]Proverbs 4:1-13, Romans 12:1-8, 1 Corinthians 12:1-31, 14:1-17 and Hebrews 12:1-17 / [6]Psalms 10:1-18, 11:1-7, Matthew 12:33-37, 1 Corinthians 13:1-13, Ephesians 4:29-32, 5:22-33, Colossians 3:12-25, James 1:19-27 and 3:1-18 / [7]Proverbs 22:29 / [8]1 Samuel 16:1-23 and 1 Peter 2:1-10 / [9]2 Chronicles 15:1-7, Proverbs 3:13-16, 14:12-16, Isaiah 55:1-13, Matthew 18:1-14, 2 Corinthians 4:1-18, Hebrews 5:12-14 and 6:1-8

Salad: [1]Exodus 20:1-6 and Psalms 101:3 / [2]Matthew 7:7-12 and Philippians 2:1-4 / [3]Proverbs 12:14-16 and 18:6-7 / [4]Proverbs 18:1-2 and Ecclesiastes 10:12-13 / [5]Proverbs 10:19-21, 17:27-28, 20:3 and 29:7-11

Fishing: [1]Proverbs 21:19 / [2]Matthew 7:13-29 and John 10:1-30 / [3]Psalms 23:1-6 / [4]John 14:1-31 / [5]Hebrews 10:1-39 / [6]Proverbs 2:1-22 / [7]Proverbs 3:1-26 / [8]Luke 5:1-11 / [9]Hebrews 12:5-11

Deer Season: [1]Leviticus 11:1-8, Proverbs 6:6-11, Matthew 15:1-20, Acts 10:1-48, Romans 14:1-23, 1 Timothy 4:1-5 and 5:8 / [2]Genesis 9:1-4 and Leviticus 17:10-16 / [3]Numbers 27:1-8, Judges 4:1-24, 1 Samuel 17:32-37, Isaiah 6:1-8 and Joel 2:28-32 / [4]Proverbs 27:10, Ecclesiastes 4:9-12, Mark 12:28-34, Romans 15:1-7 and 1 John 3:16-24 / [5]Leviticus 19:32-34, Ecclesiastes 4:7-8, Luke 10:25-37, Romans 13:8-10, 1 Timothy 5:1-2 and 1 Peter 5:5-7 / [6]Proverbs 6:1-5, 6:20-35, 7:1-27, 27:12, Matthew 4:1-11, 1 Corinthians 10:1-13, Ephesians 6:10-20, Hebrews 4:12-16 and 2 Peter 2:1-22 / [7]Psalms 119:104-105, Proverbs 1:1-9, 3:1-12, 4:1-13, 12:15, 15:5, 19:20-21 and 22:6 / [8]Exodus 31:1-11, Psalms 18:32-42, 144:1-2 Proverbs 14:30, 17:22, Ecclesiastes 4:4, 1 Corinthians 1:18-31, 13:1-13, Galatians 5:13-26, Philippians 4:1-9, Hebrews 5:12-14, James 3:13-18 and 4:10

Bruises: [1]Proverbs 17:6 / [2]Proverbs 12:4, 21:9, 21:19, 27:15-16 and 1 Peter 3:1-6 / [3]1 Peter 3:7 / [4]Proverbs 12:8 and 14:1 / [5]Proverbs 6:12-19, 11:22, 24:1-2 and 31:10-31 / [6]Psalms 127:1-5 / [7]Proverbs 16:27 and 26:20-25 / [8]Proverbs 16:28 / [9]1 Corinthians 13:1-13 / [10]Exodus 20:16, Leviticus 18:1-18, Proverbs 3:29-35, 19:9, Matthew 5:21-26,

John 8:37-59, Romans 13:8-14, 14:10-13, 1 Corinthians 6:9-11, Galatians 5:12-26, 1 Peter 4:1-6, 1 John 2:1-11 and Revelation 20:11-15 and 21:1-8 / [11]Proverbs 15:1-9, Matthew 10:34-39, 18:1-14, Luke 6:45, Romans 3:10-26, Ephesians 4:17-32, 5:1-14, Titus 3:1-11, James 3:1-18 and 1 Peter 3:8-17 / [12]Matthew 15:1-20 and Luke 8:19-21 / [13]Exodus 23:7, Proverbs 12:10, 26:28, Isaiah 49:1-26, Ephesians 5:15-21 and Hebrews 10:26-39 / [14]Deuteronomy 32:30-43, Psalms 11:1-7 and 140:1-13 / [15]Proverbs 12:25 and 16:24 / [16]John 8:31-34 / [17]Romans 13:1-7 / [18]Ephesians 6:1-20 / [19]Proverbs 26:26-27/ [20]Proverbs 19:18-19

Doom: [1]Proverbs 26:20-28, Titus 1:1-16 and 2:1-8 / [2]Proverbs 11:10, 24:17-20, Isaiah 55:1-11, Jeremiah 29:11-14 and Matthew 5:43-48 / [3]Proverbs 2:1-22, 3:1-26, 4:1-13, Matthew 19:16-30 and Romans 3:1-18 / [4]Proverbs 1:20-33, 4:14-27, 12:16, 18:17 and 2 Timothy 2:1-26 / [5]Ecclesiastes 7:9 and 2 Timothy 3:1-17 / [6]1 Kings 18:1-46, 19:1-21, Job 1:1-12, Proverbs 16:2-4, Ecclesiastes 7:13-29, Ezekiel 3:16-21 and 33:1-20

Alice Was Right: [1]Psalms 111:1-10, Proverbs 2:1-22, 4:1-13, 8:1-36, 11:8-9, 13:10, 15:33, 16:16-23, 19:8 and 24:13-14 / [2]Proverbs 3:29-35, 4:14-27, 5:1-23, 6:12-15, 9:1-18, 16:27-30, 30:20, Jeremiah 17:5-14, Matthew 23:1-39, Romans 13:1-10, 1 Corinthians 3:16-23, Galatians 5:13-26, Philippians 2:1-16, James 1:13-27 and Revelation 21:7-8 / [3]Proverbs 6:16-19, 30:32-33, Luke 8:16-21, 1 Corinthians 6:9-11, James 3:1-18 and 4:1-12 / [4]Ecclesiastes 5:10-20, Matthew 6:19-34, 19:16-30, Mark 7:1-23, Luke 12:13-21, Philippians 4:4-9, Colossians 3:1-17, 1 Timothy 6:1-21, 2 Timothy 1:7-14 and 1 John 2:15-17 / [5]Proverbs 3:13-26, 13:20, 24:1-22 and Daniel 12:1-13 / [6]Matthew 17:14-21, Luke 1:26-37 and 18:18-27 / [7]Psalms 18:1-36, 27:1-14, 37:1-40, Proverbs 3:1-12, Isaiah 53:1-12, 55:1-13, Jeremiah 33:1-3, Matthew 6:1-18, Mark 5:1-20, 11:12-26, Luke 4:16-30, 6:27-49, 18:1-14, Romans 8:1-39, Hebrews 10:12-39, 11:1-6, James 1:1-12 and 5:7-20

Loophole: [1]Proverbs 17:1, 21:9, 21:19, 27:15-16 and Matthew 10:34-38 / [2]Psalms 116:1-19, Jeremiah 33:1-3, Micah 7:1-20, Matthew 4:1-4, Philippians 4:4-9, 1 John 5:14-15 and Revelation 3:18-20 / [3]Titus 1:1-16 and 2:1-15 / [4]Psalms 5:1-12, 18:1-42, 34:1-22, Jeremiah 17:5-11, 29:8-14 and Ephesians 6:10-20 / [5]Exodus 20:12 and Matthew 18:1-14 / [6]Proverbs 31:10-31, Matthew 19:13-15, Ephesians 6:1-9, 2 Thessalonians 3:10-15 and 1 Peter 3:8-16 / [7]Proverbs 26:18-28 and 2 Timothy 3:1-17

The Backslider Prayer List: [1]Exodus 5:1-8 and Matthew 23:1-39 / [2]Exodus 6:1-8, 12:31-32, Nehemiah 4:1-5, Acts 5:16-29 and 1 Timothy 5:8 / [3]Exodus 20:12, Matthew 19:13-14 and Ephesians 6:1-20 / [4]1 Corinthians 12:1-31 / [5]2 Chronicles 15:1-7, 1 Corinthians

9:24-27 and 2 Timothy 2:1-26 / [6]Psalms 18:1-50, 23:1-6, Isaiah 28:23-29, 40:25-31 and Philippians 4:6-13 / [7]Matthew 6:19-21 and Hebrews 10:19-25 / [8]Psalms 91:1-16, Ecclesiastes 4:9-12 and Isaiah 41:8-20 / [9]Isaiah 49:8-16 and 1 Corinthians 13:1-13 / [10]Proverbs 16:24 and 27:17 / [11]Jeremiah 29:11-14, Galatians 6:1-10 and Hebrews 12:1-13 / [12]Proverbs 14:14, Isaiah 57:1-21, Jeremiah 3:6-17, 8:1-19, 14:1-22, 15:1-21, 24:1-10, Hosea 14:1-9, Hebrews 5:12-14, 6:1-12 and 2 Peter 2:1-22 / [13]Proverbs 31:9 / [14]Psalms 68:1-6, Matthew 6:24-34, 10:27-31, 25:31-46 and Luke 14:7-14 / [15]Isaiah 64:1-12 / [16]Matthew 7:1-5 and Ephesians 4:1-6 / [17]Proverbs 25:2-3, Isaiah 1:1-20, Matthew 18:1-14, Ephesians 4:7-32 and Philippians 2:1-16 / [18]Matthew 7:7-12 and Romans 8:11-30 / [19]Matthew 5:38-48 / [20]Psalms 27:1-14, 31:1-24, Isaiah 61:1-11, Matthew 7:13-29 and James 1:1-12, Revelation 19:1-21, 20:1-15, 21:1-8 and 22:1-21

Spunky: [1]Exodus 20:12, Deuteronomy 28:1-14, 1 Samuel 15:16-23, John 14:10-21 and Ephesians 6:1-9 / [2]James 2:14-26 / [3]Proverbs 15:3-4, 15:16-17, 15:24, 21:9, 21:19, 27:15-16, 31:10-31, Matthew 7:7-27, 10:21-39 and 18:1-14 / [4]1 Corinthians 13:1-13 and 1 Timothy 5:1-21 / [5]Proverbs 3:27, 18:17, Matthew 7:1-5 and Galatians 6:1-5 / [6]Matthew 10:40-42, Romans 5:1-5, Galatians 6:6-10 and Philippians 4:10-13 / [7]Proverbs 15:1-2 / [8]Proverbs 15:15, 15:23, 15:30 and 16:20-24

Checkmate: [1]Psalms 35:1-28 and John 15:16-27 / [2]Exodus 20:12, Ephesians 6:1-9 and Colossians 3:20-25 / [3]Romans 15:1-3, Galatians 6:1-6, Philippians 2:1-16 and Hebrews 10:19-25 / [4]Proverbs 16:24, 18:20-21 and Matthew 5:13-16 / [5]Genesis 1:27-31, Proverbs 14:30, Mark 12:28-34, Romans 15:4-7, Galatians 5:13-26 and James 2:1-13 / [6]Proverbs 27:17, Ecclesiastes 4:9-12 and Isaiah 40:28-31 / [7]Proverbs 31:10-31 and Matthew 19:16-30 / [8]Proverbs 1:10-33, 3:29-35, 4:14-27, 6:12-19, 19:18 and 29:27 / [9]Deuteronomy 32:18-43, Romans 8:12-18, 12:9-21, 2 Corinthians 12:9-10, Galatians 6:7-10, Colossians 3:1-15, Hebrews 10:26-39 and 1 John 3:10-15 / [10]Psalms 133:1-3 and 1 Corinthians 13:1-13 / [11]Deuteronomy 15:7-11, Psalms 112:1-10, Proverbs 14:31, 28:27, Matthew 25:31-46, Acts 20:32-35, James 2:14-26, 1 John 3:16-24 and 4:19-21 / [12]Proverbs 11:24-31, 29:23, Matthew 6:1-4, Luke 6:38 and 2 Corinthians 9:6-15 / [13]Proverbs 3:27, 19:17, 22:9 and Luke 3:7-17 / [14]Proverbs 19:18, 21:19 and 29:25 / [15]Matthew 10:28-31, Philippians 4:6-9, 2 Timothy 1:7 and 1 John 4:13-18 / [16]Daniel 6:18-23, Matthew 7:7-11, John 14:12-14 and 2 Timothy 4:16-18

Two Storms: [1]Exodus 20:16, Proverbs 3:30, 10:6-12, 11:5, 15:1-4, 16:28-30, 21:4, 22:24-25, Ecclesiastes 7:9, Luke 6:43-45, Colossians 3:1-11 and James 1:19-27 / [2]Proverbs 3:31-32, 4:1-27, 8:1-36, 10:19, 11:9, 16:32, 21:8, James 1:12-18 and 1 Peter 3:1-17 /

[3]Proverbs 10:18, 11:3, 11:22, 15:12, Matthew 5:10-12, 7:6, 12:33-37 and 2 Timothy 3:1-9 / [4]Exodus 20:12, Proverbs 10:23, 16:27, 21:9, Isaiah 5:18-24, Matthew 10:34-39, 2 Corinthians 10:1-6, Colossians 3:12-25, 2 Timothy 3:10-17, 2 Peter 3:1-18 and Jude 1:3-25 / [5]Proverbs 10:20, 21:2, 25:26, 26:9, 27:15-16, Matthew 7:1-5, Philippians 2:1-16 and Hebrews 12:1-3 / [6]Proverbs 9:1-18, 21:10, 21:19, Matthew 23:1-39 and 1 Peter 2:1-25 / [7]Ephesians 4:1-16 and 2 Timothy 4:1-5 / [8]Acts 9:1-22 and 1 Corinthians 2:1-16 / [9]Matthew 7:13-23, John 14:23-26, 1 Corinthians 6:9-20, 13:1-13, Ephesians 4:17-32 and 5:1-21 / [10]Romans 10:1-21, Galatians 6:7-9 and 1 John 2:1-11 / [11]Ezekiel 33:1-20, John 14:10-14, Acts 19:11-12, 1 Corinthians 12:1-31 and 1 John 4:1-6 / [12]Judges 6:1-16, Psalms 18:1-42, 144:1-15, Jeremiah 1:4-10, 1 Corinthians 1:25-31, 1 Timothy 4:12-16 and 2 Timothy 2:1-7 / [13]Genesis 40:1-22, Daniel 2:17-20 and Joel 2:28-32 / [14]Hebrews 4:11-13 / [15]Deuteronomy 10:20-21, 11:22-25, Joshua 23:6-13, Psalms 91:1-16, Proverbs 10:25, Isaiah 41:1-20, 43:1-13, 54:10-17, Matthew 7:24-27 and Luke 8:4-15 / [16]Psalms 31:1-24, 34:1-22, 63:1-11 and Isaiah 29:17-24 / [17]Exodus 33:7-17, Isaiah 45:2-7, 49:13-19, 57:1-21 and Romans 8:18-39

Section 6

Fire: [1]Proverbs 10:31-32, 18:6-7, 18:20-21, Luke 6:43-45, Galatians 5:19-26, James 3:1-18 and 1 Peter 3:10-12 / [2]Proverbs 10:19, 11:9, 17:27-28, Matthew 7:1-5, 15:7-20, Luke 12:1-3 and Romans 2:1-11 / [3]Proverbs 4:23-27, 5:1-14, 13:3, Matthew 12:33-37 and Ephesians 4:29-32 / [4]Proverbs 18:17 and 31:8-9 / [5]Deuteronomy 8:1-6, Psalms 37:1-40, Proverbs 10:29, Isaiah 35:1-10, 54:10-17, 55:1-13, 61:1-11, Matthew 10:34-39, Luke 4:16-21 and Romans 8:18-39 / [6]Psalms 12:1-8, Proverbs 20:1, 26:23-28, 1 Corinthians 6:9-12 and Ephesians 5:18-21 / [7]Proverbs 27:12 / [8]Proverbs 11:3, Matthew 6:12-15, 7:12-27, 18:1-14, Luke 16:19-31, John 3:13-21, Romans 12:17-21, 1 Peter 3:8-9, 2 Peter 2:1-22, Revelation 20:12-15 and 21:6-8 / [9]Genesis 1:27-31, Isaiah 45:1-11, Ezekiel 18:1-32, Joel 2:23-32, Acts 2:1-40, 10:1-28 and Galatians 3:27-29 / [10]Isaiah 5:11-19 and 28:1-22 / [11]Proverbs 12:22, 17:10-12, 17:26, 21:2, Jeremiah 17:9-10, Matthew 23:1-39, Mark 7:20-23, John 8:37-59, Romans 6:11-23 and 1 John 1:5-10 / [12]Psalms 120:1-7, Proverbs 10:7-9, Isaiah 5:20-24, Daniel 12:1-13 and Ephesians 5:1-17 / [13]Psalms 34:1-22, 97:1-12, Matthew 18:15-17 and Luke 12:4-7

First Bedroom to the Left: [1]Proverbs 26:11 and 27:12 / [2]Genesis 19:1-26, Exodus 20:1-17, Deuteronomy 28:1-68, 2 Chronicles 7:12-14, Psalms 2:1-12, Jeremiah 17:1-13, Matthew 5:1-20, 24:3-51, Luke 13:22-35, John 15:18-25, Romans 1:18-32, Galatians 5:1-26, 2 Timothy 4:1-5, Revelation 13:1-18, 14:1-13, 18:1-24, 19:11-21 and 20:1-15 /

[3]Romans 13:1-7 and 1 Peter 2:13-17 / [4]Matthew 18:1-14 and 1 Peter 2:1-12 / [5]Matthew 10:12-31, 1 Corinthians 10:1-13 and Ephesians 6:10-20 / [6]Genesis 9:18-29, Leviticus 18:1-30, Proverbs 20:1, 21:15-19, 1 Corinthians 5:1-13, 6:9-20, Ephesians 5:1-21, Titus 2:1-5, Hebrews 4:12-16 and Revelation 3:14-22 / [7]2 Corinthians 4:1-18, 10:3-6 and Philippians 4:8-9 / [8]Matthew 23:1-36

Just a Game: [1]Matthew 7:1-21, Romans 1:18-32, 2:1-11, 2 Corinthians 9:6-7 and Galatians 5:13-26 / [2]1 Samuel 16:7, John 7:24, Acts 10:34-46, Romans 10:8-13 and Revelation 7:9-10 / [3]Proverbs 21:2, John 3:16-21, 1 Corinthians 9:24-27, 13:1-13, 1 Timothy 6:1-19, Titus 2:1-15, 2 Peter 2:1-22 and Revelation 20:11-15 / [4]1 Peter 3:3-4 / [5]Psalms 146:1-10, Mark 8:23-25, 10:46-52, Luke 4:18-19, John 9:1-11, 20:24-31, 2 Corinthians 5:1-9 and 1 John 3:21-24 / [6]Exodus 20:1-17, Deuteronomy 28:1-68, Joshua 6:17-19, 7:1-25, Hosea 4:1-14 and 2 Timothy 2:1-26 / [7]Romans 12:1-13 / [8]Matthew 5:33-37 and Hebrews 12:1-17 / [9]Luke 12:1-7 and Romans 14:4 / [10]Psalms 34:1-22, Proverbs 3:1-8, Matthew 5:38-48, Romans 12:14-21, Ephesians 4:1-32, James 1:12-27, 3:1-18, 4:1-12 and 1 Peter 3:8-17 / [11]Proverbs 19:19 / [12]Proverbs 10:6, 11:9, 15:1, 15:4, 18:6, Ecclesiastes 10:1-4 and 1 Thessalonians 5:15-21 / [13]Proverbs 1:10-9 / [14]Ecclesiastes 4:9-12 / [15]Psalms 82:1-8, Ecclesiastes 8:11-13, Isaiah 1:10-20, Zechariah 7:9-13, 2 Timothy 4:1-5 and James 2:14-20 / [16]Exodus 20:16, Proverbs 6:16-19, John 8:31-44 and Romans 16:17-20 / [17]Proverbs 25:2 and James 2:1-13 / [18]Revelation 21:1-8 / [19]Proverbs 17:15 and 17:26 / [20]Psalms 37:1-40, Proverbs 1:20-33, 19:5, 24:17-20, Ecclesiastes 10:11-15, Galatians 6:1-10 and 1 Peter 5:2-10

A Second Generation: [1]Proverbs 15:4, 18:21, 25:24, 27:15-16 and Ecclesiastes 10:11-14 / [2]Exodus 20:12, Luke 8:19-21, Ephesians 6:1-9 and Colossians 3:20-25 / [3]Proverbs 10:18-21 / [4]Psalms 120:1-7 / [5]Luke 18:1-8 / [6]Proverbs 12:25 / [7]Proverbs 26:24-28 and 29:5 / [8]Exodus 20:14-17, Psalms 5:1-12, 12:1-8, Proverbs 4:1-27, 5:1-23, 6:12-35, 7:1-27, 10:16, 10:23, 15:6, 18:2, 27:7-8, 29:3, Ecclesiastes 7:24-29, 10:8 and 2 Timothy 3:1-17 / [9]Proverbs 14:1, Matthew 12:33-37, 1 Corinthians 6:9-20 and James 3:1-18 / [10]2 Samuel 11:1-27, 12:1-14, Proverbs 10:6, 10:17-19, 13:3, 13:5-6, 18:3, 18:6, 18:17, 28:23, Ecclesiastes 10:1-3, Jeremiah 1:4-19, Luke 12:1-5, Romans 16:17-20, 1 Corinthians 3:9-23, Ephesians 5:1-33, 1 Timothy 4:12-16 and Jude 1:3-25 / [11]Proverbs 4:24-27 / [12]Genesis 37:1-36, 42:1-24, 45:1-15, 49:22-33, 50:15-26, Deuteronomy 32:35, 1 Samuel 24:1-20, Proverbs 10:24, 10:31, 12:13, 12:20-21, John 3:16-21, Romans 12:9-21, Ephesians 4:25-32, 2 Thessalonians 1:3-12 and Hebrews 10:26-39 / [13]2 Chronicles 7:12-14, Psalms 25:1-22, Proverbs 10:17, 10:27, 26:20-23, Matthew 7:1-5, Romans 1:18-32, 2:1-16, James 4:1-12 and Revelation 20:11-15

Goody-Goody: [1]Psalms 68:1-6 and Matthew 18:10 / [2]1 Corinthians 7:32-40 / [3]Ezekiel 33:1-20, 1 Corinthians 6:9-20, Galatians 5:13-26, 6:1-10, Colossians 3:1-17 and 2 Timothy 2:1-26 / [4]Ecclesiastes 4:9-12 / [5]Deuteronomy 22:13-21, 22:28-29, Jeremiah 17:5-10, John 8:1-11 and Hebrews 13:4 / [6]Proverbs 1:20-33 / [7]Psalms 37:1-40 / [8]Proverbs 6:12-26, 25:28 and 2 Timothy 3:1-17 / [9]Proverbs 5:1-14, 7:1-27, 8:1-36, 9:1-18, 17:10-11, 24:1-14, 31:8-9, Matthew 5:27-30, 1 Corinthians 10:1-13 and 1 John 2:15-17

Defend Yourself: [1]1 Samuel 16:7, Romans 5:1-5, 1 Corinthians 9:24-27, 2 Corinthians 4:6-18, Galatians 6:9 and Hebrews 12:1-13 / [2]Psalms 133:1-3, Matthew 18:18-20 and Hebrews 10:23-25 / [3]1 Corinthians 1:9-18, 6:9-11 and Galatians 5:16-26 / [4]Proverbs 6:12-19, Matthew 12:34-37, Romans 12:1-21, 16:17-20, 1 Corinthians 1:19-31, 12:4-31, 13:1-13, Ephesians 4:1-32, 2 Thessalonians 3:5-15, James 1:19-27, 2:1-26 and 3:1-18 / [5]Proverbs 12:26 / [6]Ecclesiastes 12:10-14 / [7]Proverbs 8:13, 11:2, 16:18, 29:22-23, Daniel 4:37, Mark 7:20-23 and 1 Peter 3:8-17 / [8]Proverbs 22:22-23, Matthew 10:16-31, John 3:12-21, Luke 3:1-17 and 1 Peter 5:8-11 / [9]Psalms 5:1-12, Jeremiah 17:1-10, Proverbs 13:20, 22:24-25, 2 Corinthians 10:3-6, 1 John 4:1-21 and Revelation 21:6-8 / [10]Psalms 37:1-40, Zechariah 2:8-13, 3:1-10 and Jude 1:4-25

Red: [1]Judges 6:1-40 and Revelation 3:7-13 / [2]Psalms 119:105, Isaiah 60:1-5, John 1:1-14, 8:12, James 1:16-17, 1 Peter 2:9-10 and 1 John 1:5-10 / [3]Ezekiel 37:1-14 and James 1:18-27 / [4]John 3:16-21 / [5]Psalms 59:1-17, 80:1-19, 119:120-150, 1 Corinthians 1:18-31 and 2 Timothy 2:1-26 / [6]Proverbs 19:22, Ezekiel 3:16-21, 1 Corinthians 13:1-13, Galatians 5:16-26, 1 Timothy 4:1-16, Hebrews 12:1-14, 1 Peter 1:3-25 and 3:8-12 / [7]2 Peter 1:4-8 / [8]Psalms 31:1-24, 37:1-40, 144:1-15, Ecclesiastes 4:9-12, Romans 8:18-39 and Philippians 3:12-21

Opportunity: [1]Romans 8:26-27 / [2]Proverbs 3:27, Matthew 18:1-14, Romans 8:28-30, 1 Corinthians 13:1-13, James 2:1-26 and 3 John 1:4-8 / [3]Psalms 27:1-14, Jeremiah 32:27, Romans 9:15-18, 2 Corinthians 10:3-6 and James 1:2-8 / [4]Exodus 20:12 and 2 Timothy 2:3-5 / [5]1 Samuel 1:1-28, 2:1-10, Psalms 3:1-8, 146:1-10 and Proverbs 13:2-3 / [6]Isaiah 43:1-21, 49:13-16, 2 Corinthians 9:5-9, James 3:1-18 and 1 Peter 5:1-11

Encourage: [1]1 Peter 3:3-4 / [2]Isaiah 6:1-8 / [3]Psalms 37:1-40, 143:1-12, Isaiah 41:8-14, Acts 4:1-13, Romans 5:1-5 and 1 Corinthians 1:25-31 / [4]Proverbs 6:12-19 / [5]Proverbs 3:11-12 / [6]Proverbs 27:17, 1 Corinthians 9:19-27, Hebrews 5:12-14 and 10:19-25 / [7]Psalms 68:1-6, Proverbs 16:24, 17:22, Romans 15:1-7, Galatians 5:13-23, 6:1-10, Ephesians 4:1-32, Colossians 1:3-15, Philippians 1:3-11, 1 Peter 2:1-12, 2 Peter 1:2-12 and 3:10-18 / [8]Proverbs 3:1-8, 11:18, 18:24, Jeremiah 17:5-8, Luke 6:20-23, 1 Timothy 4:1-16 and Revelation 3:7-22

Female: [1]Deuteronomy 8:1-6, Proverbs 1:1-9, 10:17, 12:1, 19:20-21, 24:5-6 and Hebrews 12:1-13 / [2]Psalms 18:1-36, 27:1-14, Matthew 18:10-14, Romans 8:28-39, 1 Corinthians 12:12-31, 13:1-13 and Hebrews 10:24-25/ [3]Isaiah 12:1-6, 41:17-20, 44:1-8, Matthew 25:31-46, 1 Corinthians 3:5-23 and 6:12-20 / [4]1 Samuel 3:1-11 / [5]1 Samuel 15:22-28, 16:1-13 and Matthew 22:1-14 / [6]2 Samuel 21:15-22, Proverbs 3:11-12, 4:1-9, 15:5, Matthew 7:6, Ephesians 6:1-4 and Colossians 3:20-21 / [7]Isaiah 55:8-9 and Jeremiah 29:11-14

Section 7

Good Eye: [1]Exodus 20:16, Proverbs 6:12-19, 14:1 and 19:5 / [2]Proverbs 14:7-8 and John 8:31-32 / [3]Psalms 15:1-5, 120:1-7, Proverbs 10:20, 14:12, 14:16, 15:4, 18:20-21, 21:4, 21:8-10, Isaiah 54:1-17, 1 Corinthians 13:1-13, Galatians 5:13-26, Titus 2:1-15, James 3:1-18 and 1 Peter 3:8-12 / [4]Proverbs 14:4 and Isaiah 49:14-16 / [5]Exodus 20:12, Proverbs 15:1-3, 16:7, Matthew 10:16-42 and John 14:23-27 / [6]Proverbs 14:2, 2 Corinthians 10:3-6 and Philippians 4:6-9 / [7]Proverbs 10:19, 13:3, 14:3, 17:27-28 and 21:23 / [8]Matthew 5:43-48 and James 1:16-27 / [9]Psalms 30:1-12, Matthew 6:24-34 and Romans 9:15-26

Fish: [1]Exodus 18:13-23 / [2]Proverbs 25:28, Matthew 20:25-28, John 13:1-17, 1 Corinthians 12:1-31, 13:1-13, Philippians 2:1-16, Colossians 4:1-6 and 1 Peter 5:2-4 / [3]1 Timothy 4:12, James 1:19-27, 3:1-18 and 2 Peter 5:5-7 / [4]Matthew 10:16-42, Ephesians 6:10-20 and James 5:19-20 / [5]Proverbs 3:5-6, 16:23-24, Luke 15:1-7, Romans 5:1-5, 2 Corinthians 4:1-18, Galatians 6:6-10, Hebrews 12:1-14, James 1:2-8, 5:7-11, 1 Peter 2:18-25 and 5:5-11

Cool It: [1]Proverbs 16:25, Romans 2:1-13, Galatians 5:13-26, James 1:19-26, 3:1-12, 4:1-6 and 4:11-12 / [2]Psalms 25:1-21, Proverbs 11:2, 25:21-22, Matthew 5:38-48, Mark 9:33-37, Romans 12:1-21, 1 Corinthians 1:25-31, 13:1-13, Ephesians 4:1-6, 6:5-9, Philippians 2:1-16, Colossians 3:1-15, James 3:13-18, 1 Peter 3:3-4 and 5:5-10 / [3]Proverbs 16:18-24, 19:19 and 2 Timothy 3:1-17 / [4]Proverbs 6:12-19 and Mark 7:14-23 / [5]1 Samuel 17:57-58, 18:1-16, Psalms 140:1-13, Proverbs 8:1-17, 16:7, 18:12, 22:4, 22:12, 29:23, Daniel 4:37, James 4:7-10 and 1 Peter 5:2-4

Nicki: [1]Isaiah 55:6-13, Joel 2:11-14, Matthew 6:5-15, 9:9-13, Luke 6:20-45, Romans 3:21-26, 12:1-21, 2 Timothy 3:1-17 and 2 Peter 3:9-18 / [2]Proverbs 15:1-4, 16:24, 18:20-21 and Isaiah 57:15-21 / [3]Proverbs 16:1-7 / [4]Psalms 32:1-11, Isaiah 1:16-20, 30:18-26, Matthew 6:1-4, 2 Corinthians 3:1-18, 12:9-10, Ephesians 2:1-22, 4:1-32, 5:1-21, 1 Peter 1:13-25 and 5:6-11 / [5]Numbers 6:22-27, Psalms 23:1-6 and Romans 8:13-39

Varsity: [1]Psalms 133:1-3, Proverbs 27:17, Ecclesiastes 4:9-12 and 1 Thessalonians 5:11-15 / [2]Matthew 7:1-5 and Galatians 6:1-10 and James 1:13 / [3]Romans 12:9-21 / [4]Matthew 12:22-37, 1 Corinthians 3:1-23, Hebrews 5:12-14 and 1 Peter 2:1-12 / [5]Proverbs 24:16-18 and 26:17

Ruby: [1]Isaiah 30:20-21, Matthew 4:1-11, Mark 8:34-38 and John 14:15-21 / [2]Proverbs 4:7-9, 13:20, 22:24-25, Matthew 10:16-20, 1 Corinthians 10:1-15 and 2 Corinthians 6:14-18 / [3]Philippians 2:1-16 and 1 Thessalonians 5:11-13 / [4]Proverbs 14:7 / [5]Proverbs 28:28 / [6]James 1:19-27 / [7]Galatians 5:13-26 and 1 Peter 5:8-10 / [8]Proverbs 28:4-5, Romans 12:1-21, 1 Corinthians 13:1-13, Galatians 6:1-5, Ephesians 4:17-32, 6:10-20, 1 Thessalonians 5:14-15, 1 Timothy 4:8-16 and Titus 2:11-15 / [9]Proverbs 28:1, 28:10 and 28:17-18 / [10]Psalms 75:1-10, Proverbs 3:1-8, 4:11-27, 28:23 and Philippians 4:6-9 / [11]Psalms 1:1-6, 18:1-42, 26:1-12, 119:92-122, Proverbs 30:32-33, Ezekiel 22:13-14 and Hebrews 10:24-39

Not Stupid: [1]Jeremiah 29:11 and Matthew 7:7-11 / [2]Matthew 20:20-28, Romans 5:1-4, Galatians 6:2 and James 2:14-20 / [3]Proverbs 13:12 and 16:21-23 / [4]Proverbs 4:5-9, 13:10, 16:24, Ecclesiastes 4:9-12, Luke 6:43-49 and 2 Corinthians 1:3-7 / [5]1 Corinthians 13:1-13, Galatians 5:16-26 and Ephesians 4:1-25 / [6]Matthew 9:35-38 and 2 Corinthians 9:6-9 / [7]Matthew 6:1-4

Mammon: [1]Genesis 2:15-17, 3:1-19, Exodus 23:8, Psalms 15:1-5, Proverbs 1:10, 10:22, 13:4-6, 13:13-16, 15:16, 16:16-17, 16:27-30, 22:1-5, 23:4-8, Matthew 4:1-11, 1 Corinthians 10:1-14, 2 Thessalonians 3:1-16 and 1 Peter 5:8-10 / [2]Psalms 37:1-20, Proverbs 16:8, 19:22, 28:18-22, 30:7-9, 31:10-31, Ezekiel 18:4-9, Matthew 26:40-41, Luke 12:13-34, 1 Corinthians 15:33, 2 Corinthians 6:1-18, Philippians 4:6-13, 1 Timothy 6:8-19, Hebrews 13:5-6 and James 4:1-10 / [3]Proverbs 27:6-7, Romans 13:9-14, Ephesians 5:1-21 and 2 Timothy 3:1-17 / [4]Proverbs 25:26 and Matthew 13:1-23 / [5]Proverbs 26:11 / [6]Proverbs 6:6-11, 14:23, 19:15, 20:13, 21:25-26, 22:7 and 24:30-34 / [7]Ezekiel 33:1-9 / [8]Proverbs 6:12-19, Isaiah 5:20-25, Matthew 6:22-24, Ephesians 2:1-10, Colossians

3:22-25, 2 Timothy 2:1-26, James 1:21-27, 1 John 2:15-29 and Revelation 22:14-15 / [9]Proverbs 10:2, Ecclesiastes 5:10-17, Romans 1:18-32, 2:1-11 and John 3:16-21

Sadie: [1]Joel 2:28-32 / [2]Isaiah 55:6-11, Jeremiah 1:4-10, Ezekiel 33:1-20, Daniel 1:17-21, Matthew 2:1-20, 27:15-19, Hebrews 5:4-14 and Revelation 21:7-8 / [3]1 Corinthians 15:33-34 / [4]Colossians 3:12-17 / [5]Proverbs 12:26, Luke 6:20-36 and 23:33-37 / [6]Matthew 7:1-5, 18:10-14, Luke 5:27-32, 15:11-32, 18:9-14, John 4:5-42, 8:1-12, 1 Corinthians 12:1-31, 13:1-13 and Hebrews 4:12-16 / [7]Genesis 37:1-28, Isaiah 6:1-13, Jeremiah 19:14-15, 20:1-2, Mark 6:17-29, John 15:1-27 and 1 Corinthians 1:18-31 / [8]Psalms 25:1-22 / [9]Exodus 20:13, Judges 7:8-22, Psalms 106:34-40, 139:1-16, Proverbs 2:1-22, 6:12-19, 13:20, 14:6-7, 20:3, 22:24-25, Ecclesiastes 11:5, Isaiah 57:1-21, Jeremiah 17:1-10, 20:7-13, 1 Corinthians 10:1-15 and 1 Thessalonians 4:1-8 / [10]Proverbs 11:22 / [11]Proverbs 15:1, 15:18 and 15:23 and Matthew 7:6 / [12]Proverbs 27:12 and 1 Peter 4:12-19

I Said It: [1]Proverbs 16:9 / [2]Exodus 4:1-17 and Judges 6:1-16 / [3]Proverbs 3:5-6, Isaiah 55:6-11, Jeremiah 29:11-12, Romans 8:28, 2 Corinthians 4:15-18 / [4]Proverbs 10:18-19 and Ecclesiastes 10:20 / [5]Isaiah 1:16-20 and 6:1-8 / [6]Psalms 52:1-9 / [7]Proverbs 15:1 / [8]Deuteronomy 20:1-8, 31:6 and Ephesians 6:10-20 / [9]1 Samuel 17:1-51, Psalms 18:1-40, Proverbs 16:32 and James 4:1-10 / [10]Matthew 6:34, 2 Peter 3:1-18 and Jude 1:3-25 / [11]Proverbs 26:17, John 15:12-13, Romans 15:1-7 and Revelation 21:6-8 / [12]Isaiah 53:1-12 and Romans 5:1-11 / [13]Proverbs 10:20-21, 17:28, 18:21, 21:23, Matthew 4:1-11, Ephesians 4:17-32, Titus 3:1-11, James 1:19-27, 3:1-18, 4:11-12 / [14]Psalms 140:1-13 / [15]Proverbs 4:1-27, 21:19, 27:12 and 27:15-16 / [16]Matthew 5:43-48 and Romans 12:1-21 / [17]Psalms 91:1-16, Proverbs 1:8-19, 6:12-19, 10:23-24, 1 Peter 2:19-25 and 3:8-17 / [18]Psalms 32:1-11, 34:1-22, 46:1-11, 118:1-29, 141:1-10, Proverbs 16:7, 30:5, Isaiah 41:8-20, 45:1-7, 54:11-17, Nahum 1:1-7, 1 Corinthians 1:18-31 and 2 Timothy 4:16-18

You'll Learn: [1]Proverbs 13:11, Matthew 24:37-51, 25:13-30, Luke 14:25-33 and 2 Thessalonians 3:1-12 / [2]Proverbs 22:29, 27:18, Matthew 6:19-24, 20:1-16, 1 Corinthians 16:13-14, Ephesians 6:5-9, Colossians 3:22-25, 4:1, Titus 2:9-15 and 1 Peter 4:1-11 / [3]Proverbs 10:22, 16:3, 1 Corinthians 15:51-58 and Ephesians 5:1-21 / [4]Ecclesiastes 3:9-13 and 5:18-20 / [5]Proverbs 12:25, 17:22 and 27:17

Mrs. Weather: [1]Matthew 25:31-46 / [2]Ecclesiastes 4:9-12 / [3]Leviticus 19:32, Acts 20:33-35, Romans 13:8-10, Ephesians 4:1-3, Philippians 2:1-4, Colossians 3:12-17, 1 Timothy 5:1-2 and 1 Peter 5:5 / [4]Proverbs 1:1-7, 3:13-18, 4:5-9, 8:1-36 and James 1:2-8 / [5]Ecclesiastes 1:1-11 / [6]Psalms 18:1-42, 32:1-11, 46:1-11 and Ephesians 6:10-20 /

[7]Jeremiah 17:5-13, Psalms 118:5-9, Song of Solomon 3:5, Matthew 19:1-12, Mark 7:14-23, Galatians 5:16-21 and 2 Timothy 2:22 / [8]Genesis 2:18-25, 3:1-24, Psalms 90:1-17, Proverbs 4:23, 11:2-5, 16:18, Ecclesiastes 12:1-7, Isaiah 46:3-4, Hosea 2:13-23, John 21:18, 1 Corinthians 7:1-40, 2 Corinthians 6:11-18, Ephesians 5:22-33, Colossians 2:8-10, 3:18-19, 2 Timothy 3:1-17, Titus 2:1-5 and 1 Peter 3:1-9 / [9]Psalms 71:1-24, Ecclesiastes 12:9-14, Jeremiah 29:11-13, Matthew 11:28-30, John 15:1-11, Ephesians 4:7-25, Philippians 1:3-6, Colossians 1:3-20, Hebrews 5:12-14, 6:1-12, 12:1-17 and 2 Peter 1:2-11

Scouts: [1]Deuteronomy 11:16-28, Proverbs 1:1-33 and 17:6 / [2]Proverbs 6:6-11, John 19:1-30, Philippians 1:4-6, 2 Timothy 4:1-8 / [3]Proverbs 3:1-27, 15:5 and 22:6 / [4]Proverbs 15:1-2, Matthew 10:16 and Titus 2:1-15 / [5]Proverbs 14:1, 21:19 and 26:20-25 / [6]Proverbs 13:10, Matthew 24:1-13, Luke 9:57-62, 1 Corinthians 9:24-27, Galatians 6:1-9, 2 Timothy 2:1-10, Hebrews 12:1-13 and Revelation 3:1-6

Lessons: [1]Matthew 18:18-20, Acts 1:12-14, 2:1-4, 2:41-43, 16:25-34, 1 Corinthians 16:19, Colossians 4:15, 2 Timothy 4:1-5, Philemon 1:1-3 and Hebrews 10:19-25 / [2]Daniel 2:20-22 and Luke 12:2-3 / [3]Romans 15:1-7 / [4]Galatians 6:1-10 / [5]Proverbs 22:3 and 27:5-9 / [6]Proverbs 15:4, 16:24, 17:1, 1 Corinthians 11:17-34 and 1 Peter 2:3-4 / [7]James 2:1-26 / [8]Proverbs 22:16 / [9]Proverbs 21:2-5, John 6:26-35 and 1 Timothy 6:17-19 / [10]Proverbs 21:7, 22:9, Matthew 25:31-46, Luke 12:22-34, 14:12-14, Ephesians 5:1-21 and 1 John 3:16-24 / [11]Proverbs 3:9-10, 13:11, 13:18, 21:20, 23:4-5, Ecclesiastes 3:9-13, 7:11-20, Isaiah 55:1-13, Luke 16:1-13 and James 5:1-8 / [12]Proverbs 11:13, 22:14, 31:1-3, Ecclesiastes 7:23-29, Jeremiah 9:1-26, 17:5-13, Ezekiel 14:1-8, Matthew 13:18-23, 18:15-17, Mark 7:20-23, Romans 1:18-32, 2:1-16, 1 Corinthians 6:9-20, 2 Corinthians 12:14-21, Galatians 5:16-26, Ephesians 4:29-32, 1 Thessalonians 5:1-11, James 3:1-18, 1 Peter 4:1-19 and 1 John 2:15-17 / [13]Proverbs 23:6-8, 26:11 and 27:12 / [14]Exodus 20:16, Proverbs 6:12-19, 14:1, Matthew 6:22-23 and 1 Peter 5:1-11 / [15]Luke 1:26-38 / [16]Psalms 12:1-8, 35:1-28, Matthew 12:33-37, 15:16-20, 1 Corinthians 13:1-13 and 2 Timothy 3:1-17 / [17]Exodus 20:12, Matthew 5:38-48, Romans 12:1-21, Ephesians 6:1-20, 2 Timothy 2:3-26 and 4:1-5 / [18]Matthew 7:1-5, 23:1-39 and Revelation 12:10-11

Mack: [1]Romans 12:1-13, 2 Corinthians 9:6-15, Philippians 4:10-14 and 1 Timothy 5:8 / [2]Luke 10:25-37 / [3]Psalms 56:1-13 and Matthew 18:1-14 / [4]Ecclesiastes 4:9-12 and 2 Corinthians 1:3-7 / [5]Matthew 25:31-46 and James 2:14-26 / [6]Matthew 6:1-15, 2 Corinthians 10:3-6 and Philippians 4:6-9 / [7]1 Corinthians 7:1-40 and Titus 2:1-8 / [8]Isaiah 49:14-16, Acts 3:17-26, Colossians 1:9-15 and Revelation 12:10-11 / [9]Matthew

9:9-13, Luke 6:27-45, 1 Corinthians 13:1-13 and Ephesians 4:29-32 / [10]Isaiah 1:15-20, 55:3-11, Joel 2:11-13, Micah 7:1-10, Acts 13:38-41, 2 Corinthians 10:12-18, Titus 2:11-15 and Hebrews 8:8-13 / [11]Luke 6:20-26

Sweet Sixteen: [1]Numbers 23:19, Proverbs 11:3, 13:4-5, 19:21-22, 24:30-34, 26:14-16, Matthew 5:33-37, Mark 7:18-23, Colossians 3:1-17, 2 Thessalonians 3:1-15 and James 4:13-17 / [2]Psalms 17:1-15, 120:1-7, Proverbs 8:13, 10:9-13, 17:10-16, 26:18-19 and James 1:17 / [3]Psalms 24:1-10, Proverbs 9:13-18, 10:22-32, 11:3, 15:4, 28:14-16, Isaiah 49:14-16, Ezekiel 11:17-21, Matthew 7:7-12 and Ephesians 4:17-25 / [4]Psalms 25:1-22, Ecclesiastes 4:9-12 and Jeremiah 17:5-14

Running Your Mouth: [1]Proverbs 14:20-21, Matthew 3:1-4, 1 Corinthians 1:25-31, 12:1-31, 13:1-13, James 2:1-13 and 4:1-10 / [2]Psalms 101:1-8, Proverbs 6:16-19, 10:18-19, 14:16, 15:4, Matthew 12:33-37, 2 Timothy 3:1-17, Titus 3:1-10 and James 4:11-12 / [3]Philippians 4:6-9 / [4]Proverbs 16:28, Matthew 18:15-17, 1 Timothy 4:7-16 and 2 Timothy 2:14-26 / [5]Proverbs 11:22 / [6]Psalms 19:1-14, 34:6-22, Proverbs 11:8-9, Romans 12:17-21 and 1 Peter 3:13-17 / [7]Psalms 51:1-19, Proverbs 9:1-18, 14:35, 16:6, 18:20-21, 20:30, 21:23, 26:20-22, Malachi 3:1-6, Luke 12:1-3, John 3:14-21, 15:1-17, Romans 12:1-16, 1 Peter 3:8-12, 1 John 1:1-10 and Revelation 3:14-22

Oliver: [1]Psalms 139:1-24, Proverbs 31:30-31 and 1 Corinthians 13:1-13 / [2]Psalms 45:1-17, Colossians 3:1-14 and 1 Peter 3:3-4 / [3]Matthew 5:38-48, Romans 12:6-21, Titus 3:1-8 and Hebrews 4:12-16 / [4]1 Samuel 16:7, Psalms 32:1-11, Proverbs 3:1-8, Jeremiah 17:9-11, 1 Corinthians 6:9-11, Galatians 6:7-10, Ephesians 4:25-32, 5:1-21, Colossians 3:23-25, James 4:4-10, 1 Peter 5:5-7 and Revelation 22:10-12 / [5]Proverbs 12:18, 12:25 and Ephesians 6:1-20 / [6]Ecclesiastes 5:18-20, Habakkuk 3:1-19, 2 Corinthians 4:1-18, Philippians 4:5-9 and 1 Peter 5:8-11 / [7]Ecclesiastes 4:9-12

Dance: [1]Mark 12:28-34 and Galatians 5:13-23 / [2]Proverbs 16:3 / [3]Matthew 18:21-35 / [4]Psalms 37:1-40, Matthew 5:14-16, John 8:12, Romans 8:14-30 and 1 Peter 2:1-12 / [5]Ruth 2:1-23, 3:1-18 and 4:1-22 / [6]Numbers 6:24-26, Deuteronomy 28:1-14, Psalms 8:1-9, 20:1-9, 149:1-9, Proverbs 10:7, 16:7, Isaiah 61:1-11, Jeremiah 17:5-10, 29:11-14, Ezekiel 34:25-31 and John 10:7-10

Section 8

Deleted: [1]Deuteronomy 7:25-26, 12:1-3, Joshua 7:7-15 and 1 Thessalonians 4:1-12 / [2]Proverbs 2:1-22, 10:19, 11:3, 11:12, 11:22, 13:3, 17:28, Matthew 7:1-5, Luke 8:17, 18:9-14, Romans 2:1-29, 12:9-21, 1 Corinthians 6:9-11, Galatians 5:13-26, Ephesians 5:1-21, 1 Timothy 1:3-17 and James 1:19-27 / [3]Matthew 5:17-30 / [4]Proverbs 21:4, Ecclesiastes 4:9-12 and 1 John 3:10-15 / [5]Exodus 20:16 and Proverbs 6:12-19 / [6]Proverbs 18:17 / [7]Exodus 34:5-7, Deuteronomy 8:5, 19:15-21, Psalms 37:1-40, 54:1-7, 121:1-8, Proverbs 3:11-12, 13:24, 22:6, 22:15, 25:2, 29:15, Isaiah 41:10-16, 43:1-2, 58:1-14, 59:1-21, Ezekiel 18:1-32, Amos 5:1-15, Romans 1:18-32, Ephesians 6:1-20, 2 Timothy 3:1-17, 4:1-5, Hebrews 12:1-17, 1 Peter 4:12-19, Revelation 21:5-8 and 22:12-15

Ditch the Girl: [1]James 4:13-16 / [2]Galatians 5:13-26 / [3]Deuteronomy 22:5, Matthew 23:1-39 and Romans 12:1-13 / [4]Psalms 139:1-18, Isaiah 60:1-2 and Malachi 4:1-3 / [5]1 Corinthians 16:13-14 / [6]Proverbs 14:30 and Luke 6:43-45 / [7]Psalms 127:1-5, Proverbs 17:6, 20:30 and 1 Corinthians 7:25-40 / [8]Proverbs 26:17 / [9]Proverbs 10:19, 13:3, 14:29, 16:32, 17:27-28 and Romans 12:14-21 / [10]Proverbs 11:22, 12:18, 15:1-4, 15:28, 16:2, 16:27-30, 18:21, 20:25, 27:6, Luke 6:20-38 and James 3:1-18

Launched: [1]Judges 6:11-16 / [2]Deuteronomy 31:6, Judges 15:11-20 and Isaiah 41:8-16 / [3]Psalms 31:1-24 and Proverbs 15:1-2 / [4]Exodus 20:16, 23:1, Leviticus 18:1-7, 19:15-18, Deuteronomy 19:18-20, Proverbs 14:1, 15:3-4, Matthew 18:1-9, Galatians 5:1-26 and Revelation 12:9-12 / [5]Exodus 20:12, Proverbs 25:24, Ephesians 6:1-20, 2 Timothy 1:7, Hebrews 12:1-29, James 1:19-26 and 1 Peter 2:1-12 / [6]1 Samuel 17:28-49, 1 Kings 18:22-46, 19:1-2, 2 Kings 9:6-10, 9:30-37, Psalms 18:1-42, 34:1-22, 35:1-28, Proverbs 18:20-21 and 24:15-16 / [7]Psalms 126:1-6, Proverbs 24:17-18, Luke 6:20-37 and 1 Timothy 4:8-16

What's Your Emergency?: [1]Proverbs 10:19-21, 18:2-3, 20:3, 25:28, Luke 6:41-42, Galatians 5:19-26 and 6:1-5 / [2]Proverbs 4:24 / [3]Proverbs 31:10-31 / [4]Proverbs 10:31-32, 29:22, Ecclesiastes 7:9, Matthew 12:33-37, Mark 7:1-23, Romans 2:1-11, 3:9-19, Ephesians 4:17-32, 1 Timothy 6:20-21, Titus 2:1-15, James 1:19-27 and 1 John 1:5-10 / [5]Proverbs 18:6, 22:24-25, 24:17-18, Matthew 5:17-22, Romans 12:17-21 and James 3:1-18 / [6]Proverbs 1:7, 15:1, 26:3-12, 29:9, Jeremiah 1:4-8 and 1 Timothy 4:12-16 / [7]Romans 13:1-7 / [8]Proverbs 18:7 / [9]1 Corinthians 10:13 / [10]Psalms 33:1-22, Proverbs 12:22, 14:5 and 28:13 / [11]Psalms 27:1-14, 34:1-22, Proverbs 14:1, Isaiah 41:8-16, 57:1-21, Jeremiah 29:11-14, Luke 12:1-5, John 8:31-44, 2 Corinthians 10:3-6, Ephesians 6:10-20 and Jude 1:4-25 / [12]Proverbs 13:20 and Luke 6:43-45 / [13]Proverbs 21:9 / [14]Deuteronomy

24:16, Judges 8:20-21, John 10:1-16, 1 Corinthians 5:9-13, 13:11 and Revelation 21:5-8 / [15]Mark 11:23-24 and Luke 6:27-40 / [16]Exodus 34:6-7, Proverbs 19:19, Jeremiah 31:28-34, Luke 6:46-49 and John 16:33

Odd: [1]Proverbs 22:1 / [2]Proverbs 6:12-19, Matthew 7:1-5, 7:12-27, 25:31-46, Luke 11:27-36, 16:19-31, Galatians 5:13-26 and 1 Peter 4:1-9 / [3]Psalms 4:1-8, John 10:1-16, 13:34-35, Ephesians 6:10-20 and Philippians 2:1-4 / [4]Leviticus 18:1-30, Psalms 51:1-19, 139:1-24, Proverbs 8:1-36, 11:2, Zechariah 7:8-14, Matthew 11:25-30, Mark 7:1-23, Luke 5:27-32, 18:9-14, Romans 1:16-32, 3:9-26, 1 Corinthians 6:9-20, 10:1-24, 2 Corinthians 10:12, Colossians 3:12-17, 1 Timothy 1:3-17, 4:1-16, 2 Timothy 2:15 and 1 John 4:20-21 / [5]Proverbs 10:12, 18:24, 29:23, Jeremiah 17:5-10, 1 Corinthians 13:1-13, 1 Peter 2:9-12 and 3:3-4 / [6]Matthew 9:35-38, Romans 12:1-21 and 1 Peter 5:1-11 / [7]Ecclesiastes 4:9-13, Jeremiah 17:13-17 and Colossians 1:9-15

Goals: [1]Joshua 1:1-9, Psalms 56:1-13, Proverbs 3:1-35, Matthew 7:13-27, Romans 12:1-2, Ephesians 6:1-20, 2 Timothy 3:16-17 and Revelation 21:1-8 / [2]Matthew 10:34-39, 13:1-23, Mark 8:34-38, Luke 12:1-12, 14:26-33 and James 4:1-10 / [3]Judges 6:1-16, 1 Samuel 2:1-10, 16:1-13, 1 Chronicles 29:10-12, Proverbs 10:22, 11:4, 11:25, 15:16, 22:4, 23:4-5, 24:1-4, Ecclesiastes 5:10-20, Jeremiah 17:1-13, Matthew 19:16-30, Luke 12:13-34, Acts 4:1-13, 1 Corinthians 1:18-31, 6:9-11, 13:1-13, 1 Timothy 6:3-21, James 3:1-18, Revelation 17:1-2 and 18:1-24 / [4]Psalms 37:1-40, Matthew 15:7-14, Philippians 4:6-9 / [5]Jeremiah 29:11-14, 2 Timothy 2:1-26, Hebrews 12:1-13 and James 4:13-16

Indifference: [1]Proverbs 15:27, 16:8, 17:23, 28:21, Matthew 7:21-27, 1 Corinthians 15:33-34, Revelation 21:5-8 and 22:10-15 / [2]Matthew 12:33-37 / [3]Proverbs 27:2, Galatians 5:7-26, Ephesians 5:1-21, Philippians 4:8-9, Colossians 3:1-17 and James 1:19-27 / [4]Psalms 1:1-6, 15:1-5, 26:1-10, 41:1-13, 82:1-8, Ecclesiastes 4:9-12, Proverbs 11:3, 19:1, 26:1-5, 27:17, 28:1-2, 31:8-9, John 15:12-13, 2 Corinthians 10:1-6, Ephesians 4:17-32 and Philippians 2:1-4 / [5]Proverbs 18:24 and 2 Timothy 2:1-10 / [6]Proverbs 27:7, 27:12, Ezekiel 14:1-11, 1 Corinthians 6:9-20, 2 Corinthians 6:12-18, 2 Timothy 3:1-9, James 4:1-10 and Jude 1:3-23 / [7]Proverbs 10:18, 11:13, 15:4 and 16:27-30 / [8]Isaiah 3:1-26, 5:13-25, Jeremiah 17:5-11, Luke 18:9-14, 1 Corinthians 13:1-13 and 1 Timothy 6:3-10 / [9]Proverbs 26:18-19, 27:6 and Philippians 3:17-19 / [10]Proverbs 3:1-35, 26:20-28, Matthew 4:1-11, 7:1-6, Romans 3:10-18, 12:1-21, 1 Corinthians 10:6-22, 2 Corinthians 10:12-18, 13:5-10, Ephesians 2:1-10, 2 Timothy 2:14-26, 3:13-17 and James 1:12-17

Peacock: [1]Proverbs 29:25 / [2]Proverbs 6:12-19, 28:13, John 1:1-5, 15:12-23, James 4:1-10, 1 Peter 1:13-16, 2:9-12, 3:3-4 and 1 John 1:5-10 / [3]Matthew 6:14-15 and Ephesians 4:25-32 / [4]Psalms 23:1-6, John 17:12-26, 2 Corinthians 12:9-10, Ephesians 2:1-10, Colossians 3:1-17, 2 Timothy 1:7 and 1 John 4:15-19 / [5]1 Timothy 5:8 and James 4:17 / [6]Exodus 20:13, Psalms 106:32-40, Matthew 7:1-5, 12:33-37, 23:1-39, Romans 2:1-11, 14:10-13, 1 Timothy 1:5-16 and 1 Peter 3:8-17 / [7]1 Corinthians 13:1-13 / [8]Luke 6:26-38, John 8:1-12 and James 4:11-12 / [9]1 Samuel 16:7, Proverbs 31:30-31, Matthew 10:29-40, Titus 2:1-5 and 1 Peter 5:1-11 / [10]Numbers 6:22-27, 2 Chronicles 7:12-14, Psalms 4:1-3, 27:1-14, 31:1-24, 103:1-22, 139:1-24, Isaiah 1:16-20, 55:1-11, Joel 2:12-13, Matthew 6:25-34, 7:7-14, 9:9-13, Luke 15:1-32, John 3:14-21, Acts 3:19-23, Romans 3:21-26, 12:1-21, Philippians 4:6-9, Titus 2:11-15, 2 Peter 3:1-9 and 1 John 2:1-11

Armageddon: [1]Matthew 5:33-37 and Jeremiah 17:5-10 / [2]Romans 12:1-16, 1 Corinthians 10:24 and Philippians 2:1-4 / [3]Romans 8:28 / [4]Exodus 22:21-24, Psalms 4:1-8, 6:1-10, 7:1-17, 10:1-18, 11:1-7, 13:1-6, 37:1-40, 68:1-6, 94:1-23, Isaiah 59:1-21 and Philippians 4:4-9 / [5]Psalms 20:1-9, Proverbs 1:10-19 and 6:12-19 / [6]Exodus 23:6-9, Psalms 12:1-8, 82:1-5, Proverbs 21:2, Jeremiah 22:1-9 and Matthew 24:12-13 / [7]Proverbs 31:8-9, Mark 7:20-23, John 2:13-17, Romans 1:16-32 and Galatians 6:1-10 / [8]Psalms 14:1-7, Proverbs 12:22, 17:28, 18:6 and Zephaniah 3:5 / [9]Matthew 26:45-56 and Revelation 21:6-8 / [10]Proverbs 1:20-33, 2:1-22, 3:1-35, 29:27, Isaiah 55:6-11, Romans 12:17-21, 1 Corinthians 1:25-31, 2 Corinthians 10:1-6, Ephesians 4:1-32, 5:1-17, 2 Timothy 2:19-26 and 1 Peter 3:8-12 / [11]Leviticus 19:15-18, Psalms 1:1-6, 3:1-8, 5:1-12, 15:1-5, Proverbs 14:29, 20:3, Ecclesiastes 4:9-12, Romans 13:8-14, Galatians 5:7-26, James 1:19-27, 1 Peter 2:1-17 and 3:8-12 / [12]James 3:1-18 / [13]Proverbs 27:17, Isaiah 49:14-19, 1 Corinthians 13:1-13, Ephesians 6:1-20 and James 4:1-10

Amin: [1]Acts 12:5-10 / [2]1 Corinthians 6:9-11, Colossians 4:5-6 and James 3:1-18 / [3]Exodus 16:1-8 and Numbers 11:1-2 / [4]Proverbs 15:16, 16:8, 21:19 and 25:24 / [5]Exodus 7:1-5, Jeremiah 17:5-10, Hebrews 3:7-15 and 4:11-16 / [6]Proverbs 12:15, 13:10, 17:13, Acts 7:51-53 and Ephesians 4:17-32 / [7]Psalms 37:1-40, 40:1-17, 84:1-12, Proverbs 18:24, Isaiah 61:1-3, Matthew 10:7-40, Luke 4:14-30, Romans 3:21-26, 5:6-11, 2 Corinthians 4:1-18, Ephesians 6:10-20, Philippians 4:6-9, 2 Timothy 1:7-11 and Revelations 3:14-22 / [8]Proverbs 27:17, 28:13-14, 29:25, Ecclesiastes 4:9-12, 1 Corinthians 7:1-40, 13:1-13, Philippians 2:1-4 and 1 John 4:10-21

Coach Gather: [1]Deuteronomy 8:5-6, Proverbs 3:11-12, 12:1, 22:6, Hebrews 12:1-13 and Revelation 3:19 / [2]Matthew 12:31-37, 15:7-20, Ephesians 4:29, 5:1-21, Colossians 3:1-17 and 4:5-6 / ³Jeremiah 29:11-14 / ⁴Ephesians 6:5-9 and Colossians 3:22-25 / ⁵Hebrews 10:24-25 / ⁶Proverbs 11:24-25, Matthew 24:45-51, Mark 10:35-45, Acts 20:32-35, 1 Corinthians 9:24-27, Philippians 2:1-4 and 1 Peter 5:1-7 / ⁷Ephesians 4:17-27 and 2 Timothy 1:7 / ⁸Proverbs 1:7, 10:8, 10:17, 12:16, 15:12, 25:28, 1 Corinthians 13:1-13 and Galatians 5:13-26 / ⁹Proverbs 15:1-4, 17:11-14, 29:11 and 1 Corinthians 10:13 / ¹⁰Proverbs 27:6, 29:2, Lamentations 3:1-66, Matthew 7:1-5, 23:1-39 and Titus 2:1-15 / ¹¹Genesis 50:20, Leviticus 19:15-18, Proverbs 6:12-19, 10:18, 11:12-13, 11:17-23, 11:27, 16:32, 18:5-8, 18:21, 18:24, 21:13, 26:20-28, 29:10, Isaiah 41:8-16, Micah 2:1, Matthew 7:15-23, 10:16-39, Romans 16:17-20, 1 Corinthians 5:9-13, 2 Thessalonians 3:1-15, 2 Timothy 2:14-26, James 4:1-12, 1 Peter 5:8-11 and 2 Peter 2:1-22 / ¹²Matthew 18:15-17 and 18:21-35 / ¹³Deuteronomy 17:2-13 and John 8:1-11 / ¹⁴Proverbs 3:1-8, 12:2-3, 16:12-15, 18:17, 21:1, 29:26, Isaiah 40:28-31, 2 Corinthians 10:3-6, 1 Timothy 4:12-16 and James 3:1-18 / ¹⁵Psalms 23:1-6, 107:1-43, 103:1-22, 133:1-3, Isaiah 55:6-11, Ezekiel 33:1-20, Matthew 25:31-46, Luke 8:16-21, 12:1-7, Romans 5:1-5, 8:18-30, 12:17-21, Ephesians 2:1-10, 6:10-20, Philippians 2:12-16, 1 Peter 1:3-9, 3:8-12 and James 1:12

Words: ¹Psalms 133:1-3 and Romans 12:1-21 / ²Proverbs 12:25, 15:23, 16:24, John 13:34-35, Philippians 2:1-4 and 1 John 3:16-24 / ³Proverbs 15:1-4, 18:2-3, 20:3, Matthew 12:34-37, Mark 7:20-23, Luke 6:39-45, Hebrews 12:14-17, James 4:11-12 and 1 John 3:10-15 / ⁴Psalms 4:1-8, Proverbs 13:2-3, 14:23, 14:29, 18:6-7, 18:21, 29:10-11, Jeremiah 17:5-13, Ecclesiastes 4:26-27, 10:11-14, Luke 12:1-5, Romans 14:16-19, 1 Corinthians 13:1-13, Ephesians 4:29-32, Colossians 3:12-17, James 3:1-18 and 1 Peter 3:8-17 / ⁵1 Corinthians 9:24-27, 2 Timothy 4:1-8, 4:17-18, Hebrews 12:1-13, James 4:1-10 and Revelation 3:7-13

Thad: ¹Proverbs 10:7, 10:24, 14:1 and 21:19 / ²Exodus 20:17, Proverbs 4:20-27, 30:32-33, Galatians 5:13-26, Philippians 2:1-4, Colossians 3:1-14 and 1 John 2:15-17 / ³Jeremiah 17:5-13 and 2 Corinthians 6:1-12

Degrading: ¹Job 31:1-12, Psalms 101:1-8, Proverbs 8:13, 10:31-32, 31:30-31 and Hebrews 13:4 / ²Leviticus 18:1-30, Matthew 5:27-30, Romans 1:16-32, 1 Corinthians 3:18-23, 6:9-20 and Galatians 5:13-26 / ³Proverbs 4:1-27, 7:1-27, Luke 8:19-21, Ephesians 5:1-21, 6:10-20 and 1 John 2:1-17 / ⁴1 Corinthians 10:13-23 / ⁵Proverbs 11:3, 15:4, 22:1, Jeremiah 17:5-13, Matthew 18:1-14, Luke 8:4-18, 1 Corinthians 15:33-34, 2 Corinthians 10:1-12, Galatians 5:1, James 4:1-10 and Revelation 21:1-8

Dear Nancy: [1]Proverbs 27:17, Ecclesiastes 4:9-12 and Matthew 5:33-37 / [2]Judges 4:1-24, Ephesians 4:26-27 and James 1:2-27 / [3]Joshua 1:5-9, 23:6-13, Psalms 18:1-50, 84:1-12, 91:1-16, Proverbs 27:1, Isaiah 54:11-17, Jeremiah 17:5-13, 2 Corinthians 10:3-6, Ephesians 6:10-20 and James 4:1-16

Welcome: [1]Philippians 2:1-4 / [2]Leviticus 19:33-34, Psalms 146:1-10 and Proverbs 16:9 / [3]Exodus 21:16, Proverbs 6:12-19, Ecclesiastes 4:9-12, Jeremiah 5:20-26 and Revelation 18:4-13

Help Us: [1]Genesis 1:1-2, Isaiah 11:1-5, Ezekiel 36:23-27, Zechariah 4:6, Matthew 12:31-32, Luke 11:11-13, John 14:15-26 and 1 Thessalonians 5:5-24 / [2]Isaiah 66:22-24, Mark 9:43-44, Luke 16:19-24 and Revelation 20:11-15 / [3]Numbers 21:6-9, John 3:1-21, Acts 2:1-41 and Romans 8:1-17 / [4]Matthew 28:18-20, Mark 16:15-20 and 1 Peter 3:18-22 / [5]Romans 10:1-21 and 2 Peter 2:1-22 / [6]Psalms 139:1-24, John 4:1-26, 10:1-30, Acts 4:1-22, 10:34-48, 19:1-6, Romans 5:1-11, Ephesians 2:1-22 and 4:1-6 / [7]Matthew 10:27-39, 13:1-23, 15:7-20, 19:23-30 and Mark 9:33-42 / [8]Isaiah 43:15-21 and Colossians 4:2-6 / [9]Proverbs 10:7, Matthew 5:43-48 and 1 Peter 3:3-4 / [10]Psalms 34:1-22, Acts 8:26-40, Romans 8:28-30, 1 Corinthians 1:10-31, Hebrews 10:19-25 and James 1:12-27

Mascot: [1]Proverbs 21:19 and 27:15-16 / [2]Proverbs 23:24 / [3]Proverbs 15:1, 15:7, 15:16-18, 27:6, 15:28, 29:11, Ephesians 6:1-4, 2 Timothy 1:7 and 1 Peter 5:5-10 / [4]Psalms 18:1-42, 68:1-6, Proverbs 10:28, 13:12, Isaiah 41:8-17, 61:1-3, Jeremiah 29:11-14, Luke 4:16-21 and 13:10-17 / [5]Matthew 5:27-30 / [6]Proverbs 16:24 / [7]Ezekiel 37:1-14 / [8]Proverbs 27:2 / [9]Matthew 19:1-12, 1 Corinthians 7:1-40 and Hebrews 13:4 / [10]Proverbs 4:14-27, Jeremiah 17:5-13, Matthew 5:13-16, 10:26-33, John 14:6, Romans 5:1-5 12:1-13, 1 Corinthians 2:1-9, 9:24-27, 10:1-24, 2 Corinthians 6:14-18, 10:3-6, Galatians 5:13-26, Ephesians 6:10-20, Philippians 4:6-9, 2 Timothy 2:3-5, Hebrews 12:1-17, 1 Peter 2:1-12 and Revelation 21:6-8

Don't Look Back: [1]Matthew 6:1-4 / [2]Genesis 19:1-26, Proverbs 4:1-27, Matthew 7:6, Luke 9:59-62, 1 Corinthians 2:9, 7:1-40, 2 Timothy 3:1-17 and 1 Peter 3:1-12 / [3]1 Samuel 16:7, Proverbs 18:17, 2 Corinthians 11:1-15, Philippians 1:9-17 and Hebrews 5:12-14 / [4]Proverbs 20:3, Matthew 5:43-48, 12:33-37, Romans 12:14-21, 1 Corinthians 13:1-13, Ephesians 4:26-32 and James 1:19-20 / [5]Proverbs 27:17 / [6]Luke 17:1-4 / [7]Proverbs 27:5 / [8]Song of Solomon 8:4, Isaiah 55:8-13, Jeremiah 17:5-10, Matthew 7:13-27, Hebrews 4:12 and James 1:21-25 / [9]Deuteronomy 8:1-20, Proverbs 12:15, 28:26 and Philippians 3:7-14